D1453515

THE HISTORY OF THE JEWISH PEOPLE
IN THE AGE OF JESUS CHRIST

THE HISTORY
OF THE JEWISH PEOPLE
IN THE AGE OF JESUS CHRIST
(175 B.C.–A.D. 135)

BY

EMIL SCHÜRER

A NEW ENGLISH VERSION
REVISED AND EDITED BY

GEZA VERMES   FERGUS MILLAR
MARTIN GOODMAN

Literary Editor
PAMELA VERMES

Organizing Editor
MATTHEW BLACK

VOLUME III, PART 2

EDINBURGH T. & T. CLARK LTD 59 GEORGE STREET

Revised English Edition

Copyright © 1987 T. & T. CLARK LTD.

SET IN MONOTYPE BASKERVILLE 10 ON 11 POINT
BY BRADLEY COMPUTING, LOWER SOUDLEY, GLOS.
ON A MONOTYPE LASERCOMP PHOTOTYPESETTER
AT OXFORD UNIVERSITY COMPUTING SERVICE

PRINTED BY PAGE BROS (NORWICH) LIMITED

BOUND BY HUNTER & FOULIS LIMITED, EDINBURGH

FOR

T. & T. CLARK LTD EDINBURGH

Schürer, Emil
The history of the Jewish people in the age of Jesus Christ.—New
English version
Vol. 3 Pt. 2
1. Jews—History—175 B.C.–135 A.D.
I. Title   II. Vermes, Geza   III. Millar, Fergus
IV. Goodman, Martin V. Geschichte des jüdischen Volkes
im Zeitalter Jesu Christi. *English*
933 DS122
        ISBN 0 567 09373 5

FIRST EDITION AND REPRINTS 1885–1924
REVISED EDITION 1987

Preface

As explained in the Preface to volume III.1, it became clear in the course of printing the third and last volume of the revised edition of Schürer's *History* that the very extensive material available had increased the bulk of the work to the point where division into two halves was essential. Volume III.1 therefore contains the larger part, namely §31 on the Diaspora, §32 on Jewish literature composed in Hebrew or Aramaic, and §33A on that composed in Greek. The editors have adopted the principle of division according to the original language of the writings, as opposed to presumed geographical provenance.

In the present volume III.2, which brings the entire work to a close, continuous page-numbering with III.1 has been retained. It contains firstly §33B, on Jewish literature whose original language of composition is uncertain, revised jointly by Geza Vermes and Martin Goodman. The text concludes with §34 on Philo, for which the entire academic responsibility belongs to Mrs Jenny Morris (Wycombe Abbey School), to whom the editors are extremely grateful. Final preparation for this section for the press was undertaken by Fergus Millar.

The volume is completed by a detailed index covering the whole work. The editors wish also to thank Dr Léonie Archer, Fellow of the Oxford Centre for Postgraduate Hebrew Studies, for carrying out this intricate and laborious task.

The editors would not like to take their leave without paying their profound respects to the memory of Emil Schürer, the supreme quality of whose scholarship is best shown by the fact that it can tolerate revision more than a century after the first edition.

1 July 1986

Contents

Abbreviations

AAAScHung	Acta Antiqua Academiae Scientiarum Hungaricae
AAB	Abhandlungen der Deutschen (Preussischen) Akademie der Wissenschaften zu Berlin
AAM	Abhandlungen der Bayerischen Akademie der Wissenschaften, München
AArchAcSc Hung	Acta Archaeologica Academiae Scientiarum Hungaricae
AfO	Archiv für Orientforschung
AIPhOS	Annuaire de l'Institut de Philologie et d'Histoire Orientales et Slaves
AJA	American Journal of Archaeology
AJAH	American Journal of Ancient History
AJPh	American Journal of Philology
AJS Review	Association for Jewish Studies Review
AJSL	American Journal of Semitic Languages and Literatures
AJTh	American Journal of Theology
ALGHJ	*Arbeiten zur Literatur und Geschichte des hellenistischen Judentums*
ALUOS	Annual of Leeds University Oriental Society
ANET	J. B. Pritchard (ed.), *Ancient Near Eastern Texts Relating to the Old Testament* (1969)
AnglThR	Anglican Theological Review
ANRW	H. Temporini (ed.), *Aufstieg und Niedergang der römischen Welt*
AP	A. Cowley, *Aramaic Papyri of the Fifth Century B.C.* (1923)
APAT	E. Kautzsch (ed.), *Die Apokryphen und Pseudepigraphen des Alten Testaments* (1900)
APO	E. Sachau, *Aramäische Papyrus und Ostraka aus einer Militär-Kolonie zu Elephantine* (1911)
APOT	R. H. Charles, *Apocrypha and Pseudepigrapha of the Old Testament* I–II (1912–13)
ARW	Archiv für Religionswissenschaft
AS	Anatolian Studies

ASTI	Annual of the Swedish Theological Institute
Ath. Mitt.	Mitteilungen des Deutschen Archäologischen Instituts, Athenische Abteilung
AWH	Akademie der Wissenschaften, Heidelberg
BA	Biblical Archaeologist
BAAJ	J. J. Collins, *Between Athens and Jerusalem* (1983)
BAC	Bulletino di Archeologia Cristiana
BAR	*British Archaeological Reports*
BASOR	Bulletin of the American Schools of Oriental Research
BASP	Bulletin of the American Society of Papyrologists
BAW	Bayerische Akademie der Wissenschaften
BBB	Bonner Biblische Beiträge
BCH	Bulletin de Correspondance Hellénique
BE	Bulletin Épigraphique, in REG
BGU	*Aegyptische Urkunden aus den Koeniglichen (Staatlichen) Museen zu Berlin, Griechische Urkunden*
Bibl	Biblica
BIFAO	Bulletin de l'Institut français d'archéologie orientale
BIOSCS	Bulletin of the International Organization for Septuagint and Cognate Studies
BJPES	Bulletin of the Jewish Palestine Exploration Society
BJRL	Bulletin of the John Rylands Library
BL	British Library
BMC	*Catalogue of the Greek Coins in the British Museum*
BO	Bibliotheca Orientalis
BP	E. G. Kraeling, *The Brooklyn Museum Aramaic Papyri* (1953)
BSAA	Bulletin de la Société d'Archéologie d'Alexandrie
BSOAS	Bulletin of the School of Oriental and African Studies
Bull. arch.	Bulletin Archéologique du Comité des Travaux Historiques et Scientifiques
BWA(N)T	Beiträge zur Wissenschaft vom Alten (und Neuen) Testament
Byz. Z	Byzantinische Zeitschrift
BZ	Biblische Zeitschrift
BZAW	Beihefte zur Zeitschrift für die Alttestamentliche Wissenschaft
BZNW	Beihefte zur Zeitschrift für die Neutestamentliche Wissenschaft
CBQ	Catholic Biblical Quarterly
CCAGr	Catalogus Codicum Astrologorum Graecorum
CCAR	Central Conference of the American Rabbis
CCL	Corpus Christianorum, series Latina
CE	Chronique d'Égypte

CERP	A. H. M. Jones, *Cities of the Eastern Roman Provinces* (²1971)
CG	P. E. Kahle, *The Cairo Geniza* (²1959)
CIG	*Corpus Inscriptionum Graecarum*
CIH	*Corpus Inscriptionum Hebraicarum*
CIHJ	A. Scheiber, *Corpus Inscriptionum Hungariae Judaicarum* (1960)
CIJ	J. B. Frey, *Corpus Inscriptionum Iudaicarum* I–II (1939, 1951)
CIL	*Corpus Inscriptionum Latinarum*
CIRB	I. Struve, *Corpus Inscriptionum Regni Bosporani* (1965)
CIS	*Corpus Inscriptionum Semiticarum*
CJZC	G. Luederitz, *Corpus jüdischer Zeugnisse aus der Cyrenaika* (1983)
CNRS	Centre National de la Recherche Scientifique
CPh	Classical Philology
CPJ	V. Tcherikover, A. Fuks, M. Stern, *Corpus Papyrorum Judaicarum* I–III (1957–64)
CPR	C. Wessely *et al.*, *Corpus Papyrorum Raineri*
CQ	Classical Quarterly
CRAI	Comptes-rendus de l'Académie des Inscriptions et Belles-lettres
CSCO	*Corpus Scriptorum Christianorum Orientalium*
CSEL	*Corpus Scriptorum Ecclesiasticorum Latinorum*
CSHB	*Corpus Scriptorum Historiae Byzantinae*
C–W	L. Cohn, P. Wendland and S. Reiter, *Philonis opera quae supersunt*
DAC(L)	*Dictionnaire d'Archéologie Chrétienne et de Liturgie*
DB	*Dictionnaire de la Bible*
DBS	*Dictionnaire de la Bible, Supplément*
DCB	*Dictionary of Christian Biography*
DF	B. Lifshitz, *Donateurs et fondateurs dans les synagogues juives* (1967)
DJD	*Discoveries in the Judaean Desert*
DOP	Dumbarton Oaks Papers
DSS	G. Vermes, *The Dead Sea Scrolls: Qumran in Perspective* (1977, 1982)
DSSE	G. Vermes, *The Dead Sea Scrolls in English* (1962, ²1975)
DThC	*Dictionnaire de la Théologie Catholique*
DWA	Denkschriften der Wiener Akademie
EB	Estudios Biblicos
EE	A. Dupont-Sommer, *Les écrits esséniens découverts près de la Mer Morte* (1959, ³1964)
EHR	Etudes sur l'Histoire des Religions

EJ	*Encyclopaedia Judaica*
ESJL	B. Z. Wacholder, *Eupolemus: A Study of Judaeo-Greek Literature* (1974)
EThL	Ephemerides Theologicae Lovanienses
EvTh	Evangelische Theologie
FGrH	F. Jacoby, *Die Fragmente der griechischen Historiker*
FHG	I. Müller, *Fragmenta Historicorum Graecorum*
FHJA	C. R. Holladay, *Fragments from Hellenistic Jewish Authors*, I: *Historians* (1983)
FIRA	S. Riccobono, *Fontes Iuris Romani Anteiustiniani*
FJB	Frankfurter Judaistische Beiträge
FPG	A.-M. Denis, *Fragmenta Pseudepigraphorum quae supersunt Graeca* (1970)
FRLANT	*Forschungen zur Religion und Literatur des Alten und Neuen Testaments*
GAQ	J. A. Fitzmyer, *The Genesis Apocryphon of Qumran Cave I: A Commentary* (1966, ²1971)
GCS	*Die Griechischen Christlichen Schriftsteller der ersten drei Jahrhunderte*
GJV	E. Schürer, *Geschichte des jüdischen Volkes im Zeitalter Jesu Christi*
GLAJJ	M. Stern, *Greek and Latin Authors on Jews and Judaism* I–III (1974–84)
GRBS	Greek, Roman and Byzantine Studies
HDB	*Hastings' Dictionary of the Bible*
Hell.	L. Robert, *Hellenica* I–XIII (1940–65)
HERE	*Hastings' Encyclopaedia of Religion and Ethics*
HJ	Historisches Jahrbuch
HSCPh	Harvard Studies in Classical Philology
HThR	Harvard Theological Review
HUCA	Hebrew Union College Annual
HZ	Historische Zeitschrift
IBM	C. T. Newton *et al.*, *The Collection of Ancient Greek Inscriptions in the British Museum*
ICC	*International Critical Commentary*
ID	*Inscriptions de Délos*
IDB	*The Interpreter's Dictionary of the Bible*
IDBS	*The Interpreter's Dictionary of the Bible, Supplementary Volume*
IEJ	Israel Exploration Journal
IG	*Inscriptiones Graecae*
IG Bulg	*Inscriptiones Graecae in Bulgaria Repertae*
IGLS	*Inscriptions grecques et latines de la Syrie*
IGR	R. Cagnat *et al.*, *Inscriptiones Graecae ad Res Romanas Pertinentes*

IGUR	*Inscriptiones Graecae Urbis Romae*
IK	*Inschriften griechischer Städte aus Kleinasien*
ILAlg	*Inscriptions latines de l'Algérie*
ILChV	*Inscriptiones Latinae Christianae Veteres*
ILS	*Inscriptiones Latinae Selectae*
Ins. Cret.	*Inscriptiones Creticae*
IOSCS	International Organization for Septuagint and Cognate Studies
IOSPE	I. Latyschev, *Inscriptiones Antiquae Orae Septentrionalis Ponti Euxini Graecae et Latinae*
IOTG	H. B. Swete and R. Ottley, *Introduction to the Old Testament in Greek* (1920)
IPGAT	A.-M. Denis, *Introduction aux pseudépigraphes grecs d'Ancien Testament* (1970)
Ist. Mitt.	Mitteilungen des Deutschen Archäologischen Instituts, Istanbuler Abteilung
JAC	Jahrbuch für Antike und Christentum
JAOS	Journal of the American Oriental Society
JBL	Journal of Biblical Literature
JBR	Journal of Bible and Religion
JDAI	Jahrbuch des Deutschen Archäologischen Instituts
JE	*The Jewish Encyclopedia*
JEA	Journal of Egyptian Archaeology
JHS	Journal of Hellenic Studies
JIH	A. Scheiber (ed.), *Jewish Inscriptions in Hungary* (1983)
JJP	Journal of Juristic Papyrology
JJS	Journal of Jewish Studies
JLBBM	G. W. E. Nickelsburg, *Jewish Literature between the Bible and the Mishnah* (1981)
JNES	Journal of Near Eastern Studies
JÖAI	Jahrbuch des Österreichischen Archäologischen Instituts
JPFC	S. Safrai and M. Stern (eds.), *The Jewish People in the First Century* I–II (1974–76)
JPOS	Journal of the Palestine Oriental Society
JPTh	Jahrbücher für Protestantische Theologie
JQR	Jewish Quarterly Review
JRAS	Journal of the Royal Asiatic Society
JRS	Journal of Roman Studies
JS	Journal des Savants
JSHRZ	*Jüdische Schriften aus hellenistischer und römischer Zeit*
JSJ	Journal for the Study of Judaism
JSS(t)	Journal of Semitic Studies
JThSt	Journal of Theological Studies

JWSTP	M. E. Stone (ed.), *Jewish Writings of the Second Temple Period* (1984)
JZWL	Jüdische Zeitschrift für Wissenschaft und Leben
KAI	H. Donner and W. Röllig, *Kanaanäische und Aramäische Inschriften* I–II (³1971–6)
LASBF	Liber Annuus Studii Biblici Franciscani
LThK	Lexikon für Theologie und Kirche
MAMA	*Monumenta Asiae Minoris Antiqua*
MDAI	Mitteilungen des Deutschen Archäologischen Instituts
MEFR	Mélanges de l'École française de Rome
MGH	*Monumenta Germaniae Historica*
MGWJ	Monatsschrift für Geschichte und Wissenschaft des Judentums
MPAT	J. A. Fitzmyer and D. J. Harrington, *A Manual of Palestinian Aramaic Texts* (1978)
MQ	L. Moraldi, *I manoscritti di Qumrān* (1971)
MRR	T. R. S. Broughton, *Magistrates of the Roman Republic* I–II
MT	Masoretic Text
MUSJ	Mélanges de l'Université St. Joseph
NA(W)G	Nachrichten der Akademie der Wissenschaften in Göttingen
NC	Numismatic Chronicle
NedThT	Nederlands Theologische Tijdschrift
NESE	Neue Ephemeris für die Semitische Epigraphik
NGGW	Nachrichten von der (Kgl.) Gesellschaft der Wissenschaften zu Göttingen
Not. d. Sc.	Notizie degli Scavi
NRTh	Nouvelle Revue Théologique
NT	Novum Testamentum
NTS(t)	New Testament Studies
NTT	Norsk Teologisk Tidsskrift
ÖAW	Österreichische Akademie der Wissenschaften
OGIS	W. Dittenberger, *Orientis Graeci Inscriptiones Selectae* I–II
OLZ	Orientalische Literaturzeitung
OTP	J. H. Charlesworth, *Old Testament Pseudepigrapha* I (1983)
PA	P. M. Fraser, *Ptolemaic Alexandria* I–III (1972)
PAAJR	Proceedings of the American Academy for Jewish Research
PBJS	G. Vermes, *Post-Biblical Jewish Studies*
PBSR	Papers of the British School at Rome
PCPhS	Proceedings of the Cambridge Philological Society
PEFQSt	Palestine Exploration Fund, Quarterly Statement
PEQ	Palestine Exploration Quarterly
PG	J.-P. Migne, *Patrum Graecorum Cursus Completus*

PGM	K. Preisendanz, *Papyri Graecae Magicae*
P. Hib.	B. P. Grenfell and A. S. Hunt, *The Hibeh Papyri* I (1906)
PIR	*Prosopographia Imperii Romani*
PL	J.-P. Migne, *Patrum Latinorum Cursus Completus*
PMRS	J. H. Charlesworth, *The Pseudepigrapha and Modern Research with a Supplement* (1981)
PRE	*Realencyclopädie für Protestantische Theologie und Kirche*
PSBA	Proceedings of the Society of Biblical Archaeology
PVTG	*Pseudepigrapha Veteris Testamenti Graeca*
QAL	Quaderni di Archeologia della Libia
Q-E	J. Maier and K. Schubert, *Die Qumran-Essener* (1973)
RA	Revue Archéologique
RAC	*Reallexikon für Antike und Christentum*
RB	Revue Biblique
RBibIt	Rivista Biblica Italiana
RBT	*Realencyclopädie für Bibel und Talmud*
RE	Pauly-Wissowa, *Realencyclopädie der classischen Altertumswissenschaft*
REA	Revue des Études Anciennes
REG	Revue des Études Grecques
REJ	Revue des Études Juives
REtSl	Revue des Études Slaves
RGG	*Religion in Geschichte und Gegenwart*
RhM	Rheinisches Museum
RHP(h)R	Revue d'Histoire et de Philosophie Religieuses
RHR	Revue de l'Histoire des Religions
RIU	L. Barkóczi and A. Mócsy, *Die römischen Inschriften Ungarns*
Riv. fil.	Rivista di filologia e d'istruzione pubblica
RN	Revue Numismatique
RPh	Revue de Philologie
RQ	Revue de Qumrân
RQCA	Römische Quartalschrift für Christliche Altertumskunde
RS(c)R	Recherches de Science Religieuse
RSem	Revue sémitique
RSPhTh	Revue des sciences philosophiques et théologiques
RS(t)O(r)	Rivista degli Studi Orientali
RThLouv	Revue Théologique de Louvain
RThPhil	Revue de Théologie et de Philosophie
SAB	Sitzungsberichte der Deutschen Akademie der Wissenschaften zu Berlin
SAM	Sitzungsberichte der Bayerischen Akademie der Wissen- schaften

SAW	Sitzungsberichte der Österreichischen Akademie der Wissenschaften
SB	F. Preisigke, *Sammelbuch griechischer Urkunden aus Ägypten*
SBFLA	Studii Biblici Franciscani Liber Annuus
SBL	Society of Biblical Literature
SC	*Sources Chrétiennes*
SCI	Scripta Classica Israelica
SCO	Studi Classici e Orientali
SEG	Supplementum Epigraphicum Graecum
SEHHW	M. Rostovtzeff, *Social and Economic History of the Hellenistic World*
SIG	W. Dittenberger, *Sylloge Inscriptionum Graecarum*[3]
SMS	S. Jellicoe, *The Septuagint and Modern Study* (1968)
SNTS(MS)	Studiorum Novi Testamenti Societas (Monograph Series)
SP	Studia Patristica
ST	*Studi e Testi*
STJ	G. Vermes, *Scripture and Tradition in Judaism* (1961, [2]1973)
Str.-B.	H. L. Strack and P. Billerbeck, *Kommentar zum Neuen Testament aus Talmud und Midrasch* (1924–28)
StTh	Studia Theologica
SVT	Supplements to Vetus Testamentum
TAM	*Tituli Asiae Minoris*
TAPhA	Transactions of the American Philological Association
TDNT	*Theological Dictionary of the New Testament*
Theol. Bl.	Theologische Blätter
ThLZ	Theologische Literaturzeitung
ThQ	Theologische Quartalschrift
ThR	Theologische Revue
ThStKr	Theologische Studien und Kritiken
ThStud	Theological Studies
ThWNT	*Theologisches Wörterbuch zum Neuen Testament*
ThZ	Theologische Zeitschrift
TLS	Times Literary Supplement
TQ	J. Carmignac, *Les textes de Qumrân* I–II (1961–63)
TQHD	E. Lohse, *Die Texte von Qumran hebräisch und deutsch* (1964, [2]1971)
TS	Y. Yadin, *The Temple Scroll* I–II (1983)
TTM	J. Maier, *Die Texte vom Toten Meer* I–II (1960)
TU	*Texte und Untersuchungen*
VC	Vigiliae Christianae
VDI	Vestnik Drevne Istorii
VT	Vetus Testamentum
VTS	Vetus Testamentum, Supplement

WUNT	Wissenschaftliche Untersuchungen zum Neuen Testament
WZKM	Wiener Zeitschrift zur Kunde des Morgenlandes
YCS	Yale Classical Studies
ZAW	Zeitschrift für die Alttestamentliche Wissenschaft
ZDPV	Zeitschrift des Deutschen Palästina-Vereins
ZKTh	Zeitschrift für Katholische Theologie
ZNW	Zeitschrift für die Neutestamentliche Wissenschaft
ZPE	Zeitschrift für Papyrologie und Epigraphik
ZRGG	Zeitschrift für Religions- und Geistesgeschichte
ZSS	Zeitschrift der Savigny-Stiftung: Romanistische Abteilung
ZTK	Zeitschrift für Theologie und Kirche
ZWTh	Zeitschrift für Wissenschaftliche Theologie

§33B. JEWISH LITERATURE OF WHICH THE ORIGINAL LANGUAGE IS UNCERTAIN

It has been shown that the Jewish literature of undoubted Greek origin has much in common with the texts composed originally in Semitic languages. The Greek writings were affected in certain ways by linguistic nuances which resulted from the use of Greek language and by the characteristics of the Greek genres in which some of their ideas were couched, but for much of the surviving literature whose Jewish authorship cannot be doubted it is not possible to assign the text to any one original language. These texts have accordingly been grouped together separately here.

Many criteria have been put forward for establishing the original language of these works but none is conclusive. Almost all the texts now survive only in Greek and translations from the Greek, a fact that is due entirely to their preservation by the early Church. The hazards of assuming Greek composition because of a text's survival in Greek have been highlighted by the finds at Qumran of Semitic versions of some texts previously known only in Greek, e.g. Tobit. The non-appearance of Qumranic material in later Jewish Semitic sources, i.e. the rabbinic texts, similarly warns against taking the silence of later Jewish sources about other texts as an indication of the Greek origin of those texts. It should be clear that identification of Palestine or the diaspora as the place of origin, even if it is possible without reference to language, is in itself only a vague indication of the language of composition, since Greek works were certainly written in Palestine and Semitic works were produced outside, especially in Syria and Mesopotamia. Identification of original language by the genre of the work is similarly unsafe. The compositions which are clearly Greek and those which are clearly Semitic in origin are in many cases too close in content and style for the attribution of, e.g., all apocalyptic writings of unknown origin to a Semitic author or all historical narrative to a Greek author. The distinction, for instance, between Greek historical writing and Semitic midrash is not in practice clear cut. Nor are more specific arguments much better. Identification of Semitic idioms in a Jewish text can rarely in itself prove a Semitic original of that text. Many such phrases are in fact imitations of the influential style of the Septuagint which, however much it took from the common Greek of the period, was nonetheless sufficiently shaped by Semitisms for it to be reasonable to posit the existence, at least in religious contexts, of a Jewish Greek which a non-Jew would find hard to comprehend (see above, §33A.I, note 25;

N. Turner, 'The Unique Character of Biblical Greek', VT 5 (1955), pp. 208–13). It is impossible to know whether other influential Bible translations, such as that of Aquila in which the Semitisms are even more striking, had the same effect on the language of Jews writing in Greek. It is anyway likely, though it cannot be proved, that non-Septuagintal Semitisms were in common use at least among Jews in areas such as Palestine, where bilingualism in Greek and a Semitic language was common. Doubtless the extent to which Jewish Greek was Semitized varied from area to area and indeed from one period to another. Nor can the existence of word plays in the extant Greek texts be taken as a decisive criterion since they may always have been inserted by an imaginative translator of a Semitic original (see below, p. 724, on the story of Susanna).

Reliable criteria for establishing the original language of a work are therefore very limited and often insufficient. A Semitic original may reasonably be posited when the extant Greek can *only* be made comprehensible by hypothesizing an original Semitic text which has been mistranslated, or when variants in the Greek texts are best understood by positing different translations of a Semitic word or phrase. Syntactical analysis demonstrates that the use of particular Greek idioms, in particular the use of prepositions, varies widely between the generality of texts known to be translated from Semitic languages and the generality of texts known to be original Greek compositions, cf. R. A. Martin, 'Some Syntactical Criteria of Translation Greek', VT 10 (1960), pp. 295–310; *idem, Syntactical Evidence of Semitic Sources in Greek Documents* (1974). However, such usage can only be a valid criterion when used over a text large enough to make the statistical variation noted significant; in particular, since occasional atypical use of such prepositions does occur, the criterion should not be treated as absolute for short passages in composite texts (see below, p. 724, on the additions to Daniel). These problems are naturally amplified when the texts concerned do not even survive in Greek but in translation from Greek into another language, e.g. 2 (Slavonic) Enoch.

For none of the works treated in this section can a Greek or Semitic origin be affirmed with certainty.

I. Revision and Completion of Biblical Literature

It has been noted (above, vol. II, pp. 314–21) that it is likely that *a* canon of the Hebrew Bible had already been fixed by the middle of the second century B.C. when the book of Daniel was incorporated into it, and that this canon was probably the same as the present one by the time of Josephus in the late first century A.D. However, the number of texts not incorporated into the present canon but found in Hebrew or Aramaic at Qumran and Masada leaves open the possibility that Jews writing in Semitic languages before Josephus, and before the establishment of a proto-Masoretic text as authoritative soon after Josephus, composed their own revisions of and additions to the canonical books. If so, they failed to achieve acceptance of their work within the Hebrew canon, for all their texts survive only in Greek or in translations almost certainly made from the Greek. It is therefore impossible to know whether these books were composed by such Semitic authors or by Jews writing in Greek. This latter possibility remains that most often advocated by scholars, but this is primarily due to the possibly fortuitous fact that the works to be considered here were preserved by Greek-speaking Christians.

If the common view is correct that Greek-speaking Jews *were* responsible for the additions to the biblical canon, it must be assumed of them too that they wrote before the second century A.D. Their favourable reception of Aquila's Greek translation of the Bible (see above, pp. 493–9) suggests that from this date they relied strictly on the same text and canon as that used by Hebrew speakers. This is confirmed by Origen's remarks in his letter to Iulius Africanus. He speaks here of all the parts of the Old Testament canon which are lacking in Hebrew, specifically of the additions to Daniel and Esther and the books of Tobit and Judith, as though they had *never* belonged to the Jewish canon, Greek or Hebrew. He considers them as the exclusive property of Christians and says simply that the Jews rejected them, without distinguishing between Hebrew Jews and Greek Jews (*Epist. ad African.* 4(2)–6(3); 19(13) (ed. De Lange, SC 302, pp. 524–8, 562)). Hence, at that time the Hebrew canon had acquired absolute validity for Greek-speaking Jews as well, though it is possible that Origen preserved traces of a slightly different *order* for the Jewish Greek canon in the mid-third century A.D.[308]

Among all Jews, then, the boundaries between canonical and non-canonical books had probably remained fluid during the two centuries B.C. and the first century A.D. when the canon was finally fixed. Hence they still added to the collection of holy writings a large number of documents which originated in the last two centuries B.C., or even in the first century A.D. Some of these writings had probably originally been written in Hebrew, whether in Palestine or elsewhere, and were later translated into Greek; others were probably original Greek compositions. That they were widely accepted as holy writings

308. N. de Lange, *Origen and the Jews*(1976), pp. 49–55; the lists preserved in Eusebius, *Hist. eccl.* vi 25, 2, and Hilary, *Tractatus super Psalmos* 15 (PL IX, 241), suggest that II Esdras and the Letter of Jeremiah were also included in the Jewish canon, but this may be due to patristic carelessness, cf. de Lange, *op. cit.*, p. 53.

among Greek-speaking Jews before the first century A.D. is clear from the fact that the Christian canon of the Old Testament had a wider and more fluctuating scope from the start than the later Jewish canon, and this can only be explained by the fact that Christianity had received the canon in precisely this form from earlier Judaism. Therefore, at the time of Christian origins, some Jews also included in their collection of Scriptures the books which are customarily called 'apocryphal', following the example of Jerome, because they were lacking in the later Hebrew canon. It should however never be forgotten that a fixed boundary generally did not exist before the end of the first century A.D.

As well as adding new documents to the Scriptures, some Jews in this period also produced midrashic revisions of the writings that already existed, in the same way that, in the earlier Hebrew Bible, the Chronicler had revised the history of the book of Kings. But, besides the composition of such separate legends placed alongside the scriptural text, in some cases it seems that the canon was sufficiently fluid in this period for large interpolations to be inserted within the text itself. Nonetheless most of the books written by Jews on religious matters in this period were never accorded scriptural authority, and have been discussed elsewhere. Here only the following are grouped together: (1) the revisions and completions of writings of which older forms became canonical in the later Jewish canon (Ezra, Esther, Daniel, the Prayer of Manasseh, which is an addition to 2 Chr. 33), and (2) certain books originally intended as holy writings and, since they were revered by the early Church as authoritative, probably accepted as such also by some Greek-speaking Jews before A.D. 100 (Baruch, the Epistle of Jeremiah).[309]

1. The Greek Ezra (also called III Ezra or I Esdras)

Of the Hebrew and Aramaic canonical Ezra there exists not only a Greek translation, but also another version in Greek covering most of the same events and differing from the canonical Ezra partly by transpositions, partly by the inclusion of more material and partly through omissions. Some of the additional material is also found in the Hebrew Nehemiah and Chronicles, but some is peculiar to I Esdras. This text did not form part of the Hebrew canon but was included in the LXX (as Esdras α′) and the Vulgate (as III Esdras); I Esdras is the usual term in the English collections of the Apocrypha and will therefore be used here. The following summary of the composition of I Esdras indicates the relation between them, though the equivalences noted are not exact.

---

309. On all these writings, see the general introductions to the Apocrypha, especially R. H. Pfeiffer, *History of N.T. Times* (1949); B. Metzger, *An Introduction to the Apocrypha* (1957).

Chap. 1 = 2 Chr. 35–6: restoration of the Temple worship under Josiah (639–609) and history of Josiah's successors until the destruction of the Temple (586).

Chap. 2:1–15 = Ezr. 1 : Cyrus permits the return of the exiles in the first year of his reign (537) and releases the Temple vessels.

Chap. 2:16–30 = Ezr. 4:7–24a : Artaxerxes (464–425) forbids the continuation of the rebuilding of (the Temple and) the walls of Jerusalem, because of a complaint against the Jews.

Chap. 3:1–5:6 : independent: Zerubbabel, after the wager of the three young bodyguards (3:1–4:63), gains the favour of Darius (521–485) and obtains his permission to repatriate the exiles.

Chap. 5:7–73 = Ezr. 2:1–4:5 : a list of those who return with Zerubbabel, Zerubbabel's activities, and interruption of the building of the Temple in the time of Cyrus (536–529) until the second year of Darius (520). (Cf. also the parallels with Neh. 7:6–73a.)

Chap. 6–7 = Ezr. 4:24b–6:22 : resumption and completion of the building of the Temple during the sixth year of Darius (516).

Chap. 8:1–9:36 = Ezr. 7–10 : return of Ezra with a column of exiles during the seventh year of Artaxerxes (458); beginning of Ezra's activities.

Chap. 9:37–55 = Neh. 7:73b–8:13 : public reading of the Law by Ezra.

I Esdras differs therefore from canonical Ezra in the following ways: (1) canonical Ezra 4:7–24 is found in an earlier place; (2) I Esdras 3:1–5:6 is a passage of unknown origin found only here; (3) 2 Chr. 35–6 is prefixed to the book; (4) Neh. 7:73–8:13 is appended at the end of the book. The book is chronologically very confused. The passage in canonical Ezra 4:7–24 is chronologically out of place, but it is even more incongruous in the context given to it in I Esdras 2:16–30; and the references to the Temple in 2:18–20, where Ezra only mentions the rebuilding of the city walls, make the incongruity even worse. The history in I Esdras goes backwards in time: events are ascribed first (2:16–30) to the reign of Artaxerxes, who only became king in 465 B.C., then (3:1–5:6) to the reign of Darius, and last (5:7–73) to the reign of Cyrus. In this last section the chronological incompetence of the author becomes finally clear from his mention that Zerubbabel returned with the exiles under Cyrus (cf. 5:8, 67–73), even though the story in 3:1–5:6 has explained in detail how Zerubbabel received permission to return through the particular favour of Darius.

In trying to decide how I Esdras came to be written in its present form, it is of primary importance to understand the relation of the text (1) to the other Greek version of the Ezra story (Esdras β′ in the manuscripts of the LXX, which follows the masoretic Hebrew text very closely) and to the LXX version of Hebrew Chronicles (*Paralipomena*);

and, even more importantly, (2) to the masoretic Hebrew text of Chronicles, Ezra and Nehemiah, which should probably be ascribed to a single author.[310] Difficulties arise in the investigation not least because it is not certain whether I Esdras is complete as it stands or is a fragment of a larger work. It may be that neither the opening nor the ending was originally in its present form. Further, the masoretic Hebrew text is itself confused, and its own chronological failings may either be due to the incompetence or ignorance of the author, or to his desire to arrange material thematically rather than chronologically. So, for example, the incorrect placing of the section in Ezra 4:7–24, already discussed above, may reflect not a mistake but rather a desire to summarize in one place all the material relevant to the author's current theme of the Jews' collisions with local imperial authority in a number of reigns. Furthermore, criticism of I Esdras on the grounds of lack of chronological accuracy is itself dubious when knowledge of the general history of the period is itself dependent on such unreliable sources.[311]

Despite these problems some points can be made with some certainty about the origins of I Esdras. It seems certain that the text is not a revision or reorganization of Esdras β', the literal LXX translation of the masoretic text of Ezra (cf. E. Nestlé, *Marginalien und Materialen* (1893), pp. 23–9). The options for explaining I Esdras are therefore restricted to the following two main possibilities.

(1) The author possessed the masoretic Hebrew text of Chronicles, Ezra and Nehemiah, or a Hebrew text very similar to it, from which he then compiled sections to form a new book in order to further some theological or other purpose of his own.[312] Quite what that purpose was

310. Single authorship of all these books is usually assumed, cf., for example, R. J. Coggins, *The First and Second Books of the Chronicles* (1976), p. 3 ; *idem, The Books of Ezra and Nehemiah* (1976), pp. 1–3. See, however, the strong arguments for the books of Ezra and Nehemiah as *not* the work of the Chronicler in S. Japhet, 'The Supposed Common Authorship of Chronicles and Ezra-Nehemiah Investigated Anew', VT 18 (1968), pp. 330–71 and H. G. M. Williamson, *Israel in the Books of Chronicles* (1977), pp. 7–82. For a summary of some of the arguments, see M. A. Throntveit, 'Linguistic analysis and the question of authorship in Chronicles, Ezra and Nehemiah', VT 32 (1982), pp. 201–16.

311. For an account of the sources and a general history of the period, see M. Noth, *A History of Israel* (²1960), pp. 300–45 ; G. Widengren in J. H. Hayes and J. M. Miller, eds., *Israelite and Judaean History* (1977), chap. 9 ; W. D. Davies and L. Finkelstein, eds., *The Cambridge History of Judaism* I (1984) ; for suggestions that I Esdras should be used as a primary source for *rewriting* that history, see below, note 316.

312. For the nature of the translation, which does not set out to be literal, see E. Bayer, *Das dritte Buch Esdras und sein Verhältnis zu den Büchern Esra-Nehemia* (1911), pp. 11–86 ; B. Walde, *Die Esdrasbücher der Septuaginta (Ihr gegenseitiges Verhältnis untersucht)* (1913), pp. 15–26. This explanation of the book is accepted by Coggins in R. J. Coggins and M. A. Knibb, *The First and Second Books of Esdras* (1979), pp. 5–6. The possibility that the compiler of I Esdras used an already existing Greek translation of the Hebrew cannot be ruled out, cf. O. Eissfeldt, *An Introduction to the O.T., etc.* (1965), p. 575 ; cf. Jellicoe, SMS, p. 291, who points out that all trace of this hypothetical earlier translation is lost.

is not entirely clear. His main aim may have been to bring together from older works a history of the Temple from the last period of the legal cultus until its reconstruction and the reinstitution of the prescribed worship, perhaps as part of a polemic against the foundation of other temples by Jews outside Jerusalem (Attridge). A second aim would be the attempt to magnify Ezra, assuming that the present abrupt ending of I Esdras is deliberate and that the author did not intend to say anything further about Nehemiah.[313] In this case, the chronological errors are due to the author's lack of concern as much as his incompetence, but it is also quite possible that he had *intended* to try to *clarify* the confused canonical account but made things worse through ignorance. For example, a Jew in the last centuries B.C. might be sufficiently ignorant to believe Artaxerxes to have ruled between Cyrus and Darius.[314] A deliberate thematic excerpting of the Hebrew text in this way was more probably done by a Hebrew compiler in the first place, so that the present Greek version would be a translation of an earlier Semitic compilation, but it is naturally impossible to prove the existence of such an original.[315] Since the unique section 3:1–5:3 clearly did not originate with the Greek author of I Esdras (see below), the original language of that section, which is itself disputed (see below), will not be decisive in fixing the original language of the compilation as a whole. In any case it is possible that, even if I Esdras is secondary to the masoretic Hebrew text from the literary point of view, it may still contain some superior textual readings for correcting the MT of Ezra and Nehemiah. Further, some of the extra material found in I Esdras and not in the MT may derive, even on this hypothesis, not from the efforts of the author of I Esdras but from his use of a different text of Ezra and Nehemiah.

(2) The second possibility is in marked contrast to the first in so far as it affirms the independent importance of I Esdras as a witness to the original Hebrew text of the Chronicler, and therefore asserts a great value for the text in clarifying the history of the period concerned. According to this view, I Esdras constitutes a separate translation of part of the original Hebrew text of the work of the Chronicler, which should thus have at least equal status to the masoretic text.[316] Some

---

313. Cf. J. M. Myers, *I and II Esdras* (1974), pp. 9–10, who points out correctly that Ezra and Nehemiah traditions developed quite separately within Judaism in the last centuries B.C. This is seen most clearly perhaps in Josephus. Coggins, *op. cit.*, p. 74, points out that there is no further material dealing with Ezra in the Masoretic Hebrew text. For the ending of I Esdras as possibly not intentional, see below, note 325.

314. Coggins, *op. cit.*, pp. 5, 21.

315. Coggins, *op. cit.*, p. 6, prefers a Greek original.

316. See most recently K.-F. Pohlmann, *Studien zum dritten Esra* (1970), with references to older scholarship, including especially the articles by H. H. Howorth which are cited below in the bibliography. For an attempt to use I Esdras as an important historical

scholars have gone further, affirming that I Esdras preserves a much better text than canonical Hebrew-Aramaic Ezra and that the canonical text was produced *from* I Esdras, by the omission of I Esdras 3:1–5:6 and other changes, at some time after Josephus, who knew only I Esdras.[317] In favour of this view may be cited the comparatively bad later Greek of the present LXX translation of Ezra (i.e. Esdras β′) compared to the good second century B.C. Greek of I Esdras,[318] though Howorth's conclusion that Esdras α′ was the work of Theodotion or Symmachus is pure hypothesis.[319] The likelihood of I Esdras reflecting part of an early Hebrew version of the Chronicler's work which existed simultaneously with but separate from the masoretic tradition has been increased by the discovery at Qumran of evidence for the contemporaneous acceptance of a plurality of textual traditions for the biblical books.[320] Nonetheless, any such view is only tenable if it is admitted that the Semitic original of I Esdras was not simply an excerpt from the Chronicler's work but had itself undergone a number of revisions which could therefore account for its hopeless chronology,[321] and furthermore that there is no reason to posit that I Esdras formed part of a translation of the *whole* of the Chronicler's work extant in the author's day.[322]

The peculiarities of the extant version, such as the clumsy addition of 'and this was Zerubbabel' at 4:13, cannot be accounted for solely by positing the use of an early recension of the Chronicler's work to which the Nehemiah material had not yet been added.[323] The suggestion by Torrey that I Esdras was literally cut out of a copy of a Greek translation of the original version written by the Chronicler, and that it

source, see R. W. Klein, 'Old Readings in I Esdras: The List of Returnees from Babylon', HThR 62 (1969), pp. 99–107; F. M. Cross, 'A Reconstruction of the Judaean Restoration', JBL 94 (1975), pp. 4–18, and further examples in Myers, *op. cit.*, pp. 15–16.

317. This was the view of Howorth (see bibliography) and of C. C. Torrey, 'A Revised View of First Esdras', *Louis Ginzberg Jubilee Volume* (1945), p. 396.

318. Jellicoe, SMS, p. 291; Myers, *op. cit.*, p. 6. The use of I Esdras by Josephus in preference to the LXX translation of the Masoretic text is irrelevant for the dating of the latter translation. It may well have existed but been ignored by Josephus because he preferred the superior Greek style of I Esdras, cf. Metzger, *op. cit.*, p. 12.

319. C. C. Torrey, *Ezra Studies* (1910), p. 17.

320. F. M. Cross, Jnr., *The Ancient Library of Qumran and Modern Biblical Studies*, rev. ed. (1961), p. 41, on *4QSam*ᵃ; Vermes, DSS, pp. 206–8.

321. So C. C. Torrey, 'A Revised View of First Esdras', *Louis Ginzberg Jubilee Volume* (1945), pp. 397–401, where the evidence for, and a history of, these detailed revisions is given.

322. Perhaps the strongest argument against I Esdras as simply a section of an original translation of the whole of the work of the Chronicler is the fact that the extant Greek of the *Paralipomena* in the LXX was composed before 150 B.C. and it is implausible that two full Greek versions of the same text were produced at so early a date, cf. Williamson, *op. cit.*, pp. 20–1.

323. See e.g. S. Mowinckel, *Studien zu dem Buche Ezra-Nehemiah*, 3 vols. (1964–5).

is wrong to expect the compiler to have had any purpose beyond that of the Chronicler himself, is therefore to be rejected.[324] It is quite possible that the same purpose should be ascribed to a compiler of I Esdras from *non*-masoretic materials as was ascribed to such a compiler when it was assumed that he had used the masoretic text as his basis,[325] but it is perhaps safer to state that if I Esdras is a translation of a text of unknown extent excerpted from an unknown text, its purpose is now beyond full recall.

The origin of the section 3:1–5:6, the story of the three bodyguards, is no more sure than that of the rest of the book. It is almost certain that it did not originate with either the Chronicler or the compiler of I Esdras (assuming that I Esdras is indeed an independent compilation[326]), since it stands in direct contradiction to the rest of the narrative, to which it is only uneasily connected by 5:4–6. The original language of the section cannot be determined, though, if the story is Persian in origin, it was presumably Aramaic.[327] The story was probably of non-Jewish origin but adapted by a Jewish author.

With regard to the date of the work, it can be stated firmly that it was composed before Josephus, who used the book in *c.* A.D. 90, cf. *Ant.* xi 1–5 (1–158), and probably before the first century B.C., because of the character of the Greek text which suggests composition in the second century B.C. (see above). Possible dependence of I Esdras on the book of Daniel may suggest a date for the text after 165 B.C.[328] However, if the arguments for a Semitic original are accepted, any date back to the time of the Chronicler would be quite possible. Since I

---

324. Torrey, *art. cit.* (note 321), p. 395.

325. This denial of Torrey's view does not require the assertion that the present text of I Esdras was original to the book. It is quite *possible* that, even if the text was a secondary compilation from the Chronicler's work, it originally continued further into the history of Nehemiah, and our present text is only a fragment of that larger work, but that cannot now be decided. Cf. Williamson, *op. cit.*, pp. 12–36. K.-F. Pohlmann, *Studien zum dritten Esra* (1970), argues that originally I Esdras preserved both the order and the ending of the Chronicler's work, extending therefore to approximately the end of Nehemiah 8, but that the original end of I Esdras has been lost. Against this, see H. G. M. Williamson, 'The composition of Ezra i–vi', JThSt 34 (1983), pp. 1–8.

326. For the evidence that it is interpolated, see R. Laqueur, 'Ephorus', Hermes 46 (1911), pp. 168–72. H. Howorth, 'A Criticism of the Sources', Transactions of the Ninth International Congress of Orientalists II (1893), pp. 68–85, argued that it was an integral part of the Chronicler's original work; W. Th. In der Smitten, 'Zur Pagenerzählung im 3. Esra (3 Esr. III 1-V 6)', VT 22 (1972), pp. 492–5, holds that the story was interpolated by the compiler of I Esdras himself.

327. So R. H. Pfeiffer, *Introduction to the Old Testament* (1948), p. 251; *contra*, O. Eissfeldt, *An Introduction to the O.T., etc.* (1965), p. 575, who thinks a Greek original more likely. Cf. F. Zimmermann, 'The Story of the Three Guardsmen', JQR n.s. 54 (1963/4), pp. 179–200; J. L. Crenshaw, 'The contest of Darius' Guards', in B. O. Long, ed., *Images of Man and God* (1981), pp. 74–88.

328. Eissfeldt, *op. cit.*, p. 576.

Esdras became accepted into the LXX, an Egyptian provenance is likely but cannot be proved.[329]

Josephus, *Ant.* xi 1–5 (1–158), entirely follows the course of I Esdras, and to some extent its vocabulary and phraseology. This may be because of the superiority of its Greek style (B. M. Metzger, *An Introduction to the Apocrypha* (1957), p. 12). For example, he places the contents of I Esdras 2:15–25 and 3:1–5:6 at the same place and in the same order, interpolated between the contents of canonical Ezra chapters one and two (*Ant.* xi 2–3 (19–74)). He does not do this however without his customary attempt at clarifying the confused historical account. He changes Artaxerxes, who appears in I Esdras at a totally impossible place, into Cambyses, thus producing a plausible sequence: Cyrus, Cambyses, Darius. He emends another historical error in I Esdras by omitting the reappearance of Cyrus after Darius but implying that the return of the exiles first occurred under Darius. Josephus thus establishes the correct order of the Persian kings, but at a price, since his account as a whole is even more historically inaccurate than that in I Esdras. Cf. on the relation of Josephus to I Esdras, K.-F. Pohlmann, *Studien zum dritten Esra* (1970), pp. 74–126; Williamson, *op. cit.*, pp. 22–9; S. Mowinckel, *Studien zu dem Buche Ezra-Nehemiah* I (1964), pp. 25–8.

In the Christian Church, as well, this book was apparently used from the start and generally. Clement of Alexandria, *Strom.* i 21, 124: Zerubbabel 'having by his wisdom overcome his opponents, and obtained leave from Darius for the rebuilding of Jerusalem, returned with Esdras to his native land', which can only refer to I Esdras 3–4. Origen, *Comment. in John.* vi 1 (GCS, Origen IV, p. 107): καὶ κατὰ τοὺς Ἔσδρα δὲ χρόνους, ὅτε νικᾷ ἡ ἀλήθεια τὸν οἶνον καὶ τὸν ἐχθρὸν βασιλέα καὶ τὰς γυναῖκας, ἀνοικοδομεῖται ὁ ναὸς τῷ θεῷ (cf. I Esdr. 4:33 ff.). *Idem, In Josuam homil.* ix 10 (GCS Origen VII, p. 357): 'et nos dicamus, sicut in Esdra scriptum est, quia: "a te, Domine, est victoria, et ego tuus servus; benedictus es Deus veritatis"' (I Esdr. 4:59–60). Cyprian, *Epist.* lxxiv 9: 'Et apud Hesdram veritas vicit, sicut scriptum est: "Veritas manet et invalescit in aeternum et vivit et optinet in saecula saeculorum etc."' (I Esdr. 4:38–40). For references in later Church Fathers, see J. M. Myers, *I and II Esdras* (1974), pp. 17–18. In the Vulgate the work was relegated to an appendix following the judgement of Jerome.

The book is sometimes described as the *first* Book of Esdras in the Greek manuscripts, sometimes as the *third* Book of Ezra, the canonical books of Ezra and Nehemiah being counted as first and second

---

329. Myers, *op. cit.*, pp. 13–14, points to linguistic parallels in the Egyptian papyri of the second century B.C.

(Jerome, *Praef. in version. libr. Ezrae*, PL xxviii, 1472), and similarly in the Vulgate.

The most important Greek manuscripts are Vaticanus and Alexandrinus, because Sinaiticus does not contain this book. The text in Alexandrinus is much superior. On the editions, cf. above, p. 490; A. E. Brooke, N. McLean, and H. St. J. Thackeray, *The O.T. in Greek according to ... Codex Vaticanus, etc.* II, part iv, *I Esdras, Ezra-Nehemiah* (1935), pp. 557–603; S. Tedesche, *A Critical Edition of I Esdras* (Diss. Yale, 1928); and especially R. Hanhart, *Esdrae liber I* (1974).

Cf. on textual criticism:

Moulton, W. J., 'Ueber die Ueberlieferung und den textkritischen Werth des dritten Esrabuchs', ZAW 19 (1899), pp. 209–58; 20 (1900), pp. 1–35.

Riessler, P., 'Der textkritische Wert des dritten Esdrabuches', BZ 5 (1907), pp. 146–58.

Torrey, C. C., 'The Greek Versions of Chronicles, Ezra and Nehemiah', PSBA 25 (1903), pp. 139–40.

Torrey, C. C., 'Apparatus for the Textual Criticism of Chronicles-Ezra-Nehemiah', *O.T. and Semitic Studies in Memory of W. R. Harper* II (1908), pp. 53–112.

Jahn, C., *Die Bücher Esra (A und B) und Nehemia text-kritisch untersucht* (1909).

Bayer, E., *Das dritte Buch Esdras und sein Verhältnis zu den Büchern Esra-Nehemia* (1911).

Jacob, A., *Septuagintastudien zu Ezra* (Diss. Breslau, 1912).

Walde, B., *Die Esrabücher der Septuaginta* (1913).

Bewer, J. A., *Der Text des Buches Ezra. Beiträge zu seiner Wiederherstellung* (1922).

Allgeier, A., 'Beobachtungen am Septuagintatext der Bücher Esdras und Nehemias', Bibl. 22 (1941), pp. 227–51.

Allrik, H. L., 'I Esdras according to Codex B and A as appearing in Zerubbabel's List in I Esdras 5, 8–23', ZAW 66 (1954), pp. 272–92.

Hanhart, R., *Text und Textgeschichte des I. Esrabuches* (1974).

Concordance

Muraoka, T., *A Greek-Hebrew/Aramaic Index to I Esdras* (1984).

Ancient translations: (1) Old Latin, preserved in two recensions, one in the manuscripts and editions of the Vulgate, the other e.g. in *Codex Colbertinus 3703*. Both texts are in P. Sabatier, *Bibliorum sacrorum Latinae versiones antiquae* III (1749) (in the appendix following the N.T., as in the Vulgate). Berger identified five manuscripts of the second (older) recension which had been given by Sabatier from *Codex Colbertinus* (Berger, *Notices et extraits des manuscrits de la Bibliothèque nationale et autres bibliotheques* XXXIV.2 (1893), p. 143). Cf. also Ph. Thielmann, SAM 1899, pt. 2, p. 240. (2) Syriac, on which cf. above, p. 184. For fragments of the Syro-Hexaplaric version, cf. C. C. Torrey, AJSL 23 (1906), pp. 65–74. This book is not included in the large Milan manuscript of the Peshitta. (3) Ethiopic, ed. by Dillmann, *Biblia Vet. Test. aethiopica* V (1894).

For exegetical works in general, cf. the following:

Lupton, J. H., in H. Wace, *The Speaker's Commentary, The Apocrypha* I (1888).

Stählin, O., 'Die Hellenistisch-Jüdische Litteratur', in W. v. Christ, O. Stählin and W.

Schmidt, *Geschichte der Griechischen Litteratur etc.*[6] II.1 (1920), pp. 535–656.
Bousset, W., and Gressmann, H., *Die Religion des Judentums im Späthellenistischen Zeitalter* (³1926), pp. 6–52.
Moore, G. F., *Judaism in the First Centuries of the Christian Era* I (1927), pp. 125–216; III (1930), pp. 40–60.
Oesterley, W. O. E., and T. H. Robinson, *A History of Israel* II (1932), pp. 111–41.
Oesterley, W. O. E., *An Introduction to the Books of the Apocrypha* (1935), pp. 133–41.
Pfeiffer, R. H., *History of N.T. Times* (1949), pp. 233–57, bibliography, p. 534.
Torrey, C. C., *The Apocryphal Literature, A Brief Introduction* (1945), pp. 43–54.
Zeitlin, S., 'Jewish Apocryphal Literature', JQR 40 (1949/50), pp. 223–50.
Metzger, B. M., *An Introduction to the Apocrypha* (1957), pp. 11–19.
Brockington, *A Critical Introduction to the Apocrypha* (1961), pp. 13–20.

Commentaries

(See general commentaries on Ezra and Nehemiah as well as the following:)
Guthe, H., in E. Kautsch, APAT I, pp. 1–23.
Cook, S. A., 'I Esdras', in Charles, APOT I, pp. 1–58.
Riessler, P., *Altjüd. Schrift.* (1928), pp. 247–54, 1281 ff.
Rudolph, W., *Esra und Nehemia samt 3-Esra* (1949).
Myers, J. M., *I and II Esdras* (1974).
Coggins, R. J., and M. A. Knibb, *The First and Second Books of Esdras* (1979).
Pohlmann, K.-F., *3. Esra-Buch* (JSHRZ I.5) (1980).

Bibliography

Treuenfels, A., 'Ueber das apokryphische Buch Esra', Fürsts Lit. des Orients (1850), nos. 15–18, 40–9; (1851), nos. 7–10.
Bissell, E. C., *The First Book of Esdras, Bibliotheca sacra* (1877), pp. 209–28; reprinted in Bissell, *The Apocrypha of the O.T.* (1880), pp. 62 ff.
Büchler, A., 'Das apokryphische Esrabuch', MGWJ 41 (1897), pp. 1–16, 49–66, 97–103.
Nestle, E., *Marginalien und Materialen* (1893).
Howorth, H. H., 'The Real Character and the Importance of the First Book of Esdras', The Academy (1893), pp. 13, 60, 106, 174, 326, 524.
Howorth, H. H., 'A Criticism of the Sources and the Relative Importance and Value of the Canonical Book of Ezra and the Apocryphal Book Known as Esdras I', Transactions of the Ninth International Congress of Orientalists, held in London, 1892 II (1893), pp. 68–85.
Howorth, H. H., 'Some Unconventional Views on the Text of the Bible. I: The Apocryphal Book Esdras A and the Septuagint', PSBA 23 (1901), pp. 147–59; 'II: The Chronology and Order of Events in Esdras A, Compared with and Preferred to those in the Canonical Ezra', *ibid.*, 305–30; 'III: The Hexapla and Tetrapla of Origen and the Light they Throw on the Books of Esdras A and B', PSBA 24 (1902), pp. 147–72; 'IV: The Septuaginta Text of Nehemiah', pp. 332–40; 25 (1903), pp. 15–22, 90–8; 'V: The Genealogies and Lists in Nehemiah', 26 (1904), pp. 25–31, 63–9, 94–100; 'VI: Chronicles', 27 (1905), pp. 267–78; 'VII: Daniel and Chronicles', 29 (1907), pp. 31 ff.; 'The Modern Roman Canon and the Book of Esdras A', JThSt 7 (1906), pp. 343–54.
Thackeray, H. St. J., 'First Book of Esdras', HDB I (1898), cols. 758–63.
Volz, P., 'The Greek Ezra', EB II (1901), cols. 1488–94.
Littmann, E., 'I Esdras', JE V (1903), cols. 219–21.
Fischer, J., 'Das apokryphe und das kanonische Esrabuch', BZ 2 (1904), pp. 351–64.
Torrey, C. C., 'The Nature and Origin of First Esdras', AJSL 23 (1907), pp. 116–41, reprinted in *idem, Ezra Studies* (1910), pp. 11–36.

Torrey, C. C., 'The Story of the Three Youths', AJSL 23 (1907), pp. 177–201 (for an Aramaic original of this section) = *Ezra Studies* (1910), pp. 37–61.

York, H. C., 'The Latin Versions of First Esdras', AJSL 26 (1910), pp. 253–302.

Laqueur, R., 'Ephorus. I. Die Proömien', Hermes 46 (1911), pp. 161–206.

Batten, L. W., *A Critical and Exegetical Commentary on the Books of Ezra and Nehemiah* (1913), pp. 6–13.

Mowinckel, S., *Statholderen Nehemia* (1916).

Mowinckel, S., *Ezra den Skriftlaerde* (1916).

Hautsch, E., 'Septuaginta (Zusätze; Esra)', RE IIA (1923), cols. 1598–9.

Humbert, P., 'Magna est veritas et praevalet', OLZ 31 (1928), cols. 148–50.

Torrey, C. C., 'A Revised View of "First Esdras"', *Louis Ginzberg Jub. Vol.* I (1945), pp. 395–410.

S(c)halit, A., 'The Date and Place of the Story about the Three Bodyguards of the King in the Apocryphal Book of Ezra' (in Hebrew), BJPES 13 (1946/7), pp. 119–28.

Rudolph, W., 'Der Wettstreit der Leibwächter des Darius 3 Esra iii,l-v,6', ZAW 61 (1945/8), pp. 176–90.

S(c)halit, A., 'Κοίλη Συρία from Mid-Fourth Century to the Beginning of the Third Century B.C.', Script. Hier. I (1954), pp. 64–77.

Allrik, H. L., '1 Esdras according to Codex B and Codex A as appearing in Zerubbabel's list in I Esdras 5:8–23', ZAW 66 (1954), pp. 272–92.

Ryan, J. K., '"Magna est Veritas et praevalebit" (3 Ezra 4, 41)', American Ecclesiastical Review 135 (1956), pp. 116–24.

Rundgren, R., 'Zur Bedeutung von ΟΙΚΟΓΕΝΗΣ in III Esr. iii,l', Eranos 55 (1957), pp. 145–52.

Lommatzsch, E., 'Die stärksten Dinge', Jahrbuch der Akademie der Wissenschaften und der Literatur in Mainz (1961), pp. 236–8.

Donner, H., 'Der "Freund des Königs"', ZAW 73 (1961), pp. 269–77.

Denter, P. Th., *Die Stellung der Bücher Esdras im Kanon des Alten Testaments* (1962).

Turner, N., 'Books of Esdras', IDB II (1962), cols. 140–2.

Zimmermann, F., 'The Story of the Three Guardsmen', JQR 54 (1963/4), pp. 179–200.

Schmid, U., *Die Priamel der Werte im Griechischen von Homer bis Paulus* (1964), pp. 110–17, 120–37.

Mowinckel, S., *Studien zu den Buche Ezra-Nehemia*, 3 vols. (1964/5), I, pp. 1–28; III, pp. 10–11.

Schneemelcher, W., 'Ezra', RAC VI (1966), cols. 598 ff.

Kellermann, U., 'Das III Esrabuch und die Nehemia-überlieferung', in *Nehemia : Quellen, Überlieferung und Geschichte* (1967), pp. 128–33.

Klein, R. W., 'Old Readings in I Esdras: The List of Returnees from Babylon (Ezra 2// Nehemiah 7)', HThR 62 (1969), pp. 99–107.

Pohlmann, K.-F., *Studien zum dritten Esra* (1970).

Goodman, W. R., *A Study of I Esdras 3,1–5,6* (Diss. Duke, 1972).

In der Smitten, W. Th., 'Zur Pagenerzählung im 3. Esra (3 Esr. III 1-V 6)', VT 22 (1972), pp. 492–5.

In der Smitten, W. Th., *Esra. Quellen, Überlieferung und Geschichte* (1973).

Mosis, R., *Untersuchungen zur Theologie des Chronistischer Geschichtswerkes* (1973).

Allen, L. C., *The Greek Chronicles* I (1974), pp. 6–17.

Cross, F. M., 'A Reconstruction of the Judaean Restoration', JBL 94 (1975), pp. 4–18.

Williamson, H. G. M., *Israel in the Book of Chronicles* (1977).

Hanhart, R., 'Zu Text und Textgeschichte des ersten Esrabuches', in A. Shinan, ed., *Proceedings of the Sixth World Congress of Jewish Studies* I (1977), pp. 201–12.

Heltzer, M., 'The Greek Text of I Esdras III,1–2—Its Date and Subordination at the Achaemenian Court', Henoch 2, 2 (1980), pp. 150–5.

Crenshaw, J. L., 'The contest of Darius' Guards', in B. O. Long, ed., *Images of Man and God* (1981), pp. 74–88.

Crenshaw, J. L., 'Wisdom and authority: sapiential rhetoric and its warrant', in J. A. Emerton, ed., *Congress Volume, Vienna 1980* (Supplement to VT, XXXII, 1981), pp. 22–28.

Hilhorst, A., 'Darius' pillow (I Esdras iii.8)', JThSt 33 (1982), pp. 161–3.

Williamson, H. G. M., 'The composition of Ezra i-vi', JThSt 34 (1983), pp. 1–30.

Japhet, S., 'Sheshbazzar and Zerubbabel against the background of the historical and religious tendencies of Ezra-Nehemiah', ZAW 95 (1983), pp. 218–29.

Cf. also O. Eissfeldt, *The O.T., An Introduction etc.* (ET 1965), pp. 571–6, with bibliography on p. 574, n. 1.

2. The Additions to Esther

The canonical book of Esther tells how a Jewish virgin by the name of Esther, the foster-daughter of Mordecai, was chosen to be the wife of the Persian King Ahasuerus (Xerxes or possibly Artaxerxes); how at the same time Haman, the prime minister of the king, issued a decree in his name for the extermination of all the Jews and was already making preparations to have Mordecai hanged; how instead Mordecai, because he had once saved the king's life, was raised to high honour and Haman was hanged on the tree prepared for Mordecai, whereat Mordecai by means of an edict issued in the king's name repealed that of Haman and permitted the Jews to destroy their enemies; and how finally the Jewish festival of Purim was instituted in memory of this wonderful deliverance.

In the Greek revision of the book a number of passages have been added into this story, i.e. Mordecai's dream, his discovery of the first conspiracy around the king, the royal edict dictated by Haman, a prayer of Mordecai, a prayer of Esther, Esther's reception by the king, the royal edict dictated by Mordecai, the interpretation of Mordecai's dream, and the date of bringing the Greek translation of Esther to Egypt. While these supplements maintain the spirit and positively increase the dramatic appeal of the original version (cf. the passage on Esther's reception by the king), they also instil a more overt religious character into the narrative (in Mordecai's dream and the prayers by him and by Esther) and attempt to bolster the historicity of the account through verbatim copies of the two royal edicts.

There continues to be debate over the original language of these insertions. The extant Aramaic and Hebrew versions of a portion of the additions are medieval (see below), and there is no mention of them in the Talmud, targumim or the Syriac translation. On the other hand, it cannot be assumed that some of the present Greek versions may not be translations of earlier Semitic works added to the Hebrew text after it had already gone into circulation in its present shorter form. There are in fact good linguistic grounds for proposing a Semitic original for all the additions, except the two edicts, which show every sign of having been composed in their present florid, rhetorical Greek.[330] For the date of composition, the only certainty is that Josephus, *Ant.* xi 6 (184–296), knew and paraphrased parts of all the additions except the dream of Mordecai and its interpretation. It is likely that these latter passages also existed in Josephus' time and were only omitted by him on the grounds that they were irrelevant to his theme.[331] A date for the translation of the main text of Hebrew Esther into Greek is fixed by the colophon, which probably indicates 114 B.C. (see above, p. 506). It is almost certain that this translation included the dream of Mordecai and its interpretation since the colophon follows immediately after the latter passage, but it cannot be certain that it also contained the other additions, particularly the two royal edicts.[332] It is highly unlikely that this translator *composed* any of the additions. If they were his compositions he would hardly have incorporated so many inconsistencies and contradictions between them and the main text (e.g. 11:3 and 12:1, which portray Mordecai as prominent at the royal court from the beginning, against 2:21). Nor would he have produced such a literal translation of the main text if he was capable of the sophisticated style of the royal edicts.[333] In that case, it is quite possible that the additions were all composed separately by different authors before insertion into the Esther narratives. This possibility is confirmed by the fact that both Josephus and the translator of the Old Latin version lacked in their manuscripts the story of Mordecai's uncovering of the conspiracy against the king and part of the prayer of Esther, which suggests a gradual accretion of the extra material rather than careful reworking of the original text.[334] In that case, the additions may have been composed at any time before or after the translation of Esther into Greek. A date after the completion of a Hebrew book of Esther is clearly necessary. The early Hellenistic period is not improbable.

330. Th. Nöldeke, EB II (1901), col. 1406; F.-X. Roiron, 'Les parties deutero-canoniques du Livre d'Esther', RSR 6 (1916), pp. 3–16; C. A. Moore, 'On the Origins of the LXX Additions to the Book of Esther', JBL 92 (1973), pp. 382–93; R. A. Martin, 'Syntax Criticism of the LXX Additions to the Book of Esther', JBL 94 (1975), pp. 65–72.

331. C. A. Moore, *Daniel, Esther and Jeremiah: The Additions* (1977), pp. 165–6. Even if Josephus' Greek text lacked these passages, they may well have been found in other manuscripts of the same period, cf. Nöldeke, EB II (1901), col. 1406. They were at any rate known to Origen in the third century A.D., cf. *Epistola ad Africanum* 5 (3) (ed. De Lange, SC 302, pp. 526–8).

332. J. B. Schildenberger, *Das Buch Esther* (1941), p. 9.

333. Moore, *op. cit.*, pp. 165–6. A compromise is to assume that the same author, Lysimachus, translated the additions from their Semitic originals along with the main text (and therefore was not responsible for the inconsistencies), so that only the edicts were included by him untouched since they came to him already written in 'official' Greek, cf. L. Soubigou, *Esther traduit et commente* (1952), p. 588.

334. Moore, *op. cit.*, p. 166.

Similarities in the themes treated in the additions to those in the book of Judith and the dreams in Daniel may suggest a date in the second century B.C.[335] For the place of composition, if the Semitic origins of some of the passages can be assumed, a Palestinian background is plausible. For the two edicts certainly composed in Greek, their sophisticated style would be quite possible for a Jew in many parts of the Mediterranean diaspora.[336]

Some late codices of Hebrew Esther contain at the end an Aramaic text of the dream and prayers of Mordecai and Esther also found in the so-called second Targum of the Book of Esther, in the Midrash on Esther, and elsewhere in rabbinic texts, but all this material belongs to the eighth century A.D. or later. Texts can be found in P. de Lagarde, *Hagiographa Chaldaice* (1873), pp. 362–5; A. Merx, *Chrestomathia Targumica* (1888), pp. 154–64; A. Jellinek, *Bet ha-Midrasch* V (1873), pp. 1–16, with further rabbinic material on pp. 17–81. Translations of some of this material into German in Wünsche, *Aus Israels Lehrhallen* II (1908), pp. 149–63, and into English in J. M. Fuller, 'The Rest of the Chapters of the Book of Esther', in H. Wace, ed., *Apocrypha of the Speaker's Commentary* I (1888), pp. 361–5. Cf. discussions of the first and second Targumim by L. B. Paton, *A Critical and Exegetical Commentary on the Book of Esther* (1908), pp. 18–24; P. Grelot, 'Observations sur les targums I et III d'Esther', *Bibl.* 56 (1975), pp. 53–73; M. H. Goshen-Gottstein, 'The "Third Targum" on Esther and Ms. Neofiti 1', *Bibl.* 56 (1975), pp. 301–42. Cf. also L. Ginzberg, *The Legends of the Jews* IV (1913), pp. 365–448; VI (1928), pp. 451–81, for all the post-biblical texts relating to the story of Esther.

Josephus generally includes the additions of the Greek revision in his

---

335. *Ibid.* A further date for the two royal edicts, which are stylistically similar and should be attributed to a single author, may be suggested by Esther 16:10, 14 (= Addition E: 10, 14 (Moore)), in which Haman is described in one version of the manuscripts as a Macedonian and it is charged that he intends to transfer control over the Persians to the Macedonians. This could only have been written after Alexander the Great, but it is probably reading too much into it to assert that it dates the two passages to before the rise of the Arsacid ruler Mithridates *c.* 130 B.C., cf. F. Altheim, 'Arsakiden und Sassaniden', *Historia Mundi* IV (1956), pp. 514–16, 524; R. Stiel, 'Esther, Judith and Daniel', in Altheim and Stiehl, *Die aramäische Sprache unter den Achaimeniden* II (1960), pp. 195–213; Eissfeldt, *Introduction*, p. 592.

336. The close similarity between the royal edict in 13:1–7 (= B 1–7 (Moore)) and the letter of Ptolemy Philopator in 3 Mac. 3:12–29 cannot be used for dating either text since it is not clear which author, if either, borrowed from which, cf. B. Motzo, 'Il Rifacimento Greco di Ester e il III Mac.', in *Saggi di Storia e Letteratura Giudeo-Ellenistica* (1924), pp. 272–90; C. A. Moore, 'On the origins of the LXX Additions to the Book of Esther', JBL 92 (1973), pp. 382–93, and *idem, Daniel, Esther and Jeremiah: The Additions* (1977), p. 198, for the general similarities between 3 Maccabees and Esther. Such similarities do, however, make an Alexandrian origin for the edicts included in Esther slightly more likely than other places in the Greek-speaking diaspora.

reproduction of the content (*Ant.* xi 6 (184–296)). The Hebrew version of the additions in the tenth century Sefer Josippon simply translates Josephus and has no independent value, cf. C. A. Moore, *Daniel, Esther and Jeremiah : The Additions* (1977), p. 154, n. 3.

Origen, *Epist. ad African.* 5 (3) (ed. De Lange, SC 302, pp. 526–8) mentions these additions and specifically names the most important of them. He also takes for granted that the book in this form (with the additions) is canonical for the Christian Church. He mentions the prayers of Mordecai and Esther inserted between chapters four and five (*De oratione* 13 and 14 (GCS, Origen II, pp. 326, 328, 331)).

On the two widely differing recensions of the Greek translation of Esther, see above, §33A.II, p. 506. They disagree with one another much less in the additions than in their translations of the canonical parts of the text. Since the so-called 'Lucianic' recension has misplaced the second royal edict and places it alongside a briefer version of the same letter, it is likely that it has borrowed its longer version from the LXX text; since the Old Latin usually agrees with the LXX, and the LXX usually provides a better reading, it is likely that the 'Lucianic' version borrowed all the additions from the LXX in the same way, though it cannot be proved that the borrowing was not in other cases in the reverse direction. Cf. C. A. Moore, *op. cit.*, p. 165; E. Tov, 'The "Lucianic" text of the canonical and the apocryphal sections of Esther : a rewritten biblical book', Textus 10 (1982), pp. 1–28. For editions of the texts of both versions, see above, pp. 490, 506. An English translation of the 'Lucianic' text of the additions may be found in E. C. Bissell, *The Apocrypha of the Old Testament* (1880), pp. 217–20.

On the ancient translations of the additions, see above, p. 506, for the book as a whole. The Old Latin, Coptic and Ethiopic are based on the LXX version, and therefore include the additions without comment, but the translation of Jerome was based, even if not very closely (see above, p. 506), on a Hebrew text which lacked the additions. He therefore placed all the Greek additions at the end of the book and marked them with an obelus (PL XXVIII, 1515–16). His Latin translation of these additions is based on the LXX and is extremely free. The Syriac translation, of which the main text was also based on the Hebrew, similarly provides a free version of the LXX when translating the additions. See above, p. 184.

For exegetical works in general, cf. above, pp. 715 f.

Commentaries

Fritzsche, O. F., *Exeget. Handbuch zu den Apokryphen* I (1851).
Fuller, J. M., in H. Wace, *The Speaker's Commentary, The Apocrypha* I (1888).
Scholz, A., *Commentar über das Buch Esther mit seinen Zusätzen und über Susanna* (1892).
Ryssel, V., in E. Kautzsch, APAT I, pp. 193–212.
Gregg, J. A. F., in Charles, APOT I, pp. 665–84.

Schildenberger, J. B., in Feldmann and Herkenne, *Die Heilige Schrift des A.T.* (1941).

Stummer, F., in *Die Heilige Schrift in deutscher Übersetzung* (1950).

Soubigou, L., *Esther traduit et commente*, (²1952).

Barucq, A., in *La Sainte Bible traduite en français sous la direction de l'École Biblique de Jérusalem* (1952). (Cf. the English translation and revision, *The Jerusalem Bible*, 1966, pp. 601–4.)

Bückers, H., in *Herders Bibelkommentar* (1953).

Stein, Menahem (Edmund), in A. Kahana, הספרים החיצונים (²1956).

Girbau, B. M., *Esther* (1960).

Gerleman, G., *Esther* (Biblische Komm. A.T., XXI.1–2, 1970–3).

Fuerst, W. J., 'The Rest of the Chapters of the Book of Esther', in J. C. Dancy, ed., *The Shorter Books of the Apocrypha* (1972).

Bardtke, H., *Zusätze zu Esther* (JSHRZ I.1) (1973), pp. 15–62.

Moore, C. A., *Daniel, Esther and Jeremiah: The Additions* (1977), pp. 151–252.

Bibliography

Langen, J., *Die deutero-kanonischen Stücke des Buches Esther* (1862).

Deane, W. J., 'The LXX Adds to the Hebrew Text', Expositor (1884).

André, L. E. T., *Les apocryphes de l'Ancien Testament* (1903), pp. 195–208.

Siegfried, 'Esther, apocr. book of', in JE V (1903), 237–41.

Friedländer, M., *Geschichte der jüdischen Apologetik* (1903), pp. 114–28.

Paton, L. B., 'A text-critical apparatus of the Book of Esther', in *O.T. and Semitic Studies in Memory of W. R. Harper* II (1908), pp. 1–52 (gives the Greek additions as well, with a copious critical apparatus).

Paton, L. B., *A Critical and Exegetical Commentary on the Book of Esther*, in the ICC series (1908), pp. 41–7.

Howorth, H. H., 'Some Unconventional Views on the Text of the Bible. VIII. The Prayer of Manasses and the Book of Esther', PSBA 31 (1909), pp. 89–99, 156–68.

Roiron, F.-X., 'Les parties deuterocanoniques du Livre d'Esther', RSR 6 (1916), pp. 3–16.

Motzo, B., 'Il Rifacimento greco di Ester e III Mac', in *Saggi di Storia e Letteratura Giudeo-Ellenistica* (1924), pp. 272–90.

Torrey, C. C., *The Apocryphal Literature etc.* (1945), pp. 57–9.

Ehrlich, E. L., 'Der Traum des Mordechai', ZRGG 7 (1955), pp. 69–74.

Saunders, E. W., 'Apocryphal Esther', in IDB II (1962), cols. 151 ff.

Brownlee, W. H., 'Le livre grec d'Esther et la royauté divine. Corrections orthodoxes au livre d'Esther', RB 73 (1966), pp. 161–85.

Moore, C. A., 'On the Origins of the LXX Additions to the Book of Esther', JBL 92 (1973), pp. 382–93.

Martin, R. A., 'Syntax Criticism of the LXX Additions to the Book of Esther', JBL 94 (1975), pp. 65–72.

Cf. O. Eissfeldt, *The O.T., An Introduction etc.* (1965), 591 f., and the introductions to the apocrypha.

3. The Additions to Daniel

The Greek text of the Book of Daniel contains the following additions. (a) The Prayer of Azariah and the Song of the Three Young Men in the Furnace. When the three companions of Daniel were thrown into the furnace for refusing to worship an image erected by King Nebuchadnezzar (Dan. 3), one of them, Azariah, also called Abednego, prayed for deliverance in return for confession. When his prayer was answered through an angel, all three joined in a hymn of praise.

(b) The Story of Susanna. A beautiful Jewess named Susanna, the wife of Joakim, was surprised during her bath by two lecherous old men who, when she called for help, slanderously accused her of having committed adultery with a youth. Susanna was condemned to death on the false witness of the old men, but was saved by the wisdom of the young Daniel, who effected a new investigation and convicted the elders of perjury in a skilful cross-examination. (c) The Story of Bel and the Dragon. This consists in reality of two independent passages both of which have the purpose of exposing the worthlessness and deception of idolatry. One of them recounts how King Cyrus (so Theodotion; the LXX does not mention the king's name) is convinced, through a cunning move made by Daniel, that the image of Bel did not itself consume the food put before it. The other passage reports how Daniel, because he had killed the dragon worshipped by the Babylonians through feeding it with cakes made of pitch, fat and hair, was thrown into the lions' den through the machinations of his enemies, but was miraculously fed there by the prophet Habakkuk brought by an angel, and after seven days was drawn from the den unhurt, his enemies being cast into it in his stead.

None of these narratives as they stand is a true completion of the canonical book of Daniel, and only minimal effort is made to relate them to the main story.[337] On the contrary, they appear to consist in an amalgam of different stories only loosely linked together, largely irrelevant to the story in Daniel, and probably complete before their insertion into the book. The Prayer of Azariah is a national song of lamentation and confession. The Song of the Three Young Men in fact consists of a short ode addressed to God (verses 29–34) followed by a separate psalm addressed to God's creation (verses 35–69).[338] The Story of Susanna belongs to the literary genre of the folk tale, combining two common motifs of the wise judge and the chaste wife who is falsely accused and repudiated on the word of a rejected suitor.[339] The two stories concern-

---

337. It has been argued that verses 23–8 of the Prayer of Azariah, or some portion of the passage, formed an original link between 3:23 and 3:24 of the canonical text, but, even if that is so (and it is much disputed, cf. C. A. Moore, *Daniel, Esther and Jeremiah: The Additions* (1977), pp. 63–5), the fact only points up the intrusive nature of the rest of the additions, which entirely swamp this and other linking passages.

338. For these two songs as originally distinct, cf. Moore, *op. cit.*, pp. 75–6.

339. G. Huet, 'Daniel et Suzanne: Note de littérature comparée', RHR 65 (1912), pp. 277–84; *idem*, 'Daniel et Suzanne', RHR 76 (1917), pp. 129–30; W. Baumgartner, 'Susanna—Die Geschichte einer Legende', ARW 24 (1926), esp. pp. 259–67 for a critique of earlier theories on the origin of the story; *idem*, 'Der weise Knabe und die des Ehebruchs beschuldigte Frau', ARW 27 (1929), pp. 187–8; Moore, *op. cit.*, pp. 88–9. For Greek versions of the Susanna story from the third century B.C., see C. Blümel, 'Drei Weitsreliefs an die Nymphen', Deutsche Beiträge zur Altertumswis. 12/13 (1960), pp. 23–8. Attempts have been made to connect the story to events in biblical or later Jewish history, cf. O. Fritzsche, *Zusätze zu dem Buche Daniel* (1851), p. 185, for a reference to Ahab

ing Bel and the Dragon probably derive from midrashic extrapolation of Jeremiah verses 51, 34–5, 44.[340] That all the stories should have been inserted into the book of Daniel is not entirely surprising given the discovery of yet others on the Daniel theme at Qumran.[341] In the text ascribed to Theodotion (see below, p. 727) the story of Susanna stands at the beginning of the book and that of Bel and the Dragon at the end. The Church Fathers (Hippolytus, Julius Africanus and Origen) followed this order despite the LXX having *both* additions after the canonical book.

It cannot be stated as certain whether any or none of the additions were originally composed in either Hebrew or Aramaic before being translated into Greek. External evidence is lacking for a Semitic original for any of the passages, for the extant Aramaic versions are based on the Greek (see below), and possible Hebraisms are not decisive since the author may have used a Hebraizing Greek. Nonetheless, a Semitic original is perfectly *possible* for all the additions,[342] and the argument put forward by Julius Africanus (*Epist. ad Orig.* 4–5) and by Porphyry (quoted by Jerome, *Prol. comment. in Daniel* (CCL LXXVA, p. 773)) that the Greek pun on σχῖνος and σχίζειν (verses 54–5) and πρῖνος and πρίειν (verses 58–9) proved that Susanna was originally written in Greek, is not convincing since it is quite possible that a translator of a Semitic text invented his own puns or, finding a different pun in the original, produced an equivalent pun

ben Kolaiah and Zedekiah ben Maaseiah in Jer. 29:21–3; N. Brüll, 'Das apokryphische Susanna Buch', Jahrbuch für jüdische Geschichte und Literatur 3 (1877), pp. 1–69, for a reference to Pharisaic defence of their court procedures against the Sadduccees; but these suggestions are not at all convincing.

340. N. Brüll, 'Die Geschichte von Bel und dem Drachen', Jahrbuch für jüdische Geschichte und Literatur 8 (1887), p. 28. Other factors may also have encouraged development of the story, whether knowledge of the Babylonian Enuma Elish epic (cf. H. Gunkel, *Schöpfung und Chaos in Urzeit und Endzeit* (1895), pp. 320–3), or the literary genre, found elsewhere in the Bible, of idol parody (cf. W. M. W. Roth, 'For Life, He Appeals to Death (Wis. 13:18): A Study of Old Testament Idol Parodies', CBQ 37 (1975), pp. 42–3; it is not however necessary to agree with Roth that the use of this genre implies composition in first century B.C. Egypt). The episode about the transportation of Habakkuk from Palestine seems to be a later addition to the story, cf. Moore, *op. cit.*, p. 125.

341. E.g. the prayer of Nabonidus and Pseudo-Daniel a, b and c. Cf. Vermes, DSS, pp. 72–3; Moore, *op. cit.*, p. 116. The Qumran discoveries are likely to reflect a long – tradition of such stories, and they provide no support for a specific date or provenance for the story of Bel and the Dragon, *contra* Moore, *op. cit.*, p. 128.

342. The best arguments for a Semitic original in fact apply to the Susanna story, where several consecutive verses of the LXX and Theodotion seem to translate the same Semitic original, cf. Moore, *op. cit.*, p. 116. Moore argues, *ibid.*, pp. 25–6, 44–5, 81–4, 119–20, for a Semitic origin of all the additions, but he also quotes, pp. 25–6, an unpublished syntactical analysis by R. A. Martin which tentatively concludes that the Theodotion of Bel and parts of the Susanna story in the LXX were originally Greek.

in his own language. For the date of the additions, the *terminus ante quem* is their incorporation into the Greek text of Daniel by the translators of the canonical book in *c.* 100 B.C. There is no reason to doubt that this inclusion was his responsibility, for no difference can be detected between the Greek of the additions and the rest of the book of Daniel.[343] The original composition of the additions may however have taken place at any date before the Greek translation and each passage may plausibly be assigned a quite separate date. The fact that they are not included in the Hebrew text of Daniel does not show that they were not already in circulation as separate narratives when that text was written in *c.* 163 B.C., though it does suggest that, if they were already extant in a Semitic language, no attempt was made until after that date to connect them with the Daniel story. The place of composition of the additions may have been different in each case, especially if some parts were written in Hebrew or Aramaic and other parts in Greek, but, apart from the original languages, the passages themselves offer no other clues to their places of origin.[344]

M. Gaster, 'The Unknown Aramaic Original of Theodotion's Additions to the Book of Daniel', PSBA 16 (1894), pp. 280–90, 312–17; 17 (1895), pp. 75–94; *idem*, *The Chronicles of Jerahmeel* (1899), pp. 1–9, held that the Aramaic text in the medieval chronicle of Jerahmeel represented the original version translated into Greek by Theodotion, but it is clear that Jerahmeel himself was simply translating the Greek and Latin versions, cf. I. Lévi, 'L'Histoire "de Suzanne et les deux vieillards" dans la littérature juive', REJ 95 (1933), pp. 157–71.

The Syriac version published in A. Neubauer, *The Book of Tobit* (1878), pp. xci ff., 39–43, and the Hebrew version of the Story of Susanna in A. Jellinek, *Bet ha-Midrasch* VI (1877), pp. 126–8, and M. Gaster, *The Chronicles of Jerahmeel*, ch. 65, are equally dependent on the Greek text.

There is a wealth of material for the history of the use and of the canonical validity of these passages in patristic literature. Cf. especially

343. The date of the LXX translation of Daniel is fixed by its probable use by the Alexandrian translator of 1 Maccabees, cf. 1 Mac. 1:54 compared to Dan. 11:31; 12:11 in the LXX version. Cf. Moore, *op. cit.*, p. 128, n. 15; J. A. Goldstein, *1 Maccabees* (1976), pp. 42–54; above, p. 500. Knowledge of at least the Song of the Three Young Men among Alexandrian Jews is confirmed by the order of the names Hananiah, Azariah and Mishael in 1 Mac. 2:59; 4 Mac. 16:21; 18:12, which is the same as that in verse 66 of the song, cf. R. H. Pfeiffer, *History of New Testament Times* (1949), p. 442.

344. The story of Susanna may quite well date from the Persian period, though this cannot be proved. The picture of Babylon is rather different from that in the canonical Daniel, which suggests a different place or time of composition. The story of Bel and the Dragon is more complex than the others, which may suggest a later date, perhaps in the second century B.C. For suggestions about the dates and place of origin of each addition, see Moore, *op. cit.*, pp. 29, 47–8, 91–2, 128, with summaries of older hypotheses.

C. Julius, *Die griechischen Danielzusätze und ihre kanonische Geltung (Biblische Studien*, ed. Bardenhewer, VI.3–4, 1901).

Justin Martyr mentions the three companions of Daniel: Hananiah, Azariah, and Mishael (*Apol.* i 46). It is not clear from this brief reference, however, whether he also knew the additions.

Irenaeus and Tertullian quote both the Story of Susanna and that of Bel and the Dragon. Irenaeus iv 26, 3: 'audient eas quae sunt a Daniele prophetatae voces', etc. (cf. Susanna, verses 56 and 52 f. in Theodotion). *Idem*, iv 5, 2: 'Quem (Deum) et Daniel prophetes, cum dixisset ei Cyrus rex Persarum: "Quare non adoras Bel?" annuntiavit dicens: "Quoniam etc."'. Tertullian, *De corona* 4 (Susanna). *Idem*, *De idololatria* 18 (Bel and Dragon); *De jejunio* 7 *fin.* (same). *Clement of Alexandria* also knew the LXX additions. Cf. O. Stählin, *Clemens Alexandrinus und die Septuaginta* (Nürnberg, *Progr.*, 1901), pp. 71–4.

In his commentary on Daniel, Hippolytus deals also with the Greek additions. Cf. G. Bonwetsch and H. Achelis, eds., GCS Hippolytus I (1897) (Greek text and German translation of the Slavonic). See also M. Lefèvre and G. Bardy, eds., *Hippolyte, Commentaire sur Daniel* (SC 14, 1947), with a French translation based on the Bonwetsch and Achelis edition, but which takes into account the important tenth-century Greek fragments published by C. Diobouniotis, in C. Diobouniotis and N. Beis, *Hippolyts Schrift über die Segnungen Jacobs: Hippolyts Daniel-commentar* with preface by G. Bonwetsch (TU XXXVIII, 1911), pp. 45–60. The order in which Hippolytus deals with the passages (and therefore in which he read them in his biblical text) is as follows: the Story of Susanna stands at the beginning; the Prayer of Azariah and the Song of the Three Young Men in the Furnace are dealt with together with ch. 3 (in the second book of Hippolytus' Commentary, which includes the exposition of Dan. 2–3). The Story of Bel and the Dragon was certainly known to Hippolytus and regarded by him as an integral part of the book of Daniel, but apparently he did not write a commentary on it, since there is no trace of one in any of the Greek or Slavic manuscripts (cf. Hippolytus, *Comm. in Dan.* ii 26, and the comments of Lefèvre and Bardy, *ad loc.*). The placing of the Story of Susanna at the beginning corresponds with its location in the oldest manuscripts of the Theodotionic text (Vaticanus, Alexandrinus, Marchalianus). Cf. in general on the use of Hippolytus' commentary for establishing the text of Daniel, J. Ziegler, *Der Bibeltext im Daniel-Kommentar des Hippolyt von Rom* (NAWG II.8, 1952), pp. 163–99; pp. 165–6 on the manuscripts.

Iulius Africanus is the only one among the older Church Fathers to have disputed the canonicity of these passages. In his *Epistola ad Origenem* (printed in editions of Origen, e.g. N. de Lange, SC 302 (1983), pp. 514–21) he calls Origen to account for appealing to the

Story of Susanna in a disputation on the basis that it was only an inauthentic addition to Daniel, cf. *Ep. ad Orig.* 2, 7.

In his reply (*Epistola ad Africanum*), Origen seeks to defend, with an abundance of scholarship, the genuineness and canonicity of the narratives, despite the fact that he knew that they were not included in the Hebrew Daniel. He mentions—as appearing in the middle of the text of Daniel—not only the stories of Susanna and of Bel and the Dragon, but also the Prayer of Azariah and the Song of the Three Young Men, and observes that all these narratives were to be found in both the LXX and Theodotion (*Epistola ad Africanum* 3(2) (ed. de Lange, SC 302 (1983), p. 524)). In the tenth book of his *Stromata* Origen discusses from the point of view of exegesis the Story of Susanna and that of Bel (cf. the extracts given by Jerome in his commentary on Daniel chapters 13–14 (Jerome, CCL LXXVA, pp. 945–50)). Whole passages are also frequently quoted by Origen following Theodotion's text: (1) Susanna: *Comm. in Joann.* xx 5 (GCS, Origen IV, p. 332); *ibid.* xxviii 5 (GCS, Origen IV, p. 394); *Comm. in Matth., Comm. ser.*, 61 (GCS, Origen XI, p. 140); *Comm. in epist. ad Rom., lib.* iv 2 (PG XIV, 969); *Fragm. in Genes.* iii 4 (PG XII, 57); *In Genes. homil.* xv 2 (GCS, Origen VI, p. 128); *In Josuam homil.* xxii 6 (GCS, Origen VII, p. 438); *Selecta in Psalmos, Ps. 36 (37) homil.* iv 2 (PG XII, 1354); *In Ezechiel. homil.* vi 3 (GCS, Origen VIII, pp. 379–80); *Selecta in Ezech.* 6 (PG XIII, 786); cf. particularly with regard to canonicity *In Levit. homil.* i 1 (GCS, Origen VI, p. 281; ed. Borret, SC 286, p. 68), against those who wish to adhere to the literal and historical meaning of the Scriptures. (2) Prayer of Azariah and Song of the Three Young Men: *Comm. in Matth.* xiii 2 (GCS, Origen X, p. 178); *Comm. in Matth., Comm. ser.*, 62 (GCS, Origen XI, p. 144); *Comm. in Epist. ad Rom., lib.* i 10 (PG XIV, 856); *ibid., lib.* ii 9 (PG XIV, 893); *ibid., lib.* vii 1 (PG XIV, 1104); *De oratione* 13 and 14 (GCS, Origen II, pp. 326, 328, 331). (3) Bel and the Dragon: *Exhortatio ad martyrium* 33 (GCS, Origen I, p. 28).

Cyprian cites the Song of the Three Young Men as a model of *publica et communis oratio* in his *De dominica oratione* 8. Cf. also *De lapsis* 31. He quotes the Story of Bel in *Ad Fortunatum* 11, and *Epist.* lviii 5.

The Greek text used by the Church Fathers from the New Testament onwards is usually that ascribed to *Theodotion*. From the mid-third century A.D., only the Theodotion text was used, and it has thus largely passed into the manuscripts and editions of the LXX (see above, p. 500, and especially J. Ziegler, *Susanna, Daniel, Bel et Draco* (1954); B. M. Vellas, *Δανιήλ* (1966)).[345] According to Jerome, *Comm. in Dan.* i 4,

---

345. Jellicoe, SMS, pp. 84–8; Moore, *op. cit.*, pp. 31–2. Most scholars assume that the additions to Daniel originated with the Theodotionic translation of the rest of Daniel, whenever that translation came about (see above, p. 500). The exception is A. Schmitt, *Stammt der sogenannte 'Θ'-Text bei Daniel wirklich von Theodotion* (MSU IX, 1966), pp. 100–12, who claims a different translator (Symmachus?) for the additions. J. Schüpphaus,

5a (CCL, LXXVA, p. 811), the decision to prefer the Theodotionic text was quite deliberate at least on the part of Origen, who also knew the LXX text but decided to ignore it. The genuine LXX text of Daniel has come down to us in only two main manuscripts: the tenth century cursive Codex Chisianus 88 (88 in Holmes and Parsons and in the Göttingen ed., 87 in Field and Swete), cf. J. A. Montgomery, *A Critical and Exegetical Commentary on the Book of Daniel* (1927), pp. 25–7 (a not very good manuscript); and the Cologne section of Chester Beatty Papyrus 967, which dates from *c.* A.D. 150 and preserves only the LXX of Daniel 5–12 together with Susanna and Bel and the Dragon, but which does not include the Prayer of Azariah or the Song of the Three Young Men, cf. A. Geissen, *Der Septuaginta-Text des Buches Daniel: Kap. 5–12, zusammen mit Susanna, Bel et Draco, sowie Esther Kap. 1,10–2,15, nach dem Kölner Teil des Papyrus 967* (Papyrologische Texte und Abhand-lungen V, 1968) (the papyrus is particularly important for the text at the beginning of the story of Susanna). These witnesses can be partially checked by: (1) the fifth-century A.D. Vienna Papyrus 29255, published by P. Sanz, *Griechische literarische Papyri christlichen Inhaltes* I (1946), pp. 52–3, no. XXX (no variants not found also elsewhere); (2) the LXX text in the Syro-Hexapla, published by Ceriani, *Codex Syro-Hexaplaris Ambrosianus photolithographice editus* (1874); (3) the Old Latin translation used by Tertullian, which was probably based on a LXX text slightly different from Origen's. Cf. F. C. Burkitt, *The Old Latin and the Itala* (1896). For all patristic citations of the LXX text, see J. Ziegler, *Susanna, Daniel, Bel et Draco* (1954), pp. 22–7. The LXX text with apparatus collated from all these sources can be found in Ziegler, *op. cit.*, pp. 81–223, printed at the foot of the page below the Theodotion text. On the LXX translation of Daniel generally, cf. A. Bludau, *Die alexandrinische Uebersetzung des Buches Daniel* (Biblische Studien, ed. Bardenhewer, II.2–3, 1897); J. A. Montgomery, *A Critical and Exegetical Commentary on the Book of Daniel* (1927), pp. 25–6.

Ancient translations. Some of the Old Latin patristic citations are gathered in the corpus of P. Sabatier, *Biblior. sacror. Latinae versiones antiquae* II (1739–49; repr. 1757). For a much fuller list of the citations of the Old Latin of Daniel, including the additions, see A. Dold, 'Konstanzer altlateinische Propheten—und Evangelien—Bruchstücke:

'Der Verhältnis von LXX- und Theodotion-Text in den apokryphen Zusätzen zum Danielbuch', ZAW 83 (1971), pp. 49–72, argues strongly that the Theodotion text of the Additions is a re-editing of the LXX text and not a new translation from a Semitic original. In either case, the existence of Theodotionic readings of Daniel before the work of Theodotion himself in the second century A.D. makes it possible that the Theodotionic text of the Additions was as old as, or only slightly younger than, the LXX text. For the relevant Theodotionic readings of Daniel in pre-Theodotion texts, see J. A. Montgomery, *A Critical and Exegetical Commentary on the Book of Daniel* (1927), pp. 46–50; R. H. Charles, *A Critical and Exegetical Commentary on the Book of Daniel* (1929), pp. liii-lvii, cxvi-cxxii.

mit Glossen', in *Texte u. Arbeiten herausg. durch die Erz. Beuron* I.7–9 (1923); Montgomery, *op. cit.*, pp. 29–32; Ziegler, *op. cit.*, pp. 36–7. The Old Latin is based on both Theodotion and the LXX; the LXX text used may have differed from that used by Origen (see above). Jerome translated the Greek additions entirely from Theodotion, marking them with an obelus and including them in his translation of Daniel from the Hebrew, cf. his remarks, PL xxviii, 1386. Cf. above, p. 184, on the editions of the common Syriac text. Ziegler, *op. cit.*, pp. 36–43, discusses the ancient versions and has full references to them in his apparatus criticus, but they shed little extra light on the Greek text.

For later rabbinic versions of the stories in the additions, cf. L. Ginzberg, *The Legends of the Jews* IV (1913), pp. 327–31, 338, 346; VI (1928), pp. 384, 414–20, 426–7, 432–6.

For exegetical works in general, cf. above, pp. 248 f.

Commentaries

Fritzsche, O. F., *Exeget. Handbuch zu den Apokryphen* I (1851).

Bissell, E. D., *The Apocrypha of the O.T.* (1880).

Ball, C. J., in H. Wace, *The Apocrypha* II (1888).

Zöckler, O., *Die Apokryphen des A.T. nebst einem Anhang über die Pseudepigraphenliteratur (Kurzgef. Kommentar zu den heil. Schriften A. und N.T.*, ed. Strack and Zöckler, IX, 1891), pp. 214–21, 231–5.

Scholz, A., *Commentar über das Buch Esther mit seinem Zusätzen und über Susanna* (1892).

Scholz, A., *Commentar über das Buch Judith und über Bel und Drache* (²1896).

Rothstein, J. W., in E. Kautzsch, APAT I (1900), pp. 172–93.

Bennett, W. H., 'The Prayer of Azariah and The Song of the Three Children', D. M. Kay, 'The History of Susanna', and T. Witton Davies, 'Bel and the Dragon', in Charles, APOT I, pp. 625 ff., 638 ff., and 652 ff.

Montgomery, J. A., *A Critical and Exegetical Commentary on the Book of Daniel* (1927).

Goettsberger, J., *Das Buch Daniel übersetzt und erklärt* (1928), pp. 10 ff., 94–100.

Charles, R. H., *A Critical and Exegetical Commentary on the Book of Daniel* (1929).

Kuhl, C., *Die drei Männer im Feur* (BZAW LV, 1930).

Lattey, C., *The Book of Daniel* (1948), pp. xl-lii, 114–19.

Delcor, M., *Le Livre de Daniel* (1971).

Plöger, O., *Zusätze zu Daniel* (JSHRZ I.1, 1973), pp. 63–87.

Moore, C. A., *Daniel, Esther and Jeremiah : The Additions* (1977).

Bibliography

Wiederholt, Th. von, ThQ (1869), pp. 287 ff., 377 ff. (Story of Susanna); ThQ (1871), pp. 373 ff. (Prayer of Azariah and Song of the Three Young Men); ThQ (1872), pp. 554 ff. (Bel and Dragon).

Brüll, N., 'Das apokryphische Susannabuch', Jahrbb. für jüd. Gesch. und Literatur 3 (1877), pp. 1–69 (also separately).

Brüll, N., 'Das Gebet der drei Männer im Feuerofen', Jahrbb. für jüd. Gesch. und Literatur 8 (1887), pp. 22–7.

Brüll, N., 'Die Geschichte von Bel und dem Drachen', Jahrbb. für jüd. Gesch. und Literatur 8 (1887), pp. 28–9.

Gunkel, H., *Schöpfung und Chaos* (1895), pp. 320–3 (on the Dragon).

Burkitt, F. C., *The Old Latin and the Itala* (1896), pp. 18 ff.

Bludau, A., *Die alexandrinische Uebersetzung des Buches Daniel* (Biblische Studien, ed. Bardenhewer, II.2–3, 1897), pp. 155–204.

Marshall, J. T., 'Bel and the Dragon', in HDB I (1898), cols. 267 ff.; 'Susanna', HDB IV

(1902), cols. 630–2; 'The Song of the Three Children', HDB IV (1902), cols. 754–6.
Julius, C., *Die griechischen Danielzusätze* (Biblische Studien, ed. Bardenhewer, VI.3–4, 1901).
André, L. E. T., *Les apocryphes de l'Ancien Testament* (1903), pp. 208–37.
Daubney, W. H., *The Three Additions to Daniel* (1906).
Howorth, H. H., 'Some unconventional views on the text of the Bible, VII : Daniel and Chronicles', PSBA 29 (1907), pp. 31–8, 61–9.
Huet, G., 'Daniel et Suzanne: Note de littérature comparée', RHR 65 (1912), pp. 277–84.
Landersdorfer, S., 'Der Drache von Babylon', BZ 11 (1913), pp. 1–4.
Huet, G., 'Daniel et Suzanne', RHR 76 (1917), pp. 129–30.
Hautsch, RE IIA.2 (1923), cols. 1601–3.
Baumgartner, W. I., 'Susanna. Die Geschichte einer Legende', ARW 24 (1926), pp. 258–80.
Baumgartner, W. I., 'Der weise Knabe und die des Ehebruchs beschuldigte Frau', ARW 27 (1929), pp. 187 f. (*Zum Alten Testament und seiner Umwelt* (1959), pp. 42–67).
Lévi, I., 'L'histoire "de Suzanne et les deux vieillards" dans la littérature juive', REJ 95 (1933), pp. 157–71.
Heller, Bernhard (= Dob), 'Die Susannaerzählung: ein Märchen', ZAW 54 (1936), pp. 281–7.
Torrey, C. C., *The Apocryphal Literature etc.* (1945), pp. 54–7.
Rowley, H. H., 'The Unity of the Book of Daniel', in *The Servant of the Lord and Other Essays on the Old Testament*, ed. Rowley (1952, ²1965), pp. 249–80.
Forderer, M., 'Der Schild des Achilleus und der Lobgesang im Feuerofen', Studium Generale, Heidelberg, 8 (1955), pp. 294–301.
MacKenzie, R. A. F., 'The Meaning of the Susanna Story', Canadian Journal of Theology 3 (1957), pp. 211–18.
Zimmermann, F., 'The Story of Susanna and its Original Language', JQR 48 (1957/8), pp. 237–41.
Zimmermann, F., 'Bel and the Dragon', VT 8 (1958), 438–40.
Katz, P., 'The Text of 2 Maccabees Reconsidered', ZNW 51 (1960), pp. 10–30, cf. 27–30: appendix: 'πρεσβυτέριον in I Tim. iv, 14 and Susanna 50'.
Frost, S. B., 'Daniel: ... The Additions', in IDB I (1962), col. 767.
Wurmbrand, M., 'A Falasha Variant of the Story of Susanna', Bibl. 44 (1963), pp. 29–35.
Schmitt, A., *Stammt der sogenannte "Θ"-Text bei Daniel wirklich von Theodotion?* (MSU IX, 1966).
Grelot, P., 'Les versions grecques de Daniel', Bibl. 4 (1966), pp. 381–402.
Jones, B. W., 'The Prayer in Daniel ix', VT 18 (1968), pp. 488–93.
Papadopoulos, N., 'The Deuterocanonical Sections of Daniel', Theologia 40 (1969), pp. 458–89; 41 (1970), pp. 340–64.
Fenz, A. K., 'Ein Drache in Babel. Exegetische Skizze über Daniel 14:23–42', Svensk Exegetisk Årsbok 35 (1970), pp. 5–16.
Schüpphaus, J., 'Der Verhältnis von LXX- und Theodotion-Text in den apocryphen Zusätzen zum Danielbuch', ZAW 83 (1971), pp. 49–72.
Roth, W. M. W., 'For Life, He Appeals to Death (Wis. 13:18): A Study of Old Testament Idol Parodies', CBQ 37 (1975), pp. 21–47.
Nickelsburg, G. W. E., JLBBM, pp. 25–30.
Milik, J. T., 'Daniel et Susanne à Qumrân?', in J. Doré et al., eds., *De la Torah au Messie: Mélanges H. Cazelles* (1981), pp. 337–59.

4. The Prayer of Manasseh

In the same way that the prayers of Mordecai and Esther are interpolated as a supplement in the Book of Esther, and the Prayer of Azariah and the Song of the Three Young Men in the Book of Daniel, so the Prayer of Manasseh, in which the king, led into captivity, humbly confesses his sin before God and begs for forgiveness, was intended to supplement 2 Chronicles. There was particular occasion to compose such a prayer because 2 Chronicles 33:18–19 mentions that the prayer of Manasseh is recorded elsewhere in the Chronicles of the kings of Israel (18), or in the Chronicle of Hozai (or, according to the Greek texts, the Chronicle of the Seers) (19). The prayer is not included in the text of Chronicles in the LXX manuscripts but is collected in most of the Greek manuscripts, from the fifth century and later, together with other prayers and hymns as an appendix to the Psalms (as e.g. in Codex Alexandrinus and in *Psalterium Turicense*). It is not mentioned in any of the ancient lists of apocryphal books, but this may be because it was considered to be canonical. It is not possible to say anything with certainty about the date, place of origin or original language of the Prayer of Manasseh, except that it was evidently extant before the third century A.D.[346]

The earliest citation of the prayer is in the third century A.D. *Didascalia* preserved in full only in Syriac translation. For a critical edition of the Syriac text, cf. P. de Lagarde, *Didascalia apostolorum Syriace* (repr. 1911); English translation: R. H. Connolly, *Didascalia Apostolorum* (1929); German translation: Achelis and Flemming, *Die syrische Didaskalia* (1904), pp. 36 ff. It is given here in full, and also in the later revised form of the Didascalia, i.e. the Apostolic Constitutions (F. X. Funk, *Didascalia et constitutiones apostolorum* I (1905; repr. 1960), pp. 84–9). The whole textual tradition, including that of the LXX manuscripts, very probably derives from this source (so Nestle and F.-N. Nau), but the tradition preserved in the psalteries should also be taken into account. It is improbable, however, that it was first composed by the author of the *Apost. Const.* as Fabricius assumed (*Liber Tobiae Judith Oratio Manasse Sapientia et Ecclesiasticus gr. et lat.*, ed. Joh. Alb. Fabricius (1691), p. 208) and F.-N. Nau (Revue de l'Orient chrétien, 1908, p. 137), both because the content of the prayer definitely indicates a Jewish origin (cf. the opening verse) and because it (verse 4) is already quoted in *Apost. Const.* 8, 7, 5, as being a well-known work. The view of Howorth ('Some Unconventional Views on the Text of the Bible, VIII', PSBA 31 (1909), pp. 89–99), that the prayer together with the story around it was taken from the genuine

---

346. On the date, cf. J. H. Charlesworth, *The Pseudepigrapha and Modern Research* (1976), p. 157: 'between 200 B.C. and A.D. 70', but Berthold, cited by V. Ryssel, in E. Kautzsch, APAT, p. 167, affirms a date only *just* before the composition of the *Didascalia* in the third century A.D. Denis, IPGAT, p. 181, asserts that the original language was certainly Greek, but C. C. Torrey, *The Apocryphal Literature* (1945), pp. 68 f., follows R. H. Charles, in Charles, APOT I, p. 614, n. 1, in preferring a Semitic original. The prayer is too short for such speculation to be resolved.

LXX text of Chronicles (corresponding to his view of the later origin of our Greek text of Chronicles, cf. above, p. 712) is idiosyncratic. The notice following the text of the prayer in *Apost. Const.*, that in answer to Manasseh's penitential confession a miraculous flame melted the iron of his chains and freed him, seems also to have been known to Iulius Africanus in the third century A.D., cf. John of Damascus, *Sacra Parallela* (PG XCV, 1436), with a slightly different text of the same passage given by Pitra, *Analecta Sacra* II (1884), p. 292. Africanus apparently believed the chains to have been broken rather than melted, but it is clear that he knew both the legend in the Didascalia and the text of the prayer, and this further legend may therefore have also been of Jewish origin.

The Latin translation which has passed into the published Vulgate is a sixteenth century version made from the Greek, cf. H. Schneider, 'Der Vulgata-Text der Oratio Manasse', BZ N.F.4 (1960), pp. 277–82. None of the other extant Latin versions is sufficiently early to be of any help for textual criticism, cf. H. Volz, 'Zur Überlieferung des Gebetes Manasse', Zeitschrift für Kirchengeschichte 70 (1959), pp. 293–307.

Editions

Funk, F. X., *Didascalia et Constitutiones Apostolarum* I (1905; repr. 1960), pp. 84–9.
Swete, H. B., *The O.T. in Greek according to the LXX* III ([4]1912), pp. 824–6 (text of Codex Alexandrinus with variants from the *Psalt. Turicense*).
Rahlfs, A., *Psalmi cum Odis* (1931), pp. 362–3 (a critical text).
Denis, FPG, pp. 115–17.
Baars, W., and H. Schneider, eds., *Peshitta* IV.6 (1972), pp. i-vii, 1–9.

Translations and Commentaries

Fritzsche, O. F., *Exeget. Handbuch zu den Apokryphen* I (1851).
Zöckler, O., *Die Apokryphen des A.T. nebst einem Anhang über die Pseudepigraphenliteratur* (*Kurzgef. Kommentar zu den heil. Schriften A. und N.T.*, eds. Strack and Zöckler, no. 9, 1891), pp. 236–8.
Ryssel, V., in E. Kautzsch, APAT I, pp. 165–71.
Ryle, H. E., 'The Prayer of Manasses', in Charles, APOT I, pp. 612–24.
Riessler, P., *Altjüdisches Schrifttum ausserhalb den Bibel, übersetzt und erläutert* (1928), pp. 348 ff.
Connolly, R. H., *Didascalia Apostolorum* (1929), pp. 72–6.
Artom, Elihu (Elia) S., in A. Kahana, הספרים החיצונים ([2]1956).
Osswald, E., *Das Gebet Manasses* (JSHRZ IV.1, 1974), pp. 15–27.

Bibliography

Nestle, E., *Septuagintastudien* III (1899), pp. 4 f., 6–22; IV (1903), pp. 5–9.
Nau, F.-N., 'Un Extrait de la Didascalie: La Prière de Manassé', Revue de l'Orient Chrétien 13 (1908), pp. 134–41 (with a critical edition of the Syriac text).
Wilkins, G., 'The Prayer of Manasseh', Hermathena 16 (1911), pp. 167–78.
Norden, E., *Agnostos Theos* (1913), p. 205.
Bardenhewer, O., *Geschichte der altkirchlichen Literatur*[2] II (1914), pp. 304–12.
Stählin, O., 'Die hellenistisch-jüdische Literatur', in W. v. Christ, O. Stählin and W.

Schmidt, *Geschichte der griech. Literatur etc.*[6] II.1 (1920), p. 555.

Hautsch, in RE IIA.2 (1923), col. 1603.

Torrey, C. C., *The Apocryphal Literature etc.* (1945), pp. 67–9.

Schneider, H., 'Die biblischen Oden im christlichen Altertum, seit dem VI. Jahrhundert, in Jerusalem und Konstantinopel, im Mittelalter, im hexaplarischen Psalter', Bibl. 30 (1949), pp. 28–65, 239–72, 433–53, 479–500; Bibl. 40 (1949), pp. 199–200 (*Studia Biblica et Orientalia* I (1959), pp. 65–75).

Volz, H., 'Zur Überlieferung des Gebetes Manasses', Zeitschrift für Kirchengeschichte 70 (1959), pp. 293–307.

Schneider, H., 'Der Vulgata-Text der Oratio Manasse', BZ 4 (1960), 277–82.

Wikgren, A., 'Prayer of Manasseh', in IDB III (1962), cols. 255–6.

Denis, IPGAT, pp. 177–81.

For Jewish legends about Manasseh, cf.

L. Ginzberg, *The Legends of the Jews* IV (1913), pp. 106–8, and VI (1928).

5. The Book of Baruch (I Baruch)

The Greek Book of Baruch belongs, strictly speaking, to the prophetic pseudepigrapha, in particular to those which are predominantly hortatory. It is placed here because it was included as canonical in the Greek Bible by some Church Fathers from the second century A.D. and after, who treated it as a supplement to the book of Jeremiah. It is possible that some Jews at an earlier period also treated I Baruch as an integral part of the Bible but, apart from the later Christian attributions of canonicity, there is no other evidence for this.

The book claims to be written by Baruch, the confidential friend and companion of the prophet Jeremiah. The contents are rather disparate and fall into two halves, the second of which comprises two further sections. The book as a whole begins with a superscription in which what follows is described as a book by Baruch written in the fifth year after the destruction of Jerusalem by the Chaldeans (1:1–2). Baruch read this book aloud to King Jeconiah and all the exiles in Babylon and it made such an impression that it was decided to send money to Jerusalem so that sacrifices and prayers might be offered there for King Nebuchadnezzar and his son Belshazzar. Jews living in Jerusalem were at the same time requested to read the accompanying work in the Temple on festival days (1:3–14). This work, which is then given in full (1:15–5:9), is clearly identical with that read out by Baruch, and hence identical to that announced in the title. The first half of this work (1:15–3:8) is a profound confession of sins by the exiles (1:15–2:5), followed by their prayers to God (2:6–3:8). They recognize that the terrible fate which has fallen on them and on the Holy City is the righteous judgement of God on their sins, and they implore him henceforth to show mercy on them. They confess in particular that their disobedience to the King of Babylon was a rebellion against God himself, for it was God's will that Israel should obey the King of Babylon (2:21–4). The second half of the book (3:9–5:9) includes instruction and comfort for the humiliated people. (a) Instruction: Israel has been humiliated because it has forsaken the source of wisdom. True wisdom is with God alone. The people must return to that wisdom (3:9–4:4). (b) Comfort: Jerusalem will not be devastated forever, and the people will not always be in captivity. They must take courage, for the scattered members will be reunited in the Holy Land (4:5–5:9).

Although the introduction (1:1–14) was presumably composed by the compiler of most, if not all, of the rest of I Baruch, it is possible to treat the other major sections as entirely independent compositions by different authors.[347] The second half has very obviously been joined quite abruptly to the first at 3:9.[348] Internal coherence exists only insofar as both halves presuppose the same historical situation, i.e. the destruction of Jerusalem and the deportation of the people into captivity. Otherwise there is no connection between them and it is indeed inconceivable that they belonged together from the start. In addition, the style and mode of expression are quite different; the first half is more Hebraistic than the second half, and basic words and phrases receive entirely different treatment.[349] It is probable that the two halves are the works of different authors, though, less plausibly, the divergences might be due to different translators into Greek. Within the second half of the book, there is every reason to suppose that the wisdom poem in 3:9–4:4 was written by a different author from the person responsible for the psalm in 4:5–5:9.[350] In the first half, it is not possible to be so dogmatic. The whole of 1:1–3:8 is stylistically a unity, though this might conceivably be the effect of a single *translator*, so that separate authors of the Semitic originals can still be postulated.[351] It has been argued that 1:3–14 is a later interpolation (so Eissfeldt and

---

347. See C. A. Moore, *Daniel, Esther and Jeremiah: The Additions* (1977), pp. 257–8, who treats I Baruch as consisting of *five* separate compositions. G. W. E. Nickelsburg, in JWSTP, pp. 140–4, asserts greater unity.

348. G. W. E. Nickelsburg, JLBBM, pp. 111, 153, suggests that 3:9–13 may have been inserted as a link by the redactor.

349. H. St. J. Thackeray, 'Notes and Studies: The Greek Translators of Jeremiah', JThSt 4 (1903), pp. 261–6; cf. A. Wifstrand, 'Die Stillung der enklitischen Personalpronomina bei den Septuaginta', Bull. de la Soc. Royale des Lettres de Lund (1949/50), p. 64; R. A. Martin, 'Some Syntactical Criteria of Translation Greek', VT 10 (1960), pp. 297–306, 309–10; E. Tov, *The Book of Baruch also called I Baruch (Greek and Hebrew)* (1975), p. 7.

350. C. A. Moore, 'Towards the Dating of the Book of Baruch', CBQ 36 (1974), pp. 312–20; idem, *Daniel, Esther and Jeremiah: The Additions* (1977), pp. 314–16, suggests further that I Baruch 5:5–9 is a late addition based on Psalms of Solomon 11. But the whole question of the relationship of I Baruch to the Psalms of Solomon is still problematic (see below).

351. The grounds put forward by Moore, *op. cit.*, pp. 257–8, 291–4, for distinguishing a number of separate authors within 1:15–3:8 are not convincing, cf. Nickelsburg, JLBBM, pp. 110, 152, notes 24 and 26, but they cannot be disproved.

others), because the story of the recitation of Baruch's book and the effect that it had comes as a break between 1:1–2 and 1:15–3:8, since after the superscription (1:1–2) the book itself is expected. Furthermore, through the interpolated story a contradiction makes itself apparent in that the book itself presupposes the destruction of the Temple (1:2; 2:26), whereas in the interpolation the sacrificial cult is portrayed as continuing (1:10, 14). However, against 1:3–14 as an interpolation is the dependence of both this passage (at 1:11–12) and the rest of the first half of the book on the book of Daniel (see below). It is probably wrong to expect too much historical accuracy of a pseudepigraph, and the whole of 1:1–14 is rather confused.[352] The question of the unity of the first half of I Baruch should thus be left open.

It is clear that any hypothesis about the original language of I Baruch needs to treat each section separately. No trace of a Semitic version of any of the sections has survived, and the fact that Origen obelized the whole book indicates than none was extant in his day, but, since it has been plausibly claimed that the Greek of *all* the sections contains Hebraisms and mistranslations of a hypothetical Semitic original, Hebrew or Aramaic composition is possible for the whole book, though the evidence is strongest for 1:1–3:8 and weakest for 4:5–5:9. [353] Nonetheless it is also possible that the second half of the book was written from the first in Greek, and it is better to leave the matter undecided.

Judgement about the place of origin of the sections of the book in their original form depends entirely on their original language which, as has been seen, is uncertain. Nonetheless, it can be asserted that the completion of most of the book in its present form was probably undertaken in Palestine since the introduction (1:1–14), which was all presumably written by such a compiler if 1:3–14 was not interpolated later (see above), was composed originally in Hebrew.[354]

For the date of composition it is again necessary to distinguish between the composition of the individual parts of I Baruch and the compilation of the whole work. Throughout 1:1–3:8 there are very close

352. So Moore, *op. cit.*, pp. 257, 275, who also points out that 2:3 also seems to refer to the siege of 586 B.C. when the Temple was destroyed. It is wrong to expect too much historical accuracy in a pseudepigraph.

353. The relevant evidence is listed by O. C. Whitehouse in Charles, APOT I, pp. 571–2, and R. R. Harwell, *The Principal Versions of Baruch* (1915), pp. 52–6. Moore, *op. cit.*, p. 260, cites further as confirmation of the probable Semitic origins of the book an unpublished syntactical analysis by R. A. Martin. For a Hebrew origin as likely for 3:9–5:9, see J. Kneucker, *Das Buch Baruch* (1879), pp. 25 ff.; R. H. Pfeiffer, *History of New Testament Times* (1949), pp. 419 ff.; D. G. Burke, *The Poetry of Baruch* (1982); for a Greek original, see E. Tov, *The Book of Baruch also called I Baruch (Greek and Hebrew)* (1975), p. 7, n. 5.

354. Cf. Moore, *op. cit.*, pp. 257, 260.

parallels with the prayer in Daniel 9:4–19, e.g. the almost verbal agreement between Dan. 9:7–10 and I Bar. 1:15–18; less close but possibly significant are similarities to other parts of Daniel, such as the placing together of Nebuchadnezzar and Belshazzar even though this is historically inaccurate in I Bar. 1:11–12 (= Dan. 5:2 ff.). Many scholars have taken this as evidence for a post-Maccabaean date for this part of I Baruch on the assumption that it has borrowed from Daniel, but, though borrowing in the opposite direction is very unlikely, it is most probable that the two texts depend on a common source consisting in the sort of prayer that might well have achieved wide circulation at any time from the fourth century B.C. onwards.[355] The similarities to Daniel are therefore only a very general indication of the approximate era of this I Baruch section. I Baruch 1:1–3:8 can however be much more firmly dated by the fact that this section was probably rendered into Greek by the same man who translated the LXX of Jeremiah. Since the whole prophetic corpus, including Jeremiah, was known to have been translated into Greek by the time of the translation of Ben Sira's work by his grandson in 116 B.C., I Baruch 1:1–3:8 must also have been composed before that date.[356]

No such fixed date is available for the second part of the book. For the wisdom section 3:9–4:4 no indications of any kind are available. For 4:5–5:9 the only relevant fact lies in the striking similarities between I Baruch 4:36–5:9 and Ps. Sol. 11. As with the relation of Daniel to the first half of Baruch, many scholars have assumed that the passage in I Baruch is dependent on the Psalms of Solomon and must therefore date after the composition of those Psalms in the first century B.C.,[357] but in fact the relationship is not at all clear, so that the borrowing may have been in the reverse direction or both texts may derive from a common

---

355. For Baruch as dependent on Daniel, see most recently B. M. Wambacq, 'Les prières de Baruch (I 15-II 19) et de Daniel (IX 5–19)', Bibl. 40 (1959), pp. 463–75. A post-Maccabaean date is accordingly accepted by O. Eissfeldt, *An Introduction to the O.T.*, etc. (1965), pp. 593 ff. For the dependence of Daniel on Baruch, see W. Stoderl, *Zur Echtheitsfrage von Baruch I–3,8* (1922). For a common source for both authors, see C. A. Moore, 'Towards the Dating of the Book of Baruch', CBQ 36 (1974), pp. 312–20; *idem*, *op. cit.*, pp. 291–3.

356. E. Tov, *The Septuagint Translation of Jeremiah and Baruch* (1976), pp. 111–33, 165, makes it clear that the similarities of the two translations are too close to dismiss them, as Schürer did in 1909, as simply the influence of the Jeremiah tranlsation on the later translation of I Baruch 1:1–3:8. Tov argues further, *op. cit.*, pp. 6, 166–7, that the present Greek text of Baruch 1:1–3:8 was changed by a later reviser who tried to bring the original translation of this part of Baruch and of Jer. 29–52 more into line with the Hebrew. This reviser probably worked before the end of the first century A.D.

357. H. E. Ryle and M. R. James, *Psalms of the Pharisees, Commonly Called the Psalms of Solomon* (1891), pp. lxxii-lxxiii, 100–3.

source.[358] Thus, in deciding *when* before 116 B.C. to date the first half of the book, and in fixing *any* time at all for the second half of the book and the compilation of the whole, the only relevant considerations lie in the tone of the contents. Unfortunately, these considerations cannot be reckoned any more decisive. In the first half of the book the author assumes the destruction of Jerusalem and the deportation of the people (1:2; 2:23, 26). In this catastrophe the people saw God's judgement on their sin, particularly for their rebellion against the gentile authority whom God himself had placed over Israel (1:21–4). The people thus hurried in repentance to offer sacrifices and to pray for their gentile ruler (1:10–11). It has seemed to some scholars (e.g. Schürer) that such views would be impossible after the Maccabaean revolt and that the first half of the book must therefore date to the beginning of the second century B.C. (Moore) or earlier. This argument is fallacious since there is much evidence that not all Jews maintained ideological opposition to gentile rule once the immediate persecution was over.[359] The second half of the book also assumes the devastation of Jerusalem and the deportation of the people (4:10–16), its purpose being to give instruction and comfort after the event. Since this half is otherwise undated, it is possible to see this background as a reference to the destruction of the Temple in A.D. 70 and to date both this section and the compilation of the whole book by the attachment of this part to the present first half of the book to the late first century A.D. or after. In that case, the compiler will have been led to put the two halves of the book together by the striking relevance of the already extant first section to conditions after A.D. 70. For the compiler, the emphasis on the need to sacrifice for the gentile ruler (1:10–11) will have then appeared to refer to the discontinuance of the daily offering for the Roman emperor which began the rebellion in A.D. 66 (*B.J.* ii 17, 2–4; cf. vol. II, pp. 310–12); the unhistorical juxtaposition of Nebuchadnezzar and Belshazzar will have seemed reminiscent of the relation between Vespasian and Titus; and the narration that parents ate the

358. For the Psalms of Solomon as dependent on I Baruch, see W. Pesch, 'Die Abhängigkeit des 11. Salomonischen Psalms vom letzten Kapitel des Buches Baruch', ZAW 67 (1955), pp. 251–63. For both texts as dependent on a common source, see among others R. H. Charles, in Charles, APOT I, pp. 573–4. C. A. Moore, in CBQ 36 (1974), pp. 312–20, cf. *idem, Daniel, Esther and Jeremiah: The Additions* (1977), pp. 314–16, argues that I Baruch 4:36–5:4 is simply based on a common source known also to the author of Psalms of Solomon 11, but suggests that I Baruch 5:4–9 *is* based directly on the Psalms of Solomon and therefore should be viewed as a later addition to the book.

359. J. A. Goldstein, 'The Apocryphal Book of Baruch', PAAJR 46–47 (1979–80), pp. 197–99, suggests that the fictional setting is intended to encourage Jews to accept the authority of Antiochus V (= Belshazzar) after the death of Antiochus IV (= Nebuchadnezzar) in 164 B.C. The suggestion is very hypothetical but has the merit of demonstrating the possibility of a Maccabaean or a later date.

flesh of their children during the misery of war (2:3), which was included in the original passage only as a literary convention in describing the horrors of wars, will have seemed uncannily accurate given Josephus' account of precisely this behaviour during the siege of A.D. 70 (*B.J.* vi 3, 4 (205–13)).[360] However, so late a date for the compilation of Baruch is not positively *required* since, as has been seen, there exists no firm criterion for dating the second half of the book which might therefore have been written considerably earlier, even as early as the second century B.C.[361] In that case it can only be said of the compilation of the whole that it presumably took place after the translation of the LXX of Jeremiah, since the second half was not included in the translation. However, although it is certain that that translation did not occur *after* 116 B.C., it may have taken place at any date in the second century before that time, in which case a second century date for the composition and compilation of the whole of I Baruch is perfectly possible, and the references to the destruction of Jerusalem throughout the work must be taken as the purely literary invention of the author in his attempt to render the pseudepigraphon historically plausible by imitating Jeremiah.[362]

Jerome denied the existence of a Hebrew text of Baruch, cf. *Prol. comment. in Jerem.* (CCL LXXIV, p. 1), *Prol. in versionem Jerem.* (PL XXVIII, 904), as did Epiphanius, *De mensuris et ponderibus* 5, but this does not prove that it never existed. In the Milan manuscript of the *Syrus hexaplaris* the remark occurs three times, 'this is not in the Hebrew' (cf. Ceriani's remarks in his edition, *Monum. sacra et prof.* I.1, 1861). (Nestle's explanation (*Septuagintastudien* IV, p. 12) that these notes refer not to a Hebrew text of Baruch but to the passages quoted there from the Old Testament is, particularly at 1:17, impossible because nothing is in fact quoted.) The notes about a Hebrew text must have been made

360. The contacts of Baruch with the Theodotionic text of Daniel 1–2 are very striking, though occasional divergences suggest that the author of Baruch may have relied on his memory, cf. J. A. Montgomery, *A Critical and Exegetical Commentary on the Book of Daniel* (1927), pp. 49 f. However, they cannot be used as firm supporting evidence for a later date given the difficulties in dating the Daniel text (see above, p. 501), though they do make a first century A.D. date somewhat more likely. Certainly, a date after A.D. 70 cannot be ruled out for the book, any more than for the Apocalypse of Baruch and IV Ezra, by its later acceptance and use by Christian authors, though this fact does make a date after A.D. 100 improbable.

361. A date before the second century B.C. is rather unlikely because of similarities between 3:9–4:4 and both Ben Sira and Wisdom of Solomon. However, it can only be certain for 3:9–5:9 that it was all written after the book of Job, on which a number of passages in both sections rely, cf. Moore, *op. cit.*, pp. 304 (for 3:9–4:4), 309 (on 4:12).

362. If I Baruch 1:3–14 is a later interpolation (see above, pp. 734 f.), it may reasonably be argued that it at least was added to the text after A.D. 70 in direct reference to the cessation of the sacrifices in A.D. 66 and the misery that followed, cf. O. Eissfeldt, *The O.T., An Introduction, etc.* (1965), p. 594.

later than Origen, for in the Hexapla the whole of Baruch was 'obelized' as not existing in Hebrew (in Codex Chisianus the following remark is found at the end of Baruch: βαρουχ ολως ωβελισται κατα τους ο', cf. *Novae Patrum Bibliothecae ab A. Maio collectae* X.3 (1905), p. 220; also in the *Syr. hexapl.*, cf. Nestle, *op. cit.*).

The Jews read Baruch and the Lamentations of Jeremiah during public worship on the tenth of Gorpiaios, according to the *Apostolic Constitutions* v 20: 'even now on the tenth day of the month Gorpiaios, when they assemble together, they read the Lamentations of Jeremiah ... and Baruch.' The main source of the late fourth-century *Apostolic Constitutions* is at this point the third century A.D. Didascalia. The Didascalia however also survives independently for this passage in Syriac translation and does *not* mention Baruch. Furthermore, it speaks of the reading of the Lamentations of Jeremiah as taking place on the ninth of Ab rather than the tenth of Gorpiaios (R. H. Connolly, *Didascalia Apostolorum* (1929), pp. 191–2). The reference in the *Apostolic Constitutions* may therefore be to the ninth of Ab, because the following paragraph deals with the day of the destruction of Jerusalem, and it is also known independently that the Lamentations of Jeremiah were read on that day (cf. 'Ab, ninth day of', in JE I (1901), cols. 23–5). It is however puzzling that the *Apostolic Constitutions* should have equated the ninth of Ab with the tenth of Gorpiaios, since otherwise it used the Syro-Macedonian calendar (v 14, 1; 17, 2; cf. 13) according to which Gorpiaios should be equivalent to Elul. It is possible that the author of *Apostolic Constitutions* meant to refer to the Day of Atonement (the tenth of Tishri) but, since there is no supporting evidence for the use of the Lamentations of Jeremiah then, it is most likely that he, like the Didascalia, intended the tenth of Ab, which Josephus, *B.J.* vi 4, 5 (250), along with some rabbis, gives as the date of the double burning of the Temple, even though this was normally commemorated on the ninth of Ab. Cf. H. St. J. Thackeray, *The Septuagint and Jewish Worship* (²1923), pp. 107–9; cf. pp. 80–107 for internal evidence within the book for a liturgical origin. Thackeray, *op. cit.*, pp. 109–11, furthermore follows G. Bickell, *Conspectus rei Syr. Lit.*, p. 7, n. 7, in considering that the remark in the *Apostolic Constitutions* is confirmed by a passage which contains a quotation from Baruch preserved in a probably sixth-century A.D. text incorrectly attributed to Ephraem (Ephraem Syrus, *Opp. Syr.* III, p. 212. A better text in Ephraem, *Sermones* II.3, CSCO 311–12 = Scriptores Syri 134–5 (1970). Transl. by J. B. Morris, *Select Works of St. Ephrem* (1847), pp. 61 ff.): 'Today let the synagogue sing this song among the people: "He has brought upon me a great mourning; the Lord has left me desolate, and the Lord has forgotten that I am his heritage, and has reckoned me as a stranger, and as a widow that is bereaved."' (For the date of this work, see Burkitt, cited by Thackeray, *loc. cit.*) It is however very dubious whether this passage really shows that Jews had a liturgical use for I Baruch in the sixth century A.D., as Thackeray claimed. The first sentence, which seems to describe such a use, is actually just a direct quotation of I Baruch 4:9 and is intended by the Christian writer to be hortatory rather than descriptive, cf. A. Sundberg, *The Old Testament in the Early Church* (1958), pp. 74–7.

Many Church Fathers, apparently intending to give the Hebrew canon, include Baruch among the canonical writings: Cyril. Jerus., in Zahn, *Gesch. des neutestamentl. Kanons* II, p. 179; Swete and Ottley, IOTG, p. 204: Ἰερεμίου [μία] μετὰ Βαροὺχ καὶ Θρήνων καὶ Ἐπιστολῆς. *Laodicene Canons* in Swete and Ottley, IOTG, p. 209: Ἰερεμίας καὶ Βαρούχ, Θρῆνοι καὶ Ἐπιστολαί (sic); Athanasius, in *ibid.*, p. 204: Ἰερεμίας καὶ σὺν αὐτῷ Βαρούχ, Θρῆνοι καὶ Ἐπιστολή; Epiphanius, *Pan. Haer.* viii 6 (ed. Holl, GCS Epiphanius I (1915), pp. 191–2): Ἰερεμίας ὁ προφήτης μετὰ τῶν Θρήνων καὶ Ἐπιστολῶν αὐτοῦ τε καὶ <τοῦ> Βαροὺχ (cf. Swete and Ottley, p. 204); Stichometr. Niceph. (in Swete and Ottley, p. 208): Ἰερεμίας προφήτης στίχ. δ´, Βαροὺχ στίχ. ψ´. But Epiphanius, *De mensuris et ponderibus* 5, who says clearly that no text survived παρ' Ἑβραίοις, shows that it would be wrong to deduce from these passages that Baruch really belonged to the *Jewish* canon.

On its use in the Christian Church, cf. the exhaustive discussion in F. H. Reusch, *Erklärung des Buchs Baruch* (1853), pp. 1–21, 268 ff., and G. H. Hoberg, *Die älteste lateinische Uebersetzung des Buches Baruch* (1902), pp. 7–19. The book is frequently quoted as a work of the prophet Jeremiah, because it was already early connected with this book. The favourite passage of the Church Fathers was that of the appearance of God on earth (Bar. 3:38: μετὰ τοῦτο ἐπὶ τῆς γῆς ὤφθη καὶ ἐν τοῖς ἀνθρώποις συνανεστράφη). It is not clear from the text what should be the subject of the verb ὤφθη. Both Greek and Latin Fathers took it to be God, who is the subject of the preceding verse, so that the verse becomes a prediction of the incarnation of Christ and is probably a rather clumsy Christian interpolation. This view is reflected in the Latin and Syriac versions, which translate '*he* appeared on earth'. However, if the subject is taken to be Wisdom, the subject of the following verse, there is no reason to reject the verse as inauthentic, cf. C. A. Moore, *Daniel, Esther and Jeremiah: The Additions* (1977), ad loc. The oldest quotation is in Athenagoras, *Leg.* 9 (ed. Schoedel, p. 20), where Bar. 3:36 is cited as a saying of a προφήτης. Irenaeus iv 20, 4, alludes to Bar. 3:38. In *ibid.* v 35, 1, he quotes Bar. 4:36–5:9, with the formula: 'significavit Jeremias propheta'. Clement of Alexandria, *Paedag.* i 10, 91–2, cites various passages as sayings of the prophet Jeremiah. In *Paedag.* ii 3, 36, he cites Bar. 3:16–19, with the formula ἡ θεία που λέγει γραφή. Hippolytus mentions in his *Contra Noetum* 2:5 (ed.

Butterworth, p. 47) that Noetus and his followers appealed amongst others to Bar. 3:36–8 as proof for their patripassian Christology. He himself then gives a sophisticated interpretation of the passage (*Contra Noetum* 5:1–5, ed. Butterworth, pp. 55–7), to escape the difficulty. Hence Baruch was a normative authority for both Noetus and Hippolytus. Origen, *In Jerem. homil.* vii 3 (GCS, Origen III, p. 54; ed. Nautin, SC 232, p. 348): γέγραπται· 'ἄκουε, 'Ισραήλ κ.τ.λ. = Bar. 3:9–13. *Idem, Selecta in Jerem.* 31 (PG XIII, 581): Γέγραπται ἐν τῷ Βαρούχ· 'τί ὅτι ἐν γῇ κ.τ.λ. = Bar. 3:10. (However, when Origen in Eusebius, *Hist. eccl.* vi 25, 2, appears to state that the Epistle of Jeremiah is canonical it is not clear whether he intended to include or exclude I Baruch. Cf. Moore, *op. cit.*, p. 262, n. 12.) Commodian., *Carmen apologet.*, 371–2 (CCL CXXVIII (1960), p. 87): 'Hieremias ait: Hic deus est etc.' = Bar. 3:36–8. Cyprian, *Testim.* ii 6: 'Item apud Hieremiam prophetam: Hic deus noster etc.' = Bar. 3:36–8.

Among the Greek manuscripts the most important are Vaticanus, Alexandrinus, Marchalianus, and finally Codex Chisianus (on which see A. Rahlfs, *Verzeichnis der griechischen Handschriften des Alten Testaments* (MSU III) (1914), pp. 278–80). Sinaiticus does not contain Baruch. The Theodotion translation of I Baruch is attested only by five readings in the Syro-Hexapla, cf. R. R. Harwell, *The Principal Versions of Baruch* (1915), pp. 6–7.

Editions

Ziegler, J., *Ieremias, Baruch, Threni, Epistula Ieremiae* (1957; [2]1976).

Tov, E., *The Book of Baruch also called I Baruch (Greek and Hebrew)* (1975) (text, a reconstruction of the Hebrew of 1:1–3:8, and translation).

Ancient Translations

(1) The Latin translation, which is extant in three different versions: (a) that which, though not by Jerome, has passed into the Vulgate and is a close rendering of the standard Greek text; (b) a shorter text found in only a few manuscripts published in P. Sabatier, *Bibliorum sacrorum Latinae versiones antiquae* II (1749), pp. 734 ff. J. J. Kneucker, *Das Buch Baruch* (1879), pp. 157 ff., argued that (b) is a later recension of (a) in which the Latin is improved and readings changed to agree with the Greek in B; against him R. R. Harwell, *The Principal Version of Baruch* (1915), pp. 29–46, argues convincingly that (b) was not reliant on (a) but rather descended independently from a Greek text which antedates the standard text of Baruch. (c) The text of *Codex Gothicus* from León, Spain, of the year 960, published by G. Hoberg, *Die älteste lateinische Übersetzung des Buches Baruch* (1902), was claimed by him and by Schürer in ThLZ (1903), pp. 374–6, as an older recension of a hypothetical original text than either of the other two versions, but it is

more likely that it represents a late attempt to conform the (b) version to the standard Greek text, cf. Harwell, *op. cit.*, pp. 47–51. Similarly late and unimportant is the manuscript published in A. Amelli, *De Libri Baruch vetustissime latina versione usque ad huc inedita in celeberrimo codice Cavensi, Monte Cassino* (1902).

(2) The two Syriac translations, on which see Harwell, *op. cit.*, pp. 5–28. (a) The Peshitta, i.e. the usual Syriac text, cf. above, p. 184. (b) The Syro-Hexaplar version, published by A. Ceriani, *Monumenta sacra et profana* I.1 (1861). Cf. the photolithographic copy of the entire manuscript published by Ceriani in 1874 (see above, p. 184).

(3) A Coptic translation published by H. Brugsch (Zeitschr. für ägyptische Sprache und Alterthumskunde 10–12 (1872–4); cf. (1876), p. 148.
A collation from a Greek text is given by Schulte, *Die koptische Uebersetzung der vier grossen Propheten* (1892), pp. 37–9. Cf. Ziegler's ed., pp. 22–6.

(4) The Ethiopic translation in Dillmann, *Biblia Vet. Test. aethiopica* V (1894), with a translation back into Greek. Dillmann did not however use the important Berlin Codex (Ms. Orient. Fol. 3067), on which see Ziegler's ed., pp. 34–7.

Commentaries

Fritzsche, O. F., *Exeget. Handb. zu den Apokryphen* I (1851).
Reusch, F. H., *Erklärung des Buchs Baruch* (1853).
Kneucker, J. J., *Das Buch Baruch, Geschichte und Kritik, Uebersetzung und Erklärung* (1879).
Gifford, E. H., in H. Wace, *The Speaker's Bible, The Apocrypha* II (1888).
Zöckler, O., 'Das Buch Baruch', in *Die Apokryphen des A.T. nebst einem Anhang über die Pseudepigraphenliteratur (Kurzgef. Kommentar zu den heil. Schriften A. und N.T.*, ed. Strack and Zöckler, no. 9, 1891), 239–49.
Rothstein, J. W., in E. Kautzsch, APAT I, pp. 213–25.
Whitehouse, O. C., 'The Book of Baruch or I Baruch', in Charles, APOT I, pp. 569–95.
Kalt, E., *Das Buch Baruch übersetzt und erklärt*, in F. Feldmann and H. Herkenne, *Die Heilige Schrift des A.T.* (1932).
Hamp, V., *Baruch*, in *Die Heilige Schrift in deutscher Übersetzung* (1950).
Schneider, H., *Baruch* (1954).
Kahana, A., הספרים החיצונים (²1956).
Wambacq, B. M., *Jeremias, Klaagliederen, Baruch, Brief van Jeremias* (1957).
Gelin, A., *Le Livre de Baruch* (1959).
Gunneweg, A. H. J., *Das Buch Baruch* (JSHRZ III.2) (1975), pp. 165–81.
Moore, C. A., *Daniel, Esther and Jeremiah: The Additions* (1977).

Bibliography

Marshall, J. T., HDB I (1898), cols. 251–4.
Toy, C. H., 'Baruch, book of', JE II (1902), cols. 556–7.
Hoberg, G. H., *Die älteste lateinische Übersetzung des Buches Baruch* (²1902).
Thackeray, H. St. J., 'The Greek Translators of Jeremiah', JThSt 4 (1903), pp. 245–66, esp. 261–6.
Nestle, E., *Septuagintastudien* IV (1903), pp. 11–16.
Harwell, R. R., *The Principal Versions of Baruch* (1915).

Stählin, O., 'Die hellenistisch-jüdische Literatur', in W. Christ, O. Stählin and W. Schmidt, *Geschichte der griechischen Litteratur*[6] II.1 (1920), pp. 555 ff.

Stoderl, W., *Zur Echtheitsfrage von Baruch i-iii, 8* (1922).

Thackeray, H. St. J., *The Septuagint and Jewish Worship* ([2]1923), pp. 80–111.

Hautsch, E., in RE IIA.2 (1923), cols. 1603–4.

Heinisch, P., 'Zur Entstehung des Buches Baruch', Theologie und Glaube 20 (1928), pp. 696–710.

Oesterley, W. O. E., *An Introduction to the Books of the Apocrypha* (1935), pp. 256–67.

Torrey, C. C., *The Apocryphal Literature etc.* (1945), pp. 59–64.

Pfeiffer, R. H., *History of N.T. Times* (1949), pp. 409–25.

Pesch, W., 'Die Abhängigkeit des 11. salomonischen Psalms vom letzten Kapitel des Buches Baruch', ZAW 67 (1955), pp. 251–63.

Wambacq, B. M., 'Les prières de Baruch (i,15-ii,19) et de Daniel (ix,5–19)', Bibl. 40 (1959), pp. 463–75.

Wambacq, B. M., 'L'unité littéraire de Baruch i-iii,8', EThL xii (1959), 455–60.

Tedesche, S., 'Baruch, Book of', IDB I (1962), cols. 362–3.

Wambacq, B. M., 'L'unité du livre de Baruch', Bibl. 47 (1966), pp. 574–6.

Bonnard, P.-E., *La Sagesse en personne annoncée et venue : Jésus-Christ* (1966), pp. 81–88.

Battistone, J. J., 'An Examination of the Literary and Theological Background of the Wisdom Passage of the Book of Baruch' (Diss. Duke Univ., 1968).

Rocco, B., 'La μάννα di Baruch I,10', Bibbia e Oriente 2 (1969), pp. 273–7.

Le Moyne, J., 'Baruch', DB suppl. VIII (1972), cols. 724–86.

Moore, C. A., 'Towards the Dating of the Book of Baruch', CBQ 36 (1974), pp. 312–20.

Tov, E., *The Septuagint Translation of Jeremiah and Baruch. A Discussion of an Early Revision of the LXX of Jeremiah 29–52 and Baruch 1:1–38* (1976).

Tov, E., 'The Relation between the Greek Versions of Baruch and Daniel', in M. E. Stone, ed., *Armenian and Biblical Studies* (1976), pp. 27–34.

Martin, R. A., *Syntactical and Critical Concordance to the Greek Text of Baruch and the Epistle of Jeremiah* (Computer Bible, 12) (1977).

Goldstein, J. A., 'The Apocryphal Book of Baruch', PAAJR 46–47 (1979–80), pp. 179–99.

Burke, D. G., *The Poetry of Baruch: a reconstruction and analysis of the original Hebrew text of Baruch 3:9–5:9* (1982).

Cf. O. Eissfeldt, *The O.T., An Introduction etc.* (1965), 592–4, and introductions to the apocrypha. Cf. above, p. 715 f.

6. The Letter of Jeremiah

The Letter of Jeremiah, which in some of the later Greek manuscripts follows immediately after I Baruch without a break, is nonetheless a quite separate work. Although it was treated as canonical by the Church Fathers from the second century A.D., being included by name in a number of canon lists and considered by others as an adjunct to the Book of Jeremiah itself,[363] it was excluded from the Hebrew canon at least by the time of Jerome, cf. *Comm. on Jeremiah, praef.* (PL XXIV, 706).

The Letter purports to be written to the exiles who were to be deported to Babylon. It is a tirade against idolatry which revolves around the theme that the images of wood, silver and gold, like the miserable, powerless and perishable creatures of man's hand, are

363. C. A. Moore, *Daniel, Esther and Jeremiah : The Additions* (1977), p. 325.

utterly unable to do either good or bad. In this way the author sought to restrain his fellow-believers from any participation in heathen cults.

This small work is extant only in Greek, and, as the discovery of a Greek fragment at Qumran demonstrates, it circulated in this language in Palestine during the first century B.C. (see below). There is quite good linguistic evidence, however, that the letter was written originally in either Hebrew[364] or Aramaic.[365] The letter could date to any time between the latest biblical passages which are its inspiration, i.e. Isaiah 44:9–20 and 46:5–7 in *c.* 540 B.C., and the date of the Qumran fragment of the Greek version in the first century B.C. It is also likely that 2 Mac. 2:1–2 alludes to this letter; the fact that 2 Mac. 2:4 states that Jeremiah gave orders about the tent and the ark, which are not mentioned in the letter, does not preclude a reference to the letter in the attack on idolatry ascribed to the prophet in 2:1–2 (cf. J. T. Marshall, 'The Epistle of Jeremy', HDB II, p. 579). In that case, the original version of the letter will have been composed before this part of 2 Maccabees, which probably dates to the second century B.C. (see above, p. 533).

The Greek used in the present text shows marked influence from the κοινή, suggesting a second century B.C. date (cf. W. Naumann, 'Untersuchungen über den apokryphen Jeremiasbrief', BZAW 25 (1913), pp. 31–44). If the original version was in a Semitic language, however, this is of little help in dating its composition.[366] There are few clues for the place of composition. It may be relevant that the idolatry attacked seems closer to Babylonian than Greek or Egyptian paganism (so Neumann, *art. cit.*, pp. 3–31; Moore, pp. 328–9), but this may have been occasioned by the fictional setting of the letter rather than the circumstances of the author.

The remark of the Targum on Jer. 10:11, designating this Aramaic verse as a copy from the Letter of Jeremiah, is not a reference to the letter, cf. Nestle, *Marginalien und Materialien* (1893), 42 ff. Origen's assertion, that Lamentations and 'the letter' are connected with the book of Jeremiah in the Hebrew canon, is surely a slip (Eusebius, *Hist. eccl.* vi 25, 2: Ἱερεμίας σὺν Θρήνοις καὶ τῇ ἐπιστολῇ ἐν ἑνί). Origen intended to say only that the writings of Jeremiah were counted as *one*

---

364. C. J. Ball, in Charles, APOT I, pp. 597–8; Moore, *op. cit.*, pp. 326–7. The Hebraisms noted are not decisive but, more significantly, corrupt and variant readings can be best explained in verses 12, 16, 21, 68 and 72 on the hypothesis of a Hebrew original.

365. C. C. Torrey, *The Apocryphal Literature* (1945), p. 66, on ἐν τῷ στέγῳ ('on the roof') in verse 11 as a mistranslation of על אגרא ('for hire') as על עיגרא ('on the roof').

366. Moore, *op. cit.*, pp. 328, 334–5, suggests tentatively that the prediction in verse 3, that Israel may have to stay in Babylon 'up to seven generations', i.e. until *c.* 317 B.C., should be taken literally; but this hypothesis should be rejected as too literalistic.

by the Jews, so that the total number of books of Scripture is twenty-two.

Christian writers do not often allude to the letter. Although he does not actually quote it, Aristides, *Apologia*, ed. J. Geffcken, *Zwei Griechische Apologeten* (1907), seems to have been much influenced by it, and brief portions are quoted by Tertullian, *De Scorpiace* 8, Cyprian, *De dominica oratione* 5, and later writers. In the Latin Vulgate the letter has been added as chapter six to the Book of Baruch.

The manuscripts, editions, ancient translations, and exegetical works are generally the same as those for I Baruch (see above, pp. 741–2). Papyrus fragments of the Greek text have been found in Cave VII of Qumran, published in M. Baillet, J. T. Milik and R. de Vaux (avec une contribution de H. W. Baker), *Les 'Petites Grottes' de Qumran* (DJD III, 1962), p. 143, plate xxx. Cf. A. Dupont-Sommer, *The Essene Writings from Qumran* (1961), p. 297.

Commentaries

Rothstein, J. W., *Der Jeremiasbrief*, in Kautsch, APAT, pp. 226–29.
Ball, C. J., in Charles, APOT I, cols. 596–611.
Hamp, V., *Der Brief des Jeremia* (1948).
Artom, Elihu S., in Kahana, הספרים החיצונים (²1956).
Gunneweg, A. H. J., *Der Brief Jeremias* (JSHRZ III.2, 1975), pp. 183–92.
Moore, C. A., *Daniel, Esther and Jeremiah : The Additions* (1977).

Bibliography

Marshall, J. T., 'The Epistle of Jeremy', HDB II (1899), cols. 578–90.
Nestle, E., *Septuagintastudien* IV (1903), pp. 16–19.
Naumann, W., *Untersuchungen über den apokryphen Jeremiasbrief* (BZAW, no. 25, 1913), pp. 1–53.
Thackeray, H. St. J., *Some Aspects of the Greek O.T.* (1927), pp. 53–64.
Artom, Elihu S., 'L'origine, la data e gli scopi dell' Epistola di Geremia', Annuario Studi Ebr. 1 (1935), pp. 49–74.
Torrey, C. C., *The Apocryphal Literature* (1945), pp. 64–7.
Robert, A., 'Jérémie, la lettre de', DB suppl. IV (1949), cols. 849–57.
Baars, W., 'Two Palestinian Syriac Texts identified as Parts of the Epistle of Jeremy', VT 2 (1961), pp. 77–81.
Lee, G. M., 'Apocryphal Cats : Baruch 6:21', VT 21 (1971), pp. 111–12.
Martin, R. A., *Syntactical and Critical Concordance to the Greek Text of Baruch and the Epistle of Jeremiah* (1977).
Nicklesburg, G. W. E., JLBBM, pp. 35–8.

Cf. also O. Eissfeldt, *The O.T., An Introduction etc.* (1965), 594 f.

II. Pseudepigraphic Apocalypses

1. 2 (Slavonic) Enoch

The Slavonic or Second Book of Enoch, known also as the Book of the Secrets of Enoch, was first published in a longer version by A. Popov in 1880, and in a shorter recension from a sixteenth century Serbian manuscript by S. Novaković in 1884. It reached the western scholarly world through the medium of an English and a German translation, which both appeared in 1896 (R. H. Charles and W. R. Morfill, *The Book of the Secrets of Enoch*; G. N. Bonwetsch, *Das slavische Henochbuch*). The most up-to-date edition of the manuscripts is that by A. Vaillant, *Le livre des secrets d'Hénoch : Texte slave et traduction française* (1952), and the latest study of the complicated textual problems is contained in F. I. Andersen's introduction in OTP I (1983), pp. 92–100, who lists twenty manuscripts transmitting the short and the long texts, or different extracts incorporated into miscellaneous collections.

The relationship between the two recensions is very complex. R. H. Charles preferred the longer text, and explained the shorter as an abridgement (APOT II, pp. 425–6: 'complete' and 'incomplete' versions). By contrast, N. Schmidt (JAOS 41 (1921), pp. 307–12), A. Vaillant (*op. cit.*) and most recent authors (U. Fischer, *Eschatologie*, pp. 37–8; Nickelsburg, JLBBM, p. 185; J. J. Collins, 'The Genre Apocalypse', *Apocalypticism*, p. 553) recognize the shorter recension as older. Owing to the lack of clarity regarding the interrelation of the various text types, it is advisable to keep all the options open and to envisage that old, and possibly even original, material has survived in the longer version (S. Pines, Enc. Jud. 6, col. 797; Andersen, OTP I, pp. 93–4).

The book has been influenced by the Ethiopic Enoch, although it cannot be defined as a free revision of it. Chapters 3–37 are related to 1 En. 12–36; chapters 38–66 to 1 En. 81, 91–105; chapters 67–73 deal with the descendants of Enoch and are partly connected with 1 En. 106–7.

2 Enoch is a midrashic expansion of Gen. 5:21–32, covering the life of Enoch and of his posterity until the flood. Part 1 (chapters 3–21) describes Enoch's journey to the seven heavens,[1] where he is led by two

---

1. The longer recension (21:6 ; 22:1) knows the eighth, ninth and tenth heavens also, as well as their Hebrew names *Mazzaloth*, *Kokhabim* and *'Araboth*. The latter designates the seventh, i.e. the highest heaven in bHag. 12b. No Hebrew source counting ten heavens has survived, except perhaps Num. R. 14:12 (on Num. 7:13), where the ten celestial spheres (reminiscent of the ten Sefiroth of the Kabbalah) are mentioned (cf. Hans

angels. It is worth noting that Paradise is located in the third heaven (8:1), which recalls 2 Cor. 12:2–4 (οἶδα ἄνθρωπον... ἁρπαγέντα ... ἕως τρίτου οὐρανοῦ ... καὶ οἶδα τὸν τοιοῦτον ἄνθρωπον... ὅτι ἡρπάγη εἰς τὸν παράδεισον).[2] •

In the second section (chapters 22–37), Enoch has to appear before God divested of his earthly clothing and wearing a heavenly garment. God reveals to him the events of the creation and the history of mankind to his own time. The story of the origins follows Gen. 1. In the longer version (30:3), the seven planets, designated by Greek names, Kronos, Aphrodite, Ares, Sun, Zeus, Hermes, Moon, are listed from the highest downwards. The history of mankind closes with the divine prediction that because of their idolatry and adultery men will be punished with the flood.

The doctrinal and ethical instructions of Enoch to his children form the last section (chapters 38–66). Brought back to the earth, Enoch emphasizes the importance of his books (366 in number according to the long recension, 360 according to the shorter: cf. 23:6 and 68:2) which contain the revelations he has received. His moral doctrine echoes that of Ben Sira. Similarity to the Ethiopic Enoch is less noticeable in this section. The book closes with a brief account of the ascension of Enoch to heaven (chapter 67), and with a short retrospect of his life (chapter 68).

The supplementary chapters (69–73) outline the priestly succession of Enoch. His office of revealer and expiator (64:5) is inherited first by Methuselah, then by Noah's younger brother Nir, and finally by the miraculously born Melkizedek. Nir's sterile wife, Sopanim, finds herself pregnant in her old age, although she no longer sleeps with her husband. Accused by him of unchastity, she suddenly dies, but a living child, Melkizedek, emerges from the dead body. The longer version ends with an allusion to the flood and to the death of Noah (73:5–9).

Apart from obvious phrases there is nothing specifically Christian in the work. Resemblances may be due to a background common to 2 Enoch and the New Testament and not, as Vaillant has claimed, to a use of the latter by the former. Neither does 2 Enoch contain any hint of the Christian concept of a redeemer (cf. Andersen, *op. cit.*, p. 96). By contrast, the full acceptance of animal sacrifice clearly favours a Jewish

---

Bietenhard, *Die himmlische Welt im Urchristentum und Spätjudentum* [WUNT 2] (1951), p. 6). The two verses have no parallels in the shorter version and are thought to be interpolations. Nevertheless, the Hebrew words may indicate an ancient source. *Mazzaloth* and *Kokhabim* are listed as the third and fourth groups of heavenly bodies, the first two are the sun and the moon, which are situated below the first heaven in 3 En. 17:6–7. Cf. P. Alexander, OTP I, p. 270. For the Hebrew text, see P. Schäfer, *Synopse zur Hekhalot-Literatur* (1981), § 858.

2. Cf. P. Schäfer, 'New Testament and Hekhaloth Literature: The Journey into Heaven in Paul and in Merkavah Mysticism', JJS 35 (1984), pp. 22–3.

origin. Reference to the binding of all four legs of the victim (59:3) suggests a practice disapproved of by the rabbis (cf. mTam. 4:1 ; bTam. 31b).

The original language of the composition cannot be determined. There is, nevertheless, an intrinsic probability that the Slavonic depends on a Greek text, one that is reinforced by the occurrence of Greek terms, such as the designation of the planets in 30:3 and the explanation of the name Adam (Ἀδάμ) by means of an anagram from Ἀνατολή, Δύσις, Ἄρκτος, Μεσημβρία (30:13; cf. also 3 Sib. 24–5). Other obvious Greek words surviving in Slavonic include *Grigori* = οἱ ἐγρήγοροι (18:1, 2, 7, 9 etc.) and Arkhas = ἀρχή (26:2). Hence a number of scholars from Charles onwards have advanced the view that 2 Enoch, or at least a great proportion of it, was written in Greek.[3] Nevertheless, even those who opt for a Greek original tend to postulate a Semitic source or sources behind the Greek (cf. Andersen, OTP I, p. 94). Leaving apart certain stylistic peculiarities, which may be identified as Semitisms but which may have resulted from a deliberate imitation of biblical idioms by a Jewish author writing in Greek, a number of Hebrew words are preserved even at the Slavonic stage, which can best be explained as relics of a Hebrew document. The most significant of these are names of the Jewish months Siwan and Tebeth (48:2), Siwan and Nisan (68:1), Iyyar and Nisan (73:5, 8). Furthermore, the longer recension gives also the Hebrew names of the eighth, ninth and tenth heavens (cf. above, n. 1). *Otanim* (20:1 in both recensions) transcribes inexactly the Hebrew אופנים. Recently N. A. Meshchersky has conjectured on the basis of Semitisms contained in it that the shorter version was made directly from the Hebrew,[4] but this seems to be an exaggeration, especially when it is recalled that most surviving Hebrew terms appear only in the longer recension. It is safer to conclude that elements belonging to 2 Enoch existed both in Greek and in Hebrew. No decisive particular proof can be advanced for dating the document, though the prevailing opinion favours the first century A.D.[5] However, the general principle establishing a *terminus ad*

3. Cf. Charles, APOT II, p. 426; Vaillant, *Hénoch*, pp. xi-xiii; Pines, 'Eschatology', p. 73; Enc. Jud. 6, cols. 797–9; Fischer, *Eschatologie*, p. 39; Nickelsburg, JLBBM, p. 185; Collins, 'The Genre Apocalypse', *Apocalypticism*, pp. 533–4; Andersen, OTP I, p. 94.

4. 'Sledy pamyatnikov Kumrana v staroslavyanskoi i drevnerusskoi literature (K izucheniya slavyanskikh versii knigi Enokha)', Trudy otdela drevnerusskoi literatury 19 (1963), pp. 130–47; 'Problemy izucheniya slavyano-russkoi perevodnoi literatury XI-XV vv.', *ibid.* 20 (1964), pp. 180–231; 'K istorii tcksta slavyanskoi knigi Enokha', Vizantiiskii vremennik 24 (1964), pp. 91–108; 'K voprosu ob istochnikakh slavyanskoi knigi Enokha', Kratkiye soobshcheniya Instituta narodov Azii 86 (1965), pp. 72–8. (Cf. Andersen, OTP I, p. 93, n. 7; p. 94, n. 9.)

5. Cf. Charles, APOT II, p. 429; G. Scholem, *Ursprung und Anfänge der Kabbala* (1962), p. 64; M. Philonenko, 'La cosmologie du Livre des secrets d'Hénoch', *Religions en Egypte*

quem for the adoption of Jewish works by Christians prior to A.D. 135 can be invoked in the case of 2 Enoch, too.[6] The final form of the text, as reflected in the Slavonic manuscripts, must have resulted from a long and complex editorial process which it is no longer possible to reconstruct with any degree of assurance (Andersen, OTP I, p. 95).

The Melchizedek legend appended to 2 Enoch contains a miraculous birth story which in its concrete details differs from any known version, but fits into the inter-Testamental speculations on the birth of his brother, Noah (1 En. 106–7); Gen. Ap. 2), and on Melchizedek's arrival in the world ἀπάτωρ ἀμήτωρ ἀγενεαλόγητος (Heb. 7:3). Its dependence on the New Testament is, however, most unlikely (Andersen, OTP I, pp. 96–7). For the Qumran Melchizedek fragments, see above, pp. 449–51.

The Greek composition is often associated with Egypt because of the mention of phoenixes and chalkydries, or brazen serpents, with lions' feet and tails and the heads of crocodiles (12:1), and because of the similarity of the author's ideas to those of Philo, Sirach and the Book of Wisdom.[7]

There is no certain reference to 2 Enoch in patristic literature. It is possible, however, that Origen's allusion to Enoch's account of the creation concerns 2 En. 24–30, since 1 En. does not discuss the subject. 'Nam et in eo libello … quem Hermas conscripsit, ita refertur. Primo omnium crede quia unus est deus, qui omnia creavit atque conposuit; qui cum nihil esset prius, esse fecit omnia … Sed et in Enoch libro his similia describuntur.' (*De Principiis* i 3, 2, ed. Koetschau, GCS 22, p. 51.)

Editions

Sokolov, M., *Materialy i zametki po starinnoj slavjanskoj literature. Vypusk tretij VII. Slavjanskaja Kniga Enoka, II. Tekst s latinskim perevodom. Cetinija*, University of Moscow (1899).
Vaillant, A., *Le livre des secrets d'Hénoch : Texte slave et traduction française* (1952, 1976).

Translations

English
Charles, R. H., and W. R. Morfill, *The Book of the Secrets of Enoch* (1896).

---

hellénistique et romaine (1969), pp. 109–16; S. Pines, 'Eschatology and the Concept of Time in the Slavonic Book of Enoch', *Types of Redemption*, ed. J. Z. Werblowsky and J. C. Bleeker [Numen suppl. 18] (1970), pp. 72–87; J. C. Greenfield, 'Prolegomenon' to H. Odeberg, *3 Enoch or the Hebrew Book of Enoch* (1973), pp. xviii-xx; U. Fischer, *Eschatologie und Jenseitserwartung im hellenistischen Diasporajudentum* [BZW 44] (1978), pp. 38–41.

6. The medieval dates assigned to 2 Enoch are generally held to be untenable. Mrs A. S. D. Maunder's claim that it is a Bogomil work ('The Date and Place of Writing of the Slavonic Book of Enoch', The Observatory 41 (1918), pp. 313–16) has been rebutted by A. Rubinstein in 'Observations on the Slavonic Book of Enoch', JJS 13 (1962), pp. 3–4. J. T. Milik's theory concerning a ninth century Byzantine authorship (*The Books of Enoch* (1976), pp. 107–16) is equally far-fetched. Cf. Collins, *art. cit.*, p. 533, n. 7.

7. Charles, APOT II, p. 426. Cf. also Fischer, *op. cit.*, p. 40; Collins, *art. cit.*, pp. 533–4.

Forbes, N., and R. H. Charles, '2 Enoch or the Book of the Secrets of Enoch', APOT II, pp. 425–69.
Andersen, F. I., '2 (Slavonic Apocalypse of) Enoch', OTP I, pp. 91–221.

French
Vaillant, A., *op. cit.*

German
Bonwetsch, G., *Die Bücher der Geheimnisse Henochs* (1922).
Riessler, P., *Altjüdisches Schrifttum* (1928), pp. 425–73, 1297–8.

Bibliography

Fotheringham, J. K., 'The Date and Place of Writing of the Slavonic Enoch', JThSt 20 (1919), p. 252.
Charles, R. H., 'The Date and Place of Writing of the Slavonic Enoch', JThSt 22 (1921), pp. 161–3.
Schmidt, N., 'The Two Recensions of the Slavonic Enoch', JAOS 41 (1921), pp. 307–12.
Lake, K., 'The Date of the Slavonic Enoch', HThR 16 (1923), pp. 397–8.
Gry, L., 'Quelques noms d'anges et d'êtres mystérieux en II Hénoch', RB 49 (1940), pp. 195–204.
Rubinstein, A., 'Observations on the Slavonic Book of Enoch', JJS 13 (1962), pp. 1–21.
Repp, F., 'Textkritische Untersuchungen zum Henoch-Apokryph des cod. slav. 125 der Österreichischen Nationalbibliothek', Wiener Slavistisches Jahrbuch 10 (1963), pp. 58–68.
Philonenko, M., 'La cosmogonie du Livre des secrets d'Hénoch', *Religions en Égypte hellénistique et romaine* (1969), pp. 109–16.
Pines, S., 'Eschatology and the Concept of Time in the Slavonic Book of Enoch', *Types of Redemption*, ed. R. J. Z. Werblowsky and C. J. Bleeker [Numen suppl. 18] (1970), pp. 72–87.
Idem, 'Enoch, Slavonic Book of', Enc. Jud. 6, cols. 797–9.
E. Turdeanu, 'Une curiosité de l'Énoch slave: Les phénix du sixième ciel', REtSl 67 (1968), pp. 53–4.
Idem, 'Dieu créa l'homme de huit éléments et tira son nom des quatre coins du monde', R. Et. Roumaines 13–14 (1974), pp. 163–94.
Fischer, U., *Eschatologie und Jenseitserwartung im hellenistischen Diasporajudentum* [BZNW 44] (1978), pp. 30–70.
Turdeanu, E., *Apocryphes slaves et roumaines de l'Ancien Testament* (1981), pp. 37–43.
Charlesworth, J. H., PMRS, pp. 103–6, 283.
Nickelsburg, G. W. E., JLBBM, pp. 185–8, 191–3.

2. The Syriac Apocalypse of Baruch (2 Baruch)

The Syriac Apocalypse of Baruch was first revealed in its entirety in 1871 when A. M. Ceriani edited it from the Codex Ambrosianus 13.21 Inf (folios 257a–265b) in his *Monumenta sacra et profana* V ii, pp. 113–80. He had issued a Latin translation of the work in 1866. Chapters 78–86 (Baruch's letter) were already included in the Paris and London Polyglots. Further Syriac excerpts are incorporated into Jacobite lectionaries. The text of the Apocalypse and the letter was published by M. Kmoskó in *Patrologia Syriaca* in 1907, and more recently by S. Dedering in the Leiden Peshitta project in 1973. A Greek papyrus fragment has preserved 12:1–13:2 (recto) and 13:11–14:2 (verso). It was edited by B. P. Grenfell and A. S. Hunt in *The Oxyrhynchus Papyri* III (1903), pp. 4–7; cf. also A.-M. Denis, FPG, pp. 118–20. An Arabic version, probably made from a different Syriac recension, still awaits publication.

The book professes to be a writing of Baruch, who relates in the first person events which he witnessed and revelations he received immediately before and after the destruction of Jerusalem. It contains, in addition to prayers and laments, apocalyptic visions and their interpretations, and a letter already alluded to which Baruch despatches by an eagle to the exiles. The work may be divided into seven sections.

I. In the twenty-fifth year of Jeconiah, God informs Baruch of the imminent downfall of Jerusalem. The city is destroyed by four angels and the Babylonians deport the Judaeans to captivity. Jeremiah follows them, but Baruch is instructed to remain there and laments over the ruins (chapters 1–12). II. After a fast of seven days, the judgement of the gentiles is foretold to Baruch. He then queries the purpose of being righteous, but is reminded of the responsibility deriving from the possession of the Torah and comforted by the prospect of ultimate justice. God promises a full revelation of the future at the end of another week of sanctification and fasting (chapters 13–20). III. Baruch's prayer is followed by a divine answer describing the end of time, divided into twelve epochs, and full of growing tribulations. The reckoning is given in a completely unintelligible form, possibly due to textual corruption, namely that the measure of that time will be in 'two parts: weeks of seven weeks' (27:2). When the calamities have affected the entire world, the age of the Messiah, culminating in the resurrection, will be revealed. Thereupon Baruch exhorts the elders of the people to prepare themselves for greater disasters (chapters 21–34). IV. In the ruins of the Holy of Holies, Baruch receives a revelation in a dream concerning a great forest, a vine, and a spring. The spring swells, carries away the mountains and, with the exception of a cedar, uproots the forest. At the end, even this last tree falls. The vine orders that it should be burned. Then the vine begins to grow and fill the valley. The dream is explained as announcing the destruction of the kingdom that has ruined Zion, and the succession of three further kingdoms. The Messiah, symbolized by the vine and the spring, is to overthrow the fourth kingdom whose head, the last cedar, will be convicted and put to death, and will inaugurate his everlasting reign. Baruch further fasts and exhorts the people (chapters 35–46). V. The tribulations of the last days are shown to him, as well as the glory of the risen and the dreadfulness of the damned (chapters 47–52). VI. In the Apocalypse of the cloud that follows, there is an alternating series of black and clear rains, six of each, but the black rain always heavier than the clear rain.

Finally lightning heals the earth, and twelve rivers arising from the sea submit themselves to the lightning. The angel Ramael expounds the vision in the form of a world history from Adam to the return from the Babylonian exile. This will be succeeded by the exceedingly dark rain of the ultimate upheaval and the brightness of salvation by God's Anointed. Subsequently Baruch is told to climb a high mountain to see the whole earth before being removed from this world, without passing through death, and being preserved until the end of times (chapters 53–76). VII. After a final address of encouragement to the people, Baruch sends two letters to the exiled Jews. The first is despatched, attached to the neck of an eagle, to the nine-and-a-half tribes of the first exile; the second is carried by three men to the brethren in Babylon. The dominating themes are judgement and salvation, together with constant obedience to the Torah (chapters 77–87).

The surviving version of the book ends here. It contains no trace of a letter to the Babylonian exiles referred to in 77:19. It may have been lost in the course of transmission, unless it corresponds to the deutero-canonical Baruch (P. Bogaert, *Apocalypse de Baruch* I (1969), p. 80), or to parts of it (1:1–3; 3:9–4:29 according to Charles, APOT II, p. 476). Baruch's survey of the earth from a mountain top and his subsequent translation, mentioned in 76:2–3, are not given in detail either. Although Charles saw in 2 Baruch a very complex book made from several documents (*The Apocalypse of Baruch*, pp. liii-lxv; APOT II, pp. 474–6), a good case for the unity of plan and composition has been presented by a number of scholars.[1] That the author of an apocalypse should have taken over and utilized sundry traditional elements is a commonly attested feature in this type of literature.

There is unanimity concerning a post-A.D. 70 dating of 2 Baruch. The principal source for this view (*pace* Charles who considers it as an interpolation) is provided by 32:2–4 where two destructions of the Temple are hinted at.[2] The vividness of shock and sorrow caused by the ruin of the Holy City and the Sanctuary, as well as 2 Baruch's close links with 4 Ezra and, to a lesser degree, with Pseudo-Philo's *Liber Antiquitatum Biblicarum*,[3] point towards a late first or early second century A.D. date. The interrelationship between the three writings,

---

1. See C. Clemen, 'Die Zusammensetzung des Buches Henoch, der Apokalypse des Baruch und des vierten Buches Esra', ThStKr 71 (1898), pp. 211–46; M. R. James, 'Pseudo-Philo and Baruch', JThSt 16 (1915), p. 405; B. Violet, *Die Apokalypsen des Esra und des Baruch in deutscher Gestalt* (1924), p. xc; P. Bogaert, *Apocalypse de Baruch* I (1969), pp. 57–91.

2. The obscure phrase in 28:2, mentioned above, cannot serve as basis for any reliable chronological deduction. See most recently A. F. J. Klijn, OTP I, pp. 616–17.

3. Cf. Violet, *op. cit.*, pp. lxxvii-lxxxi; L. Gry, 'La date de la fin des temps selon les révélations ou les calculs du Pseudo-Philon et de Baruch (Apocalypse syriaque)', RB 48 (1939), pp. 337–56.

and more particularly between 4 Ezra and 2 Baruch, is impossible to determine precisely because all the criteria at the end turn out to be subjective.[4] Since it is possible that 2 Bar. 61:7 is cited in the Epistle of Barnabas 11:9 (a document dated to about A.D. 120–130), and since it seems to be unaware of the war under Hadrian, the *terminus ante quem* for its composition may safely be set at A.D. 130. Among the scholars prepared to offer a more precise date, B. Violet and L. Gry suggest A.D. 116 and P. Bogaert A.D. 95.[5] One cannot go far wrong by assigning the composition of the book to about A.D. 100.

The Syriac text of 2 Baruch stems from the Greek. The Ambrosian manuscript itself displays the heading: 'The Book of the Apocalypse of Baruch the son of Neriah translated from the Greek into Syriac.' The Oxyrhynchus fragment (see above, p. 751) provides a concrete proof of this thesis.[6] P. Bogaert concludes that Greek was probably the original language of the composition, which was destined for the western diaspora (*op. cit.*, pp. 378–80).[7] Nevertheless the arguments set out by R. H. Charles and others in favour of Hebrew or Aramaic still appear to be preferable.[8]

The reference to Βαρούχ, Ἀμβακούμ, Ἐζηκιὴλ καὶ Δανιὴλ ψευδε-πίγραφα in the Stichometry of Nicephorus and in the Pseudo-Athanasian Synopsis does not necessarily allude to 2 Baruch; it may concern 3 Baruch or the Paralipomena of Jeremiah. The same applies to the Origen quotation, *De Principiis* ii 3, 6. The only patristic evidence that may testify to the knowledge of 2 Baruch comes from the Epistle of

4. The priority of 4 Ezra has been defended by A. Dillmann, H. Gunkel, B. Violet, L. Gry, O. Eissfeldt, etc. The opposite view has been advanced by C. Clemen, J. Wellhausen, E. Schürer, P. Bogaert, etc. Charles and Nickelsburg declined to opt one way or the other because of the composite nature of both books, or the tenuousness of the relationship between them. Klijn conjectures a common source to both, rather than mutual dependence, but considers 2 Baruch younger than 4 Ezra because of its 'advanced stage of theological development' (OTP I, p. 617).

5. Violet, *op. cit.*, p. xcii, identifies the earthquake mentioned in 2 Bar. 70:8 with that which struck Antioch in A.D. 115. For the theory of L. Gry, see *art. cit.* [in n. 3 above], pp. 345–56. Bogaert's argument is set out in *L'Apocalypse de Baruch* I (1969), pp. 291–5. For further details, see *ibid.*, pp. 270–1.

6. Cf. Denis, IPGAT, pp. 182–6.

7. Among earlier scholars favouring Greek, mention should be made of I. Langen, *Commentatio qua Apocalypsis Baruch ... illustratur* (1867), pp. 8–9; A. Dillmann, 'Pseudepigraphen des Alten Testaments', RE/Prot. Theol. und Kirche XII (²1883), pp. 356–8.

8. Charles, *Apoc. of Bar.*, pp. xliv-liii; APOT II, pp. 472–4; J. Wellhausen, *Skizzen und Vorarbeiten* VI (1899), pp. 234–41; L. Ginzberg, 'Baruch', JE II, p. 555; Violet, *op. cit.*, pp. lxxiii, 344–50; F. Zimmermann, 'Textual Observations on the Apocalypse of Baruch', JThSt 40 (1939), pp. 151–66; 'Translation and Mistranslation in the Apocalypse of Baruch', M. Ben Horin *et al.* (eds.), *Studies and Essays in Honor of A. A. Neuman* (1962), pp. 580–7.

Barnabas 11:9: καὶ πάλιν ἕτερος προφήτης λέγει· Καὶ ἦν ἡ γῆ τοῦ Ἰακὼβ ἐπαινουμένη παρὰ πᾶσαν τὴν γῆν = 2 Bar. 61:7: 'And the land, which was then beloved because its inhabitants did not sin, was praised more than all lands.'[9]

It may also be noted that a work similar to 2 Baruch is cited by Cyprian in *Testimonia* iii 29 (PL 4, 752 B–C): 'Item in Baruch: "*Veniet enim tempus et quaeretis me et vos et qui post vos fuerint audire verbum sapientiae et intellectus, et non invenietis* (cf. 2 Bar. 48:36). Nationes autem cupient videre sapientem, et non continget eis; non quia deerit aut deficiet sapientia huius saeculi terrae, sed neque deerit sermo legis saeculo. *Erit enim sapientia in paucis vigilantibus et taciturnis* (cf. 2 Bar. 48:33) et quietis sibi confabulantes, quoniam quidam eos horrebunt et timebunt ut malos. Alii autem nec credunt verbo legis Altissimi. Alii autem ore stupentes non credent, et credent, et contradicentes erunt contrarii et impedientes spiritum veritatis. *Alii autem erunt sapientes ad spiritum erroris et pronuntiantes sicut Altissimi et fortis edicta* (2 Bar. 48:34). Alii autem personales fidei. Alii capaces et fortes in fide Altissimi, et odibiles alieno."' Cf. 2 Bar. 48:33–6. See Charles, *The Apocalypse of Baruch*, pp. 77–8; APOT II, p. 506.

Editions

Syriac
Ceriani, A. M., 'Apocalypsis syriaca Baruch', *Monumenta sacra et profana* V, 2 (1871), pp. 113–80.
Kmoskó, M., *Liber Apocalypseos Baruch filii Neriae Patrologia syriaca* (Pars prima) II (1907), cols. 1056–1305.
Dedering, S., 'Apocalypse of Baruch', *Peshitta* IV.3 (1973), pp. i–iv, 1–50.

Greek
Grenfell, B. P., and Hunt, A. S., *The Oxyrhynchus Papyri* III (1903), pp. 4–6.
Charles, R. H., APOT II, pp. 487–90.
Denis, A. M., FPG, pp. 118–20.

Translations

Latin
Ceriani, A. M., *Monumenta sacra et profana* I.2 (1866), pp. i–iv, 73–98.

English
Charles, R. H., *The Apocalypse of Baruch* (1896), APOT II, pp. 470–526.
Idem, *The Apocalypse of Baruch* (1918).
Klijn, A. F. J., '2 (Syriac Apocalypse of) Baruch', OTP I, pp. 615–52.

9. The theory was first proposed by F. Perles, 'Notes sur les Apocryphes et les Pseudépigraphes. I. Traces des Apocryphes et des Pseudépigraphes dans la liturgie juive', REJ 73 (1921), p. 183. Cf. Bogaert, *op. cit.* I, pp. 272–5 (suggesting in addition a citation in Barn. 16:6 (γέγραπται γάρ· Καὶ ἔσται τῆς ἑβδομάδος συντελουμένης οἰκοδομηθήσεται ναὸς θεοῦ ἐνδόξως ἐπὶ τῷ ὀνόματι Κυρίου) of 2 Bar. 32:4 ('And after that it [the building of Zion] must be renewed in glory and perfected forever').

German

Ryssel, V., APAT II, pp. 402–46.

Violet, B., *Die Apokalypsen des Esra und Baruch* [GCS 32] (1924).

Riessler, P., *Altjüdisches Schrifttum*, pp. 55–113, 1270–2.

Klijn, A. F. J., *Die syrische Baruch-Apokalypse* [JSHRZ V.2] (1976), pp. 103–91.

French

Bogaert, P., *Apocalypse de Baruch : Introduction, traduction du syriaque et commentaire* I-II [SC 144/5] (1969).

Bibliography

Rosenthal, F., *Vier apokryphische Bücher aus der Zeit und Schule R. Aqibas : Assumptio Mosis, das vierte Buch Esra, die Apokalypse Baruch, das Buch Tobi* (1885).

Clemen, C., 'Die Zusammensctzung des Buches Henoch, der Apokalypse des Baruch und des vierten Buches Esra', ThStKr 71 (1898), pp. 211–46.

Wellhausen, J., 'Zur apokalyptischen Literatur', *Skizzen und Vorarbeiten* VI (1899), pp. 215–49.

Ginzberg, L., 'Baruch', JE II, pp. 551–6.

Sigwalt, C., 'Die Chronologie der syrischen Baruchapokalypse', BZ 9 (1911), pp. 397–8.

James, M. R., 'Notes on Apocrypha. i. Pseudo-Philo and Baruch', JThSt 16 (1915), pp. 403–5.

Frey, J.-B., 'Apocryphes de l'Ancien Testament', DBS I, cols. 418–23.

Gry, L., 'La date de la fin des temps selon les révélations ou les calculs du Pseudo-Philon et de Baruch (Apocalypse syriaque)', RB 48 (1939), pp. 337–56.

Zimmermann, F., 'Textual Observations on the Apocalypse of Baruch', JThSt 40 (1939), pp. 151–6.

Gry, L., 'La ruine du Temple par Titus', RB 55 (1948), pp. 215–26.

Lods, A., *Histoire de la littérature hébraïque et juive* (1950), pp. 998–1005.

Zimmermann, F., 'Translation et Mistranslation in the Apocalypse of Baruch', M. Ben Horin et al., *Studies and Essays in Honor of A. A. Neuman* (1962), pp. 580–7.

Baars, W., 'Neue Textzeugen der syrischen Baruchapokalypse', VT 13 (1963), pp. 476–8.

Hadot, J., 'La datation de l'Apocalypse syriaque de Baruch', Semitica 15 (1965), pp. 79–97.

Eissfeldt, O., *Introduction* (1965), pp. 627–30.

Thoma, C., 'Jüdische Apokalyptik am Ende des ersten nachchristlichen Jahrhunderts : Religionsgeschichtliche Bemerkungen zur syrischen Baruchapokalypse und zum vierten Esrabuch', Kairos 11 (1969), pp. 134–44.

Harnisch, W., *Verhängnis und Verheissung der Geschichte : Untersuchungen zum Zeit- und Geschichtsverständnis im 4. Esra und in der syrischen Baruchapokalypse* (1969).

Denis, IPGAT, pp. 182–6.

Klijn, A. F. J., 'The Sources and the Redaction of the Syriac Apocalypse of Baruch', JSJ 1 (1970), pp. 65–76.

Grintz, Y. M., 'Baruch, Apocalypse of (Syriac)', Enc. Jud. 4, cols. 270–2.

Nickelsburg, G. W. E., 'Narrative Traditions in the Paralipomena of Jeremiah and 2 Baruch', CBQ 35 (1973), pp. 60–8.

Bogaert, P.-M., 'Le nom de Baruch dans la littérature pseudépigraphique : l'apocalypse syriaque et le livre deutérocanonique', W. C. van Unnik (ed.), *La littérature juive entre Tenach et Mishna* (1974), pp. 56–72.

van Koningsveld, P. S., 'An Arabic Manuscript of the Apocalypse of Baruch', JSJ 6 (1975), pp. 205–7.

Dautzenberg, G., 'Das Bild der Prophetie im 4. Esra und im syr Bar', *Urchristliche Prophetie* [BWANT VI.4] (1975), pp. 90–8.

Charlesworth, J. H., PMRS, pp. 83–6.

Nickelsburg, G. W. E., JLBBM, pp. 281–7, 305–8.
Licht, J., 'An Analysis of Baruch's Prayer (Syr. Bar. 21)', JJS 33 (1982), pp. 327–31 [=
    Y. Yadin Festschrift].

III. BIBLICAL MIDRASH

1. The Life of Adam and Eve (Apocalypse of Moses)

Among the various midrashic accounts of the story of the first man and woman, pride of place belongs to a composition preserved in a Greek recension under the misnomer *Apocalypse of Moses*,[1] in a Latin account known as *Vita Adae et Evae*, and in a Slavonic version. They all survive in Christian recensions, but depend on original compositions which are thought to be Jewish.[2] Whether they correspond to works mentioned in early Christian sources remains uncertain.[3]

The Greek, Latin and Slavonic recensions all represent a story of the life and death of Adam and Eve with details of the temptation and the fall, for which Eve bears the main responsibility. The work testifies to a firmly established belief in a general resurrection of the dead (cf. *Apoc. of Moses* 41:3; 43:2) and represents Seth as the agent for the transmission of revelations entrusted by God to Adam.

Of the three versions, the Greek reflects the earliest form of the narrative. The Latin and the Slavonic are best understood as additions

---

1. Chosen by C. Tischendorf, it derives from the title of the work appearing in the manuscripts: 'Story and life of Adam and Eve, the first creatures, ἀποκαλυφθεῖσα παρὰ θεοῦ Μωϋσῇ.'

2. External evidence regarding a Jewish 'Book of Adam' is unsubstantial. Though alluded to in a few rabbinic dicta, it appears to represent midrashic speculation on Gen. 5:1, זה ספר תולדות אדם. The rabbis mentioning it seem to envisage, not so much an account of the life of Adam, as a history of mankind. The clearest reference is attributed to the third century Palestinian Amora, Simeon Resh Laqish: 'It is written, "This is the book of the generations of Adam" (Gen. 5:1). Did Adam, the first man, have a book? This teaches that the Holy One, blessed be He, showed the first Adam every generation and its masters, every generation and its sages, every generation and its leaders' (bAZ 5a). When Judah the Prince sought to ordain his physician, Samuel the Astronomer, the latter resisted him, saying: 'I saw written in the Book of Adam that Samuel the Astronomer would be called a sage, but not a rabbi, and that Rabbi's cure would be effected by him' (bBM 85b–86a). The King Messiah will not arrive, according to R. Tanhum, until all the souls planned by God have been created. 'And these are the souls mentioned in the Book of Adam: "This is the book of the generations of Adam"' (BR 24:4, Theodor, p. 231; cf. also Ex.R. 40:2).

3. The *Apostolic Constitutions* vi 16, 3 lists an apocryphal Ἀδάμ together with works on Moses, Enoch and Isaiah. A *Liber qui appellatur poenitentia Adae* figures in the *Decretum Gelasianum* § 6, 2, v. 297 (ed. E. von Dobschütz, 1912, pp. 304–5). The Apocrypha catalogue of the Sixty Books and that of the Armenian Mechithar open their lists of Jewish writings by an apocryphal *Adam*. The Gnostic composition entitled Ἀποκαλύψεις τοῦ Ἀδάμ was known to Epiphanius (*Haer.* xxvi 5, 1: PG 41, 340A). A Life of Adam is hinted at in George Syncellus (ed. Dindorf CSHB I, p. 18) and quoted by George Cedrenus (ed. I. Bekker, CSHB I, pp. 17–18; cf. M. R. James, *The Lost Apocrypha* (1920), p. 2).

to the Greek form of the story. It can also be argued that the *Life* was
unknown to the editor of the *Apocalypse* but that, by contrast, the
Apocalypse is presupposed by the arrangement of the *Life*.[4]

Although all the recensions have passed through the hands of
Christian editors, the doubts advanced formerly by Schürer among
others concerning the Jewishness of the original work appear to be
ill-founded.[5] To begin with, the obviously Christian additions are
patently different from the rest of the work. It is enough to consider the
doxologies at the end of the *Apocalypse of Moses* (43:4–5), or the insertion
of the *Gospel of Nicodemus* 19 into *Life* 42:2–5. Furthermore, both
compositions contain typically Jewish features. Both the *Apocalypse*
(43:3) and the *Life* (51:2) stress the importance of the Sabbath, and its
connection with the resurrection whose symbol it is, according to
bSanh. 97a. Reference to the Merkabah (*Life* 25:3), to the paradise in
the third among the seven heavens (*Apocalypse* 37:5; 40:1; 35:2), and
the identification of the wicked as men who refused to love God's law
(*Life* 29:7), are further indications of Jewishness. The idea of the world's
destruction first by water, then by fire (*Life* 49:3) is a doctrine
paralleled in Josephus, *Ant.* i 2, 3 (70), where Adam foretells a
conflagration and a deluge; the same idea is attested also in 2 Pet.
3:5–7. The fiery end of the world is alluded to repeatedly in Sib.
3:83–7; 5:512–31 as well as in the Qumran *Hodayoth* 3:29–34.[6] The two
tables on which the life of Adam and Eve were to be recorded, one of
stone, the other of clay, one to survive the flood and the other, the
conflagration (*Life* 50:1–2), derive from a Jewish legend attested also by
Josephus, *Ant.* i 2, 3 (70–71).

The original language of the writings remains uncertain. Since the
Apocalypse is preserved in Greek and the *Life* is undoubtedly dependent
on a Greek text, a reasonable case can be made out that they both were

---

4. See Fuchs in APAT II, pp. 508–9; L. S. A. Wells, in APOT II, pp. 128–9;
Nickelsburg, JLBBM, pp. 253–7. The contents of the two works are listed in parallel
columns:

	Apoc			Life
a)		—	Penance, fall of Satan, birth of Cain	1:1–22:2
b)		1:1–5:1a	Birth of Abel, Seth	22:3–24:2
c)		—	Adam's revelations to Seth	25–29
d)		5:1b–14:3	Adam's sickness, his journey to paradise	30–44
e)		15–30	Eve's story	—
f)		31:1–42:2	Adam's death and burial	45–48
g)		—	Eve's testament	49:1–50:2
h)		42:3–43:4	Eve's death and burial	50:3–51:3

5. Cf. *Geschichte* ([4]1909), III, p. 399.

6. Cf. G. Vermes, 'La secte juive de la Nouvelle Alliance d'après ses hymnes
récemment découverts', Cahiers Sioniens 4 (1950), pp. 192–3.

composed in Greek (Denis, IPGAT, p. 7). Biblical quotations follow the Septuagint, and Hebrew concepts such as 'garden of Eden' and 'Gehenna' are rendered as παράδεισος and Ἀχερουσία (APAT II, pp. 511–12; APOT, p. 130). On the other hand, it has been remarked that the Greek text is full of Hebraisms (APAT II, p. 511; APOT II, pp. 129–30), from which it is inferred that earlier Semitic (Hebrew or Aramaic) sources underlie the Greek version (cf. *ibid.* and J.-B. Frey, DBS I, c. 105). Moreover, as L. Ginzberg indicated, many of the themes appearing in the Adam literature are paralleled in rabbinic writings (JE I, pp. 179–80). Nevertheless, neither of these arguments is decisive. In particular, Semitisms in Jewish Greek can be seen as part of a literary style, without necessarily implying servile translation. If, instead of a Semitic original, it is assumed that the author of a Greek apocryphon utilized cognate Hebrew or Aramaic documents, it may reasonably be suggested that the author was a Jewish Hellenist.

The work contains no direct evidence for firm dating. A possible faint historical allusion occurs in *Life* 29:6, with its reference to the rebuilding of a sanctuary that will outshine the previous one. If this new Temple is that built by Herod, the *terminus post quem* is the end of the first century B.C. and, since its destruction is not mentioned, the passage predates A.D. 70. On the other hand, the allusion may point to the messianic Temple.[7] It is mainly on general grounds that a first or early second century A.D. date appears to be most likely.

Editions

Greek
Tischendorf, C., *Apocalypses apocryphae Mosis, Esdrae, Pauli, Iohannis, item Mariae dormitio* (1866), pp. 1–23.
Ceriani, A. M., *Monumenta sacra et profana* V, 1 (1868), pp. 19–24.
    For the manuscripts, see Denis, IPGAT, pp. 3–5.

Latin
Meyer, W., 'Vita Adae et Evae', AAM XIV, 3 (1878), pp. 187–250.

Slavonic
Jagič, V., *Slavische Beiträge zu den biblischen Apokryphen. I. Die altslavischen Texte des Adamsbuches* [Denkschriften AW 42] (1893).
Lieberman, S., 'Neglected Sources', Tarbiz 62 (1972), pp. 42–54 (Hebr.).

Armenian
Josepheanz, H. S., *Treasury of Ancient and Modern Fathers* (1896) [in Armenian].
Preuschen, E., 'Die apokryphen gnostischen Adamschriften aus dem Armenischen übersetzt', *Festgruss B. Stade* (1900), pp. 168–209.
Issaverdens, J., *The Uncanonical Writings of the Old Testament found in Armenian Manuscripts of the Library of St. Lazarus* (1901), pp. 43–8.

Coptic-Sahidic (Apoc. 31:2–32:2)
Crum, W. E., *Catalogue of the Coptic Manuscripts in the Collection of the John Rylands Library* (1909), p. 40.

7. Cf. Eissfeldt, *Introduction*, p. 637; Denis, IPGAT, pp. 6–7.

Translations

(a) *English*
Wells, L. S. A., 'The Books of Adam and Eve', APOT II, pp. 123–54.

(b) *German*
Fuchs, C., 'Das Leben Adams und Evas', APAT II, pp. 506–28.
Riessler, P., 'Apokalypse des Moses', *Altjüdisches Schrifttum*, pp. 138–55, 1273–4.

French
J.-P. Migne, *Dictionnaire des apocryphes* I (1856), cols. 240–94.

Bibliography

Ginzberg, L., 'Adam, Book of', JE I, pp. 179–80.
Kabisch, R., 'Die Entstehungszeit der Apokalypse Mose', ZNW 6 (1905), pp. 109–34.
James, M. R., *The Lost Apocrypha of the Old Testament* (1920), pp. 1–8.
Mozley, J. H., 'The Vita Adae', JThSt 30 (1929), pp. 121–49.
Torrey, C. C., *The Apocryphal Literature* (1945), pp. 131–3.
Eissfeldt, O., *Introduction*, pp. 636–7.
Denis, IPGAT, pp. 1–14.
Bianchi, U., 'La rédemption dans les livres d'Adam', Numen 18 (1971), pp. 1–8.
Nickelsburg, G. W. E., 'Some related Traditions in the Apocalypse of Adam, the Books of Adam and Eve and I Enoch', in B. Layton (ed.), *The Rediscovery of Gnosticism* II (1980), pp. 515–39.
Idem, JLBBM, pp. 253–7, 274.
Charlesworth, J. H., PMRS, pp. 74–5, 273.

Appendix

A number of further writings are related to the Adam literature. They are all Christian or Gnostic compositions whose Jewish roots, if any, are impossible to determine.

1. *The Cave of Treasures* is a collection of legends from the time of Adam and Eve until Jesus. It has been preserved in Syriac and Arabic recensions. They were edited by C. Bezold, *Die Schatzhöhle* (1888). Cf. E. A. Wallis Budge, *The Book of the Cave of Treasures* (1927). See also Denis, IPGAT, pp. 8–9.

2. *The Conflict of Adam and Eve* is a biblical history similar to the *Cave of Treasures*. The extant Ethiopic version was made from the Arabic. See A. Dillmann, *Das christliche Adambuch des Morgenlandes* (1853); E. Trumpp, *Der Kampf Adams (gegen die Versuchungen des Satans) oder Das christliche Adambuch des Morgenlandes*, AAM XV, 3 (1880); S. C. Malan, *The Book of Adam and Eve also called The Conflict of Adam and Eve with Satan* (1882); J.-P. Migne, *Dictionnaire des apocryphes* I (1856), cols. 290–392. Cf. also Denis, IPGAT, p. 9.

3. *The Penance of Adam* (Liber qui appellatur poenitentia Adae), is referred to in the *Decretum Gelasianum* (cf. above, n. 3).

4. *The Testament of Adam* consists of revelations entrusted by Adam to Seth. It has survived in Syriac, Arabic, Ethiopic and Greek. See E. Renan, *Fragments du livre gnostique intitulé Apocalypse d'Adam, ou Pénitence*

d'Adam, ou Testament d'Adam (1854); C. Bezold, 'Das arabisch-äthiopische Testamentum Adami', in *Orientalische Studien Th. Nöldeke gewidmet* II (1906), pp. 893–912; M. Kmosko, 'Testamentum Adae', in R. Graffin (ed.), *Patrologia Syriaca* II (1907), pp. 1309–60; F. Nau, 'Apotelesmata Apollonii Tyanensis', *ibid.*, pp. 1362–92 (Greek text); S. E. Robinson, *The Testament of Adam : An Examination of the Syriac and Greek Traditions* (1982); *idem*, 'Testament of Adam', in J. H. Charlesworth (ed.), OTP I (1983), pp. 989–95.

5. *The Apocalypse of Adam* is a gnostic document containing revelations to Seth. Its text in the Sahidic dialect of Coptic was discovered in 1946 at Nag Hammadi in a codex (Codex V) dating to the second half of the fourth century A.D. The original language is assumed to be Greek. See A. Bölig and P. Labib, *Koptisch-gnostische Apokalypsen aus Codex V von Nag Hammadi im Koptischen Museum zu Alt-Kairo* (1963), pp. 86–117; R. Kasser, 'Bibliothèque gnostique V: Apocalypse d'Adam', RThPhil 17 (1967), pp. 316–33; G. MacRae and D. M. Parrott, 'The Apocalypse of Adam (V, 5)', in J. M. Robinson (ed.), *The Nag Hammadi Library in English* (1977), pp. 256–64; G. MacRae, 'The Apocalypse of Adam', in D. M. Parrott (ed.), *Nag Hammadi Codices V, 2–5 and VI with Papyrus Berilonensis 8502, 1 and 4* (1979), pp. 151–95; *idem*, 'Apocalypse of Adam', OTP I, pp. 707–19.

2. *The Testament of Abraham*

The testament genre provides only the structure for this narrative about the death of Abraham since, despite the characteristic setting around the hero's deathbed, the patriarch does not in fact make his testament. Indeed, in the longer recension of the work (A), which probably best preserves its original form, the essence of the story is the hero's refusal to accept his death as commanded by God's messengers, and he provides himself with no opportunity to dispense ethical advice of the kind normal in this genre. The lesson of the work, according to the long recension A, lies instead in the apocalyptic vision vouchsafed to Abraham of the judgement of the souls of the dead and in his growing insight into the nature of death.

The archangel Michael is sent by God to tell Abraham to prepare for death by making his testament (A1). Abraham greets Michael with hospitality (A2–5) but, when Michael reveals his identity and mission (5–7), tries to postpone death. In the long recension A, Abraham is portrayed as positively refusing to die. Michael, at God's behest, persists in his demand (A8–9), so Abraham delays matters by asking to see the inhabited world (so the long recension (A9), πᾶσαν τὴν οἰκουμένην; the short recension (B7) refers to all God's creation, τὰ κτίσματα ἃ ἐκτίσατο κύριος ὁ θεός μου ἐν οὐρανῷ καὶ ἐπὶ γῆς). Abraham is granted this vision but is so appalled by the wickedness he perceives that he calls down destruction on the sinners (A10). A further vision of the careful recording and accurate weighing of men's deeds and the judgement of their souls by Abel (A11–13) demonstrates God's compassion in forgiving the penitent, and persuades Abraham to pray, successfully, for the revival of those he had condemned (A14). In the short recension B, the patriarch's survey of the sinfulness of the world (B12) does not precede but follows his vision of the judgement (B10–11) and, since his moral attitude towards sinners is unchanged by what he has seen, the judgement scene, which is here comparatively briefly described, plays a more minor literary role.

On his return home, Abraham remains unwilling to prepare for death and Michael returns to heaven in despair (A15). God then sends a second messenger, Death, with the same summons. He is more abrupt and eventually succeeds. Abraham's sullen unwillingness to accept his instructions is greeted by persistence and a grisly vision of various forms of death (A17). When Death has explained both that sudden death is a good thing in so far as it precludes further punishment for wrongdoing (A18) and that this form of demise is common (A20), the patriarch is himself led to death, tricked, according to the long recension A, into kissing the hand of Death in the mistaken hope of receiving life and strength thereby. His soul is immediately transported to heaven by Michael (A20).

The story presupposes an interest in, and admiration for, Abraham as a pious man. It was evidently intended for a Jewish audience. The interest of the author in universal moral qualities and the fate of all humanity after death does not necessarily show that he espoused a universalistic form of Judaism (*contra* Sanders) but may simply reflect his literary aim: his main teaching is not the nature of piety (which is taken for granted) but the inevitability of death and the operation of divine judgement. Such a theme is not well suited to the testament genre or the traditional picture of Abraham, and at times the author comes close to parodying both the genre and the hero. Abraham's qualities of hospitality and righteousness are taken from the biblical account, but his willingness to condemn sinners is in marked contrast to his intercession over the fate of Sodom and Gomorrah (Gen. 18:23–33), and his disobedience when commanded to die contrasts with his unquestioning faith in the biblical version as shown by his willingness to sacrifice Isaac (Gen. 22:1–14). Some elements of the picture of Abraham have been transferred to him from other biblical figures, most strikingly in the adoption of the resistance to death usually ascribed in Jewish texts to Moses, cf. S. Loewenstamm in G. W. E. Nickelsburg, ed., *Studies on the Testament of Abraham* (1976), pp. 219–25.

The book now survives in two distinct Greek recensions (see below, p.

764) and later versions made from the Greek. It is probable that Greek was the language of its original composition. The many Hebrew idioms used in the long recension (A) led earlier scholars to assume that it has been translated from Hebrew (Kohler, Ginzberg), but nothing in this recension *requires* a semitic original and it is more likely that it was composed in a Jewish Greek. There are stronger grounds for believing that the short recension (B) is based directly on a Hebrew original (so, most recently, Schmidt), since its simple language is close to that of the Septuagint translations of the early narrative sections of the Bible. It is however possible here too that the author wrote in a Greek deliberately made appropriate to his subject matter and therefore took the style direct from the Septuagint.[1]

There are no certain indications of the place of writing. An Egyptian origin for the long recension (A) is often posited on the grounds that some of the Greek is similar to that in the later, Alexandrian books of the Septuagint (Delcor). It is also possible that particular motifs, such as aspects of the personification of death and the weighing of the souls of the dead, have been borrowed from Egyptian religion (Schmidt), but these ideas, even if they cannot be directly paralleled in Jewish or Greek sources, can easily have derived from those traditions, and an Egyptian influence need not be assumed. Nothing points specifically to a Palestinian background (*contra* Janssen), though that would not be impossible even if the work was composed in Greek. If the short recension B was written first in Hebrew that would make Palestine plausible as its provenance, but if both recensions were Greek compositions an origin anywhere in the diaspora would be possible.

The work should be accepted as Jewish even though the more particular elements of Jewish piety are not stressed. The Christian interpolations, which are more numerous in the long recension (A) than in the short (B), can be easily excised without affecting the coherence of the narrative,[2] and nothing in the narrative would be

1. On the problems in ascertaining the original language see N. Turner, *The Testament of Abraham* (Ph.D. diss., London, 1953); *idem*, 'The "Testament of Abraham": Problems in Biblical Greek', NTSt 1 (1954–5), pp. 222–3; R. A. Martin, 'Syntax criticism of the Testament of Abraham', in G. W. E. Nickelsburg (ed.), *Studies on the Testament of Abraham* (1976), pp. 95–120, with the remarks on his method by R. A. Kraft, *ibid.*, pp. 121–37. E. P. Sanders in Charlesworth, OTP I, pp. 873–4, remarks that any Hebrew original must presumably have been composed in deliberately archaic Hebrew if its Greek translation looks so similar to the Septuagint, and that there is no evidence of composition in early forms of Hebrew in this period.

2. E. P. Sanders in Charlesworth, OTP I, p. 875. On the interpolations in the judgement scene in the long recension see Nickelsburg in G. W. E. Nickelsburg (ed.), *Studies on the Testament of Abraham* (1976), pp. 29–37. See also N. Turner, NTSt 1 (1954–5), pp. 220–1; *idem*, *The Testament of Abraham* (Ph.D. diss., London, 1953), pp. 14–48, on extensive Christian influence on the *vocabulary* of the Testament. It is possible that resemblances to passages in the New Testament (A 11:2 = Mt. 7:13 ff.; A 11:11 =

unlikely for a Jewish writer. There are no grounds for seeing the Testament, which promotes a generalised morality, as the product of any sectarian group.[3]

The date of composition is hard to determine since there are no references to historical events within the work and no certain witnesses to the work itself before the Middle Ages (see below). Its adoption by Christians makes a date before *c.* A.D.150 probable. It is unlikely to be a very early work because it presupposes the popularity of both the testament genre and apocalyptic. This would not however preclude composition in the late second or the first century B.C.

St. Paul may have used the Testament of Abraham, A 13:13, at 1 Cor. 3:13–14, cf. C. W. Fishburne, 'I Corinthians III.10–15 and the Testament of Abraham', NTSt 17 (1970), pp. 109–15, but this is denied by Sanders, in Charlesworth, OTP I, p. 878, note 54, who believes that the relationship is the reverse.

The late Christian apocryphal Apocalypse of Paul 4–6 contains the same motif as Testament of Abraham A 10:14 = B 12:13, but is not necessarily dependent upon it. The lost Apocalypse of Peter may quote the Testament, according to M. R. James, *The Testament of Abraham* (1892), pp. 23–4. The Apocalypse of Sedrach, a confused late Christian collection of Jewish traditions (cf. Denis, IPGAT, pp. 97–9) borrowed directly from the Testament of Abraham, cf. M. R. James, *The Testament of Abraham* (1892), pp. 31–3, 66.

Const. Apost. 6, 16, 3 may refer to the Testament in the fourth century in citing apocryphal books 'of the three patriarchs'. See below, p. 805, on the Testaments of Isaac and Jacob.

The Stichometry of Nicephorus and the Synopsis of Ps.-Athanasius note a work called 'Of Abraham' among the apocryphal works of the Old Testament, cf. Denis, IPGAT, pp. XIV and 31, but this may refer to the Apocalypse of Abraham (see above, p. 288).

Priscillian, *Liber de Fide et de Apocryphis* 58 (ed. Schepss, CSEL XVIII, pp. 45–6) speaks of a prophecy of Abraham and probably refers to this work since it is connected by him with prophecies of Isaac and Jacob (see below).

The book exists in two clearly separate recensions which, because of their frequent agreements in narrative and vocabulary, must ultimately derive from a single source. However, they differ so considerably in their present form that their precise relationship can no longer be

---

Mt. 7:13 ff. and Mt. 25:46; A 13:13 = 1 Cor. 3:13 ff.) show use of the Testament by the authors of the New Testament, but it is more likely that these are Christian interpolations, which are particularly common in the long recension A; see below, p. 765.

3. Sanders, *op. cit.*, p. 876, rightly dismisses the assertions by Kohler, Schmidt and Delcor that the Testament is an Essene work.

established. The longer recension (A) may preserve the original form of the story better than the short recension (B), since some elements of the narrative, such as the judgement scene, serve an important function in A but, though present, are not significant in B (Nickelsburg). The long recension, however, contains more signs of Christian editing and more words of demonstrably late Greek of the fifth or sixth century A.D., cf. N. Turner, NTSt 1 (1955), pp. 221–2, so it remains possible that the comparatively simple, clear account in the short recension (B) may be closer to the original (Turdeanu). At the least, B may retain more of the original vocabulary. On the relation between the recensions see the articles in G. W. E. Nickelsburg (ed.), *Studies in the Testament of Abraham* (1976), pp. 23–137.

The most important manuscripts for the long recension (A) are the fourteenth century Paris Fonds grec. 770 and the fifteenth century Jerusalem manuscript, Patr. S. Sepulchri 66. Primary for the short recension (B) are the fifteenth century Paris Fonds grec. 1613 and especially Milan Ambros. gr. 405, which dates to the eleventh or twelfth century. Cf. in general Denis, IPGAT, pp. 32–3; F. Schmidt, *Le Testament d'Abraham* I (Ph.D. diss., Strasbourg, 1971), pp. 1–20, for the importance of Ambros. gr. 405; S. Agourides, 'The Testament of Abraham: an unpublished Modern Greek manuscript', Deltion Biblion Meleton 1 (1972), pp. 238–48.

Ancient Versions

The book exists in many ancient versions, of which the most important are the following.

(1) *Two Rumanian versions.* One of these is an abridgement of the long Greek recension A, cf. edition and translation by M. Gaster, 'The Apocalypse of Abraham, From the Roumanian Text', Translations of the Society of Biblical Archaeology 9 (1887), pp. 195–226 (= *Studies and Texts in Folklore, etc.* I (1925), pp. 92–124). The other is closer to the short recension B. Cf. É. Turdeanu, 'Le *Testament d'Abraham* en slave et en roumain', Oxford Slavonic Papers 10 (1977), pp. 1–38.

(2) *Slavonic.* This version is closest to recension B. Cf. Turdeanu, *art. cit.*, and *idem*, 'Notes sur la tradition littéraire du Testament d'Abraham', in *Silloge bizantina ... S. G. Mercati* (1957), pp. 405–9. Cf., on both the Rumanian and the Slavonic, É. Turdeanu, *Apocryphes slaves et roumains de l'Ancien Testament* (1981).

(3) *Coptic.* This version is close to recension B. Edited by I. Guidi, 'Il testo copto del testamento di Abramo', Rendiconti della Reale Accademia dei Lincei, Classe sc. mor. stor. filol. V, 9 (1900), pp. 158–80.

(4) *Arabic and Ethiopic.* These are based on the Coptic, cf. Denis,

IPGAT, p. 34; M. Gaguine, *The Falasha Version of the Testaments of Abraham, Isaac and Jacob* (Ph.D., Manchester, 1965). Cf. on the versions in general M. Delcor, *Le Testament d'Abraham* (1973), pp. 15–22.

The Coptic, Arabic and Ethiopic versions link the Testament of Abraham with the Testaments of Isaac and Jacob. This seems to have been a late phenomenon, perhaps in response to the mention in *Const. Apost.* 6, 16, 3 of apocryphal books τῶν τριῶν πατριαρχῶν. The Testaments of Isaac and Jacob are largely derived from the Testament of Abraham. In their present form they are Christian writings, and it is impossible to tell whether they are based on earlier Jewish works, see below, p. 805.

Editions

James, M. R., *The Testament of Abraham* (1892).
Schmidt, F., *Le Testament d'Abraham* (Ph.D. diss., Strasbourg, 1971). (The short recension B, taking account of the manuscript Ambros. gr. 405, which was not known to James.)
Stone, M. E., *The Testament of Abraham: The Greek Recensions* (1972). (James's text with English translation.)

Translations and Commentaries

English
Box, G. H., *The Testament of Abraham* (1927).
Sanders, E. P., 'Testament of Abraham', in Charlesworth, OTP I, pp. 871–902.

French
Delcor, M., *Le Testament d'Abraham* (1973). (A full commentary.)

German
Janssen, E., *Das Testament Abrahams* (JSHRZ III.2) (1975), pp. 193–256.
Riessler, P., *Altjüdisches Schrifttum* (1928), pp. 1332–3.

Bibliography

Kohler, K., 'The Pre-Talmudic Haggada II: The Apocalypse of Abraham and its Kindred', JQR 7 (1895), pp. 581–606.
Riessler, P., 'Das Testament Abrahams, ein jüdisches Apokryphon', ThQ 106 (1925), pp. 3–22.
Turner, N., *The Testament of Abraham* (Ph.D. diss., London, 1953).
Turner, N., 'The "Testament of Abraham": Problems in Biblical Greek', NTSt 1 (1954–5), pp. 219–23.
Piatelli, E., 'Il testamento di Abramo', Annuario di Studi Ebraici 2 (1964–5), pp. 111–22.
Delcor, M., 'De l'origine de quelques traditions contenues dans le Testament d'Abraham', in P. Peli (ed.), *Proceedings of the Fifth World Congress of Jewish Studies* I (1969), pp. 192–200. (Reprinted with corrections in *Religion d'Israël et Proche Orient Ancien* (1976), pp. 241–50.)
Denis, IPGAT, pp. 31–9.
Fishburne, C. W., 'I Corinthians III.10–15 and the Testament of Abraham', NTSt 17 (1970), pp. 109–15.
Schmidt, F., *Le Testament d'Abraham* (Ph.D. diss., Strasbourg, 1971).
Schmidt, F., 'Traditions relatives à Abraham dans la littérature hellénistique juive', École Pratique des Hautes-Études, Section: Religion, Annuaire 82 (1973), pp. 191–4.

Schmidt, F., 'Le monde à l'image du bouclier d'Achille', RHR 185 (1974), pp. 122–6.
Kolenkow, A. B., 'What is the role of testament in the Testament of Abraham?', HThR 67 (1974), pp. 182–4.
Nickelsburg, G. W. E. (ed.), *Studies on the Testament of Abraham* (1976).
Nickelsburg, JLBBM, pp. 248–53.
Collins, BAAJ, pp. 226–8.
Nickelsburg, G. W. E., in JWSTP, pp. 60–4.

3. The Testaments of the Twelve Patriarchs

The Testaments of the Twelve Patriarchs form a pseudepigraphic work in which the main constituent feature is direct exhortation. The work is preserved in its entirety in Greek, first published by J. E. Grabe in *Spicilegium SS. Patrum ut et Haereticorum saeculi post Christum natum* I, II & III (Oxford, 1698), after having circulated from the beginning of the sixteenth century in a Latin translation prepared by Robert Grosseteste in the thirteenth century.[1]

The extant Greek text of the book contains numerous direct references to the doctrine of the Incarnation and for this reason was considered by its first students to be the work of a Christian. It can however be argued that Jewish documents underlie the composition issued by a Christian editor.

The book, as its title indicates, belongs to the category of testamentary literature inspired by the 'death-bed' discourses of Jacob (Gen. 49) and Moses (Deut. 33), and contains the spiritual 'testaments' left by the twelve sons of Jacob. Three elements may be distinguished in each Testament. 1. The patriarch recounts his life-story, bewailing his sins and commending his virtues. The biographical data, though generally in line with the biblical narrative, are considerably enriched with fresh haggadic detail. 2. The patriarchal autobiography is followed by appropriate admonitions which stress the need to avoid the ancestor's sin or to emulate his virtue. 3. Towards the end of each Testament, predictions concerning the future of the tribe are given at some length, with the exception of the Testament of Gad, where this section is foreshortened. A patriarch may foretell his descendants' apostasy from God (or, which seems at times to be quasi-synonymous, their rebellion against Levi and Judah) and that, as a result, they will incur punishment, particularly captivity and dispersion. Such a prophecy is frequently accompanied by an exhortation to hold fast to the tribes of Levi and Judah. Brief Christian allusions to salvation are linked to these prophecies in the Testaments of Simeon, Levi, Zebulun, Dan, Naphtali, Asher, Joseph and Benjamin.

1. Cf. S. H. Thomson, *The Writings of Robert Grosseteste, Bishop of Lincoln 1235–1253* (1940), pp. 42–4; H. J. de Jonge, 'La bibliothèque de Michel Chomatès et la tradition occidentale des Testaments des XII Patriarches', in M. de Jonge, *Studies on the Testaments of the Twelve Patriarchs* (1975), pp. 97–106.

The ideas contained in the Testaments are very varied. Many of them appear to be explicable only on the hypothesis of a Jewish author. The story of the patriarchs is told wholly in the style of haggadic midrash. The writer displays a lively interest in the Jewish tribes as such; he laments their apostasy and dispersion; he encourages them to accept Levi and Judah as their leaders appointed by God;[2] he hopes for their final repentance and deliverance. Moral precepts dominate his outlook. He condemns envy, avarice, wrath, falsehood and unchastity; he calls for the practice of the various virtues. He also lays special emphasis on the priestly sacrificial cult as a divinely ordained institution, and provides details which go beyond the Bible.[3] He attaches much weight to the levitical character of the priesthood. On account of its sacred office, the tribe of Levi precedes all the others, even that of Judah. The children of Levi are especially exhorted to study the Torah. They must unremittingly read the Law of God and thus be sought after and honoured and served by men desiring to hear the Law from them.[4] There are also frequent admonitions to observe the Law and to obey the commandments.[5] By contrast, many passages can only have been written by a Christian, proclaiming universal salvation (a doctrine not un-Jewish in itself), but through a God incarnate. Indeed in one instance several textual witnesses allude to St. Paul (TBen. 11). The Christology presupposed appears to be Patripassian in character.[6]

The first editor, Grabe, explained these contradictory features by assuming that the book was written by a Jew but subsequently interpolated by a Christian. Later scholars, however, beginning with J. A. Fabricius (*Codex pseudepigraphus Veteris Testamenti*, 1713), advanced the thesis that the Testaments were written by a Christian in Greek,[7] and the only argument for the next century and a half was whether the author's standpoint was Jewish-Christian or Gentile-Christian, with

---

2. See TReub. 6:7; TSim. 5:6; 7:1; TLevi 2:11; TJud. 21:3; 25:2; TIss. 5:7; TDan 5:4; TNapht. 5:13; 8:2. In all these passages Levi comes first. The reverse order figures in TDan 5:10; TJos. 19:11; TBen. 11:2.

3. Cf. for example TLevi 9:11 : καὶ πρὸ τοῦ εἰσελθεῖν σε εἰς τὰ ἅγια, λούου· καὶ ἐν τῷ θύειν σε νίπτου. καὶ ἀπαρτίζων πάλιν τὴν θυσίαν, νίπτου (see vol. II, p. 294 and n. 10). See further 9:12, determining that only the wood of twelve evergreen trees may be used for the fire of burnt-offerings. Cf. also Jub. 21:12–16 and the detailed ritual prescriptions contained in the Bodleian Genizah fragments of TLevi cols. c and d and the corresponding Greek version. On these, see below, pp. 775–6.

4. TLevi 13:2–4; cf. Ecclus 39.

5. TReub. 6:8; TLevi 13:1; TJud. 13:1; 26:1; TZeb. 5:1; 10:2; TDan 5:1; TNapht. 3:2; TGad 3:2; TAsh. 6:1, 33; TJos. 11:1; 18:1; 19:11; TBen. 3:1; 10:3, 11.

6. TSim. 6:5, 7; TLevi 4:1; TIss. 7:7; TZeb. 9:8; TDan 5:13; TNapht. 8:3; TAsh. 7:3; TBen. 10:7–9.

7. For a survey of the early stages of Testaments research, see H. D. Singerland, *The Testaments of the Twelve Patriarchs: A Critical History of Research* (1977), pp. 5–33. Full bibliographical details may be found there.

appropriate Gentile-Christian or Jewish-Christian interpolations to account for the discrepant features. F. Schnapp was the first to investigate systematically the problem of whether the whole work had not undergone a thorough re-working. He argued that only the biographical notices and the exhortations attached and closely corresponding to them belonged to the original Jewish composition. The apocalyptic predictions were added to it by a Jewish hand, and further Christian interpolations were introduced at a later stage. Schnapp's work set in motion a swing of the pendulum, and scholarship at the turn of the century re-adopted the theory of a basic Jewish document subjected to Christian revision. Such was the opinion of F. C. Conybeare, E. Preuschen, W. Bousset *et al.* R. H. Charles, author of *The Greek Versions of the Testaments of the Twelve Patriarchs* and *The Testaments of the Twelve Patriarchs translated from the Editor's Greek Text*, both published in 1908, sought to establish the literary history of the work through a careful study of the textual evidence. According to his theory, the Greek manuscripts, nine of which were available to him, represent two recensions, *a* and *β*, of which *a*, although containing manifest omissions, is preferable to *β* because it is freer from Christian interpolations. The superiority of *a* is confirmed by the Armenian version, which is also devoid of many of the Christian additions present in the Greek *β* recension (on which the Armenian otherwise actually depends). To further complicate matters, Charles did not simply suggest that the shorter (only slightly Christianized) Greek recension *a* reflected an original Jewish document written in Hebrew, but postulated two separate Hebrew recensions from which the Greek *a* and *β* ultimately derived.

The discovery of fragments from an Aramaic Testament of Levi in the Cairo Genizah and of a corresponding Greek version in an Athos manuscript, and the publication of a medieval Hebrew midrash akin to the Testament of Naphtali (see below, pp. 776–7), did not affect substantially the theories arrived at from the study of the Greek Testaments. These texts were thought to have derived from a source (in the case of the Testament of Naphtali, an indirect source) of the Greek document.[8]

A new phase of scholarship began with the Qumran finds of Aramaic remains of a Testament of Levi, Hebrew fragments of the Testament of Naphtali, and possibly of other Testaments (see below, pp. 775–6). The new documents have reinforced the prevailing thesis concerning the Jewishness of the Testaments. In particular, several messianic passages, especially those reflecting the notion of a priestly and a royal redeemer, which many earlier scholars identified as Christian, have

---

8. Charles, *Testaments*, pp. lxvii, lxix–lxx.

been recognized by a number of writers as parallel to Qumran messianism. [9]

Apart from the impact of Qumran, the most significant changes in Testaments studies has resulted from a fresh examination of the textual evidence, especially the Greek and Armenian manuscript data. Charles's assessment of the Greek texts and his preference for recension α, already criticized by F. C. Burkitt and J. W. Hunkin,[10]has been exposed as incorrect by M. de Jonge,[11] whose views are supported in regard to the Armenian version by C. Burchard[12] and M. E. Stone.[13]

The principal corollary of de Jonge's findings, as opposed to those of Charles, is that passages described as Christian interpolations can no longer be distinguished on the basis of text-critical evidence. Indeed, de Jonge has reverted to the pre-Schnapp-Charles stage of development; for him, the Testaments are a Christian composition, albeit dependent on earlier Jewish works. To complete the merry-go-round, J. T. Milik has opined that the Testaments are probably of *Jewish-Christian* origin. [14]

Following this totally chaotic *status questionis*, in the light of de Jonge's textual theory which appears to be established and represented in his two editions of the Greek text, three questions remain to be formulated and answered.

(1) Are the Testaments a Jewish work with Christian additions; or are they a Christian writing utilizing Jewish documents?

(2) Are they a translation into Greek from Semitic originals, or a Greek composition with Semitic antecedents?

(3) Bearing in mind the solutions given to the first two questions, how does one date the Testaments?

(1) As far as their Jewish or Christian identity is concerned, four kinds of elements may theoretically be distinguished in a work such as the Testaments: (a) neutral, i.e. either Jewish or Christian elements; (b) fully Christian elements; (c) Jewish-Christian elements; and (d)

---

9. Cf. A. Dupont-Sommer, *Nouveaux aperçus sur les manuscrits de la Mer Morte* (1953), pp. 78–83; A. S. van der Woude, *Die messianischen Vorstellungen der Gemeinde von Qumran* (1957); M. Philonenko, *Les interpolations chrétiennes des Testaments des Douze Patriarches* (1960); A. Hultgård, *L'eschatologie des Testaments des Douze Patriarches* I (1977), pp. 304–6, etc.

10. Burkitt, JThSt 10 (1908), pp. 135–41; Hunkin, *ibid.* 16 (1914), pp. 80–97.

11. M. de Jonge first argued his case in *The Testaments of the Twelve Patriarchs* (1953), and has developed it in a number of subsequent studies including an *editio minor* and an *editio maior* of the Greek text. Cf. below.

12. 'Die armenische Überlieferung der Testamente der zwölf Patriarchen', in W. Eltester, *Studien zu den Testamenten der zwölf Patriarchen*, pp. 1–29.

13. *The Testament of Levi: A First Study of the Armenian Manuscripts* (1969).

14. RB 62 (1955), p. 406; *Ten Years of Discovery in the Wilderness of Judaea* (1959), pp. 34–5.

strictly Jewish elements. Of these (a) is of no significance for the
determination of the nature of the work. As regards (b), the passages
indisputably belonging to this category are limited in quantity;[15] figure
only in predictions; are grouped, when they extend beyond single
sentences or sentence clauses; and usually interrupt the flow of the
narrative. [16] In the face of these facts, the inescapable conclusion is that
the fully Christian units are secondary and must be (*pace* de Jonge)[17]
recognized as superimposed on an earlier Judaeo-Christian or Jewish
composition. The many allusions to the importance of obedience to
God's Law (TReub. 6:8; TLevi 9:6–7; 14:4; TJud. 26:1; TDan. 6:10,
etc.), generally represented as a source of morality, may testify to (c),
i.e. Jewish Christianity, but more probably to Judaism (= d),
especially since the Testaments include a number of features scarcely

15. The passages which are unquestionably Christian represent in all less than two
printed pages in M. de Jonge's *editio minor* where the Testaments *in toto* cover 86 pages.

16. The following passages may be identified as Christian.
TSim. 6:5: ὅτι Κύριος ὁ θεὸς μέγας τοῦ Ἰσραὴλ φαινόμενος ἐπὶ γῆς ⌈ὡς ἄνθρωπος⌉. (The
last two words are omitted in manuscript *a*. Charles noted that this may be simply a
theophany. Cf. *Testaments*, p. lxi.) TSim. 6:7: ὅτι θεὸς σῶμα λαβὼν καὶ συνεσθίων
ἀνθρώποις ἔσωσεν ἀνθρώπους. TSim. 7:2: θεὸν καὶ ἄνθρωπον. οὗτος σώσει πάντα τὰ ἔθνη καὶ
τὸ γένος τοῦ Ἰσραήλ. TLevi 4:4: πλὴν οἱ υἱοί σου ἐπιβαλοῦσι χεῖρας ἐπ᾽ αὐτόν, τοῦ
ἀποσκολοπίσαι αὐτόν. *Ib.* 10:2: εἰς τὸν σωτῆρα τοῦ κόσμου. *Ib.* 14:2: οἵτινες ἐπιβαλοῦσι
χεῖρας αὐτῶν ἐπὶ σωτῆρα τοῦ κόσμου (cf. 4:4). *Ib.* 18:7: πνεῦμα ... καταπαύσει ἐπ᾽ αὐτὸν ἐν
τῷ ὕδατι (The last three words which constitute the Christian element are missing from
manuscript *e*.)
TZeb. 9:8: καὶ ὄψεσθε θεὸν ἐν σχήματι ἀνθρώπου (cf. above TSim. 6:5).
TNapht. 8:3: ὀφθήσεται ὁ θεὸς κατοικῶν ἐν ἀνθρώποις (cf. above TSim. 6:5).
TAsh. 7:3: [ὁ ὕψιστος] ἐλθὼν ὡς ἄνθρωπος, μετὰ ἀνθρώπων ἐσθίων καὶ πίνων. TJos.
19:6 (11): ἀνατελεῖ ὑμῖν [ὁ ἀμνὸς τοῦ θεοῦ], χάριτι σώζων [πάντα τὰ ἔθνη καὶ] τὸν Ἰσραήλ.
(The words between square brackets are absent from the Armenian version.)
TBen. 3:8: περὶ τοῦ ἀμνοῦ τοῦ θεοῦ καὶ σωτῆρος τοῦ κόσμου. *Ib.* 9:3–5: κύριος
ὑβρισθήσεται, καὶ ἐξουθενωθήσεται καὶ ἐπὶ ξύλου ὑψωθήσεται. καὶ ἔσται τὸ ἅπλωμα τοῦ ναοῦ
σχιζόμενον, καὶ μεταβήσεται τὸ πνεῦμα τοῦ θεοῦ ἐπὶ τὰ ἔθνη ὡς πῦρ ἐκχυνόμενον. καὶ ἀνελθὼν
ἐκ τοῦ ᾅδου ἔσται ἀναβαίνων ἀπὸ γῆς εἰς οὐρανόν· ἔγνων δὲ οἷος ἔσται ταπεινὸς ἐπὶ γῆς καὶ οἷος
ἔνδοξος ἐν οὐρανῷ. *Ib.* 10:7: προσκυνοῦντες τὸν βασιλέα τῶν οὐρανῶν τὸν ἐπὶ γῆς φανέντα
μορφῇ ἀνθρώπου ταπεινώσεως. TBen. 11:1: καὶ οὐκέτι κληθήσομαι λύκος ἅρπαξ διὰ τὰς
ἁρπαγὰς ὑμῶν ἀλλ᾽ ἐργάτης κυρίου διαδίδους τροφὴν τοῖς ἐργαζομένοις τὸ ἀγαθόν (St. Paul?).
For a more detailed discussion of the Christian passages, see Charles, *Testaments*, pp.
lxi–v; M. Philonenko, *Les interpolations chrétiennes des Testaments des douze patriarches et les
manuscrits de Qoumrân* (1960); J. Jervell, 'Ein Interpolator interpretiert. Zu der christlichen
Bearbeitung der Testamente der zwölf Patriarchen', in W. Eltester (ed.), *Studien zu den
Testamenten der zwölf Patriarchen* (1969), pp. 30–61; A. Hultgård, *L'eschatologie des
Testaments des Douze Patriarches* II (1982), pp. 228–38.

17. M. de Jonge declares that, from a methodological point of view, the presence of
Christian material in a work is a *prima facie* argument in favour of the Christian character
of neutral sections as well ('Christian Influence in the Testaments of the Twelve
Patriarchs', NT 4 (1960), pp. 182–235, esp. 185–8). This principle can safely be adopted
only if one ignores the early Christian tendency towards doctrinal adaptation and
assimilation, and in the absence of definitely non-Christian (= Jewish) elements in the
writing under consideration. Neither condition applies in the case of the Testaments.

characteristic of any form of Christianity. Among these may be singled out the stress, throughout the Testaments, on the leadership of Levi and Judah, and the consequent duty to remain attached to these tribes. Such superiority recalls more the Qumran milieu than any kind of Christianity. Moreover, such an emphasis on both Levi and Judah echoes also the doctrine of their pre-eminence in the purely Jewish context of Jubilees 31:4–22. The important role attributed to the Book of Enoch deserves special mention, too.[18] For even though Enoch is quoted once in the New Testament, in Jude 14–15, the reverential use of his book in the Testaments rather recalls the Jubilees-Qumran milieu. The Testaments are, therefore, best defined as a Jewish work, related to, but not necessarily deriving from, Qumran, which has survived in a Christian version incorporating a limited amount of easily recognizable editorial modifications and glosses.

(2) The question of the original language of the Testaments has never been satisfactorily resolved. The extant evidence,[19] sporadic though it may be, suggests three possibilities: *i*. The Greek Testaments have been translated from a Semitic (Hebrew/Aramaic) text. *ii*. They are an original Greek composition, using as models for the whole work or for some parts of it pre-existing individual Testaments written in Hebrew or Aramaic. *iii*. The Testaments are a Greek re-working of one of the Semitic recensions in circulation among Jews.

i. Irrespective of the final conclusion whether or not the Greek Testaments should be characterized as a translation, it can firmly be stated that in no sense can they be recognized as rendering any of the *surviving* Semitic texts. The latter are in general longer than the corresponding Greek accounts.[20] Consequently, the case for an underlying Semitic original entirely depends on a linguistic analysis of the extant Greek version, more precisely on the 'Semitisms' identified in

18. TSim. 5:4; TLevi 10:5; 14:1; TJud. 18:1; TZeb. 3:4; TDan 5:6; TNapht. 4:1; TBen. 9:1; 10:6.

19. The Semitic material consists of the following: the Hebrew Midrash *Wa-yissa'u* related to TJud.; a Hebrew Testament of Naphtali; Aramaic fragments from the TLevi discovered in the Cairo Genizah; Aramaic fragments from TLevi found in Qumran Caves 1 and 4; Hebrew fragments from TNapht. from 4Q. The minute remains of an Aramaic TJud. from 4Q, of a Hebrew TJud. from 3Q and of an Aramaic TJos. from 4Q possibly belong to the Testaments material, but the scrappiness of the evidence precludes any firm identification. For a fuller description of these texts, see below, pp. 775–7. The reference to a Hebrew work ascribed in CD 4:14–18 to Levi the son of Jacob may not correspond to a *Testament*. If it does, it is not identical with the known version. It would be therefore superfluous to speculate whether the indirect quotation in CD derives from a Hebrew original or is the Hebrew summary of an Aramaic text.

20. The Greek additions to manuscript *e* (Athos, Monastery of Koutloumous, Cod. 39) at TLevi 2:3 and 18:2 which echo the Aramaic of the Genizah fragments constitute the only exception. Cf. M. de Jonge *et al.* (eds.), *The Testaments of the Twelve Patriarchs* (1978), p. xvii.

it, and on alleged mistranslations from the Hebrew or Aramaic. R. H. Charles compiled a list of Hebraisms[21] and A. Hultgård has recently produced an impressive series of Hebraisms and Aramaisms.[22]

The arguments in favour of a Semitic original must however be viewed against the evidence favouring a Greek composition. Also, it must be remembered that Semitisms in a Jewish-Greek text do not necessarily betray the incompetence of a translator; they may reflect a deliberate stylistic device aiming at the production of a Semitic flavour in a Greek text.[23]

ii. The thesis of a Greek original relies on three main grounds: dependence on the Septuagint, the use of typically Greek concepts and that of a Greek homiletic style.[24] It may be pointed out, however, that many differences from the LXX appear in Bible quotations, that the Greek text may have been revised to bring it closer to the LXX, and that a LXX-type Greek biblical citation may be a rendering from an Egyptian Hebrew recension of Scripture. As for the Hellenistic terminology and style, they may be secondary, corresponding to improvements introduced by Jewish-Greek editors of the Testaments.[25]

iii. The intermediate solution between a direct translation from a Semitic original and a Greek composition assumes that a work such as the Testaments does not proceed from a single author but depends on multiple antecedents, each of which has evolved separately and without a final editorial unification. In favour of this hypothesis may be cited the several recensions of the text of the Bible itself prior to its 'canonization'; the notable differences between the Hebrew and the Greek Ben Sira, and the recensional diversity attested for instance in the case of 1 Enoch or the Damascus Rule.[26] As regards the Testaments, and leaving out of consideration the late midrashic 'parallels' to the Testaments of Judah and Naphtali, the first peculiarity disclosed by the Genizah and Qumran evidence concerns the use of two languages. TLevi survives in both places in Aramaic and TNaphtali in

---

21. *Testaments*, pp. xliii-vii.

22. *L'eschatologie des Testaments* II (1982), pp. 173–81.

23. In the present state of documentation relating to the Testaments, J. Becker is probably correct in reaching the conclusion that they were written in 'semitisierendes Griechisch'. Cf. *Untersuchungen zur Entstehungsgeschichte der Testamente der zwölf Patriarchen* (1970), pp. 169–72; *Die Testamente* (JSHRZ III/1, 1974), p. 25.

24. Cf. e.g. M. de Jonge, *Testaments* (1953), pp. 118, 163; J. Becker, *Entstehungsgeschichte* (1970), pp. 187, 193–4, 209–10, 221–2, 401, etc.

25. Cf. Hultgård, *op.cit.* II, pp. 165–71.

26. These are questions which precede the problem of actual translation in antiquity. On the latter, see J. Barr, 'The Typology of Literalism in ancient biblical translations', NAG Nr. 11 (1979), pp. 279–325; S. P. Brock, 'Aspects of Translation Technique in Antiquity', Greek, Rom. & Byz. St. 20 (1979), pp. 69–87.

Hebrew. If, moreover, Milik's theory concerning fragments belonging to TJudah and TJoseph (cf. p. 776) turns out to be correct, not only will these relics confirm the linguistic duality, but they may also indicate that, like the canonical Daniel and 4Q Tobit (cf. above, pp. 224–5, 246–7), the same work has been transmitted fully or partly in Aramaic as well as in Hebrew. From the different languages used, it would be logical to infer that TLevi and TNaphtali originated independently from one another; and bearing in mind the relative unimportance of Naphtali compared, say, with Levi, Joseph or Judah, it is equally reasonable to suppose that several Testaments came to be written in Semitic languages, leading no doubt progressively to the formation of a twelve-fold composition.

To account both for the Semitic substratum and for the genuine Hellenistic features of the Greek Testaments, as well as for the similarities and substantial differences between the textual witnesses, the best explanation seems to be that the Greek Testaments have resulted from an abbreviation and free re-working by Greek-speaking Jews of one, if not several, of the recensions of the Semitic Testaments. It goes without saying that it was on the Greek version(s) that Christian editorial activity was subsequently exercised.

(3) Considering the highly complex redactional development of the Testaments,[27] and the absence of any definite historical pointer in the text itself, dating is bound to be problematic. The Christian revision, reflecting the influence of the Fourth Gospel,[28] is most likely to have been effected in the course of the second century A.D. The polemical sections relating to priesthood and kingship best fit the Maccabaean-Hasmonaean era, and attempts have been made to identify allusions in TLevi 8:14–15 to John Hyrcanus I,[29] and to Alexander Jannaeus in TLevi 14:5.[30] The redaction of the Testaments should therefore be placed in the Hasmonaean age, and since no reference to the Romans figures anywhere,[31] a pre–63 B.C. dating is advisable.[32] If the view suggested above concerning a Greek redaction of the work is accepted, it should also fall within the 100–63 B.C. period.

27. See, e.g., Becker, *Entstehungsgeschichte*, pp. 373–7.

28. Cf. TJos. 19:6 (11); TBen. 3:8.

29. E.g. Charles, *Testaments*, pp. lii-iii.

30. Charles, *ibid.*, p. lviii; Hultgård II, p. 226.

31. See especially TNapht. 5:8, where the Syrians are placed to the end of the series of enemies.

32. Scholars dating the Testaments to the second half of the second century B.C. include R. H. Charles (*Testaments*, p. lii), W. Bousset (ZNW I (1900), pp. 197–202), H. C. Kee (OTP I, p. 778, but NTSt 24 (1978), p. 269: *c.* 100 B.C.). P. Sacchi assigns the two main stages of redaction to the middle of the second century B.C., and to 40–30 B.C. (*Apocrifi dell'A.T.*, p. 739). A. Hultgård (II, p. 227) may well be right in proposing the first half of the first century B.C.

The Semitic antecedents of the Testaments are to be traced to the second century B.C. 4Q TLevi appears to belong to an early layer of Qumran palaeography, and J. T. Milik assigns it to the end of the second or the beginning of the first century B.C.[33] In his view, the original TLevi is a Samaritan work 'composed in the course of the third century [B.C.], if not towards the end of the fourth'.[34] As the proof for this early dating will not be forthcoming before the promised edition of the Aramaic TLevi, a single mention should now suffice. Somewhat less adventurously, E. Bickerman, J. Thomas and J. Becker select the first quarter of the second century B.C. for the origin of the Testaments.[35] On the whole, the second century B.C. provides the most suitable background for the origins of the Semitic Testaments. Any further precision would be too speculative.

Only a schematic discussion is possible regarding the provenance of the Testaments. An early second century B.C. dating of the Semitic antecedents would bring to mind the pietistic (Hasidic) circles of the pre-Maccabaean age. The presence among the Dead Sea Scrolls of the Testaments of Levi and Naphtali (as well as perhaps those of Judah and Joseph) witnesses the popularity of this type of literature at Qumran. Respect for, and criticism of, the priesthood, the influence of the doctrine of the two spirits and two ways,[36] and the attestation of both distinct and joint royal and priestly redeemer figures,[37] indicate either the impact of the Testaments on Qumran thought, or a Qumran stage in the development of the Testaments. Whether the Greek editor of the work was a Palestinian or a diaspora Jew cannot be decided on the basis of the available data, though the special interest in Joseph may point to an Egyptian origin.[38]

The Semitic material cognate to the Greek Testaments includes *(a)*

33. RB 62 (1955), p. 399.
34. *Enoch* (1976), p. 24.
35. Bickerman, 'The Date of the Testaments of the Twelve Patriarchs', JBL 69 (1950), pp. 245–60; revised in *Studies in Jewish and Christian History* II (1980), pp. 1–23. From an allusion in TJos. 16:4–5 to the equivalence between a standard gold coin and a didrachm, he deduces that the period envisaged must be 200–150 B.C. (*ibid.*, pp. 12–14). J. Thomas, in W. Eltester, *Studien* (1969), pp. 83–6; J. Becker, *Entstehungsgeschichte*, p. 376; JSHRZ III/1, p. 25.
36. Cf. especially TJud. 20:1; TAsh. 1:3–9—1QS 3:13–4:26.
37. Cf. TJud. 1:6; 24:1–6; TJos. 19:4; TDan 5:10; TGad 8:1—1QSa 2:11–21; CD 11:23; 14:19; 19:10; 20:1.
38. See J. Becker, *Entstehungsgeschichte*, p. 374; H. C. Kee, OTP I, p. 778.
Charles identified the author as a Pharisee (*Testaments*, p. xv), P. Riessler (*Altjüdisches Schrifttum*, p. 1335) as an Essene. A Qumran-Essene provenance has been proposed by, among others, A. Dupont-Sommer (*Essene Writings*, pp. 301–5), M. Philonenko (*Les interpolations chrétiennes des Testaments des Douze Patriarches et les manuscrits de Qoumrân*, 1960), O. Eissfeldt (*Introduction*, p. 633). A. Hultgård attributes the composition to levitical *ḥᵃkāmîm* (*Eschatologie* II, pp. 219–22).

Qumran fragments; *(b)* Genizah texts; and *(c)* rabbinic midrashim.

(a) Qumran Caves 1 and 4 have yielded remains belonging to an Aramaic Testament of Levi. *1Q21*[39] points towards TLevi 8, and is related to the Bodleian Genizah fragment, col. a. *4QTLevi ar*[a] (earlier designated *ar*[b]) cols. 1–2, corresponds to Bodl. col. a and the addition attested in the Greek manuscript e after TLevi 2:3;[40] col. 3 is related to TLevi 14 and is parallel to Bodl. col. d and Cambridge cols. e-f.[41]

A Hebrew Testament of Naphtali has survived in Cave 4, containing a longer version of TNapht. 1:6–12. Only a single sentence, dealing in the etymology of the name Bilha (*4QTest Napht.* 1 ii 45 = TNapht. 1:12) has so far been published.[42]

The more doubtful identifications include an Aramaic Testament of Judah (*4Q A Ju* 1 a-b) pertaining to the context of TJud. 12:11–12; and a Hebrew version of the same Testament (*3Q H Ju*) which may be linked with TJud. 25:1–2. Small fragments of an Aramaic Testament of Joseph (*4Q A Jo* 1 a-b and 2 a-b) may reflect TJos. 14:4–5; 15:1; 16:4–5; 17:1–2.[43]

(b) Fragments of an Aramaic Testament of Levi have been yielded by the Cairo Genizah. The Cambridge material is represented by T-S 16.94 and that of the Bodleian Library in Oxford by Ms Heb c 27 f 56. Dating to the eleventh, or possibly the tenth century A.D.,[44] they extend approximately from TLevi 9 to 13, and closely resemble the extant parallel passages in the Qumran manuscripts. The Greek Ms e (Athos, Monastery of Koutloumous, cod. 39 of the eleventh century) contains the translation of Bodl. col. b-d, of four further columns lost in Aramaic, as well as of Cambr. col. c, lines 3–13. For the original editions, see the Bibliography. All the texts appear in Appendix III of Charles, *The Greek Versions*, pp. 243–56.[45]

(c) Rabbinic literature has preserved two midrashic works related to the Testaments.

(i) The Hebrew Testament of Naphtali was printed by S. A. Wertheimer in 1890 and edited by M. Gaster from the Bodleian

---

39. J. T. Milik, DJD I, pp. 87–91.
40. Milik, RB 62 (1955), pp. 398–406.
41. Milik, *Enoch*, p. 23.
42. *Ibid.*, p. 198.
43. J. T. Milik, 'Ecrits préesséniens de Qumrân', in M. Delcor, *Qumrân* (1978), pp. 97–102. Milik's *3Q H Ju* equals *3Q7* in M. Baillet, DJD III, p. 99. The fragment, if correctly identified as TJos. 16:4–5, would supply an Aramaic basis for Bickerman's numismatic argument mentioned in n. 35 above.
44. M. Beit-Arié quoted by J. C. Greenfield and M. E. Stone, RB 86 (1979), p. 216.
45. A list of revised readings by J. C. Greenfield and M. E. Stone has been published in RB 86 (1979), pp. 229–30.

manuscript of the Chronicles of Yerahmeel in 1894.[46] The Bodleian text is included in Charles, *Greek Versions*, Appendix II, pp. 239–44. (ii) The Hebrew *Midrash Wa-yissa'u*, dealing with the wars of the Patriarchs, is related to the Testament of Judah. Edited by A. Jellinek, בית המדרש III (1855), pp. 1–3, it is reprinted as Appendix I in Charles, *Greek Versions*, pp. 235–8.[47]

Concerning the relationship between the Testaments and ancient Jewish literature, the frequent references to the Book of Enoch should be noted (TSim. 5:4; TLevi 10:5; 14:1; TJud. 18:1; TZeb. 3:4; TDan 5:6; TNapht. 4:1; TBen. 9:1). None of the allusions can, however, be identified as quotations from the extant versions of Enoch. In the biographical portions are numerous contacts with the Book of Jubilees.[48] The Aramaic fragments also display many similarities with Jubilees.

A possible citation of the Testament of Levi in Hebrew has been noticed in the Damascus Rule 4:14–18.

The Testaments are specifically quoted by Origen, *In librum Iesu Nave homilia* xv 6 (ed. W. Baehrens, GCS VII/2, p. 392): 'Sed et in aliquo quodam libello, qui apellatur testamentum duodecim patriarcharum, quamvis non habeatur in canone, talem tamen quendam sensum invenimus, quod per singulos peccantes singuli satanae intelligi debeant' (cf. TReub. 2–3). Jerome, *Tractatus de Psalmo XV* (ed. Morin, CCL 78, p. 376): 'In Libro quoque Patriarcharum, licet inter apocryphos computetur, ita inveni, ut quomodo fel ad iracundiam sic renes ad calliditatem et ad astutiam sint creati. Πανουργία autem id est calliditas, ut vel in bonam vel in malam partem accipiatur ...' (cf. TNapht. 2:8). In the Stichometry of Nicephorus, the Πατριάρχαι are specified under the ἀπόκρυφα, along with Enoch, the Assumption of Moses, and similar writings with 5,100 στίχοι. The present form of the Testaments is about half that size.[49] See also the *Synopsis Athanasii* and in the anonymous list of Sixty Books.

The following Greek manuscripts are extant:

a Oxford, Bodleian Library Baroccio 133 (*c*. 1270);
b Cambridge, University Library Ff. I. 24 (late 10th century);
c Vatican Library Cod. Graec. 731 (13th century);
d Vatican Library Cod. Graec. 1238 (end of 12th century);

---

46. S. A. Wertheimer, בתי המדרש I (1890), pp. 199–203; M. Gaster, 'The Hebrew Text of one of the Testaments of the Twelve Patriarchs', Proc. Soc. Bibl. Arch. 16 (1894), pp. 33–49, 109–17. M. de Jonge, *Testaments* (1953), pp. 52–60; J. Becker, *Entstehungsgeschichte* (1970), pp. 105–13; Th. Korteweg, 'The Meaning of Naphtali's Vision', in de Jonge, *Studies* (1975), pp. 269–90; A. Hultgård, *Eschatologie* II, pp. 128–35, 288–98.

47. Cf. H. L. Strack and G. Stemberger, *Einleitung in Talmud und Midrash* (⁷1982), p. 300. T. Alexander and J. Dan, 'The Complete *Midrash Vayissa'u*', Folklore Research Center Studies 3 (1972), pp. 67–76; Hultgård, II, pp. 123–7.

48. Cf. Charles, *Testaments*, p. 238.

49. Cf. H. J. de Jonge in M. de Jonge, *Studies* (1975), p. 66.

e Athos, Monastery of Koutloumous Cod. 39 (11th century);
f Paris, Bibliothèque Nationale, Fonds grec 2658 (11th century);
g Patmos, Monastery of St. John the Theologian, Ms. 411 (15th century);
h Mt. Sinai, Monastery of St. Catharine, Cod. Graec. 547 (17th century);
i Mt. Sinai, Mon. St. Cath. (not earlier than 17th century);
j Mt. Sinai, Mon. St. Cath. Cod. Graec. 2170 (18th century);
k Venice, Biblioteca Nazionale di S. Marco, Cod. Gr. Z 494 (mid–13th
century);
l Athos, Library of the Laura, Laura I 48 (16th–17th century);
m Ankara, Türk Tarih Kurumu MS Gr. 60 (16th century);
n Athos, Monastery of Vatopedi Cod. 659 (14th century).

For a full description, see M. de Jonge, *The Testaments* (1978), pp.
xi-xxv. Charles used the first nine codices in his 1908 edition. His
arrangement of these into two families, α (= Mss c, h, i) and β (= Mss
a, b, d, e, f, g, j), has been proved erroneous by M. de Jonge *et al.* who
propose, instead, a family I (b, k) and a family II (the rest of the Greek
manuscripts as well as the Armenian, Slavonic and Serbian versions (cf.
op. cit., pp. xxxiii-xli)).

Editions

1. Greek Testaments

Charles, R. H., *The Greek Versions of the Testaments of the Twelve Patriarchs* (1908, repr.
1966).
Jonge, M. de, *Testamenta XII Patriarcharum edited according to Cambridge University Library
MSF f 1.24* (1964, ²1970).
Jonge, M. de, in cooperation with Hollander, H. W., Jonge, H. J. de, Korteweg, Th., *The
Testaments of the Twelve Patriarchs* (1978).

2. Aramaic and Hebrew fragments
a) Qumran
Milik, J. T., DJD I (1955), pp. 87–91 (TLevi).
Idem, 'Le Testament de Lévi en araméen: Fragments de la grotte 4 de Qumrân', RB 62
(1955), pp. 398–406.
Idem, The Book of Enoch (1976), p. 23 (4Q Levi ar). *Ibid.*, p. 198 (4Q TestNapht).
Idem, 'Les écrits préésséniens de Qumrân: d'Hénoch à Amram', in Delcor, M., *Qumrân:
sa piété, sa théologie et son milieu* (1978), pp. 97–102.
Fitzmyer, J. A., and Harrington, D. J., *A Manual of Palestinian Aramaic Texts* (1978), no.
20 (*1QTLevi ar*), pp. 80–8, 202–3; no. 21 (*4QTLevi ar*), pp. 88–91, 203–4.

b) Cairo Genizah
Pass, H. L., and Arendzen, J., 'Fragment of an Aramaic Text of the Testament of Levi',
JQR 12 (1900), pp. 651–61 (Cambridge fragm.).
Charles, R. H. and Cowley, A., 'An Early Source of the Testaments of the Patriarchs',
JQR 19 (1907), pp. 566–83.
Lévi, I., 'Notes sur le texte araméen du Testament de Lévi récemment découvert', REJ
54 (1907), pp. 166–80.
Idem, 'Encore un mot sur le texte . . .', *ibid.*, pp. 285–7.
Grelot, P., 'Le Testament araméen de Lévi est-il traduit de l'hébreu?', REJ 14 (1955),
pp. 91–9.
Idem, 'Notes sur le Testament araméen de Lévi', RB 63 (1956), pp. 391–406.
Greenfield, J. C., and Stone, M. E., 'Remarks on the Aramaic Testament of Levi from
the Geniza', RB 86 (1979), pp. 214–30.

Versions

1. *Armenian*

Yovsēp'eanç, S., *T'angaran hin ew nor naxneaç I. Ankanon girk' hin ktakaranaç* (1896), pp. 27–151.

Preuschen, E., 'Die armenische Übersetzung der Testamente der zwölf Patriarchen', ZNW 1 (1900), pp. 106–40.

Stone, M., *The Testament of Levi. A First Study of the Armenian MSS of the XII Patriarchs in the Convent of St. James, Jerusalem* (1969).

Burchardt, Chr., 'Zur armenischen Überlieferung der Testamente der zwölf Patriarchen', in Eltester, W., *Studien zu den Testamenten der zwölf Patriarchen* (1969), pp. 1–29.

Jonge, M. de, 'The Greek Testaments of the Twelve Patriarchs and the Armenian Version', in *Studies on the Testaments of the Twelve Patriarchs* (1975), pp. 120–39.

Stone, M., *The Armenian Version of the Testament of Joseph* (1975).

Idem, 'The Armenian Version of the Testaments of the Twelve Patriarchs: Selection of Manuscripts', Sion 49 (1975), pp. 207–14.

Idem, 'New Evidence for the Armenian Version of the Testaments of the Twelve Patriarchs', RB 84 (1977), pp. 94–107.

2. *Slavonic*

Tichonravov, N. S., *Pamjatniki otrecennoj russkoj literatury* I (1863), pp. 146–232.

Turdeanu, E., 'Les Testaments des Douze Patriarches en Slave', JSJ 1 (1970), pp. 148–84.

Gaylord, H. E., and Korteweg, Th., 'The Slavic Versions', in de Jonge, M., *Studies* (1975), pp. 140–3.

3. *Syriac*

Wright, W., *Catalogue of Syriac Manuscripts in the British Museum* II, p. 997. [This is a small fragment corresponding to the end of the Aramaic Genizah fragment, col. d. It is printed in Charles, *Greek Versions*, p. 254.]

Translations

English

Sinker, R., *Ante-Nicene Christian Library* XXII (1871), pp. 13–79.

Charles, R. H., *The Testaments of the Twelve Patriarchs* (1908).

Idem, APOT II (1913), pp. 282–367.

Kee, H. C., OTP I (1983), pp. 775–828.

German

Schnapp, F., APAT II (1900), pp. 458–506.

Riessler, P., *Altjüdisches Schrifttum* (1928), pp. 1149–1250, 1335–8.

Becker, J., JSHRZ III/1 (1974), pp. 1–163.

Italian

Sacchi, P., *Apocrifi dell'Antico Testamento* (1981), pp. 727–948.

Bibliography

Geiger, A., 'Apokryphen zweiter Ordnung', JZWL 7 (1869), pp. 116–35.

Sinker, R., *The Testaments of the XII Patriarchs: An Attempt to estimate their Historic and Dogmatic Worth* (1869).

Schnapp, F., *Die Testamente der zwölf Patriarchen untersucht* (1884).

Conybeare, F. C., 'A Collation of Sinker's Text of the Testaments of Reuben and Simeon with the Armenian Version', JQR 8 (1896), pp. 260–8.

Idem, 'A Collation of Armenian Texts of the Testaments ...', *ibid.*, pp. 471–85.

Bousset, W., 'Die Testamente der XII Patriarchen', ZNW 1 (1900), pp. 141–75, 187–209.

Kohler, K., 'Testaments of the Twelve Patriarchs', JE XII (1906), pp. 113–18.

Hunkin, J. W., 'The Testaments of the Twelve Patriarchs', JThSt 16 (1914), pp. 80–97.

Messel, N., 'Über die textkritisch begründete Ausscheidung vermutlicher christlicher Interpolationen in den Testamenten der zwölf Patriarchen', BZAW 33 (1918), pp. 355–74.

Eppel, R., *Le piétisme juif dans les Testaments des douze patriarches* (1930).

Beasley-Murray, G. R., 'The Two Messiahs in the Testaments of the Twelve Patriarchs', JThSt 48 (1947), pp. 1–12.

Manson, T. W., 'Testaments of the XII Patriarchs: Levi VIII', *ibid.*, pp. 59–61.

Black, M., 'The Messiah in the Testament of Levi XVIII', ET 60 (1948–9), pp. 321–2.

Bickerman, E., 'The Date of the Testaments of the Twelve Patriarchs', JBL 69 (1950), pp. 245–60 [= *Studies in Jewish and Christian History* II (1980), pp. 1–23].

Rabin, C., 'The Teacher of Righteousness in the Testaments of the Twelve Patriarchs', JJS 3 (1952), pp. 127–8.

Otzen, B., 'Die neugefundenen hebräischen Sektenschriften und die Testamente der zwölf Patriarchen', StTh 7 (1953), pp. 125–57.

Jonge, M. de, *The Testaments of the Twelve Patriarchs: A Study of their Text, Composition and Origin* (1953).

Idem, 'Christian Influence in the Testaments of the Twelve Patriarchs', NT 4 (1960), pp. 182–235.

Braun, F.-M., 'Les Testaments des douze patriarches et le problème de leur origine', RB 67 (1960), pp. 516–49.

Philonenko, M., *Les interpolations chrétiennes des Testaments des Douze Patriarches et les manuscrits de Qoumrân* (1960).

Jonge, M. de, 'Once more: Christian Influence...', NT 5 (1962), pp. 311–19.

Smith, M., 'The Testaments of the Twelve Patriarchs', IDB IV (1962), pp. 575–9.

Eissfeldt, O., *Introduction* (1965), pp. 631–6, 775.

Jervell, J., 'Ein Interpolator interpretiert. Zu der christlichen Bearbeitung der Testamente der zwölf Patriarchen', in Eltester, W. (ed.), *Studien zu den Testamenten der zwölf Patriarchen* (1969), pp. 30–61.

Thomas, J., 'Aktuelles im Zeugnis der zwölf Väter', *ibid.*, pp. 62–150.

Becker, J., *Untersuchungen zur Entstehungsgeschichte der Testamente der zwölf Patriarchen* (1970).

Denis, IPGAT (1970), pp. 49–59.

Flusser, D., 'Testaments of the Twelve Patriarchs', Enc. Jud. 13 (1971), cols. 184–6.

Grelot, P., 'Quatre cents trente ans (Ex 12, 40): Note sur les Testaments de Lévi et d'Amram', *Homenaje a J. Prado* (1975), pp. 571–84.

Jonge, M. de (ed.), *Studies on the Testaments of the Twelve Patriarchs* (1975).

Nickelsburg, G. W. E. (ed.), *Studies on the Testament of Joseph* (1975).

Charlesworth, J. H., 'Reflections on the SNTS Pseudepigrapha Seminar at Duke on the Testaments of the Twelve Patriarchs', NTSt 23 (1977), pp. 296–304.

Slingerland, D., *The Testaments of the Twelve Patriarchs: A Critical History of Research* (1977).

Idem, 'The Testament of Joseph: A Redaction-Critical Study', JBL 96 (1977), pp. 507–16.

Kee, H. C., 'The Ethical Dimensions of the Testaments of the XII Patriarchs as a Clue to Provenance', NTSt 24 (1978), pp. 259–70.

Jonge, M. de, 'The Main Issues in the Study of the Testaments of the Twelve Patriarchs', NTSt 26 (1980), pp. 508–24.

Charlesworth, J. H., PMRS (1981), pp. 211–20, 305–7.

Nickelsburg, G. W. E., JLBBM (1981), pp. 231–41, 273.

Grelot, P., 'Le Livre des Jubilés et le Testament de Lévi', Casetti, P., et al. (eds.), *Mélanges D. Barthélemy* (1981), pp. 110–33.

Jonge, M. de, 'Levi, the Sons of Levi and the Law, in *Testament Levi* X, XIV-XV and XVI', *De la Tôrah au Messie. Mélanges H. Cazelles* (1981), pp. 513–23.

Hultgård, A., *L'eschatologie des Testaments des Douze Patriarches* I. *Interprétation des textes*; II.
Composition de l'ouvrage, textes et traductions (1977, 1982).

4. *The Book of Jannes and Jambres*

The Book of Jannes and Jambres is a midrash based on Exod. 7:8 ff.,
viz. on the story of two Egyptian magicians who competed
unsuccessfully with Moses and Aaron. The names Jannes and Jambres
are not mentioned in the Old Testament, but appear relatively early in
Jewish and pagan writings, in the New Testament and Christian
documents. The Greek texts have predominantly Ἰαννῆς καὶ Ἰαμβρῆς
and the Latin spelling is 'Iannes' or 'Iamnes' and 'Mambres'. Targum
Pseudo-Jonathan reads ינים וימבריס (Ex. 7:11). The Talmud and
Midrash, on the other hand, speak of יוחני וממרא,[1] whereas the
Damascus Rule refers to יחנה and his brother (CD 5:18). Whatever the
original form, the names are almost certainly Semitic.[2]

The book survives in Greek fragments,[3] and is mentioned by Origen,
Ambrosiaster, and the *Decretum Gelasii*. A fragment in Latin and Anglo-
Saxon, in which Mambres invokes the soul of his dead brother Jamnes
and the latter confesses that he is deservedly suffering in the underworld, may also derive from the same source. As the name of Jannes
was already known both to Pliny and to the author of the Damascus
Rule, the work, or at least the traditions on which it is based, must
antedate 100 B.C.

For Jannes and Jambres in rabbinic literature, see K. Kohler, JE
VII, pp. 587–8; Str.-B. III, pp. 660–4; Renée Bloch, 'Moïse dans la
tradition rabbinique', *Moïse, l'homme de l'Alliance* (1955), pp. 105–6; H.
Odeberg, TDNT III, pp. 192–3; M. Stone, Enc. Jud. 9, col. 1277.

Amongst the Latin and Greek writers, Pliny and Apuleius are
familiar with Jannes, the Neoplatonic Numenius with both Jannes and
Jambres. 1. Pliny, *NH* xxx 1, 11: 'Est et alia magices factio a Mose et
Ianne et Lotape ac Iudaeis pendens, sed multis milibus annorum post
Zoroastren.' 2. Apuleius, *Apologia* (or *De magia*) 90 (ed. Hildebrand):
'Ego ille sim Carinondas vel Damigeron vel is Moses vel Iannes vel
Apollonius vel ipse Dardanus, vel quicumque alius post Zoroastren et
Hostanen inter magos celebratus est.' 3. Numenius, in Eusebius, *Praep.
ev.* ix 8, 1: Τὰ δ' ἑξῆς Ἰαννῆς καὶ Ἰαμβρῆς Αἰγύπτιοι ἱερογραμματεῖς,

1. Other Targumic and rabbinic variants are יונים, יונוס, יוחנא on the one hand and ימריס
and יומברוס on the other: cf. J. Levy, *Chaldäisches Wörterbuch* I, p. 337; Str.-B. III,
p. 660; H. Odeberg, TDNT III, p. 192.

2. The first name echoes various Aramaic forms of יוחנן; the second the biblical ממרא
(Gen. 14:13, 24). The Greek Ἰαμβρῆς probably represents an alliterative contamination.
For the insertion of β between μ and ρ in Greek transcriptions, see Μάμβρη and Νέμβροδ
in the LXX Gen. 13:18, 14:13 and 10:8.

3. Cf. A. Pietersma, 'Greek and Coptic Inedita in the Chester Beatty Library', BIOSCS
7 (1974), pp. 15–17; P. Maraval, 'Fragments grecs du livre de Jannès et Jambré', ZPE 25
(1977), pp. 199–207.

ἄνδρες οὐδενὸς ἥττους μαγεῦσαι κριθέντες εἶναι, ἐπὶ Ἰουδαίων ἐξελαυνομ-
ένων ἐξ Αἰγύπτου. Μουσαίῳ γοῦν τῷ Ἰουδαίων ἐξηγησαμένῳ, ἀνδρὶ
γενομένῳ θεῷ εὔξασθαι δυνατωτάτῳ, οἱ παραστῆναι ἀξιωθέντες ὑπὸ τοῦ
πλήθους τοῦ τῶν Αἰγυτίων οὗτοι ἦσαν, τῶν τε συμφορῶν ἃς ὁ Μουσαῖος
ἐπῆγε τῇ Αἰγύπτῳ, τὰς νεανικοτάτας αὐτῶν ἐπιλύεσθαι ὤφθησαν δυνατοί.
With reference to this, Origen says of Numenius, *Contra Celsum* iv 51:
ἐκτίθεται καὶ τὴν περὶ Μωϋσέως καὶ Ἰαννοῦ καὶ Ἰαμβροῦ ἱστορίαν. In the
New Testament 2 Tim. 3:8 refers to the clash of Jannes and Jambres
with Moses: Ἰάννης καὶ Ἰαμβρῆς ἀντέστησαν Μωϋσεῖ. There are further
passages occurring among Greek Christian writers, *Evang. Nicodemi* (=
Acta Pilati) 5; *Acta Petri et Pauli* 55; *Constitut. apostol.* viii 1, and later
Church Fathers. Among Latin writers, see *Evang. Nicodemi* (= *Gesta
Pilati*) 5; Cyprian, *De unitate ecclesiae* 16; *Decretum Gelasianum* (ed. E. von
Dobschütz, pp. 306–7), and later Church Fathers.

The Book of Jannes and Jambres (or Mambres) is mentioned in the
following: 1. Origen, *Comm. in Matth.* 27:9 (ed. Klostermann, CGS 38,
p. 250): 'quod ait: "sicut Iannes et Mambres restiterunt Mosi" non
invenitur in publicis scripturis, sed in libro secreto, qui suprascribitur:
Iannes et Mambres liber.' 2. Origen, *Comm. in Matt.* 23:37 (ed.
Klostermann, p. 51) cites 2 Tim. 3:8: 'sicut Iannes et Mambres
restiterunt Mosi, sicut et isti restitunt veritati' as a proof that the New
Testament refers sometimes to apocryphal writings. 'Nec enim scimus
in libris canonizatis historiam de Ianne et Mambre resistentibus Mosi.'
3. Ambrosiaster on 2 Tim. 3:8 (PL 17, 494AB): 'Exemplum hoc de
apocryphis est; Iannes enim et Mambres fratres erant magi vel venefici
Aegyptiorum, qui arte magiae suae virtutibus Dei, quae per Moysen
agebantur, aemulatione commentitia resistere se putabant. Sed cum
Moysis virtus in operibus cresceret, humiles facti, confessi sunt cum
dolore vulnerum Deum in Moyse operatum.' 4. *Decretum Gelasianum* (ed.
E. von Dobschütz, pp. 306–7): 'Liber, qui appellatur Poenitentia
Jamne et Mambre apocryphus.' 5. Philostorgius, *Hist. Eccl.* ix 2 (ed. J.
Bidez, GCS 21, p. 116): Μωσῆς, φησίν, τοὺς περὶ Ἰαννὴν καὶ Ἰαμβρὴν ἐν
ἕλκεσι κολασάμενος, καὶ τὴν θατέρου τούτων μητέρα τῷ θανάτῳ
παρεπέμψατο (cf. Denis, FPG, p. 69).[4]

Alleged quotations from Jannes and Mambres appear in the Greek
Acts of St. Catherine. Cf. J. Viteau, *Passions des saints Ecaterine et Pierre
d'Alexandrie* (1897), pp. 7, 30; G. B. Bronzini, 'La Leggenda di S.

---

4. In addition to this Greek fragment, an Aramaic quotation from the Book of Jannes
and Jambres figures, according to K. Koch, in Targum Pseudo-Jonathan on Ex. 1:15,
where the two magicians interpret Pharaoh's dream concerning a lamb that outweighs
the whole of Egypt as representing Moses. Cf. 'Das Lamm des Ägypten vernichtet. Ein
Fragment aus Jannes und Jambres und sein geschichtlicher Hintergrund', ZNW 57
(1966), pp. 79–93. However, the Targumist is just as likely to have freely supplied the
words rather than to have borrowed them from a written source.

Caterina d'Alessandria', AANL 9 (1960), pp. 261–73; Denis, IPGAT, p. 148. There is also a bilingual Latin/Anglo-Saxon manuscript dating to the eleventh century. Cf. M. R. James, 'A Fragment of the "Penitence of Jannes 'and Jambres"', JThSt 2 (1901), pp. 572–7; *idem*, *The Lost Apocrypha* (1920), pp. 32–3.

Bibliography

Denis, IPGAT, pp. 146–9.
Charlesworth, PMRS, pp. 133–4, 291.
Pietersma, A., and Lutz, R. T., 'Jannes and Jambres' in OTP II (forthcoming).

5. The Book of Eldad and Modad.

Under the names of two Israelites אלדד and מידד (LXX Ἐλδὰδ καὶ Μωδάδ), who according to Numbers 11:26–9 prophesied in the camp during the wandering in the wilderness, a book was in circulation which in addition to being mentioned in the Stichometry of Nicephorus as consisting of 400 verses, is also quoted in the mid-second-century Shepherd of Hermas as a genuine prophetic writing.

According to Targum Neofiti and Targum Pseudo-Jonathan on Numbers 11:26–9, the prophecies related mainly to the last assault of Gog and Magog against the community of Israel. It is however very doubtful whether this indicates the precise contents of the book.

Shepherd of Hermas, *Vis.* ii 3, 4 (ed. M. Whittaker, p. 7; Denis, FPG, p. 68): Ἐγγὺς Κύριος τοῖς ἐπιστρεφομένοις ὡς γέγραπται ἐν τῷ Ἐλδὰδ καὶ Μωδάτ, τοῖς προφητεύσασιν ἐν τῷ ἐρήμῳ τῷ λαῷ.

Bibliography

Beer, G., 'Eldad und Medad im Pseudojonathan', MGWJ 6 (1857), pp. 346–50.
Aberbach, M., 'Eldad and Medad', Enc. Jud. 6, cols. 575–6.
Denis, IPGAT, pp. 142–4.
Vermes, G., *Jesus the Jew* (1973), p. 113.
Le Déaut, R., *Targum du Pentateuque* III. *Nombres* (1979), pp. 110–11.

6. The Lives of the Prophets

A collection of non-biblical traditions supplementing the scriptural stories of the prophets survives in several Greek recensions. The text has been known since 1622, when D. Petavius published Ms. Paris 1115 (reprinted in PG 43, cols. 393–413). The prophets' number and order varies, but Isaiah, Jeremiah, Ezekiel, Daniel and the Twelve are always included. In certain recensions, Nathan, Ahijah the Philonite, Joed, Zechariah the son of Jehoiada, Azariah the son of Oded, as well as

Elijah and Elisha figure also.[1] Particular attention is paid to their deaths and to their places of burial.[2] Six prophets, viz Isaiah, Jeremiah, Ezekiel, Micah, Amos and Zechariah the son of Jehoiada, are said to have been murdered.[3] Haggadic elements serve to enrich the portraits, and to link them with other biblical figures.[4]

The author of the Lives mentions a number of Palestinian geographical names otherwise unknown when indicating the birth-places of prophets, e.g. Σαρίρα (Ezekiel), Βηθαχαράμ (Obadiah), Καριαθμαοῦς (Jonah), Σαβαραθά (Zephaniah), Σωφᾶ (Malachi) and Συβαθά (Azariah). It is suggested that his point of view is that of an inhabitant of Jerusalem. This conclusion does not however apply to the life of Jeremiah, which seems to have come from Egypt.[5]

The original language of the composition cannot be determined with any degree of certainty. It may have been Greek with Semitic colouring,[6] or the Greek may have derived from the Hebrew.[7] It is equally plausible to postulate a Semitic source, freely re-worked by a Hellenistic Jew.

The dating is as usual highly problematic. One of the principal arguments in favour of the late first century A.D. is the location of Gilead, home of Elijah, in the land of the *Arabs* (ἐκ γῆς Ἀράβων), the Nabataean kingdom.[8] Similarly, the prediction of the end of the Temple by Zechariah may point to a post-A.D. 70 period.

The composition has been expanded by Christian editors, and in its final form is undoubtedly Christian. The section that appears to have been substantially re-worked is the life of Jeremiah. In the most characteristic Christian passage (verses 7–8), he is said to have announced to the Egyptian priests that their man-made deities would collapse when a virgin mother and her child of divine appearance (σὺν

---

1. Cf. C. C. Torrey, *The Lives of the Prophets* (1946), p. 8.

2. Cf. J. Jeremias, *Heiligengräber in Jesu Umwelt* (1958).

3. Traditions regarding the persecution and murder of prophets are attested in the Gospels (Mt. 5:12—Lk. 6:23; Mt. 23:30–31—Lk. 20:48; Mt. 23:37—Lk. 13:34), as well as in the Martyrdom of Isaiah (see above, pp. 335–41) and in rabbinic literature. Cf. H.-J. Schoeps, 'Die jüdischen Prophetenmorde', *Aus frühchristlicher Zeit* (1950), pp. 126–43.

4. E.g. Obadiah is described as a pupil of Elijah, and identified with the officer of Ahab who saved one hundred prophets, a tradition echoed also in Sifre on Num. 27:1 (133) and bSanh. 39b. Jonah, settled in Tyre after his Nineveh adventure, is also associated with Elijah (cf. also PRE 33).

5. Torrey, *op. cit.*, pp. 10–11. Cf. also the Appendix ('Jeremiah and the Reptiles of Egypt') on pp. 49–52.

6. T. Schermann, *Prophetarum vitae fabulosae* (1907), p. x; *Die Vitae Prophetarum*, TU XXXI (1907), pp. 122, 131–3; E. Nestle, *Marginalien und Materialen* II.1 (1893), p. 46.

7. H. A. Hamaker, *Commentatio in libellum de vita et morte prophetarum* (1833); Torrey, *op. cit.*, pp. 1, 7, 16–17.

8. Torrey, *op. cit.*, pp. 11–12.

βρέφει θεοειδεῖ) arrived in their country. Whilst awaiting the fulfilment of this prophecy, the Egyptians would honour a virgin mother and worship a child lying in a manger.[9]

The Lives have survived in five Greek recensions, designated A-E in Schermann's edition. Recension A, preserved in medieval manuscripts and dating to the sixth century A.D., has been transmitted as a work of Epiphanius. Recension B, from the third or fourth century according to Schermann, has circulated under the name of Dorotheus of Tyre or Antioch, a martyr under Diocletian. The sixth century recension C, also attributed to Epiphanius, is shorter and older than B, and derives from D. The latter is conserved in the sixth century Codex Marchalianus (Vat. Graec. 2125). It is the oldest recension (probably from the third century), free of the many interpolations detectable in the other versions. Equally from the sixth century comes Recension E, called after Hesychius of Jerusalem, and attested again in medieval codices. For a full description, see Schermann, *Prophetarum vitae fabulosae* (1907), pp. xiii-xxxi; cf. also Denis, IPGAT, pp. 85–7. Denis (*ibid.*, pp. 87–8) further mentions a sixth recension contained in Christian hagiography (*synaxaria* and *menologia*).

The *Vitae prophetarum* are represented also in various forms in Syriac, mostly dependent on Recension D and normally attributed to Epiphanius.[10] There are, moreover, Armenian, Ethiopic and Arab versions.[11]

No explicit reference is made to the Lives of the Prophets in the ancient lists of apocrypha, except possibly in the Armenian catalogue of Sarcavag, mentioning a book entitled The Deaths of the Prophets (Denis, *op. cit.*, p. 85). Origen's information on the deaths of Isaiah, Zechariah and Ezekiel is contained 'in scripturis non manifestis': *Comm. Ser. 28 in Matth. 23:37–39* (ed. E. Klostermann [GCS 38], p. 50).

Prophetic legends may also be found in rabbinic literature.[12]

---

9. Torrey, *op. cit.*, p. 9, explains this passage as a Christian story borrowed by the Jewish compiler of the Lives probably before A.D. 80 (p. 11). A less fanciful interpretation would see in the Life of Jeremiah a Christian recasting of an earlier Jewish narrative.

10. Cf. Denis, *op. cit.*, p. 88. In an unpublished supplement, prepared for a re-edition of IPGAT by S. P. Brock, the Syriac recensions are grouped under three headings: (1) the text edited by E. Nestle; the Ambrosian Syro-Hexapla manuscript (Milan, C. 313 Inf.) and the lives in the west Syrian chronicles; (2) a later Nestorian recension of (1); (3) abbreviated texts.

11. Denis, IPGAT, pp. 88–9 and notes 21–4. M. A. Knibb, 'The Ethiopic Version of the Lives of the Prophets Ezekiel and Daniel', BSOAS 43 (1980), pp. 197–206.

12. Cf. above, notes 3–4, and especially L. Ginzberg, *Legends of the Jews* IV, pp. 193–340; VI, pp. 316–429.

Editions

Greek
Schermann, Th., *Prophetarum vitae fabulosae, Indices apostolorum discipulorumque Domini* [Bibl. Teuberiana] (1907).
Torrey, C. C., *The Lives of the Prophets. Text and Translation* [JBL Monogr. Ser. 1] (1946).

Syriac
Nestle, E., *Porta linguarum orientalium V. Grammatica syriaca* (^{2}1888), pp. 86–107 of the chrestomathy.
Chabot, J.-B., *Chronique de Michel le Syrien* I (1899), pp. 63–102.
Ebied, R. Y., 'Some Syriac Manuscripts from the Collection of Sir E. A. Wallis Budge', Or. Christ. Analecta 197 (1974), pp. 523–4.
Hall, I. H., 'The Lives of the Prophets', JBL 7 (1887), pp. 28–40.

Translations

English
Torrey, *op. cit.*

German
Riessler, P., *Altjüdisches Schrifttum* (1928), pp. 871–80.

Bibliography

Schermann, Th., *Propheten und Apostellegenden* [TU 31, 3] (1907).
Bernheimer, R., 'Vitae prophetarum', JAOS 55 (1935), pp. 200–3.
Jeremias, J., *Heiligengräber in Jesu Umwelt (Mt. 23, 29; Lk. 11, 47). Eine Untersuchung zur Volksreligion zur Zeit Jesu* (1958).
Jonge, M. de, 'Christelijke elementen in der Vitae Prophetarum', NedThT 16 (1962), pp. 161–78.
Negoita, A., 'La vie des prophètes selon le synaxaire de l'église grecque', *Studia semitica, philologia necnon philosophica Ioanni Bakos dicata* (1965), pp. 173–92.
Denis, IPGAT (1970), pp. 85–90.
Stone, M. E., 'Prophets, Lives of the', Enc. Jud. 13, cols. 1149–50.
Charlesworth, J. H., PMRS (1981), pp. 175–7.

APPENDIX: WORKS OF UNCERTAIN (JEWISH OR CHRISTIAN) ORIGIN

*1. The Odes of Solomon**

The forty-two short lyrical hymns known as the 'Odes of Solomon' are now generally regarded as a product of early Christianity, although date, milieu and original language all remain uncertain. A. Harnack and H. Grimme indeed maintained that the Odes were of Jewish origin and written in Hebrew (between 50 B.C. and A.D. 67), but then reworked by a Christian about A.D. 100. Though the theory of a Jewish provenance has now been abandoned, the possibility of a Hebrew original still remains alive among scholars who see some link with the Qumran community (Ode 5 opens with the words 'I give thanks to thee, Lord, because ...', as do many of the *Hodayoth*) : J. Carmignac in particular has argued that the author was a member of the community who had converted to Christianity.[1] Others, impressed by phraseology and imagery common to the Odes and the Gospel of John (as well as to the Qumran literature), have supposed that both the Odes and John emanate from the same circles; it is just as possible, however, to see the Odist as drawing freely on Johannine motifs.

Parallels with certain of the Nag Hammadi texts (notably the Gospel of Truth) have led some scholars to characterize the Odes as 'Gnostic' (the term 'knowledge' occurs nineteen times), but this is only justifiable if one understands the term 'Gnostic' in such an attenuated sense that its application to the Odes becomes hardly meaningful.

Many of the images in the Odes can be seen as conveying allusions to themes connected with baptism, and much is to be said for the view that the Odes represent celebrations of the continuing experience of the baptismal life, where the baptized Christian at times even identifies his own experience with that of Christ and so speaks in his name.[2]

There is still as great an uncertainty about the original language and the date as there is about the milieu out of which the Odes emerged. While most scholars now prefer Syriac, the possibility that Greek was the original language has by no means been ruled out (the possibility of an underlying Hebrew or Aramaic is much more remote). On the matter of dating, opinions range from the late first century A.D. to the

---

* By Dr S. P. Brock (University of Oxford).

1. J. Carmignac, 'Les affinites qumraniennes de la onzième Ode de Salomon', RQ 3 (1961/2), pp. 71–102. Any such links are denied by K. Rudolf, 'War der Verfasser der Oden Salomos ein "Qumran-Christ"', RQ 4 (1963/4), pp. 523–55.

2. They should not, however, be described as 'hymns of the catechumens', as J. H. Bernard claimed, *The Odes of Solomon* [Texts and Studies VIII.3 (1912)].

second half of the third century. For those who opt for an early date the links between the Odes and the Gospel of John are of particular significance; the fairly sophisticated Christology of the Odes, however, makes such an early dating improbable, and if anti-Marcionite polemic is really present it will be ruled out.[3] A third-century dating rests of the supposition (by no means certain) that Ode 38 is anti-Manichaean.[4] On the whole a late second century date seems to have most to be said in its favour.

Although a Syrian or North Mesopotamian provenance seems most likely, attempts to pin the Odes down to a particular town (Antioch, Edessa) or author (Valentinus, Bardaisan) are unconvincing.

The Odes of Solomon come down most nearly complete in Syriac, in two manuscripts, London, B.L. Add. 14538 of the tenth century (first identified in 1912), containing Odes 17:7b-end, and Manchester, Rylands Syr. 9 of the fifteenth century (first published 1909), containing Odes 3-end.

Five Odes (nos. 1, 5, 6, 22 and 25) are also preserved in Coptic (first published in 1812), where they have been incorporated into the Gnostic work Pistis Sophia (in B.L. Add. 5114) and given a Gnostic interpretation.

Ode 11 is also transmitted in Greek, in Papyrus Bodmer IX, of the third century (featuring between the Apocryphal letter of Paul to the Corinthians and the Letter of Jude).

The specific attribution to Solomon is found in all these witnesses, and Lactantius (*de Divin. Inst.* iv 12) too quotes Ode 19:6–7 as being by 'Salomon in Ode undevicesima'. The two Syriac manuscripts in fact transmit the Odes along with the Psalms of Solomon, giving a continuous numeration (thus Ps. Sol. 1 is numbered 43). The fact that the Pistis Sophia quotes one of the two Odes which are missing from the Syriac manuscripts as 'Ode 19' suggests that the Psalms of Solomon were also transmitted with the Odes in Coptic, but in the reverse sequence, with the eighteen Psalms of Solomon there featuring first.

Editions

(a) *Syriac*

Harris, J. R., and Mingana, A., *The Odes and Psalms of Solomon re-edited* (1916, 1920), two volumes.

Charlesworth, J. H., *The Odes of Solomon* (1973; revised edition 1977). (With bibliography to *c.* 1971.)

3. H. J. W. Drijvers, 'Die Oden Salomos und die Polemik mit den Markioniten im syrischen Christentum', Orientalia Christiana Analecta 205 (1978), pp. 39–55 (reprinted in his *East of Antioch* (1984), ch. VII).

4. H. J. W. Drijvers, 'Odes of Solomon and Psalms of Mani', in *Studies in Gnosticism and Hellenistic Religions presented to G. Quispel* (1981), pp. 117–30 (reprinted in his *East of Antioch* (1984), ch. X).

Lattke, M., *Die Oden Salomos in ihrer Bedeutung für Neues Testament und Gnosis* (Orbis Biblicus et Orientalis 25/1, 1a, 2 (1979–80)). (With concordance in vol. II.)

Charlesworth, J. H., *Papyri and Leather Manuscripts of the Odes of Solomon* (1981). (Photographic edition of the Syriac, Greek and Coptic manuscripts.)

(b) *Greek*

Testuz, M., *Papyrus Bodmer X-XII* (1959), pp. 49–69.

(c) *Coptic*

Schmidt, C. (tr. Macdermot, V.), *Pistis Sophia* (Nag Hammadi Studies IX; 1978), pp. 114–15, 117, 132–3, 151–2, 157–8.

Translations

English

Harris-Mingana, *op. cit.* (with commentary).
Charlesworth, *op. cit.* (with notes).

French

Labourt, J., and Batiffol, P., *Les Odes de Salomon : une oeuvre chrétienne des environs de l'an 100–120* (1911) (with commentary).

German

Lattke, *op. cit.*

Italian

Tondelli, L., *Le Odi di Salomone : Cantici cristiani degli inizi del II secolo* (1914).

Modern Greek

Fanourgakis, V., *Hai Odai Solomontos* (Analekta Vlatadon 29; 1979).

Select Bibliography

Segelberg, E., 'Evangelium Veritatis: a confirmation homily and its relations to the Odes of Solomon', Orientalia Suecana 8 (1959), pp. 3–42.

Daniélou, J., 'Odes de Salomon', DBS 6 (1960), cols. 677–84.

Emerton, J. A., 'Some problems of text and language in the Odes of Solomon', JThSt n.s. 18 (1967), pp. 372–406.

Chadwick, H., 'Some reflections on the character and theology of the Odes of Solomon', in *Kyriakon : Festschrift Johannes Quasten* I (1970), pp. 266–70.

Charlesworth, J. H., 'Qumran, John and the Odes of Solomon', in his *John and Qumran* (1972), pp. 107–36.

Idem, 'The Odes of Solomon and the Gospel of John', CBQ 35 (1973), pp. 298–322.

Drijvers, H. J. W., 'Odes of Solomon', in his *East of Antioch* (1984), ch. VII-X.

Pierce, M., 'Themes in the Odes of Solomon and other early Christian writers and their baptismal character', Ephemerides Liturgicae 98 (1984), pp. 35–59.

See also the references in notes 1 and 2 above.

2. The Greek Apocalypse of Baruch (3 Baruch)

This apocalypse, known conventionally as 3 Baruch to distinguish it from the Syriac apocalypse 2 Baruch (see above, p. 750) and the Book of Baruch (see above, p. 734), narrates briefly the grief of Baruch at Nebuchadnezzar's destruction of Jerusalem and its Temple and then tells at length how an angel comforted him, once he had agreed to end his complaints, by leading him through the five heavens. In the first of these, he sees the punishment of the enemies of God who had built a tower in hostility to him. They appear in the strange form of hybrid animals with faces like cows (Chapter 2). In the second heaven, Baruch witnesses the punishment of those who had instigated the tower building. They are evidently a separate group and also appear as hybrid animals, but with dog-like faces (Chapter 3). In the third heaven, Baruch witnesses a variety of strange sights. He sees a dragon or serpent whose belly is compared or identified with Hades, and a phoenix which shelters the earth from the sun's rays with its wings. The way in which the sun and the moon function is explained to him (Chapters 4–9). While in this heaven, Baruch enquires about the tree which caused Adam to err and is warned at length about the evil propensities of the vine, which causes men to sin (4:8–17). In the next heaven (presumably the fourth, although the Greek text at 10:1 reads 'third'), Baruch finds exotic birds ensconced next to the pool where the souls of the righteous assemble; since, according to the Slavonic (10:5), these birds ceaselessly sing the praises of God, they are probably to be identified with the righteous souls themselves (Chapter 10). In the long climax (Chapters 11–16), Baruch watches angels bringing to the gate of the fifth heaven baskets containing the offerings of men to God. The empty baskets of the wicked are contrasted to the full ones of the virtuous and the partially filled ones of the morally indeterminate. Baruch is then returned to earth to tell his fellow men about his vision and to offer praises to God (Chapter 17).

In contrast to other apocalypses, Baruch does not here reach God's throne but witnesses God's work only through a variety of angels. The visions are presented as consolation for the loss of the Temple. Baruch is made to contemplate God's beneficent and just rule and to realize, implicitly, that Jerusalem was destroyed because of the people's sins, but that consideration of the rest of creation should teach that Jerusalem's destruction is not totally disastrous. The visions show how punishment by God is always appropriate to the sin. Punishment appears to be immediate; only at 1:7 does Baruch refer to a future day of judgement. The categories of sinners in the different heavens may be specific; the builders of the tower may be Greek sophists (Picard) or the Roman conquerors of Jerusalem (Nicklesburg), but this cannot be certain.

The work is a Christian composition in its present form. An obvious Christian passage can be found in the Greek version at 4:15 where, contrary to the general condemnation of the vine, its fruit is said to become the blood of God; but there may be further Christian rewriting in this passage (4:8–17) and throughout Chapters 11–16 (Hughes), as in the paraphrase of Mt. 25:23 at 15:4 in the Greek version (cf. H. F. D. Sparks, *The Apocryphal Old Testament* (1984), pp. 899–900 for further parallels in this section with Mt. 24–25). The structure of the composition should therefore be accepted as Jewish but it is impossible to say how much of the detail has been altered.

It is unlikely that a Jewish apocalypse would have been accepted into Christian circles after the second century A.D., but no specific indication of the date of 3 Baruch can be found except for its general similarity to 2 Baruch and 4 Ezra and to elements in 2 Enoch and the Testament of Abraham. Its relation to these and to the other extant writings about Baruch cannot be determined. There are some parallels with the Syriac apocalypse of Baruch and the Paraleipomena of Jeremiah, but dependence in either direction cannot be demonstrated in any passage apart from the description of Baruch in verse 2 of the Prologue in the Greek text of 3 Baruch. This description, which appears to refer directly to the Paraleipomena, is probably a late interpolation (James); it is not found in the Slavonic text. All the other parallels may be due to use of common traditions by the authors of the various works about Baruch (Sparks). This is particularly likely because the interests of the author of this apocalypse seem to be rather different from those of the writer of 2 Baruch or the Paraleipomena (Gaylord). The work is unlikely to date to much before the first century A.D. since it presupposes the apocalypse genre but, although the opening theme of the destruction of the first Temple would have special relevance after A.D. 70, the same motif may also have been used before that date.

3 Baruch survives in Greek and a Slavonic version of the Greek. Nothing requires a Semitic original but that would be quite possible. Attribution to the Egyptian diaspora on the grounds of the mention of the phoenix and aspects of Egyptian mythology (Picard, Nickelsburg, and others) is hypothetical. Composition in Syria has been suggested (Rost), on no strong grounds. The fact that the work suggests that the destruction of Jerusalem is not as disastrous as might be thought may make an origin in Palestine less likely; alternatively, the theology propounded might seem all the more relevant in that country, especially if the book was composed after A.D. 70.

The relation between the Greek and the Slavonic versions of 3 Baruch is not clear. The differences are not crucial to the meaning of the apocalypse. The Greek text is longer than the Slavonic, but it too appears to have been abridged to some extent, and the Slavonic both contains some possibly genuine material which is absent in the Greek and omits some patent late Christian interpolations which are found in the Greek. Cf. H. Gaylord in Charlesworth, OTP I, pp. 655–7.

The Greek text is based on the fifteenth or sixteenth century manuscript BM MS Add. 10073 and the early fifteenth century manuscript 46 of the Monastery of the Hagia, Andros. Both probably derive from the same original, cf. J. C. Picard, *Apocalypsis Baruchi Graece* (1967), p. 69. The Slavonic text is found in at least twelve manuscripts which can be divided into two main families. The earliest and often the best of these manuscripts is a thirteenth century manuscript from Sinai which has been split into four parts of which three are now in Leningrad, cf. B. M. Zagrebin, in *Iz istorii rukopisnych i staropechatnych sobranii otdela rukopisei i redkich knig GPB* (1979), pp. 61–80. It can be supplemented by two later manuscripts of the same family and by a larger number of manuscripts of the other family, cf. E. Turdeanu, 'L'Apocalypse de Baruch en slave', Revue des études slaves 48 (1969), pp. 23–48; *idem*, *Les apocryphes slaves et roumaines de l'Ancien Testament* (1981), pp. 372–85; H. E. Gaylord in Charlesworth, OTP I, pp. 654–5, 661; *idem*, *The Slavonic Version of 3 Baruch* (forthcoming).

It is possible that Origen, *De principiis* ii 3, 6 (GCS Origen V, pp. 122–3; ed. Crouzel and Simonetti, SC 252, p. 268) refers to 3 Baruch as evidence for the existence of seven worlds or heavens. If so, Origen's text must have been longer than the surviving version, which mentions only five. Alternatively, Origen refers to another work altogether which is now lost since it seems improbable that the present work ever described more than five heavens (Picard).

The Stichometry of Nicephorus and the Synopsis of Ps.-Athanasius mention a work entitled 'Baruch', but this may refer to 2 Baruch.

A Latin version of 3 Baruch may have been extant in the seventh century, but it does not survive, cf. M. R. James, JThSt 16 (1915), p. 413.

Editions

Greek text:
James, M. R., 'The Apocalypse of Baruch', in J. A. Robinson, ed., *Apocrypha Anecdota* II (1889), pp. 83–94.
Picard, J.-C., *Apocalypsis Baruchi Graece* (1967).

Slavonic text:
Novakovič, S., 'Otkrivene Varuhovo', Starine 18 (1886), pp. 203–9.
Tichonravov, N., 'Otkrovenie Varuka', Sbornik otd. russk. jas. i slov. 58 (1894), pp. 48–54.
Sokolov, M. I., 'Apokrificheskoe Otkrovenie Varukha', Drevnosti i trudy Slavyanskoi Komisii Imperatorskogo Moskovskogo arkheologicheskogo obshchestva 4 (1907), pp. 201–58.
Ivanov, I., *Bogomilski knigi i legendi* (1925), pp. 193–200.
Hercigonia, E., ' "Videnye Varuhovo" u Petrisovu Zborniky 12 1468 Godine', Zbornik za filologiyu i lingvistiku n.s. 7 (1964), pp. 63–93.
Gaylord, H. E., *The Slavonic Version of 3 Baruch* (forthcoming).

Translations and Commentaries

English:
Morfill, W. R., in J. A. Robinson, ed., *Apocrypha Anecdota* II (1889), pp. 95–102 (based on Slavonic ms. N).

Hughes, H. M., 'The Greek Apocalypse of Baruch', in Charles, APOT II, pp. 527–41 (an eclectic text).

Gaylord, H. E., '3 Baruch', in Charlesworth, OTP I, pp. 653–79 (parallel translations of Slavonic and Greek).

Sparks, H. F. D., *The Apocryphal Old Testament* (1984), pp. 897–914 (a revised version of Hughes's translation).

German:

Bonwetsch, N., 'Das slavisch erhaltene Baruchbuch', NGGW (1896), pp. 91–101 (based on Slavonic ms. N).

Ryssel, V., in Kautzsch, APAT II, pp. 448–57.

Riessler, P., *Altjüdisches Schrifttum* (1928), pp. 40–54, 1269 ff.

Hage, W., *Die griechische Baruch-Apokalypse* (JSHRZ V.1) (1974), pp. 15–44 (based on Slavonic ms. 5).

Hebrew:

Artom, E. S., in A. Kahana, ed., הספרים החיצונים I (1936), pp. 408–25.

Artom, E. S., הספרים החיצונים (1967).

Concordance

Denis, A.-M., with Y. Janssens, *Concordance de l'Apocalypse grecque de Baruch* (1970).

Bibliography

James, M. R., in J. A. Robinson, ed., *Apocrypha Anecdota* II (1889), pp. li–lxxi.

Ginsberg, L., 'Greek Apocalypse of Baruch', JE II (1902), pp. 549–51.

Lüdtke, W., 'Beiträge zu slavischen Apokryphen: 2. Apokalypse des Baruch', ZAW 31 (1911), pp. 219–22.

James, M. R., 'Notes on Apocrypha vi: Traces of the Greek Apocalypse of Baruch in other writings', JThSt 16 (1915), pp. 410–13.

Turdeanu, E., 'Apocryphes bogomiles et apocryphes pseudo-bogomiles', RHR 69 (1950), pp. 177–81.

Turdeanu, E., 'Les apocryphes slaves et roumains: leur apport à la connaissance des apocryphes grecs', Studi bizantini e neoellenici 8 (1953), pp. 50–2.

Goodenough, E. R., *Jewish Symbols in the Greco-Roman Period* VI (1956), p. 131; VIII (1958), pp. 42, 69 ff.

Turdeanu, E., 'L'Apocalypse de Baruch en slave', Revue des études slaves 48 (1969), pp. 23–48.

Picard, J.-C., 'Observations sur l'Apocalypse grecque de Baruch I: Cadre historique fictif et efficacité symbolique', Semitica 20 (1970), pp. 77–103.

Denis, IPGAT, pp. 79–84.

Guggenheim, J. Y., 'Baruch, Greek Apocalypse of', Enc. Jud. IV (1971), cols. 273–4.

Rost, L., *Einleitung in die alttestamentlichen Apokryphen und Pseudepigraphen* (1971), pp. 86–8.

Jacobson, H., 'A note on the Greek Apocalypse of Baruch', JSJ 7 (1976), pp. 201–3.

Fischer, U., *Eschatologie und Jenseitserwartung im hellenistischen Diasporajudentum* (1978), pp. 71–84.

Nickelsburg, JLBBM, pp. 299–303.

Collins, BAAJ, pp. 232–6.

3. Apocryphon of Ezekiel

The Byzantine author, George Nicephorus, included in his list of the apocrypha of the Old Testament a work attributed to Ezekiel, and the same book is mentioned in the synopsis of Pseudo-Athanasius. It is likely that at least some of the material attributed to Ezekiel in the early Christian writings belonged to this book.

A long fragment of a parable quoted by Epiphanius, *Adv. Haer.* 64, 70, 6–17 (ed. Holl and Dummer, GCS (^{2}1980), pp. 515–17), is explicitly attributed by him to an apocryphon which passed under the name of Ezekiel. This parable concerned the story of the blind man and the lame man who combined to rob the orchard of a king. The tale is a common one and it is possible to find parallels in Persian and Indian sources[5] as well as in the Greek anthology (cf. *Anth. Pal.* ix 11–13). More significantly, the same narrative is found in rabbinic texts (bSanh. 91 a-b; Mekh. Shirata, 2; Lev. R. 4:5) in a somewhat garbled form which may suggest dependence upon the original text of the apocryphon cited by Epiphanius.[6] According to him, the parable was intended to demonstrate the interdependence of the body and the soul when judgement after death was at issue. It is possible that he continues to paraphrase the same text at *Pan. Haer.* 64 (ed. Holl and Dummer, GCS Epiphanius II (^{2}1980), pp. 515, 517).

The other fragments attributed to Ezekiel are much shorter. A passage concerning repentance in the style of biblical prophecy, quoted by Clement of Rome, *Ep. i ad Cor.* 8 3, is also given in part by Clement of Alexandria, *Paedagogus* i 10, 91, 2 = GCS, Clement I, p. 143, lines 20–1, where it is specifically attributed to Ezekiel. Clement of Alexandria, *Quis Dives Salv.* 39, 2 = GCS, Clement III, p. 185, quotes the same passage, but without reference to Ezekiel. A small prophetic fragment about the imposition of judgement on each individual is found in Clement of Alexandria, *Quis Dives Salv.* 40, 2 = GCS, Clement III, p. 186, PG ix, 645, and is assigned to Ezekiel by Evagrius, who reproduces it in the Latin translation of Athanasius, *Vita Antonii* 18 (PG XXVI, 869). The sentence, 'and the heifer shall bear and they shall say, "She has not borne"', is frequently quoted in early Christian texts as a witness to the virgin birth of Jesus, e.g. Clement of Alexandria, *Strom.* vii 16; *Acta Petri* 29; Epiphanius, *Pan. Haer.* 30, 30, 1 (GCS 25 (1915), p. 374). It is quoted by them always as a prophecy, and is assigned by Tertullian, *De Carne Christi* 23 (PL II, 790 C), to Ezekiel. Finally, Chester Beatty Papyrus 185, of the fourth century A.D., contains three fragments of a prophetic text similar to Ezekiel 34. This text is not paralleled in the MT or LXX, but one passage is probably quoted by Clement of Alexandria, *Paedagogus* i 9, 84, 2–4 (= GCS 12 (1936), p. 139) as deriving from Ezekiel.

It is possible but not at all certain that all these passages stem from a

---

5. Cf. Denis, IPGAT, p. 188.

6. M. R. James, 'The Apocryphal Ezekiel', JThSt 15 (1914), pp. 238–9.

single book.[7] The sentence relating to the heifer has probably been excerpted from a narrative, possibly a parable rather than a prophecy, and it may therefore belong with the apocryphon quoted by Epiphanius. The other sections are similar to the prophetic passages of the canonical book of Ezekiel and may have been composed as additions to that book.[8]

The Jewish origin of the *story* of the long parable about the lame man and the blind man is very probable, given the rabbinic parallels. It is less clear whether the text as it now stands in Epiphanius is a Jewish work. There is no reason to suppose that the language of the apocryphon has been preserved verbatim. It is impossible to tell, either, whether it was originally Greek or Semitic or whether apparently Christian elements of the phraseology are due to Epiphanius or to his source.[9] The other fragments could also be either Jewish or Christian, though repentance and judgement would be natural topics for a Jewish apocryphon.[10] There is no indication of the date of any of the passages, except that they must have been written before their first citation, i.e. the fourth century A.D. in the case of the parable,[11] and the second or third century A.D. for the other texts. It has been argued that the reference in Josephus, *Ant.* x 5, 1 (79), to *two* books of the prophet Ezekiel demonstrates the existence of an apocryphon by the mid-first century A.D.,[12] but it is likely that Josephus only refers here to the canonical book.[13] It is also not possible to postulate a *terminus post quem* since the term *'paganus'* used frequently in the parable, and taken by some to indicate a date in the Roman period, may have been introduced by Epiphanius.[14]

7. In favour of this, cf. K. Holl, 'Das Apokryphon Ezekiel', in *idem, Gesammelte Aufsätze zur Kirchengeschichte* II (1928), pp. 33–43; Denis, IPGAT, pp. 187–91.

8. Cf. M. R. James, *art. cit.*, p. 240, for both these arguments. Only the version in Epiphanius has the verb in the future.

9. Cf. Holl, *op. cit.*, p. 39, for possible Christian phrases. Holl asserts that they are due to Epiphanius himself, which is possible but not necessary.

10. Holl, *op. cit.*, p. 39, argues that a Christian would not have written an apocryphon to an Old Testament book, but this assertion begs the question. M. R. James, *The Lost Apocrypha of the Old Testament* (1920), p. 67, suggests that the use of the heifer quotation to prove the virgin birth indicates a Christian origin, but this Christian *use* does not preclude Jewish *composition*, which would also be possible, cf. Denis, IPGAT, p. 189.

11. Note that the rabbinic texts cited above as apparently dependent on Epiphanius' apocryphon may all have been compiled after that date, and that the attribution of the stories to earlier, i.e. second century A.D., rabbis, does not prove the earlier existence of the apocryphon. If Origen, *Comm. ser.* 28 (GCS XXXVIII (1933), p. 50, lines 24–5), refers to this work of Ezekiel, that would push the date back into the third century A.D.

12. Denis, IPGAT, p. 190.

13. Cf. R. Marcus, Loeb ed., *ad loc.*; H. St. J. Thackeray, *The Septuagint and Jewish Worship* (²1923), p. 37, on the practice of dividing biblical works into two parts.

14. For this as a dating criterion, see Denis, IPGAT, p. 190.

Other texts associated with Ezekiel probably have nothing to do with the present fragments. The legends about Ezekiel in Pseudo-Epiphanius, *Vitae Prophetarum*, may have derived from the lost apocryphon since material from the Martyrdom of Isaiah and Paralipomena Jeremiae were used there in this way, but this is uncertain, cf. M. R. James, *The Lost Apocrypha of the Old Testament* (1920), pp. 68–70. There is no reason to connect the anonymous story about a precious stone, given in Georgius Cedrenus (PL CXXI, 225 C–226 B), with the Ezekiel apocryphon, cf. Denis, IPGAT, pp. 188, 302–3, *contra* M. R. James, JThSt 15 (1914), pp. 241–2.

Editions

Holl, K., 'Das Apokryphon Ezechiel', in *Aus Schrift und Gesch. Theol. Abhandlungen A. Schlatter dargebr.* (1922), pp. 85–98 = *idem, Gesammelte Aufsätze zur Kirchengeschichte* II, *Der Osten* (1928), pp. 33–43 (without the Chester Beatty Papyrus 185 text).
Papyrus text in C. Bonner, *The Homily on the passion by Melito, Bishop of Sardis, with some Fragments of the Apocryphal Ezekiel* (1940), pp. 183–5.
Full text in Denis, FPG, pp. 121–8.

Translations

English:
James, M. R., *The Lost Apocrypha of the Old Testament* (1920), pp. 64–8.
Mueller, J. R., and S. E. Robinson in Charlesworth, OTP II (forthcoming).

German:
Riessler, P., *Altjüd. Schrift.* (1928), pp. 334–6, 1288–9.
Eckart, K. G., *Das Apokryphon Ezechiel* (JSHRZ V, 1974), pp. 45–55.

Bibliography

Resch, A., *Agrapha Aussercanonische Schriftfragmente* ... (²1906), pp. 305, 322 ff., 381–4.
James, M. R., 'The Apocryphal Ezekiel', JThSt 15 (1914), pp. 236–43.
James, M. R., *The Lost Apocrypha of the Old Testament* (1920), pp. 64–70.
Kutsch, E., 'Ezechiel, Apokryphon', in RGG II (³1958), col. 844.
Stone, M. E., EJ VI (1971), col. 1099.
Denis, IPGAT, pp. 187–91.
Guillaumont, A., 'Une Citation de l'apocryphe d'Ezéchiel dans l'exégèse au sujet de l'âme (Nag Hammadi II, 6)', *Essays on the Nag Hammadi Texts in Honour of Pahor Labib*, ed. M. Krause (1975), pp. 25–39.
Scopello, M., 'Les *Testimonia* dans le traité de l'exégèse de l'âme (*Nag Hammadi* II, 6)', RHR 191 (1977), pp. 159–71.
Stroker, W. D., 'The Source of an Agraphon in the Manichaean Psalm-Book', JThSt 28 (1977), pp. 114–18.

4. Lost Pseudepigrapha

In addition to the extant prophetic pseudepigrapha (cf. §32.V), many other similar works circulated in the ancient Church, as is known partly from the canon lists, partly from the incidental quotations of the Church Fathers. In most cases, it can no longer be determined with any certainty whether they were of Jewish or Christian origin. Since, however, in the earliest period of Christianity this branch of literary production chiefly flourished amongst the heretical groups and was only later appropriated by the main Church circles, those Old Testament pseudepigrapha which the earliest Church Fathers, up to and including Origen, mention with especial respect, *may* well have been inherited from Judaism. It is possible to combine this criterion with another. Several canon lists exist in which the Old Testament apocrypha are enumerated very fully. Amongst the writings named there, those which are extant (e.g. Enoch, Assumption of Moses, Psalms of Solomon) are unquestionably of Jewish origin. This justifies the conjecture that the remainder are also of the same provenance. The canon lists in question are as follows.

(1) The *Stichometry of Nicephorus*, i.e. a list of the canonical and apocryphal writings of the Old and New Testaments, with an estimate of the number of verses in each book, which is appended to the *Chronographia compendiaria* of Nicephorus of Constantinople (about 800 A.D.) but is certainly considerably older. Printed in an appendix to G. Dindorf's edition of *Georgius Syncellus et Nicephorus Constantinopolitanus* [*Corp. Scrip. Hist. Byz.*] (1829); Migne, PG 100, col. 1060; Th. Zahn, *Geschichte des N.T. Kanons* II, 1 (1890), pp. 297–301; Denis, IPGAT. The list of Old Testament Apocrypha runs as follows:

α' Ἐνώχ στίχων, δω' (4800). β' Πατριάρχαι στίχων, ερ' (5100). γ' Προσευχὴ Ἰωσήφ στίχων, αρ' (1100). δ' Διαθήκη Μωϋσέως στίχων, αρ' (1100). ε' Ἀνάληψις Μωϋσέως στίχων, αυ' (1400). ς' Ἀβραὰμ στίχων τ' (300). ζ' Ἐλὰδ (sic) καί Μωδὰδ στίχων υ' (400). η' Ἠλία προφήτου στίχων τις' (316). θ' Σοφονίου προφήτου στίχων χ' (600). ι' Ζαχαρίου πατρὸς Ἰωάννου στίχων φ' (500). ια' Βαρούχ, Ἀμβακούμ, Ἰεζεκιὴλ καὶ Δανιὴλ ψευδεπίγραφα.

(2) The so-called *Synopsis Pseudo-Athanasii* exclusively reproduces, in the portion concerning the apocrypha, the Stichometry of Nicephorus, but without any estimate of the number of verses. Cf. Migne, PG 28, col. 432B; J. A. Robinson, 'Collation of the Pseudo-Athanasian Synopsis', *Texts and Studies* III, 3 (1895), pp. 105–20.

(3) Related to this is an anonymous medieval canon list, sometimes called the Sixty Books. Cf. Th. Zahn, *Geschichte des N.T. Kanons* II, 1 (1890), pp. 290–2; E. Preuschen, *Analecta*, pp. 158–60; Denis, IPGAT, pp. xi-xv. The complete list of the Old Testament Apocrypha runs as follows: α' Ἀδάμ β' Ἐνώχ γ' Λάμεχ δ' Πατριάρχαι ε' Ἰωσήφ προσευχή ς' Ἐλδὰμ καὶ Μωδάμ (al. Ἐλδὰδ καὶ Μωδάδ) ζ' Διαθήκη Μωσέως η' Ἡ ἀνάληψις Μωσέως θ' Ψαλμοὶ Σαλομῶντος ι' Ἠλίου ἀποκάλυψις ια' Ἡσαίου ὅρασις ιβ' Σοφονίου ἀποκάλυψις ιγ' Ζαχαρίου ἀποκάλυψις ιδ' Ἔσδρα ἀποκάλυψις.

The main body of this list is identical with that of the Stichometry of

Nicephorus.[15] The first ten items are repeated in their entirety, with the single exception of no. 6, Abraham. Moreover, these ten numbers are all probably prophetic pseudepigrapha, i.e. writings claiming either to have been written by the relevant men of God themselves, or to contain revelations alleged to derive from them; and it is presumably to this circumstance that they are indebted for their relatively wide circulation in the Church. The last of these identifies itself by its title Ζαχαρίου πατρὸς 'Ιωάννου as a Christian apocryphon.[16] Six of the others (Enoch, the Testaments of the Patriarchs, the Testament and Assumption of Moses, the Apocalypse of Moses, and Eldad and Modad) have already been discussed (cf. pp. 250–68, 767–81, 278–88, 757–60, 781). The remaining three (Prayer of Joseph, Elijah, and Zephaniah) are all quoted with respect, either by Origen or by still older Church Fathers, and may therefore with some degree of probability be regarded as Jewish products, and deserve to be more fully considered here.

(1) *The Prayer of Joseph*

The Προσευχὴ 'Ιωσήφ consists of 1,100 verses according to Nicephorus. It is well known, particularly through several quotations in Origen, who calls it 'a writing not to be despised' (οὐκ εὐκαταφρόντον γραφήν), and states specifically that it was in use among the Jews (παρ' 'Εβραίοις). In the passages cited, Jacob appears as speaker throughout, describing himself as the firstborn of all the living, that is to say, as the chief captain of the angels. When he comes out of Mesopotamia, Uriel encounters him, wrestles with him and claims that he is the first among the angels. Jacob however rebukes him and tells him, Uriel, that he is eighth in rank after him. In another passage, Jacob says that he has read the destinies of men recorded in heavenly tables.

Origen, *In Ioannem II* xxxi 25 (189–90), ed. E. Preuschen, GCS 10, pp. 88–9 (Denis, FPG, p. 61): εἰ δέ τις προσίεται καὶ τῶν παρ' 'Εβραίοις φερομένων ἀποκρύφων τὴν ἐπιγραφομένην 'Ιωσὴφ προσευχήν, ἄντικρυς τοῦτο τὸ δόγμα καὶ σαφῶς εἰρημένον ἐκεῖθεν λήψεται, ὡς ἄρα οἱ ἀρχῆθεν ἐξαίρετόν τι ἐσχηκότες παρὰ ἀνθρώπους, πολλῷ κρείττους τυγχάνοντες τῶν λοιπῶν ψυχῶν, ἀπὸ τοῦ εἶναι ἄγγελοι ἐπὶ τὴν ἀνθρωπίνην καταβεβήκασι φύσιν. φησὶ γοῦν ὁ 'Ιακώβ·'Ο γὰρ λαλῶν πρὸς ὑμᾶς ἐγὼ 'Ιακὼβ καὶ 'Ισραὴλ ἄγγελος θεοῦ εἰμι ἐγὼ καὶ πνεῦμα ἀρχικόν, καὶ 'Αβραὰμ καὶ 'Ισαὰκ προεκτίσθησαν πρὸ παντὸς ἔργου· ἐγὼ δὲ 'Ιακώβ, ὁ κληθεὶς ὑπὸ ἀνθρώπων 'Ιακώβ, τὸ δὲ ὄνομά μου 'Ισραήλ, ὁ κληθεὶς ὑπὸ θεοῦ 'Ισραήλ, ἀνὴρ ὁρῶν θεόν, ὅτι ἐγὼ πρωτόγονος παντὸς ζῴου ζωουμένου ὑπὸ θεοῦ.' καὶ

15. Concerning a Slavonic version, see A. Berendts, *Studien über Zacharias-Apokryphen und Zacharias-Legenden* (1895), pp. 3 ff.; W. Lüdtke, 'Beiträge zu slavischen Apokryphen', ZAW 31 (1911), pp. 230–5. On a kindred Armenian list, see Th. Zahn, *Forschungen zur Geschichte des N.T. Kanons*, part V (1893), pp. 115–48.

16. There is no positive evidence that πατρὸς 'Ιωάννου is a later addition. See Berendts, *op. cit.*, p. 10.

ἐπιφέρει·Ἐγώ δὲ ὅτε ἠρχόμην ἀπὸ Μεσοποταμίας τῆς Συρίας, ἐξῆλθεν
Οὐριὴλ ὁ ἄγγελος τοῦ θεοῦ, καὶ εἶπεν ὅτι κατέβην ἐπὶ τὴν γῆν κ καὶ
κατεσκήνωσα ἐν ἀνθρώποις, καὶ ὅτι ἐκλήθην ὀνόματι Ἰακώβ· ἐζήλωσε καὶ
ἐμαχέσατό μοι, καὶ ἐπάλαιε πρός με, λέγων προτερήσειν ἐπάνω τοῦ
ὀνόματός μου τὸ ὄνομα αὐτοῦ καὶ τοῦ πρὸ παντὸς ἀγγέλου. καὶ εἶπα αὐτῷ
τὸ ὄνομα αὐτοῦ καὶ πόσος ἐστὶν ἐν υἱοῖς θεοῦ· Οὐχὶ σὺ Οὐριὴλ ὄγδοος ἐμοῦ,
κἀγὼ Ἰσραὴλ ἀρχάγγελος δυνάμεως κυρίου καὶ ἀρχιχιλίαρχός εἰμι ἐν υἱοῖς
θεοῦ; οὐχὶ ἐγὼ Ἰσραὴλ ὁ ἐν προσώπῳ θεοῦ λειτουργὸς πρῶτος, καὶ
ἐπεκαλεσάμην ἐν ὀνόματι ἀσβέστῳ τὸν θεόν μου;' εἰκὸς γὰρ τούτων ἀληθῶς
ὑπὸ τοῦ Ἰακὼβ λεγομένων καὶ διὰ τοῦτο ἀναγεγραμμένων.

Origen, fragment from *In Genesim (1:14)* iii 9 = Eusebius, *Praep. ev.*
vi 11, 64 (ed. K. Mras, p. 356, 23–4; Denis, FPG, p. 62): Διόπερ ἐν τῇ
προσευχῇ τοῦ Ἰωσὴφ δύναται οὕτω νοεῖσθαι τὸ λεγόμενον ὑπὸ τοῦ Ἰακώβ·
'Ἀνέγνων γὰρ ἐν ταῖς πλαξὶ τοῦ οὐρανοῦ, ὅσα συμβήσεται ὑμῖν καὶ τοῖς
υἱοῖς ὑμῶν.' Cf. also *ibid.* iii 12 (*Philocalia* 23, 19, ed. J. Robinson, p. 208;
PG 12, p. 81BC), where the contents of the detailed fragment first
quoted are given more succinctly.

For the history of the tradition concerning the fight between Jacob and
an angel, see J. Z. Smith, *op. cit.* (1978), p. 66. Cf. also G. Vermes, 'The
Archangel Sariel', *Christianity, Judaism and Other Greco-Roman Cults* III
(1975), pp. 159–66.

Bibliography

Denis, IPGAT, pp. 125–7.
Charlesworth, PMRS, pp. 140–2.
Smith, J. Z., 'The Prayer of Joseph', *Religions in Antiquity: Essays in Memory of E. R.
Goodenough*, ed. J. Neusner (1968), pp. 253–94. Reprinted with an afterword in
Smith, *Map is not Territory: Studies in the History of Religions* (1978), pp. 24–66.

(2) *The Apocalypse of Elijah*

The prophet Elijah has this in common with Enoch, that he was
translated into heaven straight from this life. He is therefore frequently
associated with Enoch in sacred legend, and must like Enoch have
seemed especially worthy to receive heavenly revelations. (For the
Enoch literature, see pp. 250–77 above.) A work under his name
(containing 316 verses according to Nicephorus) is mentioned in the
Constit. apostol. vi 16 and in patristic quotations simply as an
apocryphon. According to the more exact titles in the apocrypha lists
(Ἠλία προφήτου in Nicephorus, Ἠλία ἀποκάλυψις in the anonymous list),
also in Ambrosiaster and Jerome, it was an apocalypse (see below).

It is mentioned by Origen as the source of Paul's quotation in 1 Cor.
2:9 (καθὼς γέγραπται: ἃ ὀφθαλμὸς οὐκ εἶδεν καὶ οὖς οὐκ ἤκουσεν καὶ ἐπὶ
καρδίαν ἀνθρώπου οὐκ ἀνέβη κ.τ.λ.). Jerome protested strongly against
the opinion that Paul is here quoting an apocryphon. It is nevertheless
quite credible since the author of the Epistle of Jude, for example,

certainly quotes from the Book of Enoch. Origen at all events knew of an Apocalypse of Elijah containing the passage cited, which he believed to be Jewish. Although, of course, the possibility of a Christian interpolation cannot be excluded (as e.g. 1 Cor. 2:9 in the Ascension of Isaiah was inserted by a Christian hand), the circumstance that 1 Cor. 2:9 is not traceable in the Hebrew Bible makes Origen's interpretation fairly probable. If it is correct, this apocalypse is pre-Pauline. (Ambrosiaster and Euthalius share Origen's reading.)

The same passage as that in 1 Corinthians is cited also by Clement of Rome, 34:8. As Clement employs non-canonical quotations elsewhere, he may similarly have used the Apocalypse of Elijah. It is more likely however that he took the citation from 1 Corinthians. On the other hand, Clement of Alexandria, *Protrept.* x 94, 4 and *Const. apost.* vii 32, 5 quote 1 Cor. 2:9 in a peculiar form which must depend on a common source which may well have been the Apocalypse of Elijah.

According to Epiphanius (*Haer.* xlii 12, 5), Eph. 5:14 (ἔγειρε κατεύδων καὶ ἀνάστα ἐκ τῶν νεκρῶν καὶ ἐπιφαύσει σοι ὁ Χριστός) also appeared in the Elijah apocryphon. The same passage is however attributed to Isaiah in a commentary by Hippolytus on Daniel 4:56 (ed. Bonwetsch and Achelis I, p. 328), and to an apocryphon of Jeremiah by Euthalius (ed. A. Gallandi, *Bibliotheca Vet. Patr. Antiq. Script. Eccl.* X, p. 260). In view of this lack of consensus, it is difficult to form an opinion. As Origen does not mention it, it is very improbable that Eph. 5:14 figured in the Apocalypse of Elijah which was known to him. Where he cites the passage, he does not name Elijah.

Origen, *Comm. in Matt. 27:9* (ed. Klostermann, p. 250): 'et apostolus scripturas quasdam secretorum profert, sicut dicit alicui: "quod oculus non vidit, nec auris audivit" (1 Cor. 2:9); in nullo enim regulari libro hoc positum invenitur, nisi in secretis Eliae prophetae.' Cf. also Origen's *Comm. in Matt. 23:37*, where Origen remarks, in connection with Jesus' statement that Jerusalem killed the prophets, that in the Old Testament only one death of a prophet in Jerusalem is recorded. He continues: 'Propterea videndum, ne forte oporteat ex libris secretioribus, qui apud Iudaeos feruntur, ostendere verbum Christi, et non solum Christi, sed etiam discipulorum eius' (cf. such accounts as Heb. 11:37) ... Fertur ergo in scripturis non manifestis serratum esse Iesaiam, et Zachariam occisum, et Ezechielem. Arbitror autem circuisse in melotis (ἐν μηλωταῖς Hebr. 11:37), in pellibus caprinis Eliam, qui in solitudine et in montibus vagabatur.' 1 Cor. 2:9 figures also among further evidence that in the New Testament reference is sometimes made to apocryphal writings. Origen finally remarks: 'Oportet ergo caute considerare, ut nec omnia secreta, quae feruntur in nomine sanctorum, suscipiamus propter Iudaeos, qui forte ad destructionem veritatis scripturarum nostrarum quaedam finxerunt, confirmantes dogmata falsa, nec omnia abiiciamus, quae pertinent ad demonstrationem scripturarum nostrarum.' The entire context makes it clear that Origen had merely Jewish apocrypha in mind. In another passage, probably belonging to an earlier date (J. A. Cramer, *Catenae in S. Pauli epistolas ad Corinthios* (1841), p. 42), Origen professes himself uncertain whether Paul in 1 Cor. 2:9 makes a free reference to Isa. 52:15 or to some lost writing. He seems therefore not to have discovered the passage in the Apocalypse of Elijah until later (Th. Zahn, *Geschichte des neutestamentlichen Kanons* II, 2, pp. 802–3).

The so-called Ambrosiaster (*Comment. in epist. Pauli*, printed among the works of Ambrosius) remarks on 1 Cor. 2:9 (PL XVII, col. 205): 'hoc est scriptum in Apocalypsi Heliae in apocryphis'.

Euthalius, in his learned statistical work on the Pauline Epistles, likewise traces 1 Cor. 2:9 to the apocryphal Elijah (A. Gallandi, *Biblioth. patrum* X, p. 258). He is followed by Syncellus, ed. Dindorf I, p. 48. On Euthalius, see J. A. Robinson, 'Euthaliana', TS III, 3 (1895); E. von Dobschütz, 'Euthaliusstudien', ZKG 19 (1899), 107–54; F. C. Conybeare, 'The Date of Euthalius', ZNW 5 (1904), pp. 39–52; A. Jülicher, RE, s.v. 'Euthalios' (2)'.

Jerome, *Epistola 57 ad Pammachium* 9: 'Pergamus ad apostolum Paulum. Scribit ad Corinthios: Si enim cognovissent Dominum gloriae ... (1 Cor. 2:8–9) ... Solent in hoc loco apocryphorum quidam deliramenta sectari et dicere, quod de apocalypsi Eliae sumptum sit ...' (Jerome then traces the quotation to Isa. 64:3). *Comm. in Iesaiam 64:3* (al. 64:4): 'paraphrasim huius testimonii quasi Hebraeus ex Hebraeis assumit apostolus Paulus de authenticis libris in epistola quam scribit ad Corinthios (1 Cor. 2:9), non verbum ex verbo reddens, quod facere omnino contemnit, sed sensuum exprimens veritatem, quibus utitur ad id quod voluerit roborandum. Unde apocryphorum deliramenta conticeant, quae ex occasione huius testimonii ingeruntur ecclesiis Christi ... Ascensio enim Isaiae et apocalypsis Eliae hoc habent testimonium.'

Clement of Rome, 34:8 (ed. Funk, Bihlmeyer and Schneemelcher, p. 154): λέγει γάρ· Ὀφθαλμὸς οὐκ εἶδεν καὶ οὖς οὐκ ἤκουσεν καὶ ἐπὶ καρδίαν ἀνθρώπου οὐκ ἀνέβη ὅσα ἡτοίμασεν τοῖς ὑπομένουσιν αὐτόν (Paul: τοῖς ἀγαπῶσιν αὐτόν). Clement of Alexandria, *Protr.* x 94, 4: ὅθεν ἡ γραφὴ εἰκότως εὐαγγελίζεται τοῖς πεπιστευκόσιν· οἱ δὲ ἅγιοι κυρίου κληρονομήσουσι τὴν δόξαν τοῦ θεοῦ καὶ τὴν δύναμιν αὐτοῦ· ποίαν, ὦ μακάριε, δόξαν; εἰπέ μοι· ἣν ὀφθαλμὸς οὐκ εἶδεν οὐδὲ οὖς ἤκουσεν, οὐδὲ ἐπὶ καρδίαν ἀνέβη· καὶ χαρήσονται ἐπὶ τῇ βασιλείᾳ τοῦ κυρίου αὐτῶν εἰς τοὺς αἰῶνας, ἀμήν.' On this passage see Denis, IPGAT, pp. 163–4 and n. 4.

Epiphanius, *Haer.* xlii 12, 3 (ed. K. Holl, pp. 179,25–180,3): Διὸ λέγει, ἔγειρε ὁ καθεύδων καὶ ἀνάστα ἐκ τῶν νεκρῶν, καὶ ἐπιφαύσει σοι ὁ

Χριστός' (Eph. 5:14). Πόθεν τῷ ἀποστόλῳ τὸ 'διὸ καὶ λέγει', ἀλλὰ ἀπὸ τῆς παλαιᾶς δῆλον διαθήκης; τούτου δὲ ἐμφέρεται παρὰ τῷ 'Ηλίᾳ. Hippolytus, *De Antichristo* 15 (ed. H. Achelis II, p. 12), cites this same passage, Eph. 5:14, with the formula ὁ προφήτης λέγει, and in a somewhat different form (ἐξεγέρθητι instead of ἀνάστα). In his commentary on Daniel 4:56 (ed. G. N. Bonwetsch and H. Achelis I, p. 328) the introductory formula reads καὶ 'Ησαΐας λέγει. Here also ἐξεγέρθητι stands in place of ἀνάστα. In both passages from Hippolytus, the quotation appears among canonical material. Ησαιας would therefore appear to be a corruption of Ηλιας. According to Euthalius, Eph. 5:14 figured in an apocryphon of Jeremiah (Gallandi, *Biblioth. patr.* X, p. 260); cf. also Syncellus (ed. Dindorf I, p. 48). It is a mistake to suppose that Origen also was acquainted with a non-canonical source for Eph. 5:14. He admittedly quotes the words as a prophetic dictum, but nothing suggests that he took them from anywhere except Eph. 5:14 (*Selecta in Psalm.*, on Ps. 3:6, PG XII, 1128A: ὁ προφήτης φησίν· ὕπνωσαν ὕπνον αὐτῶν καὶ οὐχ εὗρον οὐδέν— = Ps. 76:6—καὶ τὸ· ἔγειρε ὁ καθεύδων...).

A Greek fragment appended to a biblical manuscript from the thirteenth century (Codex Paris gr. 4, fol. 228) attributes to the prophet Elijah a description of Antichrist:

' Εμφέρεται ἐν ἀποκρύφοις ὅτι 'Ηλίας ὁ προφήτης εἶπε περὶ τοῦ 'Αντιχρίστου· οἷος μέλλῃ τότε φαίνεσθαι· ἡ κεφαλὴ αὐτοῦ φλὸξ πυρός· ὁ ὀφθαλμὸς αὐτοῦ ὁ δεξιός κέκραται αἵματος. 'Ο δὲ εὐώνυμος χαροπὸς ἔχων δύο κόρας, τὰ δὲ βλεφ[αρα] αὐτοῦ λευκά, τὰ δὲ χεῖλος αὐτοῦ τὸ κάτω μέγα· ὁ δεξιὸς αὐτοῦ μηρὸς λεπτός, καὶ οἱ πόδες αὐτοῦ πλατεῖς, τέθλασται δὲ ὁ μέγας δάκτυλος τοῦ ποδὸς αὐτοῦ.

The text was published by F. Nau, 'Révélations et légendes. II. Saint Clément de Rome. Le Portrait de l'Antéchrist (Paris, ms. grec n° 4, fol. 228 r°)', JA 9 (1917), p. 458.

There are Coptic fragments, both Akhmimic and Sahidic, of an Apocalypse of Elijah closely related to the Apocalypse of Zephaniah (cf. no. 3 below). The text has been edited by G. Steindorff, *Die Apokalypse des Elias. Eine unbekannte Apokalypse und Bruchstücke der Sophonias-Apokalypse* (1899). For an English translation see H. P. Houghton, 'The Coptic Apocalypse ... The Apocalypse of Elias', Aegyptus 39 (1959), pp. 179–210. For a German translation, see P. Riessler, *Altjüdisches Schrifttum*, pp. 114–25, 1272. Cf. also P. Lacau, 'Remarques sur le manuscrit akhmimique des Apocalypses de Sophonie et d'Élie', JA 254 (1966), pp. 169–95; A. Pietersma, 'Greek and Coptic Inedita of the Chester Beatty Library', BIOSCS 7 (1974), pp. 17–18. The Chester Beatty papyrus has subsequently been published by A. Pietersma, S. T. Lomstock and H. W. Attridge, *The Apocalypse of Elijah based on Pap. Chester Beatty 2018* (1981).

A Latin fragment, a poor translation from Greek, figures in an

Epistula Titi discipuli Pauli. It is introduced as a vision of the prophet Elijah ('testatur propheta Helias vidisse') and depicts the torments of the damned in hell. Cf. D. de Bruyne, 'Nouveaux fragments des Actes de Pierre, de Paul, de Jean, d'André, et de l'Apocalypse d'Élie', Rev. Bénédictine 25 (1908), pp. 149–60; 'Epistula Titi discipuli Pauli', *ibid.* 37 (1925), pp. 47–72; M. R. James, *The Lost Apocrypha of the Old Testament* (1920), p. 55.

The Coptic Christian Apocalypse of Elijah is dated to the second half of the third century A.D. (cf. J. M. Rosenstiehl, *L'apocalypse d'Élie* (1972), p. 75; O. S. Wintermute, OTP I, pp. 729–30). Whatever Jewish ingredients it may contain are likely to go back to the previous century at least.

The work of the Hellenist Eupolemus, περὶ τῆς Ἡλίου προφητείας (Eusebius, *Praep. ev.* ix 30, 1) has nothing to do with our apocryphon. See p. 517 above. On Elijah legends amongst the Gnostics, see Epiphanius, *Haer.* xxvi 13.

Among rabbinic writings is an Apocalypse of Elijah published by A. Jellinek, *Bet ha-Midrasch* III (1855), pp. xvii–xviii, 65–8, and M. Buttenweiser, *Die hebräische Eliasapokalypse und ihre Stellung in der apokalyptischen Litteratur des rabbinischen Schrifttums und der Kirche* (1897). The work is probably post-Talmudic despite Buttenweiser's claim that it belongs to the second half of the third century A.D. On Talmudic allusions to sayings of Elijah (bSanh. 97b; bYom. 19b), see I. Lévi, 'Apocalypses dans le Talmud', REJ 1 (1880), pp. 108–10.

Bibliography

Zahn, Th., *Geschichte des neutestamentlichen Kanons* II, 2 (1892), pp. 801–10.
Denis, IPGAT, pp. 163–9.
Charlesworth, PMRS, pp. 95–8.
Rosenstiehl, J.-M., *L'Apocalypse d'Élie* (1972).
Stone, M. E., and J. Strugnell, *The Books of Elijah*, Parts 1–2 (1979).
Wintermute, O. S., 'Apocalypse of Elijah', OTP I, pp. 722–53.

(3) *The Apocalypse of Zephaniah*

Apart from the Stichometry of Nicephorus, which credits it with 600 verses, and the anonymous Apocrypha list, this work is known only through a citation in Clement of Alexandria, but possibly an Apocalypse of Zephaniah preserved in Coptic may be connected with that cited by Clement.

Clement of Alexandria, *Strom.* v 11, 77, 2 (ed. O. Stählin and L. Früchtel, p. 377): Ἀπ' οὐχ ὅμοια ταῦτα τοῖς ὑπὸ Σοφονία λεχθεῖσι τοῦ προφήτου; 'καὶ ἀνέλαβέν με πνεῦμα καὶ ἀνήνεγκέν με εἰς οὐρανὸν πέμπτον καὶ ἐθεώρουν ἀγγέλους καλουμένους κυρίους, καὶ τὸ διάδημα αὐτῶν ἐπικείμενον ἐν πνεύματι ἁγίῳ καὶ ἦν ἑκάστου αὐτῶν ὁ θρόνος ἑπταπλασίων φωτὸς ἡλίου ἀνατέλλοντος, οἰκοῦντας ἐν ναοῖς σωτηρίας καὶ ὑμνοῦντας θεὸν ἄρρητον ὕψιστον.'

A Coptic Apocalypse of Zephaniah preserved partly in Akhmimic, partly in Sahidic fragments, dating to the fourth and fifth centuries, has been edited by G. Steindorff, *Die Apokalypse des Elias ... Bruchstücke der Sophonias-Apokalypse* (1899). Cf. also H. P. Houghton, 'The Coptic Apocalypse', Aegyptus 39 (1959), pp. 42–67, 76–83, 87–91 for an English translation.

The text restored by Steindorff falls into two long sections, between which there is no very close connection. In the first, designated an anonymous Apocalypse (pp. 1–18 of the Akhmim recension) the prophet is instructed by various angels concerning the abode in the future world of the righteous and the ungodly, and concerning the fate of both. In the second section, Steindorff's Apocalypse of Elijah, the prophet is first commissioned to preach repentance, with a reference to God having sent his son. Wars between Assyrian and Persian kings are then prophesied to take place in Egypt, and finally the appearance and defeat of Antichrist are described. Steindorff saw in this portion a Christian revision of the old Apocalypse of Elijah known to Origen. This is however unlikely because this Coptic Apocalypse is widely interspersed with New Testament reminiscences. The work as it stands is therefore Christian. If a Jewish proto-document is to be assumed, it must be reduced to a very modest dimension. If it existed at all, it was the work of a Hellenized Jew produced between the redaction of the Greek Susanna (referred to in 6:10) and the quotation of the work by Clement of Alexandria, say between 100 B.C. and A.D. 175. Cf. O. S. Wintermute, 'Apocalypse of Zephaniah', OTP I, pp. 500–1.

Bibliography

Denis, IPGAT, pp. 192–3.
Charlesworth, PMRS, pp. 220–3.
Wintermute, O. S., 'Apocalypse of Zephaniah', OTP I, pp. 497–515 (with an English translation).
Lacau, P., 'Remarques sur le manuscrit akhmimique des apocalypses de Sophonie et d'Élie', JA 254 (1966), pp. 169–95.

With the apocalypses described here, the number is by no means exhausted of those in circulation in the ancient Church. At the close of the Stichometry of Nicephorus ψευδεπίγραφα of Baruch, Habakkuk, Ezekiel and Daniel are mentioned. Euthalius knew, as has been noted, an apocryphon of Jeremiah. Jerome refers to a Hebrew apocryphon of Jeremiah containing Matthew 27:9.[17]

---

17. Jerome, *ad Matth. 27:9:* 'Legi nuper in quodam Hebraico volumine, quod Nazaraenae sectae mihi Hebraeus obtulit, Ieremiae apocryphum, in quo haec ad verbum scripta reperi.'

The Jewish origin of these and similar writings is questionable, especially in view of their late attestation in the Church. Even the four pseudepigrapha mentioned at the end of the Stichometry of Nicephorus are manifestly a later addition to the original list.

The apocryphal *Jacob's Ladder*, preserved in various Slavonic recensions and edited with a German translation by N. Bonwetsch, 'Die apokryphe Leiter Jakobs', NGGW, philol.-hist. Kl. (1900), pp. 76–87, deserves also a brief mention here. It gives various revelations associated with Gen. 28:10 ff. A work dealing with those verses circulated among the Ebionites according to Epiphanius, *Haer.* xxx 16, 7: ἀναβαθμοὺς δέ τινας καὶ ὑπηγήσεις δῆθεν ἐν τοῖς ἀναβαθμοῖς Ἰακώβου ὑποτίθεναι, ὡς ἐξηγουμένου κατά τε τοῦ ναοῦ καὶ τῶν θυσιῶν, κατά τε τοῦ πυρὸς τοῦ ἐν τῷ θυσιαστηρίῳ καὶ ἄλλα πολλὰ κενοφωνίας ἔμπλεα. Nevertheless, the identity of the 'Ladder of Jacob' and the 'Ascents of Jacob' of Epiphanius is uncertain according to M. R. James, *The Lost Apocrypha of the Old Testament* (1920), pp. 102–3, and H. Weinel, 'Die spätere christliche Apokalyptik', *Gunkel Festschrift* (1923), pp. 172–3. The Slavonic texts include no such polemic against the Temple cultus. On the other hand, they show points of contact with Enoch, 4 Ezra and the Apocalypse of Abraham. Thus Jewish material of one kind or another may underlie this document; but marked divergences among the Slavonic recensions testify to a considerable editorial freedom. The texts are presumably late. Cf. H. G. Lunt, OTP II (forthcoming).

Of an equally late date and highly problematic Jewish provenance are the Greek *Apocalypse of Esdras* (cf. Denis, IPGAT, pp. 91–6; Charlesworth, PMRS, pp. 116–17; M. E. Stone, OTP I, pp. 561–79); the *Testament of Isaac* (Denis, IPGAT, p. 34; Charlesworth, PMRS, pp. 123–5; W. F. Stinespring, OTP I, pp. 903–11); the *Fifth Book of the Maccabees* (Charlesworth, PMRS, pp. 153–8); the *Apocalypse of Sedrach* (Denis, IPGAT, pp. 97–9; Charlesworth, PMRS, pp. 178–82; S. Agourides, OTP I, pp. 605–13); and the *History of the Rechabites* in the Apocalypse of Zosimus (Charlesworth, PMRS, pp. 223–8; *idem*, *The History of the Rechabites. Volume I: The Greek Recension* (1982)).

5. Small Fragments of Anonymous Jewish Literature in Christian Texts

Many anonymous quotations in the writings of the early Church are presented as deriving from earlier authoritative books, or even Scripture, though it is impossible to find the words cited in any of the scriptural texts now extant. Some may have been excerpted from earlier Jewish books other than those so far described, but it is very difficult to be certain in identifying such fragments. Since all these texts are, by definition, congenial to the Christian authors who use them, their contents may also often have been composed by earlier Christian authors; the line between Jewish authorship and that of some of the very early Christians is furthermore often impossible to establish by content alone, and there is much evidence of an extensive Christian apocryphal literature. Other quotations which some scholars are tempted to assign to new pseudepigrapha turn out on closer inspection to consist in nothing more than the citation of variant readings in biblical and other extant texts or composite quotations from a number of such texts. This practice seems to have been particularly common in the early Church because of the use of testimonia and florilegia of biblical texts both by Jews and by early Christians, in which scriptural citations might be subtly modified for polemical purposes.[18] Other apparent pseudepigraphical citations may be simple allusions or inexplicit quotations of already known texts, or they may form new parts of other identified works. The following citations almost certainly derive from lost Jewish books.[19]

(1) Clement of Rome, *Ep. i ad Gr.* (ed. A. Jaubert, SC 167, 1971) 23, 3–4, attributes to Scripture a passage relating to those who hesitate but eventually convert. The passage is given with an extra verse in Clement, *Ep.* ii 11, 2–4, where it is introduced as a prophetic saying. None of the suggested attributions to known pseudepigrapha is convincing, cf. Denis, IPGAT, pp. 286–7.

(2) Clement of Rome *Ep.* i 17, 6 (= Clement of Alexandria, *Strom.* iv 17/106, 4) states: 'I am the vapour that comes from the pot.' It is sometimes assigned to the Assumption of Moses, but for no good reason (see above, p. 278).

(3) Clement of Alexandria, *Protrept.* x 98, 1 (GCS XII (1936), p. 71; ed. Mondésert and Plassart, SC 2, 3rd ed., p. 166), mentions a certain prophecy: 'Therefore matters here below will go badly so long as one puts confidence in statues.' Cf. Denis, IPGAT, p. 294.

(4) Hippolytus, *de Antichristo* 15 and 54 (GCS I.2 (1897), pp. 12, 36) cites a prophecy that the Antichrist will have a victorious army over all

---

18. See J. R. Harris, *Testimonia* I-II (1916–20); B. P. W. Stather Hunt, *Primitive Gospel Sources* (1951); modifications in R. A. Kraft, 'Barnabas' Isaiah Text and the "Testimony Book" Hypothesis', JBL 79 (1960), pp. 336–50; P. Prigent, *Les Testimonia dans le Christianisme primitif, L'Epître de Barnabé I-XVI et ses sources* (1961), pp. 16–28. Christian testimony books were apparently anti-Jewish. The function of earlier Jewish collections may have varied, cf. the fragments from Qumran Cave 4. Cf. N. Walter, JSHRZ IV.3 (1983), pp. 248–50.

19. In ascribing such quotations to lost works, each quotation must be taken individually. For the identification of many such lost works, see A. Resch, *Agrapha, Aussercanonische Schriftfragmente* (1906); M. R. James, *The Lost Apocrypha of the Old Testament* (1920). For a more sceptical treatment see Denis, IPGAT, pp. 284–303, where good arguments are given against ascribing to Jewish literature many fragments tentatively so assigned by Resch, James, and others. These fragments are accordingly ignored in the following survey, following Denis.

the land and sea. Cf. M. R. James, *The Lost Apocrypha* (1920), p. 92, and above, p. 802; but see also Denis, IPGAT, p. 298, n. 33, for the possibility that Hippolytus had a Christian text on this subject and was using it here.

(5) *Const. Apost.* iv 1, 2 (ed. Funk, p. 219, lines 14–15), cites a quotation that: 'He whom the holy ones have not eaten, the Assyrians will eat.' No known origin can be posited.

(6) *Const. Apost.*, books vii-viii (ed. Funk, pp. 386–594), may contain remnants of Jewish prayers in only slightly altered form. The biblical quotations used in them are from the LXX, which suggests composition in Greek. Cf. K. Kohler, 'Ueber die Ursprünge und Grundformen der synagogalen Liturgie: Eine Studie', MGWJ IV.F. 1 (1893), pp. 441–51, 489–97; W. Bousset, 'Eine jüdische Gebetssammlung im siebenten Buch der apostolischen Konstitutionen', NGGW *Philologische-historische Klasse 1915* (1916), pp. 438–85; K. Kohler, 'The Essene Version of the Seven Benedictions as Preserved in the VII Book of the Apostolic Constitutions', HUCA 1 (1924), pp. 410–25; E. R. Goodenough, *By Light, Light!* (1935), pp. 306–508; J. H. Charlesworth, *The Pseudepigrapha and Modern Research with a Supplement* (1981), Supplement, pp. 288–9. English translations by W. Whiston in the *Ante-Nicene Fathers* VII (1868, reprinted 1970), pp. 385–508; E. R. Goodenough, *By Light, Light!*, pp. 306 ff.; D. A. Fiensy and D. R. Darnell in Charlesworth, OTP II (forthcoming).

(7) Sozomen, *Hist. Eccl.* ix 17, 4–5 (GCS L (1960), p. 408, 3–9), describes a non-canonical Jewish book which narrated the burial in royal vestments of the son of Joash, King of Judah, explaining the boy's death as divine chastisement of the king for the assassination of the prophet Zachariah. Cf. Denis, IPGAT, pp. 302–3.

(8) Georgius Hamartolus, *Chronicon* (ed. C. de Boor, IV, 11, pp. 216–18 = PG CX, 268 C–269 B), and Georgius Cedrenus (ed. I. Bekker, pp. 193–4 = PG CXXI, 225 C–226 B), preserve a story about alms-giving which concerns a wealthy woman deprived of her riches who spends her last money on a stone which turns out to belong to the vestments of Aaron and is bought for a high price by the high priest. Cf. M. R. James, 'The Apocryphal Ezekiel', JThSt 15 (1914), pp. 241–2; above, p. 796.

(9) Mention should also be made here of fragments of probably Jewish works found in papyri of the fourth century A.D. and later. (a) P. Oxy. 2069 (end of fourth century A.D.) contains five fragments of an apocalyptic heavenly vision of, among other things, the Red Sea, cf. A. S. Hunt, *The Oxyrhynchus Papyri* XVII (1927), pp. 6–8. (b) P. Lond. 113 (13 a) and 113 (12 b), of the sixth or seventh centuries A.D., contains a midrash on the arrival in Egypt of Jacob and his sons (Gen. 41:39–42:38). Published by H. J. M. Milne, *Catalogue of the Literary*

Papyri in the British Museum (1927), pp. 187–90, nos. 226 and 227, as the 'History of Joseph', it may also be represented by further papyri, i.e. Louvre Gr. Pap. 7738 a; Bodleian Gr. th. f. 15 [P] and Gr. th. e. 9 [P], and further papyrus fragments which are announced by G. Zervos in J. H. Charlesworth, *The Pseudepigrapha and Modern Research with Supplement* (1981), suppl. p. 293. An English translation of all the papyri possibly connected with this work will be presented by Zervos in Charlesworth, OTP II (forthcoming).

It can be said of all these fragmentary texts that they may be Jewish since nothing about them makes a Christian or other origin necessary. None can be dated more accurately than to before the time that they are first quoted. Except for the prayers preserved in *Const. Ap.*, insufficient survives of each of these works for the original language of the text to be known.

No full study of such citations has yet been made. Information and texts must therefore be culled from the editions and indices of the Christian authors concerned and from the general discussions noted in the bibliography.

Bibliography

Krauss, S., 'The Jews in the Works of the Church Fathers', JQR 5 (1893), pp. 122–57.
Resch, A., *Agrapha, Aussercanonische Schriftfragmente* (1906).
James, M. R., *The Lost Apocrypha of the Old Testament, their Titles and Fragments* (1920).
Denis, IPGAT, pp. 284–303.

§ 34. THE JEWISH PHILOSOPHER PHILO

BY JENNY MORRIS

Bibliography[1]

Dähne, A. F., *Geschichtliche Darstellung der jüdisch-alexandrinischen Religions-Philosophie* (1834).

Gfrörer, A., *Philo und die jüdisch-alexandrinische Theosophie* ([2]1835).

Siegfried, C., *Philo von Alexandria als Ausleger des Alten Testaments an sich selbst und nach seinem geschichtlichen Einfluss betrachtet. Nebst Untersuchungen über die Gräcität Philos* (1875).

Ritter, B., *Philo und die Halacha : eine vergleichende Studie* (1879).

Drummond, J., *Philo Judaeus or the Jewish-Alexandrian Philosophy in its Development and Completion* (1888; repr. 1969).

Massebieau, L., *Le Classement des oeuvres de Philon* (*Bibliothèque de l'École des Hautes Études, Sciences Religieuses* I, 1889), pp. 1–91.

Wendland, P., *Philo und die kynisch-stoische Diatribe* (1895).

Cohn, L., Prolegomena to *Philonis Opera* I (1896), pp. i-lxxxix (on mss.).

Cohn, L., 'Kritisch-exegetische Beiträge zu Philo', Hermes 32 (1897), pp. 107–48.

Cohn, L., 'Einteilung und Chronologie der Schriften Philos', Philologus, Suppl. Bd. 7 (1899), pp. 389–436.

Friedländer, M., *Geschichte der jüdischen Apologetik* (1903), pp. 192–328.

Massebieau, L. and Bréhier, E., 'Essai sur la Chronologie de la vie et des oeuvres de Philon', RHR 53 (1906), pp. 25–64, 164–85, 267–89. (Also published separately.)

Bousset, W., *Die Religion des Judentums im neutest. Zeitalter* ([2]1906), pp. 503–24; ([3]1926, repr. 1966, ed. H. Gressmann), pp. 438–55.

Bréhier, E., *Les idées philosophiques et religieuses de Philon d'Alexandrie* (1907; [2]1925, repr. 1950).

Wendland, P., *Die hellenistisch-römische Kultur in ihren Beziehungen zu Judentum und Christentum* (*Handbuch zum N.T.* I.2) (1907), pp. 114–17; ([2/3]1912; [4]1972), pp. 205–11.

Bentwich, N., *Philo of Alexandria* (1910). (Introductory discussion.)

Bousset, W., *Jüdisch-christlicher Schulbetrieb in Alexandria und Rom* (1915), pp. 8–154.

Billings, Th. H., *The Platonism of Philo Judaeus* (1919).

Christ, W. von, Schmid, W., and Stählin, O., *Geschichte der griechischen Literatur* II.1 ([6]1920), pp. 625–56.

Zeller, E., *Die Philosophie der Griechen* III.2 ([5]1923, repr. 1963), pp. 385–467.

Adler, M., *Studien zu Philon von Alexandreia* (1929).

Goodenough, E. R., *The Jurisprudence of the Jewish Courts in Egypt. Legal Administration by the Jews under the Early Roman Empire as described by Philo Judaeus* (1929).

Lewy, H., *Sobria Ebrietas : Untersuchungen zur Geschichte der antiken Mystik* (1929).

Pascher, J., Ἡ βασιλικὴ ὁδός. *Der Königsweg zu Wiedergeburt und Vergottung bei Philon von Alexandreia* (1931).

Broughton, J. S., *The Idea of Progress in Philo Judaeus* (1932).

---

1. To supplement this general bibliography of Philo's works and thought, consult the bibliographies listed below, p. 812. Assessments of major studies are generally included. The older literature can be found in H. L. Goodhart and E. R. Goodenough, *Bibliography* (below, p. 812), and in Schürer, GJV III ([3]1909), pp. 633–4, 696–8. Further literature on individual works and topics in the discussions below.

Heinemann, I., *Philons griechische und jüdische Bildung. Kulturvergleichende Untersuchungen zu Philons Darstellung der jüdischen Gesetze* (1932, repr. 1962).[2]

Goodenough, E. R., *By Light, Light! The mystic Gospel of Hellenistic Judaism* (1935, repr. 1969).[3]

Goodenough, E. R., 'Literal Mystery in Hellenistic Judaism', *Quantulacumque: Studies Presented to K. Lake* (1937), pp. 227–41.

Idem, *The Politics of Philo Judaeus. Practice and Theory* (1938, repr. 1967).

Völker, W., *Fortschritt und Vollendung bei Philo von Alexandrien. Eine Studie zur Geschichte der Frömmigkeit* (1938).[4]

Meyer, A., *Vorsehungsglaube und Schicksalsidee in ihrem Verhältnis bei Philo von Alexandria* (1939).

Belkin, S., *Philo and the Oral Law. The Philonic Interpretation of Biblical Law in Relation to the Palestinian Halakah* (1940).[5]

Leisegang, H., 'Philon', RE XX.1 (1941), cols. 1–50.

Pohlenz, M., 'Philon von Alexandreia', NAWG, N.F. 135 (1942), pp. 409–87 = *Kleine Schriften* I (1965), pp. 305–83.

Wolfson, H. A., *Philo: Foundations of Religious Philosophy in Judaism, Christianity and Islam* (1947).[6]

Katz, P., *Philo's Bible: The Aberrant Text of Biblical Quotations in Some Philonic Writings and its Place in the Textual History of the Greek Bible* (1950).

Bréhier, E., 'Philo Judaeus', in *Études de philosophie antique* (1955), pp. 207–14.

Sandmel, S., *Philo's Place in Judaism: A Study of Conceptions of Abraham in Jewish Literature* (1956; [2]1971).

Daniélou, J., *Philon d'Alexandrie* (1958). (Introductory discussion.)

Arnaldez, R., 'Introduction Générale', in *Les Oeuvres de Philon d'Alexandrie* I (1961), pp. 17–112.

Colpe, C., 'Philo', RGG V ([3]1961), cols. 341–6.

Smallwood, E. M., Introduction to *Philonis Alexandrini, Legatio ad Gaium* (1961), pp. 3–43.

Goodenough, E. R., *An Introduction to Philo Judaeus* ([2]1962).

Jaubert, A., *La Notion d'Alliance dans le Judaïsme aux abords de l'ère chrétienne* (1963), pp. 375–442, 477–98.

Boyancé, O., 'Études Philoniennes', REG 76 (1963), pp. 64–110.

Theiler, W., 'Philo von Alexandria und der Beginn des kaiserzeitlichen Platonismus', in *Parusia, Festgabe für J. Hirschbergert*, ed. K. Flasch (1965), pp. 199–218 = *Untersuchungen zur antiken Literatur* (1970), pp. 484–501.

Borgen, P., *Bread from Heaven. An Exegetical Study of the Concept of Manna in the Gospel of John and the Writings of Philo* (1965).

Mondésert, C., Cadiou, R., Ménard, J. E., and Arnaldez, R., 'Philon d'Alexandrie ou Philon le Juif', DB Supp. VII (1966), cols. 1288–348.

Chadwick, H., 'Philo', in A. H. Armstrong, ed., *The Cambridge History of Later Greek and Early Medieval Philosophy* (1967), pp. 133–57.

2. See review by A. Posner, REJ 93 (1932), pp. 89–102; and I. Heinemann, MGWJ 76 (1932), pp. 267–9. For further reviews of important Philo studies see ANRW II.21.1 (1984), pp. 93–6.

3. On Goodenough's approach see S. Sandmel, *Philo of Alexandria* (1979), pp. 140–7. Goodenough summarizes his own position and reviews the other major studies of Philo of the 1930s and 1940s in *An Introduction to Philo Judaeus* ([2]1962), pp. 11–29.

4. See Goodenough, *op. cit.*, pp. 14–16.

5. See review by E. R. Goodenough, JBL 59 (1940), pp. 420–3.

6. For criticisms and assessments of Wolfson's methodology see E. R. Goodenough, 'Wolfson's Philo', JBL 67 (1948), pp. 87–109; A. Mendelson, 'A Reappraisal of Wolfson's Method', SP 3 (1974–5), pp. 11–26.

Arnaldez, R., ed., *Philon d'Alexandrie*, Colloques nationaux du CNRS VII (1967).
Früchtel, U., *Die kosmologischen Vorstellungen bei Philo von Alexandrien* (1968).
Christiansen, I., *Die Technik der allegorischen Auslegungswissenschaft bei Philo von Alexandrien* (1969).
Delling, G., 'Wunder–Allegorie–Mythus bei Philon von Alexandreia', in *Studien zum Neuen Testament und zum hellenistischen Judentum. Gesammelte Aufsätze* (1970), pp. 72–129.
Maddalena, A., *Filone Alessandrino* (1970).
Williamson, R., *Philo and the Epistle to the Hebrews* (1970).
Baer, R., *Philo's Use of the Categories Male and Female* (1970).
Amir, Y., 'Philo Judaeus', EJ XIII (1971), cols. 409–15.
Nock, A. D., 'Philo and Hellenistic Philosophy', in *Essays on Religion and the Ancient World*, ed. Z. Stewart, I-II (1972), pp. 559–65.
Dillon, J., *The Middle Platonists. A Study of Platonism 80 B.C. to A.D. 220* (1977), pp. 139–83.
Nikiprowetzky, V., *Le Commentaire de l'Écriture chez Philon d'Alexandrie* (1977).
Sandmel, S., *Philo of Alexandria. An Introduction* (1979).
Mendelson, A., *Secular Education in Philo of Alexandria* (1982).
Amir, Y., *Die hellenistische Gestalt des Judentums bei Philon von Alexandrien* (1983).
Cazeaux, J., *La trame et la chaîne, ou les structures littéraires et l'Exégèse dans cinq des traités de Philon d'Alexandrie* (1983).
Haase, W., ed., ANRW II.21.1 : *Religion (Hellenistisches Judentum in Römischer Zeit : Philon)* (1984).
Terian, A., *From Biblical Exposition to Apologetics : Literary Tendencies in Philo of Alexandria* (1984).

Editions and Translations[7]

Mangey, T., Φίλωνος τοῦ Ἰουδαίου τὰ εὑρισκόμενα ἅπαντα. *Philonis Judaei opera quae reperiri potuerunt omnia. Textum cum Mss contulit, quamplurima etiam e Codd. Vaticano, Mediceo et Bodleiano, scriptoribus item vetustis, necnon catenis graecis ineditis, adjecit, interpretationemque emendavit, universa notis et observationibus illustravit* (1742). (Standard edition until Cohn-Wendland-Reiter.)
Richter, C. E., *Philonis Iudaei opera omnia* (1828–30). (Includes Latin for Armenian.)
Cohn, L., Wendland, P., and Reiter, S., *Philonis opera quae supersunt* I-VI (1896–1930, repr. 1962), Editio maior. (Standard edition.) (Abbreviated C-W henceforth.)
Cohn, L., and Wendland, P., *Philonis opera quae supersunt* I-VI (1896–1915), Editio minor.
Cohn, L., *et al.*, *Die Werke Philos von Alexandria in deutscher Übersetzung* I-VII (1909–64).
Colson, F. H. (and Whitaker, G. H. for I-V), *Philo* I-X (1929–62) [Loeb Classical Library]. (Uses text of Cohn-Wendland-Reiter with minor changes and variant readings.)
Marcus, R., *Philo Supplements* I and II (1953). (Translation, with notes, of Armenian version of *Quaestiones*.) (Loeb Classical Library.)
Arnaldez, R., *et al.*, *Les oeuvres de Philon d'Alexandrie publiées sous le patronage de l'Université de Lyon* I-XXXV (1961- ; XXXVI forthcoming).

Indexes and Concordance

Leisegang, H., *Indices ad Philonis Alexandrini Opera* (vol. VII of C-W, 1926–30).

7. Full details of the older editions and of many translations are given in H. L. Goodhart and E. R. Goodenough, *Bibliography*, pp. 187–210. Details of editions, translations and bibliography of individual works will be found in the notes to discussion of works below.

Marcus, R., 'An Armenian-Greek Index to Philo's *Quaestiones* and *De Vita Contemplativa*', JAOS 53 (1933), pp. 257–82.
Earp, J. W., *Indices to Philo* (in Colson, vol. X, 1962).
Borgen, P., and Skarsten, R., *Complete KWIC-Concordance of Philo's Writings* (magnetic tape) (1973). (Includes all Greek works and identified Greek fragments and provides context.)
Mayer, G., *Index Philoneus* (1974). (Based on Cohn-Wendland, ed. minor, and omitting most fragments.)

Bibliographies and Research Surveys

Cohn, L., 'The Latest Researches on Philo of Alexandria (1830–1892)', JQR 5 (1893), pp. 24–50.
Marcus, R., 'Recent Literature on Philo', in Baron, S. W., and Marx, A., eds., *Jewish Studies in Memory of George A. Kohut* (1935), pp. 463–91.
Goodhart, H. A., and Goodenough, E. R., *A General Bibliography of Philo Judaeus* (1937, repr. 1967). (Lists mss., editions, translations and literature by topic with references to reviews.)
W. Völker, *Fortschritt und Vollendung* (1938), pp. 1–47. (Kritischer Überblick über die bisherige Philo-Forschung, die Aufgabe, methodische Bemerkungen.)
Thyen, H., 'Die Probleme der neueren Philo-Forschung', Theologische Rundschau 23 (1955), pp. 230–46.
Pouilloux, J., 'Philon d'Alexandrie: recherches et points de vue nouveaux', RHR 161 (1962), pp. 135–7.
Feldman, L., *Studies in Judaica: Scholarship on Philo and Josephus (1937–62)* (1963), pp. 3–26. (Arranged by topic, and includes assessment and reference to reviews.)
Hamerton-Kelly, R. G., 'Sources and Traditions in Philo Judaeus: Prolegomena to an Analysis of his Writings', SP 1 (1972), pp. 3–26.
Nazzaro, A. V., *Recenti Studi Filoniani (1963–70)* (1973).
Delling, G., and Maser, R. M., *Bibliographie zur jüdisch-hellenistischen und intertestamentarischen Literatur 1900–1970* (TU CVII, 1975).
Radice, R., *Filone di Alessandria: bibliografia generale 1937–1982* (1983).
Hilgert, E., 'Bibliographia Philoniana 1935–81', ANRW II.21.1 (1984), pp. 47–97. (See also Hilgert's bibliographies and abstracts in SP 1–6 (1972–80).)
Borgen, P., 'Philo of Alexandria. A critical and synthetical survey of research since World War II', ANRW II.21.1, pp. 98–154. (See other articles in ANRW II.21.1 for specialized bibliography and summaries of research on particular topics.)

Abbreviations

(Following *Les Oeuvres de Philon*, except *Anim.*)

Abr.	*De Abrahamo*
Aet.	*De aeternitate mundi*
Agric.	*De agricultura*
Anim.	*De animalibus (Alexander)*
Cher.	*De Cherubim*
Confus.	*De confusione linguarum*
Congr.	*De congressu eruditionis gratia*
Contempl.	*De vita contemplativa*
Decal.	*De Decalogo*
Deter.	*Quod deterius potiori insidiari soleat*

Deus.	*Quod deus sit immutabilis*
Ebr.	*De ebrietate*
Flacc.	*In Flaccum*
Fug.	*De fuga et inventione*
Gig.	*De gigantibus*
Her.	*Quid rerum divinarum heres sit*
Hypoth.	*Hypothetica (Apologia pro Iudaeis)*
Ios.	*De Iosepho*
Legat.	*Legatio ad Gaium*
Leg. i, ii, iii	*Legum allegoriae* i, ii, iii
Migr.	*De migratione Abrahami*
Mos. i, ii	*De vita Mosis* i, ii
Mutat.	*De mutatione nominum*
Opif.	*De opificio mundi*
Plant.	*De plantatione*
Poster.	*De posteritate Caini*
Praem.	*De praemiis et poenis, de exsecrationibus*
Prob.	*Quod omnis probus liber sit*
Prov.	*De Providentia*
Quaest. Gen.	*Quaestiones et solutiones in Genesim*
Quaest. Ex.	*Quaestiones et solutiones in Exodum*
Sacrif.	*De sacrificiis Abelis et Caini*
Sobr.	*De sobrietate*
Somn. i, ii	*De somniis*
Spec. i, ii, iii, iv	*De specialibus legibus* i, ii, iii, iv
Virt.	*De virtutibus*

For discussion of the titles of individual works see the notes to pp. 826–70 below.

I. Life and Works

None of the Greek-Jewish writers occupies so prominent a position as Philo of Alexandria. The volume of his extant works alone makes him the most significant; none of the others can be nearly so clearly pictured as Philo as regards their thought, or their literary and philosophical endeavours. But he is also, in his own right, the most obviously outstanding of those who sought to marry Jewish faith with Hellenic culture, to retail Greek culture to the Jews and Jewish religious knowledge to the Greeks.[8] Philo was probably more deeply steeped in Greek wisdom than any other known Jewish author writing in Greek;

8. Whilst there are those who regard Philo's synthesis as a conscious process of self-definition, others would now regard the sharp differentiation between Judaism and Hellenism as a construct of modern historians rather than as part of Philo's own outlook. For the former approach see A. Mendelson, *Secular Education in Philo of Alexandria* (1982), pp. xvii–xxv; for the latter, T. Rajak, *Josephus* (1983), pp. 8–9. For a detailed survey of

certainly he made more impact on history than any of the others. The immense influence he exercised on later times testifies to this, particularly his influence on Christian theology, some aspects of which may be traced back to elements of Hellenistic-Jewish thought.[9] His importance in relation to Jewish traditions is harder to assess, due to neglect by the rabbis on the one hand, and to the sparsity of evidence for contemporary Alexandrian Jewish traditions on the other.[10] Philo's status as a philosopher is even more controversial: some regard him as a philosophic compiler or preacher, whilst others see him not only as an original and systematic philosopher but as the initiator of a philosophic tradition.[11]

Little can be firmly stated about Philo's life. The *testimonia* are meagre.[12] Jerome's statement that he was of priestly descent finds no

the way in which scholarship on Philo has been preoccupied with the attempt to separate his Judaism from his Hellenism, see V. Nikiprowetzky, *Le Commentaire de l'Écriture* (1977), pp. 12–49; G. Pfeifer, 'Zur Beurteilung Philons in der neuerer Literatur', ZAW 77 (1965), pp. 212–14. On the question of Philo's audience see below, pp. 817, 840, 853–4, 855, 878, 889.

9. Eusebius calls Philo πλεῖστος ἀνὴρ οὐ μόνον τῶν ἡμετέρων ἀλλὰ καὶ τῶν ἀπὸ τῆς ἔξωθεν ὁρμωμένων παιδείας ἐπισημότατος (*H.E.* ii 4, 3). For Philo's influence on Christian writers see below, p. 889. The quest for the origins of Christianity was responsible for many of the early studies of Philo, and has continued to stimulate interest in him although there are now other perspectives. For the interests of nineteenth-century Philonists see A. Momigliano, JThSt n.s. 21 (1970), pp. 149–53. Goodenough's approach derived from an interest in gentile Christianity and its origins rather than in the Hellenized Alexandrian Jews whose influence on Christianity exercised the German Philonists. See n. 3 above.

10. For Philo's relationship to contemporary and later Palestinian Jewish thought see below, pp. 871–89. The character and traditions of the Alexandrian Jewish community before the time of Philo can barely be reconstructed from the literature of possible or probable Alexandrian provenance which has survived. W. Bousset's attempt to trace a pre-Philonic Alexandrian tradition is founded on insufficient evidence: *Jüdisch-christlicher Schulbetrieb* (1915); see B. Mack, ANRW II.21.1, pp. 241–5. See further pp. 470–704 above. The evidence for Philo's own time derives almost exclusively from his works. Recent interest in the context of Philo's works in the Alexandrian synagogue has thrown some light on exegetical practices, but we still know too little to determine Philo's relationship to his contemporaries in this community. See p. 877 below

11. See pp. 871–80 below. The most systematic assertion of Philo's philosophical importance and influence is found in the work of H. A. Wolfson; see n. 6 above.

12. C-W, vol. I, pp. lxxxxv-cxiii. Josephus' brief description of Philo is the only reference that is a near contemporary. Josephus introduces Philo as the leader of the embassy to Gaius, *Ant.* xviii 8, 1 (259), where he is described as ἀνὴρ τὰ πάντα ἔνδοξος Ἀλεξάνδρου τε τοῦ ἀλαβάρχου ἀδελφὸς ὢν καὶ φιλοσοφίας οὐκ ἄπειρος. He gives no other explicit information about Philo's writings. The other testimonia are from lexicographers (the Suda and Photius) or Christian authors (Clement of Alexandria, Origen, Ps.-Justin, Anatolius, Ps.-Chrysostom, Eusebius, Jerome, Basil, Ambrose, Epiphanius, Augustine, Theodoret, the Armenian translator of Philo's works, Sozomenus, Isidore of Pelusium, Anastasius the Sinaite, the author of the *Sacra Parallela* attributed to John of Damascus (see n. 17 below), Arethas, and Theodorus Metochita).

Their testimony to Philo's works is more useful than their sparse ·and dubious references to his life; see n. 17 below.

substantiation in the earlier sources:[13] even Eusebius knows nothing of it. According to Josephus he was a brother of Alexander the Alabarch; so he belonged to one of the leading families of Alexandrian Jewry.[14] The

13. *De vir. ill.* 11: 'Philon Iudaeus, natione Alexandrinus, de genere sacerdotum.' On Jerome's account see A. Ceresa-Gastaldo, 'The Biographical Method of Jerome's *De viris illustribus*', *Studia Patristica* XV.1, ed. E. A. Livingstone (TU XXVIII, 1984), pp. 54–68). Cf. Photius, Cod. 105: ἔστι δὲ τὸ γένος ἐξ ἱερέων καταγόμεος. For Schwartz's suggestions regarding Philo's descent see next note.

14. For attempts to reconstruct Philo's life and family see E. Zeller, *Die Philosophie der Griechen* III.2 (⁵1923), p. 385, n. 2 (using the evidence then available); J. Schwartz, 'L'Égypte de Philon', in *Philon D'Alexandrie*, ed. R. Arnaldez, pp. 35–44; *idem*, 'Note sur la famille de Philon d'Alexandrie', AIPhHOS 13 (1953) = *Mélanges Isidore Lévy* (1955), pp. 591–602. Schwartz builds upon the evidence for Philo's family by attempting to place the details known in a historical context, and presents the following conclusions. (1) Philo's grandfather was probably rewarded with Roman citizenship by Julius Caesar, as Antipater had been, and his settling in Egypt coincided with Augustus' conquest. (2) Philo's father was probably ἐπίτροπος of Claudius' mother's estates before Philo's brother Alexander. (3) Philo's family may have been of Hasmonean descent, since Philo's nephew Marcus Iulius Alexander married Berenice, daughter of Agrippa I, and Herodian women normally married royalty or those of royal descent. These points have all been challenged; see S. S. Foster, 'A Note on the "Note" of J. Schwartz', SP 4 (1976/7), pp. 25–32.

The evidence for members of Philo's family is extensive compared with that for Philo himself. Josephus (*loc. cit.*) associates Philo with his brother Alexander. This brother (whom Goodhart regards as younger than Philo: see E. R. Goodenough, *Introduction* (²1962), p. 8) lent Agrippa money, Jos. *Ant.* xviii 6, 3 (159–60), and managed Antonia's estates, Jos. *Ant.* xix 5, 1 (276), cf. xx 5, 2 (100). He also decorated the Temple gates with silver and gold, Jos. *B.J.* v 5, 3 (205), and might be the Alexander who, according to tradition, had all the names of God in his copy of the Pentateuch overlaid with gold (H. Graetz, 'Alexander and his gold-lettered Scroll', JQR 2 (1890), pp. 102–4, on the tradition in *Massechet Soferim* 1:2, cf. 2:7; and *Massechet Sefer Torah* 1:10). It is just possible that Alexander the Alabarch was also the estate owner Gaius Iulius Alexander, mentioned in papyri of A.D. 26 (CPJ II, no. 420a) and 28/9 (420b).

Alexander's sons, Philo's nephews, are also documented. Marcus married Berenice, Jos. *Ant.* xix 5, 1 (276–7); see CPJ II, no. 419; A. Fuks, 'Marcus Iulius Alexander (Relating to the History of Philo's Family)', Zion 13–14 (1948–9), pp. 10–17 (Hebr.). For evidence relating to his commercial activities in the Thebaid, see E. G. Turner, 'Tiberius Iulius Alexander', JRS 44 (1954), p. 59.

Tiberius Iulius Alexander's career is well known and documented from Josephus, Tacitus, inscriptions and papyri (notably the edict of A.D. 68) and possibly an allusion in Juvenal; for an account of this evidence and Tiberius' career in its historical context see E. G. Turner, *op. cit.*, pp. 54–64; also V. Burr, *Tiberius Iulius Alexander* (1955); PIR² I 139. Tiberius Iulius is the Alexander with whom Philo discusses providence and the rationality of animals in the dialogues *Prov.* and *Anim.* (see below, pp. 864–6) and possibly the dedicatee of the spurious *De mundo* (see pp. 868–9 below); see A. Terian, 'Introduction to Philo's Dialogues', ANRW II.21.1 (1984), pp. 272–94, esp. pp. 290–1; note also M. Hadas-Lebel, *De Providentia, Oeuvres* XXXV (1973), pp. 40–5. *Anim.* 54 might suggest that Tiberius was one of the ambassadors to Gaius in A.D. 39/40; see A. Terian, *Philonis Alexandrini De Animalibus* (1981), *ad loc.* Turner (P.Oxy. XXV, p. 104) links the embassy mentioned there with that of *Anim.* 54, dating it to A.D. 13, and regarding the Alexander in question as the Alabarch; cf. J. Schwartz, 'L'Égypte de Philon', in *Philon d'Alexandrie*, ed. R. Arnaldez (1967), p. 40; M. Hadas-Lebel, *op. cit.*, pp. 40–1.

only date in his life which can be chronologically fixed is that of his participation in the embassy to Caligula in A.D. 39–40 which his own *Legatio ad Gaium* describes. Since he was then already of advanced years, he may have been born between about 20 and 10 B.C.[15] Otherwise there are few unequivocal biographical hints in his works.[16] The Christian legend that he met Peter in Rome during the time of Claudius is historically worthless.[17]

Despite the uncertainties surrounding Philo's career and the precise historical context of each of his works, the environment in which he lived can be described in the light of the historical evidence, chiefly

Another member of the family is introduced in *Anim.*, a Lysimachus whom Terian identifies as the son of a daughter of Alexander the Alabarch, betrothed to Tiberius' daughter; he might be the Iulius Lysimachus whose representatives are with Tuscus the Prefect at a tribunal in A.D. 63 according to a Fouad papyrus. See Terian, *op. cit.*, pp. 281–3. See further, for the documentary evidence, CPJ II, nos. 418–20.

15. For the date of the embassy see E. M. Smallwood, *Philonis Alexandrini, Legatio ad Gaium* (1961), pp. 47–50; *idem*, *The Jews under Roman Rule* (1976), pp. 242–6. For the view that the embassy departed in the winter of 38/9 see P. J. Sijpesteijn, 'The Legationes ad Gaium', JJS 15 (1964), pp. 87–96; cf. vol. I, pp. 393–8. For the *Legatio* see below, pp. 859–64. Philo gives little preamble to the mission, simply changing to the use of 'we' at 29 (174). Josephus tells us that Philo was the leader of the deputation, *Ant.* xviii, 1 (259). Strangely, Philo tells us nothing about the other ambassadors, except that there were five, *Legat.* 46 (370); Josephus thought there were three members of each deputation, *Ant.* xviii 8, 1 (257). Philo's brother, Alexander, and his nephew, Tiberius Iulius Alexander, might well have been amongst the five. (For Alexander see E. G. Turner, *art. cit.*, p. 58; he was imprisoned by Gaius in Rome: Jos. *Ant.* xix 5, 1 (276). For Tiberius, see n. 14 above, and p. 866 below.)

Philo mentions his age twice in *Legat.*: at the beginning he implies that he was γέρων when he wrote the work, 1 (1); later he implies that he was the oldest member of the deputation, 28 (182). (If Alexander the Alabarch *was* one of the party, this would reinforce Goodhart's view that Philo was older than his brother; see above, n. 14.)

For considerations of the influence of Philo's family background on his attitudes see V. A. Tcherikover, CPJ I, p. 67; and n. 22 below. For views on the relative chronology of Philo's works, see below, n. 116.

On Philo's date of birth see A. Nazzaro, 'Il problema cronologico della nascita di Filone Alessandrino', *Rendiconti della Accademia di archeologia, lettere e belle arti*, Napoli n.s. 38 (1938), pp. 129–38 (places Philo's date of birth between 15 and 10 B.C.).

16. Note however his pilgrimage to Jerusalem, *Prov.*, Fr. 2, 64.

17. Eusebius, *H.E.* ii 17, 1; 18, 8; Jerome, *De vir. ill.* 11; Photius, *Cod.* 105; the Suda, s.v. Φίλων (following the Greek translation of Jerome). See J. E. Bruns, 'Philo Christianus: The Debris of a Legend', HThR 66 (1973), pp. 141–5. Bruns adds an account of Philo's baptism from the *Acta Johannis* of Ps.-Prochorus (ed. Th. Zahn, 1880, pp. 110–12) to the Christian *testimonia* assembled in C-W; he traces a Philo legend according to which he was baptised by John, made a second visit to Rome under Claudius, met Peter, and wrote the book of Wisdom. Eusebius seems to imply a written document, for which Bruns suggests Hegesippus as author. For portraits of Philo as a Christian saint from the Greek Codex of John Damascenus see E. R. Goodenough, *The Politics of Philo Judaeus* (1938, repr. 1967), p. v. For Philo in Christian thought see below, p. 889.

papyrological.[18] The strife between Greeks and Jews in Philo's Alexandria (which Philo describes in *Flacc.* and the *Legat.*) is also illuminated by the evidence of the papyri.[19] The only incontestably apologetic work of Philo's—the *Hypothetica*—should be seen in the context of the anti-semitism known from Josephus' *Against Apion*.[20] The question of Philo's audience for the sections of his *oeuvre* generally regarded as exoteric must now be set in a framework which takes account of the realities of Philo's situation vis-à-vis pagan contemporaries and the feasibility of proselytism, as well as the characteristics of the works in question.[21]

In the light of Philo's position as a well-born provincial with Roman citizenship, as well as a Jew, his works have been scrutinized for indications of his attitudes towards Rome. Philo expresses lavish praise of Augustus, and opposition to the Principate is only obliquely expressed, if indeed it is discernible at all.[22] The character of his works suggests rather that his concerns were focused largely on the important

---

18. See pp. 50, 127–9 above.

19. See e.g. E. M. Smallwood, *The Jews Under Roman Rule* (1976), pp. 235–50.

20. See pp. 866–8 below. For reflections on papyrus of Alexandrian anti-semitism see esp. CPJ II, nos. 154–9 (the 'Acts of the Alexandrian Martyrs'); H. A. Musurillo, *The Acts of the Pagan Martyrs* (1954). See vol. I, pp. 39–40.

21. There is no direct evidence as to whom Philo was addressing, or which contemporaries read (or heard) his works; see below, pp. 888–9. Assumptions on this question derive from judgements regarding the character of the works. Even the *Hypothetica*, which Eusebius describes as addressed πρὸς κατήγορους αὐτῶν lacks (in the extant sections) the explicit confrontation with the Jews' critics which characterizes *Contra Apionem*. V. Tcherikover has questioned the feasibility in principle of proselytizing literature, see 'Jewish Apologetic Literature Reconsidered', Eos 48 (1956), pp. 169–93.

22. Praise of Augustus: *Legat.* 21 (143)–22 (151). See G. Delling, 'Philons Enkomion auf Augustus', Klio 54 (1972), pp. 175–87. For the upper-class provincial point of view towards Augustus and its historiographical manifestations see E. Gabba, 'The Historians and Augustus', in F. Millar and E. Segal (eds.), *Caesar Augustus* (1984), pp. 61–88, esp. pp. 63–4. Since none of Philo's works are political tracts it is difficult to extrapolate political opinions. Even in passages where issues such as the relation of the individual to a regime are at issue, Philo's views on the Roman principate are hard to pinpoint. Goodenough maintained that Philo set out to criticize Roman rule, but covertly, and mainly in treatises destined for an esoteric audience; see *The Politics of Philo Judaeus* (1938, repr. 1967); idem, *An Introduction* ([2]1962), pp. 52–74. See *contra* A. H. M. Jones's review of Goodenough, *Politics*, JThSt 40 (1939), p. 183, pointing out the complexity of the relationship of an Alexandrian Jew to the imperial government; note also A. Momigliano, review of *An Introduction*, JRS 34 (1944), pp. 163–5, on Goodenough's interpretation of *Somn.* ii 12–13 (81–92) and *Dec.* 1–2 (4–9).

Philo's puzzling concept of democracy, which represents his ideal constitution, is hardly to be equated with Roman republicanism; see E. Langstadt, 'Zu Philos Begriff der Demokratie', in *Gaster Anniversary Volume* (1936), pp. 349–64; Wolfson, *Philo* II, pp. 382–3; A. Momigliano, *op. cit.*; J. Dillon, *The Middle Platonists* (1977), p. 154. On Philo's politics see in general R. Barraclough, 'Philo's Politics: Roman Rule and Hellenistic Judaism', in ANRW II.21.1, pp. 417–553.

Alexandrian Jewish community of which he was a member. Apart from his participation in the embassy to Rome, late in life (and possibly an earlier period of reluctant political involvement[23]), his interests lay chiefly within the context of the Alexandrian Jewish *politeuma* and synagogue. The style of his works (particularly of the sequence known as the *Exposition*) might indicate a concern with education and preaching. The *Quaestiones* are thought by some to reflect Alexandrian synagogue lections.[24] Further afield, Philo clearly knew the community of Therapeutae, and had made a pilgrimage to Jerusalem,[25] though the extent of his familiarity with Jewish thought and practice in contemporary Palestine (if indeed they differed markedly from those of Alexandria) remains open to dispute. Attempts to link his accounts of Jewish legal principle to the practice of local Jewish tribunals, on the

23. The view that Philo was politically active at some point before his leadership of the embassy to Gaius is held by those who (a) regard the passage at the beginning of *Spec.* iii (see below, p. 843) as autobiographical rather than literary, and (b) assume that Philo could not have written all that follows this passage after A.D. 40, since he was already an old man. See further pp. 844, 849–50 below. For the chronology and order of Philo's works see below, pp. 841–4. Philo's participation in local politics is claimed by Goodenough to have been extensive and life-long; see 'Philo and Public Life', JEA 12 (1926), pp. 77–9. He suggests that Philo was involved in some capacity with the Jewish courts; see further p. 848 and esp. pp. 874–5, n. 13 below. There is little except the wider activities of his family to suggest that Philo's public duties might have taken him beyond the Jewish *politeuma* into responsibilities in the Alexandrian *polis*.

24. Those treatises in which minimal knowledge of Jewish history and scripture is presupposed, and in which the style is relatively simple, might have been composed for educational or paraenetic purposes within the community, possibly to counter apostasy. On the homiletic character of the treatises see P. Borgen, *Bread from Heaven* (1965), pp. 28–58; V. Nikiprowetzky, *Le Commentaire de l'Écriture chez Philon d'Alexandrie* (1977), pp. 174–80; F. Siegert, *Drei hellenistische-jüdische Predigten* (1980), pp. 6–8. For a synagogue context for the *Quaestiones* see below, p. 830; for such a context for Philo's allegorical writings as a whole, R. Barraclough, ANRW II.21.1, pp. 447–8. Whilst Philo gives vent only to a generalized denunciation of paganism, his criticism of Jewish exegetes, allegorists, literalists and apostates evokes the Jewish environment in which his interests were focused. Philo does not name those whose approach he criticizes, but his testimony is indicative of a diversity of exegetical traditions in his own community. See M. J. Shroyer, 'Alexandrian Jewish Literalists', JBL 55 (1936), pp. 261–84; S. Belkin, *Philo and the Oral Law* (1940), pp. 11–18; H. A. Wolfson, *Philo* I (1947), pp. 55–86; S. Sandmel, 'Philo's Environment and Philo's Exegesis', JBR 22 (1954), pp. 248–53; B. L. Mack, 'Exegetical Traditions in Alexandrian Judaism', SP 3 (1974–5), pp. 71–112; D. M. Hay, 'Philo's References to other Allegorists', SP 6 (1979–80), pp. 41–75; P. Borgen, ANRW II.21.2, pp. 126–8. For a summary of studies on Philo's testimony to Alexandrian exegesis and the importance of the issue see B. Mack, 'Philo Judaeus and Exegetical Traditions in Alexandria', ANRW II.21.1, pp. 227–71. For allegorical interpretation see pp. 876–7 below.

25. Philo's knowledge of the Therapeutae: Colson, Loeb vol. IX, p. 106, n.a. See further p. 857 below. Pilgrimage to Jerusalem: *Prov.* Fr. 2, 64 (possibly a repeated occurrence; see Colson, vol. IX *ad loc.*).

other hand, have not been generally accepted.[26] As in the case of his references to pagan institutions, and indeed in some of his biographical remarks, it is difficult to determine the force of literary convention; literary tradition, whether scriptural or pagan, might account for references to certain aspects of life, and these should not be taken as firm evidence either for Philo's own experience, or for characteristics of the Judaism of his environment.[27] The works of Philo are illuminated by other historical evidence, then, but at least in the case of the treatises relating to scriptural material, they provide little historical evidence in their own right.[28]

Of Philo's numerous works many have been lost.[29] Yet thanks to his popularity with the Church Fathers and with Christian theologians, it would seem that the greater part, at least, has been preserved.[30] The standard edition of his works is that of Cohn, Wendland and Reiter (see above, p. 811, Editions), though this does not include many Greek

26. For a survey of the scholarship on the relationship between Philo's disquisitions on the laws and Palestinian halakha see S. Belkin, *Philo and the Oral Law* (1940), pp. vii-x, and below, pp. 874-5, n. 13. The most radical attempt to link Philo's position with an Alexandrian Jewish legal system is that of E. R. Goodenough, *The Jurisprudence of the Jewish Courts in Egypt* (1929); see further p. 848 below.

27. Participation in banquets: *Leg.* iii 53 (156); *Fug.* 5 (28-9); *Spec.* iv 74-5; theatres: *Prob.* 20 (141); sports: *Prov.*, Fr. 2, 58; *Prob.* 5 (26). Philo's participation in pagan social activities, particularly sport in which veneration of Hermes was involved, has been denied by those who regard these as incompatible with his Jewishness. See H. A. Wolfson, *Philo* I, pp. 78-86. The Alexandrian Jews' association with the gymnasium is evidenced in the edict of Claudius of A.D. 41, see CPJ II, no. 153, lines 92-3. For Philo's allusions to athletics see H. A. Harris, *Greek Athletics and the Jews* (1976), ch. 3. For *Spec.* iii 1 see below pp. 843, 844, 849-50.

Even if Philo's references to pagan social activities are regarded as literary only (or as references to Jewish, not Greek institutions), his education was certainly partly secular and Greek; see further p. 871 below. The discussion of *encyclios paideia* in *Congr.* not only reflects direct knowledge of the Greek education system but also includes an autobiographical passage, 14 (74-6). Wolfson considers this a Stoic *topos* (*Philo* I, pp. 78-81); but the prevalence of references to the *encyclia* elsewhere in Philo's works, and indeed the general nature of his *paideia*, dispose others to accept the passage as autobiography. See P. Borgen, *Bread from Heaven* (1965), pp. 99-121; M. Alexandre, *De Congressu* (*Oeuvres* XVI, 1967), pp. 41-7; 79-82; A. Mendelson, *Secular Education in Philo of Alexandria* (1982), esp. pp. 25-6. For the view that the 'philosophical' (non-scriptural) treatises date from a period close to Philo's Greek education see below, n. 116 and n. 188.

28. The importance of establishing a historical context for Philo's works is urged by V. Tcherikover, 'Jewish Apologetic Literature Reconsidered', Eos 48 (1956), pp. 169-93; cf. P. Borgen, *Bread from Heaven* (1965), pp. 111 ff.; G. Delling, 'Perspektiven der Erforschung des hellenistischen Judentums', HUCA 45 (1974), pp. 133-76.

29. For the lost works see below, p. 868. D. Barthélemy, 'Est-ce Hoshaya Rabba qui censura le 'Commentaire Allegorique?', *Philon d'Alexandrie*, ed. R. Arnaldez (1967), p. 59, n. 9, suggests that the greater part of the corpus might have already been lost before Eusebius.

30. For Philo and the Church see below, pp. 888-9.

fragments, or compositions extant only in Armenian.[31] Work on the location and identification of the Greek fragments has progressed since Harris's collection of 1886, but it remains incomplete.[32] The valuable Armenian versions of works otherwise lost were translated into Latin by Aucher in the 1820s. They are now receiving critical attention, as are the Armenian versions of works which have also survived in Greek.[33]

31. For details of the earlier editions see H. L. Goodhart and E. R. Goodenough, *Bibliography*, pp. 197–94. The *editio princeps* is Φίλωνος Ἰουδαίου εἰς τὰ τοῦ Μωσέως κοσμοποιητικά, ἱστορικά, νομοθετικά. Τοῦ αὐτοῦ Μονοβίβλια. *Philonis Judaei in libros Mosis de mundi opificio historicos, de legibus. Ejiusdem libri singulares. Ex bibliotheca regia.* Parisiis, ex officina Adriana Turnebi, 1552. Contributions to the completion of this very imperfect edition were made by D. Höschel, *Philonis Judaei opuscula tria*; and *Philo Judaeus de septenario ejusdem fragmenta II, e libro de providentia* (Goodhart and Goodenough, *Bibliography*, nos. 397 (1587), 399 (1614)). Collective editions also appeared in 1613 (no. 398), 1640 (no. 402), and 1691 (a reprint, at Frankfort, of the 1640 edition). Mangey's edition (no. 404; see above, p. 811) marked an important advance. It was not only more complete than earlier editions, but was the first to have been based upon an extensive comparison of manuscripts. The edition of A. F. Pfeiffer (1785–92; no. 407) remained incomplete; it contained only the contents of Mangey's vol. I and vol. II, 1–40. On the deficiencies of the editions of Mangey and Pfeiffer see F. Creuzer, 'Zur Kritik der Schriften des Juden Philo', ThStKr 5 (1832), pp. 5–17. For details, and reviews of the Cohn-Wendland-Reiter Editio Maior see Goodhart and Goodenough, *Bibliography*, pp. 194–6, no. 431.

32. Collection of the Greek fragments was begun by A. Mai in the following works: (1) *Philo et Virgilii interpretes*, containing *Philonis Judaei de cophini festo et de colendis parentibus cum brevi scripto de Jona* (1818) (Goodhart and Goodenough, *Bibliography*, no. 412); (2) *Classicorum auctorum e Vaticinis codicibus editorum* IV (1831) (*De cophini festo, de honorandis parentibus*, *Philonis ex opere in Exodum selectae quaestiones*) (no. 414); (3) *Scriptorum veterum nova collectio e Vaticanis codicibus* (1833) (no. 415) (contains specimens from a Florilegium of Leontius and Johannes with numerous smaller fragments of Philo); (4) *Philonis Judaei, Porphyrii philosophi, Eusebii Pamphili opera inedita*, containing *Philonis Judaei de virtute ejiusque partibus* (1816) (no. 411). C. G. L. Grossman contributed *Questiones ad Exodum* ii 62–8, in *Anecdoton Graecum Philonis Judaei de Cherubinis, Exod. XXV, 18* (1856) (no. 421) (in fact this supposed Anecdoton from the Cod. Vat. n. 379 was already printed by Mai, in (2) above). O. Tischendorf published *Philonea, inedita altera, altera nunc demum recte ex vetere scriptura eruta* in 1868 (no. 422). J. B. Pitra's *Analecta sacra spicilegio Solesmensi parata* II (1884) gives fragments from the Florilegium of the Codex Coislinianus 276 and details of Vatican manuscripts. The out-dated collection of fragments by J. Rendel Harris, *Fragments of Philo Judaeus* (1886), has not been superceded, but a critical edition of fragments to supplement the Cohn-Wendland-Reiter text is in preparation by James Royse. More Greek fragments are published in P. Wendland, *Neu entdeckte Fragmente Philos* (1891); K. Praechter, 'Unbeachtete Philonfragmente', Archiv für Geschichte der Philosophie 9 (1896), pp. 415–26; H. Lewy, 'Neue Philontexte in der Überarbeitung des Ambrosius. Mit einem Anhang: Neu gefundene griechische Philonfragmente', SAB, Phil.-hist. Kl. (1932), pp. 23–84. The fragments preserved in Eusebius are the best known and best edited; these include fragments of *Contempl.* (see F. Conybeare, *Philo about the Contemplative Life* (1895), pp. 181–7) as well as the otherwise lost *Hypothetica*. See further pp. 866–8 below. For fragments of the *Quaestiones* see pp. 826–30 below.

33. (1) *Philonis Iudaei sermones tres hactenus inediti I et II. De providentia, et III De animalibus, ex armena versione antiquissima ab ipso originali textu graeco ad verbum stricte exequuta, nunc primum in Latium fideliter translati*, per P. Jo. Baptistam Aucher (1822); (2) *Philonis Iudaei*

Some Latin fragments have been of value in the establishment of modern editions.[34] The texts and translations in the Loeb and Université de Lyon series (*Les Oeuvres de Philon*) are based upon the Cohn-Wendland-Reiter edition, but modifications to the text are suggested in both.

Details of the numerous manuscripts are supplied by Goodhart and Goodenough, *Bibliography*, pp. 136–87, and an analysis is provided in C-W.[35] The whole tradition, direct and indirect, probably derives, in

---

Paralipomena armena. Libri videlicet quatuor in Genesin. Libri duo in Exodum. Sermo unus de Sampsone. Alter de Jona. Tertius de tribus angelis Abraamo apparentibus. Opera hactenus inedita ex armena versione antiquissima ab ipso originali textu graeco ... *nunc primum in Latium fideliter translata per P. Jo. Baptistam Aucher* (1826). On Aucher see H. Lewy, *The Pseudo-Philonic De Jona* I (*Studies and Documents*, ed. K. and S. Lake, VII, 1936), pp. 1–3. Armenian extracts of works also extant in Greek were published by the Mechitarists: *Sermons of Philo the Hebrew, translated by our Ancestors, the Greek text of which has come down to us* (1892) (Armenian only); details in C. Mercier, *Quaestiones et Solutiones in Genesim I et II e versione armeniana* (*Oeuvres* XXXIVA, 1979), pp. 16–17. For details of the Armenian translations of Philo see H. Lewy, *op. cit.*, pp. 4–8 (manuscripts), 9–16 (date and provenance), 16–24 (the Armenian translator). Lewy regards the translator of all the Philonic and Ps.-Philonic works as belonging to the school of translators founded in Byzantium soon after 570 (p. 16). Cf. Aucher, *Sermones*, pref., pp. iii-iv; F. Conybeare, *Philo about the Contemplative Life* (1895), pp. 154–5; R. Marcus, *Questions on Genesis* (Loeb, Supplement to Philo, vol. I, 1953), pp. vii-viii; F. Petit, *L'ancienne version latine des Questions sur la Genèse de Philon d'Alexandrie* I: *Édition critique*, II: *Commentaire* (TU CXIII-IV, 1973), vol. I, pp. 7–15; C. Mercier, *op. cit.*, pp. 26–9; F. Siegert, *Drei hellenistisch-jüdische Predigten* (1980), pp. 2–4; A. Terian, *Philonis Alexandrini De Animalibus* (1981), pp. 3–25; S. Arevšatyan, 'The Date of the Armenian Version of the Works of Philo', Banber Matenadarani 10 (1971), pp. 7–18 (Armenian; abstract in *Revue d'études arméniennes* n.s. 9 (1972), pp. 482–3). Of the works in Armenian, fragments of *Prov.* and of the *Quaestiones* are also available in Greek (see below pp. 864–5 and 826–30). For *Anim.* see below pp. 865–6. For *De Deo* see p. 839; for *De Sampsone* and *De Jona* see p. 869. There are also Armenian fragments of *Leg.*, *Abr.*, *Spec.*, and *Dec.*; see C. Mercier, *op. cit.*, pp. 16–17; *idem*, 'La version arménienne du Legum Allegoriae', in *Armeniaca* (1969), pp. 9–15. For the Armenian manuscripts see Goodhart and Goodenough, *Bibliography*, pp. 182–5.

There are also manuscripts of ancient Armenian Philo commentaries in the State Library of Ancient Manuscripts, Erevan: G. Grigorian, 'The Armenian Commentaries on the works of Philo of Alexandria', Banber Matenadarani 5 (1960), pp. 95–115 (Armenian; abstract, SP 2 (1973), p. 57).

34. There are ancient Latin versions (which Petit dates to the fourth century and attributes to the same, rather poor translator, *op. cit.* pp. 7–13) of *Quaestiones ad Genesim* and the *Contempl.* See F. Conybeare, 'The Lost Works of Philo', The Academy 38 (1890), p. 32; *idem*, *Philo about the Contemplative Life* (1895), pp. 139–45; C-W vol. I, pp. l-lii; R. Marcus, *Questions on Exodus* (Loeb, Suppl. to *Philo* II), pp. 267–8. On the Latin translation of *Quaestiones ad Genesim* see below p. 829, n. 50; also A. Siegmund, *Die Überlieferung der Griechischen Christlichen Literatur in der Lateinischen Kirche bis zum zwölften Jahrhundert* (1949), pp. 127–8. For the Latin manuscripts see Goodhart and Goodenough, *Bibliography*, pp. 177–81.

35. In addition to the manuscript surveys in the Prolegomena to C-W vol. I and at the beginning of successive volumes, see the following studies of the history of the text: L. Cohn, 'Zur indirekten Überlieferung Philos und der älteren Kirchenväter', Jahrbücher

the main, from the library at Caesarea. This view is supported not only by a note in the Codex Vindobonensis, but chiefly by the fact that the tradition nowhere extends beyond the limits known to Eusebius. No certain trace exists of the compositions no longer familiar to him apart from references to them in the extant works.[36] In addition to the

---

für protestantische Theologie 18 (1892), pp. 475–90 (with Nachtrag by P. Wendland, pp. 490–2); *idem*, 'Die Philo-Handschriften in Oxford und Paris', Philologus 51 (1892), pp. 266–75; *idem*, 'Kritisch-exegetische Beiträge zu Philo', Hermes 31 (1896), pp. 107–48; *idem*, 'Kritisch-exegetische Beiträge zu Philo', Hermes 32 (1897), pp. 107–48 (on C-W vol. I); P. Wendland, 'Kritische und exegetische Bemerkungen zu Philo', RhM NF 52 (1897), pp. 465–504; 53 (1898), pp. 1–36; L. Cohn and P. Wendland, 'Zur neuen Philo-Ausgabe', Philologus 59, NF 13 (1900), pp. 521–36; L. Cohn, 'Beiträge zur Textgeschichte und Kritik der philonischen Schriften', Hermes 38 (1903), pp. 498–545 (on vol. IV); *idem*, 'Ein Philo-Palimpsest', SAB (1905), pp. 36–52 (on Cod. Vat. gr. 316); *idem*, 'Neue Beiträge zur Textgeschichte und Kritik der philonischen Schriften', Hermes 43 (1908), pp. 177–219 (on vol. V); *idem*, 'Kritische Bemerkungen zu Philo', Hermes 51 (1916), pp. 161–88. Six manuscripts not classified or not used in C-W are listed in Goodhart and Goodenough, pp. 153–4. See also P. J. Alexander, 'A Neglected Palimpsest of Philo Judaeus', *Studia Codicologica*, ed. K. Treu (TU CXXIV, 1977), pp. 1–14. Alexander reports preliminary study of Cod. Athen. 880, which represents none of the lost works (though it should be emphasized that one page remains undeciphered; see p. 4, n. 2); but it contains all or part of *Sacrif., Deter., Poster., Gig., Deus, Agric., Ebr., Sobr., Confus., Somn., and Virt.* Alexander suggests a date in the last quarter of the tenth or the first part of the eleventh century; he also notes similarities with Codex Vindobonensis Theologicus Graecus 29 (see below, n. 36). A collation of this text for *Agric.* with the other codices suggested that the Athenensis shared the mistakes of the UF class (see C-W vol. I, pp. xix-xxvii). The palimpsest yields some readings for the last sections of *Poster.* for which there is only one other manuscript (U) (see below, pp. 834–5). The title of *Ebr.* is fuller than elsewhere (see below, p. 836), and there are one or two marginal glosses of value. Alexander maintains that 'in a number of places the palimpsest reproduces the fourth century archetype of the Philonic tradition [see below, n. 36] more faithfully than do its closest relatives (U and F) or indeed any of the manuscripts' (p. 11).

36. For Codex Vindobonensis Theologicus Graecus 29 see Goodhart and Goodenough, *Bibliography*, p. 152, no. 112; L. Cohn, *Philonis Alexandrini libellus de opificio mundi* (1889), pp. i-vii; F. Conybeare, 'The Lost Works of Philo', The Academy 38 (1890), p. 32 (correcting Cohn's misleading account of the codex); C-W vol. I, pp. iii-iv, xxxv-xxxvii (with facsimile of f. 153 at end of volume); P. Alexander, 'A Neglected Palimpsest of Philo Judaeus', *Studia Codicologica*, ed. K. Treu (TU CXXIV, 1977), pp. 7–8 (with further bibliography, p. 8, n. 1). The codex contains only about a half of *Opif.* and breaks off in mid-sentence. It is prefaced, however, by a contents list and this is of value in itself, since details of titles of partially lost works (those surviving mainly in Armenian, see below, nn. 46–7) are supplied. The value of the codex lies chiefly in the cruciform inscription accompanying this list, copied from the archetype by the scribe and recording Εὐζοίος ἐπίσκοπος ἐν σωματίοις ἀνενεώσατο. That Euzoios (bishop of Caesarea *c.* A.D. 370) had the works transferred from papyrus to parchment for his library is confirmed by Jerome, *De vir. ill.* 113: 'Euzoius ... adolescens Caesareae eruditus est, et eiusdem postea urbis episcopus plurimo labore corruptam iam bibliothecam Origenis et Pamphili in membranis instaurare conatus est.' Cf. *Ep.* 34 *ad Marcellam* 1: 'quam ex parte corruptam Acacius dehinc et Euzoius eiusdem ecclesiae sacerdotes in membranis instaurare conati sunt.' Origen's library was brought to Caesarea by Pamphilus Martyr from Alexandria early in the fourth century. Euzoius had his text made in the 370s. Doubts have been raised regarding Origen's library as the source of the tradition; see G. Heinrici, reviews of

manuscripts, there are two papyri, probably from the third century, and belonging to the same exemplar represented in the Caesarea library a century later.[37]

For textual restoration, and the reconstruction of the corpus, the following indirect sources in particular have to be taken into account

---

C-W, ThLZ 22 (1897), col. 213; 25 (1900), col. 658. The thesis is supported, however, by Eusebius' catalogue of Philo's works, based on the collection of the Caesarea library, *H.E.* ii 18, 1–7; ii 5, 1; see p. 825 below. Although some of the works mentioned are now lost (see below, p. 828), it is more significant that of the works alluded to within the corpus but not known to Eusebius, none has since reappeared, suggesting that our tradition does, indeed, depend upon the Caesarea collection. See D. Barthélemy, 'Est-ce Hoshaya Rabba qui censura le "Commentaire allégorique"?', in *Philon d'Alexandrie*, ed. R. Arnaldez (1967), pp. 59–60. For a summary of the transmission of the text see M. Hart, *Quis Rerum Divinarum Heres Sit* (*Oeuvres* XV, 1966), pp. 154–61.

37. Of the two papyri of Philo, one has been known since 1893, and contains *Heres* and *Sacrif.*, and the other is a codex from Oxyrhynchus containing a selection of works. See R. A. Pack, *The Greek and Latin Literary Texts from Greco-Roman Egypt* ([2]1965), p. 79 (also listing an anonymous fragment of the fourth or fifth century which *may* be part of *Deus*). The first papyrus, Parisinus suppl. gr. 1120, found at Coptos, was first thought to belong to the sixth century, but is now dated to the third. See O. P. Scheil, 'Traités réédités d'après un Papyrus du VIe siècle environ', Mémoires publiés par les membres de la Mission archéologique française au Caire 9 (1893), pp. 149–215; F. G. Kenyon, *Paleography of Greek Papyri* (1897), p. 145; A. S. Hunt, *The Oxyrhynchus Papyri* IX (1912), p. 16; C-W vol. I, pp. xli–ix (reporting U. Wilcken's criticism of Scheil's date); vol. III, pp. iii–xl; M. Harl, *Quis rerum divinarum heres sit* (*Oeuvres* XV, 1966), pp. 154–5; J. van Haelst, *Catalogue des papyrus littéraires juifs et chrétiens* (1976), no. 695; cf. E. G. Turner, *Greek Papyri* ([2]1980), pp. 22, 200.

The Oxyrhynchus codex, dating from the third century, preserves some material lost in the manuscripts, and can be partially reconstructed to show its original contents, although it has been published in fragments; see van Haelst, *Catalogue*, no. 696 (who gives an erroneous date). The fragments are published as P.Oxy. IX, no. 1173; XI, no. 1356; PSI XI, no. 1207; P.Oxy. XVIII, no. 2158; P.Haun. 8. See W. G. Waddell, 'On the Oxyrhynchus Papyrus of Philo (P.Oxy. IX, 1173; XI, 1356)', Études de Papyrologie 1 (1932), pp. 1–6; L. Früchtel, 'Zum Oxyrhynchos-Papyrus des Philon (Ox.-Pap. XI 1356)', Philologische Wochenschrift 58 (1938), pp. 1437–9; J. Royse, 'The Oxyrhynchus Papyrus of Philo', BASP 17 (1980), pp. 155–65 (attempts a reconstruction of the content). For the relationship between the papyri and Euzoios' parchment text see D. Barthélemy, *art. cit.*, pp. 59–60, who points out that the papyri were copied by Christians, and that the first author to have drawn upon Philo and whose works we possess was Clement. He concludes that it is likely that 'ce fut au didascalée d'Alexandrie, sous Pantène ou sous Clément, que l'oeuvre de Philon, ou du moins ce que l'on en put regrouper, fut sauvée de l'abandon où les juifs hellénophones la laissaient' (p. 60). (On the Christian interest in Philo and Jewish neglect, see below, pp. 888–9.) Barthélemy maintains that 'tout se passe comme si *deux* éditions du Commentaire Allégorique, chacune amputée de certains traités, avaient quitté par deux voies différentes le scriptorium de la bibliothèque de Césarée. L'une de ces éditions ... avaient subi les retouches clandestines d'un rabbin orthodoxe de faible culture grecque, ... l'autre édition ... offrait un texte sans retouches juives : celui qu'attestent les papyrus égyptiens et les citations de Clément, Origène et Eusèbe' (p. 65).

alongside the manuscript tradition.[38] (1) The Armenian translations, both of lost and of extant works.[39] (2) The so-called *Sacra Parallela*; this is a selection from patristic works, but also including Philo's, arranged according to rubrics, probably by John Damascenus. The original has not survived, but there are extracts and revisions which, despite their secondary form, still provide valuable material for the history of the transmission of Philo's works.[40] (3) The *Catenae*: these are exegetical

38. For surveys of this material see P. Wendland, *Neu entdeckte Fragmente Philos* (1891); H. Lewy, 'Neu gefundene griechische Philonfragmente', SAB, Phil.-hist. Kl. (1932), pp. 72–84; C-W vol. I, pp. lii-lxx; II, pp. x-xvii; III, pp. xii-xvi; IV, pp. xxi-xxviii; V, pp. xii-xviii; VI, pp. ii-iv, xl-xlvii.

39. See above, p. 820, and below, pp. 826–30.

40. PG XCV, col. 1041-XCVI, col. 544. According to the extant preface, the original work was composed of three books. The first dealt with God and divine matters, the second dealt with men and human relations, and the third, known as the παράλληλα, dealt with 'parallel' virtues and vices. The first book is in its original arrangement, but is much abridged, in the Cod. Coislinianus 276 in Paris (Goodhart and Goodenough, *Bibliography*, no. 50); the second, which is also in its original arrangement but even more drastically abridged, is in Cod. Vaticanus 1553 (Goodhart and Goodenough, *Bibliography*, no. 52; the title of the work is recorded as Λεοντίου πρεσβυτέρου καὶ Ἰωάννου τῶν ἱερῶν βιβλίον δεύτερον); the third book has not survived in its original form. The arrangement of the sections within the first two books is alphabetical. This alphabetical sequence for the headings became the main organizing principle of the later recensions; here the division into books was abandoned and the headings from all three books were assembled according to the letters of the alphabet. Lequien published one of these recensions from Vaticanus gr. 1236 as *Johannis Damasceni opera* II, pp. 274–730 (see Goodhart and Goodenough, no. 58). More valuable is another alphabetically arranged recension, the Berolinensis gr. 46 (formerly known as Rupefucaldinus, Claromontanus 150, Meermannianus 94 and Phillippicus 1450; Goodhart and Goodenough, no. 57); Lequien published extracts from it: II, pp. 730–90. (Mangey published fragments from the *Sacra Parallela* in vol. II, pp. 648–60, and listed further fragments under the heading 'Johannes Monachus ineditus', pp. 660–70; these are actually identical with those of the Berolinensis gr. 46; see Harris, *Fragments*, pp. xix-xx.)

The numerous citations of Philo in these *Sacra Parallela* are valuable for three reasons: (1) they frequently supply good readings for the extant works of Philo; (2) they yield many fragments of the lost works; (3) they provide several hints as to the original arrangement of Philo's works from their precise information as to their titles. It must be acknowledged that this precise information concerning the titles is effaced or much abridged in most of the later recensions, preserved in the main in Coislinianus 276, Vaticanus 1553, and in Berolinensis gr. 46. As will be seen below, our knowledge of the titles of the treatises is much enriched from these sources. See further F. Loofs, *Studien über die dem Johannes von Damaskus zugeschriebenen Parallelen* (1892); L. Cohn, 'Zur indirekten Überlieferung Philos und der älteren Kirchenväter', Jahrbücher für protestantische Theologie 18 (1892), pp. 480–90; C-W vol. I, pp. lxiii-lxx; II, pp. xi-xiv; III, pp. xiv-xv; V, p. xvii; VI, pp. xl-xlvi; K. Holl, *Die Sacra Parallela des Johannes Damascenus* (TU XVI.1 = NF I.1, 1896); idem, *Fragmente vornicänischer Kirchenväter aus den Sacra Parallela* (TU XX.2, 1899); Harris, *Fragments*, pp. vii-xxiii; Goodhart and Goodenough, *Bibliography*, pp. 142–3, 156–7; M. Jugie, 'Jean Damascène', DThC VIII (1924), cols. 702–3; B. Studer, *Die Theologische Arbeitsweise des Johannes von Damaskus* (1956), p. 26.

Closely related to the *Sacra Parallela* of John of Damascus are the similar works of Maximus Confessor and Antonius Melissa, the difference being that in addition to

collections of excerpts from Philo and the Church Fathers. For Philo the great *Catena* on the Octateuch, extant in various recensions, merits particular attention.[41]

A reasonably complete catalogue of the works of Philo was drawn up by Eusebius in his *Ecclesiastical History*.[42] Unfortunately, however, it is so lacking in structure that it affords no clue to the correct classification of the works. For this we are almost entirely dependent upon the contents of the works themselves, including one or two internal references permitting the establishment of a partial relative chronology. Both the classification into groups or sequences and the chronology or the works (especially in relation to Philo's journey to Rome) have been

citations from patristic literature these contain citations from pagan authors. On the *Florilegia* and *Gnomologia* and their relationship to the *Sacra Parallela* see C. Wachsmuth, *Studien zu den griechischen Florilegien* (1882); R. Cadiou, 'Sur un florilège philonien', REG 70 (1957), pp. 93–101; 71 (1958), pp. 55–60; M. Richard, 'Florilèges grecs', *Dict. de Spiritualité* V (1962), cols. 475–512 = M. Richard, *Opera Minora* I (1976), no. 1; H. Chadwick, 'Florilegium', RAC VII (1969), cols. 1131–60; F. Petit, *L'ancienne version latine*, pp. 25–8; idem, *Quaestiones in Genesim et in Exodum* (*Oeuvres* XXXIII), pp. 21–8; idem, 'En marge de l'édition des fragments de Philon (Questions sur la Genèse et l'Exode), les florilèges damascéniens', *Studia Patristica* XV.1 (TU CXXVIII, 1984), pp. 20–5; cf. C-W, vol. I, p. xvii; IV, pp. xxiv-v; V, p. xvii; VI, pp. xi-vi; Goodhart and Goodenough, *Bibliography*, pp. 44–5.

41. A recension of this *Catena* was published under the title Σειρὰ ἑνὸς καὶ πεντήκοντα ὑπομνηματιστῶν εἰς τὴν ὀκτάτευχην καὶ τὰ τῶν βασιλειῶν, ἐπιμελείᾳ Νικηφόρου... (1772–3); see F. Petit, 'Les fragments grecs du livre VI des Questions sur la Genèse de Philon d'Alexandrie', Le Muséon 89 (1971), pp. 105–6, n. 55; for the relationship between this text and Procopius of Gaza's *Commentary* see Goodhart and Goodenough, *Bibliography*, pp. 164–5. All previous Greek editions are combined in PG LXXXVII. On the *Catenae* see further Harris, *Fragments*, pp. 4–5; C-W vol. II, pp. xv-xvii; III, pp. xv-xvi; IV, pp. xxii-iv; V, p. xvi. See also e.g. H. Achelis, *Hippolytusstudien* (TU XVI.4, 1897), pp. 94–110; G. Karo and J. Lietzmann, 'Catenarum Graecarum Catalogus', NGGW, Phil.-hist. Kl. (1902), pp. 1–66, 229–350, 559–620; A. Rahlfs, *Verzeichnis der griechischen Handschriften des Alten Testaments* (1914), pp. 377–8; R. Devresse, 'Chaînes exégétiques grecques', DB Supp. I (1928), cols. 1084–8; idem, 'Anciens commentateurs grecs de l'Octateuque', RB 44 (1935), pp. 166–91; 45 (1936), pp. 201–20; *Les anciens commentateurs grecs de l'Octateuque et des Rois* (1959); F. Petit, 'Les chaînes exégétiques grecques sur la Genèse et l'Exode. Programme d'exploration et d'édition', *Studia Patristica* XVII (TU CXV, 1975), pp. 46–50; idem, 'Une chaîne exégétique grecque peu connue? Sinai gr. 2. Descriptions et analyse', *Studia Codicologica*, ed. K. Treu (TU CXXIV, 1973), pp. 341–50.

42. Eusebius, *H.E.* ii 18. See K. Lake, Eusebius, *The Ecclesiastical History* (Loeb, 1953), pp. xl-xliv; C-W, vol. I, pp. xi,·xxxxviii-ci; II, pp. x-xi; IV, p. xxvi; V, p. xviii; VI, pp. ii-iii, xlvii. On the relationship between this catalogue and the manuscript tradition see above, p. 822. Jerome's information rests entirely upon Eusebius' catalogue: *De vir. ill.* 11 (C-W vol. I, pp. ci-ciii). The catalogue in the Suda (s.v. Φίλων) is in turn copied from the Greek translation of Jerome, with only a few additions (C-W vol. I, pp. cx-cxi). Some independent material is provided by Photius, *Bibliotheca* (ed. R. Henry, 1962), Cod. 103, 104, 105 (C-W vol. I, pp. cix-cx). The extensive fragments from various works of Philo quoted in Eusebius' *Praeparatio Evangelica* are also extremely valuable. See below, pp. 856, 866–8; F. Conybeare, *Philo about the Contemplative Life* (1895), pp. 181–91.

reconstructed in several different ways. What does emerge, however, is that a careful consideration reveals more coherence in Philo's *oeuvre* than might appear from the superscriptions in the editions. The majority of his works can, in fact, be seen as sub-divisions of a few large major works. Starting from the distinction between works on the Pentateuch and others, the former category comprises more than three-quarters of all that has been preserved of Philo's works; it consists of three major series, the *Quaestiones* (pp. 826–30), the *Legum Allegoria* (pp. 830–40), and the *Exposition* (pp. 840–54).[43]

Quaestiones et Solutiones (Ζητήματα καὶ λύσεις)

These form comparatively brief catechetical expositions of the Pentateuch in the form of questions and answers.[44] Our extant fragments of the work are confined to the *Quaestiones* on Exodus and Genesis, and are incomplete. Even when account is taken not only of the basic Armenian text, but also of the Latin additions and the Greek fragments from various sources, it remains uncertain whether Philo

43. The scholarship on the classification and relative chronology of the works of scriptural commentary is surveyed by V. Nikiprowetzsky, *Le Commentaire*, pp. 192–202. See also below, n. 55 and pp. 841–4. The *Quaestiones* and *Legum Allegoria* are both exegetical commentaries; the latter is more extensive (see below, n. 55) and is generally agreed to consist of *Leg.* i, ii, iii, *Cher., Sacrif., Deter., Poster., Gig.* and *Deus, Agric.* and *Plant., Ebr., Sobr., Confus., Migr., Heres., Congr., Fug., Mutat.*, and *Somn.* (discussed in this order below). For a different view on the content of the *Legum Allegoria* see E. Lucchesi, *L'usage de Philon dans l'oeuvre exégétique de Saint Ambroise* (ALGHJ IX, 1977), p. 123. The *Exposition* (which is not Philo's title) contains *Opif., Abr., Jos., Dec., Spec.* i-iv, *Virt., Praem.* (taken in this order; for the position of *Opif.* see below, pp. 832 and 844–5). There is disagreement regarding the classification (and in some cases the authenticity) of the remaining works, which are discussed in the following order below: *Mos., Prob., Vit., Aet., Legat.* and *Flacc., Prov., Anim., Hypoth. (Apologia).* (Note that Schürer, GJV III (⁴1909), pp. 687 ff., considered *Vit.* and *Aet.* under the heading of spurious works.)

It is generally agreed that the division of the series into books is Philo's, even if in some cases the original division has been distorted in transmission. See E. Lucchesi, 'La division en six livres des *Quaestiones in Genesim* de Philon d'Alexandrie', Muséon 89 (1976), p. 393; cf. J. Royse, SP 4 (1976-7), pp. 77–8. See further below, p. 835.

44. On the form and character of the *Quaestiones* see P. Borgen and R. Skarsten, '*Quaestiones et Solutiones:* Some Observations on the Form of Philo's Exegesis', SP 4 (1976-7), pp. 1–15; R. Marcus, *Questions on Genesis* (Loeb Philo Suppl. I), pp. ix-xv; F. Petit, *L'ancienne version*, pp. 2–3; S. Sandmel, 'Philo's Environment and Philo's Exegesis', JBR 22 (1954), p. 249 (the *Quaestiones* as preliminary notes); P. Borgen, ANRW II.21.1, pp. 134–7; S. Belkin, 'The Midrash Quaestiones et Solutiones in Genesim et in Exodum of Philo Alexandrinus and its Relation to the Palestinian Midrash', Horeb 14 (1960), pp. 1–74 (Hebr.); *idem*, 'The Earliest Source of the Rabbinic Midrash—Quaestiones et Solutiones in Genesim et Exodum of Philo Alexandrinus', *Abraham Weiss Jubilee Volume*, Hebrew section, ed. S. Belkin (1964), pp. 579–633.

For V. Nikiprowetzky's view that the *Quaestiones* method of exegesis is central to Philo's approach, see 'L'Exégèse de Philon d'Alexandrie', RHPR 53 (1973), pp. 309–29; *idem*, *Le Commentaire*, pp. 170–80. For the relation between the *Quaestiones* and the *Allegory of the Laws* see below, n. 55.

completed the series for the rest of the Pentateuch, or even planned to do so.[45] The work was available to Eusebius only for Genesis and Exodus (*H.E.* ii 18, 1 and 5); and the extant texts and numerous citations in the *Sacra Parallela* extend almost exclusively to these two books. Of the exposition of Genesis six books can be certainly traced, but they extend only to Gen. 28.[46] Since there is no trace of any sequel,

45. See J. Royse, 'The Original Structure of Philo's Quaestiones', SP 4 (1976–7), pp. 41–78. It is highly unlikely that the *Quaestiones* originally covered the entire Pentateuch. To do so it would have been very extensive, and it is inherently unlikely that a work of this length would have suffered such losses by the time of Eusebius. The evidence for *Quaestiones* on books other than Genesis and Exodus is not decisive. It consists of: (1) In Codex Vaticanus 1553 of the *Sacra Parallela* there are three citations with the lemma Φίλωνος τῶν ἐν τῷ Λευιτικῷ ζητημάτων. This occurs at f. 133ʳ, I.9 (on the text διάβολαι ... ἀλλότριαι); at f. 202ʳ, I.20 (on the text μείζονα ... πτωχεύσαντας); and at f. 224ʳ, I.3–4 (on the text μηδενὶ ... εὑρεθῇς). The last citation adds ὡς ἀπὸ Κράτητος. (For the second citation see Harris, *Fragments*, p. 75. Schürer noted that the inadequate edition of A. Mai, *Scriptorum veterum nova collectio* VII (1833), pp. 74–109 (= PG LXXXVI.2, cols. 2017–2100) only printed the second citation. Harris followed Mai. Royse has verified the references through microfilm of Vat. gr. 1553.) (2) The same manuscript has, in one case, the lemma Φίλωνος ἐκ τῶν ἐν τῷ νόμῳ ζητημάτων, f. 276ᵛ, I.4–5 (on the text ὡς ... παραδοθέν). (3) In *Spec.* i 269, on Numbers 19:1–9, Philo says: τίνα δὲ διὰ τούτων ὡς διὰ συμβόλων αἰνίττεται, δι' ἑτέρων ἠκριβώσαμεν ἀλληγοροῦντες. Cohn, 'Einteilung', p. 403, took this as an allusion to a lost set of *Quaestiones* on Numbers. (4) In *Quaest. Gen.* iv 123 Philo remarks, in connection with the discussion of Gen. 24:36, 'But what the principle of these things is will be explained when we enquire into the blessings' (trans. R. Marcus). This might be taken as a reference to the blessings in Deut. 33.

All four pieces of evidence can be challenged: the lemmata of Vat. gr. 1553 are unreliable, like all those in the *Sacra Parallela*; see Royse, p. 43; on Vat. gr. 1553, M. Richard, 'Florilèges spirituels, III. Florilèges grecs', *Dictionnaire de Spiritualité* V (1962), col. 478. The discussion of Numbers 19:1–9 could have occurred at some point in the *Allegorical Commentary* (but now lost), rather than in a lost *Quaestiones* on Numbers. The reference in *Quaest. Gen.* iv 123 might be to the blessings in Gen. 49; the extant text of the Armenian version of *Quaest. Gen.* does not extend this far, but it is perhaps more plausible to suppose the loss of part of *Quaest. Gen.* than of *Quaestiones* extending as far as Deuteronomy. See Royse, *art. cit.*, p. 42 (with references to other views). Finally, it remains possible that Philo did, indeed, plan to continue the *Quaestiones* for the entire Pentateuch, but did not in fact proceed beyond Genesis (cf. Sandmel, 'Philo's Environment', p. 249). Not only did Eusebius know nothing of *Quaestiones* on Numbers, Leviticus and Deuteronomy, but nor does it appear that any such works were used by authors of the *florilegia* (with the dubious exceptions of the texts from Vat. gr. 1553), by Procopius, the authors of the *Catenae*, or the Armenian and Latin translators. See E. Lucchesi, 'La division en six livres des *Quaestiones in Genesim* de Philon d'Alexandrie', *Le Muséon* 89 (1976), pp. 383–95; C. Mercier, *Quaestiones et Solutiones in Genesim I et II* (1979), pp. 25–6; Royse, *art. cit.*; J. C. M. van Winden, 'The first fragment of Philo's Quaestiones in Genesim', VC 33 (1979), pp. 313–18.

46. Eusebius does not tell us how many books comprised the exposition of Genesis. In Codex Vindobonensis theol. gr. 29 (see above, n. 36) the catalogue of Philo's works itemizes τῶν ἐν γενέσει ζητημάτων καὶ λύσεων α', β', γ', δ', ε', ζ' (see C-W I, p. xxxvi). The same number of books is cited in the *Sacra Parallela* and the same number, again, is contained in Armenian translation, for what appears as book iv in the Armenian actually represents books iv, v, and vi; this is shown by the length of book iv in the Armenian and

it remains open to question whether such a thing ever existed. According to Eusebius the exposition of Exodus comprised five books (*H.E.* ii 18, 5; likewise Jerome).[47] His testimony is supported by the catalogue of Philo's works in the Codex Vindobonensis gr. 29. But three of these five books must have been lost soon after Eusebius, for our other information knows of only two books, which are probably identical with the original second and fifth. The extant sections are : (1)

---

by the citations in the *Sacra Parallela*. The citations with the lemma ἐκ τοῦ δ' τῶν ἐν γενέσει ζητημάτων come from the Armenian book iv 33–76 (on Genesis 19:2–23:6); the citations with the lemma ἐκ τοῦ ε' τῶν ἐν γενέσει ζητημάτων are from the Armenian book iv 99 and 104 (on Genesis 24:16 and 24:18) and those with the citations ἐκ τοῦ ζ' τῶν ἐν γενέσει ζητημάτων are from the Armenian book iv 204 and 206 (on Gen. 27:6 and 27:18). See Harris, *Fragments*, pp. 32–46. The Armenian translation breaks off with the exposition of Gen. 29:8–9. Procopius' use of the *Quaestiones* ceases a little before this point. There are no citations from later books. (The lemma ἐκ τοῦ θ' τῶν ἐν γενέσει ζητημάτων given with *Quaest. Gen.* iv 104 by Mai was a misreading of ε'; see Royse, pp. 73–4, n. 78; Petit, *Quaestiones*, p. 178.)

For the sixth book of *Quaest. Gen.* see Harris, *Fragments*, pp. 69–72; F. Petit, 'Les fragments grecs du livre VI des Questions sur la Genèse de Philon d'Alexandrie', Le Muséon 89 (1971), pp. 93–150; *idem, Quaestiones*, p. 214; Royse, pp. 51–3. For the Latin version, which begins with iv 154 (of the Armenian) see F. Petit, *L'ancienne version*; Royse, *art. cit.*, pp. 44–5.

47. Codex Vindobonensis theol. gr. 29 lists τῶν ἐν ἐξόδῳ ζητημάτων καὶ λύσεων (α' deleted) β' καὶ ε' (C-W I, p. xxxvi; see also Royse, *art. cit.*, pp. 54, 74 for reading). So the manuscript from which this catalogue was copied had contained books ii and v. (The codex itself did not contain them, however; see above, n. 36.) The Armenian version also preserved just two books, but here they are marked as books i and ii. Again, in the *Sacra Parallela* only a first and a second book are cited—the same books, in fact, as those preserved in Armenian. (See Harris, *Fragments*, pp. 47–68. For one fragment referring to a fourth book, see Royse, p. 54.) For the second book we find both the lemma ἐκ τοῦ β' τῶν ἐν ἐξόδῳ ζητημάτων (Berolinensis gr. 46 (Rupefuc.) fol. 72ᵛ, 110ʳ, 114ʳ, 277ʳ, Coislinianus fol. 119ᵛ, 183ʳ, 196ᵛ, 208ʳ, 259ᵛ, Vaticanus fol. 150ʳ) and ἐκ τοῦ τελευταίου τῶν ἐν ἐξόδῳ ζητημάτων (Berolinensis (Rupefuc.) fol. 22ᵛ, 51ʳ, 110ʳ, Coislinianus fol. 34ᵛ, 44ᵛ, 120ʳ, 155ʳ⁻ᵛ, 157ʳ, 183ʳ, 245ʳ, 254ʳ, Vaticanus fol. 168ʳ, 182ᵛ, 212ᵛ); see Wendland, 'Neu entdeckte Fragmente', pp. 103–4; Royse, *loc. cit.* The Armenian second book went up to Exod. 28; the citations in the *Sacra Parallela* also appear only to extend this far. There is no trace of any continuation. The two books preserved in Armenian and cited in the *Sacra Parallela* as books i and ii are identical to the original books ii and v. The first Armenian book (which is just a fragment, as its length indicates) deals with Exod. 12, and the second with Exod. 22–8. Eusebius lists εἰς τὴν ἔξοδον ζητημάτων καὶ λύσεων α', β', γ', δ', ε' καὶ τὸ περὶ τῆς σκηνῆς (*H.E.* ii 18, 5). This is most probably a reference to the conclusion of *Quaest. Ex.* (see Royse, pp. 54–5). If we are to understand Eusebius as having added these words to his reference to the fifth book (rather than as a reference to a separate book altogether) then this provides further evidence for the hypothesis that our second book was originally the fifth book, for the account of the tabernacle is in our second book. It is possible that a false numeration could have prevailed when Acacius and Euzoius revised the library at Caesarea (see above, n. 36); only books ii and v of the *Quaest. Ex.* were available and so the new enumeration was adopted and came to prevail. Codex Vindobonensis theol. gr. 29 has preserved the original enumeration for us. For further discussion of the structure of the *Quaest. Ex.* and alternatives to this view, see Royse, pp. 53–62.

the six books on Genesis in an Armenian version,[48] where they are numbered as four. There is a lacuna, however, between the second and third books, since the exposition of Gen. 10:10–15:6 is missing. Has a complete book been lost here? Of the exposition of Exodus there are extant in Armenian a fragment of one book (probably the second) and another book (probably the fifth) substantially complete. (2) A large part of the *Quaestiones et solutiones in Genesim* is preserved in an old Latin version, printed several times at the beginning of the sixteenth century, but comparatively neglected until recent times.[49] It can be dated to the last quarter of the fourth century, and consists of the last third of the Armenian book iv—that is, in fact, the sixth book. (3) A host of small fragments of the Greek text in the different recensions of the *Sacra Parallela* and the *Catenae*.[50] (4) With the aid of the Armenian text it can also now be established that Ambrose was one of the Church Fathers who transcribed passages from the *Quaestiones* almost word for word without mentioning Philo's name.[51] The attempted reconstructions of

48. The Armenian version was first published by Aucher, with a Latin translation, see above, p. 820. R. Marcus produced an English translation from the Armenian: *Questions and Answers on Genesis* (Loeb, Philo Supp. I, 1953); *Questions and Answers on Exodus* (Supp. II, 1953). Charles Mercier has provided a French translation, based on a reexamination of the Armenian text; Aucher's Latin is printed alongside the French translation: C. Mercier, *Quaestiones et Solutiones in Genesim I et II e versione armeniaca* (*Oeuvres* XXXIVA, 1979). On the character of the Armenian version see R. Marcus, 'A note on Philo's *Quaestiones in Gen.* ii 31', CPh 39 (1944), pp. 257–8; *idem*, 'Notes on the Armenian Text of Philo's Quaestiones in Genesim Bk. I-III', JNES 7 (1948), pp. 111–15; G. Bolognesi, 'Postille sulla traduzione armena della Quaestiones et Solutiones in Genesim di Filone', Archivo Glotologico Italiano 55 (1970), pp. 52–77.

49. *Philonis Iudaei centum et duae quaestiones et totidem responsiones morales super Genesin* (1520). A second edition was published at Basel in 1527 (and subsequently reprinted) as *Philonis Judaei Alexandrini, libri antiquitatum, quaestionum et solutionum in Genesin, de Essaeis, de nominibus Hebraicis, de mundo*. Aucher printed the Old Latin text of *Quaest. Gen.* iv 154–245 from the 1538 edition beneath his Armenian text with Latin translation, pp. 362–443 (also in Richter, VII, pp. 212–61). For the manuscripts of the Old Latin version, see Goodhard and Goodenough, *Bibliography*, pp. 177–81. See F. Petit, *L'ancienne version latine des Questions sur la Genèse de Philon d'Alexandrie*. I: *Édition critique*. II: *Commentaire* (TU CXIII-IV, 1973). See also A. Siegmund, *Die Überlieferung der griechischen christlichen Literatur in der lateinischen Kirche bis zum zwölften Jahrhundert* (1949), pp. 127–8; R. Marcus, *Questions on Exodus*, Appendix B: 'Additions in the Old Latin Version', pp. 267–75. On the Latin versions of Philo see above, n. 34.

50. See F. Petit, *Quaestiones in Genesim et in Exodum: fragmenta graeca* (*Oeuvres* XXXIII, 1978), for the reassembly of fragments from the *Catenae*, the *Epitome* of Procopius of Gaza, the *Florilegia*, a small fragment on Genesis in Eusebius, *Praep. ev.* vii 13, from Byzantine chroniclers and from John Lydus; see Petit, *op. cit.*, pp. 14–34; *idem*, 'Les fragments grecs du livre VI des Questions sur la Genèse de Philon d'Alexandrie', Le Muséon 89 (1971), pp. 93–150. There is a direct textual tradition for just one short section of *Quaest. Ex.* ii 62–8; this is contained in the manuscript Vaticanus gr. 379, fol. 385^v–388^v (C-W I, pp. xxv-xxvii).

51. H. Lewy, 'Neue Philontexte in der Überarbeitung des Ambrosius. Mit einem Anhang: Neu gefundene griechische Philonfragmente', SAB Phil.-hist. Kl. (1932), pp.

the design, extent and methodology of the *Quaestiones* are of some consequence for the interpretation of Philo's work as a whole, in so far as it has been suggested that these treatises reflected Alexandrian Sabbath lections. If this hypothesis is accepted, and if the pattern of Philo's selection of biblical texts for the *Quaestiones* can be discerned, some progress is achieved towards an insight into the practices of the Alexandrian synagogue.[52]

Legum Allegoria (Νόμων ἱερῶν ἀλληγορία)[53]

The scriptural texts treated in the form of short expositions with philosophical and allegorical elaboration in the *Quaestiones* are dealt with at greater length in the long sequence entitled *The Allegory of the Laws*. Some regard this as Philo's *magnum opus*. It is an allegorical commentary on selected passages of Genesis.[54] There are frequent correspondences between the *Quaestiones* and the *Allegorical Commentary* in content, since both present allegorical exegesis, though this is perhaps more thoroughgoing in the latter.[55] Here, the deeper

---

28–84; E. Lucchesi, 'L'usage de Philon dans l'oeuvre de Saint Ambroise' (ALGHJ IX, 1977); H. Savon, *Saint Ambrose devant l'exégèse de Philon le Juif* (1977); idem, 'Ambroise et Jérôme, lecteurs de Philon', ANRW II.21.2 (1984), pp. 737–44.

52. See Royse, pp. 62–3. This hypothesis was originally suggested by R. Marcus, *Questions on Genesis*, pp. xiii-xv. Royse (p. 82) suggests that textual features of the *Quaestiones* confirm Marcus's view that 'Philo is not following a cycle which was peculiar to him, or to some sectarian group, but rather than this division was sufficiently in the mainstream of Jewish practice of that time that a division very much like it became the established norm'.

53. This title is also given in Eusebius, *H.E.* ii 18, 1; Photius, *Bibliotheca* cod. 103; cf. Origen, *Comm. in Matt.* xvii 17 (GCS XL, p. 635); *Contra Celsum* iv 51. The singular ἀλληγορία prevails as the designation of the *Allegorical Commentary* throughout the citations in the *Sacra Parallela* (ἐκ τοῦ α' τῆς νόμων ἱερῶν ἀλληγορίας etc.). In general the tradition alternates between singular and plural.

54. On the *Allegorical Commentary* in general see L. Cohn, 'Einteilung', pp. 393–402; M. Adler, *Studien zu Philon von Alexandreia* (1929), pp. 1–67, esp. pp. 8–24; Goodenough, *Introduction*, pp. 46–8; idem, *By Light, Light!*, pp. 245–55; S. Sandmel, *Philo of Alexandria*, pp. 76–8. For a list of the treatises and biblical texts covered see S. Sandmel, *loc. cit.*; F. Petit, *L'ancienne version*, p. 3. E. Lucchesi defines the *Allegory of the Laws* differently, so that it comprises *Opif.*, *Leg.* i, ii, iii, *Cher.*, *Sacrif.*, *Deter.* and *Poster.*; see above, n. 45. For the position of *Opif.*, see below, pp. 832, 844–5.

55. On the relationship between the *Quaestiones* and the *Allegory* see V. Nikiprowetzky, 'L'Exégèse de Philon', in D. Winston and J. Dillon (eds.), *Two Treatises of Philo of Alexandria* (1983), pp. 5–75, esp. pp. 67–9. Cf. S. Sandmel, *Philo of Alexandria*, pp. 79–80. The suggestion that the *Quaestiones* represented a catechetical treatment of material pursued in a more scholarly fashion in the *Allegory*, Schürer, GJV III (⁴1909), pp. 648 ff., is now generally regarded as misleading; the method of the *Quaestiones* is employed in the *Allegory* (and even in the *Exposition*) and there is overlap of content too. V. Nikiprowetzky regards the form of the *Quaestiones* as the key to Philo's method of composition throughout his expository works; see also above, n. 44. It is difficult to determine the chronological relationship of the *Quaestiones* and the *Allegorical Commentary*. Disagreement arises from the difficulty of identifying clear cross-references in Philo's works (see further below, pp. 841–4,

allegorical meaning of Holy Scripture is established in a wide-ranging and detailed discussion, which often seems to stray from the text with copious citations of parallel passages.[56] There are some affinities with Midrash in Philo's method here.[57] For all its apparent arbitrariness, this allegorical interpretation does have rules and laws; once an allegorical meaning is established for a particular biblical person, theme or event, this meaning is maintained through the *Commentary* with some consistency.[58] In particular, there is a fundamental notion which underlies the exposition as a whole: the history of mankind, as narrated in Genesis, amounts in essence to a large-scale psychological and ethical theory. The different characters, good and bad, who make their appearance, represent the different states of the soul (τρόποι τῆς ψυχῆς) which are found in men.[59] The underlying aim of the *Allegorical Commentary* appears to be the analysis of these types in their variety and in their relationship both to one another and to God and the world of the senses, and from this to draw out moral instruction. It might even be said that Philo's interests in this work lay in the human soul and in morality, rather than in speculative theology.[60]

At the beginning, the commentary follows the text of Genesis verse by verse. Later, particular sections are selected, and some are treated in such detail that they extend to monograph length. So, for example, the story of Noah gives Philo the opportunity to write two books on drunkenness (*Ebr.*, see below, p. 836). The series as it stands begins with

845, 855). For some of the passages at issue, and references to literature on the problem, V. Nikiprowetzky, *op. cit.*, pp. 67–8. From references to the lost work *On numbers* in *Quaest. Gen.* iv 110 (and Fr. 9 of the ancient Latin version) and (?) in *Mos.* ii 11 (115), it can be suggested that at least part of the *Quaestiones* followed *Mos. Mos.* itself is difficult to place, however (see below, pp. 854–5). If the reference to a proposed work on the tetrad in *Opif.* 16 (52) is taken as an announcement of the forthcoming work *On numbers*, we could say, further, that part of the *Quaestiones* followed *Opif.* But since it is doubtful whether *Opif.* was part of the *Allegorical Commentary*, this relationship only indicates that the *Quaestiones* was not among Philo's earliest works. Possible references to discussions in the *Allegory* are found at *Quaest. Gen.* ii 4 and 34 (see R. Marcus *ad loc.*). The view that at least part of *Quaestiones* was composed earlier than the *Allegorical Commentary* is found in Grossman, *De Philonis Judaei operum continua serie et ordine chronologico comment.* II (1842), pp. 14–17; cf. Massebieau, 'Essai sur la Chronologie de la vie et des oeuvres de Philon', RHR 53 (1906), pp. 279–87; L. Cohn, 'Einteilung', pp. 430–2.

56. On the allegorical method see further below, pp. 876–8.

57. See further below, pp. 874–5. For Midrash see vol. I, pp. 90–9. For the *Quaestiones* as Midrash see esp. S. Belkin, *Philo and the Oral Law* (1940).

58. Consult indexes listed above, p. 811, and note J. W. Earp, 'Index of Names', in Colson, Loeb Philo vol. X, pp. 269–433.

59. See A. Mendelson, *Secular Education in Philo of Alexandria* (1982), pp. 47–65. For Philo's moral theory see further pp. 886–8 below.

60. Schürer claimed that Philo's ultimate intention was not to be a speculative theologian but a psychologist and moralist; see GJV III (⁴1909), p. 649. For the view that he was neither, but rather a scriptural commentator, see V. Nikiprowetzky, *Le Commentaire*, pp. 181–3, and *passim*.

Gen. 2:1 : καὶ συνετελέσθησαν ὁ οὐρανὸς καὶ ἡ γῆ. The creation of the world was evidently not discussed. The treatise *Opif.* which precedes the *Legum Allegoria* in the editions is not an allegorical commentary on the story of creation so much as the creation story itself. What is more, the first book of the *Leg.* is not attached in any way to *Opif.*; it begins with Gen. 2:1, while the creation of man has already been treated in *Opif.* Most likely, then, *Opif.* was not written to begin the *Allegorical Commentary.* It may be asked whether Philo did not also write an allegorical commentary on Gen. 1 which has not survived. But it is perfectly plausible that he did not, and that the sequence actually begins with *Leg.* i; the *Allegorical Commentary* deals principally with the history of mankind, which only begins in Gen. 2:1. The abrupt beginning of *Leg.* i need cause no surprise, since this method of starting directly with the text to be expounded is found in the later books of Philo's commentaries, and appears also in Rabbinic Midrash.[61] In the textual tradition the title Νόμων ἱερῶν ἀλληγορία, which belongs to the whole series, is only given for the first books. The later books all bear individual titles, which gives the impression that they were independent works. The *Allegorical Commentary* comprises:[62]

Legum Allegoriae i (Νόμων ἱερῶν ἀλληγορίας τῶν μετὰ τὴν ἐξαήμερον τὸ πρῶτον) on Gen. 2:1–17.

Legum Allegoriae ii (Νόμων ἱερῶν ἀλληγορίας τῶν μετὰ τὴν ἐξαήμερον τὸ δεύτερον) on Gen. 2:18–3:1a.

Legum Allegoriae iii (Νόμων ἱερῶν ἀλληγορίας τῶν μετὰ τὴν ἐξαήμερον τὸ τρίτον)[63] on Gen. 3:8b–19.

The difference in the lengths of books i and ii suggests the conjecture that they are actually one book, and in fact the division has no manuscript authority.[64] *Legum Allegoriae* therefore consists of two books. There is however a lacuna between the two, since a commentary on Gen. 3:1b–8a is missing. A commentary on Gen. 3:20–23 is also absent, since the following book (*Cher.*) begins with 3:24. As Philo was still following the text step by step in these early books, it might be assumed that these missing sections were each treated in a separate book—which is fairly certain for the second missing section.[65] The

---

61. See further pp. 844–5 below.

62. In the discussion of the separate treatises making up the *Allegorical Commentary* which follows, the first note will provide in each case brief references to the main editions and translations (listed in full, p. 811 above), and select bibliographical items relevant to each.

63. C-W vol. I, pp. 61–169; E. Bréhier, *Philon: Commentaire allégorique des saintes lois après l'oeuvre des six jours: texte grec, traduction française* (1909); Loeb vol. I (1929), pp. 139–473; C. Mondésert, *Legum Allegoriae I–III* (*Oeuvres* II, 1962). See C. Mercier, 'La version arménienne du Legum Allegoriae', *Armeniaca* (1969), pp. 9–15.

64. In C-W the division is retained merely on grounds of practicality; see vol. I, p. lxxxvi; cf. Mondésert, p. 18.

original *Leg. All.* might therefore be reconstructed as follows : Book i on Gen. 2:1–3:1a; Book ii on Gen. 3:1b–3:8a; Book iii on Gen. 3:8b–19; Book iv on Gen. 3:20–23. The citations in the *Sacra Parallela* are in line with this reconstruction. In particular the third book (the commentary on Gen. 3:8b–19) is frequently quoted with the lemma ἐκ τοῦ γ' τῆς νόμων ἱερῶν ἀλληγορίας.[66] This third book is described in the manuscripts as ἀλληγορία δευτέρα,[67] but this could be explained by the assumption that in the archetype of these manuscripts the real second book was already lacking.

De Cherubim (Περὶ τῶν Χερουβίμ)[68]

The treatise *On the Cherubim* covers Genesis 3:24 and 4:1. From this point in the series, the individual books are no longer transmitted under the general title νόμων ἱερῶν ἀλληγορία but under special headings. According to the reconstruction of the *Leg.* suggested above, the present treatise would be the fifth book, though it might have formed the fourth combined with the (lost) commentary on Gen. 3:20–23.[69]

De sacrificiis Abelis et Caini (Περὶ ὧν ἱερουργοῦσιν Ἄβελ καὶ Κάϊν)[70]

On Gen. 4:2–4. Until Cohn's restoration, there was a lacuna in the

---

65. The remark in *Sacrif.* 12 (51): τί δέ ἐστι τὸ γῆν ἐργάζεσθαι, διὰ τῶν προτέρων βίβλων ἐδηλώσαμεν seems to be a reference to this lost commentary on Gen. 3:23. *Agric.* 1 (2) has been suggested as the allusion, see A. Méasson, *De sacrif.* (*Oeuvres* IV, 1966), p. 117, n. 3; but this is unlikely in view of the priority of *Sacrif.* in the sequence of books in the *Commentary*. An allusion to *Quaest. Gen.* is possible, though it is perhaps unlikely that Philo would refer to a separate work (rather than a separate treatise within a work) with the words διὰ τῶν προτέρων βίβλων.

66. See C-W vol. I, notes on pp. 114, 115, 123, 128, 129, 130, 136, 148, 153, 162. There appear to be only two citations from our book i in the *Sacra Parallela* which give a book number. The first is introduced with the lemma ἐκ τοῦ δευτέρου τῆς νόμων ἱερῶν ἀλληγορίας (C-W, n. on p. 72); the other with the lemma ἐκ τοῦ α' τῆς νόμων ἱερῶν ἀλληγορίας (C-W, p. 74). The first citation must therefore be a mistake (but see Cohn's alternative explanation, p. lxxxvi). Citations with the lemma ἐκ τοῦ δ' τῆς νόμων ἱερῶν ἀλληγορίας are to be found in the *Sacra Parallela* as follows: Codex Berolinensis gr. 4 (Rupefuc.) fol. 29ᵛ, Codex Laurentianus VIII, 22 fol. 69ᵛ, Codex Coislinianus fol. 126ᵛ, Codex Vaticanus 1553 fol. 57ᵛ, 93ʳ, 111ʳ, 115ᵛ, 252ʳ⁻ᵛ. See Harris, *Fragments*, pp. 6–8.

67. See C-W vol. I, p. 113.

68. C-W vol. I, pp. 170–201; Loeb vol. II (1929), pp. 1–85; J. Gorez, *De Cherubim* (*Oeuvres* III, 1963).

69. The full title reads: περὶ τῶν Χερουβὶμ καὶ τῆς φλογίνης ῥομφαίας καὶ τοῦ κτισθέντος πρώτου ἐξ ἀνθρώπου Κάϊν.

70. C-W vol. I, pp. 202–57; Loeb Philo II (1929), pp. 87–139; A. Méasson, *De Sacrificiis Abelis et Caini* (*Oeuvres* IV, 1966); idem, 'Le *De Sacrificiis Abelis et Caini* de Philon d'Alexandrie', Bull. de l'Ass. G. Budé 25 (1966), pp. 309–16; J. V. Vernhes, 'Philon d'Alexandrie, *De sacrificiis Abelis et Caini*', Revue de Philologie 94 (1968), pp. 298–305. *Sacrif.* 31–32 is on P.Oxy. IX, no. 1173; *Sacrif.* 42–43/45 is on P.Oxy. XI, no. 1356.
The title given is the conventional one in the editions, and is presented in some of the manuscripts. But the better manuscript tradition has περὶ γενέσεως Ἄβελ καὶ ὧν αὐτός τε καὶ ὁ ἀδελφὸς αὐτοῦ Κάϊν ἱερουργοῦσιν (restored by Cohn; see C-W, p. 202, n.). In the *Sacra Parallela* the title is abbreviated to read περὶ γενέσεως Ἄβελ or simply εἰς τὸν Ἄβελ

earlier editions, from 21–32. This came about through the composition of the spurious treatise *de mercede meretricis* (see below, p. 849) from parts of two different Philonic works. Section 1 of the work is taken from *Spec.* i, and 2–4 from *Sacrif.* After these apparently homogeneous sections had been combined, the corresponding passages in *Spec.* i and *Sacrif.* were deleted. Wendland discovered that this had happened by considering the better manuscript tradition, and confirmation was yielded by the papyrus codex from Coptos.[71] *Sacrif.* was used extensively by Ambrose in his *De Cain et Abel.*[72]

Between *Sacrif.* and the next treatise in the series the exposition of Gen. 4:5–7 is missing. It will have formed either the conclusion of this book or a separate book.

Quod deterius potiori insidiari soleat (Περὶ τοῦ τὸ χεῖρον τῷ κρείττονι φιλεῖν ἐπιτίθεσθαι)[73]
On Gen. 4:8–15. In the *Sacra Parallela*, this treatise is often introduced by the formula ἐκ τοῦ ζ' καὶ η' τῆς νόμων ἱερῶν ἀλληγορίας.[74] The curious formula ἐκ τοῦ ζ' καὶ η' might mean that the sixth book was also called the seventh, according to a different reckoning ; ἐκ τοῦ ζ' τοῦ καὶ η' would thus be more accurate. According to the usual reckoning, then, *Deter.* was the sixth book in the Allegorical Commentary ; but it was also sometimes counted as the seventh, probably as a result of the positioning of *Opif.* at the head of the series.[75]

De posteritate Caini (Περὶ τῶν τοῦ δοκησισόφου Κάϊν ἐγγόνων)[76]
On Gen. 4:16–25. This treatise survives only in two manuscripts,

---

(see C-W, notes to pp. 207, 238, 247).

71. P. Wendland, *Neu entdeckte Fragmente* (1891), pp. 125–45 ; for the papyrus from Coptos see above, n. 37.

72. CSEL XXXII.1 ; see A. Méasson, p. 53, and n. oo above.

73. C-W vol. I, pp. 258–98 ; Loeb Philo II (1929), pp. 197–319 ; I. Feuer, *Quod Deterius Potiori insidiari soleat* (*Oeuvres* V, 1965). *Deter.* 51–2, 53–5, 56–7 is on P.Oxy. IX, no. 1173. For *Deter.* in Codex Athen. 880 see P. Alexander, *op. cit.* in n. 35 above. The treatise was already cited under this special title by Origen, *Comm. in Matt.* xv 3 (GCS XL, p. 355). Eusebius mistakenly quotes several passages from *Confus.* under the same title (*Praep. ev.* xi 15).

74. See C-W vol. I, notes on pp. 259, 266, 289 for references. On one occasion the lemma ἐκ τοῦ ζ' τῶν αὐτῶν is found (see C-W vol. I, n. on p. 272). The lemma ἐκ τοῦ ζ' καὶ η' τῆς νόμων ἱερῶν ἀλληγορίας is used twice in Vaticanus 1553, referring not to *Deter.* but to the following book, *Poster.* (see C-W vol. II, notes on pp. 3 and 33). This is evidently a mistake. (On Vat. 1553 see above, n. 40.).

75. On the position of *Opif.* see below, pp. 844–5. See also V. Nikiprowetzky, *Le Commentaire*, p. 199.

76. C-W vol. II, pp. 1–41 ; Loeb Philo II (1929), pp. 321–439 ; R. Arnaldez, *De Posteritate Caini* (*Oeuvres* VI, 1972). See P. Wendland, 'Zu Philos Schrift *de posteritate Caini* (Nebst Bemerkungen zur Rekonstruktion der Septuaginta)', *Philologus* 57 (1898), pp. 248–88. *Post.* 37–40/40–44 is on P.Oxy. XI, no. 1356 ; *Post.* 31–32/4 on PSI X, no. 1207. The full title is περὶ τῶν τοῦ δοκησισόφου Κάϊν ἐγγόνων καὶ ὡς μετανάστης γίνεται.

Vaticanus 381 (first published from this by Mangey[77]) and Atheniensis Bibl. Nat. 880.[78] In both, it follows *Deter.*, whilst in the papyrus it follows *Ebr.*, probably because the order of the papyrus is in disarray.[79] Codex Atheniensis Bibl. Nat. 880 yields valuable readings for the last sections of *Poster.* Like the preceding book, *Poster.* is cited in the *Sacra Parallela* with the formula ἐκ τοῦ η′ καὶ θ′ τῆς νόμων ἱερῶν ἀλληγορίας.[80] Eusebius, in his catalogue in *H.E.* ii 18, does not use the special titles of the books from the *Allegorical Commentary* listed above, whereas he does use these titles for the books which follow. This is presumably because for him the former were included under the general title νόμων ἱερῶν ἀλληγορία, whilst the latter were not. It may be added that in the *Sacra Parallela*, also, it is only up to this point that citations are given under the general title. It is possible that Philo himself issued the following books with special titles, but not those above. (On the authenticity of the book divisions, see above, n. 46.) There is justification for this, insofar as in the books which follow it is no longer the uninterrupted text but only selected passages which are commented upon. The exegetical method, however, remains uniform throughout.

De gigantibus (Περὶ γιγάντων)
On Gen. 6:1–4.

Quod deus sit immutabilis (Ὅτι ἄτρεπτον τὸ θεῖον)[81]
On Gen. 6:4–12.

Although these two sections stand separately in the manuscripts and editions, they really form a single book. The *Sacra Parallela* cite passages from *Deus* with the formula ἐκ τοῦ περὶ γιγάντων;[82] Eusebius refers to the work as περὶ γιγάντων ἢ περὶ τοῦ μὴ τρέπεσθαι τὸ θεῖον (*H.E.* ii 18, 4). A few citations with the formula ἐκ τοῦ περὶ γιγάντων cannot be traced, so it would appear that a passage is missing.[83] Massebieau conjectured that there is a reference to a lost commentary on Gen. 5:32 in *Sobr.* 11 (52): ἔφαμεν πάλαι ὅτι Σήμ ἐπώνυμός ἐστιν ἀγαθοῦ. Between *Gig.* / *Deus* and *Agric.* he also inserted the two lost books περὶ διαθηκῶν to which

77. For details of subsequent textual work by Tischendorf, Wendland and Holwerda see C-W vol. II, pp. xix ff.

78. For *Poster.* in Cod. Athen. 880 see P. Alexander, 'A Neglected Palimpsest', pp. 10–11 (n. 36 above).

79. See J. Royse, 'The Oxyrhynchus Papyrus', p. 159, n. 8.

80. Five references are given in C-W vol. II, nn. to pp. 5, 6, 13, 21, 31.

81. C-W vol. II, pp. 42–5, 55–94; Loeb Philo II-III (1929–30); A. Mosès, *De Gigantibus, Quod Deus Sit Immutabilis* (*Oeuvres* VII-VIII, 1963). See esp. D. Winston and J. Dillon, *Two Treatises of Philo of Alexandria : A Commentary on De Gigantibus and Quod Deus Sit Immutabilis* (1983). For *Gig.* and *Deus* in Cod. Athen. 880 see P. Alexander, 'A Neglected Palimpsest' (n. 36 above).

82. See C-W vol. II, nn. to pp. 57, 65, 66, 67, 70, 71 and xxi.

83. See Harris, *Fragments*, p. 9; C-W vol. II, p. xxii, n. 1.

Philo refers in *Mutat.* (see below, p. 839).[84]

De agricultura (Περὶ γεωργίας)
On Gen. 9:20a.

De plantatione Noe (Περὶ φυτουργίας Νῶε τὸ δεύτερον)[85]
On Gen. 9:20b.

These are probably to be considered as the two books περὶ γεωργίας to which Eusebius refers, *H.E.* ii 18, 2 (cf. Jerome, *De vir. ill.* 11 : 'de agricultura duo'). Eusebius, *Praep. ev.* vii 13, 3–4: ἐν τῷ περὶ γεωγίας προτέρῳ ... ἐν τῷ δευτέρῳ. The end of the second book is perhaps missing, for at 37 (149) Philo announces that he intends to discuss the two opposing views ὅτι ὁ σοφὸς μεθυσθήσεται and ὅτι οὐ μεθυσθήσεται, but the plan is only carried out for the first view, 37 (150)–42 (175). For the second view, only the πρῶτος καὶ δυνατώτατος λόγος is presented in 42 (176), and the rest appears to be missing.[86]

De ebrietate (Περὶ μέθης)[87]
On Gen. 9:21. According to Eusebius, *H.E.* ii 18, 2 and Jerome, *De vir. ill.* 11, Philo wrote two books περὶ μέθης. It is disputed whether the extant book is the first or second. Neither the internal evidence from the treatises themselves, nor the labels in the manuscripts and the *Sacra Parallela* are entirely conclusive. The oldest evidence, from a papyrus, seems to indicate that the extant book is the second.[88]

84. *Le Classement*, pp. 21–3; C-W vol. II, p. xxii; Cohn, 'Einteilung', pp. 397, 430–1.

85. C-W vol. II, pp. 95–132, 133–69; Loeb Philo III (1930); J. Pouilloux, *De agricultura* (*Oeuvres* IX, 1961); *idem, De plantatione* (*Oeuvres* X, 1963). See H. von Arnim, *Quellenstudien zu Philo von Alexandria* (1888), pp. 101–40 (for Philo's philosophic sources); R. G. Hamerton-Kelly, 'Some Techniques of Composition in Philo's Allegorical Commentary with Special Reference to *De Agricultura*—A Study on the Hellenistic Midrash', in *Jews, Greeks and Christians. Religious Cultures in Late Antiquity*, ed. R. G. Hamerton-Kelly and R. Scroggs (1976), pp. 45–56.

86. See C-W vol. II, p. xxvii. For *Agric.* in Cod. Athen. 880 see P. Alexander, 'A Neglected Palimpsest' (n. 36 above).

87. C-W vol. II, pp. 170–214; Loeb Philo III (1930); J. Gorez, *De ebrietate. De sobrietate* (*Oeuvres* XI-XII, 1962). See H. von Arnim, *Quellenstudien*, pp. 101–40; M. Adler, 'Bemerkungen zu Philos Schrift περὶ μέθης', Wiener Studien 42 (1922–3), pp. 92–6; 44 (1924–5), pp. 220–3; 45 (1926–7), pp. 117–20; 245–8.

Ebr. 8–11; 11–13; 14; 17–18; 219–21; 221–3 is on P.Oxy. IX, no. 1173; *Ebr.* 223 is on PSI XI, no. 1207; *Ebr.* 1–4, 4–8 is on P.Haun., no. 8. For *Ebr.* in Cod. Athen. 880 see P. Alexander, 'A Neglected Palimpsest' (n. 36).

88. The arguments for supposing the extant book to be the first are: (1) The opening words of our book, τὰ μὲν τοῖς ἄλλοις φιλοσόφοις εἰρημένα περὶ μέθης, ὡς οἶόν τε ἦν, ἐν τῇ πρὸ ταυτῆς ὑπεμνήσαμεν βίβλῳ refer to the conclusion of *Plant.* (2) Near the beginning of our book, 2 (4), an outline of the topic is presented, from which one expects that the final subject for discussion will be wine as σύμβολον εὐφροσύνης and γυμνότητος. Since these sections are not present in the argument, it might be argued that they formed the lost second book, a commentary on Gen. 9:21b–23. The opening of the following treatise, *Sobr.*, appears to confirm this: τὰ περὶ μέθης καὶ τῆς ἐπομένης αὐτῇ γυμνότητος εἰρημένα τῷ νομοθέτῃ διεξεληλυθότες πρότερον. See Massebieau, *Le Classement*, pp. 24 ff.; and esp. C-W

De sobrietate (Περὶ τοῦ ἐξένηψε Νῶε)[89]
On Gen. 9:24–27. The unusual brevity of this treatise has led to the suggestion that a considerable part of it is missing.[90] Cohn thought that *Sobr.* and *Confus.* originally formed one book.[91] This supposition gains support from the fact that in the *Sacra Parallela* a sentence from *Confus.* is cited with the formula ἐκ τοῦ περὶ τοῦ νήψας ὁ νοῦς εὔχεται.[92]

De confusione linguarum (Περὶ συγχύσεως διαλέκτων)[93]
On Gen. 11:1–9. Eusebius quotes several passages from this work in *Praep. ev.* xi 15, with the erroneous statement that they are from περὶ τοῦ τὸ χεῖρον τῷ κρείττονι φιλεῖν ἐπιτίθεσθαι.

De migratione Abrahami (Περὶ ἀποικίας)[94]
On Gen. 12:1–6.

Quis rerum divinarum heres sit (Περὶ τοῦ τίς ὁ τῶν θείων πραγμάτων κληρονόμος)[95]
On Gen. 15:2–18.

---

vol. II, pp. xxvi-viii; M. Adler, *Studien* (1929), pp. 53–66. The evidence afforded by the *Sacra Parallela* is not decisive, since it proves that another (lost) book existed, but the lemmata are unreliable; see C-W, *loc. cit.* The texts are given by P. Wendland, *Neu entdeckte Fragmente Philos* (1891), pp. 22–5 (but 9 and 11 should be discounted; see J. Royse, 'The Oxyrhynchus Papyrus', p. 161, n. 10). However, the evidence from the papyrus appears to prove the opposite view, since at P.Haun. fol. 2ʳ, just before the beginning of *Ebr.*, there is [...] β′, which appears to be designating the extant book as the second; see T. Larsen, *P.Haun.* I, p. 50. P.Oxy., fr. 4 and P.Haun., fr. 1, would then be fragments of the lost book i. See further J. Royse, *art. cit.*, pp. 160–1.

89. C-W vol. II, pp. 215–28; Loeb Philo III (1930), pp. 437–81; J. Gorez, *op. cit.* For *Sobr.* in Cod. Athen. 880 see P. Alexander, 'A Neglected Palimpsest' (n. 36 above). Instead of the title given here, Eusebius, *H.E.* ii 18, 2, has περὶ ὧν νήψας ὁ νοῦς εὔχεται καὶ καταρᾶται. Jerome, *De vir. ill.* 11 has: 'de his quae sensu precamur et detestamur'. Similarly two of the four manuscripts (including Cod. Athen. 880) and the Cod. Coisl. of the *Sacra Parallela*; see C-W vol. II, p. xxx and n. to p. 261. Cod. Athen. 880 gives the fullest version of the title: πε(ρὶ) ὧν νήψας ὁ νοῦς εὔχεται καὶ καταρᾶται κ(αὶ) πε(ρὶ) ἰσχύος...ίας (P. Alexander, 'A Neglected Palimpsest', p. 5). Only one manuscript has the title given above, περὶ τοῦ ἐξένηψε Νῶε, which has prevailed in the editions (see C-W, n. to p. 215). Another has Νῶε in the margin. Despite the weak attestation, Νῶε is probably to be taken into the title in view of the fact that Philo does not usually indicate the allegorical interpretation in the titles.

90. Massebieau, *Le Classement*, p. 25; C-W vol. II, p. xxxi.

91. 'Einteilung', p. 399.

92. C-W vol. II, p. 261, n.

93. C-W vol. II, pp. 229–67; Loeb Philo IV (1932), pp. 1–119; J.-G. Kahn, *De confusione linguarum* (*Oeuvres* XIII, 1963). For *Confus.* in Cod. Athen. 880 see P. Alexander, 'A Neglected Palimpsest' (n. 36 above). The same title is found in Eusebius, *H.E.* ii 18, 2.

94. C-W vol. II, pp. 268–314; Loeb Philo IV (1932), pp. 121–267; R. Cadiou, *La migration d'Abraham* (SC XLVII, 1957); J. Cazeaux, *De migratione Abrahami* (*Oeuvres* XIV, 1965). See *idem*, *La trame et la chaîne ou les Structures littéraires et l'Éxégèse dans cinq des Traités de Philon d'Alexandrie* (1983), pp. 38–152. The same title is found in Eusebius, *H.E.* ii 18, 4.

95. C-W vol. III, pp. 1–71; Loeb Philo IV (1932), pp. 269–447; M. Harl, *Quis rerum*

In Codex Berolinensis gr. 46 (Rupefucaldinus) fol. 137ʳ this treatise is cited with the formula ἐκ τοῦ περὶ κοσμοποιίας, which led some scholars to conclude that this was a more comprehensive title under which a considerable number of Philo's writings were subsumed. But more probably it is merely an error of citation, for this passage is adduced in the same manuscript fol. 44ᵛ with the correct formula τίς ἐστιν ὁ τῶν θείων κληρονόμος.[96] In the prologue of this book, reference is made to an earlier work in the words ἐν μὲν τῇ πρὸ ταύτης βίβλῳ περὶ μισθῶν ὡς ἐνῆν ἐπ' ἀκριβείας διεξήλθομεν. This treatise is not *Migr.*, since this does not deal with rewards but with δωρεαί, Gen. 12:1–3. The περὶ μισθῶν was probably the commentary on Gen. 15:1 which has not survived.[97]

De congressu eruditionis causa (Περὶ τῆς πρὸς τὰ προπαιδεύματα συνόδου)[98] On Gen. 16:1–6. This treatise is of great importance for its use of allegory,[99] the view of παιδεία and for Philo's conception of wisdom in general. Its influence on Christian thinkers was considerable,

---

divinarum heres sit (*Oeuvres* XV, 1966). See D. Hay, 'Philo's Treatise on the Logos-Cutter', SP 2 (1973), pp. 9–22; J. Cazeaux, *op. cit.*, pp. 154–354. *Heres* has survived on most of the Philo manuscripts and on the papyrus from Coptos; see M. Harl, *op. cit.*, pp. 154–7. Eusebius, *H.E.* ii 18, 2, gives the title περὶ τοῦ τίς ὁ τῶν θείων ἐστὶ κληρονόμος ἢ περὶ τῆς εἰς τὰ ἴσα καὶ ἐναντία τομῆς. Jerome, *De vir. ill.* 11, makes two works out of this double title: 'De herede divinarum rerum liber unus, De divisione aequalium et contrariorum liber.' Cf. the Suda s.v. Φίλων. The Coptos papyrus gives exactly the same title, in its superscription, as that of the Greek manuscripts of Eusebius. The same title is found once in the *Sacra Parallela* (Cod. Reg. 923: Harris, *Fragments*, p. 91; see C-W vol. III, p. 14, n.) and in some of the manuscripts. In other manuscripts and in most of the quotations in the *Sacra Parallela* the second half of the title is omitted (see C-W, nn. to pp. 2, 3, 22, 24). The linking of the two halves by καί is probably more correct than by ἤ (so only Eusebius and the papyrus), since the treatise deals first with the one theme, then with the other (C-W vol. III, p. xvi). See also M. Harl, *op. cit.*, pp. 18–19.

96. See e.g. Mangey, I, p. 473, n. On other errors of citation see C-W vol. III, p. xvi, n. 3.

97. See Massebieau, *Le Classement*, pp. 27 ff., n.; L. Cohn, 'Einteilung', p. 400; M. Harl, *op. cit.*, p. 18, n. 1.

98. C-W vol. III, pp. 72–109; Loeb Philo IV (1932), pp. 449–551; M. Alexandre, *De congressu eruditionis causa* (*Oeuvres* XVI, 1967). See P. Borgen, *Bread from Heaven* (1965), pp. 99–121; J. Cazeaux, *op. cit.*, pp. 356–80; B. L. Mack, 'Weisheit und Allegorie bei Philo von Alexandrien: Untersuchungen zum Traktat *De Congressu eruditionis*', SP 5 (1978), pp. 57–105; A. Mendelson, *Secular Education in Philo of Alexandria* (1982).

In Eusebius, *H.E.* ii 18, 2, the title runs: περὶ τῆς πρὸς τὰ παιδεύματα συνόδου. But the προπαιδεύματα transmitted in the manuscripts of Philo is to be preferred, for the fact that Abraham first consorted with Hagar before he had offspring by Sarah means, according to Philo, that a man must first make himself familiar with the lower propaedeutic sciences before he can ascend to the higher wisdom, and obtain the fruits of it in the form of virtue. Cf. also Philo's own reference in the prologue of the next book, *Fug.*: εἰρηκότες ἐν τῷ προτέρῳ τὰ πρέποντα περὶ τῶν προπαιδευμάτων καὶ περὶ κακώσεως. For the conventional Latin title see Colson, Loeb IV, p. 449.

99. On the importance of Philo's use of allegory see pp. 876–8 below.

particularly in the context of the relationship between the Church and classical culture.[100]

De fuga et inventione (Περὶ φυγῆς καὶ εὑρέσεως)[101]
On Gen. 16:6–14. *Fug.*, like *Congr.*, represents many of the characteristic features of Philo's philosophic and religious outlook, being concerned principally with the relationship between man and God. This treatise was used extensively by Ambrose in *De fuga saeculi*.[102]

De mutatione nominum (Περὶ τῶν μετανομαζομένων)[103]
On Gen. 17:1–22. At 6 (53) Philo refers to a work now lost: τὸν δὲ περὶ διαθηκῶν σύμπαντα λόγον ἐν δύσιν ἀναγέγραφα συντάξεσιν. This work was already missing in Eusebius' time: *H.E.* ii 18, 3.[104]

De deo[105]
On Gen. 18:2.

De somniis i and ii (Περὶ τοῦ θεοπέμπτους εἶναι τοὺς ὀνείρους)[106]
On Gen. 28:12 ff. and 31:11 ff. (the two dreams of Jacob) and Gen. 37

100. See M. Alexandre, *op. cit.*, pp. 83–97.

101. C-W vol. III, pp. 110–55; Loeb Philo V (1934), pp. 1–125; E. Starobinski-Safran, *De fuga et inventione* (*Oeuvres* XVII, 1970); J. Cazeaux, *op. cit.*, pp. 381–473. *Fug.* is extant in two manuscripts only. Venetus gr. 40 has the title περὶ φυγάδων which was given in the editions before C-W. The title above, περὶ φυγῆς καὶ εὑρέσεως, is given in Palatinus 248; cf. Eusebius, *H.E.* ii 18, 2, and the *Sacra Parallela* (see C-W vol. III, nn. to pp. 141, 143, 146). This is certainly the correct title, for the treatise deals with the flight and finding of Hagar. Eusebius' title soon underwent corruption. Jerome was already reading φύσεως for φυγῆς (*de natura et inventione*). Nicephorus has the double title ὁ περὶ φυγῆς καὶ αἱρέσεως· ἔτι δὲ ὁ περὶ φύσεως καὶ εὑρέσεως. See E. Starobinski-Safran, *op. cit.*, pp. 30–3.

102. CSEL XXXII.1.

103. C-W vol. III, pp. 156–203; Loeb Philo V (1934), pp. 127–281; R. Arnaldez, C. Mondésert and J. Pouilloux, *De mutatione nominum* (*Oeuvres* XVIII, 1964); J. Cazeaux, *op. cit.*, pp. 475–580. The title is the same in Eusebius, *H.E.* ii 18, 3. In the *Sacra Parallela* the treatise is frequently cited with the lemma ἐκ τοῦ περὶ τῶν μετανομαζομένων or ἐκ τῶν μετανομαζομένων. See C-W vol. III, p. xviii, nn. to pp. 157, 158, 160, 163, 164, 165, 166, 185, 188, 193, 194, 198. Sometimes this lemma is used erroneously with passages from other treatises of Philo. See Harris, *Fragments*, pp. 24 ff. (one passage in *Quaest. Gen.* and another in *Leg.* iii).

104. In *Quaest. Ex.* ii 34 (Aucher, p. 493), Philo refers to an earlier discussion *De divino testamento*. This could be another reference to the lost work περὶ διαθηκῶν (see C-W vol. II, p. xxii; Massebieau, *Le Classement*, p. 23); but it might equally well refer to an earlier (and lost) chapter of the *Quaestiones*.

105. Among the works surviving only in Armenian is a small fragment *De Deo*, giving an exposition of Genesis 18:2 (Aucher II, pp. 613–19 = Richter VII, pp. 409–14). Massebieau considered this to be a fragment of the lost commentary on Gen. 18 ff., which would have occupied this position in the *Allegorical Commentary*; see Massebieau, *Le Classement*, p. 29; see M. Adler, 'Das philonische Fragment De deo', MGWJ 80 (1936), pp. 163–70; M. Harl, 'Cosmologie grecque et représentations juives chez Philon', in *Philon d'Alexandrie*, ed. R. Arnaldez (1967), pp. 191–203; F. Siegert, *Drei hellenistisch-jüdische Predigten* (1980), pp. 84–93.

106. C-W vol. III, pp. 204–58, 259–306; Loeb Philo V (1934), pp. 283–579; P. Savinel, *De somniis I-II* (*Oeuvres* XIX, 1962). See P. Wendland, 'Eine doxographische

and 40–1 (the dreams of Joseph, Pharaoh's chief butler and chief baker, and Pharaoh himself). According to Eusebius, *H.E.* ii 18, 4, and Jerome, *De vir ill.* 11, Philo wrote five books on dreams, so three must be lost. From the beginning of the extant books, it appears that Philo distinguished three types of dreams.[107] The extant books deal with the second and third kinds. Our first book was preceded by another, in which τὸ πρῶτον εἶδος was discussed, namely those dreams in which God himself speaks with the dreamer. This would be a suitable context for the dream of Abimelech in Gen. 20:3, which might, therefore, have been dealt with here.[108] Nothing certain can be stated with regard to the content of the remaining lost books.[109] The section on Jacob's ladder (Gen. 28:12 ff.) from the first of the extant books is mentioned by Origen, *C. Celsum* vi 21.

The Exposition

The third main group of Philo's writings on the Pentateuch is a systematic presentation of the Mosaic legislation.[110] Allegorical interpretation is, in fact, occasionally used in this group as a whole as well as in the *Allegory of the Laws*. But in the main, these are genuinely historical descriptions: a systematic exposition of the great legislative work of Moses, whose content, value and significance the author intends to clarify, probably for a wider readership than was envisaged for the *Allegorical Commentary*. For the presentation here is more popular, while the great *Allegorical Commentary* is an esoteric work.[111]

Quelle Philos', SAB (1897), pp. 1074–9. For *Somn.* in Cod. Athen. 880 see P. Alexander, 'A Neglected Palimpsest' (n. 36 above). For the chronological issues surrounding *Somn.* see below, p. 843.

107. Philo was probably influenced by the Stoic classification here. According to Cicero, *De Div.* i 64, Posidonius 'tribus modis censet deorum adpulsu homines somniare, uno quod provideat animus ipse per sese, quippe qui deorum cognatione teneatur, altero, quod plenus aer sit inmortalium animorum, in quibus tamquam insignitae notae veritatis appareant, tertio, quod ipsi di cum hominibus colloquantur.' Cf. *Somn.* i 1–2; ii 1–2. See Colson, Loeb Philo V, pp. 593–4; M. Petit, 'Les songes dans l'oeuvre de Philon d'Alexandrie', in *Mélanges d'histoire des religions offerts à Henri-Charles Puech* (1974), pp. 151–9. For bibliography on the influence of Stoicism (including Posidonius) on Philo, see below, pp. 872–3, n. 9.

108. So Massebieau, *Le Classement*, p. 30.

109. Massebieau, *Le Classement*, p. 31, suggested that Philo dealt with the views of other philosophers about dreams in two preceding books, making the two extant books the fourth and fifth. Cf. *idem*, 'Essai', pp. 34–69, 164–70; C-W vol. III, pp. xix ff.; L. Cohn, 'Einteilung', p. 402.

110. On the general character of this series (known by convention as the *Exposition*) see S. Sandmel, *Philo of Alexandria* (1979), pp. 47–76; E. R. Goodenough, 'Philo's Exposition of the Law and the De Vita Mosis', HThR 26 (1933), pp. 109–25; *By Light, Light!*, esp. pp. 121–52.

111. The distinction between the *Allegorical Commentary* as an esoteric and the *Exposition* as an exoteric work is widely accepted, but Goodenough's further argument that the treatises forming the *Exposition* were written for gentiles lacks sufficient evidence. This

The treatises constituting this group are varied, and seem to be independent works, grouped together. Philo's own statements put it beyond doubt, however, that they belong together and form a coherent work.[112] As to its construction, the *Exposition* falls into three parts. (a) The beginning, which also constitutes an introduction to the group, comprises a description of the creation of the world (*Opif.*).[113] Moses set this at the beginning because his legislation was truly in conformity with nature, adjusting itself to the order of nature. He who follows it acts πρὸς τὸ βούλημα τῆς φύσεως. Thus in the first place the order of nature itself is described, as it came into existence through the Creation.

This introduction is followed by (b) the narratives of the lives of virtuous men (*Abr., Jos.*). These appeared in history before the revelation of the written law, for they are the unwritten laws, so to speak (ἔμψυχοι καὶ λογικοὶ νόμοι, *Abr.* 1 (5); νόμοι ἄγραφοι, *Dec.* 1 (1)).[114] As distinct from the written particular laws, these represent general ethical norms (τοὺς καθολικωτέρους καὶ ὡσὰν ἀρχετύπους νόμους, *Abr.* 1 (3)). Finally, the third part is formed by (c) the description of the legislation proper, which again falls into two divisions: (1) the description of the ten principal components of the Law (*Dec.*), and (2) the description of the Special Laws which belong to each of these ten principal components (*Spec.*). By way of appendix, there then follow a couple of treatises about some cardinal virtues and about the rewards of the good and the punishment of the wicked (*Virt., Praem.*).

This survey of the contents of the series also serves to show that it is Philo's intention to present his readers with the entire content of the Pentateuch, complete in all its essentials, in a lucid exposition. His conception is, however, an authentically Jewish one, in that for him all this falls under the notion of νόμος.[115]

Opinions still differ widely as to the chronological relationship

---

assumption underlies all of Goodenough's work; see especially 'Philo's Exposition of the Law', HThR 27 (1933), pp. 109–25; *Politics*, pp. 42–63 (comparing *Somn.* and *Jos.*). On the question of audience see further p. 817 above and p. 889 below.

112. Cross-references and programmatic statements testify to the overall design of the work; see e.g. below, p. 842.

113. For the controversy over the position of *Opif.* see above, p. 832, and below, pp. 844–5.

114. On the notion of νόμος ἔμψυχος see E. R. Goodenough, 'The Political Philosophy of Hellenistic Kingship', YCS 1 (1928), pp. 53–102. On ἄγραφος νόμος see R. Hirzel, ''Αγραφος νόμος', Abhandl. der philolog.-hist. Classe der König. Sächsischen Gesellsch. der Wiss. XXI (1900); J. Heinemann, 'Die Lehre vom ungeschriebenen Gesetz', HUCA 4 (1927), pp. 149–71; E. M. Smallwood, *Philonis Alexandrini Legatio ad Gaium* (1961), pp. 208–9; A. Mosès, *De Specialibus Legibus* (*Oeuvres* XXV, 1970), pp. 360–1.

115. On Philo's conception of νόμος in relation to the Mosaic Law see V. Nikiprowetzky, *Le Commentaire*, pp. 117–55; E. R. Goodenough, *By Light, Light!*, pp. 48–94, 370–413. On Philo and Halakha see below, p. 874.

between the *Exposition* and the *Allegorical Commentary*.[116] Of those who
have attempted to piece together a relative chronology for Philo's
works, Cohn, whose views are generally accepted, considered the
Allegorical Commentary to be the earlier work;[117] Massebieau, postulating
an intellectual evolution for Philo, preferred the reverse order.[118] The
criteria for determining the order are twofold: internal references in
Philo's text to other works—references which are often ambiguous—
and assessments of the character of the works, together with some
assumption of an intellectual development. Much also depends on the
interpretation of Philo's reference to his own political involvement in
Spec. iii.[119] Reconstruction of a sequence is precarious in that a decision
on such questions as the position of *Opif.* or of the relationship of *Vita
Mosis* to the *Exposition*[120] can vitiate the whole schema.

Cohn based his opinion that the *Allegorical Commentary* preceded the
Exposition principally upon two cross-references in the text. Firstly, in
Dec. 20 (101)—part of the *Exposition*—Philo refers to an allegorical
interpretation of the Creation story given earlier ($\mu\epsilon\mu\dot\eta\nu\upsilon\tau\alpha\iota$ $\delta\iota\dot\alpha$ $\tau\hat\omega\nu$
$\dot\alpha\lambda\lambda\eta\gamma\upsilon\rho\eta\theta\dot\epsilon\nu\tau\omega\nu$ $\dot\epsilon\nu$ $\dot\epsilon\tau\dot\epsilon\rho o\iota\varsigma$). But this may refer to *Opif.*, just as well as to
the *Allegorical Commentary*, and *Opif.* belongs, most probably, to the
Exposition. Secondly, in *Sacr.* 40 (136) he expresses the intention of
dealing later in detail with the prescriptions in Lev. 3:3 ff. This may
however very well refer to a *projected* section of the *Allegorical Commentary*,

---

116. On the order and chronology of Philo's works the most important early studies
were A. Gfrörer, *Philo und die jüdisch-alexandrinische Theosophie* I ([2]1835), pp. 1–113; A. F.
Dähne, 'Einige Bemerkungen über die Schriften des Juden Philo, angeknüpft an eine
Untersuchung über deren ursprüngliche Anordnung', ThStKr 6 (1883), pp. 984–1040;
C. Grossmann, *De Philonis Judaei operum continua serie et ordine chronologico commentatio*
(1841–2); H. Ewald, *Geschichte des Volkes Israël* VI (1868), pp. 257–312; C. Siegfried,
'Abhandlung zur Kritik der Schriften Philos', ZWTh 17 (1874), pp. 562–6. Now
fundamental are L. Cohn, 'Einteilung und Chronologie der Schriften Philos', Philologus,
Suppl.-Bd. 7 (1899), pp. 389–436; L. Massebieau, *Le classement des oeuvres de Philon*
(*Bibliothèque de l'École Practique des Hautes Etudes, Sciences Religieuses* I, 1889), pp. 1–91; L.
Massebieau and E. Bréhier, 'Essai sur la chronologie de la vie et des oeuvres de Philon',
RHR 53 (1906), pp. 25–64, 164–85, 267–89; M. Adler, *Studien zu Philo von Alexandreia*
(1929), pp. 66–72 (criticism of Massebieau on chronology of *Legum Allegoria*). See also W.
Völker, *Fortschritt und Vollendung* (1938), pp. 16–18, esp. n. 2. The issues and literature
(including subsequent contributions, chiefly made in the context of other topics) are
surveyed in V. Nikiprowetzky, *Le Commentaire*, pp. 192–235. For a refutation of the view
that Philo wrote philosophical works in his youth, later turning to theological exegesis in
maturity, see A. Terian, ANRW II.21.1, pp. 292–4.

117. L. Cohn, 'Einteilung', pp. 432–4.

118. Massebieau, 'Essai', pp. 24–64, 164–70 (on the context of the *Exposition*); pp.
170–85 (on the context of the *Allegorical Commentary*); pp. 267–79 (on the relationship
between the two works in the context of Philo's attitudes towards political life).

119. See below, pp. 843, 849–50.

120. On these issues see below, pp. 844–5 (*Opif.*), and pp. 854–5 (*Mos.*). Grossmann's
position is generally considered erroneous because of his views on these two treatises.

and does not prove that the *Exposition* followed later.[121]

Massebieau, whose studies were edited after his death by Bréhier, attached little importance to the cross-references in Philo, since they are generally ambiguous and never specific.[122] Instead, he produced a painstaking and penetrating analysis aimed at discovering the circumstances underlying the two groups of writings. In the *Exposition*, the beginning of *Spec.* iii is particularly crucial:[123] here Philo complains bitterly that he, who otherwise concerned himself with philosophy, has been drawn into political life through the unhappy circumstances of the time (εἰς μέγα πέλαγος τῶν ἐν πολιτείᾳ φροντίδων). There are also possible references to persecutions of the Jews in later sections of the *Exposition* (e.g. *Spec.* iv 178–86; *Praem.* 169–72 (*Exsecr.* 8)).

Massebieau connects these allusions with the early period of Tiberius, when, under the influence of the all-powerful Sejanus, measures were adopted against the Jews.[124] Massebieau divides treatises of the *Allegorical Commentary* into four groups, according to whether they reflect times of peace or periods of hostility. The first books, up to and including *Gig.* and *Deus*, belong to a tranquil period, namely from the fall of Sejanus to the death of Tiberius (A.D. 31–7). The second group, he postulates, would belong in the period of persecution under Caligula, the third in the peaceful time under Claudius, while in his opinion the books *De Somniis* precede all the others in the *Allegorical Commentary*, and ought to be placed as early as the time of Sejanus.[125] Massebieau finds confirmation for his chronological reconstructions in the attitudes in the two main groups of writings towards political life. In consequence of his practical experiences, it is suggested, Philo set a higher value upon political life than he had earlier. It now became a necessary means for ascending to what he always regarded as the highest level: the 'contemplative life'. The earlier point of view is expressed in the *Exposition*, the later in the *Allegorical Commentary*.[126]

It is open to question, however, whether there really is such a difference between the two main groups of works in their assessment of the political life.[127] A more fundamental weakness of Massebieau's position is the fact that he is compelled to assume harassment and oppression of the Jews in the first period of Tiberius in order to explain the bitter complaint at the beginning of *Spec.* iii and the allusions to

121. See, against Cohn's view, Massebieau, 'Essai', pp. 286 ff.

122. There is a brief consideration of the cross-references at the end of the study, pp. 284–7. For a summary of what can reasonably be deduced from cross-references see V. Nikiprowetzky, *Le Commentaire*, pp. 194–5.

123. See below, pp. 849–50.

124. 'Essai', p. 64.

125. *Ibid.*, pp. 174–80.

126. *Ibid.*, pp. 267–79.

127. See above, n. 23, and below, n. 129.

persecution in the later sections of the work. But such oppression is only attested in respect of the Jews of Rome, not of Alexandrian Jews.[128] The Jews of Alexandria had no known reason to be dissatisfied with the government of Tiberius. The troubles under Gaius, on the other hand, did force Philo to take part in political life: he had to travel to Rome at the head of a Jewish embassy (vol. I, pp. 390–8; above, p. 816). This is a suitable background to explain the complaints in *Spec.* iii.[129] If this passage is taken to refer to the stormy years in Alexandria described in *Flacc.* and *Legat.*, then the last sections of the *Exposition* at least would have been written late in Philo's life. It might then be suggested that Philo could hardly have produced the *Allegorical Commentary* after these remaining works in the *Exposition*, at so late a stage of life.[130]

De opificio mundi (Περὶ τῆς κατὰ Μωϋσέα κοσμοποιΐας)[131]
By convention, this treatise is placed at the beginning of Philo's works in the editions, before *Leg.* i.[132] Although *Opif.* can usefully be read as the introduction to the *Allegorical Commentary*, and some still maintain that Philo intended it to be considered as such, there are good grounds for linking it closely with *Abr.*, and placing it at the head of the

128. See E. M. Smallwood, 'Some Notes on the Jews under Tiberius', Latomus 15 (1956), pp. 314–29; *idem, Philonis Alexandrini Legatio ad Gaium* (1961), pp. 243–4; *idem, The Jews under Roman Rule* (1976), pp. 200–16. Cf. E. T. Merrill, 'The expulsion of the Jews from Rome under Tiberius', CPh 14 (1919), pp. 365–72; E. C. Abel, 'Were the Jews Banished from Rome in 19 A.D.?', REJ 127 (1968), pp. 383–6. See above, pp. 75–6.

129. So Cohn, 'Einteilung', pp. 433 ff. Goodenough, seeing Philo's involvement in political life as more or less continuous, considered this reference as occasioned by the context of the treatise rather than by contemporary biographical circumstances; see 'Philo and Public Life', JEA 12 (1926), pp. 77–9; cf. *The Jurisprudence of the Jewish Courts in Egypt* (1929, repr. 1968), p. 9; *Politics*, pp. 66–8. It has also been suggested that the passage is entirely literary, and as such provides no evidence either for Philo's career or for the relative chronology of his works. See Colson, Loeb VII, pp. 631–2; A. Mosès, *De Specialibus Legibus III et IV (Oeuvres* XXV, 1970), pp. 11 and 52–4, nn. 1–2.

130. The 'philosophical' treatises do seem to have been written in Philo's old age, however; see A. Terian, *Philonis Alexandrini De Animalibus* (1981), p. 34; *idem*, ANRW II.21.1, pp. 291–4. This raises the possibility that Philo accomplished most of his writing as an elderly man. See further A. Terian, ANRW II.21.1, pp. 292–4.

131. C-W vol. I, pp. 1–60; Loeb Philo I (1929), pp. 1–137; R. Arnaldez, *De opificio mundi (Oeuvres* I, 1961). Cf. J. G. Müller, *Des Juden Philo Buch von der Weltschöpfung* (1841); L. Cohn, *Philonis Alexandrini libellus de opificio mundi* (1889, repr. 1967); C. Kraus Reggiani, *Filone Alessandrino. De opificio mundi. De Abrahamo. De Josepho* (1979), pp. 19–50. Note E. Grumach, 'Zur Quellenfrage von Philos De opificio mundi §1–3', MGWJ 83, NF 47 (1939), pp. 126–31; P. Boyancé, 'Études philoniennes', REG 76 (1963), pp. 64–110. Instead of κατὰ Μωϋσέα the majority of the manuscripts wrongly give Μωϋσέως. The correct reading was restored by Cohn from Codex Vindobonensis and the *Sacra Parallela* (see C-W vol. I, p. lxxxv).

132. It is placed at the head of the *Exposition* in L. Cohn et al., *Die Werke Philos*, however. The problem is surveyed in V. Nikiprowetzky, *Le Commentaire*, pp. 197–9; cf. R. Arnaldez, *op. cit.*, pp. 124–5.

Exposition.[133] As has been suggested above (p. 832), the character of *Opif.* distinguishes it from the *Allegorical Commentary*, and the prologue of the treatise itself indicates that it was conceived as an introduction to the exposition of the legislation. The strongest grounds for placing *Opif.* at the head of the *Exposition* are the words at the beginning of *Abr.*: ὃν μὲν οὖν τρόπον ἡ κοσμοποιΐα διατέτακται, διὰ τῆς προτέρας συντάξεως, ὡς οἷόν τε ἦν, ἠκριβώσαμεν. It is impossible to relate this remark to the entire *Allegorical Commentary*, rather than to *Opif.*, both because of the expression κοσμοποιΐα and also because of the singular διὰ τῆς προτέρας συντάξεως. The matter is further complicated by the fact that *Opif.* seems to have been set at the head of the *Allegorical Commentary* at some time in antiquity (some say by Philo himself) to replace a missing commentary on Gen. 1. This might account for the fact that Eusebius (*Praep. Ev.* viii 12, 384d, ed. Gifford) cites a passage from this document with the formula ἀπὸ τοῦ πρώτου τῶν εἰς τὸν νόμον. It would also explain the omission of *Opif.* in the catalogue of Eusebius, *H.E.* ii 18, insofar as he understands it to be one part of the νόμων ἱερῶν ἀλληγορία; likewise the strange formulae of citation mentioned above (ἐκ τοῦ ζ' καὶ η' / η' καὶ θ' τῆς νόμων ἱερῶν ἀλληγορίας; see pp. 834–5 above).[134]

133. Cf. V. Nikiprowetzky, *op. cit.*, p. 199.

134. Cohn, 'Einteilung', p. 407, however understood Eusebius at this point to be citing *Opif.* quite correctly as the first book of the *Exposition*. But the phrase εἰς τὸν νόμον must mean that Eusebius was referring to the *Commentary* on the Law. Eusebius gives another citation from *Opif.*, introducing it with the lemma λέγει δ' οὖν ὁ Ἑβραῖος Φίλων τὰ πάτρια διερμηνεύων αὐτοῖς ῥήμασιν (*Praep. ev.* xi 23–4). Siegfried's theory was that the *Allegory* was interpolated between *Opif.* and *Abr.* by Philo himself. See 'Philo und der überlieferte Text der LXX', ZWTh 16 (1873), pp. 217–38, 411–28, 522–40; cf. V. Nikiprowetzky, *Le Commentaire*, pp. 199–200. The arrangement of the two major series of Philo's works would thus take the following form: (1) Creation of the world (*Opif.*); (2) *Allegorical Commentary*; (3) Legislation (*Exposition*). Two passages have been taken to suggest this arrangement. (a) *Mos.* ii 8 (46–7), where it is said of the Holy Scriptures which Moses composed: τούτων τοίνυν τὸ μὲν ἱστορικὸν μέρος, τὸ δὲ περὶ τὰς προστάξεις καὶ ἀπαγορεύσεις, ὑπὲρ οὗ δεύτερον λέξομεν τὸ πρότερον τῇ τάξει πρότερον ἀκριβώσαντες. ἔστιν οὖν τοῦ ἱστορικοῦ τὸ μὲν περὶ τῆς τοῦ κόσμου γενέσεως, τὸ δὲ γενεαλογικόν, τοῦ δὲ γενεαλογικοῦ τὸ μὲν περὶ κολάσεως ἀσεβῶν, τὸ δ' αὖ περὶ τιμῆς δικαίων. Here Philo divides the contents of the Mosaic writings initially into two groups, the historical and the legislative. He then says that he will treat the latter, having already treated the former in some detail. It might be argued that the ἱστορικὸν μέρος refers to the *Allegorical Commentary*, since the βίοι σοφῶν treat only of the good, not good and bad. This statement would then indicate that the delineation of the Mosaic legislation was later than the *Allegorical Commentary*. He goes on to subdivide the historical section into two: (1) περὶ τῆς τοῦ κόσμου γενέσεως, and (2) τὸ γενεαλογικόν. This tells us that *Opif.* was already written by the time *Mos.* was composed, but it does not reveal the order of Philo's works. (b) *Praem.* i 1 (1–3). Here Philo divides the revelations (λόγια) imparted by means of Moses into three categories (ἰδέαι): (1) περὶ κοσμοποιΐας; (2) τὸ ἱστορικὸν μέρος; (3) τὸ νομοθετικὸν μέρος. Philo says that he has discussed all these in preceding treatises. But this, again, provides no testimony to the order of Philo's writings (except that these works had been composed by the time *Praem.* was begun): the order relates to the Pentateuch, not to

De Abrahamo (Βίος σοφοῦ τοῦ κατὰ διδασκαλίαν τελειωθέντος ἢ νόμων ἀγράφων [αʹ], ὅ ἐστι περὶ Ἀβραάμ).[135]

This treatise belongs to the group of the νόμοι ἄγραφοι, that is, the βίοι σοφῶν, *Dec.* 1 (1), the description of the lives of the virtuous men who through their exemplary conduct represent the general types of morality. There were two groups of such types, with three in each group, namely (1) Enos, Enoch, Noah, and (2) Abraham, Isaac, and Jacob. Enos represents ἐλπίς, Enoch μετάνοια καὶ βελτίωσις, Noah δικαιοσύνη, *Abr.* 2–5 (7–30). The second triad stands on a higher level: Abraham is the symbol of the διδασκαλικὴ ἀρετή (virtue acquired by learning), Isaac of the φυσικὴ ἀρετή (inborn virtue), Jacob of the ἀσκητικὴ ἀρετή (virtue obtained by practice), see *Abr.* 11 (52), *Jos.* 1 (1). The first three are dealt with only briefly. The greatest part of *Abr.* is concerned with Abraham himself.

De Iosepho (Βίος πολιτικοῦ ὅπερ ἐστὶ περὶ Ἰωσήφ)[136]

After the life of Abraham one expects the biographies of Isaac and

---

Philo's works.

In fact it is doubtful whether τὸ ἱστορικὸν μέρος should be taken to refer to the *Allegorical Commentary* in either passage. In *Mos.* ii 8 (46–7) the programmatic statement can be taken as no more than a description of *Mos.* itself, in which book i covers the historical material, whilst book ii is concerned with legislation. (The objection to this, that *Mos.* does not accomplish this plan, may be answered by assuming the loss of a section at the end of book ii.) Alternatively, the announcement can be considered as a plan for the *Exposition* as a whole—a theory which carries implications for the relationship between *Mos.* and the *Exposition*; see E. R. Goodenough, 'Philo's Exposition of the Law and his De Vita Mosis', HThR 27 (1933), pp. 109–25, esp. p. 112. In *Praem.*, the plan seems to be confined to the *Exposition*, since τὸ νομοθετικὸν μέρος can hardly refer to the *Allegorical Commentary* either.

135. C-W vol. IV, pp. 1–60; Loeb Philo VI (1935), pp. 1–135; J. Gorez, *De Abrahamo* (*Oeuvres* XX, 1966). See C. Kraus Reggiani, *op. cit.*, pp. 162–81; A. Priessnig, 'Die literarische Form der Patriarchenbiographien des Philo von Alexandrien', MGWJ 73 (1929), pp. 143–55; W. Richardson, 'The Philonic Patriarchs as Nomos Empsychos', *Studia Patristica* I (TU LXIII, 1957), pp. 512–25; S. Sandmel, *Philo's Place in Judaism: A Study of Conceptions of Abraham in Jewish Literature* (²1971); G. Mayer, 'Aspekte des Abrahambildes in der hellenistisch-jüdischen Literatur', EvTh 32 (1972), pp. 118–27. An Armenian version of *Abr.* (as The Life of the Wise Man) was published by the Mechitarists in 1892 (pp. 33–104); see above, n. 33. In Eusebius, *H.E.* ii 18, 4, the title runs [περὶ] βίου σοφοῦ τοῦ κατὰ δικαιοσύνην τελειωθέντος ἢ νόμων ἀγράφων. Here δικαιοσύνην instead of the διδασκαλίαν presented by the manuscripts of Philo must be an error. For Abraham is indeed the type of the διδασκαλικὴ ἀρετή. After ἀγράφων the number αʹ is probably to be inserted, since our book is only the first about the unwritten laws. In the *Sacra Parallela* our book is cited with the formula ἐκ τοῦ περὶ βίου σοφοῦ. See C-W vol. IV, p. 59, n.

136. C-W vol. IV, pp. 61–118; Loeb Philo VI (1935), pp. 137–271; J. Laporte, *De Iosepho* (*Oeuvres* XXI, 1964). See C. Kraus Reggiani, *op. cit.*, pp. 257–94. The title varies in the manuscripts between βίος πολιτικοῦ and βίος πολιτικός. The first, however, is better attested (see C-W vol. IV, p. 61, n.). Eusebius, *H.E.* ii 18, 6, has ὁ πολιτικός. Photius, *Bibl.*, cod. 103: περὶ βίου πολιτικοῦ. The Suda s.v. Ἀβραάμ: Φίλων ἐν τῷ τοῦ πολιτικοῦ βίῳ

Jacob to follow on immediately. That Philo wrote these lives is known from the prologue to *De Iosepho*, but they seem to have been lost at an early date, since no trace of them has survived. The prologue of *De Iosepho* also makes clear that it is to be included at this point in the series; this is strange, however, since the number of exemplary βίοι might have been thought complete with the triad Abraham, Isaac and Jacob. But Joseph is added to the sequence here because the examples of Abraham, Isaac and Jacob relate only to an ideal cosmopolitan world, not to the empirical world with its varied constitutions. The life of Joseph is therefore intended to show how the wise man is to conduct himself in public life as it is in practice.[137]

De Decalogo (Περὶ τῶν δέκα λογίων οἳ κεφάλαια νόμων εἰσί)[138]
With this treatise the exposition of the legislation proper begins, τῶν ἀναγραφέντων νόμων, *Dec.* 1 (1); indeed it is the ten chief commandments which are first described, commandments given by God himself without the intervention of Moses.

De specialibus legibus i–iv (Περὶ τῶν ἀναφερομένων ἐν εἴδει νόμων εἰς τὰ συντείνοντα κεφάλαια τῶν δέκα λόγων α', β', γ', δ'.)[139]
In this work Philo makes an extremely interesting attempt to bring the

(in the article Φίλων the Suda has περὶ ἀγωγῆς βίου, following Jerome's Greek translator). In the *Sacra Parallela* the book is cited with the lemma ἐκ τοῦ εἰς τὸν Ἰωσήφ (C-W vol. IV, p. 79, n.).

137. After *Ios.* the editions give *Mos.*, which is, indeed, appropriate to this group in terms of its literary character. But there is no indication in the work (or in other treatises) that it belongs with the other lives, and it is in fact quite independent. Its presence would disrupt the series, for Moses, as law-giver, stands apart and thus is not a generally acknowledged 'type' of ethical conduct, nor is he portrayed as such. See further pp. 854–5 below.

138. C-W vol. IV, pp. 180–209; Loeb Philo VII (1937), pp. 1–95; V. Nikiprowetzky, *De decalogo* (*Oeuvres* XXIII, 1965). See S. Sandmel, 'The Confrontation of Greek and Jewish Ethics: Philo, *De Decalogo*', CCAR Journal 15 (1968), pp. 54–63 (repr. in *Two Living Traditions: Essays on Religion and the Bible* (1972), pp. 279–90).
In the title of *Decal.* the text varies between λογίων ἃ and λογίων οἳ. The first form predominates in the titles of the four books *De specialibus legibus* and is confirmed by Eusebius, *H.E.* ii 18, 5: περὶ τῶν δέκα λογίων. The *Sacra Parallela* cite the treatise with the lemma ἐκ τοῦ εἰς τὸν [or τὴν] δεκάλογον (C-W vol. IV, pp. 280, 287, 290, 299, 300). Jerome has *de tabernaculo et decalogo libri quattuor* as a result of a careless abbreviation of Eusebius' text. The Vatican palimpsest (Cod. Vat. gr. 316), still not used in C-W, is not of serious importance for the text of *Decal.* (It has λόγων οἳ in the superscription; see L. Cohn, 'Ein Philo-Palimpsest', SAB (1905), p. 40.)

139. C-W vol. V, pp. 1–265; Loeb Philo VII (1937), pp. 97–641; VIII (1939), pp. 1–155; S. Daniel, *De specialibus legibus i–ii* (*Oeuvres* XXIV, 1975); A. Mosès, *De specialibus legibus iii–iv* (*Oeuvres* XXV, 1970). See esp. S. Daniel, 'Le Halacha de Philon selon le premier livre des "Lois spéciales"', in *Philon d'Alexandrie*, ed. R. Arnaldez (1967), pp. 221–41; R. Hecht, 'Preliminary Issues in the Analysis of Philo's *De Specialibus Legibus*', SP 5 (1978), pp. 1–55. An Armenian version of parts of *Spec.* (under different titles) was published by the Mechitarists in 1892; see C. Mercier, *Quaestiones et Solutiones in Genesim I et II*, pp. 16–17.

Mosaic special laws into a systematic arrangement according to the ten rubrics of the Decalogue.[140] Thus in connection with the First and Second Commandments (worship of God) he describes the whole legislation regarding the priesthood and sacrifice; in connection with the Fourth (celebration of the Sabbath) all the laws relating to the festivals; in the context of the Sixth (prohibition of adultery) the law of marriage; and under the other headings the whole of civil and criminal law. There has been considerable debate regarding the relation between the legislative details contained in the Special Laws and Palestinian Halakha. Goodenough claimed that Philo was here basing his account on the laws of the local Alexandrian Jewish courts; others trace affinities with Palestinian law.[141]

According to the testimony of Eusebius (*H.E.* ii 18, 5), the complete work comprised four books, which seem to have been preserved complete; in the early editions they were in disorder and had to be restored by Cohn.[142] The manuscripts divide the work into small sections with sub-titles, which are grouped together into the four books in modern editions.[143]

Spec. i[144]

The book comprises the following sections: *De circumcisione*: 1–2 (1–12); *De monarchia*[145] 1 and 2: 3–11 (13–65) and 12–26 (66–130); *De praemiis sacerdotum*: 27–32 (131–161); *De victimis*: 33–47 (162–256); *De sacrificantibus* or *De victimas offerentibus*: 48–63 (257–345). The division of the book into separate sections with special titles appears to be fairly

The above is the title given by Eusebius, *H.E.* ii 18, 5. The manuscripts of Philo concur, except that instead of εἰς τὰ συντείνοντα κεφάλαια the particular content of each of the four books is specified (e.g. εἰς τρία γένη τῶν δέκα λογίων, τὸ τρίτον, τὸ τέταρτον, τὸ πέμπτον etc.).

140. For the relationship between *Spec.* and *Dec.* see V. Nikiprowetzky, *De decalogo*, pp. 1–34; A. Mosès, *op. cit.*, pp. 14–17.

141. On Philo and Halakha in general see pp. 874–5, n. 13 below. On the legal disquisitions in *Spec.* and their relationship with Jewish legal theory and practice both in Palestine and the Diaspora see E. R. Goodenough, *The Jurisprudence of the Jewish Courts in Egypt* (1929); I. Heinemann, *Philons griechische und jüdische Bildung* (1932); S. Daniel, 'Le Halacha de Philon' (n. 139).

142. The text was improved by Cohn's use of the Vatican palimpsest (Vat. gr. 316), which contains the whole of book i and more than a third of book ii. See L. Cohn, 'Ein Philo-Palimpsest', SAB (1905), pp. 36–52; C-W vol. V, pp. v–vii; L. Cohn, 'Neue Beiträge zur Textgeschichte und Kritik der philonischen Schriften', Hermes 43 (1908), pp. 177–219.

143. For details see Colson, Loeb Philo VII, p. xviii; VIII, p. xxiv.

144. Three manuscripts have the full title: περὶ τῶν ἀναφερομένων ἐν εἴδει νόμων εἰς δύο κεφάλαια τῶν δέκα λογίων, τό τε μὴ νομίζειν ἔξω τοῦ ἑνὸς θεοὺς ἑτέρους αὐτοκρατεῖς καὶ τὸ μὴ χειρόκμητα θεοπλαστεῖν. See S. P. Wendland, 'Neu entdeckte Fragmente Philos', p. 136; C-W vol. V, p. xix (mentioning only two; the third is Vat. 379; for this see C-W vol. I, pp. xxv ff.).

145. The beginning of this is also in Eusebius, *Praep. ev.* xiii 18, 12 ff.

old. In the manuscripts it is carried even further than in the editions. Thus in some manuscripts *De monarchia* is divided into two sections περὶ ἱεροῦ and περὶ ἱερέων.[146] The treatise *De victimis* is mentioned by Eusebius as a separate document: περὶ τῶν εἰς τὰς ἱερουργίας ζῴων καὶ τίνα τὰ τῶν θυσιῶν εἴδη (*H.E.* ii 18, 5). In the older texts of *De victimis* a considerable portion was missing; Wendland published it from a neglected manuscript, and Cohn also supplied it from the Vatican palimpsest which he rediscovered.[147] On the basis of these two sources the section was incorporated into the text in Cohn's edition: 35 (177–93). It deals with the offerings for the feast days (according to Num. 28–9 and Lev. 16 and 23).

A passage is also missing in the older texts of *De sacrificantibus*: 51 (280–4); it was combined with a passage from *Sacrif.* to form the treatise known as *de mercede meretricis*.[148] This treatise does indeed consist of genuine Philonic material, but does not derive directly from Philo in its present form. Wendland demonstrated the original position of the separate passages from it on the basis of the better manuscripts, and the Vatican palimpsest (Vat. gr. 316) confirmed his findings.

Spec. ii[149]

The early editions of this book did not include the sections *de septenario*: 10 (39)–33 (214); *de colendis parentibus*: 38 (224)–48 (262), which in fact belong together with the sections on the Third Commandment, 1 (1)–9 (38), and on the basket rite, 34 (215)–37 (223).[150]

Spec. iii[151]

Here Philo deals with the Sixth and Seventh Commandments, considering legislation to do with sexual offences and with murder and other acts of violence. The famous opening of the book, in which Philo reflects on his own career and attitude to the contemplative life and to

146. P. Wendland, 'Neu entdeckte Fragmente', pp. 136 ff.; C-W vol. V, pp. 17, 20. The title περὶ τοῦ ἱεροῦ is also found in the *Sacra Parallela* (Harris, *Fragments*, p. 83 = Cod. Vat. 1553 fol. 179^r).

147. Wendland, 'Neu entdeckte Fragmente', pp. 1–14. On the Vatican palimpsest see above, n. 00.

148. So in ed. by Mangey II, pp. 164–9.

149. Full title: περὶ τῶν ἀναφερομένων ἐν εἴδει νόμων εἰς τρία γένη τῶν δέκα λογίων, τὸ τρίτον, τὸ τέταρτον, τὸ πέμπτον, τὸ περὶ εὐορκίας καὶ σεβασμοῦ τῆς ἱερᾶς ἑβδόμης καὶ γονέων τιμῆς.

150. Mangey gave just a small portion of the book (II, pp. 270–7) and followed it with *de septenario* as a separate piece (II, pp. 277–98), but with the text incomplete; *de colendis parentibus* was entirely missing, moreover. Most of what was missing was given by Mai, *De cophini festo et de colendis parentibus* (1818) and in *Classicorum auctorum* IV, pp. 402–29. The complete text of the entire book was first given by Tischendorf, *Philonea*, pp. 1–83. See Colson in Loeb Philo VII, pp. xv-xvii.

151. Full title: περὶ τῶν ἀναφερομένων ἐν εἴδει νόμων εἰς δύο γένη τῶν δέκα λογίων, τὸ ἕκτον καὶ τὸ ἕβδομον, τὸ κατὰ μοίχων καὶ παντὸς ἀκολάστου καὶ τὸ κατὰ ἀνδροφόνων καὶ πάσης βίας.

political involvement, has been taken to mark a division of some sort between books i and ii on the one hand, and iii and iv on the other. Whether this is merely a stylistic marker, or a sign of a division of content or approach, or whether the passage has wider reference to Philo's career and *oeuvre* as a whole, is uncertain.[152]

As to the text, it has been suggested that 31 (169)–32 (180) is an interpolation, possibly from *De virtutibus* (*De fortitudine*); alternatively it might be a displaced section of text from the *Spec.* but belonging in a different position from its present context.[153]

Spec. iv[154]

This book completes the discussion of the Commandments, dealing rather more cursorily with the Eighth, Ninth and Tenth Commandments than with the previous seven. At 25 (132) Philo changes his approach to the Laws; having concluded the survey in terms of the Ten Commandments, he now proceeds to consider the Laws under the headings of particular virtues. Although the sections 14 (79)–25 (135) and 26 (136)–28 (150) are entitled, respectively, *De concupiscentia* and *De iustitia*, these sections belong in fact with Book iv; they provide a transition to the next treatise, *De virtutibus*, but the words νυνὶ δὲ περὶ τῆς ... δικαιοσύνης λεκτέον at 25 (135) suggest that *De iustitia* should none the less be attached to *De specialibus legibus*. So, indeed, does the superscription of the whole book, in which it is expressly indicated that this book deals also: περὶ δικαιοσύνης, ἣ πᾶσι τοῖς ἱ λογίοις ἐφαρμόζει.[155]

De virtutibus (Περὶ τριῶν ἀρετῶν ἃς σὺν ἄλλαις ἀνέγραψε Μωϋσῆς περὶ ἀνδρείας καὶ φιλανθρωπίας καὶ μετανοίας).[156]
The work as we have it comprises four distinct sections, entitled *De*

152. See pp. 843, 844 above.
153. See A. Mosès, *op. cit.*, pp. 355–6.
154. This book was first published by Mangey from Codex Seldenianus = Bodleianus 3400. (On this manuscript see C-W vol. V, pp. viii ff.) Full title: περὶ τῶν ἀναφερομένων ἐν εἴδει νόμων εἰς τρία γένη τῶν δέκα λογίων, τὸ η′ καὶ τὸ θ′ καὶ τὸ ι′, τὸ περὶ τοῦ μὴ κλέπτειν καὶ ψευδομαρτυρεῖν καὶ μὴ ἐπιθυμεῖν καὶ περὶ τῶν εἰς ἕκαστον ἀναφερομένων καὶ περὶ δικαιοσύνης, ἣ πᾶσι τοῖς ἱ λογίοις ἐφαρμόζει, ὅ ἐστι τῆς συντάξεως. Some such word as τέλος is missing at the end.
155. On the sub-titles and enumeration of chapters in C-W see Colson, Loeb Philo VIII, p. xxiii. For the relationship between *Spec.* and *De iustitia* see A. Mosès, *op. cit.*, pp. 17–21.
156. C-W vol. V, pp. 266–335; Loeb Philo VIII (1939), pp. 157–305; R. Arnaldez, P. Delobre, M.-R. Servel and A.-M. Verilhac, *De virtutibus* (*Oeuvres* XXVI, 1962). The title of the book as given here is found in the Codex Seldenianus; see C-W vol. V, pp. viii and 266, n. It is confirmed by Eusebius, *H.E.* ii 18, 2: περὶ τῶν τριῶν ἀρετῶν ἃς σὺν ἄλλαις ἀνέγραψε Μωϋσῆς. Cf. Jerome, *De vir. ill.* 11: 'de tribus virtutibus liber unus'. The title περὶ τριῶν ἀρετῶν also occurs in the *Sacra Parallela*: Cod. Rupefuc. fol. 212ᵛ: τοῦ αὐτοῦ ἐκ τοῦ περὶ τριῶν ἀρετῶν (τριῶν in the manuscript). The passage cited is *Virt.* 3 (9): ὁ σπουδαῖος ὀλιγοδεής etc. See also Codex Vaticanus 1553 fol. 73ʳ: Φίλωνος ἐκ τοῦ περὶ γ′ ἀρετῶν (there is uncertainty as to whether the reading is γ′ or τ̄ = τῶν). On the other

fortitudine, 1 (1)–8 (50); *De humanitate* or *De caritate*, 9 (51)–32 (174); *De paenitentia*, 33 (175)–34 (186); and *De nobilitate*, 35 (187)–41 (227). In the prologue, reference is made to *De iustitia*, the final section of *Spec*. iv, of which the continuation is here presented: περὶ δικαιοσύνης καὶ τῶν κατ᾽ αὐτὴν ὅσα καίρια πρότερον εἰπών, μέτειμι τὸ ἑξῆς ἐπ᾽ ἀνδρείαν.

Virt. is thus a sort of appendix to *Spec*. In this work, the Mosaic laws are brought together which do not belong under the ten rubrics of the Decalogue, but under that of particular cardinal virtues; they are, however, only to be fully realized through the observance of the Decalogue as a whole.[157] It may have been technical factors which made Philo allocate part of this Appendix to Book iv of *Spec*. and the rest to a separate work; he may, that is, have wished to produce books of roughly uniform size.

There is disagreement about the components of *Virt*., in that some argue that certain sections belong elsewhere in Philo's works, and there is also uncertainty as to whether a lost περὶ εὐσεβείας once formed part of the work. The various rearrangements suggested arise because the title in Eusebius (*H.E.* ii 18), and in most other sources, refer to *three* virtues, rather than to four or five, if account is taken of a lost περὶ εὐσεβείας. So some of the sections must either be removed from *Virt*. altogether, or else it must be assumed that some were subordinate to three main headings. To begin with the lost treatise, its existence is known not only from three fragments attributed explicitly to the work,[158] but also from the manuscript titles of *Virt*. in which it is included (but in one case as the sub-title to *De humanitate*).[159] This would seem to lead to the conclusion that περὶ εὐσεβείας formed part of *Virt*.[160] A clue to its precise position might be afforded by the opening

hand a number of manuscripts have περὶ ἀρετῶν ἤτοι περὶ ἀνδρείας καὶ εὐσεβείας καὶ φιλανθρωπίας καὶ μετανοίας. Wendland mentions seven manuscripts giving this title: Hermes 31, p. 436; cf. Cohn, Philologus 51, p. 268; C-W, p. 266, n.; Loeb Philo VIII, p. 440. On περὶ εὐσεβείας see below, n. 160.

157. So *Spec*. iv 25 (133–4).

158. See Harris, *Fragments*, pp. 10–11. J. Royse, 'The Oxyrhynchus Papyrus', pp. 162–3, suggests that P.Oxy. fr. 10ʳ, 9–10 fits with the line of thought in one of these extracts, Coislinianus 276, fol. 269ʳ (11), 12–19.

159. See above, n. 000, and Colson, Loeb Philo VIII, pp. xiii-xiv.

160. Schürer, GJV III⁴, p. 671, n. 101, advanced the following reasons against the view that περὶ εὐσεβείας had originally occupied this position. (1) The reference at the close of *De concupiscentia*, *Spec*. iv 25 (135), to an earlier treatment of εὐσέβεια makes it unlikely that he was about to write on this topic again. (This reference is probably to the discussion of the first four commandments in *Spec*.) (2) Εὐσέβεια might be considered a different sort of virtue, the source of all other virtues, and so unlikely to be put on a par with ἀνδρεία and φιλανθρωπία. (3) The attestation of the form of the title with περὶ τριῶν is far stronger than that for four virtues. (4) Clement used *De fortitudine* and *De humanitate* as if the one followed the other: *Strom*. ii 81–98; see Wendland in Hermes 31 (1896), pp. 444 ff. (5) The opening of *De humanitate* need not mean that περὶ εὐσεβείας was between *De*

words of *De humanitate*: τὴν δ' εὐσεβείας συγγενεστάτην καὶ ἀδελφὴν καὶ δίδυμον ὄντως ἑξῆς ἐπισκεπτέον φιλανθρωπίαν. If this implies that piety was considered before humanity, then περὶ εὐσεβείας would have been between *De fortitudine* and *De humanitate*. As to the size of this work, a tentative attempt to identify περὶ εὐσεβείας with a fragmentary papyrus and calculate the work's length by the arrangement of the papyrus as a whole has suggested one roughly the same as that of *De fortitudine*.[161]

As to the existing sections of *De virtutibus*, there have been four attempts to reduce the number to three sections, to agree with Eusebius' description.[162] The earliest solution was to exclude *De humanitate* and *De paenitentia* and join them to *Mos.* as an appendix.[163] The fact that the books περὶ τοῦ βίου Μωϋσέως are mentioned in the prologue to *De humanitate* is insufficient reason to suppose that this treatise stands in a literary relation to *Mos.*[164] Another, more radical view is that which regards *De fortitudine* as the closing section of *Spec.*, and the other treatises at present in *Virt.* as belonging together as an entirely separate work.[165] The main reason for rejecting this suggestion is the fact that Clement attached his extracts from *De fortitudine* to those from *De humanitate*.[166]

Perhaps the most plausible alteration to the present arrangement of *Virt.* is that according to which *De paenitentia* and *De nobilitate* are merely elaborations of the virtue *humanitas*;[167] the three virtues would then be

---

fortitudine and *De humanitate*. The predicate τὴν εὐσεβείας συγγενέστατην serves only to characterize the high value of φιλανθρωπία (it is directly related to εὐσέβεια, the source of all virtues). The titles mentioning a treatise περὶ εὐσεβείας could have been given because of a misunderstanding of this passage. (6) The citations in the *Sacra Parallela* testify only to the existence of a treatise, but tell us nothing as to its position.

161. So Royse, *op. cit.*, pp. 163–4; cf. also Colson, Loeb Philo VIII, p. xi.

162. Or to four, if περὶ εὐσεβείας is included.

163. Massebieau, *Le Classement*, pp. 38–41, 49–54, following Gfrörer and Dähne; see Wendland, Hermes 31 (1896), pp. 435–56.

164. E. R. Goodenough, 'Philo's Exposition', pp. 110–11.

165. Massebieau, *Le Classement*, pp. 39–41. (1) Philo says at the end of *De concupiscentia*, *Spec.* iv 25 (135), that he has already treated εὐσέβεια and intends to treat δικαιοσύνη, which is what he does. If then this treatise is added, the circle of the four Stoic cardinal virtues, which Philo frequently names as such (φρόνησις, σωφροσύνη, δικαιοσύνη, ἀνδρεία), is complete and no further continuation seems possible. (2) In the prologue of *Praem.*, which forms the epilogue to the entire *Exposition* (see below, p. 853), Philo says, 1 (3), that in his work he has dealt with all the separate laws and also with the virtues in peace and war: προσέτι τῶν ἀρετῶν ἃς ἀπένειμεν εἰρήνῃ τε καὶ πολέμῳ. This seems to be a reference to the treatises *De iustitia* and *De fortitudine*, which would therefore have to be treated as the conclusion of the work.

166. See above, n. 160. Further objections can be made. (1) The prologue of *De humanitate* (n. 160 above) shows beyond doubt that Philo knows other cardinal virtues in addition to the four stoic cardinal virtues. (2) Wendland, Hermes 31 (1896), p. 439, showed that according to Philo δικαιοσύνη is not exclusively a virtue for a time of peace nor is ἀνδρεία exclusively one for war, but both have to stand the test in both situations.

167. C-W vol. V, pp. xxvi-xvii. Cf. Colson, Loeb Philo VIII, pp. xv-xvi.

courage, piety and humanity. A remaining alternative is to regard *De paenitentia*, as an adjunct to *De humanitate* and *De nobilitate*,[168] as belonging elsewhere—either as an independent treatise, as part of another treatise, or as part of the otherwise very short section *De paenitentia*. This last possibility is probably to be preferred; in three manuscripts *De nobilitate* follows *De paenitentia* (in Clement, *Strom.* ii 98–9, the excerpts from *De nobilitate* are attached to those from *De humanitate*).[169] As regards content, there is an affinity between *De paenitentia* and *De nobilitate*: the former invites the pagan to turn to the true God, but *De nobilitate* affirms the equal rights of the proselyte, since true nobility does not rest on birth.

De praemiis et poenis (Περὶ ἄθλων καὶ ἐπιτιμίων)

De exsecrationibus (Περὶ ἀρῶν)[170]

These treatises are attached to the *Exposition* as a kind of epilogue.[171] In the prologue Philo says that after he has dealt in his earlier writings with the three principal categories of the Mosaic revelation—the κοσμοποιΐα, the ἱστορικόν and the νομοθετικόν (n. 134 above)—he wishes now to pass over to the rewards destined for the good and the punishments in store for the wicked. Although *De exsecrationibus* is treated as a separate work in three of the four manuscripts, it follows naturally from the last section of *De praemiis*, which deals with the 'blessings' (εὐχαί or εὐλογίαι).[172] A considerable lacuna occurs in the text at 13 (78), before the beginning of the section on blessings,[173] for the discussion *De poenis* begins at 12 (67) but is evidently far from complete. The work falls into two pairs of sections: (1) on rewards and punishments, and (2) on blessings and curses, Lev. 26, Deut. 28.[174] The transition from the first half to the second falls in the lacuna.

Goodenough regarded the *Exposition* as a whole as directed towards

---

168. On the position of *De nobilitate* see Wendland, Hermes 31 (1896), pp. 442–3.

169. See Colson, Loeb Philo VIII, pp. xvii–xviii.

170. C-W vol. V, pp. 336–65, 365–76; Loeb Philo VIII (1939), pp. 307–423; A. Beckaert, *De praemiis et poenis. De exsecrationibus* (Oeuvres XXVII, 1967). See J. Cazeaux, 'Système implicite dans l'exégèse de Philon. Un example: le *De praemiis*', SP 6 (1979–80), pp. 3–33.

171. The two sections are separated rather crudely. Eusebius, *H.E.* ii 18, 5, refers to περὶ τῶν προκειμένων ἐν τῷ νόμῳ τοῖς μὲν ἀγαθοῖς ἄθλων, τοῖς δὲ πονηροῖς ἐπιτιμίων καὶ ἀρῶν. The title περὶ ἄθλων καὶ ἐπιτιμίων also appears in the *Sacra Parallela*: Cod. Rupefuc. fol. 128ᵛ, 131ʳ, 284ᵛ; see C-W vol. V, nn. to pp. 340, 347, 351, 357. Περὶ εὐχῆς καὶ εὐλογίων is also found: Cod. Rupefuc. fol. 276ʳ (= *Praem.* 17), see C-W vol. V, p. 359, n.

172. For the view that the sections on blessings and curses formed a separate work see E. R. Goodenough, 'Philo's Exposition', pp. 118–25.

173. See C-W vol. V, p. 353.

174. C-W vol. V, pp. xxviii–ix, adopts a threefold division: περὶ ἄθλων καὶ ἐπιτιμίων καὶ ἀρῶν (but note the twofold division in Eusebius and the single title in the *Sacra Parallela*, above, n. 171).

gentiles, and yet found the second section of the work, 14 (79)–20 (126), 'explicable only as designed for Jews'. His opinion that this section did not originally belong at the end of the *Exposition* was justified chiefly in terms of the content, and involved the hypothesis that the present ending was inserted by a copyist to replace a lost original. Such a solution allowed Goodenough to preserve his conviction that the *Exposition* was for gentiles, but the hypothesis has not commanded assent. [175]

In addition to these three great works on the Pentateuch, Philo also wrote several separate treatises, of which the following are extant, some complete and some fragmentary.

De vita Mosis i-ii (Περὶ τοῦ βίου Μωϋσέως) [176]
Although, strangely, this work is missing from Eusebius' catalogue, its authenticity is no longer in doubt.[177] It was already cited by Clement, *Strom.* i 23 (153): ᾗ φησι Φίλων ἐν τῷ Μωϋσέως βίῳ, cf. *Strom.* ii 19 (100). There are also references to the *Life of Moses* in other treatises. These references, and the character of *Mos.* itself, have given rise to differing theories as to its relation to the *Exposition*.[178] At first sight, the *Mos.* is similar in literary character to the lives of the σόφοι which form the first part of the *Exposition*; but there are several reasons why it cannot be grouped formally with these.[179] First, the work makes no reference to preceding βίοι in its opening sections.[180] Secondly, its design and

175. See Goodenough, *op. cit.*, but cf. Colson, Loeb Philo VIII, p. xix.

176. C-W vol. IV, pp. 119–268; Loeb Philo VI (1935), pp. 273–595; R. Arnaldez, C. Mondésert, J. Pouilloux and P. Savinel, *De vita Mosis* (*Oeuvres* XXII, 1967). See e.g. B. Botte, 'La vie de Moïse par Philon', in 'Moïse, l'homme de l'Alliance', Cahiers Sioniens (1954), pp. 55–62; E. Starobinski-Safran, 'La prophétie de Moïse et sa portée d'après Philon', in *La Figure de Moïse*, ed. R. Martin-Achard *et al.* (1978), pp. 67–80. The title περὶ Μωϋσέως βίου is found in the *Sacra Parallela*, e.g. Cod. Rupefuc. fol. 27br, 74r, 114r, 119r, 141br, 274r; see C-W vol. IV, pp. 124, 128, 133, 134, 145, 158, 175, 187, 188, 201, 242.
Mangey divided the work into three books (II, pp. 80–179), and this division is already found in the manuscripts, but is certainly wrong, as is shown by the following quotation from *De humanitate* = *Virt.* 9 (52): δεδήλωται πρότερον ἐν δυσὶ συντάξεσιν, ἃς ἀνέγραψα περὶ τοῦ βίου Μωϋσέως (Mangey's reading τρισί instead of δυσί has little support, see C-W vol. V, p. 280, app. crit.). In the Catena Barberini passages from the so-called third book are cited with the lemma ἐκ τοῦ περὶ τοῦ βίου Μωϋσέως λόγου δευτέρου (C-W vol. IV, pp. 241, 254). The books once called ii and iii are thus actually only one book, as indeed their length also shows. However, Massebieau, *Le Classement*, pp. 42 ff, suggested that a portion is missing at the conclusion of what used to be called book ii, i.e. at ii 12 (65). But the length of the missing part need not have been significant, see Wendland, Hermes 31 (1896), p. 440, n. 2.

177. See R. Arnaldez *et al.*, *op. cit.*, pp. 11–12.

178. See Nikiprowetzky, *Le Commentaire*, pp. 194–5.

179. See S. Sandmel, *Philo of Alexandria*, pp. 47–52.

180. In fact the rather polemical tone of the opening links *Mos.* with *Hyp.*, *Flacc.* and *Legat.*

approach are different from those of *Abr.* and *Ios.*[181] Thirdly, *Mos.* does not form part of the scheme announced at the beginning of *Abr.* Finally, there is the inherent anomaly of the lawgiver himself being presented as a νόμος ἔμψυχος.

Nevertheless, there are reasons for linking *Mos.* with the *Exposition* as a whole, even if it does not form part of the sequence of lives of σοφοί. Firstly, it is referred to in *Praem.* 9 (53) as if it were essential to the argument of the *Exposition*. In *Virt.* 52 (= *De humanitate* 1) Philo refers explicitly to 'a work of two books which I wrote on the Life of Moses', and proceeds to supplement this account. There is also the consideration that the lives of the great prophets in the *Exposition* would seem incomplete without an account of Moses (even if this were provided out of sequence, as a companion piece, introduction or supplement to the *Exposition*). A passage in the second book of *Mos.* itself has been interpreted in a way which might explain the relationship between the books on Moses and the *Exposition*: at ii 8 (45–7) Philo distinguishes between the historical and the legislative parts of the works of Moses. He then surveys the historical parts in a way which follows the pattern of the *Exposition* itself, mentioning the creation of the world as one component (*Opif.*) and the account of 'particular persons' as another (the βίος of Abraham, etc.). The reference to the legislative parts of Moses' writings would be taken as an announcement, or summary, of *Spec.* Such a summary of the outline of the *Exposition* might suggest that *Mos.* was composed as some sort of companion piece—probably as an introduction—since the reference to the books on Moses in *Virt.* 52 suggests that *Mos.* was written earlier.

Some take the survey in *Mos.* ii (45–6) as no more than a synopsis of the content of the treatise itself. But only part of what is announced here is presented in *Mos.* as we have it, for the legislative part of the Pentateuch is not discussed. It is, however, possible that such a discussion stood originally at the end of ii 12 (65) and that there is a lacuna at this point.[182]

The mode of presentation of the life of Moses has often been considered evidence that the work was written for gentiles, even as a proselytizing tract. Affinities with Graeco-Roman literary genres, an absence of complex allegorical exegesis, and some conceptual affinities with pagan works are insufficient to prove the point. It can, however, be said that Philo envisaged an exoteric audience for this work.[183]

181. See e.g. Colson, Loeb Philo VI, pp. xiv–xv.

182. See Colson, Loeb Philo VI, pp. 606–7, and above, n. 176, for further discussion of this passage.

183. For the presentation of Moses see R. Arnaldez *et al.*, *De vita Mosis*, pp. 14–17; B. Botte, *op. cit.* Goodenough saw the work as an introduction to Judaism for interested gentiles; *op. cit.*, pp. 110, 124. For pagan views of Moses, see J. G. Gager, *Moses in*

Quod omnis probus liber (Περὶ τοῦ πάντα σπουδαῖον εἶναι ἐλεύθερον)[184]

This is really only one half of a larger work which considered the topic announced in the title in terms of its two opposed aspects. Philo himself refers to the lost first half, περὶ τοῦ δοῦλον εἶναι πάντα φαῦλον, at the beginning of the extant second half. Eusebius lists the work as follows: περὶ τοῦ δοῦλου εἶναι πάντα φαῦλον, ᾧ ἑξῆς ἐστιν ὁ περὶ τοῦ πάντα σπουδαῖον ἐλεύθερον εἶναι (*H.E.* ii 18, 6). He also reproduced a considerable portion of the work—the description of the Essenes, 12 (75)–13 (91)—in *Praep. ev.* viii 12. Ambrose paraphrased the work in his thirty-seventh letter.[185] Though the work's authenticity has been questioned, it is now generally accepted.[186] Stoic influence on the treatise is obvious not only in the thesis at issue, but also in the arguments presented.[187] There is comparatively little reference to scripture, and many allusions to Greek literature.[188] The description of the Essenes, and its relationship to Philo's account of the same people in *Hypothetica* and of the Therapeutae has been discussed in vol. II, pp. 555–74.

De vita contemplativa (Περὶ βίου θεωρητικοῦ ἢ ἱκετῶν ἀρετῶν)[189]

The treatise is devoted to a favourable description of a religious

---

Greco-Roman Paganism (1972).

184. C-W vol. VI, pp. 1–45; Loeb Philo IX (1941), pp. 1–101; M. Petit, *Quod omnis probus liber sit* (*Oeuvres* XXVIII, 1974).

185. Cf. C-W, apparatus, esp. pp. 16–17.

186. See C-W vol VI, pp. iv-v. For the older literature on the *Echtheitsfrage* see Schürer, GVJ III⁴, p. 676, n. 115. Wendland's studies lead to the conclusion that the work is authentically Philonic, but with the use of a Stoic Vorlage, 'Philos Schrift Περὶ τοῦ πάντα σπουδαῖον εἶναι ἐλεύθερον', Archiv für Gesch. der Philosophie 1 (1888), pp. 509–17. Cf. Massebieau, *Le Classement*, pp. 79–87, arguing for authenticity. The *Florilegia* do not include *Prob.*; see F. Petit, *Studia Patristica* XV (1984), p. 21, n. 4.

187. The main theme of *Prob.* is a fundamental tenet of Stoicism. It is also found in Philo's *Poster.* 41 (138): ὁ σοφὸς μόνος ἐλεύθερός τε καὶ ἄρχων. See P. Wendland and O. Kern, *Beiträge zur Gesch. der griech. Philosophie und Religion* (1895), p. 51.

188. Some suggest that this aligns *Prob.* with Philo's early works, but see A. Terian, ANRW II.21.1, pp. 292–4, for a refutation of this view of Philo's philosophical development.

189. C-W vol. VI, pp. 46–71; Loeb Philo IX (1941), pp. 103–69; F. Daumas and P.-J.-L. Miquel, *De vita contemplativa* (*Oeuvres* XXIX, 1963). See F. Conybeare, *Philo About the Contemplative Life* (1895); P. Geoltrain, *Le traité de la Vie Contemplative de Philon d'Alexandrie* (1960); vol. II, pp. 562–74. Conybeare also prints the extracts from Eusebius, the Armenian and the Old Latin. The Old Latin translation exists in two recensions, and there is also a more recent Latin version dating from the Renaissance. Instead of the above title Eusebius twice gives περὶ βίου θεωρητικοῦ ἢ ἱκετῶν (*H.E.* ii 18, 7 and 17, 3). Most manuscripts add ἀρετῶν τὸ δ', or ἀρετῆς τὸ τέταρτον after ἱκετῶν. The Cod. Paris. 435 only has ἱκέται ἢ περὶ ἀρετῶν δ' (see Conybeare, p. 25, textual note). The designation as the fourth book of the ἀρεταί is missing not only in Eusebius but also in the Armenian version, and is certainly a later addition; see Schürer, ThLZ (1895), p. 395; Cohn, 'Einteilung', pp. 420 ff.

The authenticity of the work was demonstrated by Conybeare, *op. cit.*, pp. 258–358,

community known as the Therapeutae (cf. vol. II, pp. 593–7). These are servants of God and physicians of souls (1) who, possessed by heavenly inspiration, abandon all their property to their relatives and withdraw into solitude (2). Philo claims that there are such people in many places, particularly in each nome of Egypt; but he knows of one colony in particular, in the neighbourhood of Alexandria, on Lake Mareotis. Here each member has his hermit's cell (*οἴκημα ἱερόν, ὁ καλεῖται σεμνεῖον καὶ μοναστήριον*) in which all alone (*μονούμενος*) he devotes himself from morning to evening exclusively to philosophical meditation with the aid of the holy scriptures. Food and drink are not brought to these *οἰκίαι*; only after sunset do the Therapeutae partake of nourishment. But many fast for three or even six days at a time. On the seventh day they assemble together for divine service in a *κοινὸς σύλλογος*. After forty-nine days—that is, on every fiftieth day—they celebrate a festal meal, but one at which only water, bread and salt with hyssop are served; this meal is followed by a *παννυχίς* with dancing and spiritual songs. (The description of this meal occupies three-fifths of the entire treatise, namely ch. 5–11.)

Eusebius identified the Therapeutae described here with Christian monks. So he saw the treatise as evidence that these already existed in Philo's time, and hence gives detailed information about its contents (*H.E.* ii 17, cf. 16, 2). Eusebius' interpretation remained the dominant one in the Christian Church.[190] The affinity between the Therapeutae and Christian monks is indeed striking, and this has sometimes given rise to the suspicion that the treatise was actually composed by someone assuming the guise of Philo in order to recommend Christian monasticism. Other reasons for doubting the treatise's authenticity have been presented: Philo does not show knowledge of the existence of this colony of Therapeutae elsewhere in his works, although mention of it might well be expected at various junctures. His philosophical outlook is not, in fact, inconsistent with the monastic ideal of *Contempl.*; the absolute renunciation of the world and the strict asceticism glorified in this treatise do however represent a more extreme viewpoint than the general admiration for a *vita contemplativa* found elsewhere in his writings, e.g. *Spec.* iii 1 (1–6). It has also been argued that the parody of

and defined by Massebieau, 'Le traité de la vie contemplative et la question des Thérapeutes', RHR 16 (1887), pp. 170–98, 284–319; 17, pp. 230–2; *Le Classement*, pp. 59–61; P. Wendland, 'Die Therapeuten und die philonische Schrift vom beschaulichen Leben', Jahrb. für class. Philol. 22, Suppl. (1896), pp. 695–772. Cf. C-W vol. VI, pp. ix–xxxi. Schürer continued to maintain its spurious character, however. His doubts are summarized above; see also ThLZ (1895), pp. 385–91.

190. Photius, *Bibl.*, cod. 104, is an exception: *ἀνεγνώσθησαν δὲ καὶ τῶν παρὰ Ἰουδαίοις φιλοσοφησάντων τήν τε θεωρητικὴν καὶ τὴν πρακτικὴν φιλοσοφίαν βίοι*. Epiphanius, *Haer.* 29, 5, cites *Contempl.* with the lemma *ἐν τῇ περὶ Ἰεσσαίων αὐτοῦ ἐπιγραφομένῃ βίβλῳ*, but is nevertheless of the opinion that it relates to Christians.

Plato's *Symposium* in *Contempl.* 7 is inconsistent with Philo's high regard for Greek philosophy, especially Platonism. Some of those who regard the work as spurious attribute it to a Jewish author, but it would perhaps be more plausible to attribute it to Christian monks. As regards language, style and range of ideas, *Contempl.* can be accepted as authentically Philonic, and it is now generally regarded as his (n. 189).

De aeternitate mundi (Περὶ ἀφθαρσίας κόσμου)[191]

Doubts may still be expressed as to the authenticity of this treatise, at least in its present form, but it has generally been accepted as part of the Philonic corpus.[192] Dispute centres upon the Stoic view of the eternity of the world presented in *Aet.*, and its relationship to Philo's cosmology. There is also disagreement regarding the stage in Philo's

191. C-W vol. VI, pp. 72–119; Loeb Philo IX (1941), pp. 171–291; R. Arneldez and J. Pouilloux, *De aeternitate mundi* (*Oeuvres* XXX, 1969). See esp. J. Bernays, 'Über die Herstellung des Zusammenhanges in der unter Philos Namen gehenden Schrift περὶ ἀφθαρσίας κόσμου durch Blätterversetzung', Monatsberichte der Berliner Akademie (1863), pp. 34–40 = *Gesammelte Abhandlungen* I (1885), pp. 283–90; *idem*, 'Die unter Philons Werken stehende Schrift über die Unzerstörbarkeit des Weltalls nach ihrer ursprünglichen Anordnung Wiederhergestellt und ins Deutsche übertragen', AAB Phil.-hist. Kl. (1876), pp. 209–78; E. Zeller, 'Der pseudophilonische Bericht über Theophrast', Hermes 15 (1880), pp. 137–46; F. Cumont, *Philonis de aeternitate mundi* (1891); E. Norden, 'Über den Streit des Theophrast und Zeno bei Philo περὶ ἀφθαρσίας κόσμου', Jahrbb. für class. Philol. 19, Supp. (1893), pp. 440–52; H. von Arnim, *Quellenstudien*, pp. 1–52; H. Leisegang, 'Philons Schrift über die Ewigkeit der Welt', Philologus N.F. 46 (1937), pp. 156–76; D. T. Runia, 'Philo's De Aeternitate Mundi: The Problem of its Interpretation', VC 35 (1981), pp. 105–51.

192. See the survey, especially of the views of Bernays, Cumont and Leisegang, in R. Arneldez and J. Pouilloux, *op. cit.*, pp. 12–37. Only one manuscript explicitly attributes the work to Philo (the Vaticanus ends Φίλωνος Ἰουδαίου περὶ ἀφθαρσίας κόσμου). It is the central theme of the work—that the world is eternal—which is regarded as unphilonic, however, and the onus on those who accept its authenticity has been to show that the sentiment is somehow consistent with Philo's thought (for which see Colson, Loeb Philo IX, p. 178), or else to demonstrate that the expression of this point of view in a particular literary context does not commit Philo to it. The most searching criticism of the work was that of Bernays. He attempted to show that the extant text had fallen into disorder through displacement of the leaves. He published the text in Greek and German according to an order restored by him, and with a commentary. E. Zeller, Hermes 15 (1880), pp. 137–46, agreed that the present text was not Philonic, as did von Arnim, *op. cit.*, who investigated the philosophic sources used. Cumont's defence of the work's authenticity has generally been accepted. Schürer remained sceptical, however. Authenticity could only be defended, he maintained, if what is set out about the eternity of the world in the extant text was only a report, which was to be followed in missing sections by a presentation of the opposite point of view. Bernays rightly rejected this explanation, Schürer felt, on the grounds that the excerpts from the writings of others are linked by incidental notes in which the author himself maintains the theory of the ἀφθαρσία τοῦ κόσμου. The note at the conclusion of the extant text: ἃ μὲν οὖν περὶ ἀφθαρσίας τοῦ κόσμου παρειλήφαμεν, εἴρηται κατὰ δύναμιν. τὰς δὲ πρὸς ἕκαστον ἐναντιώσεις ἐν τοῖς ἔπειτα δηλωτέον does not imply that what has preceded is report and that now the author's own opposed views are to follow, but that the author now intended to go into the objections against this view which he has up to this point expressed.

career at which the work was composed, if its authenticity is accepted.[193]

In Flaccum (Εἰς Φλάκκον)
De legatione ad Gaium (Περὶ ἀρετῶν καὶ πρεσβείας πρὸς Γάιον) [194]
In these two works Philo relates the history of the persecutions which the Jews had to suffer in the time of Gaius, particularly in Alexandria. The narrative is so detailed and graphic that it could only have come from a man who had involved himself personally in the events described. This makes the two works a prime source for Philo's life, for the history of the Jews at this period, and also for the reign of Gaius.

The original extent of Philo's historical works, and the relationship of *Flacc.* and the *Leg.* to this complete sequence of historical works, are problems on which no consensus has been reached.[195] That Philo originally wrote more on this subject than the two extant treatises is certain.[196] *Flacc.* begins, 1 (1): δεύτερος μετὰ Σηιανὸν Φλάκκος Ἀουίλλιος διαδέχεται τὴν κατὰ τῶν Ἰουδαίων ἐπιβουλήν. The book we have was therefore preceded by another, recording the persecutions inflicted on

---

193. Cf. p. 856 above on *Prob.*

194. *Flacc.*: C-W vol. VI, pp. 120–54; Loeb Philo IX (1941), pp. 293–403; H. Box, *Philonis Alexandrini In Flaccum* (1939, repr. 1979); A. Pelletier, *In Flaccum (Oeuvres* XXXI, 1967).

Legat.: C-W vol. VI, pp. 155–223; Loeb Philo X (1962), pp. i-xxxi; 1–187; E. M. Smallwood, *Philonis Alexandrini Legatio ad Gaium* (1961); A. Pelletier, *Legatio ad Gaium (Oeuvres* XXXII, 1972). See esp. F. Delauney, *Philon d'Alexandrie. Écrits historiques. Influences, lettres et persécutions des Juifs dans le monde romain* (²1890); H. Leisegang, 'Philons Schrift über die Gesandtschaft der alexandrinischen Juden an den Kaiser Gaius Caligula', JBL 57 (1938), pp. 377–405; P. J. Sijpesteijn, 'The Legationes ad Gaium', JJS 15 (1964), pp. 87–96; C. Kraus Reggiani, 'I rapporti tra l'impero romano e il mondo ebraico al tempo di Caligula secondo la "Legatio ad Gaium" di Filone Alessandrino', ANRW II.21.1, pp. 554–86.

The tradition regarding the titles is very uncertain which complicates the difficulties surrounding the original character of the works (see below, n. 207). For the titles given here see C-W vol. I, pp. xiii, xxv, xxxii, xxxv. There are also prolix and worthless expansions: ἱστορία πάνυ ὀφέλιμος καὶ τῷ βίῳ χρήσιμος τὰ κατὰ τὸν Φλάκκον ἤτοι περὶ προνοίας and ἱστορία πάνυ χρήσιμος καὶ ὀφέλιμος περὶ τῶν κατὰ τὸν Γάιον καὶ τῆς αἰτίας τῆς πρὸς ἅπαν τὸ Ἰουδαίων ἔθνος ἀπεχθείας αὐτοῦ. For these see C-W vol. I, pp. v, ix, xi. The *Sacra Parallela* normally use the lemma ἐκ τοῦ or ἐκ τῶν κατὰ Φλάκκον and ἐκ τῆς πρὸς Γάιον πρεσβείας. Photius, *Bibl.* 105, records ἀνεγνώσθη δὲ αὐτοῦ καὶ λόγος οὗ ἡ ἐπιγραφὴ Γάιος ψεγόμενος καὶ Φλάκκος ἢ Φλάκκων ψεγόμενος (ἐν οἷς λόγοις κ.τ.λ.). (The title Φλάκκος ψεγόμενος is also found in Codex Palatinus 248 (C-W vol. I, p. xxxv).) Similarly Eusebius in the *Chronicle*, ed. Schoene II, pp. 150–1. The text runs (a) according to Jerome: 'Refert Filo in eo libro qui "Flaccus" inscribitur'; (b) according to the Armenian: 'Philon in eo libro, quem ipse ad Flaccum scripsit, refert'; (c) according to Syncellus: Φίλων ἱστορεῖ ἐν τῷ ἐπιγεγραμμένῳ λόγῳ Φλάκκῳ. The correct text of Eusebius is preserved in (c). On the title mentioned in Eusebius, *H.E.*, see below.

195. See Smallwood, *op. cit.*, pp. 36–43; Kraus Reggiani, *op. cit.*, pp. 555–9, 571–6.

196. The author of the *Sacra Parallela* seems already, like Photius, to have known only the two extant books (see above, n. 194).

860 §34. *The Jewish Philosopher Philo*

the Jews by Sejanus. The *Leg.* closes with the words: εἴρηται μὲν οὖν κεφαλαιωδέστερον ἡ αἰτία τῆς πρὸς ἅπαν τὸ Ἰουδαίων ἔθνος ἀπεχθείας Γαΐου. λεκτέον δὲ καὶ τὴν παλινῳδίαν.¹⁹⁷ A further book will therefore have followed, or at least been planned, in which Philo related this. It is possible to reconstruct a sequence of historical works, on the basis of these and other allusions to lost parts, so that *Flacc.* and *Leg.* form parts of one sequence, or rather are two books of a five-book work. This reconstruction is made as follows. It is known from a note in the *Chronicle* of Eusebius that the persecutions under Sejanus were recounted in the second book of the complete work to which he refers.¹⁹⁸ This would imply that *Flacc.* must have been the third book in the work. Since we also have *Leg.* and know that it had a sequel, this would give a total of at least five books, which is confirmed by the definite statement in Eusebius, *H.E.* ii 5, 1: καὶ δὴ τὰ κατὰ Γάιον οὗτος Ἰουδαίοις συμβάντα πέντε βιβλίοις παραδίδωσι. The brief survey which Eusebius gives of the contents of the work also agrees precisely with the reconstruction proposed so far. He says that Philo here relates how in the time of Tiberius, Sejanus displayed great zeal in Rome in the effort to annihilate the whole people; but in Judaea, Pilate threw the Jews into great agitation because he wanted to adopt some course, in regard to the Temple, which conflicted with their ordinances.¹⁹⁹ After the death of Tiberius, Gaius, who now came to the throne, behaved in general in a highly arrogant fashion, but most of all brought harm upon the entire Jewish people.²⁰⁰ Now what is said here about Sejanus and Pilate cannot relate to the occasional isolated remarks in the extant books,²⁰¹ for these deal only with the time of Gaius. According to the statements of Eusebius referred to above, however, the oppression by Sejanus and Pilate must have been narrated in a separate section of the work, before events under Gaius.

As to the character of this reconstructed work, *Flacc.* and the final remarks of *Leg.* clearly show that here Philo intends to describe not only

197. On the meaning of παλινῳδία see Smallwood, *op. cit.*, pp. 324–4; Kraus Reggiani, *op. cit.*, pp. 575–6.
198. Eusebius, *Chron.*, ed. Schoene II, pp. 150–1: (1) According to Jerome: 'Seianus praefectus Tiberii, qui aput eum plurimum poterat, instantissime cohortatur, ut gentem Judaeorum deleat. Filo meminit in libro legationis secundo.' (2) According to the Armenian: 'Seianus Tiberii procurator, qui intimus erat consiliarius regis, universim gentem Judaeorum deperdendam exposcebat. Meminit autem huius Philon in secunda relatione.' (3) According to Syncellus: Σηιανὸς ἔπαρχος Τιβερίου Καίσαρος περὶ τελείας ἀπωλείας τοῦ ἔθνους τῶν Ἰουδαίων πολλὰ συνεβούλευε τῷ Καίσαρι, ὡς Φίλων Ἰουδαῖος ἐξ Ἀλεξανδρείας διάγων ἱστορεῖ ἐν τῇ δευτέρᾳ τῆς περὶ αὐτοῦ πρεσβείας.
199. *H.E.* ii 5, 7: πρῶτον δὴ οὖν κατὰ Τιβέριον ἐπὶ μὲν τῆς Ῥωμαίων πόλεως ἱστορεῖ Σηιανὸν... ἄρδην τὸ πᾶν ἔθνος ἀπολέσθαι εἰσαγηοχέναι, ἐπὶ δὲ τῆς Ἰουδαίας Πιλᾶτον...
200. *H.E.* ii 6, 1: μετὰ δὲ τὴν Τιβερίου τελευτὴν Γάιον τὴν ἀρχὴν παρειληφότα... πάντων μάλιστα τὸ πᾶν Ἰουδαίων ἔθνος οὐ σμικρὰ καταβλάψαι.
201. But see Loeb Philo X, pp. xviii-xix.

how the Jews were persecuted, but also what a dreadful end was prepared for their persecutors by the avenging hand of God.[202] In *Flacc.*, the description of his punishment occupies as much space as the account of his measures against the Jews; the παλινῳδία appears to have occupied a complete book, and if it contained an account of the Jews' restored fortunes it will have concluded this work on their vindication. The basic idea of the work will thus have been similar to that of Lactantius' *De mortibus persecutorum*:[203] the persecutors of the pious meet with a frightful end. The enemies of the Jews with whom Philo deals did in fact all meet with a violent death: Sejanus, Flaccus, Gaius. Pilate's fate is recorded only in legend (vol. I, p. 387). On this hypothesis, the complete work can be reconstructed as follows. Book i presumably contained a general introduction. Book ii will have related the persecutions in the time of Tiberius, by Sejanus in Rome and by Pilate in Judaea, together with the violent end of these two enemies of the Jews.[204] Book iii is the extant *Flacc.* (not in fact against Flaccus, but about him). It records how through the pressure of the Alexandrian rabble and the desire to win Gaius' favour he allowed himself to be carried away into a merciless persecution of the Jews, in defiance of all law, and how he himself was then overtaken by the condemnation he deserved.[205] Book iv is *Legatio*. The title is hardly appropriate, for the aim is not to narrate the mission of the Alexandrian Jews to Gaius as such, but to recount the persecution of the Jews by him; the demented emperor's scornful treatment of the embassy sent to Rome also belongs to this topic, of course. Book v dealt with the παλινῳδία, that is, one might assume, the downfall of Gaius and the favourable turn in Jewish affairs which this brought about. It is also possible that *Legatio*

202. See Massebieau, *Le Classement*, pp. 65–78.

203. See now the edition, commentary and translation by J. L. Creed (1984). Comparison might also be made with the 'Acts of the Pagan Martyrs'; see vol. I, pp. 39–40.

204. The expulsion of the Jews from Rome in A.D. 19 is attested by Tacitus, *Ann.* ii 85 = GLAJJ II, no. 284; Suetonius, *Tib.* 36 = GLAJJ II, no. 306; Jos. *Ant.* xviii 3, 5 (83–4); ?Seneca, *Ep.* 108, 22 = GLAJJ I, no. 189; Dio lvii 18, 5a = GLAJJ II, no. 419. See pp. 75–6 above. None of these authors however attributes responsibility for this to Sejanus. Philo is therefore our only evidence for an 'anti-Jewish' policy on Sejanus' part: see *Leg.* 24 (159–60) with Smallwood's comments. Furthermore, in *Flacc.* 1 (1) he says that Flaccus continued Sejanus' machinations against the Jews. *Leg.* 38 (299–305), part of the letter of Agrippa to Gaius, also records Pilate's conflict with the population of Jerusalem over the episode of the gilded shields, without however making any link with a supposed wider policy, on the part of Sejanus or anyone else. For Pilate's governorship see vol. I, pp. 383–7; cf. J.-P. Lémondon, *Pilate et le gouvernement de la Judée : textes et monuments* (1981).

205. In the *Sacra Parallela* a passage is cited which is not in the extant treatise (Cod. Rupefuc. fol. 80ᵛ = Cod. Coislinianus, fol. 111ʳ = Harris, *Fragments*, p. 10). See Massebieau, *Le Classement*, p. 66, on the defectiveness of our text of *Flacc.*

comprises the original Book iv and a part of Book v, so that only some portion of the latter would be missing. The *Legatio* is unusually long, and even so appears to have many lacunae.[206]

If this plan for the work is accepted, it also serves to explain the repetitions in the extant parts of the work. It is beyond doubt that the persecution of the Alexandrian Jews portrayed in *Flacc.* 5–11 (25–96) is the same as that recounted in *Legat.* 18–20 (120–39). The extended repetition of the same events within the same work seems very strange. For this reason, and also on the grounds that there are no cross-references between the two descriptions, many scholars are of the opinion that *Flacc.* should be regarded as an entirely separate document, and not part of the historical work in five books mentioned by Eusebius. From the perspective of this work outlined above, however, such repetition is not only explicable but necessary. Philo was not intending to write a coherent history of the persecutions, so much as to deal with the persecutors, each individually. The persecution in Alexandria therefore had to be dealt with both in the story of Flaccus and in that of Gaius, in the one case in so far as Flaccus was responsible, in the other in so far as it was instigated by Caligula.

The title of this reconstituted historical work is problematic, since Eusebius' statements create difficulties. According to the passage from the *Chronicle*, the whole work appears to have been designed ἡ πρεσβεία. Again, when summarizing the contents of the complete work in the *Ecclesiastical History*, Eusebius says that all this is written ἐν ᾗ συνέγραψε πρεσβείᾳ (*H.E.* ii 5, 6). But then at the end of this summary review of the contents, he writes that Philo tells of a thousand other sufferings which befell the Jews in Alexandria ἐν δευτέρῳ συγγράμματι ᾧ [*or* ὧν] ἐπέγραψε περὶ ἀρετῶν. From this it would appear (with the reading ᾧ)[207] that Philo wrote two works dealing with these events, one of

206. See Massebieau, *Le Classement*, pp. 65–78; Cohn, 'Einteilung', p. 422; Box, *op. cit.*, pp. xxxv-xxxvii.

207. Box, *op. cit.*, p. xxxvii; Smallwood, p. 39. An alternative is to adopt the reading ὧν and translate 'in the second book of the work ὧν ἐπέγραψεν περὶ ἀρετῶν' (cf. Rufinus: 'in secundo operis sui de virtutibus libro'). Now if the persecutions under Caligula were already dealt with by book ii of the complete work, Philo must have used the remaining three books to describe the embassy to Gaius and the παλινῳδία. This would mean that our *Legat.* must have sizeable lacunae and it must cover the material from the original books ii to iv. That is possible, but complications ensue in reconciling this view with Eusebius' remark in *Chron.* (n. 198, above) that the persecutions of Sejanus were dealt with in the second book of the πρεσβεία. It seems unlikely that Philo would have dealt both with this and with the persecutions under Caligula in one and the same book. What is more, if we assume that both the reference here to the persecutions under Sejanus and that at the start of *Flacc.* are allusions to the same treatment of the topic, then *Flacc.* must have been the third book of the work; this is incompatible with the statement of Eusebius, *H.E.* ii 6, 3, if the reading ὧν is given. If one regards *Flacc.* as an entirely separate work (see below) then we must understand there to have been two treatments of the

which was entitled ἡ πρεσβεία and the other περὶ ἀρετῶν. However, not only is this intrinsically improbable, but Eusebius only mentions the latter title in his main catalogue of Philo's works (*H.E.* ii 18). There he says that Philo gave the name περὶ ἀρετῶν to the work dealing with the godless deeds of Gaius in irony (*H.E.* ii 18, 8). No other work on these events is listed, and the catalogue here is generally quite complete. A possible solution to this anomaly is the assumption that δευτέρῳ is the gloss of a scribe who could not make the different titles in ii 5, 6 and ii 6, 3 tally. Both would, in fact, relate to the same work. In the Old Syriac version of Eusebius, the words ἐν δευτέρῳ συγγράμματι ᾧ ἐπέγραψε περὶ ἀρετῶν are missing altogether. We cannot draw any certain conclusions from this translation for the criticism of the text, however, since omissions are quite common in it.

The title περὶ ἀρετῶν seems to apply to the entire historical work and to originate from Philo himself. It was not meant ironically, but was intended to suggest that virtue ultimately still gains the victory over godlessness. The title πρεσβεία, which can hardly derive from Philo, does not even fit the part dealing with Gaius, still less the work as a whole. Even if we were to take it in the sense of 'Apology' (cf. Athenagoras' πρεσβεία περὶ Χριστιανῶν), it would not correspond to the content of the work.[208]

If *Flacc.* is regarded as a separate work,[209] and not part of the five-book work, the reconstruction of the latter will be different. It is not only the absence of cross-references and the presence of repetitions between *Flacc.* and *Legat.* which lead some scholars to conclude that *Flacc.* is a separate treatise; the references to it in Eusebius' *Chronicle* and in later writers distinguish between *Flacc.* and the work of which *Legat.* forms a part. Eusebius here mentions the 'treatise entitled "Flaccus"',[210] and the 'Embassy' is referred to separately.[211] Photius also distinguishes between works censuring Gaius and Flaccus respectively. Two distinct works are also mentioned in the references given for extracts from the two works in the *Sacra Parallela*. The only other evidence comes from the manuscript titles: in these, *Flacc.* is not presented as part of περὶ ἀρετῶν. In the codices the two works are usually side by side, but separate. If it is supposed, then, that *Flacc.*, together with the lost prefatory section (or book) on Sejanus, is to be considered apart from περὶ ἀρετῶν, the structure of this work in relation to *Legat.* has still to be reconstructed. This has been done in several ways, according to

persecutions under Sejanus.

208. See Box, *op. cit.*, p. xxxviii; Smallwood, pp. 39–40.

209. This view is more widely accepted than that outlined in the previous paragraphs; see Box, p. xxxvii; Smallwood, pp. 40–3; Kraus Reggiani, *op. cit.*, pp. 555–7.

210. For the title of *Flacc.* see Box, pp. xxxvii, xxxviii.

211. See Smallwood, pp. 38–9.

whether one regards the *Legat.* as constituting a small part, or alternatively as representing most of, the original five books, compressed. Eusebius' references to persecution by Sejanus and Pilate (*H.E.* ii 5, 6–7) have been taken to imply that lacunae occur in *Legat.*, for which these topics supply the content.[212] If the short passages in *Legat.* on these subjects, 24 (159–61) and 38 (299–305), are all that Eusebius was referring to, however, and if the abrupt changes of subject in *Legat.* are regarded as a consequence of the theme of invective against Gaius, then *Legat.* is almost complete (the 'palinode' however is still missing).[213]

A remaining possibility is the thesis that neither *Flacc.* nor *Legat.* represent Philo's original compositions; they are later compilations assembled from the original five books mentioned by Eusebius. The compiler would in each case have selected material from these books around a persecutor figure, namely Flaccus and Gaius. Since abridgements and compilations often supersede complete works, it would be plausible that in this case two such works should have replaced the originals in the manuscripts.[214]

De Providentia (Περὶ προνοίας)[215]

The work is extant in full only in Armenian, and was first published by Aucher, with a Latin translation, from which the modern translations have all been made, rather than from the Armenian.[216] Two Greek fragments, one slight and one extensive, are given in Eusebius, *Praep. ev.*

212. Smallwood, pp. 41–3.

213. This is Colson's theory, see Loeb Philo X, pp. xvi-xxvi; cf. Smallwood, pp. 42–3.

214. So Pelletier, *Legatio*, p. 21.

215. *Armenian text:* Aucher, *Philonis Judaei Sermones tres hactenus inediti* (1822) (Latin translation of Armenian); C. E. Richter, *Philonis Judaei opera omnia* VIII (1828–30), pp. 45–100 (reprinted in stereotype ed., 1851–3, vol. VIII, pp. 52–113) (Latin translation); *Die Werke* VII (1964), pp. 322–62 (German translation by L. Früchtel from Aucher); M. Hadas-Lebel, *De Providentia* (*Oeuvres* XXXV, 1973) (Aucher's Latin with French translation).

Greek fragments: Mangey II, pp. 625–6, 634–47 (Eusebius' fragments) (not in C-W); Loeb Philo IX (1941), pp. 443–507 (Eusebius, using Gifford's text of *Praep. ev.*); M. Hadas Lebel, *op. cit.* (using text of Eusebius by K. Mras; also includes fragments from *Florilegia*). See also Harris, *Fragments*, pp. 75–6.

See esp. P. Wendland, *Philos Schrift über die Vorsehung, ein Beitrag zur Geschichte der nacharistotelischen Philosophie* (1892); *idem*, *Die philosophischen Quellen des Philo von Alexandria in seiner Schrift über die Vorsehung* (1892); A. Terian, 'A Critical Introduction to Philo's Dialogues', ANRW II.21.1, pp. 272–94.

The title is given by Eusebius, *H.E.* ii 18, 6; *Praep. ev.* vii 20, 336a; viii 13, 385d; and in the *Sacra Parallela*: Codex Vaticanus 1553 fol. 260^{r-v}; ἐκ τοῦ περὶ προνοίας α' (mistake for β'?); Cod. Coislinianus fol. 215^v; Cod. Rupefuc. fol. 27^{br}; fol. 114^{r-v}. See Harris, *Fragments*, pp. 75–6; Wendland, *Philos Schrift*, pp. 88 ff.; M. Hadas-Lebel, *De Providentia*, pp. 355–6.

216. For the Armenian Philo see p. 820 above. There is no modern edition or direct translation of the Armenian of *Prov.*

vii 21 and viii 14;[217] there are also some short fragments in the *Sacra Parallela*.

The Armenian text comprises two books, but the first of these is preserved only in an abbreviated and partially edited form. Eusebius quotes only the second book,[218] and introduces it twice with the formula ἐν τῷ περὶ προνοίας. In the *Ecclesiastical History*, also, the title τὸ περὶ προνοίας is more generally attested (only one manuscript has τά). Indeed, at this very point Eusebius reckons the document among the μονόβιβλα. He thus cannot have known the first book. Wendland's study of the thought, language and style of the work has convinced most subsequent scholars of its authenticity.[219] Either Book i has been altered in form since its composition by Philo,[220] or Philo composed a work in which different literary forms were adopted in the two parts, a procedure not without parallel in classical literature.

In the two treatises, Philo upholds belief in the workings of providence in the world, whilst 'Alexander', Philo's nephew, presents sceptical counter-arguments. The dialogue form is only found in Book ii, as the work now stands, though it might originally have been used in both books. Although it is more concerned with Greek philosophic concepts than Philo's scripturally-based works, there are still indications of its Jewish character, not only because of the position taken up by its author.[221] The influence of Stoicism is very pronounced, and Alexander's responses appear to have been derived from the New Academy.[222] Like the following work, *Prov.* probably belongs to the end of Philo's life.[223]

De animalibus (ὁ Ἀλέξανδρος ἢ περὶ τοῦ λόγον ἔχειν τὰ ἄλογα ζῷα)[224]

This work survives only in the Armenian translation, though there are

217. The first fragment (vii 21) is from the middle of the second book (Aucher, pp. 80–2; ii 50–1 in the ed. by M. Hadas-Lebel, ed.); the second, viii 14, consists of several large portions extending throughout the second book and forming a selection from it (see Hadas-Lebel, p. 21: Concordance). Hödschel also published two small fragments from *Prov.*

218. All the quotations in the *florilegia* also derive from the second book: see M. Hadas-Lebel, *De Providentia*, pp. 355–6.

219. On the question of authenticity see most recently Hadas-Lebel, *op. cit.*, pp. 22–46.

220. On the first book see Massebieau, *Le Classement*, pp. 87–91 (expressing doubts as to authenticity); Wendland, *Philos Schrift*, pp. 38 ff.

221. See A. Terian, ANRW II.21.1, p. 283, and cf. P. Borgen, *ibid.*, p. 119.

222. A. Terian, *ibid.*, pp. 277–81; cf. M. Hadas-Lebel, *op. cit.*, pp. 58–117. Note also P. Barth, 'Die Stoische Theodizee bei Philo', *Philosophische Abhandlungen, Max Heinze zum 70. Geburtstage gewidmet* ... (1906), pp. 14–33.

223. See n. 227 below, on *Anim.*

224. J. B. Aucher, *Philonis Judaei sermones tres hactenus inediti* (1822); A. Terian, *Philonis Alexandrini De Animalibus. The Armenian Text with an Introduction, Translation and Commentary* (1981). See *idem*, 'An Introduction to Philo's Dialogues', ANRW II.21.1, pp. 272–94. The Greek title is given by Eusebius, *H.E.* ii 18, 6. Cf. Jerome, *De vir. ill.* 11: 'De

fragments in the *Sacra Parallela*. There are two sections to the discussion of the rationality of animals; during the first Alexander discourses on the rationality of animals, and he is refuted by Philo in the second. The influence of Stoicism and Academic criticism of Stoicism is again thoroughgoing, and *Anim.* is clearly linked to *Prov.* as regards context and content;[225] thus even though *Anim.* lacks explicit references to Judaism, its authenticity is assured.[226] Two references in *Anim.* can be dated, though neither provides incontrovertible evidence for the date of composition.[227] The celebrations mentioned in ch. 27 were probably those given in A.D. 12 by Germanicus, but this allusion does not mean that the work must be dated immediately thereafter. The embassy mentioned in ch. 54 would provide firmer evidence for the late composition of *Prov.* and *Anim.* if it could be assumed to refer to the Alexandrian Jewish embassy to Gaius of A.D. 39–40; this is likely but not beyond question.

Hypothetica (Apologia pro Iudaeis) (Ὑποθετικά)[228]

Knowledge of this treatise rests almost entirely on the fragments which Eusebius quotes in *Praep. ev.* viii 6–7, introducing them (viii 5, 11) with the words Φίλωνος... ἀπὸ τοῦ πρώτου συγγράμματος ὧν ἐπέγραψεν ὑποθετικῶν, ἔνθα τὸν ὑπὲρ Ἰουδαίων ὡς πρὸς κατηγόρους αὐτῶν ποιούμενος λόγον ταῦτά φησιν. The meaning of the title is obscure.[229] 'Suppositions

---

Alexandro et quod propriam rationem muta animalia habeant.' (Some editions and manuscripts of Jerome have 'De Alexandro dicente quod ...' etc.) The Greek fragments are contained in Codex Vaticanus 1553 fol. 129ᵛ.

225. Eusebius, *H.E.* ii 18, 6, links the two works; cf. Harris, *Fragments*, p. 11.

226. Massebieau considered the work to have been brought into disorder by a redactor, *Le Classement*, pp. 87–91; cf. Terian, ANRW II.21.1, pp. 283–9.

227. On the question of date see Terian, ANRW II.21.1, pp. 289–91; M. Hadas-Lebel, *De Providentia*, pp. 38–45. For the embassy vol. I, pp. 390–8, and p. 818 above. The relevant section reads in Latin translation: 'ego etiam quando per legationem adii Romam' (Aucher, p. 152). The speaker is 'Alexander'; Terian, p. 290, takes this as evidence for Tiberius Iulius Alexander's participation in the embassy to Gaius. See above, n. 15.

Surveying *Prov.* and *Anim.*, Terian, p. 291, concludes that 'the internal evidence for a late date for the composition of the dialogues is overwhelming indeed. Consequently they are to be ascribed to the closing years of the author's life (ca. A.D. 50) and placed at the end of the corpus of his works.' Cf. also M. Pohlenz, *Philon von Alexandreia*, pp. 412–15; E. G. Turner, 'Tiberius Iulius Alexander', p. 56.

228. For the text of the fragments see Eusebius, *Praep. ev.* viii 6–7 (GCS VIII.1, ed. K. Mras, 1954, pp. 427–33). In editions of Philo: ed. Mangey II, pp. 626–32; ed. Cohn, ed. min. VI, pp. 189–200; Loeb Philo IX (1941), pp. 407–37; M. Petit, *Hypothetica* (*Oeuvres*, forthcoming). See esp. M. Petit, 'A propos d'une traversée exemplaire du désert du Sinaï selon Philon (*Hypothetica* vi 2–38): texte biblique et apologétique concernant Moïse chez quelques écrivains juifs', Semitica 26 (1976), pp. 137–42; L. Troiani, 'Osservazioni sopra l'apologia di Filone: gli Hypothetica', Athenaeum 56 (1978), pp. 304–14.

229. See esp. J. Bernays, 'Philons Hypothetica und die Verwünschungen des Buzyges in Athen', Monatsberichte der Berliner Akademie (1876), pp. 589–609, esp. p. 599 (repr.

about the Jews' is unlikely, even if understood to mean suppositions presented for the assessment of an audience on the question of Jewish origins. Such a title would only fit the initial parts of the work. Bernays suggested 'counsels, recommendations'. Ὑποθετικοὶ λόγοι are those treatises which contain moral advice or recommendations, as distinct from strictly theoretical investigations of ethical questions. 'As the extant fragments already enable us to see, Philo will have shifted the emphasis of his work to the discussion of such Jewish commandments as he could recommend for observance to a non-Jewish circle of readers, to whom the document is unmistakeably directed.' A further point in favour of this explanation seems to be the fact that Philo not infrequently uses the word ὑποθῆκαι in the sense of 'counsels, admonitions, teaching', synonymous with παραινέσεις;[230] Josephus also says that the subsidiary books of the Old Testament contained 'precepts for the conduct of life': ὑποθήκας τοῦ βίου, *C. Ap.* i 8 (40).

The remark of Eusebius quoted above and the content of the fragments quoted under the heading *Hypothetica* show that the treatise was essentially apologetic, however: a defence of the Jews against slanders and unfavourable criticism.[231] The title as understood by Bernays would hardly be in keeping with this approach. Perhaps, then, it is to be explained as 'imputations', false opinions about the Jews, which are here refuted.[232] In favour of this interpretation the following remark of Philo's should be particularly noted (Euseb. *Praep. ev.* viii 6, 6): ἢ τοὺς μὲν ἀπολέμους καὶ ἀνάνδρους εἶναι καὶ παντελῶς ὀλίγους ὑποθώμεθα. This being the character of *Hypothetica*, it might be identified with the Ὑπὲρ Ἰουδαίων ἀπολογία from which Eusebius reports the description of the Essenes later in the *Praep. ev.* (viii 11); this, again, must the the work περὶ Ἰουδαίων which Eusebius lists in *H.E.* ii 18, 6.[233] The fact that Eusebius refers to the work first as *Hypothetica* (viii 5, 11), and then later in the same book as ἡ ὑπὲρ Ἰουδαίων ἀπολογία (10, 19), need not lead to the supposition that the treatises were separate; it is feasible that in introducing the first extracts he deliberately used Philo's

in *Gesammelte Abhandlungen* I (1885), pp. 262–82). See also Colson in Loeb Philo IX, pp. 410–11.

230. *Somn.* ii 10 (73); *Spec.* i 8 (299); iii 5 (29); *Virt.* 3 (70).

231. It is, in fact, the only work of Philo's which could be described as apologetic, and it is perhaps to be linked to Josephus' *Contra Apionem* in genre. For the account of the Mosaic laws in the *Hypothetica* see I. Heinemann, *Philos griechische und jüdische Bildung* (1932), pp. 352–8. Cf. Colson, Loeb Philo IX, pp. 407–8, n.

232. So Massebieau, *Le Classement*, pp. 54–9 (who also offers a different interpretation); cf. P. Wendland, Jahrbb. für class. Philologie 22 Suppl. (1896), pp. 714 ff. Cf. Cohn, 'Einteilung', p. 418.

233. The identity of the *Hypothetica* and the περὶ/ὑπὲρ Ἰουδαίων was disputed by Massebieau, *Le Classement*, pp. 54–65. For the account of the Essenes see vol. II, pp. 555–74. The authenticity of Philo's account has been challenged, but is generally accepted; see Massebieau, *op. cit.*, pp. 59–65; Wendland, *op. cit.*, p. 702.

own title, but in the second citation he merely described the work by reference to its content, which Philo's title did not, perhaps, make clear. The reference to the work περὶ Ἰουδαίων in H.E. ii 18, 6 is problematic, however, for Eusebius lists it as among the μονόβιβλα, whereas it is known that the ὑποθετικά had several books (Praep. ev. viii 5, 11: ἀπὸ τοῦ πρώτου συγγράμματος ὧν ὑπέγραψεν ὑποθετικῶν). A firm conclusion as to the identity or otherwise of these apologetic works cannot be reached.

Lost Works

If the works above are known only by fragments or Armenian versions, the following books and works, most of which have been referred to in the survey above, are certainly lost; in view of a number of unattributed fragments there may well have been other works whose titles have disappeared without trace. It is difficult, moreover, to be sure whether Philo actually completed all the projected works to which he refers.[234]

(1) Of the *Quaestiones et solutiones* more than three books on Exodus (and possibly others on the rest of the Pentateuch; see above pp. 828–30).

(2) Probably two books of the *Legum Allegoriae* (pp. 832–3).

(3) The other book *De ebrietate* (probably the first; p. 836).

(4) The book περὶ μισθῶν (p. 838).

(5) The two books περὶ διαθηκῶν (pp. 835–6, 839).

(6) Three of the five books *De somniis* (p. 840).

(7) The two biographies of Isaac and Jacob (pp. 846–7).

(8) Probably a work περὶ εὐσεβείας (pp. 851–2).

(9) The treatise περὶ τοῦ δοῦλον εἶναι πάντα φαῦλον (p. 856).

(10) Possibly several books from the work on the persecutors of the Jews. Possibly one or two works on Sejanus (pp. 859–64).

(11) A treatise περὶ ἀριθμῶν, to which Philo refers in the *Vita Mosis* and elsewhere (p. 831 n. 55).[235]

The following works have been wrongly attributed to Philo.

(1) *De mundo* (Περὶ κόσμου)[236]

The spurious character of this treatise has long been acknowledged. It is a collection of excerpts from other Philonic works, in particular from *De*

---

234. For example, Philo says in *Prob.* 3 (20): ἀλλ' ὁ μὲν περὶ τῆς ἀρχῆς τοῦ σοφοῦ λόγος εἰς καιρὸν ἐπιτηδειότερον ὑπερκείσθω. But we do not know whether this project came to fruition or not. It was also thought that Philo wrote—or intended to write—a dialogue on Isaac and Ishmael, on the distinction between true wisdom and sophistry; but the reading of *Sobr.* 2 (9) now preferred (ἐν τοῖς ἰδίᾳ λόγοις instead of ἔν τισι διαλόγοις) need not refer to a specific work on this topic, but merely to some discussion of it; see Cohn, 'Einteilung', p. 425.

235. See K. Stähler, *Die Zahlenmystik bei Philon von Alexandreia* (1931).

236. See the ed. by Mangey II, pp. 601–24. Its spurious nature was already recognised by W. Budäus, who translated the work into Latin in 1526. See also Mangey II, p. 601, n.

aeternitate mundi. The compiler has copied his models so exactly that his text may be of value for the passages taken from Philo.[237]

(2) De Sampsone ; De Jona[238]

These two treatises, extant only in Armenian, were first published by Aucher in Armenian and Latin. There is general agreement that neither is by Philo.

(3) Interpretatio Hebraicorum nominum

A work on this subject, apparently anonymous, is mentioned by Origen, *Com. in Ioann.* ii 33 (27) (GCS *Origenes* IV, p. 90) : εὕρομεν τοίνυν ἐν τῇ ἑρμηνείᾳ τῶν ὀνόματων. Eusebius says that it was ascribed to Philo, but the way in which he speaks of it shows that he too knew it only as an anonymous work, *H.E.* ii 18, 7 : καὶ τῶν ἐν νόμῳ δὲ καὶ προφήταις Ἑβραϊκῶν ὀνομάτων αἱ ἑρμηνεῖαι τοῦ αὐτοῦ σπουδὴ εἶναι λέγονται. Jerome writes that according to Origen's testimony, Philo was the author. Thus for Jerome, too, the work was evidently anonymous. He himself intended to translate it into Latin, but found the text so corrupt that he considered it necessary to undertake a thorough new recension. In the preface to this work, he expresses himself in the following terms on the history of this *Onomasticon* : 'Philo, vir disertissimus Iudaeorum, Origenis quoque testimonio conprobatur edidisse librum hebraicorum nominum eorumque etymologias iuxta ordinem litterarum e latere copulasse. Quo cum vulgo habeatur a Graecis et bibliothecas orbis inpleverit, studii mihi fuit in latinam eum linguam vertere. Verum tam dissona inter se exemplaria repperi et sic confusam ordinem, ut tacere melius iudicaverim quam reprehensione quid dignum scribere. Itaque ... singula per ordinem scripturarum volumina percucurri et vetus aedificium nova cura instaurans fecisse me reor quod a Graecis quoque adpetendum sit ... Ac ne forte consummato aedificio quasi extrema deesset manus, Novi Testamenti verba et nomina interpretatus sum, imitari volens ex parte Originem, quem post apostolos ecclesiarum magistrum nemo nisi imperitus negat. Inter cetera enim ingenui sui praeclara monimenta etiam in hoc laboravit, ut quod Philo quasi Iudaeus omiserat hic ut christianus inpleret.' Jerome's final words here imply that Origen had already undertaken a completion of the older work by adding the New Testament material. Perhaps he also revised the older material in the process, so that the entire work now passed as his. It is mentioned under his name by the author of the work

---

237. See C-W vol. II, pp. vi-x.

238. J. B. Aucher, *Paralipomena Armena* (1826), pp. 549–611. See now H. Lewy, *The Pseudo-Philonic de Jona. Part 1 : The Armenian Text with a Critical Introduction* (*Studies and Documents* VII, 1936) ; F. Siegert, *Drei hellenistisch-jüdische Predigten* (1980) (German translation of *De Jona, De Sampsone, De Deo*).

wrongly attributed to Justin Martyr, *Quaestiones et responsiones ad ortho-doxos, Quaest.* 82 and 86 (ed. Otto, V, pp. 122 and 130).

It is thus possible to distinguish three stages in the history of this lexicon: the original work was anonymous, but evidently composed by a Jew, since it was restricted to the Old Testament. A Christian supplement was undertaken by Origen, and a new recension in Latin by Jerome.[239] Origen's contribution does not appear to have been important, for his name did not become firmly attached to the work. Eusebius says no more than that the work was said to be Philo's, and even Procopius of Gaza (*c.* A.D. 500) cites it anonymously as ἡ τῶν Ἑβραϊκῶν ὀνομάτων ἑρμηνεία. The extant catalogues of this kind are also anonymous.[240] It is scarcely possible to determine whether the underlying treatise actually derives from Philo. We can, indeed, assemble from his works an extensive list of explanations of Hebrew proper names, from which we can judge what is Philonic material and what is not.[241] But since there is no certain way back to the archetype, whether from Jerome or from the similar catalogues elsewhere, we cannot discover whether this archetype was Philonic or not.[242]

(4) A *Liber antiquitatum biblicarum* was frequently printed under Philo's name in the sixteenth century (first in 1527). See above, pp. 325–31.

(5) Of a different kind is the Pseudo-Philonic *Breviarium temporum*, one of the forgeries published by Annius of Viterbo, probably in full confidence of their authenticity.[243]

(6) On the treatise *De virtute eiusque partibus*, published by Mai under Philo's name, see above, n. 32.

(7) On *De mercede meretricis* see above, pp. 834, 849.

---

239. This *Onomasticon* by Jerome (*Liber interpretationis hebraicorum nominum*) is in Vallarsi's edition of Jerome's works, III, cols. 1–120, and in P. Lagarde, *Onomastica Sacra* (1870), pp. 1–81; (²1887), pp. 25–116 = CCL LXXII (1959), pp. 57–161. See F. Wutz, *Onomastica sacra. Untersuchungen zum Liber interpretationis nominum hebraicorum des H. Hieronymus* I-II (TU XLI.1–2, 1914–15), esp. vol. I, pp. 13–29.

240. For various Greek and Latin *Onomastica* of scriptural names, see Vallarsi, *Hieronymi Opera* III, cols. 537 ff.; Lagarde, *Onomastica sacra*, pp. 161 ff.

241. Such collections are found in Vallarsi, *Hieronymi Opera* III, cols. 731–44; Siegfried, *Philo von Alexandria* (1875), pp. 364–8.

242. The work *de nominibus Hebraicis* printed in a Latin translation of Philo at Basel in 1527 (Goodhart and Goodenough, *Bibliography*, no. 445) is simply the *Onomasticon* of Jerome.

243. On Joannes Annius da Viterbo (Giovanni Nanni) see Goodhart and Goodenough, *Bibliography*, pp. 319–20.

II. PHILO'S PHILOSOPHICAL THOUGHT

The preceding survey of Philo's works demonstrates the many-sidedness of his cultural background and of his literary undertakings. The combination of features of both Jewish and Greek culture found in Hellenistic Jewish authors in general is particularly characteristic of Philo.[1] His Greek philosophical background is perhaps most immediately striking. He was immersed in the thought of the Greek philosophic schools, having apparently availed himself of all the educational facilities of his time.[2] His language is modelled on that of classical authors; the works of Plato, in particular, have influenced his vocabulary and phraseology.[3] He was at home with the major Greek

1. On modern works framed in terms of assessments of the relative importance of Philo's Greek and Jewish backgrounds see p. 813, n. 8 above. Schürer's discussion of Philo's thought involved some distortion; his conviction that Philo's Jewishness amounted to merely a universalized, negated Judaism (see below, n. 25), led him to concentrate upon the traditional topics of Greek philosophy, to the neglect of both Philo's cultural context and the exegetical structure of his works (see below, p. 880). Although some modifications have been made to the initial discussion (pp. 871–80) Schürer's account of Philo's thought on these topics has been preserved in the main for its intrinsic value. The modern literature listed will indicate areas of Philo's thought and historical importance not fully considered here.

2. On Philo's education see above, p. 817, n. 27. It should be noted that Philo tells us little about his Jewish education; perhaps because this would be familiar to his audience? Its influence, at any rate, is self-evident, but see below, p. 874, on Philo's ignorance of Hebrew. It is generally assumed that after the ἐγκύκλιος παιδεία Philo attended the gymnasium. For the cultural importance of the gymnasium in Alexandria and the issue of Jewish participation in gymnasium activities cf. pp. 128–9, 138–9 and 819 above.

3. On Philo's literary style see e.g. C. Siegfried, *Philo von Alexandria* (1875), pp. 31–141; T. Billings, *The Platonism of Philo Judaeus* (1919), pp. 88–103 (Platonic similes); M. Adler, *Studien zu Philon von Alexandreia* (1929); A. Michel, 'Quelques aspects de la Rhétorique chez Philon', in *Philon d'Alexandrie*, ed. R. Arnaldez (1961), pp. 81–103; E. F. Trisoglio, 'Apostrofi, parenesi e preghiere in Filone d'Alessandria', Rivista Lasalliana 31 (1964), pp. 357–410; 32 (1965), pp. 39–79; E. J. Barnes, 'Petronius, Philo and Stoic Rhetoric', Latomus 32 (1973), pp. 787–98; J. Leopold and T. Conley, 'Philo's Style and Diction', in D. Winston and J. Dillon (eds.), *Two Treatises of Philo of Alexandria* (1983), pp. 129–78; T. Conley, 'Philo's Rhetoric: Argumentation and Style', ANRW II.21.1, pp. 343–71; J. Cazeaux, *La trame et la chaîne ou les structures littéraires et l'Exégèse dans cinq des Traités de Philon d'Alexandrie* (1983); idem, 'Philon d'Alexandrie, exégète', ANRW II.21.1, pp. 156–226. Although Philo's language and literary style are thoroughly Greek, the literary genres he adopts are less obviously so. (Cf. J. Leopold and T. Conley, *op. cit.*, p. 141: 'In his own time, Philo is unique.')

On Philo and the diatribe see P. Wendland, 'Philo und die kynisch-stoische Diatribe', in P. Wendland and U. Kern, *Beiträge zur Geschichte der griechischen Philosophie und Religion* (1895), pp. 1–75; R. Bultmann, *Der Stil der Paulinischen Predigt und die kynisch-stoische Diatribe* (*Forschungen zur Religion und Literatur des Alten und Neuen Testaments* XIII, 1910); H. Thyen, *Der Stil der jüdisch-hellenistischen Homilie* (*Forschungen zur Religion und Literatur des Alten und*

poets—Homer, Euripides, and others—and he occasionally quotes them.[4] But it was the philosophers who meant most to him.[5] He calls Plato 'great'.[6] Parmenides, Euripides, Zeno, and Cleanthes were 'divine', and formed a 'sacred society'.[7]

More than anything else, however, it is Philo's own conception of the world and of human life which manifests how much he respected the Greek philosophers. In many crucial points his outlook follows the great teachers of the Greeks. Indeed, Philo has absorbed Greek thought so fully—and worked it into a new approach—that from one point of view he can himself be regarded as belonging to the succession of Greek philosophers.[8] His thought as a whole may be described as eclectic, with Platonic, Stoic and Neopythagorean doctrines featuring most prominently. At different times he has been called a Platonist and a Pythagorean, according to which aspect was singled out for emphasis. He might just as reasonably be called a Stoic, for the influence of Stoicism upon him is just as pronounced as his Platonism or Neopythagoreanism.[9]

Neuen Testaments LXV, 1955); G. Kustas, 'The Diatribe in Ancient Rhetorical Theory', *Centre for Hermeneutical Studies*, Berkeley, *Colloquy* XXII (1976).

For *Mos.* as a biography see above, p. 855. The group of philosophical treatises *Aet.*, *Prob.*, *Prov.* and *Anim.* are somewhat easier to align with Graeco-Roman genres, especially where dialogue is employed; see above, pp. 856, 858–9, 864–6.

4. For citations of classical authors by Philo see e.g. L. Siegfried, *Philo von Alexandria* (1875), pp. 137 ff.; C-W vol. VII, pp. 3–26 (Index nominum). See M. Alexandre, 'La culture profane chez Philon', in *Philon d'Alexandrie*, ed. R. Arnaldez (1967), pp. 105–30; P. Boyancé, 'Echo des exégèses de la mythologie grecque chez Philon', *ibid.*, pp. 169–88. For Philo's attitude to classical literature see M. Alexandre, *De congressu* (*Oeuvres* XVI, 1967), pp. 56–61; A. Mendelson, *Secular Education* (1982), pp. 5–7. For Philo's references to Homer, and the possibility of similar rabbinic references, see E. M. Smallwood, *Philonis Alexandrini Legatio*, pp. 195, 230 (noting that Philo mentions or quotes Euripides (most frequently), Hesiod, Aeschylus, Sophocles, and Menander).

5. See esp. Wolfson, *Philo* I, pp. 93–4. Much of the earlier work on Philo was devoted to Quellenforschung; see e.g. H. von Arnim, *Quellenstudien zu Philo* (1888).

6. *Prov.* ii 42 (trans. Aucher): 'magnus Plato'; cf. *Prob.* 2 (13): τὸν ἱερώτατον Πλάτωνα (following Cod. Mediceus, one of the best manuscripts). See also Leisegang, Index s.v. Πλάτων. Others have λιγυρώτατον, which Colson prefers (see note *ad loc.* in Loeb Philo IX). Cf. C-W *ad loc.*

7. *Prov.* ii 48 (trans. Aucher): 'Parmenides, Empedocles, Zeno, Cleanthes, aliique divi homines, ac velut verus quidam proprieque sacer coetus.' Cf. *Prob.* 1 (2): τὸν τῶν Πυθαγορείων ἱερώτατον θίασον.

8. See e.g. H. Chadwick in A. H. Armstrong (ed.), *Cambridge History of Later Greek and Early Medieval Philosophy* (1967), pp. 137–57; S. Dillon, *The Middle Platonists* (1977), pp. 139–83; B. Mack, 'Philo and Exegetical Traditions in Alexandria', ANRW II.21.1, pp. 227–71.

9. The well known proverb, ἢ Πλάτων φιλωνίζει ἢ Φίλων πλατωνίζει testifies to his reputation as a Platonist (Jerome, *De vir. ill.* 11; Suda, s.v. Φίλων; Photius, *Bibl.*, cod. 105). Cf. Jerome, *Epist.* 70 *ad Magnum oratorem* 3: 'quid loquar de Philone quem vel alterum vel Iudaeum Platonem critici pronuntiant?' Clement of Alexandria calls him a Pythagorean, and does so in the two passages in which he is characterizing his philosophical tendencies: *Strom.* i 15 (72, 4); ii 19 (100, 3). *Strom.* ii 19 (100): ὥς φησιν ὁ

Despite the thoroughgoing influence of Greek philosophy, Philo remained a Jew.[10] The wisdom of the Greeks did not make him unfaithful to the religion of his forefathers. His Jewish cultural heritage ought not to be ignored in the face of his Greek philosophical culture, impressive as the latter might appear. Most of his treatises are, after all, expositions of scripture. It is, however, beyond question that he read the Old Testament primarily, and perhaps exclusively, in Greek translation. [11] His knowledge of Hebrew seems to have been superficial

Πυθαγόρειος Φίλων. Eusebius mentions both his Platonism and his Pythagoreanism : *H.E.* ii 4, 3 : μάλιστα τὴν κατὰ Πλάτωνα καὶ Πυθαγόραν ἐζηλωκὼς ἀγωγήν. Assessments of Philo's philosophical position in relation to contemporary Greek philosophic thought include : H. von Arnim, *Quellenstudien zu Philo von Alexandria* (1888) ; P. Wendland, *Die philosophischen Quellen des Philo von Alexandria in seiner Schrift über die Vorsehung* (1892) ; E. Norden, 'Über den Streit des Theophrast und Zeno bei Philo περὶ ἀφθαρσίας κόσμου', in *Beiträge zur Geschichte der griechischen Philosophie* (Jahrbücher für classische Philologie, Suppl. XIX.2, 1893), pp. 440–52 ; P. Wendland, 'Eine doxographische Quelle Philos', SAB (1897), pp. 1074–9 ; J. Horovitz, *Untersuchungen über Philons und Platons Lehre von der Weltschöpfung* (1900) ; P. Barth, 'Die stoische Theodizee bei Philo', *Philosophische Abhandlungen, Max Heinze zum 70. Geburtstage gewidmet von Freunden und Schülern* (1906), pp. 14–33 ; P. Wendland, *Die hellenistisch-römische Kultur in ihren Beziehungen zu Judentum und Christentum* (²/³1912) (Handbuch zum N.T. I.2), pp. 203–11 ; M. Apelt, *De rationibus quibusdam quae Philoni Alexandrino cum Posidonio intercedunt* (1907) ; Th. Billings, *The Platonism of Philo Judaeus* (1919) ; W. Theiler, *Die Vorbereitung des Neoplatonismus* (1930) ; E. R. Goodenough, 'A Neo-Pythagorean Source in Philo Judaeus', YCS 3 (1932), pp. 115–64 ; I. Heinemann, *Philons griechische und jüdische Bildung* (1932, repr. 1962) ; M. Muehl, 'Zu Posidonios und Philo', Wiener Studien 60 (1942), pp. 28–36 ; M. Pohlenz, 'Philon d'Alexandreia', NGG Phil.-hist. Kl. (1942), pp. 409–87 ; *idem, Die Stoa : Geschichte einer geistigen Bewegung* I (1948), pp. 369–78 ; II (1949), pp. 180–4 ; W. Theiler, 'Philo von Alexandria und der Beginn der kaiserzeitlichen Platonismus', in *Parusia. Festgabe für J. Hirschberger* (1965), pp. 199–217 ; U. Früchtel, *Die kosmologischen Vorstellungen bei Philo von Alexandrien. Ein Beitrag zur Geschichte der Genesisexegese* (ALGHJ II, 1968) ; J. Dillon, *The Middle Platonists. A Study of Platonism 80 B.C. to A.D. 220* (1977), pp. 139–83.

Especially important are assessments of Philo in the light of recent work on Middle Platonism ; see J. Dillon, *op. cit.*, pp. 139–83 ; survey in P. Borgen, ANRW II.21.1, pp. 147–50.

10. See esp. the survey of this issue in P. Borgen, ANRW II.21.1, pp. 138–54.

11. Philo tells the story of the translation of the Torah in *Mos.* ii 5–7 (25–44). In doing so he is justifying the use of the LXX in the Alexandrian synagogue—note the festival held to commemorate the translation, 7 (41)—and in his own works. His use of the LXX (chiefly the Pentateuch) has given rise to wide interest amongst Septuagint scholars, since he sometimes departs from the LXX readings. (On the Septuagint see above, pp. 474–93.) See e.g. C. Siegfried, 'Philo und der überlieferte Text der LXX', ZWTh 16 (1873), pp. 217–38, 411–28, 522–40 ; F. C. Conybeare, 'Upon Philo's Text of the LXX', Expos. 4.4 (1891), pp. 456–66 ; F. Conybeare, 'On the Philonean Text of the Septuagint', JQR 5 (1892–3), pp. 246–80 ; 8 (1895–6), pp. 88–122 ; H. E. Ryle, *Philo and Holy Scripture* (1895) ; W. L. Knox, 'A Note on Philo's use of the O.T.', JThSt 41 (1940), pp. 30–4 ; F. H. Colson, 'Philo's Quotations from the O.T.', JThSt 41 (1940), pp. 237–51 ; R. Marcus, 'A Textual-exegetical note on Philo's Bible', JBL 69 (1950), pp. 363–5 ; P. Katz, *Philo's Bible* (1950) ; *idem* (Walters), *The Text of the Septuagint : Its Corruptions and their Emendation*, ed. D. W. Gooding (1973) ; S. Jellicoe, 'Aristeas, Philo and the Septuagint Vorlage', JThSt N.S. 12 (1961), pp. 261–71 ; G. E. Howard, 'The "Aberrant" Text of Philo's Quotations

at best. It has been argued that his Hebrew etymologies indicate first-hand knowledge of the language, but others regard the spurious nature of these etymologies as proof of Philo's ignorance of Hebrew; it is possible that he relied on some sort of etymological handbook.[12] Philo certainly did not possess an accurate, formal knowledge of Palestinian Halakhah, but a general familiarity with it might be suggested by one remark, and especially by his work *On the Special Laws*.[13] As to haggadic

---

Reconsidered', HUCA 44 (1973), pp. 197–209; Y. Amir, 'Philo and the Bible', SP 2 (1973), pp. 1–8; V. Nikiprowetzky, *Le Commentaire* (1977), pp. 51–2; D. Gooding and V. Nikiprowetzky, 'Philo's Bible in the *De Gigantibus* and *Quod Deus*', in D. Winston and J. Dillon (eds.), *Two Treatises*, pp. 89–125.

12. There has been much controversy on the question of Philo's knowledge of Hebrew. Of the older studies see especially J. B. Carpzovius, *Sacrae exercitationes in S. Paulli epistolam ad Hebraeos ex Philone Alexandrino. Praefixa sunt Philoniana prolegomena, in quibus de non adeo contemnenda Philonis eruditione hebraica, de convenientia stili Philonis cum illo D. Paulli in epistola ad Hebraeos, et de aliis nonnullis varii argumenti, exponitur* (1750), pp. xxii-lii; see S. Siegfried, *Philo von Alexandria*, p. 142, nn. 1–3 for other early discussions; *ibid.*, pp. 142–59 (Philo probably did know Hebrew). Wolfson, *Philo* I, pp. 88–90 ('while he did not know enough of the language to write his interpretations of Scripture in Hebrew, he knew enough of it to read Scripture in the original and to check up on the Greek translation whenever he found it necessary'). S. Belkin, *Philo and the Oral Law* (1940), pp. 29–48 (Philo either used the Hebrew Bible directly, or had been informed by 'Alexandrian adepts of Hebrew scripture', p. 35); I. Heinemann, *Philons griechische und jüdische Bildung*, pp. 524 ff.; and V. Nikiprowetzky, *Le Commentaire*, pp. 50–81 (with full bibliography), conclude that Philo knew no Hebrew. See also S. Sandmel, 'Philo's Knowledge of Hebrew', SP 5 (1978), pp. 107–11 (pointing out some incentives to scholarly bias in the issue).

Much of the recent debate has concentrated on Philo's etymologies and whether they testify to direct knowledge of Hebrew, or indirect use of Hebrew word-lists; see e.g. S. Belkin, 'The Interpretation of Names in Philo', Horeb 12 (1956), pp. 3–61 (in Hebrew); A. D. Mantel, 'Did Philo Know Hebrew?', Tarbiz 32 (1962–3), pp. 98–9 (in Hebrew); J.-G. Kahn, 'Did Philo know Hebrew? The Evidence of the Etymologies', Tarbiz 34 (1965), pp. 337–45 (in Hebrew); A. Hanson, 'Philo's Etymologies', JThSt 18 (1967), pp. 128–39; A. V. Nazzaro, 'Filone Alessandrino e l'ebraico', Rendiconti d. R. Accademia di archeologia, lettere e belle arti di Napoli 42 (1968), pp. 61–79; D. Rokeah, 'A New Onomasticon Fragment from Oxyrhynchus and Philo's Etymologies (P.Oxy. 2263, saec. 2, graeca)', JThSt 19 (1968), pp. 70–82; D. Gooding, 'Philo's Knowledge of Hebrew underlying the Greek', in D. Winston and J. Dillon, *Two Treatises*, pp. 119–25 (Philo neither had any awareness of the Hebrew underlying the Greek which he quotes, nor shows evidence of having access to the meaning of the Hebrew). The importance of the question for assessing Philo's Jewishness has perhaps been overemphasized. See Sandmel, 'Philo's Knowledge of Hebrew', SP 5 (1978), pp. 107, 111; cf. P. Borgen, ANRW II.21.1, p. 123.

13. See esp. *Hypoth.* 7, 6 (= Eusebius, *Praep. ev.* viii 7, 6): Philo proceeds to give several of the commandments by way of example, and then says: μυρία δὲ ἄλλα ἐπὶ τούτοις, ὅσα καὶ ἀγράφων ἐθῶν καὶ νομίμων κἂν τοῖς νόμοις αὐτοῖς. For a discussion of the Mosaic laws in *Hypoth.* compared with *Spec.* see I. Heinemann, *Philons griechische und jüdische Bildung*, pp. 352–8; A. Mosès, *De Specialibus Legibus III-IV*, pp. 24–5. There is still little agreement amongst scholars concerning Philo's relationship to Palestinian Halakhah (on which see vol. I, pp. 70–90; II, pp. 339–46). The question is of importance in so far as Philo's works provide virtually the only testimony to Jewish legal principles as expressed in Alexandria; it remains uncertain how far, if at all, these works reflect Alexandrian practice.

interpretation of scripture, Philo does introduce non-scriptural material, but this does not prove that he follows Palestinian traditions. As regards its form, his *Allegorical Commentary* on Genesis might be considered in its entirety as an application of the methods of Palestinian midrash to the field of Hellenism. There are also some similarities of content, even though they are slighter than the methodological affinity. For the legendary embellishment of the life of Moses, Philo explicitly appeals to oral tradition passed down by the Elders: 'for I have always sought to weave together what is read with what is said'.[14]

It is significant that Philo nowhere provides a systematic presentation of his thought. At most he develops particular aspects with some coherence, such as the theory of the creation of the world. As a rule, however, he presents his theories in conjunction with an Old Testament text. This is connected with the formal principle of this entire theology: the underlying presupposition of the absolute authority of the Mosaic Law. Like all Jews, Philo regarded the Torah of Moses as the supreme authority, indeed the sole authority; it was absolutely binding, constituting a perfect revelation of divine wisdom. Everything set down in the holy writings of Moses was divine utterance.[15] Every word,

---

Controversy arises partly because of the difficulties in dating Palestinian Halakhah and Haggadah; see vol. I, pp. 68–118. Important studies of Philo and the Halakhah include: B. Ritter, *Philo und die Halacha* (1879); J. Z. Lauterbach, 'Philo Judaeus—His Relation to the Halakhah', JE X (1905), pp. 15–18; E. R. Goodenough, *The Jurisprudence of the Jewish Courts in Egypt* (1929) (regards parallels with Greek and Roman legal procedure as evidence that Philo was describing Jewish law as practised in Jewish tribunals in Egypt; see criticisms in Heinemann, *op. cit.*; S. Belkin, *The Alexandrian Halakhah in the Apologetic Literature of the First Century C.E.* (1936); *idem, Philo and the Oral Law* (1940, repr. 1970; rev. by Goodenough, JBL 59 (1940), pp. 420–3); S. Daniel, 'La Halacha de Philon selon le premier livre des "Lois spéciales"', in *Philon d'Alexandrie*, ed. R. Arnaldez (1967), pp. 221–41; cf. *eadem, De Specialibus Legibus I-II* (1975); A. Mosès, *De Specialibus Legibus II-IV* (1970), pp. 23–42, 360–1; G. Alon, 'On Philo's Halakha', in *Jews, Judaism and the Classical World. Studies in Jewish History in the Times of the Second Temple and Talmud*, trans. I. Abrahams (1977), pp. 89–137; D. Daube, 'Jewish Law in the Hellenistic World', in *Jewish Law in Legal History and the Modern World*, ed. B. S. Jackson (1980), pp. 45–60. Note the survey of recent discussions by P. Borgen, ANRW II.21.1, pp. 124–6.

14. *Mos.* i 1 (4). See Wolfson, *Philo* I, pp. 189–94. On Wolfson's tendency to align Philo with Palestinian traditions without consideration of the difficulties of dating the Palestinian material, see B. Bamberger, 'The Dating of Aggadic Materials', JBL 68 (1949), pp. 115–23; cf. S. Sandmel, *Philo's Place in Judaism*, pp. 13–26; *idem*, ANRW II.21.1, pp. 34–6. Philo's non-scriptural embellishments can be traced from the index in vol. VII of L. Ginzberg, *Legends of the Jews* (1909–38); but see the cautionary remarks of S. Sandmel, *Philo of Alexandria*, p. 133. See also B. Bamberger, 'Philo and the Aggadah', HUCA 48 (1977), pp. 153–85; and earlier L. Treitel, 'Agada bei Philo', MGWJ 53 (1909), pp. 28–45, 159–73, 286–91 = *Philonische Studien*, ed. M. Braun (1915), pp. 85–113.

15. *Mos.* ii 35 (188): οὐκ ἀγνοῶ μὲν οὖν ὡς πάντα εἰσὶ χρησμοὶ ὅσα ἐν ταῖς ἱεραῖς βίβλοις ἀναγέγραπται, χρησθέντες δι' αὐτοῦ (i.e. Moses).

therefore, had a specific significance.[16] The works of the other prophets, too, linked to those of Moses, also contained divine revelation. For all prophets were God's interpreters, and He used them as instruments for the revelation of His will.[17] Connected with this formal principle that the holy scripture, and especially the Mosaic law, had absolute authority, is the further presupposition that this same source of all knowledge also contains all true wisdom. In other words, Philo formally derived from the Old Testament all the philosophical doctrines which in practice he appropriated from the Greek philosophers. The most profound and perfect instruction on matters human and divine was to be found pre-eminently in the works of Moses, not those of Plato, Pythagoras or Zeno. The Mosaic writings already contained all that was good and true—things which were later to be taught by the Greek philosophers. [18] So Moses was the real teacher of mankind, and the Greek sages simply derived their doctrines from him—a view which Philo shared with Aristobulus.[19]

The methodological procedure which enabled Philo to reinforce these assumptions and sustain them was allegorical interpretation.[20]

16. Note that Philo explains that the expression θανάτῳ θανατοῦσθαι in *Fug.* 10 (54) worried him, because he knew very well that Moses does not use a superfluous word. Cf. *Cher.* 16 (55); *Agric.* 1 (2). This conviction applies equally to the LXX; see above, n. 11.

17. The precise extent of Philo's Canon cannot be determined, but it is certain that the Torah of Moses (the Pentateuch) had an importance quite apart from that of the rest of holy scripture for him. However, the most important of the Nebiim and Kethubim are quoted by him as prophetic and sacred writings. On the divine inspiration of the prophets see *Spec.* i 2 (65): ἑρμηνεῖς γάρ εἰσιν οἱ προφῆται θεοῦ καταχρωμένου τοῖς ἐκείνων ὀργάνοις πρὸς δήλωσιν ὧν ἂν ἐθελήσῃ. Cf. *Spec.* iv 8 (49); *Her.* 53 (266). See e.g. C. F. Horneman, *Observationes ad illustrationem doctrinae de canone Veteris Testamenti ex Philone* (1775); H. E. Ryle, *Philo and Holy Scripture* (1895), pp. xvi-xxxv; P. Katz, 'The Old Testament Canon in Palestine and Alexandria', ZNW 47 (1956), pp. 191–217, esp. 209–12; and bibliography in n. 12 above. Note also H. A. Wolfson, 'The Veracity of Scripture from Philo to Spinoza', n *Religious Philosophy* ([2]1961), pp. 217–45.

18. On this principle as applied to Heraclitus see *Leg.* i 33 (108); *Her.* 43 (214); *Prob.* 8 (57). Cf. Borgen, ANRW II.21.1, p. 152.

19. On Aristobulus see esp. M. Hengel, *Judaism and Hellenism* I (1974), pp. 164–6, and above, p. 579. On the general notion that Greek philosophers drew their wisdom from the patriarchs and Moses, as traced through Ps.-Eupolemus, Eupolemus, Aristobulus, Artapanus, Josephus, and the Church Fathers, see Hengel, *op. cit.*, pp. 86, 90, 92, 129 ff., 165 ff. On Aristobulus and allegorical interpretation see below, n. 22. For the notion of Judaism as a philosophy, which is perhaps most pronounced in Philo's thought, see M. Hengel, *op. cit.*, pp. 255–61; V. Nikiprowetzky, *Le Commentaire*, esp. pp. 100 ff.; C. Elsas, 'Das Judentum als philosophische Religion bei Philo von Alexandrien', in *Altes Testament— Frühjudentum—Gnosis. Neue Studien zu 'Gnosis und Bibel'*, ed. K. W. Tröger (1980), pp. 195–220.

20. For older studies of Philo's use of allegory see Goodhart and Goodenough, *Bibliography*, pp. 248–9. The major discussions of the relative importance of Greek and Jewish exegesis as influences on Philo are Z. Frankel, *Über den Einfluss der palästinischen Exegese auf die alexandrinische Hermeneutik* (1851); C. Siegfried, *Philo von Alexandria als Ausleger des Alten Testaments* (1875, repr. 1970), pp. 160–97; L. Treitel, 'Ursprung, Begriff

Philo did not invent this method; it had been practised by Greeks and Jews before him. In the Greek context, the need to harmonize the mythological representations of Homer and of popular belief with the philosophical convictions of the educated led to the allegorical reinterpretation of Homer. Philo undoubtedly learnt from these Greek precursors. [21] But he was not the first to practise allegorical interpretation in a Jewish context either. Aristobulus had already employed it.[22] Philo himself mentions earlier exegetes in connection with his interpretation of biblical matters, but unfortunately without ever identifying them.[23] Indeed for him this procedure is taken completely

---

und Umfang der allegorischen Schrifterklärung', MGWJ 55 (1911), pp. 543–54; E. Stein, *Die allegorische Exegese des Philo aus Alexandreia* (1929); V. Nikiprowetzky, 'À propos de l'histoire de l'exégèse allégorique: l'absurdité, signe de l'allégorie', *Studia Patristica* I (1957), pp. 395–413; J. Pépin, *Mythe et allégorie. Les origines grecques et les contestations judéo-chrétiennes* (1958; ²1977); R. P. C. Hanson, *Allegory and Event* (1959); idem, 'Le "challenge" Homère-Moïse aux premiers siècles chrétiens', RScR 29 (1964), pp. 105–22; I. Christiansen, *Die Technik der allegorischen Auslegungswissenschaft bei Philon von Alexandrien (Beiträge zur Geschichte der bibl. Hermeneutik* VII, 1969); G. Delling, 'Wunder— Allegorie—Mythus bei Philon von Alexandria', in *Studien zum Neuen Testament und zum hellenistischen Judentum. Gesammelte Aufsätze* (1970), pp. 72–129; V. Nikiprowetzky, *Le Commentaire* (1977); B. L. Mack, 'Weisheit und Allegorie bei Philon von Alexandrien', SP 5 (1978), pp. 57–105.

21. On Greek exegesis and its relation to Philo's allegorizing see (in addition to the works in note 20 above) J. Tate, 'Plato and Allegorical Interpretation', CQ 23 (1929), pp. 142–54; 24 (1930), pp. 1–10; idem, 'On the History of Allegorism', CQ 28 (1934), pp. 105–14; F. Buffière, *Les mythes d'Homère et la pensée grecque* (1956); H. Dörrie, 'Zur Methodik antiker Exegese', ZNW 65 (1974), pp. 121–38; Y. Amir, 'The Allegory of Philo Compared with Homeric Allegory', Eshkoloth 6 (1970), pp. 35–45 (Hebrew); J. C. H. Lebram, 'Eine stoische Auslegung von Ex. 3.2 bei Philo', *Das Institutum Judaicum der Universität Tübingen in den Jahren 1971–1972* (1972), pp. 30–4; J. A. Coulter, *The Literary Microcosm: Theories of Interpretation of the Later Neoplatonists* (1977); D. A. Russell, *Criticism in Antiquity* (1981), esp. pp. 95 ff.

For two examples of Stoic works giving allegorized interpretations of Homer see Cornutus, *De natura deorum* (see RE Suppl. V, cols. 995–1005, s.v. 'Kornutos') and the *Quaestiones Homericae* of Heraclitus (ed. and trans. F. Buffière, 1962); both probably belong to the first century A.D.

22. On Jewish allegorical exegesis see (in addition to the works in n. 20 above) L. Ginzberg, 'Allegorical Interpretation', JE I (1901), pp. 403–11; R. Loewe, 'The "Plain" Meaning of Scripture in Early Jewish Exegesis', *Papers of the Institute of Jewish Studies, London*, ed. J. G. Weiss (1964), pp. 140–85, esp. pp. 146–52. H. A. Wolfson, *Philo* I, pp. 117–38, argues that Philo's allegorizing was essentially Jewish in character.

The most immediate influences on Philo's exegesis probably came from his predecessors in the Greek-speaking synagogue and from his Alexandrian contemporaries. Aristobulus (see pp. 579–87 above) did practise allegorical interpretation, and presents the earliest example of this in Alexandria, but it appears to have been a restrained method of allegorizing compared with that of Philo; see N. Walter, *Der Thoraausleger Aristobulus*, pp. 124–49, esp. 141–9. See also P. M. Fraser, *Ptolemaic Alexandria* (1972), pp. 695–6 and nn.

23. For Philo's allusions to earlier exegetes, which are tantalizing for their hints of controversy and a multiplicity of approaches to scripture, see esp. E. Zeller, *Die Philosophie der Griechen* III.2 (⁵1923, repr. 1963), pp. 285–8. See also M. Shroyer, 'Alexandrian

for granted; he no longer considers it necessary to justify it, though he occasionally emphasises its value and indispensability. With the aid of allegorical interpretation he could see how to read profound philosophical theories out of the early history of Genesis, especially in the fields of psychology and ethics, theories which actually had their true roots in Greek philosophy. In his hands, the surface events of the biblical narrative become profound lessons in the supreme problems of human existence.

This method enabled Philo to fulfil a two-fold mission. Through allegorical interpretation he transmitted Greek philosophic culture to his co-religionists, with whom he shared the presupposition of the authority of the Mosaic Law. He showed them that Moses had taught precisely those things which seemed right and valuable to him in Greek philosophy. Conversely, by the same method he could prove to the Greeks that all the knowledge and insights which formed the fundamentals on which they prided their own philosophers could be found in the works of Moses.[24] It was not a Greek philosopher, but Moses, who was not only the first lawgiver but also the first and greatest philosopher. These two tendencies are clearly identifiable as the mainsprings of Philo's comprehensive literary undertaking. Being both Jewish and Greek himself, he sought to employ strains of thought from both cultural backgrounds. His religious presuppositions are first and foremost those of Judaism with its belief in revelation. These religious presuppositions were not so much modified by his adoption of elements of Greek philosophy as wrought into a new approach. Since he united both strains of thought in his own background and outlook, this harmonization of Greek and Jewish elements does not need to be interpreted as the product of a conscious programme; little of his extant oeuvre could be described as overtly apologetic or propagandist.

There is undoubtedly a universalizing element in Philo's presentation of Judaism, whereby Jewish beliefs are set in a wider context transcending their origin in Jewish national history and religious observance; but the scriptural framework of Philo's works, and the very difficulty of extrapolating his views on Greek philosophical topics,

---

Jewish Literalists', JBL 55 (1936), pp. 261–84; S. Sandmel, 'Philo's Environment and Philo's Exegesis', JBR 22 (1954), pp. 248–53; B. Mack, 'Exegetical Traditions in Alexandrian Judaism: A Program for the Analysis of the Philonic Corpus', SP 3 (1974–5), pp. 71–112; D. Hay, 'Philo's References to Other Allegorists', SP 6 (1979–80), pp. 41–75; see further p. 818, n. 24 above.
24. On the question of a possible pagan audience for some of Philo's works see above, pp. 814, 817–18, 840, 855, 889.

should make it clear that the Jewish elements in his thought and approach are not to be minimized.[25]

One cannot properly speak of a close-knit Philonic system. The elements forming his outlook are too diverse to form such a thing; philosophically speaking, there are inconsistencies and repetitions in his works which make the formulation of any coherent Philonic theories difficult. This is principally because of the character of his literary enterprise: in the majority of his treatises he does not set out to outline a philosophical position, but rather takes a scriptural text as his point of

---

25. Philo has been interpreted as striving to make propaganda on both sides (so GJV III[4], p. 703). Most scholars would now regard this as an overstatement in view of the rather muted character of Philo's preaching; it also assumes a clear-cut distinction between the Greek and the Jewish aspects of Philo's thought, a distinction which Philo would hardly have recognized. Most of his works, moreover, were probably intended for Jews, so that even when Philo sets out to advocate respect for Jewish traditions within a broadly Greek outlook, one can hardly regard his mission as overtly propagandist. It is possible, however, that he was involved in controversy within the synagogue; see P. Borgen, ANRW II.21.1, pp. 126 ff.

Schürer justified his concentration, in the ensuing sections, on Philo's (Greek) philosophical thought on the grounds that his outlook could be presented without reference to any Jewish, particularistic notions; Philo only embraced these Jewish particularist notions in a form tantamount to denying them. He reduced Philo's Judaism to the sole underlying assumption that the Jewish people were in possession of the highest religious knowledge through the Mosaic revelation. If Philo is approached as if he were a systematic philosopher in the Greek tradition, Schürer's conclusion follows reasonably enough (though Wolfson's study belies it). (Cf. B. Mack, ANRW II.21.1, p. 230.) There are sufficient indications in Philo's works, however, to belie the view that his intention was to reduce Judaism to a Greek philosophy with one additional underlying premise. Not only did Schürer distort the question of Philo's Jewishness by seeming to conflate Judaism and particularism, but he also overlooked the scriptural context of most of the treatises, and the insistence upon adherence to Jewish tenets and observances throughout Philo's work. His Judaism consisted, in fact, in far more than an assumption regarding Judaism as a revealed religion. Philo adhered firmly to the obligations of the Mosaic law. He regarded it as the most perfect, just and reasonable law; its moral demands were always the purest, its social institutions the best and most humane, its religious ceremonies the most consistent with the divine intelligence. He also upheld ritual observances such as circumcision, the Sabbath, and dietary laws. Indeed he is extremely censorious of those who wish to treat these ritual laws as σύμβολα and not to observe them in the literal sense, *Mig.* 16 (89), see Wolfson, *Philo* I, p. 127. There is certainly a tendency in his thought towards the universalizing of Jewish laws, an attempt to demonstrate their cosmopolitan application; see S. Sandmel, *Philo's Place*, pp. xx ff.; V. Nikiprowetzky, *Le Commentaire*, esp. pp. 117–31; A. Mosès, *De Specialibus Legibus II-IV*, pp. 34–42. But Philo is far from denying the Jewish origins of such principles and practices. He also adheres to the principle that the Jews have prerogatives as the privileged people of God, and he repeatedly points to a distinction between Jews and others. The Jews owe their privileged position to their own and their ancestors' virtues. Judaism is thus presented as the best religion, in Philo's thought, and as one which happens to be cosmopolitan or capable of being universalized; it is not presented as the best religion *because* it is cosmopolitan (so Schürer). For a summary of these issues see P. Borgen, ANRW II.21.1, pp. 150–4.

departure. A slightly different emphasis, or sometimes even a radically different philosophical position, might be appropriate to different scriptural texts or different exegetical contexts. If, moreover, one regards his works as written with different audiences in mind, the mode of exposition might be partly determined by the prospective audience. It might be profitable to regard him as an exegete rather than as a philosopher.[26] Nevertheless, it is possible to discern individual notions pursued with some consistency throughout his *oeuvre*; certain philosophical positions are repeatedly taken up in the course of what are essentially scriptural disquisitions. Since Philo's apparently unique contribution lies in the combination of these doctrines with Jewish presuppositions and scriptural texts, the following account of his thought is arranged in terms of these topics; it should not be overlooked that Philo only presents them in the course of an exposition of the Mosaic Law.[27]

(1) God [28]

As a Jew, Philo emphasizes monotheism and the worship of God without images. Obviously this view stands in opposition to the polytheism of the pagan religions, but it can be harmonized quite closely with the conception of God found in Greek philosophic thought,

26. See V. Nikiprowetzky, *Le Commentaire* (1977), *passim*. For the fundamental questions involved, note also B. Mack, 'Philo and Exegetical Traditions in Alexandria', ANRW II.21.1, pp. 227–71.

27. For systematic presentations of Philo's thought as a product of Greek philosophy see e.g. E. Zeller, *Die Philosophie der Griechen* III.2 (⁵1923, repr. 1963), pp. 385–467, and above all H. A. Wolfson, *Philo* (1947).

28. See esp. Wolfson, *Philo* I, pp. 200–94; II, pp. 73–164; *idem*, 'The Philonic God of Revelation and his Latter-Day Deniers', in *Religious Philosophy* (1961), pp. 1–26; *idem*, 'Answers to Criticisms of my Discussions of the Ineffability of God', HThR 67 (1974), pp. 186–90. Note also E. Bréhier, *Les Idées*, pp. 69–82; A. Marmorstein, 'Philo and the Names of God', JQR N.S. 22 (1931–2), pp. 295–306; E. R. Goodenough, *By Light, Light!*, pp. 11–47, 340–1; E. Vanderlinden, 'Les divers modes de connaissance de Dieu selon Philon d'Alexandrie', *Mélanges de Science religieuse* IV (1947), pp. 285–304; S. Cohen, 'The Unity of God: A Study in Hellenistic and Rabbinic Theology', HUCA 26 (1955), pp. 425–79, esp. 433–6; A. Altmann, '*Homo Imago Dei* in Jewish and Christian Theology', JR 48 (1968), pp. 235–59; H. Braun, *Wie man über Gott nicht denken soll, dargelegt an Gedankengängen Philos von Alexandria* (1971); E. Mühlenberg, 'Das Problem der Offenbarung in Philo von Alexandrien', ZNW 64 (1973), pp. 1–18; P. Boyancé, 'Le dieu très haut chez Philon', *Mélanges d'histoire des religions offerts à Henri-Charles Puech* (1974), pp. 139–49; J. Dillon, 'The Transcendence of God in Philo', *Centre for Hermeneutical Studies, Berkeley, Colloquy XVI* (1975); S. Sandmel, *Philo of Alexandria*, pp. 89–101; J. McLelland, *God the Anonymous. A Study in Alexandrian Philosophical Theory* (Patristic Monograph Series IV, 1976), esp. pp. 23–44; Y. Amir, 'Die Begegnung des biblischen und des philosophischen Monotheismus als Grundthema des jüdischen Hellenismus', EvTh 38 (1978), pp. 2–19; J. Dillon, 'The Nature of God in the *Quod Deus*', in D. Winston and J. Dillon (eds.), *Two Treatises of Philo of Alexandria* (1983), pp. 217–27.

without serious modification of the Jewish conception. The basic conception from which Philo sets out is that of the dualism of God and the world. God alone is good and perfect; the finite as such is imperfect. All determining attributes appropriate to finite beings are therefore to be denied of God. He is eternal, unchangeable, simple, free, self-sufficient.[29] He is not only free from human errors, but also exalted above all human virtues, and better than the Good and the Beautiful.[30] Indeed, he is quite simply lacking in attributes, ἄποιος without any ποιότης,[31] since any qualification would be a limitation; his nature, then, is beyond definition. It can only be said that he is, not what he is.[32]

Philo does allow some positive affirmations about the nature of God, however. In God all perfection is united and all perfection derives from him. He fills and encompasses all things.[33] All perfection in the creation derives entirely from him, and from him alone.[34]

(2) The Intermediary Beings and the Logos[35]

Since he is absolutely perfect, God cannot enter into direct contact with

29. Eternal, ἀίδιος: *Opif.* 2 (12); *Virt.* 10 (65); unchangeable, ἄτρεπτος: *Cher.* 6 (19); *Leg.*i 15 (51); and in general *Deus*; simple, ἁπλοῦς: *Leg.* ii 1 (2); free: *Somn.* ii 38 (253); self-sufficient, χρῇζων οὐδενὸς τὸ παράπαν, ἑαυτῷ ἱκανός, αὐταρκέστατος ἑαυτῷ, *Leg.* ii 1 (1); 4 (28); *Virt.* 3 (9).

30. *Opif.* 2 (8): ὁ τῶν ὅλων νοῦς—εἰλικρινέστατος καὶ ἀκραιφνέστατος, κρείττων ἢ ἀρετὴ καὶ κρείττων ἢ ἐπιστήμη καὶ κρείττων ἢ αὐτὸ τὸ ἀγαθὸν καὶ αὐτὸ τὸ καλόν.

31. *Leg.* i 13 (36): ἄποιος; *ibid.* i 15 (51): ὁ γὰρ ἢ ποιότητα οἰόμενος ἔχειν τὸν θεὸν ἢ μὴ ἕνα εἶναι ἢ μὴ ἀγένητον καὶ ἄφθαρτον ἢ μὴ ἄτρεπτον, ἑαυτὸν ἀδικεῖ οὐ θεόν. *Deus* 11 (55): men who are lovers of the soul have dissociated God from every category or quality (ἐκβιβάζειν ... πάσης ποιότητος).

32. *Mos.* i 14 (75): ὁ δέ, τὸ μὲν πρῶτον λέγε, φησίν, αὐτοῖς ὅτι ἐγώ εἰμι ὁ ὤν, ἵνα μαθόντες διαφορὰν ὄντος τε καὶ μὴ ὄντος προσαναδιδαχθῶσιν ὡς οὐδὲν ὄνομα τὸ παράπαν ἐπ' ἐμοῦ κυριολογεῖται, ᾧ μόνῳ πρόσεστι τὸ εἶναι. *Deus* 13 (62): ὁ δ' ἄρα οὐδὲ τῷ νῷ καταληπτός, ὅτι μὴ κατὰ τὸ εἶναι μόνον· ὕπαρξις γὰρ ἔσθ' ἣν καταλαμβάνομεν αὐτοῦ, τῶν δέ γε χωρὶς ὑπάρξεως οὐδέν. *Mut.* 2 (11); *Somn.* i 40 (231).

33. *Leg.* i 14 (44): τὰ μὲν ἄλλα ἐπιδεᾶ καὶ ἔρημα καὶ κενὰ ὄντα πληρῶν καὶ περιέχων, αὐτὸς δὲ ὑπ' οὐδενὸς ἄλλου περιεχόμενος, ἅτε εἷς καὶ τὸ πᾶν αὐτὸς ὤν. Cf. *ibid.* iii 2 (4); 17 (51); *Confus.* 27 (136); *Migr.* 35 (192); *Somn.* i 11 (63).

34. *Leg.* i 3 (5): παύεται γὰρ οὐδέποτε ποιῶν ὁ θεός, ἀλλ' ὥσπερ ἴδιον τὸ καίειν πυρός, καὶ χιόνος τὸ ψύχειν, οὕτως καὶ θεοῦ τὸ ποιεῖν· καὶ πολύ γε μᾶλλον, ὅτῳ καὶ τοῖς ἄλλοις ἅπασιν ἀρχὴ τοῦ δρᾶν ἐστιν.

35. For the older literature see Goodhart and Goodenough, *Bibliography*, pp. 262–6. See esp. Wolfson, *Philo* I, pp. 217–89; Goodenough, *Introduction*, pp. 100–10; Bréhier, *Les idées*, pp. 167–75. Note also e.g. A. Aall, *Der Logos. Geschichte seiner Entwicklung in der griechischen Philosophie und der christlichen Literatur* I-II (1896–9), esp. I, pp. 184–231; L. Cohn, 'Zur Lehre vom Logos bei Philo', *Judaica: Festschrift zu Hermann Cohens siebzigstem Geburtstage* (1912), pp. 303–31; M.-J. Lagrange, 'Le Logos de Philon', RB 32 (1923), pp. 321–71; H. Ringgren, *Word and Wisdom. Studies in the Hypostatization of Divine Qualities and Functions in the Ancient Near East* (1947), esp. pp. 124–5; K. Bormann, *Die Ideen und Logoslehre Philons von Alexandrien* (1955); W. Kelbe, *Die Logoslehre von Heraklit bis Origenes* (1958, repr. 1976), pp. 95–130; G. Pfeifer, *Ursprung und Wesen der Hypostasenvorstellungen im Judentum* (*Arbeiten zur Theologie* 1 Reihe 31, 1967), esp. pp. 47–59; I. G. Kidd, 'Stoic

matter. Any such contact would defile him.[36] Therefore any operation upon the world and in the world by God is only possible through the agency of intermediate causes, or mediating powers, which restore communication between God and the world. For the closer definition of these intermediary beings Philo had at his disposal four conceptions, two belonging to the philosophical realm and two to the religious: the Platonic doctrine of Ideas (Forms) as the original patterns of all particular things, the Stoic recasting of this doctrine according to which the ideas are active causes, the Jewish doctrine of angels,[37] and the Greek of daemons.[38] All these doctrines contribute to Philo's doctrine of the intermediary beings. The Stoic doctrine of the active causes was also influential. Before the creation of the perceptible world, Philo teaches, God created the spiritual archetypes of all things.[39] These archetypes of ideas are at the same time to be conceived of as active causes, however, as powers which bring the disordered material into order.[40] By means of these spiritual powers God is active in the world. They are his servants and representatives, the emissaries and mediators between him and finite things,[41] the λόγοι of the universal reason.[42] In

Intermediaries and the End for Man', in A. A. Long (ed.), *Problems in Stoicism* (1971), pp. 150–72; R. G. Hamerton-Kelly, *Pre-Existence, Wisdom and the Son of Man. A Study in the Idea of Pre-Existence in the New Testament* (SNTSMS XXI, 1973), esp. pp. 20–1, 120–1, 145–7; L. K. K. Dey, *The Intermediary World and Patterns of Perfection in Philo and Hebrews* (1975); W. Reister, 'Die Sophia im Denken Philons', in B. Lang, *Frau Weisheit. Deutung einer biblischen Gestalt* (1975), pp. 161–4; G. D. Farandos, 'Kosmos und Logos nach Philon von Alexandria', Elementa 4 (1976), pp. 231–75; R. A. Horsley, 'Spiritual Marriage with Sophia', VC 33 (1979), pp. 30–54; R. Bigatti, 'Sui significati del termine "Logos" nel trattato "Le Allegorie delle Leggi" di Filone di Alessandria', Rivista di filosofia neoscolastica 72 (1980), pp. 431–51.

36. *Spec.* i 60 (329): ἐξ ἐκείνης γὰρ [τῆς ὕλης] πάντ' ἐγέννησεν ὁ θεός, οὐκ ἐφαπτόμενος αὐτός· οὐ γὰρ ἦν θέμις ἀπείρου καὶ πεφυρμένης ὕλης ψαύειν τὸν εὐδαίμονα καὶ μακάριον.

37. For Jewish angelology in this period see P. Schäfer, *Rivalität zwischen Engeln und Menschen: Untersuchungen zur rabbinischen Engelvorstellung* (1975), and the bibliography, pp. 243–54.

38. See e.g. RE Supp. III (1928), cols. 267–322, s.v. 'Daimon'; P. Boyancé, 'Les deux démons personnels dans l'Antiquité grecque et latine', Rev. de Philol. 61 (1935), pp. 189–202; RAC IX, cols. 546–797, s.v. 'Geister (Dämonen)'; J. Z. Smith, 'Towards Interpreting Demonic Powers in Hellenistic and Roman Antiquity', ANRW II.16.1 (1978), pp. 425–39.

39. *Opif.* 4 (16): προλαβὼν γὰρ ὁ θεὸς ἅτε θεός, ὅτι μίμημα καλὸν οὐκ ἄν ποτε γένοιτο δίχα καλοῦ παραδείγματος, οὐδέ τι τῶν αἰσθητῶν ἀνυπαίτιον, ὃ μὴ πρὸς ἀρχέτυπον καὶ νοητὴν ἰδέαν ἀπεικονίσθη, βουληθεὶς τὸν ὁρατὸν κόσμον τουτονὶ δημιουργῆσαι προεξετύπου τὸν νοητόν, ἵνα χρώμενος ἀσωμάτῳ καὶ θεοειδεστάτῳ παραδείγματι τὸν σωματικὸν ἀπεργάσηται.

40. *Spec.* i 60 (327): ταῖς ἀσωμάτοις δυνάμεσιν, ὧν ἔτυμον ὄνομα αἱ ἰδέαι, κατεχρήσατο πρὸς τὸ γένος ἕκαστον τὴν ἁρμόττουσαν λαβεῖν μορφήν. Cf. *ibid.* 8 (48).

41. *Abr.* 23 (115): ἱεραὶ καὶ θεῖαι φύσεις, ὑποδιάκονοι καὶ ὕπαρχοι τοῦ πρώτου θεοῦ. Cf. *Somn.* i 22 (142–3).

42. *Leg.* iii 62 (177): τοὺς ἀγγέλους καὶ λόγους αὐτοῦ. *Somn.* i 12 (69): τοὺς ἑαυτοῦ λόγους ἐπικουρίας ἕνεκα τῶν φιλαρέτων ἀποστέλλει. Cf. *ibid.* 21 (127): ψυχαὶ δ' εἰσὶν ἀθάνατα οἱ λόγοι οὗτοι.

the books of Moses they are called angels, among the Greeks daemons.[43] If this suggests that they are thought of as independent hypostases, and even as personal beings, other statements forbid them being taken unambiguously as such. It is said explicitly that they exist only in the divine thought.[44] They are described as the infinite powers of the infinite God,[45] but in such a way as to be an inseparable part of the divine nature. But equally it would be mistaken to deny outright the hypostatisation of the λόγοι or δυνάμεις. The fact is that Philo thought of them both as independent hypostases and also as immanent manifestations of the divine nature. The function of the intermediaries requires this ambivalent position, in so far as the powers must be identical with God if they are to be the means of participation in the deity for the finite, and yet they must be distinct from God if he is to remain outside all contact with the world.[46] With this ambiguous view of the nature of the δυνάμεις the question of their origin must also remain uncertain. Philo does actually sometimes express himself in emanationist terms, but he never comes to the point of a definite formulation of the doctrine of emanation.[47] The number of the δυνάμεις is in itself unlimited.[48] Yet Philo gives enumerations now and again, subsuming the individual powers under certain generic concepts.[49] Most commonly, he distinguishes two supreme powers, Goodness and Authority,[50] which again are united by the divine Logos. The latter, in so far as it is reckoned among the powers at all, is the highest of them all, the root from which the rest derive, the universal mediator between

43. *Somn.* 19 (115): ἀθανάτοις λόγοις, οὓς καλεῖν ἔθος ἀγγέλους. Cf. *ibid.* 22 (141): ταύτας (pure souls) δαίμονας μὲν οἱ ἄλλοι φιλόσοφοι, ὁ δὲ ἱερὸς λόγος ἀγγέλους εἴωθε καλεῖν. *Gig.* 2 (6): οὓς ἄλλοι φιλόσοφοι δαίμονας, ἀγγέλους Μωϋσῆς εἴωθεν ὀνομάζειν· ψυχαὶ δ' εἰσὶ κατὰ τὸν ἀέρα πετόμεναι.

44. *Opif.* 5 (20): just as the ideal city whose plan the designer has conceived is only existent in his own mind, τὸν αὐτὸν τρόπον οὐδ' ὁ ἐκ τῶν ἰδεῶν κόσμος ἄλλον ἂν ἔχοι τόπον ἢ τὸν θεῖον λόγον τὸν ταῦτα διακοσμήσαντα. Cf. *ibid.* 6 (24): εἰ δέ τις ἐθελήσειε γυμνοτέροις χρήσασθαι τοῖς ὀνόμασιν, οὐδὲν ἂν ἕτερον εἴποι τὸν νοητὸν κόσμον εἶναι, ἢ θεοῦ λόγον ἤδη κοσμοποιοῦντος.

45. *Sacrif.* 15 (59): ἀπερίγραφος γάρ ὁ θεός, ἀπερίγραφοι δὲ καὶ αἱ δυνάμεις αὐτοῦ.

46. So Zeller, *Philosophie der Griechen* III.2 (⁵1923), p. 413.

47. See e.g. *Fug.* 36 (198); God is ἡ πρεσβυτάτη [πηγή], καὶ μήποτ' εἰκότως· τὸν γὰρ σύμπαντα τούτου κόσμον ὤμβρησε. Cf. *Somn.* ii 32 (221).

48. *Sacrif.* 15 (59): ἀπερίγραφοι αἱ δυνάμεις. *Confus.* 34 (171): εἰς ὦν ὁ θεὸς ἀμυθήτους περὶ αὐτὸν ἔχει δυνάμεις.

49. *Fug.* 18 (95): he enumerates six in all, that is, exclusive of the θεῖος λόγος, the following five: ἡ ποιητική, ἡ βασιλική, ἡ ἵλεως, ἡ νομοθετική... (the last, or penultimate, is missing due to a lacuna).

50. Ἀγαθότης and ἀρχή: *Cher.* 9 (28); *Sacrif.* 15 (59); εὐεργεσία and ἡγεμονία, or ἡ χαριστική and ἡ βασιλική, both in *Somn.* 26 (162); ἡ εὐεργέτις and ἡ κολαστήριος, *Spec.* i 56 (307); also ἡ ποιητική and ἡ βασιλική (because God created the world because of his goodness): *Abr.* 24 (121); *Mos.* ii 20 (99).

God and the world, that in which all the activities of God are concentrated. [51]

The Logos is the active divine reason, described as the Idea which embraces all other ideas, the Power which includes all other powers.[52] It is neither uncreated, nor created as finite things are.[53] It is the representative and emissary of God,[54] the angel or archangel who transmits the revelations of God,[55] the instrument by which God created the world.[56] So it is also identified with the creative Word of God. [57] But it is the mediator not only from God to the world, but also, conversely, from the world to God. It is the High Priest who intercedes with God on behalf of the world.[58] The dilemma regarding the metaphysical status of the intermediaries in general applies to the Logos too. Philo does not comment on the ambivalence of the Logos, in that it is neither personal nor impersonal. For him the Logos is both a person distinct from God and a designation of God in a particular relation—that of his activity. The Logos as mediator must be both distinct from both parties, and yet also be in some way like both parties, and this contradiction is unresolved.[59]

It seems that Philo was the first to postulate such an intermediary entity between God and the world under the name of Logos. The inspiration for this doctrine comes from Jewish theology as well as from Greek philosophy. In Jewish theology Philo could have been influenced by the doctrine of the Wisdom of God, in the first place, and secondly that of the Spirit and of the Word of God.[60] From Platonic philosophy

51. *Fug.* 18 (94–5) ; *Quaest. Ex.* ii 68.

52. So Zeller, *op. cit.* III.2, pp. 418–19.

53. *Heres.* 42 (206) : οὔτε ἀγένητος ὡς ὁ θεὸς οὔτε γενητὸς ὡς ἡμεῖς, ἀλλὰ μέσος τῶν ἄκρων, ἀμφοτέροις ὁμηρεύων.

54. *Heres.* 42 (205) : πρεσβευτὴς τοῦ ἡγεμόνος πρὸς τὸ ὑπήκοον.

55. *Leg.* iii 62 (177) : τὸν ἄγγελον, ὅς ἐστι λόγος. *Confus.* 28 (146) : τὸν πρωτόγονον αὐτοῦ λόγον, τὸν ἀγγέλων πρεσβύτατον, ὡς ἂν πολυώνυμον ὑπάρχοντα. *Somn.* i 41 (241) ; *Heres.* 42 (205) ; *Quaest. Ex.* ii 13.

56. *Leg.* iii 31 (96) : σκιὰ θεοῦ δὲ ὁ λόγος αὐτοῦ ἐστιν, ᾧ καθάπερ ὀργάνῳ προσχρησάμενος ἐκοσμοποίει. *Cher.* 35 (127) : εὑρήσεις γὰρ αἴτιον μὲν αὐτοῦ [τοῦ κόσμου] τὸν θεόν, ὑφ᾽ οὗ γέγονεν· ὕλην δὲ τὰ τέσσαρα στοιχεῖα, ἐξ ὧν συνεκράθη· ὄργανον δὲ λόγον θεοῦ, δι᾽ οὗ κατεσκευάσθη.

57. *Leg.* i 8 (19) ; *Sacrif.* 3 (8).

58. *Gig.* 11 (52) : ὁ ἀρχιερεὺς λόγος ἐνδιατρίβειν ἀεὶ καὶ ἐνσχολάζειν τοῖς ἁγίοις δόγμασι δυνάμενος (see J. Dillon and D. Winston, *Two Treatises*, p. 264). See also *Migr.* 18 (102) : τὸν ἀρχιερέα λογον. *Fug.* 20 (108) : λέγομεν γὰρ τὸν ἀρχιερέα οὐκ ἄνθρωπον ἀλλὰ λόγον θεῖον εἶναι. Cf. *Heres.* 42 (205) ; *Mos.* ii 26 (134).

59. See Zeller, *op. cit.*, pp. 426–9.

60. In the Wisdom of Solomon (pp. 560–79 above) the Divine Word is certainly once personified (18:14–16), as elsewhere Wisdom is. But this is merely a poetical personification, not an actual hypostatization. In Jewish thought the Memra plays a role analogous to that of the Logos of Philo. See K. Kohler, 'Memra', JE VIII (1904), pp. 464 ff. The relationships between hokmah, Torah, sophia and logos in Jewish thought of the

he made use of the theory of Forms and the concept of the World-soul. The Stoic doctrine of the deity as Reason operative in the world is also close to Philo's thought here. The pantheism of the Stoic logos doctrine is not, of course, a feature of the Philonic Logos: his Logos is separate from the deity; it is also separate from created matter, so that it differs from the materialism of the Stoic concept.

(3) Creation and Preservation of the World[61]

Despite the intermediary beings, not everything that exists can be traced back to God. For evil, which is the imperfect, cannot have its ground in God in any way, even indirectly. Evil derives from a second principle, matter (ὕλη, or, in Stoic terms, οὐσία). This is the lifeless, motionless, and disordered mass, without form or property, from which God formed the world by the agency of the Logos and the divine powers.[62] For in Philo there can be talk only of a formation of the world, not of creation in the true sense, since matter does not have its origin in God but is set beside him as a second principle. Like the

---

Hellenistic period present profound problems, although some influence of Greek on Jewish concepts is generally acknowledged. See e.g. Wolfson, *Philo*, ch. 5; M. Hengel, *Judaism and Hellenism*, pp. 153–75; B. Mack, *Logos und Sophia. Untersuchungen zur Weisheitstheologie im hellenistischen Judentum* (SUNT X, 1973); idem, 'Weisheit und Allegorie bei Philo von Alexandrien: Untersuchungen zum Traktat "De Congressu eruditionis"', SP 5 (1978), pp. 57–105; H. Bietenhard, 'Logos-Theologie im Rabbinat. Ein Beitrag zur Lehre vom Worte Gottes im rabbinischen Schrifttum', ANRW II.19.2 (1979), pp. 580–618.

61. See e.g. J. Horovitz, *Untersuchungen über Philons und Platons Lehre von der Weltschöpfung* (1900); H. Leisegang, *Die Begriffe der Zeit und Ewigkeit bei Philon. Die Begriffe der Zeit und Ewigkeit in späteren Platonismus* (1913), pp. 10–14; H. A. Wolfson, *Philo* I, pp. 295–359; G. Lindeskog, *Studien zum neutestamentlichen Schöpfungsgedanken* (1952); L. Wächter, 'Der Einfluss platonischen Denkens auf rabbinische Schöpfungsspekulationen', Zeitschrift für Religions- und Geistesgeschichte 14 (1962), pp. 36–56; H. A. Wolfson, 'Two Comments Regarding the Plurality of Worlds in Jewish Sources', JQR 56 (1965–6), pp. 245–7; H. F. Weiss, *Untersuchungen zur Kosmologie des hellenistischen und palästinischen Judentums* (TU XCVII, 1966), pp. 18–74; A. Ehrhardt, *The Beginning. A Study in the Greek Philosophical Approach to the Concept of Creation from Anaximander to St. John* (1968), pp. 188–9, 196–8, 202–5; U. Früchtel, *Die kosmologischen Vorstellungen bei Philo von Alexandrien. Ein Beitrag zur Geschichte der Genesisexegese* (ALGHJ II, 1968); R. Arnaldez, *De Aeternitate Mundi* (*Oeuvres* XXX, 1969), esp. pp. 38–69; D. Winston, 'Philo's Theory of Cosmogony', in *Religious Syncretism in Antiquity: Essays in Conversation with Geo Widengren*, ed. B. A. Pearson (1975), pp. 157–71; G. Reale, 'Filone de Alessandria e la prima elaborazione filosofica della dottrina della creazione', in *Paradoxos politeia. Studi patristici in onore di Giuseppe Lazzati*, ed. R. Cantalamessa and L. F. Pizzolato (*Studia Patristica Mediolanensia* X, 1979), pp. 247 ff.; D. Winston, 'Philo's Theory of Eternal Creation: De Prov. 1.6–9', PAAJR 46–7 (1980), pp. 593–606. See P. Borgen, ANRW II.21.1, pp. 147–9.

62. *Opif.* 5 (22): [ἡ οὐσία]... ἦν μὲν γὰρ ἐξ αὑτῆς ἄτακτος ἄποιος ἄψυχος, ἑτεροιότητος ἀναρμοστίας ἀσυμφωνίας μεστή. *Heres.* 27 (140): τήν τε ἄμορφον καὶ ἄποιον τῶν ὅλων οὐσίαν. *Fug.* 2 (8): τὴν ἄποιον καὶ ἀνείδεον καὶ ἀσχημάτιστον οὐσίαν. *ibid.* 2 (9): ἡ ἄποιος ὕλη. *Spec.* i 60 (328): ἄμορφος ὕλη. Cf. *ibid.* i 60 (329); iv 35 (187).

formation of the world, its preservation is also mediated through the Logos and the divine powers. Indeed the latter process is fundamentally nothing but a continuation of the former; and what we call the laws of nature are only the totality of the orderly divine operations.

(4) Theory of Man, and Ethics[63]

In Philo's theory of man, in which he chiefly follows Platonic theory, the dualistic basis of the system comes most sharply to light. Here he starts from the presupposition that the whole atmosphere is full of souls. Of these, the souls living on a higher level are the angels or daemons who mediate God's dealings with the world.[64] On the other hand, those which stand nearer the earth are attracted by sensuality and descend into mortal bodies.[65] Accordingly the soul of man is simply one of those divine powers, those effluences of divinity, which in their original condition are called angels or daemons. Procreation only brings into being the life-breath of the soul, nourishing it and giving it perception, and this comes from the spiritual constituents of the seed. Reason,

---

63. For older literature see Goodhart and Goodenough, *Bibliography*, pp. 267–8. See esp. P. Wendland, *Philo und die kynisch-stoische Diatribe (Beiträge zur Geschichte der griechischen Philosophie*, 1895); H. Windisch, *Die Frömmigkeit Philons und ihre Bedeutung für das Christentum* (1909); I. Heinemann, 'Philos Lehre vom Eid', in *Judaica. Festschrift für H. Cohen* (1912), pp. 109–13; T. Billings, *The Platonism of Philo Judaeus* (1919), pp. 47–87; H. Lewy, *Sobria Ebrietas* (1929); I. Heinemann, *Philons griechische und jüdische Bildung* (1930, repr. 1962); F. Geiger, *Philo von Alexandreia als sozialer Denker (Tübinger Beiträge zur Altertumswissenschaft* XIX, 1932); W. Völker, *Fortschritt und Vollendung bei Philo von Alexandrien* (1938), esp. pp. 126–54; E. R. Goodenough, 'Philo on Immortality', HThR 39 (1946), pp. 85–108; J. Giblet, 'L'homme image de Dieu dans les commentaires littéraires de Philon d'Alexandrie', *Studia Hellenistica* V (1948), pp. 93–118; Wolfson, *Philo* I, pp. 360–455; II, pp. 165–303; A. Levi, 'Il problema dell'errore in Filone d'Alessandria', Rivista critica di storia della filosofia 5 (1950), pp. 281–94; L. Bréhier, *Les Idées*, pp. 177–310; C. Kannengiesser, 'Philon et les Pères sur la double creation de l'homme', in *Philon d'Alexandrie*, ed. R. Arnaldez (1967), pp. 277–96; R. Arnaldez, 'La Dialectique des Sentiments chez Philon', *ibid.*, pp. 299–330; A. Pelletier, 'Les passions à l'assaut de l'âme d'après Philon', REG 78 (1965), pp. 52–60; A. Dihle, 'Ethik', RAC VI (1966), cols. 646–796, esp. 698–700; A. Maddalena, 'L'ἔννοια e l'ἐπιστήμη θεοῦ in Filone Ebreo', Rivista di filologia 96 (1968), pp. 5–27; M. Fiedler, 'Δικαιοσύνη in der diaspora-jüdischen und intertestamentlischen Literatur', JSJ 1 (1970), pp. 120–43; S. Sandmel, 'The Confrontation of Greek and Jewish Ethics: Philo, De Decalogo', in *Judaism and Ethics*, ed. D. J. Silver (1970), pp. 163–76; R. A. Baer, *Philo's Use of the Categories Male and Female* (ALGHJ III, 1970); W. Warnach, 'Selbstliebe und Gottesliebe im Denken Philons von Alexandrien', in *Wort Gottes in der Zeit. Festschrift Karl Schelkle*, ed. H. Field and J. Nolte (1973), pp. 189–214; U. Fischer, *Eschatologie und Jenseitserwartung im hellenistischen Diasporajudentum* (BZNW XLIV, 1978); R. Melnick, 'On the Philonic Conception of the Whole Man', JSJ 11 (1980), pp. 1–32; D. A. Carson, 'Divine Sovereignty and Human Responsibility in Philo', NT 23 (1981), pp. 148–64; D. Winston, 'Philo's Ethical Theory', ANRW II.21.1 (1984), pp. 372–416.

64. *Somn.* i 22 (140); see pp. 882–3 above.

65. *Gig.* 2 (11).

however, comes into man from an external source.[66] The human πνεῦμα is thus an effluence of divinity: God has breathed his spirit into man.[67] The body, as the animal side of man, is the source of all evil, the prison in which the spirit is confined,[68] the corpse which the soul drags around with it,[69] the coffin or tomb out of which it will once again awaken to true life.[70] Since sensuality as such is evil, sin is innate in man.[71] No one can keep himself free from it, even if he lives only for one day.[72]

In accordance with these assumptions regarding the nature of man, the highest principle of ethics is obviously the utmost possible renunciation of sensuality, the eradication of desire and passion. Stoicism must, therefore, have offered the most congenial philosophical system as regards ethics. Philo adheres primarily to Stoicism; not only in the basic idea of the extermination of sensuality, but also in particular prescriptions, such as in the doctrine of the four cardinal virtues,[73] and the four passions.[74] Like the Stoics he teaches that there is only one good, morality;[75] like them he demands freedom from all emotions,[76] and the utmost possible simplicity of life;[77] like them, he is a cosmopolitan.[78] Yet for all its affinities, Philo's view of ethics remains fundamentally different from the Stoic view. The Stoics referred a man to his own resources; according to Philo, man lacks the capacity to set himself free from sensuality, since he is a sensual creature; for this he requires the help of God. It is God who plants and fosters the virtues in man's soul. Only the man who honours God and surrenders himself to

---

66. *Opif.* 22 (67): ἡ δ' [ἡ φύσις] οἷα τεχνίτης ἢ κυριώτερον εἰπεῖν ἀνεπίληπτος τέχνη ζωοπλαστεῖ τὴν μὲν ὑγρὰν οὐσίαν εἰς τὰ τοῦ σώματος μέλη καὶ μέρη διανέμουσα, τὴν δὲ πνευματικὴν εἰς τὰς τῆς ψυχῆς δυνάμεις τήν τε θρεπτικὴν καὶ τὴν αἰσθητικήν· τὴν γὰρ τοῦ λογισμοῦ τανῦν ὑπερθετέον διὰ τοὺς φάσκοντας θύραθεν αὐτὸν ἐπεισιέναι θεῖον καὶ ἀΐδιον ὄντα.

67. *Deter.* 22 (80): πνεῦμά ἐστιν ἡ ψυχῆς οὐσία. Cf. *Opif.* 46 (134–5); *Spec.* iv 24 (123); *Heres.* 11 (56)–12 (57); *ibid.* 38 (184).

68. Δεσμωτήριον: *Ebr.* 26 (101); *Leg.* iii 14 (42); *Migr.* 2 (9).

69. Νεκρὸν σῶμα: *Leg.* iii 22 (69); *Gig.* 3 (15): ὧν οὐδὲν εἰς τὸ κράτιστον τῶν ἐν ἡμῖν, ψυχὴν ἢ νοῦν, ἀναφέρεται, πάντα δὲ ἐπὶ τὸν συμφυᾶ νεκρὸν ἡμῶν, τὸ σῶμα. Cf. *Agr.* 5 (25).

70. Λάρναξ ἢ σορός: *Migr.* 3 (16); σῆμα: *Leg.* i 33 (108).

71. *Mos.* ii 29 (147): παντὶ γενητῷ, κἂν σπουδαῖον ᾖ, παρόσον ἦλθεν εἰς γένεσιν, συμφυὲς τὸ ἁμαρτάνειν ἐστίν.

72. *Mut.* 6 (48): τίς γαρ, ὡς ὁ Ἰὼβ φησι, καθαρὸς ἀπὸ ῥύπου, καὶ ἂν μία ἡμέρα ἐστὶν ἡ ζωή;

73. Φρόνησις, σωφροσύνη, ἀνδρεία, δικαιοσύνη: *Leg.* i 19 (63). See also C-W vol. VII, Index s.vv.

74. *Leg.* iii 47 (139).

75. *Poster.* 39 (133): μόνον εἶναι τὸ καλὸν ἀγαθόν.

76. *Leg.* iii 11 (68): ὁ δὲ ὄφις ἡ ἡδονὴν ἐξ ἑαυτῆς ἐστι μοχθηρά· διὰ τοῦτο ἐν μὲν σπουδαίῳ οὐχ εὑρίσκεται τὸ παράπαν, μόνος δ' αὐτῆς ὁ φαῦλος ἀπολαύει. Ibid. iii 45 (129): Μωϋσῆς δὲ ὅλον τὸν θυμὸν ἐκτέμνειν καὶ ἀποκόπτειν οἴεται δεῖν τῆς ψυχῆς, οὐ μετριοπάθειαν, ἀλλὰ συνόλως ἀπάθειαν ἀγαπῶν.

77. *Somn.* i 20 (120–6); ii 7 (48–53); *Leg.* iii 48 (115); *Deter.* 10 (33–4).

78. So Zeller, *Philosophie* III.2 (⁵1923), p. 453.

his influence can attain to perfection.[79] True morality, as Plato teaches, is imitation of the deity.[80] In this religious justification for ethics, Philo differs quite decisively from the Stoics. Political activity, and practical morality in general, is of value only in so far as it is a necessary means for resisting evil. But knowledge ought to serve this sole end, and ethics is therefore the most important part of philosophy.[81]

Nevertheless, even the purity of life which such knowledge brings about is still not the ultimate and highest aim of human development. Instead, since the origin of man is transcendent, the goal of his development is also transcendent. As he has become ensnared in this sensual life through falling away from God, so he is to struggle upwards out of it again to the direct vision of God. This aim is attainable even in this earthly life. The truly wise and virtuous man, that is to say, becomes lifted up above himself and out of himself, and in this state of ecstasy he beholds and recognizes the deity itself. His own consciousness is swallowed up and vanishes in the divine light. The spirit of God dwells in him and stirs him like the strings of a musical instrument.[82] The man who has attained to the contemplation of the divine by this path has reached the highest stage of earthly blessedness. Above it there lies only the complete deliverance from this body, the return of the soul to its original bodiless condition, which is the reward of those who have kept themselves free from attachment to this sensual body.[83]

Philo's ultimate influence was considerable,[84] but not, as far as one can discern, on Jewish thought, and certainly not on any group of Alexandrian proselytes—if indeed proselytism can be regarded as Philo's aim. Jewish literature written in Greek was to be of minimal

79. *Leg.* i 15 (48): πρέπει τῷ θεῷ φυτεύειν καὶ οἰκοδομεῖν ἐν ψυχῇ τὰς ἀρετάς. *Ibid.* i 26 (82): ὅταν ἐκβῇ ὁ νοῦς ἑαυτοῦ καὶ ἑαυτὸν ἀνενέγκῃ θεῷ, ὥσπερ ὁ γέλως Ἰσαάκ, τηνικαῦτα ὁμολογίαν τὴν πρὸς τὸν ὄντα ποιεῖται. ἕως δὲ ἑαυτὸν ὑποτίθεται ὡς αἴτιόν τινος, μακρὰν ἀφέστηκε τοῦ παραχωρεῖν θεῷ καὶ ὁμολογεῖν αὐτῷ. Cf. *ibid.* iii 77 (219).

80. *Opif.* 50 (144); *Decal.* 15 (73); *Virt.* 31 (168); *Migr.* 23 (131); 31 (175). For *philanthropia* as the imitation of God see also D. Winston in ANRW II.21.1, p. 398.

81. *Mut.* 10 (73): καθάπερ γὰρ δένδρων οὐδὲν ὄφελος, εἰ μὴ καρπῶν οἰστικὰ γένοιτο, τὸν αὐτὸν δὴ τρόπον οὐδὲ φυσιολογίας, εἰ μὴ μέλλοι κτῆσιν ἀρετῆς ἐνεγκεῖν. Cf. *Agr.* 3 (12–16).

82. *Heres.* 14 (69–70): (addressing his soul) σαυτὴν ἀπόδραθι καὶ ἔκστηθι σεαυτῆς, ὥσπερ οἱ κατεχόμενοι καὶ κορυβαντιῶντες βακχευθεῖσα καὶ θεοφορηθεῖσα κατά τινα προφητικὸν ἐνθειασμόν. Cf. *Heres.* 51 (249). See DAC IV (1959), cols. 944–87, s.v. 'Ekstase', and M. Harl, *Quis rerum divinarum heres sit* (*Oeuvres* XV, 1966), esp. pp. 27–30, 39–44, 103–50.

83. *Abr.* 44 (258): τὸν θάνατον νομίζειν μὴ σβέσιν ψυχῆς, ἀλλὰ χωρισμὸν καὶ διάζευξιν ἀπὸ σώματος, ὅθεν ἦλθεν ἀπιούσης. ἦλθε δέ, ὡς ἐν τῇ κοσμοποιίᾳ δεδήλωται, παρὰ θεοῦ. *Leg.* i 33 (108): εὖ καὶ ὁ Ἡράκλειτος κατὰ τοῦτο Μωϋσέως ἀκολουθήσας τῷ δόγματι, φησὶ γάρ, ζῶμεν τὸν ἐκείνων θάνατον, τεθνήκαμεν δὲ τὸν ἐκείνων βίον, ὡς νῦν μέν, ὅτε ζῶμεν, τεθνηκυίας τῆς ψυχῆς καὶ ὡς ἐν σήματι τῷ σώματι ἐντετυμβευμένης, εἰ δὲ ἀποθάνοιμεν, τῆς ψυχῆς ζώσης τὸν ἴδιον βίον καὶ ἀπηλλαγμένης κακοῦ καὶ νεκροῦ συνδέτου τοῦ σώματος.

84. For full bibliography on Philo's influence, from the New Testament onwards, see Goodhart and Goodenough, *Bibliography*, pp. 290–316.

interest to the rabbinic schools of Palestine after the fall of the Temple. [85] As to any hypothetical pagan audience, [86] the only reason for believing that Hellenistic Judaism found an interested pagan readership is the success of Christianity in a gentile environment; some regard this as having been facilitated by the existence of large numbers of pagans for whom the LXX, and perhaps also Hellenistic Jewish literature, had already served as a *praeparatio evangelica*. [87] It is, in fact, amongst Christian thinkers that Philo's most powerful and enduring influence is to be traced, in a direction which still lay entirely beyond his horizon—the development of Christian dogma. The New Testament already shows traces of Philonic thought; [88] and almost all Greek theologians of the first centuries—the Apologists as well as the Alexandrians, the Gnostics as well as their opponents, and also the great Greek theologians of later centuries—drew from Philo, to greater or lesser degrees, directly or indirectly, consciously or unconsciously. [89] But to pursue these traces further lies beyond the scope of this work.

85. On Josephus and Philo see vol. I, p. 49. For other Jews in Palestine who might possibly have read Philo see e.g. S. Freudenthal, *Hellenistische Studien* (1875), pp. 65–77; L. Finkelstein, 'Is Philo Mentioned in Rabbinic Literature?', JBL 53 (1934), pp. 142–9; C. Siegfried, *Philo von Alexandreia* (1875), pp. 278–302; D. Barthélemy, 'Est-ce Hoshaya Rabba qui censura le "commentaire allégorique"?', in *Philon d'Alexandrie*, ed. R. Arnaldez (1967), pp. 45–78. On the status of Greek in Palestine, and consequently the possible role of Jewish literature in Greek there, see vol. II, pp. 52–80, esp. 74–80. On the LXX and LXX-related literature, see pp. 474–504 above.

86. For Philo's possible audience or audiences, see above, pp. 814, 817–18, 840, 853–4, 878. No pagan work has yet come to light showing the unmistakeable influence of Philo. The only case of possible influence is a passage in Heliodorus, *Aethiopica* ix 9, 2–3, which is reminiscent of *Mos.* ii 24 (195). But see Goodhart and Goodenough, *Bibliography*, p. 250, n. 1. For traces of Philo in Judeo-Arabic works see e.g. H. Hirschfeld, 'The Arabic Portion of the Cairo Genizah at Cambridge', JQR 17 (1905), pp. 65–8; S. Poznanski, 'Philon dans l'ancienne litterature judéo-arabe', REJ 50 (1905), pp. 10–31.

87. For this possibility see the recent study by J. Gager, *The Origins of Anti-Semitism: Attitudes to Judaism in Pagan and Christian Antiquity* (1983).

88. For a survey of the issues, S. Sandmel, *Philo of Alexandria*, pp. 148–63; *idem*, 'Philo Judaeus', ANRW II.21.2 (1984), pp. 3–46, esp. 36–46. Note esp. various studies of Philo's relation to the fourth gospel, to Paul, and to Hebrews. See e.g. H. Chadwick, 'St. Paul and Philo of Alexandria', BJRL 48 (1966), pp. 286–307; A. W. Argyle, 'Philo and the Fourth Gospel', ET 63 (1951), pp. 385–6; R. McL. Wilson, 'Philo and the Fourth Gospel', *ibid.* 65 (1953), pp. 47–9; C. Spicq, 'Le Philonisme de l'Épitre aux Hebreux', RB 56 (1949), pp. 542–72; 57 (1950), pp. 212–42; R. Williamson, *Philo and the Epistle to the Hebrews* (ALGHJ IV, 1970); L. K. K. Dey, *The Intermediary World and Patterns of Perfection in Philo and Hebrews* (1974). For further bibliography see ANRW II.21.1, pp. 723–6.

89. Exhaustive bibliographies on Philo and the Church Fathers can be found in F. Trisoglio, 'Filone Alessandrino e l'esegesi cristiana. Contributo alla conoscenza dell'influsso esercitato da Filone sul IV secolo, specificatamente in Gregorio di Nazianzo', ANRW II.21.1, pp. 588–730, and H. Savon, 'Saint Ambrose et saint Jérôme, lecteurs de Philon', *ibid.*, pp. 731–59. Note also B. A. Pearson, 'Philo and Gnosticism', *ibid.*, pp. 295–342.

INDEX

COMPILED BY
LÉONIE J. ARCHER

MAIN INDEX

Figures in **bold** immediately following a main heading indicate either a special section devoted to the subject in question, or those pages where the subject appears most frequently within the general text. Where appropriate, this principal reference is then broken down into detailed sub-entries, together with additional references. Sub-entries are listed according to volume and page number, in ascending numerical order. The letter *n*. tacked onto a page reference indicates that the subject is only to be found in the footnote(s) of the given page. Appended to the Main Index are separate Greek, Hebrew and Aramaic word lists.

A

Aaron: eponymous ancestor of priests, II. 253.

Aaron, sons of: **II. 251–253**; made distinct from Levites by Ezekiel, II. 251–253; concept and genealogy, II. 252–253n.; and sons of Zadok, II. 252–253n.

Ab, ninth of: II. 351, III. 328, 739.

'Abadim, minor talmudic tractate: position and subject treated, I. 80.

Abba Areka (Rab), disciple of Judah ha-Nasi: takes Mishnah to Babylon, I. 79.

Abba Saul: II. 380.

Ab-beth-din: title, II. 215, 217.

Abila: various places of this name, II. 136, 137n.

Abila, capital of tetrarchy: **I. 567–569**; history of tetrarchy, I. 567–569; location, I. 567.

Abila, city of Decapolis: **II. 136–137**; liberated by Pompey, II. 94, 137; as member of the Decapolis, II. 127, 136.

Abila in Peraea: toparchy, II. 194–195; location, II. 195n.

'Abodah Zara, Mishnah tractate: position and subject matter, I. 73.

'Aboth: see *Pirke 'Aboth*.

Abraham, patriarch: according to Artapanus, the father of astrology, II. 349, III. 611; in *haggadah* generally, II. 349–350, III. 521, 527, 528–529; work about by Pseudo-Hecataeus, II. 349, III. 671, 674–675; *Apocalypse of*, III. 288–292; in the *Genesis Apocryphon* from Qumran, III. 319–320; in writings of Philo, III. 542, 846, 847; *Testament of Abraham*, III. 761–767.

Abtalion: identity, II. 357, **362–363**.

Acco: see Ptolemais.

Acmonia, in Phrygia: evidence for Jews living there, III. 30–32; synagogue of Iulia Severa, III. 30–31.

Acra in Jerusalem: **I. 154–155n.**; fortress built by Antiochus Epiphanes, I. 154; location, I. 154–155n., 193; siege of by Jonathan Maccabee, I. 181–182; captured by Simon the Maccabee, I. 192.

Acrabatta, toparchy of Judaea: **II. 7**,

Antonia, mother of Claudius: freedmen of (Pallas and Felix), I. 460.

Antonia, wife of Drusus: friend of
Berenice I, I. 443.

Antoninus Pius, emperor: permits Jews
alone to circumcise, I. 539, 555, III.
123.

Antonius Julianus: see Julianus,
Antonius.

Antonius, M.: **I. 250–253, 278**; as
young man distinguishes himself in
Egyptian campaign, I. 245; conflict
with Octavian, I. 250, 253–254;
first meets Cleopatra, I. 250; Syria
under his domination, I. 250–253,
278; Parthian campaigns, I. 251–
252; life with Cleopatra, I. 252, 253;
battle of Actium, I. 253; suicide, I.
254; conflict with Brutus and
Cassius, I. 276; appoints Phasael
and Herod tetrarchs, I. 278; battle
of Philippi, I. 278; frees those
enslaved by Cassius, I. 278;
relations with Herod, I. 281, 283,
296, 28, 300, 301; gifts to Cleopatra
of parts of Syria, Phoenicia,
Palestine and Arabia, I. 287, 288,
298, 565, II. 92, 107; children by
him and Cleopatra, I. 461n.; use
of Ituraeans as his bodyguard, I.
562.

Apama, mother of Antiochus I:
Apamea founded in honour of, III.
28.

Apamea in Phrygia: **III. 28–30**;
evidence for Jews living there, III.
28–30; foundation of, III. 28;
localisation of Noah legend, III.
28–30; coinage, III. 29–30; known
as *Kibotos*, III. 29.

Apamea in Syria: siege of Bassus there,
I. 249; census of Quirinius, I. 405,
II. 146–147n.; also called Pella, II.
146–147n.; synagogue and mosaic
inscription, III. 14.

Aphaerema (= Ephraim), district of
Samaria: joined to Judaea in time of
Maccabees, I. 141, 142, 182;
location, I. 182n.

Aphrahat: allusions to *Liber Antiquitatum Biblicarum*, III. 329.

Aphrodisias: evidence for Jews living
there, III. 25; inscription from, III.
25–26, 166, 175.

Aphrodite (Astarte): worship of in
Gentile cities of Palestine, II. 30,
31–32, 35, 36, 38, 43, 44; origin and
nature of cult, II. 31; worship of in
Athens, III. 156.

Apion, grammarian: **III. 604–607**;
anti-Jewish writings of, I. 5–6, II.
35, III. 151, 605–606, 611, 612,
615n.; and Alexandrian embassy to
Caligula, I. 392, III. 605; use of
anti-Jewish writings by Mnaseas,
III. 597–598; nickname of, III. 604;
personal history, III. 604–605;
refutation of by Josephus, III.
604–605, 606–607, 610; other works
by, III. 605; literature on, III. 607.

Apocalypse of Abraham: **III. 288–292**.

Apocalypse of Baruch: see *Baruch,
Apocalypse of*.

Apocalypse of Ezra: see *Ezra, Fourth Book
of*.

Apocalypse of Moses: **III. 457–460**.

Apocalypse of Paul: III. 764.

Apocalypse of Zephariah: **III. 803–804**.

Apocalyptic literature: **III. 177–180** *et
passim*; character and theology in
general, II. 348, 353, 510–512, III.
177–180 *et passim*, 240–244, 308,
505–508, 706–708 *et passim*, 746ff,
796–798, 799ff; for individual
works, see under separate titles.

Apocrypha of the Old Testament: **III.
177–180** *et passim*; character and
theology in general, II. 498–501,
III. 177–180, 308 *et passim*, 505–508,
706–708; for individual works, see
under separate titles.

Apocryphon of Ezekiel: **III. 793–796**.

Apocryphon of Moses: III. 285.

Apollo: Jewish worship of in Dora, I.
5–6, II. 35; worship of in Gentile
cities of Palestine, II. 30, 32, 35, 37,
38; worship of by Idumaeans, III.
597–598.

Arca in north Lebanon: location and history, I. 478.

Archaeology, of Palestine: literature on, I. 6–7.

Archelais, city: founded by Archelaus, I. 355; location, I. 355n.

Archelais, village: location, I. 355n.

Archelaus, king of Cappadocia 36 BC–17 AD: effects reconciliation between Herod and his sons, I. 293, 322; daughter marries Alexander son of Herod, I. 321; census along Roman lines in his realm, I. 414.

Archelaus, son of Herod: **I. 353–356**; dismissal and exile of, I. 259, 356, 327; supported by Ptolemy, Herod's finance minister, I. 311n.; Herod names him his successor, I. 326; struggles to get Herod's will confirmed, I. 330–333; assigned Judaea, Samaria and Idumaea by Augustus, I. 333, 354, II. 92; coins of, I. 354; tyrannical rule, I. 354–356; unlawful marriage with Glaphyra, I. 354–355; building projects, I. 355; military arrangement in kingdom, I. 363; appointment of High Priests, II. 229–230.

Archiatri: see doctors.

Archigerousiarches, as Jewish official: III. 81, 98.

Archisynagogos: **II. 434–436, III. 100–101**; officer in Synagogue, II. 428, 434–436, 450, 451; position in Jewish congregation and duties of, II. 434–435, III. 100–101; title given to women and children, II. 435, III. 25, 101, 107; in gentile cults, II. 436n.; inscriptional references to from various diaspora communities, III. 14, 22, 23, 32, 34, 68, 73, 82.

Architecture, in Palestine: **II. 56–58**; Greek style, II. 56–58; of Temple (see alo under Temple), II. 57–58; of domestic buildings, II. 58; of synagogues, II. 441–443.

Archives, genealogical, in Jerusalem: I. 411–412, 507, **II. 240–242**, III. 186n.

Archon, Jewish: **III. 98–101**; of congregation, office different from that of *archisynagogos*, II. 435, III. 100–101; inscriptional references to title in various diaspora communities, III. 13, 26, 61, 92, 93, 94, 95; *archontes* in Alexandrian community, III. 92, 93; function and appointment of in Roman community, III. 98–100, 102.

Archontes, municipal: at head of council of Tiberias, II. 180.

Ares: worship of in Trachonitis, Batanaea, Auranitis, II. 43.

Aretas I, Nabataean ruler: I. 576–577.

Aretas III, Nabataean king: **I. 578–579**; seizes Coele Syria and Damascus, I. 135, 578, II. 128; defeats Alexander Jannaeus at Adida, I. 226, 578; supporter of Hyrcanus II against Aristobulus II, I. 235, 578–579; defeated by Aristobulus II, I. 236; limited subjugation by Scaurus, I. 244, 279, 579; whether identical with Erotimus, I. 577; coins of, I. 578–579.

Aretas IV, Nabataean king: **I. 582–583**; hostilities with Antipas after repudiation of daughter, I. 342, 344, 350–351, 581; sides with Hyrcanus against Aristobulus, I. 579; conflict with Herod Antipas, I. 581; inscriptions, coinage, I. 582–583; dominion over Damascus, II. 129.

Areus I, king of Sparta: friendly relations with Onias I, I. 184–185n.

Argos: evidence for Jews living there, III. 5, 64, 66.

Ariarathes V, king of Cappadocia: supporter of Alexander Balas, I. 177n.

Aristeas, Letter of: **III. 677–687**; source for Josephus, I. 50, III. 684; evidence for Jewish settlement in Egypt, III. 40, 41; evidence for Greek translation of Bible (*Septuagint*), III. 474–476, 677–679;

negotiations with Vitellius, I. 350–351.

Artapanus, Hellenistic Jewish writer: **III**. 509, 510, **521–525**; influence on Josephus, I. 49; presents Abraham as founder of astrology, I. 349, III. 611; *haggadic* style, II. 348, 349, 350, III. 521–522; glorification of Moses, II. II 350, III. 138, 521–522, 523; general character of his work, III. 522–523; personal history, III. 523–524; literature on, III. 524–525.

Artavasdes, king of Armenia: battles with M. Antonius, I. 298.

Artaxerxes II Ochus: settles Jewish prisoners in Hyrcania, III. 6, 218n.; actions against the Jews not the setting for the book of *Judith*, III. 217–218.

Artemidorus, historian from Ascalon: II. 49.

Artemis: worship of in Gentile cities of Palestine, II. 30, 37, 38, 43–44.

As (assarius), coin: value of, II. 63, 65, **66**.

Ascalon, city: **II. 105–108**; coins of Alexander the Great minted there, I. 144, II. 106; not subjugated by Alexander Jannaeus, I. 227, 228n., II. 91, 106; eighty women hanged there, I. 231; tradition that here was birth place of Antipater, I. 234n.; public buildings of Herod, I. 308, II. 107; Roman garrison there, I. 365; Greek culture, II. 3, 31–32, 46, 49, 51, 107–108; breaks away from Seleucid kingdom and establishes own calendar, II. 91, 103, 106; free city and sanctuary under Rome, II. 94, 106, 107; location, II. 105; coins of, II. 106–107; under Ptolemies and Seleucids, II. 106–107; traditional hostility to Jews, II. 107; importance in trade, II. 108.

Asceticism: Jewish tradition of fasting (see also under Fast days), II. 483–484; of Essenes (see also under Essenes), II. 560, 593, 594; at

Qumran (see also under Qumran Community), II. 578; of Therapeutae (see also under Therapeutae), II. 592, 593. See also Celibacy.

Ashdod: see Azotus.

Asher, patriarch, Testament of: see *Testaments of the XII Patriarchs*.

Ashtaroth, city: location, I. 336n.

Asia Minor: evidence for Jewish communities (see also under individual districts and cities), III. 4–5, 17–36, 141.

Asinaus, Babylonian Jew: III. 7n.

Asinius Pollio, works of: **I. 23–24**.

Asochis, town in Galilee: I. 220.

Asophon (Asaphon), town on the Jordan: I. 220.

Ass: legend of Jews worshipping, III. 151.

Assembly, synagogal ('congregation'), use and meaning of term: **II. 429–431, 439–440, 445**. See also Community; Synagogue.

Assembly, the Great: **II. 358–359**; historicity, II. 358–359; men of, II. 358–359.

Assidaeans: see Hasidim.

Assumption of Moses: **III. 278–288**; messianic hope in, II. 506, 526, III. 280–281, 283–284n.; content of, III. 278–281; date of composition, redactional layers, III. 281–283; provenance, III. 23–284; Greek and Latin texts, III. 284, 286–287; original language Hebrew/Aramaic, III. 284; also called *Testament of Moses*, III. 286–287; editions, translations, literature on, III. 287–288; translation into Greek, III. 505.

Asteria, mother of Heracles: worship of at Philadelphia, II. 39.

Astrology, Jewish: Abraham the father of, II. 349, III. 611; general character and examples of, III. 364–366, 367–368, 369–372, 373. See also Magic.

Atargatis: cult of at Ascalon, II. 31–32;

worshipped at Ptolemais, II. 36; worshipped in Batanaea, II. 41.

Athenaeus, general of Antigonus: conflict with Nabataeans, I. 576.

Athenaeus, historian: use of Posidonius of Apamea, I. 20, 21.

Athene: worship of in Gentile cities of Palestine, II. 37, 43.

Athenion: general of Cleopatra, I. 300.

Athenobius, officer of Antiochus Sidetes: I. 198.

Athens: inscriptions for Herod and his family, I. 308; bronze statue to Hyrcanus, II. 52–53n.; trade with Palestine, II. 61, II. 121, 143n.; tribute to by Dora, II. 119; evidence for Jews living there, III. 65, 141; corporations of aliens resident there, III. 109–110; decree in honour of king Straton of Sidon, III. 109; oriental cults there, III. 156.

Athribis in Egypt: evidence for Jews living there, synagogue, III. 49, 88, 104.

Atonement, Day of: method of calculating when feast should occur, I. 591; preparation for by High Priest, II. 214, 216; duties of High Priest, II. 275–276, 277; sacrifices, II. 276, 308; children gradually accustomed to the fast, II. 420; reckoning of in *Jubilees*, III. 310.

Attalus II, king of Pergamum: promotes Alexander Balas as pretender to Syrian throne, I. 177n.

Attica: evidence for Jews living there, III. 5, 64, 65.

Atticus: whether to be identified with T. Claudius Atticus Herodes, governor of Judaea, I. 516.

Augoustesioi: name of Jewish community in Rome, III. 96.

Augustine: on *Enoch*, III. 263.

Augustus: Nicolaus' biography of, I. 31; *Res Gestae Divi Augusti*, I. 66–67; history and governors of Syria during his reign, I. 253–260;

division of provinces between himself and senate, I. 255; appoints M. Agrippa his delegate in the East, I. 256; gives Trachonitis, Batanaea and Auranitis to Herod, I. 291; involvement in Herod's domestic strife, I. 293, 294, 323; Herod presents himself repeatedly to, I. 301–302, 318–320; temples to at Panias, city renamed Caesarea, I. 305–306n., II. 40, 169; decisions regarding Herod's will, I. 330–333; encourages Antipas to marry Herodias, I. 342; imperial census in his time, I. 406–411, 426; and constitutional position of Herod as client king, I. 413–416; reduces Samaritans' taxation, I. 417; and emperor worship, II. 34–35, 45; temple to at Samaria, II. 39; gifts of cities to Herod, II. 92, 104, 116, 131, 134, 302; establishment of military colonies in Palestine, II. 96; antipathy to Judaism, II. 311, 312; gifts to Jerusalem Temple, II. 312, 313; introduces *gerousia* to Jewish community in Alexandria, III. 92–93; a Jewish community in Rome named after, III. 96; edicts of toleration in favour of Jews, III. 116–117, 119n., 121; symbolised as eagle's wing in *IV Ezra*, III. 299; for early history see Octavian.

Auranitis, district: **I. 337–338n.**; given to Herod by Augustus, I. 291, 319; location, I. 337–338n.; mixed population, I. 338, II. 14–15; Hellenisation, II. 15, 41–44.

Aureus, coin: value of, II. 64–65.

Autonomy, of cities: reality of the title *autonomos*, **II. 93–96**.

Auxiliary troops, in provinces general, and Judaea (6–70 AD): **I. 362–367**. See also Military.

Avillius Flaccus: see Flaccus, A. Avillius.

Azariah: Jewish commander in time of Maccabees, I. 165.

Azariah, Prayer of: in the Additions to

Daniel, III. 722–723, 724–725, 726, 727, 278.

Azizos: cult of at Batanaea, II. 41.

Azizus, king of Emesa: marriage to Drusilla, submits to circumcision, I. 462, 475, 449.

Azotus (Ashdod), city: **II. 108–109**; bequeathed to Salome I by Herod, I. 333, II. 109; worship of Dagon, II. 32–33; liberated by Pompey, II. 91, 109; rebuilt by Gabinius, subject to Herodians, then part of imperial estate, II. 92, 109; location, II. 108–109.

B

Baal (Baalsamin): worship of in Canatha, II. 41.

Baaru, place of warm springs: location, I. 326n.

Baba Bathra, Mishnah tractate: position and subject matter, I. 73.

Baba Kamma, Mishnah tractate: position and subject matter, I. 73.

Baba Mezi'a, Mishnah tractate: position and subject matter, I. 73.

Babas: sons of killed by Herod, I. 304.

Babata, archive of: II. 25, 79, III. 16.

Babylonia: Babylonian era (Seleucid chronology) (see also under Chronology), I. 18, 19, 125–128; history of and evidence for Jewish settlement there (see also under individual place names), III. 5–6, 7, 8–9.

Bacchides, Syrian commander: **I. 173–176**; installs Alcimus as High Priest, I. 169; subjugation of Palestine and battles with Maccabees, I. 173–176; peace with Jonathan Maccabee, I. 176.

Bagoas, general of Artaxerxes Ochus: III. 218.

Bagoas, the eunuch: in prophesy of the Pharisees, II. 505.

Balsam: **I. 298–300n.**; Jericho plantations given to Cleopatra by M.

Antonius, I. 288–289, 298–300; crop from region of Jericho, uses and fame, I. 298–300n., II. 194n.

Bamidbar Rabbah: I. 94.

Baptism: required for converts to Judaism, III. 173, 174, 642; in the *Sibylline Oracles*, III. 642; in Christian *Odes of Solomon*, III. 787.

Bar-Jesus, Jewish magician in *Acts*: III. 343.

Bar Kokhba: **I. 542–552**; literature on documents of, I. 118, 122; Roman governors during the revolt, I. 518–519; causes of great revolt, I. 535–542; history of revolt, I. 542–552; meaning of his name, I. 543–544; regarded as Messiah, I. 543–545, II. 551; coins of, I. 544, 545, 603, 606; official title 'Prince of Israel', I. 544; administration of Palestine under, I. 546–547; death, I. 552; language of documents of, II. 25–26, 27–28; Greek and Latin personal names in documents of, II. 74n.; aftermath of revolt, II. 552–557; whether hidden treasure of is referred to in Qumran *Copper Scroll*, III. 467–468.

Bar-Mizwah: II. 421.

Barabbas (of the Gospels): concerning the name, I. 385n.; involvement with insurrectionists, I. 385, 439.

Barnabas, Letter of: regarding legend that Jerusalem Temple was to be rebuilt under Hadrian, I. 535–536; contains earliest Christian allusion to *IV Ezra*, III. 301.

Baruch, Apocalypse of (= *Chronicles of Jeremiah*): **III. 292–294**, 505.

Baruch, Book of (*I Baruch*): **III. 733–743**; similarities with *Daniel*, II. 736; original language of, III. 705–708, 735; canonicity of, seen as supplement to *Jeremiah*, III. 733, 740; contents, III. 733–734; composite authorship of, III. 734–735; date of composition, III. 735–738; place of origin, III. 735; whether made use of the *Psalms of Solomon*, III. 736,

737n.; reading of on 9 *Ab*, III. 739;
use of in Christian Church, III.
740–741; ancient translations of,
III. 741–742; literature on, III.
742–743.

Baruch, Apocalypse of (II Baruch): **III.
750–756**; messianism, II. 510–511,
514 *et passim*, 536, 538, III. 751–752;
original language of, III. 705–708,
753; contents, III. 751–752; date of
compostion, III. 752–753; patristic
evidence for, III. 753–754; editions,
translations, literature on, III.
754–756.

Baruch, Apocalypse of (III Baruch): **II.
789–793**; contents, III. 789–790;
extensively re-written as Christian
work, III. 790–791; date and
provenance, III. 791; relation to
other writings about Baruch, III.
791; editions, literature on, III.
792–793.

Barzaphranes, Parthian satrap: friendship with Antigonus, I. 279.

Bascama (Basca): site of Jonathan
Maccabee's death, location, I. 187.

Bashan: see Batanaea.

Bassus, P. Ventidius: see Ventidius.

Bassus, Q. Caecilius: see Caecilius.

Bassus, S. Lucilius: see Lucilius.

Batanaea, district: **I. 336–338n.**; given
to Herod by Augustus, I. 291, 319;
and tetrarchy of Philip, I. 326, 333;
extent of ancient Bashan, I. 336–
337n.; extent of territory (in Philip's
tetrarchy), I. 336–337; mixed
population, I. 338, II. 14–15;
freedom from taxation conferred by
Herod, I. 416, 419–20; colony of
Babylonian Jews settled by Herod,
I. 419, II. 14; forms part of territory
of Agrippa II, I. 472, II. 7n.; passes
into Roman control, I. 479n.,
482n.; Hellenisation of, II. 14, 41,
44; syncretistic cults of, II. 41–44.

Bath (*Mikveh*), Jewish ritual: amount
and type of water permissible, II.
477–478; in Essene community, II.
564, 569, 570; at Qumran, II.

569n., 577n., 582; ablution necessary for conversion (baptism), III.
173, 174.

Bath houses, Greek, in Palestine: II. 55.

Bathyra, village: founded by
Babylonian Jews in Batanaea,
location, II. 14n.

Behemoth: to be consumed in messianic
age, II. 534n.

Beirut: evidence for Jews living there,
III. 14, 15.

Bekhoroth, Mishnah tractate: position
and subject matter, I. 73.

Beki'in: see *Peki'in*.

Bel and the Dragon: story of in
Additions to *Daniel*, III. 722,
724–725, 725, 727, 728.

Belchîra, Samaritan, enemy of Isaiah:
III. 336, 338n.

Belial/Beliar, satanic figure: III. 390n.,
399, 450, 459, 640–641.

Belshazzar, king of Babylon: in *Daniel*,
III. 245–246.

Ben Azzai: see Simon ben Azzai.

Ben Gamla: see Jesus ben Gamaliel.

Ben Sira, Wisdom of (Ecclesiasticus): **III.
190–212**; about the author, I.
145n., III. 201–202; Greek translation by the grandson, I. 145n., III.
477, 506–507; attitude to the
Samaritans, II. 19; held in high
esteem by Church Fathers, II.
207–208; popularity of in rabbinic
circles, II. 319, III. 205, 206; and
history of the *Shemoneh 'Esreh*, II.
459n.; and messianism, II. 498–500;
no belief in after-life, II. 500;
teachings and theology of, III. 139,
199–201; first to identify divine
wisdom with Torah, III. 199–200;
against Hellenistic liberalism, III.
200–201; exaltation of Simon and
High Priesthood, III. 200–201; date
of composition, III. 202; originally
written in Hebrew, III. 202–203;
regarding the title of, III. 202,
206–207; manuscript discoveries at
Qumran and Masada, III. 203–
204, 206; Hebrew fragments from

Qumran, III. 204, 507; *Alphabet of Ben Sira*, III. 206; manuscript, editions, literature on, III. 208–212; not a part of the Hebrew canon, III. 247; grandson's knowledge of the *Septuagint*, III. 477.

Benedictions: priestly, II. 448, 450, 453–454; and the *Shema'* (see also *Shema'*), II. 454–455; before meals, II. 482–483; the Eighteen, see *Shemoneh 'Esreh*. See also under Prayer.

Benjamin, patriarch, Testament of: see *Testaments of the XII Patriarchs*.

Berakhoth: see Benedictions.

Berakhoth, Mishnah tractate: position and subject matter, I. 71.

Berea (Beerzath/Berzatho): location, I. 173n.; site of final defeat of Judas Maccabaeus, I. 173.

Berenice I, daughter of Salome I: married to Aristobulus IV, I. 321; in Rome, I. 443.

Berenice II, daughter of Agrippa I: **I. 474–476, 479**; in inscription from Athens, I. 308n., 452n., 479n.; marriage with Polemon II of Pontus, I. 450n., 474; statue in Caesarea, I. 451; bad reputation of, I. 474, 475; power over Agrippa II, I. 474; as Nazirite in Jerusalem, I. 475, 476; affair with Titus, I. 479, III. 79n.; petitions Florus on Jews' behalf, I. 485; marriage to Herod of Chalcis, I. 571–572; marriage to Marcus Iulius Alexander, I. 571, 572n., III. 815n.

Berenice in Cyrenaica: Jewish *politeuma* there, III. 61, 88, 91, 94–95; Jewish inscription in honour of Roman official, III. 104.

Bereshith Rabbah: date, edition, literature on, **I. 93–94**.

Beroea: evidence for Jews living there, III. 65, 67, 68, 141.

Berossus, chronographer: fusion of his work by a Jew with other chronicles, III. 699.

Beryllus, secretary to Nero: I. 467.

Berytus: buildings of Herod, I. 308; as Roman colony founded by Augustus, I. 323–324n., II. 96; buildings of Agrippa I, I. 451; gifts of Agrippa II, I. 474; public games there, II. 46n., 47; gains independence from Seleucids and starts own calendar, II. 91; community of Berytians in Delos, III. 108; community of Berytians in Puteoli, III. 111.

Beth Alpha: synagogue of, II. 442n., 443.

Beth Av/Beth Avoth: sub-divison priestly course, II. 245, 248–249, 292; sub-division levitical course, II. 255.

Beth Bassai, town: I. 176.

Beth Din: use of term, II. 205, 207, 209. See also Courts; Council; *Gerousia*; Sanhedrin.

Bethel, town: location, I. 175n.; Syrian garrison under Bacchides, I. 175; subjugated by Vespasian, I. 500.

Bether, mountain fort: last refuge of Bar Kokhba, I. 551–552.

Beth ha-Kerem, town: III. 320n.

Beth-haram (Bethramphtha), city: **II. 176–178**; renamed Julias (Livias), I. 342, II. 176–177; location, II. 176, 178. See also Julias.

Beth ha-Sefer: in system of Jewish education, II. 418–419. See also under Education.

Beth-Horon, town: location, I. 159n.; Syrian garrison under Bacchides, I. 175.

Bethlehem, town: journey thither of Joseph and Mary (census of Quirinius), I. 407, 411–413, 421, 422, 426–427; expected place of origin of Messiah, II. 518, 524.

Bethletepha: **II. 193–194n.**; toparchy of Judaea, II. 191, 195; variations on name, II. 191n.; location, II. 193n.

Beth Mashku, place known only from Bar Kokhba letters: I. 546.

Beth Midrash: in system of Torah

scholarship, II. 419. See also under Education.

Betholethephene: see Bethletepha.

Bethramphtha: see Beth-haram.

Bethsaida, town: **II. 171–172**; rebuilt and renamed Julias by Philip, I. 339, II. 171–172; location, II. 171–172. See also Julias.

Beth Shean (Scythopolis), city: **II. 142–145**; Greek cults of, II. 38, 48, 143; chief commodities of, II. 68n.; location, II. 142; regarding the ancient name, II. 142; origin of name Scythopolis, II. 143; coinage and era, II. 144; history, II. 144–145; massacre of Jews there by Gentiles, II. 144; extent of territory, II. 145. See also Scythopolis.

Beth Shearim, town: synagogue of, II. 442n.; various inscriptions from the necropolis of (diaspora), III. 9, 14, 15, 16, 33.

Bethulia, town so named in *Judith*: III. 216.

Beth-Zachariah, town: location, I. 166n.

Beth-Zur, town: **I. 161n.**; garrisoned by Judas Maccabaeus, I. 161, II. 2; location, I. 161n.; refortified by Bacchides, I. 175, II. 2; Jewish garrison installed by Simon Maccabee, I. 184, II. 2; furthest outpost of Judaism up until the Maccabaeans, II. 2.

Betrothal, Jewish: differences in custom between Galilee and Judaea, II. 14; forbidden on Sabbath, II. 472; forbidden on fast days, II. 484; at Qumran, II. 579n. See also under Marriage.

Bezah (Yom Ṭob), Mishnah tractate: position and subject matter, I. 72.

Bezetha, suburb of Jerusalem: fired by Gallus, I. 488; location, I. 488n., 503.

Bible (Scripture): literature on biblical chronology, I. 9; history of the canon, dignity and authority, II. 314–321, III. 187, 706–708 *et passim*;

touching scrolls defiles hands, II. 318–319, 320; exegesis at Qumran (see also under Qumran Community), II. 348, 354n., 580n., 586, III. 392, 420–421 *et passim*; cyclical reading in Synagogue, II. 448, 450, 450–453; Aramaic translation of in synagogue readings (see also *Targums*), II. 452–453; permitted language of reading, III. 142–143; the Septuagint (see also under Septuagint), III. 474–493; Origen's Hexapla, III. 480–484, 493–494, 495, 499–500; non-Septuagint Greek translations of (Aquila and Theodotion), III. 493–504; Philo's mode of allegorical interpretation, III. 876–878; for individual books, see under separate titles, IIII. See also Torah; *Halakhah*; *Haggadah*, etc.

Bibulus, L. Calpurnius: governor of Syria, I. 253.

Bibulus, M. Calpurnius: governor of Syria, I. 247.

Bikkurim: see First-Fruits.

Bikkurim, Mishnah tractate: position and subject matter, I. 72.

Bithynia: evidence for Jews living there, III. 4, 35–36.

Blessings: see Benedictions.

Blood: ritual use in consecration of priests, II. 244.

Boeotia: evidence for Jews living there, III. 5, 64, 65.

Boethus: High Priestly family of, II. 234.

Boethus, father-in-law of Herod, High Priest: I. 320n., II. 229.

Bologna: evidence for Jews living there, III. 84.

Boreum, city in Cyrenaica: evidence for Jews living there, III. 62.

Bosporus: evidence for Jews living there, III. 36–38.

Bostra, city: capital of the province of Arabia, I. 585–586, II. 183; not included in tetrarchy of Philip, I. 337–338n.; road *via Traiana* built between it and Petra, I. 586, II. 157, 158n.

Boule: see Council.

Brescia, city in Italy: evidence for Jews living there, III. 84.

Brigands: in Galilee, time of Herod, I. 295; label given to Fourth Philosophy by Josephus, II. 600.

Brutus, M.: I. 249, 250, 276.

Buka, village: location, II. 10.

Burial-practices, Jewish: inscriptions from Marisa, II. 4–5n.; High Priest forbidden to participate in mourning ritual, II. 242; evidence from Hieropolis, III. 27–28; *heroon*, III. 28, 33; necropolis at Carthage, III. 62; catacombs of Rome, III. 79–81, 142, 144, 167; use of incantation bowls and amulets in tombs, III. 353, 358. See also Death; Funerary Inscriptions.

Burnt-offering (*Ha-tamid*): **II. 295–296, 299–301**; altar of, I. 162n.; and priestly dues, II. 261, 268n., 274; history and ritual, II. 295–296, 299–301, 302, 303, 307; accompanied by daily offering of High Priest, II. 301–302; on Sabbath, II. 307; at feasts, II. 308; by gentiles, II. 310; ceased after AD 70, III. 328. See also Sacrifice.

'Burrus': see Beryllus.

Business: transactions with Gentiles by Jews proscribed in religious law, I. 82–84.

Byblos, city: buildings of Herod, I. 308; evidence for Jews living there, III. 14, 15.

C

Caecilius Bassus, (illegal) governor of Syria: **I. 248–250**.

Caecilius, Jewish orator from Calacte: **III. 701–704**; history and writings, III. 701–704; not to be confused with earlier quaestor of same name, III. 701, 703.

Caesar, C. Julius, grandson of Augustus: governor of Syria, I. 259.

Caesar, Julius: in writings of Nicolaus of Damascus, I. 31; and triumvirate, I. 246; civil war, I. 247, 248, 276; *aera Caesariana* adopted in cities of Syria, I. 248; campaigns in Egypt and Asia Minor, I. 248, 271; given military assistance by Hyrcanus and Antipater, I. 270–271; confirms Antipater as procurator, I. 271; establishes Hyrcanus as hereditary ethnarch and high priest, I. 271, 272–274; document concerning the Jews in Josephus, I. 272–274n.; restores Joppa to the Jews, I. 274, II. 113; decrees favourable to Jews outside of Palestine, I. 275, III. 116–117, 128; death, I. 276; symbolised as eagle's wing in *IV Ezra*, III. 299.

Caesar, Sextus Julius, governor of Syria: I. 248, 276.

Caesarea (Straton's Tower): **II. 115–118**; buildings of Herod, I. 306, II. 34, 116; refounded and named as such by Herod, I. 306, II. 93, 116; public games, I. 309, II. 45, 46–47; residence of Roman procurators and principal garrison of Judaea, I. 361, 363–365, II. 117; conflict between Jews and Gentiles over civic rights, I. 364, 465, 467, II. 117, 183; Roman garrison comprised native gentile troops (see also Sebastenians), I. 364–365, 367, II. 95; hatred among non-Jews of Agrippa I, I. 451, II. 117; place of Agrippa I's death, I. 452–453; made into Roman Colony by Vespasian, I. 520, II. 117–118; benefactions of Hadrian, I. 542; coins, II. 34, 116, 117, 118; cult of Augustus and Rome, II. 34–35, 46–47; as Roman colony exempt from taxation, II. 96; under a *strategos* in time of Agrippa I, II. 97, 117; founded by Sidonian king Straton, II. 115.

Capharsaba, city: location, I. 226n.; site for foundation by Herod of Antipatris, I. 306.

Capharsalama, place so-called: location, I. 169n.

Capital punishment: **I. 370–372, II. 219–220n., 431n.**; administration of in Roman provinces, I. 370–372, II. 219–220n., 221–222; whether Sanhedrin entitled to execute capital punishment independent of Rome, I. 378, II. 218–223; hanging as method of execution among Jews, III. 410, 414, 416–417, 431n., 432n.

Capito: see Herennius Capito.

Capitolias, city: formally constituted a *polis* AD 97, I. 521, II. 94, 183; location, I. 521n., II. 138.

Cappadocia: evidence for Jews living there, III. 4.

Captain, of Jerusalem Temple: see *Sagan.*

Capua: evidence for Jews living there, III. 83.

Carabas: lunatic used in Alexandria to ridicule Agrippa I, I. 390.

Caria: evidence for Jews living there, III. 4n., 24.

Carmel, Mount: worship conducted on, II. 35.

Carthage: evidence for Jews living there, III. 62–63.

Carus, L. Aemilius: governor of Arabia, II. 154, 158.

Cassiodorus: and Latin translation of Josephus, I. 58–59.

Cassius, C. Longinus, companion of Brutus: **I. 247, 249–250**; first administration of Syria (53–51 BC), I. 247, 270, 494n.; second administration of Syria (44–42 BC), I. 249–250, 276–277, 494n.; battle of Philippi, I. 250, 278; death, I. 250; alliance with Parthians, I. 251; relations with Herod, I. 277.

Cassius, C. Longinus, jurist and governor of Syria: **I. 264**, 361n., 456.

Cassius Dio: see Dio Cassius.

Castel Porziano: inscription from Jewish community there, III. 82.

Castor of Rhodes, chronographer: writings of, date, source for Josephus, I. 42, 43.

Castra Iudaeorum, in Egypt: III. 41, 48–49.

Castration: banned by Domitian, Hadrian, etc., I. 538.

Catacombs, Jewish: of Rome, III. 79–81, 142, 144, 167; at Venosa in southern Italy, III. 83.

Cedrenus, Byzantine chronicler: use of *Jubilees*, III. 308–309, 316; regarding the names of Moses, III. 329.

Celaenae, town: inhabitants moved for foundation of Apamea, III. 28; location, III. 28.

Celebrations, among Jews and Gentiles of royal births and accessions: **I. 346–348n.**

Celendris, fortress: occupied by Piso, I. 261.

Celibacy: among the Essenes (see also under Essenes), II. 568, 570, 578, 593, 594; at Qumran (see also under Qumran Community), II. 578; as practised by the Therapeutae (see also under Therapeutae), II. 591, 593, 594. See also Marriage.

Celsus: witnesses to popularity of *Sibylline Oracles*, III. 651.

Cendebaeus, general of Antiochus VII: defeated by Maccabeans, I. 198–199.

Census: **I. 399–427**; of Quirinius in Judaea (see also Quirinius), I. 258, 259, 381, 414, 399–427, II. 599, 602, 603; Jews' antipathy to, I. 381, II. 599, 602, 603; use of for taxation purposes by Rome, I. 401–404, 410; by Archelaus of the Cietae, I. 414.

Cerealis, Sextus Vettulenus: destroys Hebron, I. 500; commander of 5th Legion in siege of Jerusalem, I. 501, 502n.; commander of garrison troops after fall of Jerusalem, I. 515.

Cerycus, sophist from Gerasa: II. 50.

Cestius Gallus, governor of Syria: **I. 265**, 487–488; expedition against Jerusalem, I. 361n., 476, 487–488; destruction of Joppa, II. 113; places Roman garrison in Sepphoris, II. 175, 176n.

Chabulon, village: location, II. 10.

Chaeremon, Egyptian Stoic philosopher: **III. 601–604**; anti-Jewish account of the Exodus from Egypt, III. 151, 601; other works by, III. 601–602; literature on, III. 603–604; personal history and date, III. 603; refutation of by Josephus, III. 610–616.

Chalcis, kingdom of: **I. 571–573**; given to Cleopatra by M. Antonius, I. 287, 288n.; centre of former Ituraean kingdom, I. 563, 564, 568, 571; history of under Herod, grandson of Herod the Great (see also Herod of Chalcis), I. 571–572; given to Agrippa II by Claudius, I. 572.

Charity: among Essenes, II. 437n., 566–567; at Qumran, II. 437n., 578; synagogal administration of alms for the poor, II. 437.

Chelkias, Jewish general: III. 48, 136.

Child-birth: offering at, II. 310.

Children, Jewish: education of boys, II. 417–422, 472; boys alone observe certain commandments, II. 420–421; obliged to observe some of the commandments, II. 420–421, 455, 456, 482.

Chios: buildings of Herod there, I. 308.

Chorazin: synagogue of, II. 442n., 443.

Christ, Jesus: see Jesus Christ.

Christianity: legends regarding Pontius Pilate, I. 137n.; Christian interpolation to text of Josephus, I. 431, 434–436, 437–438, 439; view of Jews as judges and executioners of Jesus, I. 433; use of Jewish exegesis and exegetical method, II. 354–55; use of the term *ecclesia*, II. 429–430n.; excommunication as punish-ment, II. 432; belief in the coming of Elijah, II. 515; and Messianism, II. 515, 516, 517, 518, 522, 547, 549, 553; theology of individual resurrection, II. 541–542, 543, 547; theories linking Christianity with Qumran community, II. 585; view of Eusebius that Therapeutae were Egyptian Christians, II. 596–597, III. 857; Christianisation of the *Lives of the Prophets*, II. 784–785; adoption and localisation of Noah legend in Apamea, III. 28–31; attitude of Christian emperors to Jews, III. 124; practice of exorcism, III. 343, 376; use of and additions to the *Sibylline Oracles*, III. 628, 632, 635, 641–642, 643, 644, 645, 650–651; a work under the name of Hystaspes not a Christian composition, III. 654; legends about Adam and Eve, III. 760–761; Christian or Jewish authorship of *Testament of XII Patriarchs*, III. 767, 768–772; baptism, III. 787; Christian authorship of *Odes of Solomon*, III. 787–788; Christian re-writing of *III Baruch*, III. 790–791; Christian authorship of *Apocalypse of Zephamiah*, III. 803–804; influence of Jewish philosopher Philo, III. 814, 819 *et passim*, 838–839, 889. See also below, Christians.

Christians: accuse Jews of being judges and executioners of Jesus, I. 433; called tribe in Josephus, I. 434; friendship of Pharisees with Jewish Christians, I. 441; take refuge at Pella during revolt (AD 66), I. 498, II. 147–148; compete for martyrdom under Trajan, I. 517–8; in Palestine persecuted by Rome, I. 528; persecuted by followers of Bar Kokhba, I. 545; language of, in Palestine, II. 79; cursing of by Jews, II. 432, 462–463; fellowship, II. 475n.; view of Eusebius that Therapeutae were Egyptian Christians, II. 596–597, III. 857;

necessary for full conversion to Judaism, III. 164, 165, 169, 170, 173, 174; attitude to among pagan authors, III. 615.

Cities, Hellenistic in Palestine: **II. 29–52, 85–183**; hostility towards Jewish citizens, I. 364, 456, 467, 364, II. 177, 183, 427, III. 132; process of conquest and Judaization under Hasmonaeans, II. 3, 9, 11–12, 16, 91; Hellenistic cults and culture, II. 29–52, 56; foundation of by Alexander the Great, II. 36; constitution, II. 86, 182–183; history under Ptolemies, Seleucids, and Romans, II. 87–97; 'liberated' by Pompey, II. 91–92, 94; under the Herodians, II. 92–93, 97, 182; different categories of and organisation under Rome, II. 93–96; bestowal of the right of sanctuary upon, II. 94–95; military service to Rome, II. 95–96; distinctive position of Roman colonies, II. 96; for the foundations of particular persons, see under person's name. See also under individual place-names.

Cities, Jewish in Palestine: **II. 184–198, 427–431**; internal organisation and administration (see also Council; Courts; Sanhedrin), II. 184–188, 427–433; distinguished from villages, II. 188–190; toparchies of Judaea, II. 190–196; not cities in Greek sense of the word, II. 196–197; subordinate to Jerusalem, II. 197–198; levitical, II. 256; synagogues, II. 439–447. See also under individual place-names.

Citizenship, Roman: privileges of, II. 219–220n., **III. 134–135**.

Claudius, emperor: **I. 398, III. 92–93, 128–129**; governors of Syria during his reign, I. 263–264; letter to the Alexandrians, toleration edict regarding Jews, I. 392, 393, 398, III. 43, 50, 77, 92–93, 128–129; permits Jews custody of High Priest's vestments, I. 456; famine in his time, I. 457; influence of freedmen, I. 460, 461; grants privileges and territory to Agrippa II, I. 471, 472; territorial gifts to Agrippa I, I. 567; grants Herod of Chalcis the right to appoint High Priest, I. 572; establishes colony at Ptolemais, II. 125; benefactions to Tiberias, II. 180; expulsion of Jews from Rome, III. 77–78, 122; friendly with alabarch Alexander, III. 78n.; symbolised as eagle's wing in *IV Ezra*, III. 299.

Claudius Paternus Clementianus, governor of Judaea: **I. 519**.

Claudius Severus: see Severus.

Cleanness, laws of ritual purity: see under Purity.

Cleanthes, philosopher: held in high esteem by Philo, III. 872.

Clearchus: account of Aristotle meeting Greek Jews, III. 17.

Clement of Alexandria: use of *Wisdom of Ben Sira*, III. 207–208; on *Tobit*, III. 227; on *Enoch*, III. 262; use of *Assumption of Moses*, III. 285–286; on *IV Ezra*, III. 301; allusions to *Liber Antiquitatum Biblicarum*, III. 329; on the writings of the Jewish-Hellenist Demetrius, III. 513, 514; on Eupolemus, III. 518, 519–520; oldest reference to *II Macc.*, III. 534; on Philo the Elder, III. 555, 559, 560; use of *Wisdom of Solomon*, III. 574; on the philosopher Aristobulus, III. 579–580, 581, 585; mistakenly credits Apion with special work against the Jews, III. 606; use of the *Sibylline Oracles*, III. 650–651; contains Jewish verses under Greek pseudonyms, III. 656, 657, 658, 661ff, 663–666, 667–670; use of *I Esdras*, III. 714; passages quoted as deriving from Ezekiel, III. 794.

Clement of Rome: use of *Judith*, III. 220.

Clementianus, Claudius Paternus:

I. 471, 473n., 474–475, 480n., 482n.

(7) Imperial coins in Palestine: at the time of the Procurators, I. 380n., II. 82.

(8) Coins of Chalcis, Ituraea and Abilene: literature on, I. 561; of Lysanias, I. 565; of Ptolemy Mennaeus, I. 565; of Zenodorus, I. 566; from 'Leucas' (= Abila?), I. 567; of Herod of Chalcis, I. 572.

(9) Coins of the Nabataean kings: literature on, I. 575; Aretas III, I. 578–579; Obodas II, I. 580; Aretas IV, I. 582; Malichus II, I. 583; Rabbel II, I. 584.

(10) Coins of the cities (Greek and Roman): Gaza, I. 100, 101–102; Ascalon, I. 144, II. 106–107; Raphia, II. 30, 98; Caesarea (Straton's Tower), II. 34, 35, 116, 117, 118; Dora, II. 35, 120; Damascus, II. 36–37, 128, 129; Ptolemais, II. 36, 121, 122–123; Gadara, II. 38, 134, 135, 136; Gerasa, II. 38, 51; Scythopolis, II. 38, 48, 144; Philadelphia, II. 39; Samaria-Sebaste, II. 39–40, 163; Panias, II. 40, 170; Joppa, II. 112; Hippus, II. 132; Abila, II. 137; Kanatha, II. 141; Pella, II. 147; Dium, II. 149; Heshbon, II. 166; Sepphoris (Diocaesarea), II. 176; Tiberias, II. 179, 180.

(11) Seleucid coins: literature on, I. 9–10; coins of the dynasts, I. 126–135.

Colchians: and practice of circumcision, I. 537.

Colonies (non-Roman): settlement of Babylonian Jews in Batanea by Herod the Great, I. 338n., 419–420, II. 14; settlement of Idumaeans in Trachonitis by Herod the Great, I. 338n., II. 14; settlement of Macedonians in Samaria by Alexander the Great, II. 16, 29. See also Cleruchies.

Colonies, Roman: of Aelia Capitolina, I. 553–554, II. 96; at Damascus, II. 37; at Berytus, II. 96; at Caesarea, II. 96; at Heliopolis, II. 96; character, status, and rights, II. 96, III. 89. See also under individual place-names.

Colophon: evidence for Jews living there, III. 22.

Comites: as advisors to Roman governors, I. 370.

Commandments, the (*mizwot*): **II. 415–421, 464–487**; elaboration of in Oral Law, II. 339–346; given to Moses, II. 350–351; central to Judaism, II. 406, 486–487, 464–467; all to be observed by adult males, II. 417–418, 420–421, 455, 456, 479–483; observance of by children, II. 420–421, 455, 456; *bar-mizwah*, II. 421; the *Shema'*, II. 454–455, 480–483; numbering of, II. 466–467; Sabbath observance (see also under Sabbath), II. 467–475; purity laws (see also under Purity), II. 475–478; *zizit*, *mezuzah*, *teffilin*, II. 479–481; benedictions at meals (see also under Benedictions), II. 482–483; fasting, II. 483–484; in world to come, II. 535–536; exposition of in writings of Philo, III. 847–850. See also *Halakhah*, Torah, and under specific subjects.

Commentarii, of Vespasian: source for Josephus, **I. 32–33**.

Commerce: see Business; Trade.

Commodus, C. Avidius Ceionius: governor of Judaea, I. 517.

Community, Jewish: **II. 429–431, III. 87–91**; various names for notion of (*politeuma, katoikia, laos*, etc.), I. 211, II. 428–430, III. 20, 24, 87–91, 114n.; sacrifices on behalf of by High Priests, II. 276, 301–302; sacrifices at Temple, II. 292–296,

Courts of the Temple at Jerusalem: who permitted access to (see also Temple), II, 284–285, 296, 299.

Courtyards: and laws of *'Erub*, II. 484–485.

Covenant: election of Israel, Chosen People, II. 464–466, 492, 494, 495, 580, III. 159, 199–200; notion of at Qumran (see also Qumran), II. 580, 582.

Crassus, M. Licinius: **I. 246**; administration of Syria and Parthian campaigns, I. 246, 269; triumvirate, I. 246; death, I. 269; robbery of Temple treasures, I. 269.

Creation, biblical story of: haggadic elaboration of, II. 348, 353. See also under Adam; Eve.

Crete: evidence for Jews living there, III. 4n., 5, 68, 71–72.

Crispus, Q. Marcius: governor of Bithynia, I. 249, 276.

Cronus: worship of in Batanaea, Trachonitis, Aurantis, II. 43.

Ctesiphon: evidence for Jews living there, III. 9.

Cult, Jewish: restoration of under Judas Maccabaeus, I. 162–163; elaboration of in oral law, II. 345; in world to come, II. 535–536; at Qumran, II. 581–582, 588–589. See also under Temple, Sacrifice, and specific subjects.

Cults, oriental: mix of oriental and Greek in Hellenistic cities of Palestine, II. 29–52; diffusion of throughout known world, III. 155–159; attractive characteristics of, III. 158–159. See also under names of individual gods.

Cumanus, procurator of Palestine: **I. 458–459**; deposition and exile, I. 361n., 459, 460 n,. 471–472; use of Sebastenian troops against Jews, I. 364; killing of Stephanus sparks off further trouble, I. 458–459; provocation of Jews at Passover, I. 458; activities of the Sicarii and Zealots, I. 459, II. 601; troubles between

Jews and Samaritans, I. 459; intercessions of Agrippa on behalf of Jews, I. 471–472, 459.

Cupa: alms money chest in synagogues, II. 437.

Cuspius Fadus: see Fadus.

Customs duties (tariffs, tolls): **I. 373–376**; in Palestine, type and method of collection, I. 373–376; in Palmyra, I. 373, 375n.; market toll at Jerusalem abolished by Vitellius, I. 374, 388.

Cuthites: name given to inhabitants of Samaria after Assyrian colonisation, II. 17.

Cybele: cult of in Roman empire, III. 157.

Cyprian: use of *I Macc.*, III. 183; use of *Tobit*, III. 227; use of *II Macc.*, III. 535; use of *Wisdom of Solomon*, III. 575; use of the Additions to *Daniel*, III. 727; on *II Baruch*, III. 754.

Cyprus: gift to Cleopatra from M. Antonius, I. 287, 288–289n.; Jewish rebellion under Trajan, I. 532, III. 68; evidence for Jews living there, III. 4n., 5, 58–69.

Cyprus, daughter of Herod and Mariamme I: I. 320.

Cyprus, fortress near Jericho: built by Herod in honour of his mother, I. 306.

Cyprus, mother of Herod: intrigues for downfall of Mariamme, I. 302; name of fortress built in her honour, I. 306.

Cyprus, wife of Agrippa I: helps Agrippa in time of trouble, I. 443.

Cyrenaica: evidence for Jews living there, III. 60–62, 94–95.

Cyrene: Jewish rebellion under Vespasian, I. 512; Jewish revolt under Trajan, I. 529, 531–532, III. 62; evidence for Jews living there, III. 4n., 60, 61; enjoyment of equal civil rights by Jews, III. 94, 113, 130.

Cyril of Alexandria: wrongly ascribed certain work to Aristobulus, III. 581.

Domitius Corbulo: see Corbulo, Cn. Domitius.

Dora, city: **II. 118–120**; as dependency of Sidonians, I. 144, II. 119; 'liberated' by Pompey, I. 240, II. 91, 120; conflict between Jews and Gentiles over emperor worship, I. 379n., 446, II. 120; Greek foundation myth, II. 51; in restoration of Gabinius, II. 5, 92, 120; right of sanctuary and autonomy under Rome, II. 94, 120; location, II. 118; besieged by Antiochus the Great, II. 119; perhaps tributary to Athens in 5th century, II. 119–120; Tryphon besieged there, II. 119–120; coins, II. 120.

Doris: first wife of Herod, I. 284n.

Dorotheus of Ascalon, grammarian: II. 49.

Dosa ben Archinos (Harkhinas), R.: II. 375.

Dositheus, companion of Ptolemy IV: III. 539.

Dositheus, Jewish general under Ptolemy VI: III. 135, 136, 539.

Dositheus, priest: takes Lysimachus' Greek translation of *Esther* to Egypt, III. 505–506.

Dough-offering (*ḥallah*): **II. 265**; and dues to priests, II. 258, 259; what the offering comprised, II. 265; not incumbent on Jews outside the land of Israel, II. 269; preparation, II. 477. See also under Priests; Sacrifice.

Drachma, coin: value of, II. 63, 65, 67n.

Drink-offerings: and Temple cult, II. 287–288, 300, 307; on feast days, II. 308; by Gentiles, II. 310. See also under Priests; Sacrifice.

Drusilla, daughter of Agrippa I: betrothal to Antiochus Epiphanes of Commagene, I. 446, 449n. 462; marriage to Azizus king of Emesa, I. 449n.; statue of in Caesarea, I. 451; marriage to Felix, I. 461–462.

Drusus the younger: friendship with

Agrippa I, I. 443.

Dualism: doctrine of at Qumran (See also under Qumran Community), II. 517n., 526, 535n., 536n., 554, 589, III. 172–173n.

Dupondius, coin: value of, II. 65.

Dura-Europos, city: **III. 10–13**; Jewish community of, III. 10–13; representational art in the synagogue, II. 443, III. 13; inscriptions from synagogue, III. 10–13, 139.

Dusares: cult of, II. 42.

E

Eagle: design on coins of Herod, I. 312n.; mounted over Temple Gate by Herod, I. 313, 325.

Ebhel rabbathi (Semaḥoth), minor talmudic tractate: position and subjects treated, I. 80.

Ecclesia: term for congregation, difference between it and *synagoge*, **II. 429–430**.

Ecclesiastes: see *Koheleth*.

Ecclesiasticus: see *Ben Sira, Wisdom of*.

Economy: see Trade.

Eden, Garden of: II. 546n. See also Paradise.

Edom, Edomites: see Idumaea, Idumaeans.

Edrei (later Adraa), city: location, I. 336n.

Education: Greek, in Palestine, II. 77.

Education, Jewish: **II. 415–422**; advanced rabbinic education (*beth midrash*, etc.), II. 332–334; formal instruction of children (boys), II. 333–334, 417–422, 472; principle that all should know Torah, II. 415–416, 464; at Qumran, II. 421n.; use of Sabbath meetings for instruction, II. 424–427, 447, 450–453. See also Torah; Rabbis; Synagogue; Commandments.

'Eduyoth, Mishnah tractate: position and subject matter, I. 73.

Egypt: **III. 38–60**; literature on calendar and chronology of, I. 8; chronology of Egyptian campaigns of Antiochus IV, I. 128–9; as third class of imperial province, I. 358, 359; system of taxation under Rome, I. 373, 375n., 402–403; the Jewish Revolt, AD 115–117, I. 529–531; custom of circumcision among Egyptians, I. 537–538, 539–540; evidence for Jews living there (see also under individual place names), III. 4, 5, 38–44, 46–60, 145–147; settlements of Phoenicians, Idumaeans, Samaritans and Arabs there, III. 44–46; settlement of Egyptians overseas, III. 108, 109, 110; story of the Jewish Exodus in anti-Jewish writings (see also under authors' names), III. 151–152, 595–596, 600–601, 605, 608n., 611; diffusion of its gods throughout known world, III. 156–157.

'Egyptian, the': false prophet at time of Felix, I. 463n., 464, II. 509.

Ekhah Rabbati: see *Midrash Ekhah*.

Ekron, city: given to Jonathan Maccabee by Alexander Balas, I. 140, 181, III. 3.

Elagabal, emperor: foundation of Nicopolis (= Emmaus), I. 521.

Elam: evidence for Jews living there, III. 10.

Elasa (Eleasa/Alasa): place so-called, location, I. 173n.; site of defeat of Judas Maccabaeus, I. 173.

Eldad, *Book of Eldad and Modad*: **III. 783**.

Elders, Jewish: **II. 200–202**; of the Bible, II. 200–201; as heads of priestly courses, II. 249, 287; synagogal councils of: authority and function, II. 427–429, 431–433, 435; as institution in diaspora communities (see also *Presbyteros*), III. 102. See also Council; Sanhedrin.

Eleazar ben Ananus, High Priest *c*. 16 AD: II. 230, 234.

Eleazar ben Arakh, R.: II. 370.

Eleazar ben Azariah, R.: president at Yavneh, I. 526; not identical with 'Priest Eleazar' of Bar Kokhba coins, I. 544n.; contact with famous contemporaries, II. 372, 376, 380; president at Yavneh, II. 373, 375.

Eleazar ben Boethus, High Priest *c*. 4 BC: II. 229, 234.

Eleazar ben Deinaeus: II. 601.

Eleazar ben Jair: II. 604.

Eleazar ben Simon: and Great Revolt, II. 601, 602, 604.

Eleazar ben Zadok (the older), R.: II. 375–376.

Eleazar ben Zadok (the younger), R.: II. 375n.

Eleazar, brother of Judas Maccabaeus: I. 166.

Eleazar, High Priest at time of Ptolemy II: his role in creation of the *Septuagint* according to Aristeas, III. 474, 678, 679.

Eleazar, Jewish exorcist mentioned by Josephus: III. 324–343, 376.

Eleazar, martyr under Antiochus Epiphanes: I. 155.

Eleazar of Modiim, R.: whether to be identified with the 'Priest Eleazar' of Bar Kokhba coins, I. 544; death, I. 552.

Eleazar, person so-called in Josephus, defender of Machaerus in first Revolt: I. 511.

Eleazar, son of Ananias and captain of Temple: refusal to sacrifice for emperor signals start of revolt, I. 469n., 486; commander in Idumaea during Revolt, I. 489.

Eleazar, son of Simon: and civil war in Jerusalem (AD 70), I. 501; defeated by John of Gischala, I. 502–503.

Eleazar, son of Yair, Sicarii leader: and last stand of Jews at Masada (AD 74), I. 382n., **511–512**.

Eleazar the Pharisee: identification with Qumran Teacher of Righteousness, III. 436n.

Eleazar the Priest, deputy to Bar Kokhba: whether to be identified with Eleazar of Modiim, I. 544; and messianism, I. 551.

Eleazar the Zealot: and troubles under Cumanus, I. 459; sent to Rome by Felix, I. 463.

Elephantine, Jewish military colony: **III. 38–40**; use of pagan oath-formulas, III. 37; Aramaic papyri from, III. 38–39, 174–175; origin of colony, III. 39; temple to Yahu, III. 39–40; Aramaic scroll of the *Story of Ahiqar* discovered there, III. 232, 235, 237.

Eleutheropolis, city founded under Septimimus Severus: II. 183, 521.

Eleutherus, river: as boundary between Ptolemaic and Seleucid territory, II. 88–89.

Eliezer b. Jacob (the elder), R.: **II. 371–372**.

Eliezer b. Jacob (the younger), R.: II. 371, 372.

Eliezer ben Hyrcanus, R.: **II. 374**; *Pirke de-Rabbi Eliezer*, I. 198; relations with Agrippa II, I. 475, 483n.; contemporary of Gamaliel II at Yavneh, I. 524; personal history and legends about, II. 375; religious teachings, II. 483, 487.

Eliezer ben Yose the Galilean, R.: and formulation of *haggadic middoth*, II. 354.

Elijah, the Prophet: **II. 515–516**; later legends about, II. 352; expected return before the Messiah, II. 515–516; as awakener of the dead, II. 516; righteousness of, II. 604; in *The Lives of the Prophets*, III. 784; *Apocalypse of Elijah*, III. 799–803.

Elionaeus ben Cantheras: High Priest *c.* 44 AD, II. 229n., 231, 234.

Elisha, envoy of Bar Kokhba: I. 546.

Ellasar (Pontus): III. 320n., 323n.

Emmatha, city: theatre of, II. 47–48.

Emmaus (later Nicopolis), city: **I. 512–513n.**; Syrian garrison under Bacchides, I. 175; inhabitants sold as slaves by Cassius, I. 277; former slaves of freed by M. Antonius, I. 278; siege of by Vespasian, I. 498, 499n.; date of foundation as Nicopolis, I. 512–513n., 521; whether military colony established here by Vespasian, I. 512–513n., 520; most westerly Jewish city before Hasmonaean expansion, II. 3; toparchy of Judaea, II. 190, 193; location, II. 193n.

Emmaus near Jerusalem: **I. 512–513n.**; to be distinguished from Emmaus-Nicopolis, I. 512–513n., II. 193n.; establishment of military colony under Vespasian, I. 512–513n.

Emperor: games and temples in honour of in Hellenistic cities of Palestine, I. 304, II. 34–35, 45, 47; worship of in provinces, I. 304; oath of loyalty by provincials, I. 314; daily sacrifices for at Jerusalem Temple, I. 379–380, 469, 486, 522, II. 311–312, III. 613; Jews exempt from worship of, I. 379, III. 121–122; honour of in diaspora, I. 380; no image of on Judaean coins, I. 380; Roman standards, with images of, not carried into Jerusalem, I. 380; Caligula demands emperor worship from the Jews, I. 389–397, III. 121–122; suspension of daily sacrifice for signals start of Great Revolt, I. 469n., 486; precious gifts of emperors to Jerusalem Temple, II. 312–313; synagogues built in honour of, III. 104–105. See also under individual names and subjects.

Engedi, town: under administration of Bar Kokhba, I. 546; as toparchy of Judaea, II. 7, 191, 194; famed for its palm and balsam groves, II. 194n.; site of Essene settlement, II. 563; earlier designation Hazezon-Tamar, III. 320n., 323n.

Enoch: inventor of astrology, II. 349, III. 261; and Noachean legend in

Phrygia, III. 30–32, 34; in writings of Philo, III. 846.

Enoch, Book of: **III. 250–277**; on the Jewish calendar, I. 590–591, 592–593; influence on *II Enoch*, I. 746; original language Aramaic, II. 21, 23, III. 254, 259, 260; Enoch as inventor of astrology, II. 349, III. 261; messianism of, II. 502–503, 505, 517, 519, 520–521, 526, 527, III. 252–253, 256–259; Book of Parables, II. 520n., III. 252–253, 256–259, 260; dates of constituent parts, II. 520n., III. 254–259, 258–259; regarding the expression 'Son of Man', II. 520–521, III. 252–253, 256–257; manuscript history, III. 250–251; much used by Church Fathers, III. 250, 261–264; used by *Jubilees*, III. 250, 256, 261; Aramaic discoveries from Qumran, III. 251–252, 254, 255, 256, 257–258, 260; Book of Noah, III. 252–253, 260; Book of Watchers, III. 252, 255, 256; character and story of (Ethiopic version), III. 252–254; Astronomical Book (3 Enoch), III. 253, 254, 256, 269–277; Book of Admonitions, III. 253, 255–256; Book of Dream-Visions, III. 253, 255; whether in part of Christian authorship, III. 256–259; use of in *Testament of XII Patriarchs*, III. 261, 777; editions, translations, literature on, III. 264–268; close association with Qumran *Genesis Apocryphon*, III. 321.

Enoch, Second Book of: **III. 746–750**; original language of, III. 705–708, 748; contents, III. 746–747; influence of *I Enoch*, III. 746; not a Christian work, III. 747–748; date of composition, III. 748–749; appended Melchizedek legend, III. 749; editions, translations, literature on, III. 749–750.

Enos: in writings of Philo, III. 846.

Epaphroditus, patron of Josephus: I. 48, 54, 55.

Ephesus, city: **III. 22–23**; evidence for Jews living there, III. 22–23, 88; synagogue and inscriptions, III. 23; citizen rights of Jews living there, III. 129–130.

Ephorus: whether a source for Nicolaus of Damascus, I. 31.

Ephraem: allusions to *Liber Antiquitatum Biblicarum*, III. 329.

Ephraim, district: see Aphaerema.

Ephraim, town: **I. 182n.**; incorporated into Judaea under Jonathan Maccabee, I. 182, II. 1–2; location, I. 182n.; subjugated by Vespasian, I. 500.

Epicrates: general of Antiochus IX, II. 144.

Epigraphy: see Inscriptions.

Epiphanius: on the 'Deuteroseis of Moses', use for chronology of Mishnah redaction, I. 77; use of *Jubilees*, III. 315; on the *Martyrdom of Isaiah*, III. 339–340; on Aquila, III. 494; on Theodotion, III. 499, 501; on *I Baruch*, III. 740; on the *Apocryphon of Ezekiel*, III. 794, 795.

Erotimus, founder of Nabataean dynasty: I. 577.

'Erub: law and practice of (see also under Sabbath), II. 472–473, **484–485**.

Esarhaddon, Assyrian king: in the *Story of Ahiqar*, III. 232–235.

Eschatology: see After-life; Messianism.

Esdras, First Book of (= *III Ezra*): **III. 708–718**; original language of, III. 705–708, 709–713; not included in Hebrew canon, but in Septuagint, III. 708, 714; contents differences from canonical *Ezra*, III. 709; relation to *Ezra*, *Chronicles*, *Nehemiah*, III. 709–713; purpose of work, III. 711; date of composition, III. 713–714; use of by Josephus, III. 713, 714; use of in Christian church, III. 714; literature on, III. 716–718.

Eshbon: see Heshbon.

Eshtemoa, town: synagogue of, II. 442n., 449n.

Essenes: **II. 555–574, 583–590**; healing powers and prophecy, II. 55, 590, 593–597; refused oath of allegiance to Herod, I. 314n.; punishment of excommunication, II. 431, 565; charity and alms giving, II. 437n., 567; community organisation and hierarchy, II. 447n., 563–567; rules of ritual purity, II. 475n., 564, 569, 570; withdrawal from Jerusalem Temple, II. 475n., 570, 572, 588–589; doctrine of immortality, II. 540n., 574; literature on, II. 555–558; etymology of name, II. 558–574, 559–560, 593; origin and history, II. 559–560, 585–587; classical sources on Essenism (see also under individual authors), II. 560–561, *et passim*; identification with Qumran community, II. 561, 563n., 564–567, 575, 583–585, 588–589, III. 380; number in community, II. 562–563; common meal, II. 565, 567, 569n., 570–571, 593; asceticism, II. 568, 570, 578, 593, 594; attitude toward and rules regarding marriage, II. 570, 578, 594; religious beliefs generally, II. 571–574, 588–590; belief in Providence, II. 572; importance of Moses, II. 572; 'sun worship', II. 573, 593; active involvement in revolt against Rome, II. 588; and Pythagoreanism, II. 589–590; compared with Therapeutae, II. 593–597; and authorship of *Apocalypse of Abraham*, III. 244, 290; authorship of *Assumption of Moses*, III. 244, 283–284; and authorship of *Jubilees*, III. 313–314; Essenism not the milieu of *Liber Antiquitatum Biblicarum*, III. 327–328; not the authors of the *Sibylline Oracles*, III. 642. See also Qumran Community.

Esther, biblical book: *Midrash Esther* and other midrashim, I. 95–96; and process of canonisation, II. 317–318n.; reading of at Purim, II. 450; translation into Greek, III. 505–506, 719–721; relation of Greek text to *III Macc.*, III. 539–540; additions to in Greek version, III. 718–722; contents and story, III. 718; later additions of Aramaic dream text (= Targum of Esther), III. 720. See also *Megilloth*.

Etam: aqueduct from there to Jerusalem built by Pontius Pilate, I. 385n.

Ethaos: cult of in Batanaea, II. 41–42.

Ethiopians: and custom of circumcision, I. 537.

Ethnarch: rank and significance of title, I. 333–334n.; as highest Jewish official in Palestine, see Patriarch.

Ethnos: use of term to denote Jewish community, III. **90**, 91, 114n. See also under Community.

Euaratus of Cos: at court of Herod, I. 311.

Eubius, Stoic philosopher of Ascalon: II. 49.

Euboea: evidence for Jews living there, III. 5, 68, 69.

Eucheion ('place of prayer'): III. 55.

Eulogius, bishop of Alexandria: III. 60.

Eumeneia: evidence for Jews living there, III. 32.

Eupolemus, head of Jewish delegation to Rome under Judas Maccabaeus: I. 145n., 171, III. 519.

Eupolemus, Jewish-Hellenistic writer: **III. 517–521**; and haggadic historiography, II. 348, 349, 350, III. 509, 517; on Enoch being the inventor of astrology, II. 349, III. 261; on Moses as inventor of alphabet, II. 350, III. 518, 611; writings of, III. 510, 517–518, 519–520; identification of a Pseudo-Eupolemus, III. 517, 528–530; date, personal history, III. 518–519; literature on, III. 520–521.

Euripides: Jewish poetry under name of, III. 656, 657, 659n., 661, 669; held in high esteem by Philo, III. 872.

Apocalypse of Ezra, III. 302; translations, literature on, III. 305–306; links with *II Baruch*, III. 752–753.

Ezra, Third Book of: see *Esdras, First Book of*.

Ezrat Nashim (women's gallery in synagogue): II. 448n.

F

Fabius, Roman commander in Damascus: II. 129;

Fadus, procurator of Judaea: I. **455–456**; offends Jews over High Priest's vestments, I. 379, 456; and false prophet Theudas, I. 456.

Faith: affirmation of, the *Shema'*, II. 454–455. See also under *Shema'*.

Falco, Q. Roscius Coelius Pompeius: governor of Judaea, I. **516–517**.

Fall, of Adam: according to *Jubilees*, III. 310. See also under Adam.

Families: priestly (24 courses), II. 245–250; Levitical, II. 254–256. See also Archives; Genealogies.

Famine: in Palestine, 25 BC, I. 291; 'universal' in time of Claudius, I. 457.

Fast-days, Jewish: II. **483–484**; public prayer on, II. 444; announced by trumpets, II. 446; voluntary and extraordinary fast days, II. 483–484; mode of observance, II. 484. See also under Asceticism.

Feasts, Jewish: *Pesiḳta* (midrash on feasts and sabbaths), I. 96; method of calculating on what days they should fall (see also Calendar, Jewish), I. 591; influx of pilgrims to Jerusalem for main feasts, II. 76; details of observance elaborated upon in oral law, II. 345; Sadducean rules regarding, II. 410–411; and synagogue liturgy, II. 452n., 454; annual celebration by Alexandrian Jews of their delivery

from Ptolemy Physcon, III. 115n., 145; celebration of by diaspora Jewry, III. 144–145; annual Alexandrian festival to mark translation of Bible into Greek, III. 145, 476, 480; observance of in Qumran community, III. 408, 413, 460–461, 466–467. See also Temple; Sacrifice; Sabbath; and under names of specific festivals.

Felix, procurator of Judaea: I. **460–465**; called procurator by Tacitus, I. 359; as influential freedman, I. 360, 460–461; imprisonment of the apostle Paul, I. 369n., 370n., 378, 465; whether administrator of Samaria and Judaea in time of Cumanus, I. 459–460n.; cruelty of his rule according to Tacitus, I. 461, 462; marriages of, I. 461–462; his rule a turning point toward revolt in Judaea, I. 462–465; and *Sicarii*, I. 463, II. 601; and 'the Egyptian', I. 464; date of his recall to Rome, I. 465–466n.; and Jewish-Gentile citizenship dispute in Caesarea, I. 465, II. 117.

Festivals: see Feasts.

Festus, procurator of Judaea: I. **467–468**; and apostle Paul, I. 370n., 378, 467; chronology of rule, I. 466n.; settlement of Jewish-Gentile dispute in Caesarea, I. 467; relations with Agrippa II and Berenice, I. 474, 475; conflict with priests, II. 313.

First-born of beasts, and priestly dues: II. 257, 258, 259, **265–267**, 270n. See also Tithes; Priests.

First-born of man: rite of redemption, II. **265**, **266**, 270n. See also Tithes; Priests.

First-Fruits (*Bikkurim*), and priestly dues: II. 257, 258, **262**, 269. See also Tithes; Priests.

Fiscus Judaicus: see Half-Shekel Tax; Temple.

Flaccus, A. Avillius, governor of Egypt: I. **389–391**; persecution of

Jews, I. 390–391; exile and death, I. 391; in writings of Philo, III. 453, 859–864.

Flaccus, L. Pomponius, governor of Syria: I. 262, 443.

Flaccus, propraetor of Asia, 61–62 BC: III. 27, 28, 75, 118.

Flavia Neapolis: see Neapolis.

Flavius Silva, governor of Palestine: I. 511–512, **515**.

Flood, the: Noah legend at Apamea, III. 28–30. See also under Noah.

Florus, procurator of Judaea: I. **470**, **485–486**; crucifixion of Jews with Roman citizenship, I. 369; malevolence of his rule sparks off Jewish revolt, I. 470, 485–486.

Food stuffs: II. **68–70**; foreign, imported to Palestine, II. 68–70; of Gentiles deemed unclean, II. 83–84.

Fortunatus, freedman in service of Agrippa I: I. 352.

Frugi, M. Tittius, commander of 15th Legion under Titus in siege of Jerusalem: I. 501, 502n.

Funerary Inscriptions (Jewish): II. **24–25n.**; language of in Palestine, II. 24–25, 79, 80; from various diaspora comunities, III. 9, 14, 15, 16, 17, 27–28, 31–32, 33, 34, 36, 37, 39, 42n., 47, 56, 61, 62, 63, 66, 70, 71, 73, 83, 89, 106; from Roman catacombs, III. 79–81, 167; language of in diaspora, III. 142.

Furniture: foreign, imported to Palestine, II. **71–72**.

Fuscianus, C. Allius, governor of Arabia: II. 154.

G

Gaba, city: II. **164–165**; fortified and colonised by Herod, I. 308, 315, II. 164; not to be confused with another Gaba, II. 165.

Gabalitis: see Gilead.

Gabara, town (=Garaba): toparchy of Galilee, II. 195n.

Gabinius, governor of Syria: I. **245–246**, 268–269; destroys fortresses of Alexandrium and Hyrcania, I. 238, 307; expedition to Egypt, I. 245–246, 269; accused *de maiestate*, I. 246; division of Judaea into five districts, I. 268–269, II. 12, 173; demolition of Machaerus, I. 511n.; campaign against Nabataeans, I. 580; rebuilding of cities of Palestine, II. 5–6, 12, 16, 33, 92, 98, 101, 104, 109, 110, 144; restoration of Kanatha and Samaria, citizens then known as 'Gabinians', II. 16, 39, 141, 162.

Gad, patriarch, Testament of: see *Testaments of the XII Patriarchs*.

Gadara, city: II. **132–136**; Hellenistic culture of, I. 144, II. 47, 49–50, 135, 138; captured by Alexander Jannaeus, I. 221, II. 133; location, I. 221n., II. 132, 136; 'liberated' by Pompey, henceforth part of the Decapolis, I. 240, II. 126, 134; not to be confused with Gadara in Peraea, I. 268n., II. 134; under Herod, I. 302, II. 92, 97, 134; after death of Herod became part of province of Syria, I. 333, II. 134; famed for its warm springs, II. 133; coins of, II. 134, 135, 136; slaughter of Jews there in first revolt, II. 134.

Gadara in Peraea: not to be confused with other Gadara, I. 268n., II. 134; garrisoned by Vespasian, I. 498, II. 134; location, II. 195n.; toparchy of Peraea, II. 195n.

Galaaditis: see Gilead.

Galatia: evidence for Jews living there, III. 34–35.

Galba, emperor: elevation and assassination, I. 477, 499; symbolised as eagle's wing in *IV Ezra*, III. 299.

Galilee: I. **141–142**, II. **7–10**, **184–190**; rescue of Jewish minority by Simon Maccabee, I. 142, 164–165, II. 8; Judaization of part by Aristobulus I, I. 217–218, II. 9–10; one of five administrative districts set up by Gabinius, I. 268, II. 190; part seized by tyrant Marion, I. 277; subdued by Herod, I. 283; Herod campaigns against brigandage there, I. 282, 295; under tetrarch Herod Antipas, I. 326, 333, 341–343; and war of Varus, I. 332; fertile region, I. 341; Tiberias as capital of, I. 342, II. 174, 180–181, 190; area of Jesus' ministry, I. 345, 349; killing of Galileans by Pilate, I. 385; parts of given to Agrippa II by Nero, I. 472–473; organisation of constitution and defences by Josephus, I. 489–490, II. 187; refugees from there join Bar Kokhba, I. 547; as part of Ituraean kingdom, I. 564; extent of Jewish Galilee according to Josephus, II. 6n., 10; history of name, II. 7, 8n.; Jews in minority before Hasmonaean period, II. 7–9, 13n.; population mainly Jewish in Roman period, II. 10, 13; legal differences between it and Judaea, II. 14; language differences between it and Judaea, II. 23; linen industry, II. 68n.; Sepphoris as capital of, II. 174–175, 190; internal Jewish organisation, II. 184–190; toparchies of, II. 194–195; synagogue architecture there, II. 441–442n. See also under specific subjects and place-names.

Gallery: for women in synagogue, II. 448n.

Gallus, Aelius: see Aelius Gallus.

Gallus, Cestius: see Cestius Gallus.

Gamala, city: **I. 495n.**; conquered by Alexander Jannaeus, I. 226; location, I. 337n., 495n.; not to be confused with Galaaditis (Gilead), I. 350n.; deserts Agrippa II for anti-Roman cause in First Revolt, I. 476, 477n.; fortified by Josephus, I. 490; captured by Vespasian, I. 495; under Herodian governor, II. 97.

Gamaliel I, R.: **II. 367–368**; speech in

Acts attributed to, I. 439n., 456–457n.; whether he had a servant called Tabi, I. 522n., 523n.; not president of Sanhedrin, II. 215, 216, 368; one of 'the pairs' (*zuggot*), II. 215, 358, 361; distinguished with title *rabban*, II. 326n.; sometimes confused with Gamaliel II, II. 367–368; in Christian legend, II. 368.

Gamaliel II, R.: **II. 372–373**; legendary questioning of by 'Hegemon Agnitus', I. 519; whether he had a servant called Tabi, I. 522n., 523n.; as head of the academy at Yavneh, I. 524, 525, II. 372–373, 374, 375; supervision of calendar, I. 525, 593; journeys to governor of Syria, I. 526n.; visits baths of Aphrodite at Akko (Ptolemais), II. 82; distinguished with title *rabban*, II. 326n.; journey to Rome, II. 372; character of his legal rulings, II. 373; controversy concerning Ammonite proselytes, III. 176.

Gamalitis, district: province of Agrippa's kingdom, large Jewish population, II. 7n.

Games, public (pagan): **II. 44–48, 54–55**; instituted by Herod in Palestine, I. 309–310; in Jerusalem and other Jewish cities, I. 309, II. 54–55; in Hellenistic cities of Palestine, II. 44–48; attitude of Pharisaic Judaism towards, II. 54–55; famous at Ascalon, II. 107.

Ganymede: worship of in Gentile cities in and around Palestine, II. 43.

Garasa: see Gerasa.

Garrisons: Syrian in Jerusalem (Acra), I. 154, 166, 192; Roman in Judaea, I. 362–367, II. 117. See also under Military.

Gate-keepers: Levitical office of in Temple, **II. 284–286**.

Gaul: evidence for Jews living there, III. 85.

Gaulana (Golan): conquered by Alexander Jannaeus, I. 226;

location, I. 226n.

Gaulanitis, district: **I. 337, 338**; name derived from Golan, I. 223n., 226n., 337n.; part of tetrarchy of Philip, I. 326, 333, 336–339; location, I. 337n.; mixed Jewish-Syrian population, I. 338, II. 7n., 14; given to Agrippa II by Claudius, I. 472, II. 7n.; on border of Jewish Galilee, II. 10.

Gaza, city: **II. 98–103**; Hellenistic culture of, I. 144, II. 3, 30, 46, 51, 103; trade with Athens in Persian period, I. 144, II. 61, 99; given to Herod by Augustus, I. 302, II. 101; joined to province of Syria by Augustus, I. 333, II. 101–102; Roman customs officers stationed there, I. 374; and benefactions of Hadrian, I. 542; captured by Alexander Jannaeus, I. 577, II. 6, 101, 103n.; 'liberated' by Pompey, II. 6, 94, 101; famed for its public games, II. 46; Greek foundation myth, II. 51; under Herodians ruled by an archon, II. 97; history before the time of Alexander the Great, II. 98–99; coins of, II. 99, 10 101–102; history under Ptolemies and Seleucids, II. 99–101; distinction between Old and New Gaza, II. 101–102n.; era of, II. 101, 103n.; becomes Roman colony, II. 103n.; own calendar, II. 103n.

Gazara, city (= Gezer): **I. 191n.**; Judaized by Simon Maccabee, I. 140, II. 5; fortifications strengthened under Bacchides, I. 175; location, I. 191n.; seized by Antiochus VII, then returned to Jews, I. 204–205; in the reorganisation of Judaea under Gabinius, I. 268n.

Gehinnom: meaning of term and location, II. 545n. See also Afterlife.

Genealogies, Jewish: **II. 240–242**; use of in Roman census, I. 411–412; archives in Jerusalem, I. 412n., II.

240–242; of priests, I. 412, II. 240–242; of non-priestly families, II. 242n.; as historical documents, III. 186n.

Genesis Apocryphon: See Qumran Community, Writings from.

Genesis, biblical book: *Bereshith Rabbah*, midrash, I. 93–94, II. 23; midrashic reworking in *Jubilees*, II. 348, III. 308–311, 798; fragments of exegesis on from Qumran, III. 421–423; midrash on in *Joseph and Asenath*, III. 546–548; in *II Enoch*, III. 747–749; in *Testament of Abraham*, III. 761–762; in *Testament of XII Patriarchs*, III. 767–768; exposition of in writings of Philo, III. 827–840.

Genoa: evidence for Jews living there, III. 84.

Gentiles: restricted access to Jerusalem Temple, I. 176n., 378, II. 80, 222, 284–285; non Jewish cities and districts in and around Palestine, II. 1–15, 29–52; considered levitically impure by Jews, II. 81, 82–84; dispute with Jews in Caesarea regarding civic rights, II. 117; rights of in Jewish towns or cities of mixed population, II. 183; offer gifts and sacrifice at Jerusalem Temple, II. 274, 309–313; and Sabbath observance, II. 470; and Israel in world to come, II. 493, 495, 500, 502, 503, 504, 506, 510–511, 525–526, 526–529, 530, 532, 533, 535, 547; hostility to Jews and Judaism, III. 131–132, 150–153, 594–616; attachment to Judaism, see God-fearers; Proselytes; Conversion; for Christian gentiles, see Christians.

Geography of Palestine: literature on, I. 7–8.

Ger, history and meaning of term: **III. 169–172.**

Gerasa (1), city: **II. 149–155**; derivation of name, I. 144, II. 150; founded by Alexander the Great, I. 144, II. 150; conquered by

Alexander Jannaeus, I. 226, II. 150; worship of Oriental and Greek gods, II. 37–38; games and theatres, II. 48, 149; famous men from, II. 49, 155; 'liberated' by Pompey, member of Decapolis, II. 126, 150, 153; location, II. 145; extensive remains, II. 149; citizens known as 'Antiochenes', II. 150, 151; not to be confused with city destroyed under Vespasian, II. 150; use of Pompeian era, II. 150, 152–153; coins of, II. 151; council (*boule*) of, II. 151–152; becomes Roman colony in 3rd century, II. 152; as city of province of Arabia, II. 153–155, 157, 158.

Gerasa (2), city: destroyed under Vespasian, not to be confused with Gerasa (1), I. 498, II. 150.

Gerim, minor talmudic tractate: position and subject treated, I. 80.

Gerizim, mount: Samaritan temple destroyed by Hyrcanus, I. 207; route of Samaritans in time of Pilate, I. 386–387; site of Samaritan temple and centre of Samaritan worship, I. 386, II. 17–19, 161, III. 71; later site of temple to Zeus, I. 521; Samaritans killed by Vespasian there, II. 163; in writings of (Pseudo-) Eupolemus, III. 529.

Germanicus, adopted son of Tiberius: I. 260.

Gerousia (Jewish): **II. 202–204, III. 92–100**; in Jerusalem, I. 139, II. 202–204, 227; referenced on coins of Hyrcanus I, I. 211; inscriptional references to *gerousiarches* from various diaspora communities, III. 14, 82, 97n., 98; in Alexandria, III. 92–94; in community at Rome, III. 95–96, 98–100. See also Council; Sanhedrin.

Gessius Florus: see Florus.

Gᵉzerah Shawah: exegetical method (Hillel), II. 344, 345n.

Gilead: expedition thither by Judas Maccabaeus to rescue Jews, I. 142,

164–165, II. 11; tribute exacted by Alexander Jannaeus, I. 223, II. 11; and boundary disputes of Antipas and Aretas, I. 350.

Girdle: worn by officiating priests, II. 293–294.

Gischala, city: **I. 496n.**; fortified by Josephus, controlled by John, I. 490; captured by Titus, I. 495–496; location and meaning of name, I. 496n.; for John of, see John of Gischala.

Giṭṭin, Mishnah tractate: position and subject matter, I. 72.

Gizbarim (temple treasurers): **II. 281–282**, 283.

Glaphyra, daughter of King Archelaus of Cappadocia: marriage to Alexander, I. 321, 354; marriage to Juba, I. 354; unlawful marriage with Archelaus, I. 354–355.

Glyeas, Byzantine chronicler: III. 308–309, 316.

Gnostics/Gnosticism: legends about Adam and Eve, III. 760–761; whether *Odes of Solomon* should be labelled gnostic, III. 787.

God: Divine Name of (Tetragrammaton), II. 306–307n.; and world to come/Messianic age, II. 493, 494, 495–496, 499, 501–502, 503, 505, 506, 512, 531–533; transcendence of, II. 495–496; kingdom of, II. 531–533; *Sabaoth* as divine name, III. 74–75; presentation of in Jewish *apologia*, III. 154; not exclusively the deity of the Jews, III. 159; fear of is the begining of Wisdom, III. 199–200; doctrine of in writings of Philo, III. 880–885; annointed of, see Messiah, the.

God, the Highest: see *Theos Hypsistos*.

Goddesses: worship of in gentile cities in and around Palestine, II. 30–32, 35, 36, 37, 38, 39, 42, 43, 44. See also under individual names.

'God-fearers': **III. 161–171**; various inscriptional references to, III. 21, 22, 24, 26, 70, 167–168; whether formed a distinct category, III. 26, 150, 165–169; Poppaea described as such, III. 78; to be found throughout Hellenistic-Roman world, III. 161–167; extent of observance of Jewish law, III. 164–165, 169; meaning of terms *sebomenoi, phoboumenoi* and *theosebeis*, III. 166–169; distinct from *ger toshab*, III. 170–171.

Gods: Greek and Oriental, worship of in Hellenistic cities of Palestine, II. 30–44. See also under individual names.

Gophna: **II. 192n.**; inhabitants sold as slaves by Cassius, I. 277, II. 192n.; slaves freed by M. Antonius, I. 278; subjugated by Vespasian, I. 499; as toparchy of Judaea, II. 190, 192; location, II. 192n.

Gorgias, Seleucid general: war against Maccabees, I. 159n., 160.

Gorgippi: evidence for Jews living there, III. 37–38.

Gorion, Joseph ben: in charge of Jerusalem defences at start of First Revolt, I. 489; opposed to Zealot party, I. 497; whether to be identified with Gorion son of Joseph, I. 497n.; death, I. 498.

Gortyn, city in Crete: evidence for Jews living there, III. 4n.

Governors, Roman: **I. 357–358** *et passim*; titles of (procurator, prefect, etc.), I. 255, 357–359, 372; confusion regarding title of in Judaea, I. 358–360; financial administration, I. 358–359, 372–376; in Judaea, place of residence, I. 361–362; judicial authority, I. 367–372, 378; advised by *consilium (comites)*, I. 370; names of in Judaea, AD 6–41, I. 382–383; in Judaea, AD 44–66, I. 455–470, 485–486; and limitations on competence of Sanhedrin, II. 219–223. See also under individual names.

Grain-offerings: given to priests, II. 258, 260, 282, 295–296n.; time of,

II. 300; of High Priest, II. 301–302; on feast days, II. 308; not accepted from gentiles after AD 66, II. 310.

Gratus, Valerius: see Valerius Gratus.

Greece: evidence for Jews living there, III. 4, 5, **64–72**.

Greek culture, spread of: see Hellenism.

Greek language: **II. 74–80**; extent of knowledge of among Jews of Palestine, I. 145, II. 74–80; loan words in Mishnah, II. 53–54, 55, 57, 60, 62, 65–66, 67, 69–73, 77; personal names among Jews of Palestine, II. 73–74; language permitted for Bible and divorce deeds, II. 77; loan words in Judaean Desert documents and Dead Sea Scrolls, II. 78–79; use of in synagogue services and prayer, III. 142–143; representations of Jews and Judaism in Greek literature, III. 150–153; Jewish literature of inter-testamental era composed in (see also under individual titles), III. 177–180, 470–473 *et passim*, 705–708; spoken by diaspora Jews, III. 475, 479, 493; non-Septuagint translations of Bible (Aquila and Theodotion), III. 493–504; translation of Bible into, see *Septuagint*.

Guilt-offerings: given to priests, II. 258, 260, 295–296; not accepted from gentiles after AD 66, II. 310.

Gymnasium, in cities of Palestine, see Games.

H

Habakkuk, biblical book: commentary on from Qumran, III. 433–436.

Habakkuk, prophet: in *The Lives of the Prophets*, III. 783–784.

Habdala, ceremony of: II. 459n.

Hadad: cult of in non-Jewish Palestine, II. 36, 41.

Hanina ben Dosa, the miracle worker: II. 370n.

Hannah, the Righteous Mother: martyrdom of her and her seven sons, I. 155–156.

Hannia, R. (Hananiah): II. 371.

Hanukkah: origin of festival, I. 162–163; letter to Egyptian Jews regarding (*II Macc.*), III. 533–534.

Ha'olam haba' (World to Come): II. 466, 492, 495, 497, 501–513, 517–523, 523–524, 526–528, 529–537, 537–538. See also Messianism; After-life.

Ḥarba de Mosheh (The Sword of Moses): III. 345, **350–352**.

Harim (Priestly Family/Course): II. 245, 246.

Ḥasidim: piety of, I. 143, 145, 157n.; self-defence permitted on Sabbath, I. 143, II. 474; defenders of Judaism against Hellenists and in Maccabaean struggle, I. 145, 157, III. 280, 282; compared with Pharisees, I. 157n., 212, II. 400–401; not to be identified with Maccabees, I. 157n., 169n.; persecution of by Alcimus, I. 169; authorship of *Jubilees*, III. 314.

Hasmonaeans, dynasty: 'Mishnah of the —', I. 77n.; coinage of, I. 190–191, 603–605, II. 63; origin of family name, I. 194n.; chronology of, I. 200–201n.; (priestly) kingship of, I. 281, II. 203–204, 215, 216, 227, 250; and Herod the Great, I. 296–298, 313, 301, 303; Judaization of regions conquered, II. 11; Hellenism of, II. 52; hope for longevity of dynasty, II. 500; relationship to the Zealots, II. 604, 605n.; portrayal of in *Psalms of Solomon*, III. 193–194; portrayal of in *Assumption of Moses*, III. 279, 281; anti-Hasmonaean bias of *II Macc.*, III. 532, 533. See also under individual names.

Hauran, mountain: I. 337, 338 (see also Auranitis).

Havdalah de Rabbi Aquiva (= Akiba):

III. 345.

Hazezon-Tamar (Engedi): III. 320n., 323n.

Hazor, town: location, I. 184n.

Ḥazzan: congregational duties of, II. 418, **438**, 447, 454.

Heaven: see Paradise.

Heave-offering (*Terumah*): **II. 262–263**; as payment in kind to priests, II. 262–263, 270; whether discharged by diaspora Jews, II. 269; ritual preparation of, II. 477.

Hebrew language: **II. 22–23, 26–28, III. 142–143**; use on coins of Palestine, I. 602–606, II. 26–27; displacement of by Aramaic, II. 20–26, 28; knowledge of in Hellenistic Palestine, II. 22–23, 26–28, 74, 77, 452–453; use in liturgy, II. 22,III 142–143; language of rabbinic schools, II. 23, 27; Jewish literature of inter-testamental era composed in (see also under individual titles), II. 26–27, III. 177–180, *et passim*, 705–708, *et passim*; Greek and Latin loan words, II. 53–54, 55, 57, 58, 60, 62, 63–66, 68–73, 74, 75–78, 78–80; knowledge of among diaspora Jews, III. 142–143, 493; Hebraisms in the *Septuagint*, III. 478–479.

Hebron, town: destroyed by Judas Maccabaeus, I. 165; destroyed in first revolt, I. 500.

Hecataeus of Abdera: **III. 671**; Jewish forgeries under his name, III. 657, 658–659, 671–677; personal history, III. 671; works of, III. 671.

Hegesippus (= Iosippus): author of Latin paraphrase of *Jewish War*, I. **58–59**.

Hekhalot literature: **III. 269–270, 273–274**; magic, theurgy in, III. 345, 361–364; *Angelic Liturgy* from Qumran, III. 462–464; mystical tendencies in *Testament of Job*, III. 554; for *Hekhalot* tracts see under individual titles. See also *Merkabah* (mysticism).

Ḥel: terrace of Temple, I. 175n.

Helena of Adiabene: **III. 163–164**; conversion to Judaism, III. 9, 163–164; gifts to Jerusalem Temple, III. 164; great family tomb in Jerusalem, III. 164.

Heliodorus, assassin of Seleucus IV: I. 128.

Heliopolis in Egypt: Jewish settlers there, III. 47–48; Jewish temple at Leontopolis, location (see also Leontopolis), III. 146.

Heliopolis in Syria, colony established by Augustus: II. 96.

Helios: worship of in non-Jewish Palestine, II. 30, 37, 44; invocation of sun by Essenes, II. 573, 593.

Hell: see *Gehinnom*.

Hellenism in Jewish Palestine: **II. 52–80**; impulse provided by Alexander the Great, I. 143–145; extent of in general, I. 145, II. 52–80; Jewish Hellenists, pre-Maccabaean revolt, I. 145, 148–150, III. 200–201; and Jewish literature of the inter-testamental period (see also under individual titles and authors), I. 145n., II. 347–355, III. 153–155, 177–180 *et passim*, 472–473 *et passim*; knowledge of Greek language among Jews, I. 145, II. 74–80; pro-Greek faction in opposition with Maccabees, I. 167–169, 170, 174, 176, 177, 178; under Herod the Great, I. 304–313, II. 13–14; Greek loan-words in Mishnaic Hebrew, II. 53–54, 55, 57, 58, 60, 62, 63–66, 68–73, 74, 75–78, 78–80; in internal administration, II. 53–54; public games, II. 54–55; architecture, II. 56–58; art, II. 58–59; music, II. 60; trade and commerce, II. 60–72; monetary system, II. 62–66; use of Greek personal names, II. 73–74; Greeks in Palestine, II. 75–76; cities seeking Greek titles, II. 123; Jewish philosophy of the Hellenistic period, III. 567–568, *et passim*.

Hellenism in non-Jewish Palestine: **II. 29–52**; impulse provided by Alexander the Great, I. 143–144; activities of Herod the Great (see also under Herod), I. 304–310, II. 13, 14–15; celebration of Greek cults in the cities, II. 29–52; public games (see also under Games), II. 44–48; illustrious men of letters, II. 49–50; adoption of Greek foundation myths by cities, II. 50–52.

Hellenism outside of Palestine: influence of on Jewish diaspora community structure and religion, III. 103–107, 138–141; and Jewish literature of the inter-testamental period (see also under individual titles and authors), III. 153–155, 177–180 *et passim*, 472–473 *et passim*; Jewish philosophy of the Hellenistic period, III. 567–568, *et passim*, 813–814, 871–873, 878.

Heracles: worship of in non-Jewish Palestine, II. 32, 38, 39, 43, 51.

Heraclides, minister of Antiochus IV: supporter of Alexander Balas, I. 177n.

Heraclitus, philosopher: certain letters attributed to, possibly of Jewish authorship, III. 694–695.

Ḥerem: II. 268, **431–433**. See also under Excommunication.

Herennius Capito: financial procurator of Jamnia under Caligula, I. 394.

Herennius Philo of Byblos: author of work on the Jews, I. 41.

Heretics: see *Minim*.

Hermeneutics: see *Middoth*.

Hermes: worship of in non-Jewish Palestine, II. 43, 51.

Hermes Trismegistus: III. 697–698.

Hermippus Callimachius: whether certain of his writings are Jewish forgeries, III. 695–696.

Hermogenes, author: III. 30.

Hermoupolite district: I. 530, 531.

Herod of Chalcis: **I. 571–572**; granted power to appoint High Priests, I.

Canatha, II. 15, 41; inclusion of coastal cities in his territory, II. 109, 110, 113; dissatisfaction of Gadarenes with his rule, II. 134; establishes veterans colony at Gaba, II. 164; administers Palestine along Ptolemaic lines, II. 186n.; portrayal of in *Assumption of Moses*, III. 279, 281–281.

Herodians: origins of family, I. 234n.; constitutional position as client kings, I. 316–319, 413–416; coinage of, I. 317, II. 63; celebration of birthdays/accessions, I. 347–348n.; hellenization of Trachonitis, Batanaea, and Auranitis, II. 14–15, 41; and representational art, II. 58; rule over Greek cities of Palestine in general (see also under place names), II. 92, 159–160, 182–183. See also under individual names.

Herodias, daughter of Aristobulus: I. **344, 351–352**; marriage to Antipas, I. 343; and downfall of Antipas, I. 344, 351–352; and John the Baptist, I. 346, 348, 349n.; goes into exile with Antipas, I. 352; helps Agrippa I, I. 443.

Herodias, supposed name also of daughter of Antipas: I. 348–349n.

Herodium, fortress: I. **307n.**; founded by Herod, I. 306; location, I. 307, II. 194n.; burial place of Herod, I. 328; in Bar Kokhba revolt, I. 547; toparchy of Judaea, II. 191, 194, 196; synagogue of, II. 441–443n.

Heroon (burial place): III. 28, 33.

Heshbon, city: II. **165–166**; military colony under Herod, I. 308, 315, II. 166; boundary to Jewish Peraea, II. 12, 166; location, II. 165; coinage of, II. 166; incorporation into province of Arabia, II. 166.

Hesychius (Egyptian bishop): his recension of the *Septuagint*, III. 484–485, 486.

Hexapla of Origen: III. **480–484**, 493–494, 495, 499–500.

Hierapolis: Jewish epitaphs from, III.

27–28, 89, 106.

High Priests: II. **227–236**; become political and royal figures in Second Temple period, I. 139, 193–194, II. 202–204, 227–228, 249–250, 275; successors of Jaddua, I. 139n.; pro-Greek, eve of Maccabaean revolt, I. 148–150, III. 200–201; pro-Greek, in opposition with Maccabees, I. 164–166, 167–170, 174, 176, 177, 178; new dynasty from time of Simon Maccabee, I. 193–194; become vassals of Rome from time of Pompey, I. 241, 377; presidents of Sanhedrin, I. 377, II. 202–204, 208, 210, 212–213, 215–216, 235, 275; vestments of seized then returned by Romans, I. 379, 388, 456, 471; robbing other priests of their dues, I. 465, 469, II. 250; appointment of by Agrippa II, I. 472; end of political and religious power after 70 AD, I. 523–524; appointment of by Herod of Chalcis, I. 572; as representative of the people, observance of Day of Atonement, II. 70n., 214, 216, 275–276, 277, 296; vestments of, II. 70n., 276; mainly Sadducees, II. 213, 235; no-one else else allowed to enter Holy of Holies, II. 221–222, 296; list of pontiffs of Herodian-Roman period, II. 229–232; continuing power of ex-High Priests, II. 232–234; wide application of title *archiereus*, II. 233–235; high priesthood the prerogative of a few families, II. 234, 249–250; 'sons of the High Priests', II. 234, 235–236; rules of marriage, II. 241; forbidden to mourn or attend funerals, II. 242–243; general cultic functions of, II. 275–277, 302–333, 307; daily grain offering, II. 276, 277, 301–302, 307; assisted by *sagan* in cultic duties, II. 277; appointment of by Herod, II. 313, 297. See also Priests.

Hilarius: use of *Enoch*, III. 263.

Hillel: II. **363–367**; and school of

Shammai, II. 342, 365–366; seven exegetical principles of (*middoth*), II. 344; in list of *zuggot*, II. 358, 361; personal history, II. 363–365; whether to be identified with the Pollio freed by Herod, II. 363; introduction of *prozbul*, II. 366–367; his epitome of the Torah, II. 467; sayings of, II. 467, 487; interpretation of law of divorce by his school, II. 485–486.

Himyar (the Yemen): Jewish opposition there to Christianity, III. 16.

Hippicus, tower on palace of Herod: I. 487, 508.

Hippodromes: in Jewish cities of Palestine (see also Games), II. 46, 48, 55.

Hippolytus: author of work about Plato attributed to Josephus, I. 55; use of *I Macc.*, III. 183; use of *Tobit*, III. 227; use of *Jubilees*, III. 315; use of *II Macc.*, III. 534; use of the Additions to *Daniel*, III. 726.

Hippus (= Susitha), city: **II. 130–132**; Gentile city, Hellenistic culture, I. 144, II. 131, 132; given to Herod by Augustus, I. 302, II. 92, 131; 'liberated' by Pompey, member of Decapolis, I. 333, II. 92, 126, 131; right of sanctuary, II. 94–95; in the first Jewish revolt, II. 131–132; location, II. 131; coinage of, II. 132.

Ḥiyya b. Abba, R.: compiler of Tosefta, I. 78.

Holophernes: in *Judith*, III. 216–218.

Holy of Holies: entered by Pompey, I. 240; entry forbidden on pain of death, II. 221–222, 296; position in Temple complex, II. 296. See also Atonement, Day of.

Homilies: see Sermons.

Ḥoni, 'the circle-drawer': see Onias the rain maker.

Honour of parents, religious duty: II. 486.

Horace, satirist: anti-Jewish writings, III. 609, 615n.

Horayoth, Mishnah tractate: position

and subject matter, I. 73.

Horus: worship of in non-Jewish Palestine, II. 32.

Hosea, biblical book: fragmentary commentary on from Qumran, III. 429.

Hoshaiah, R.: joint compiler of Tosefta, I. 78.

Hotam Gadol, magical work: III. 345.

Ḥullin, Mishnah tractate: position and subject matter, I. 73.

Human Images: see Art, representational.

Hyksos, the: identified with the Jews by Manetho, III. 595–596; explanation of name in Josephus, III. 596n.

Hyllarima: evidence for Jews living there, III. 24.

Hypaepa: evidence for Jews living there, III. 22.

Hyparchoi: at Tiberias, I. 343, II. 180.

Hypsicrates, author: quoted in Strabo, I. 24.

Hyrcania, fortress: history and location, I. 268n., 307n., 315.

'Hyrcanian Plain' in Lydia, location: III. 17n.

Hyrcanus I: I. **200–215**; precepts of ('Mishnah of the Hasmonaeans'), I. 77n.; meaning of name, I. 201–202n.; war with Antiochus VII, I. 201–202n., 202–207; mother of killed by Ptolemy, I. 202; conquests of, I. 207, 209, 215, II. 11, 16; subjugation and conversion of Idumaeans, I. 207, II. 3–6; constitution of Jewish state under, I. 209, 211; destruction of Samaria and Gerizim temple, I. 209–210, II. 16, 18–19; severs ties with Syria, I. 209; coins of, I. 210–211, 603; prophetic character of, I. 210, 215; relations with Pharisees and Sadducees, I. 211–214, II. 390, 394, 401; title of, I. 211; happy reign, I. 215; decree of friendship with Pergamum, III. 18; non-extant Chronicle of, III. 185–186.

Hyrcanus II: I. **267–280**; high priest during reign of Alexandra, I. 229, 232, 233; conflict with Aristobulus, I. 233–242; under the influence of Antipater, I. 233–234, 271, 275, 278; made high priest by Pompey, I. 241; constitutional position with respect to Rome, I. 267, 268, 278, 316n., 272–274; relations with Caesar, I. 270–274; established as High Priest and ethnarch by Caesar, I. 271–272; decrees of Caesar favouring Jews, I. 272–275; relations with Herod, I. 275–276, 297; captured by Parthians and mutilated, I. 279–280; death, I. 301; coinage of, I. 604; portrayal of in *Psalms of Solomon*, III. 193–194.

Hyrcanus, son of Joseph son of Tobias: built fortress at Arâk el-Emir, I. 150n., II. 59; in *The Saga of the Tobiads*, III. 558.

Hystaspes, Greek work under this name: III. 654–656.

I

Iamblichus, king of Emesa: I. 449n.

Iasus, town in Caria: evidence for Jews living there, III. 24, 25, 138.

Iconium: synagogue there, III. 34; evidence for Jews living there, III. 141.

Idumaea: Idumaean ancestry of Herodians, I. 234n.; in administrative reorganisations of Gabinius, I. 268; assigned by Augustus to Archelaus, I. 333; early settlement of Edomites, II. 2n.; as toparchy of Judaea, II. 7, 191, 194.

Idumaeans (Edomites): Judaism of, I. 27, 447n.; subjugation and conversion of by John Hyrcanus, I. 207, 538, II. 3–6, 10; ancestry of Herodians, I. 234n.; 3,000 settled by Herod in Trachonitis, I. 338n., II. 14; allegiance with Zealots

during first revolt, I. 497–498; serving in Ptolemaic army, III. 42; settlement in Memphis, Egypt, III. 45–46; worship of Apollo, III. 597–598.

Ilasios, *archisynagogos* of Antioch: III. 14.

Immer, priestly course: III. 245–246.

Immortality: doctrine of at Qumran, II. 539n., 542n., 545n., 582–583; various Jewish beliefs regarding, II. 539–540, 541, 542, 543, 544, 546, 574, III. 590; doctrine of among Essenes, II. 540n., 574. See also Soul; Resurrection.

Incense: altar of at Jerusalem Temple, II. 296–297, 305; offerings, II. 302, 305–306, 307.

Individualism: development of concept and theology, II. 492, 494, **546–547**.

Inscriptions (general): as source for period as a whole (collections, literature on), I. 11–16.

Inscriptions (Jewish): use in establishing chronology of Seleucid kings, I. 126 *et passim*; funerary, language of in Palestine (see also Funerary Inscriptions), II. 24–25, 79, 80; from Gerasa, II. 149, 151–152; of various kinds from various diaspora communities (see also under individual place names), III. 9, 10–13, 14, 15, 16, 17, 19, 20, 21–22, 23, 24, 25–26, 27–28, 30–32, 33, 34, 35, 36, 37, 40, 46–47, 48, 49, 50, 61, 63, 64, 65–66, 67–68, 69, 70–71, 72, 73, 79, 81–82, 79–81, 84–85, 87, 88, 89, 94, 95, 97, 98, 101, 103, 104, 105, 142, 144, 166, 167; from Aphrodisias, III. 25–26, 166, 175; epitaphs from Hieropolis, III. 27–28; synagogal from Stobi, III. 67–68.

Intercisa: evidence for Jews living there, III. 73.

Iosippus: see Hegesippus.

Iotape, daughter of Sampsigeramus: marriage to Aristobulus, I. 449n.

Ipsus: battle of, II. 87.

J

Jacob, patriarch: encounter with the angel Uriel in the *Prayer of Joseph*, III. 798–799; *Ladder of*, apocryphal work, III. 805; in writings of Philo, III. 846, 847.

Jacob, son of Judas the Galilean, Zealot: crucified for anti-Roman activities, I. 382n., 457, II. 600.

Jaddua, High Priest: I. 139n.

Jambres: see Jannes.

Jambri, sons of: name of tribe of brigands, I. 174.

James, son of Judas the Galilean: see Jacob, son of Judas the Galilean.

James son of Zebedee: executed by Agrippa I, I. 448.

James, the brother of Jesus: in account of Josephus, I. 430, 431, 432, 441; execution under Ananus, I. 430n., 441, 468, II. 222; leader of Jerusalem community, I. 430–431.

Jamnia (Yavneh), city: **II. 109–110**; bequeathed to Salome I by Herod, I. 333, II. 110; Jewish-Gentile friction at time of Caligula, I. 394; captured by Vespasian in revolt, I. 498, II. 110; becomes centre of Jewish learning after AD 70, I. 521, 524–526, II. 110, 369, 372; after AD 70, its Academy becomes supreme Jewish court, I. 525–526; preponderantly Jewish in time of Jesus, II. 3, 6–7, 33, 110; 'liberated' by Pompey, II. 91, 110; rebuilt by Gabinius, II. 92, 110; harbour of, II. 109; not part of Jewish territory till Alexander Jannaeus, II. 110; as toparchy of Judaea, II. 191, 193.

Jannes, *Book of Jannes and Jambres*: **III. 781–783**.

Jason, High Priest in Maccabaean Age: **I. 148–150**; appointed High Priest by Antiochus, I. 148; leader of Jerusalem Hellenising party, I. 148–149, II. 123; conflict with Menelaus, I. 149–150.

Jason of Cyrene: **I. 19–20, III. 531–537**;

author of non-extant history of Maccabaean revolt, epitomised in *II Macc.*, I. 19–20, III. 60, 509, 531–537; date of his composition, III. 532; sober nature of his historiography, III. 532–533.

Jedaiah, priestly course: priesthood at time of Ezra, II. 245–246, 247.

Jerahmeel, Chronicles of: III. 326, 330.

Jeremiah, biblical book: and process of canonisation, II. 317–318n; exegesis in *Daniel* of the seventy years prophecy, III. 248–249; *I Baruch* written as pseudepigraphic supplement to, III. 733, 738, 740; reading of *Lamentations* of Jeremiah on 9 *Ab*, III. 739; separate work entitled the *Letter of Jeremiah*, III. 743–745.

Jeremiah, prophet: *The Chronicles of* (2, 3, or 4 *Baruch*), III. 292–294; in *The Lives of the Prophets*, III. 783–784.

Jericho, city: **I. 298–300n.**; fortified by Bacchides, I. 175; in reorganisation of Gabinius, I. 268, II. 190, 194n., 204; region given to Cleopatra by M. Antonius, I. 288, 298–300; palm groves of, fertility of region, I. 298–300n., 355n.; given to Herod by Augustus, I. 302; garrisoned by Vespasian, I. 365, 499; as toparchy of Judaea, II. 191, 194; location, II. 194n.; synagogue of, II. 442n.; and siting of Essene settlement, II. 563.

Jerome: use of *I Macc.*, III. 182, 183; knowledge of the *Wisdom of Ben Sira*, III. 202–203; use of *Judith*, III. 219, 221; use of Aramaic *Tobit*, III. 224, 229–230; translation and commentary on *Daniel*, III. 247n., 729; on *Enoch*, III. 263; attitude to *IV Ezra*, III. 302; on *Jubilees*, III. 315; on the *Martyrdom of Isaiah*, III. 340; on Aquila's Greek translation of the Bible, III. 494–495, 496; on Theodotion and his translation of the Bible, III. 499, 500–501, 503–504; wrongly ascribes *IV Macc.* to Josephus, III. 590, 591; on *I Esdras*, III. 714; on *I Baruch*, III. 738; on the

Testament of XII Patriarchs, III. 777; testimony regarding Philo of Alexandria, III. 814–815, 869.

Jerusalem: literature on archaeology of, I. 7; Jews forbidden to enter after Bar Kokhba revolt, I. 38, 553, 556–557; topography and layout (biblical times), I. 42, 154–155n.; Jewish Hellenists seek title Antiochenes, I. 123, 148; gymnasium and games there time of Jason, I. 148, II. 44, 45, 54–55; and Hellenising programme of Antiochus IV, I. 148–149, 152–154, 155, II. 44; destruction of Syrian fortress by Simon Maccabaeus, I. 154, 192n.; location of the Acra, I. 154–155n., 193; and reconquests of Judas Maccabaeus, I. 162, 166; fortified by Bacchides, I. 175; siege of Acra by Jonathan Maccabaeus, I. 181–182; siege of by Antiochus VII, I. 202–203; siege of by Pompey, I. 239, 242; siege and conquest of by Herod and Sosius, I. 252, 284–286; permission given by Caesar to rebuild city walls, 47 BC, I. 272, 273n.; plundered by Parthians time of Antigonus, I. 279; auxiliary cohort stationed there, AD 6–70, I. 361–362, 362; *praetorium* of Roman governors, I. 361–362, 366; siege and capture of by Titus, I. 430n., 501–508, 520; building of new wall by Agrippa I, I. 448; paved with marble by Agrippa II, I. 476; under governorship of Florus, outbreak of revolt, I. 485–486; civil war at outbreak of revolt against Rome, I. 486–487, 496–498, 501, 502–503, 601, 602; repulse of Gallus at start of revolt, I. 487–488; defence arrangements at start of war against Rome, I. 489, 491; topography and layout (AD 70), I. 503; Roman garrison camp after AD 70, I. 367, 508, 509n., 515, 520,; destroyed, and refounded as Aelia by Hadrian (see also Aelia Capitolina), I. 521, 537, 540–541, 542, 550, 553–554; 'liberated' in Bar Kokhba revolt, I. 545–546; paganised under Hadrian, temple to Jupiter Capitolinus, I. 554–555; journeys thither by pilgrims to celebrate feasts, II. 76, II. 147, 148–149; various diaspora communities settled there, II. 76, III. 33; whether it was a *polis*, II. 183, 197–198, 204–206; as a toparchy, II. 190, 192, 197–198; in reorganisation of Gabinius, II. 190, 204; authority over the rest of Judaea (see also Council; Sanhedrin), II. 197–198, 204–206; synagogues of, II. 445, III. 133; in Messianic age, II. 495, 500, 501–502, 503, 511, 512, 513, 529–530; Qumran doctrine of the New Jerusalem, II. 529, 535, III. 427–428; monumental tomb of Helena and Izates of Adiabene, III. 164; eulogy on by Philo the Epic Poet, III. 559–560; fortress of as descrbed by Aristeas, III. 681; Sanhedrin, see under Sanhedrin, the Great; Temple, see Temple.

Jesus: many persons of that name in Josephus, I. 431.

Jesus, brother-in-law of Justus of Tiberias: I. 431n.

Jesus Christ: **I. 428–441**; relations with Herod Antipas, I. 341–342, 349–350; ministry in Galilee, I. 345, 349, II. 345, 349; women followers of, I. 345n.; arrest of, I. 372, II. 221n.; birth of, chronology, I. 424, 426, 427, II. 292; possible links with Zealot movement, I. 426, 439, 441, 457n.; Josephus' account of, I. 428–441; regarding the title 'Christos', I. 431–432, 434–435; trial of, I. 433–434, 438, 441, II. 216, 218, 219; relations with Pharisees, I. 441, II. 468, 474n., 486, 549; a cousin of, Simon son of Cleopas, I. 516; and House of David, I. 528; in time of Hadrian statues to pagan gods erected on grave and crucifixion sites, I. 555; knowledge of Greek, II. 79; on prayer, II. 99, 482n., 483; alleged statue of at Panias, II. 170, 171n.; called *rabbôni*, II. 326; preaching in synagogues, II. 434, 452; in *Apocalypse of Abraham*, III. 289; in the *Martyrdom of Isaiah*, III. 336, 337; casting out evil spirits, III. 343; identification with Qumran Teacher of Righteousness, III. 436n.; for 'Son of Man' theology, see under Messiah.

Jesus Sirach: see *Ben Sira, Wisdom of*.

Jesus, son of Ananias: I. 431n.

Jesus son of Damnaeus, High Priest: called 'son of Damnai' in Josephus, I. 431; street battle with Jesus ben Gamaliel, I. 469; appointed by Agrippa II, II. 232, 234.

Jesus son of Gamaliel, High Priest: to be identified with Ben Gamla, I. 431n., II. 232n.; distingushed from predecessor of same name in Josephus, I. 431; street battle with Jesus ben Damnai, I. 469; killed by Zealots, I. 497; active in the Revolt, II. 232, 233; appointed by Agrippa II, II. 232, 234; introduces system of primary education, II. 419.

Jesus son of Phiabi (Phabi), High Priest: appointed by Herod, I. 431n., II. 229, 234; regarding the spelling of the patronym, II. 229n.

Jesus son of Sapphias: archon of Tiberias at time of first revolt, I. 431n. II. 180n., 181; appointed commander in Idumaea at start of revolt, I. 489.

Jesus son of Seë, High Priest: appointed by Archelaus, I. 431n., II. 230, 234.

Jesus son of Thebuh: I. 431n.

Jesus, the rival of Josephus (= Jesus the Galilean?): I. 431n.

Jews (particularly in Palestine): coinage of (see also coins), I. 11, 602–606; own internal community organisation (see also Council; *Gerousia*; Sanhedrin), I. 138–140,

376–381, 525–526, II. 184–190, 197–198, 427–439; persecution under Antiochus IV, I. 150–158; revolt against Hellenisers and Antiochus IV (see also under Maccabaean Revolt), I. 158–163, 164 *et passim*; relations with the Spartans, I. 184–185; religious sensibilities offended by procurators, I. 331–332, 356–357, 378–381, 384, 386, 455–470, 485–486; and 'War of Varus', I. 331–332; attitude towards representational art, I. 342–343, 380–381, 384, 386, 490, II. 58–59, 81–82, 443–444 III. 154; civil and religious jurisdiction after AD 70 (see also Sanhedrin; Jamnia; Rabbis), I. 525–526; exempt from Roman military service (see also Military), I. 362–363, II. 474–475, III. 120–121; and emperor worship (see also under Emperor; Sacrifice), I. 379, 380, 389–397, II. 311–312; and census at time of Quirinius, I. 381, 400, 441, 405–427, II. 600, 602, 604–605; trouble under Caligula, I. 389–397; poll-tax to Rome (see also Taxes; Tribute), I. 402–403; part played in death of Jesus Christ, I. 433–434, 438, 440–441; first revolt against Rome, I. 485–513; religious reorganisation / reassessment after AD 70, I. 521–528; Torah observance and the commandments (see also under *Mizwot*; Torah; and specific subjects), I. 527–528, II. 314–315, 321,.323, 414–416, 424–425, 464–487, 535–536; persecution of Davidic line under Vespasian, I. 528; second revolt against Rome (Bar Kokhba), I. 534–557; practice of circumcision banned by Hadrian, I. 537–540, 555; geographic spread and increase of under Maccabees and Hasmonaeans, II. 1–14; attitude to Samaritans, II. 6–7n., 17, 19–20, III. 59, 327, 640; numbers of in Galilee, II. 7–10, 13;

in lands east of the Jordan, II. 10–13; in province of Samaria, II. 16; language of (see also Hebrew; Greek etc.), II. 20–28; Jewish prisoners killed in games under Titus, II. 47, 48; influence of Hellenism (see also under Hellenism), II. 52–84, III. 470–473, 567–568 *et passim*; use of Greek and Latin names, II. 73–74; contact with non-Jews to be limited, II. 82–84; civic rights in gentile cities of Palestine, II. 117, 183, 427; half-shekel tax to Temple, II. 271–272, 282, 295; literature of in the inter-testemental era (see also under individual titles), II. 347–355, III. 177–180 *et passim*, 472–473 *et passim*; cursing Christians, II. 432, 462–463; Chosen people, covenant, II. 464–466, 492, 494, 495, 580, III. 159, 199–200; Sabbath observance (see also Sabbath), II. 467–475, 484–485; decree of friendship with Pergamum, III. 18; for various groupings of (Essenes, Sadducees etc.) see under separate headings; study of Torah, see Education; Torah. See also Judaea; Judaism; Palestine.

Jews, diaspora: **III. 1–176**; Jewish proselytizers in Rome, I. 197; helped by influence of Herod the Great, I. 319; exempt from Roman military service (see also Military), I. 362–363, II. 474–475, III. 22–23, 120–121; persecution under Caligula in Alexandria, I. 389–393; community organisation, extent of own jurisdiction, I. 526, II. 427, III. 21, 90, 87–125; revolts in Egypt, Cyrene, and Mesopotamia under Trajan, I. 529–533, III. 7, 149; travel to Jerusalem for feasts, II. 76, III. 147, 148–149; causes of dispersion, III. · 3–4; extent and geographic spread of diaspora (see also under separate countries and place names, and below), III. 3–85;

of Babylonia, III. 5–6, 7, 8–9; opposition to Christianity in Arabia, III. 16; hostility to Christians in Smyrna, III. 19–20; protection of religious practices by Rome, III. 21, 23, 24, 25, 27, 93, 116–125, 131–132; sending dues to Temple in Jerusalem, III. 21, 23, 27, 118–119, 140, 147–148; send dues to Patriarch in Palestine, III. 34, 67, 124–125, 148; geographic spread of in Egypt, III. 38–44, 46–60, 145–147; military service, Elephantine, III. 39–40; *castra Iudaeorum* in Egypt, III. 41, 48–49; of Alexandria, III. 42–44, 50, 88–89, 92–94, 113, 126n., 127–129, 135–137, 138, 145, 153; 2-drachma tax imposed after AD 70, III. 54, 58, 122–123; evidence for in North Africa, III. 60–64; geographic spread of in Greece, III. 64–72; community in Rome, extent and organisation, III. 73–81, 95–100, 113, 116–118, 121, 132–133; geographic spread of in Italy, III. 73–84; various terms for notion of 'community' (*laos, politeuma*, etc.), III. 87–91, 114n.; community structure influenced by pagan models, III. 103–107; comparison with non-Jewish diaspora communities, III. 107–113; different constitutional positions of the various communities, III. 107–125; whether held citizenship of Rome and of Greek cities, III. 126–137; of Asia Minor, III. 129–134, 141; hostility to them among gentiles, III. 131–132, 150–153, 594, 607–608, 609–616; religious practices of including elements of syncretism, III. 138–149; language of, III. 142–143, 475, 479, 493; replacement of Temple sacrifice by communal meals, III. 144–145; messianic expectations of, III. 149; literature of in the inter-testamental era (see also under individual titles), III. 177–180 *et passim*, 472–473 *et passim*; extent of Hellenisation, III. 567–568, 813–814, 871–873, 878; anti-Jewish literature, III. 594–616. See also Jews (above); Judaism.

Joazar, son of Boethus, High Priest: supporting census of Quirinius, I. 381; deposition, I. 425; appointed by Herod, then Archelaus, II. 229, 230, 234.

Job: identification in midrash with Jobab, III. 525, 552; *Testament of Job*, III. 525, 552–555.

Job, biblical book: inclusion in canon, II. 317–318n.; in the *Septuagint* and writings of Aristeas, III. 525.

John, brother of Judas Maccabaeus: death, I. 174.

John, Gospel of: links with the *Odes of Solomon*, III. 787–788.

John Malalas: account of martyrdom of Christians, I. 517–518.

John of Antioch: account of martyrdom of Christians, I. 517–518.

John of Gischala: I. **490–491**, **496** *et passim*; conflict with Josephus, I. 490–491; as leader of Zealots in Jerusalem, I. 496–498, 501–502, 503; defeated by Titus, I. 496; during siege of Jerusalem, I. 503–508; prisoner in Titus' triumph, I. 508, 509.

John, son of Simon Maccabee: appointed governor of Gazara, I. 191.

John, tax-collector of Caesarea: I. 374, 376.

John, the Apostle: trial of before Sanhedrin, II. 219.

John the Baptist: I. **345–348**; account of in Josephus and the Gospels, I. 345, 346; imprisonment and execution by Herod Antipas, I. 345–348; aged twelve at time of Quirinius' census, I. 420–421; Josephus' use of term *epikaloumenos Baptistes*, I. 420–421; identification with Qumran Teacher of Right-

eousness, III. 436n.

John the Essene, Jewish general in the first revolt: I. 588.

Joiarib, priestly course: primacy of in Josephus' day, II. 247, 249–250; Hasmonaean priests belonged to, II. 250.

Jonathan bar Ba'ayan: commander in Engedi during Bar Kokhba revolt, I. 546, II. 79.

Jonathan ben Uzziel: not to be identified with Theodotion, III. 499, 502.

Jonathan, Maccabee: I. **174–188**; given three districts of Samaria by Demetrius II, I. 141, 182, II. 2; avenges death of his brother John, I. 174–175; establishes rival government in Michmash, I. 177; as head of the Jewish people, I. 178–187; made High Priest by Alexander Balas, I. 178; foreign policy with respect to Syria, I. 180–187; formally made governor of Judaea by Alexander Balas, I. 180; attacks on various cities, policy of annexation, I. 182, 184, 185, II. 101, 106, 109, 116; letter to the Spartans, I. 184–185; treaty of friendship with Rome, I. 184, III. 74; killed by Tryphon, I. 187, II. 587; buried at Modein, I. 188; identification with Qumran 'Wicked Priest', I. 188n., II. 587, III. 435, 438; date of death, I. 189n.

Jonathan, son of Ananus, High Priest: supporter of Felix, I. 459–460, 463, II. 233; killed by *sicarii*, I. 463, II. 233; appointed by Vitellius, II. 230, 234.

Joppa, city: II. **110–114**; site of Andromeda myth, I. 144, II. 33–34, 111; Judaized by Simon Maccabee, I. 187, II. 3, 6–7, 112; captured and then returned to Jews by Antiochus VII, I. 204–205, II. 112; ceded to Jews by Caesar, I. 274–275, II. 113; returned to Herod by Augustus, I. 302, II. 92, 113; Greek culture and

427, II. 599, 603–605; procurators, AD 44–46, I. 455–470; history of during first revolt against Rome, I. 484–513; as private possession of Vespasian, I. 512, 521; list of Roman governors after AD 70, I. 515–519; revolt under Bar Kokhba, I. 534–557; Hebrew coinage, I. 602–606; religious differences with Galilee, II. 13–14; language different to that of Galilee, II. 23; trade and commerce, II. 60–72, 68n.; financial administration of under the procurators, II. 372–376; history under the Hasmonaeans and Herodians, see under individual names. See also under specific rulers, place-names and subjects, and under Jews; Palestine.

Judaean desert, literary finds: **I. 118–122, II. 78–79**; secondary literature, editions, translations, I. 118–122; evidence for history of Bar Kokhba revolt, I. 543, 546–547; Babatha archive, II. 25, 79, II. 16; language of, II. 78–79. See also Masada; Murabba'at; etc.

Judaeo-Christians: see Nazarenes.

Judah bar Manasse: leader of Arabaya during Bar Kokhba revolt, I. 546.

Judah ben Bethera, R.: II. 380.

Judah ben Tema, R.: II. 487.

Judah ha-Nasi, R.: traditionally ascribed composition of Mishnah, I. 76–77; first President of Sanhedrin to carry title 'Nasi', II. 217; teachings of regarding proselytes, III. 176.

Judah, patriarch: Testament of, see *Testaments of the XII Patriarchs.*

Judah, Patriarch, 4th century AD: III. 34.

Judaism: imagelessness of, attitude towards representational art, I. 342–343, 380–381, 384, 386, 490, 556n., II. 58–59, 81–82, III. 139, 154; reorganisation / reassessment after AD 70, I. 521–528; = Torah observance (see also Torah), I.

527–528, II. 314–315, 321, 323, 415–416, 424–425, 464–467; Hadrian's ban on circumcision (see also Circumcision), I. 537–540, 542, 555; differences in practice between Judaea and Galilee, II. 13–14; influence of Hellenism (see also Hellenism), II. 52–53, 54–55, 58–59, 81–84, III. 470–473, 567–568 *et passim*; covenant, Jews = Chosen People, II. 323, 464–466, 492, 494, 495, 580, III. 159, 199–200; literature of in the inter-testamental era (see also under individual titles), II. 347–355, III. 177–180 *et passim*, 472–473 *et passim*; Sabbath observance, II. 467–475, 484–485; laws of purity (see also Purity), II. 475–478; *zizit, mezuzah*, and *tefillin*, II. 479, 480–481; prayer (see also Prayer), II. 481–483; practice of fasting, II. 483–484; legalism of, II. 486; spirituality, II. 487; messianic hopes and doctrines (see also Messianism), II. 492–554; in world to come, II. 535–536; doctrines of after-life, II. 539–540, 541–544, 544–547; political tolerance of Jewish religion by Ptolemies, Seleucids and Rome, III. 21, 23, 24, 25, 27, 76, 77, 116–125, 131–132; misunderstanding of and hostility to among gentiles, III. 131–132, 150–153, 611–615; religious practices of diaspora Jewry, III. 138–149; apologetic literature and propaganda (see also under individual titles; Apologetic literature; Proselytes), III. 150, 153–155, 159, 471–473, 548, 552, 617–618 *et passim*; proselytes and God-fearers (see also under those entries and Conversion), III. 150, 159–176; universalistic tendancies, III. 159–160; condemnation of magical practices (see also Magic), III. 342 346; for various groupings within (Sadducees, Essenes, etc.) see under separate headings. See also Jews; Temple; Synagogue; *Halakhah*; etc.

Judaization: forced of various people, see Conversion.

Judas Maccabaeus: **I. 158–173**; etymology of name 'Maccabaeus', I. 158; uprising against Antiochus IV, I. 158–163; restoration of Temple and cult, I. 162–163; as head of the Jewish people, I. 164–173; battles against various cities, I. 164, 165, II. 110, 112; rescuing Jews of land east of Jordan, I. 164–165, II. 11; obtains religious freedom for nation from Syria, I. 167–168; siege of Syrian garrison in Jerusalem, I. 166; conflict with pro-Greek faction, time of Demetrius, I. 168–170; hostilities against Demetrius I, I. 168–173; defeat of Nicanor, feast of 'Nicanor's Day' instituted, I. 170; not appointed High Priest, I. 170; treaty with Rome, I. 171–172, III. 74; death, and burial at Modein, I. 173.

Judas of Gamala, son of Ezekias: **II. 599–606**; leader of Galilean revolt in 'War of Varus', I. 332; revolt over census of Quirinius, I. 381–382, 414, 417, 418, 425, II. 599, 603–604; family prominent anti-Romans, I. 382n., II. 600; origin of nickname 'the Galilean', I. 414; possible links with followers of Jesus Christ, I. 426, 439, 441, 457n.; founder of the fourth philosophy, I. 439, 381–382, II. 599–606; characterisation of in Josephus, I. 441, II. 600, 602, 604–605; whether to be identified with Judas the Galilean, II. 600n.

Judas, son of Sapphoraeus, R.: executed by Herod, I. 294, 325, 330.

Judas, son of Simon Maccabee: defeat of Cendebaeus, I. 198; assassination of, I. 199.

Judas the Essene: prophet at time of

Aristobulus I, II. 574, 587; identification with Qumran Teacher of Righteousness, III. 436n.

Judas the Galilean: see Judas of Gamala.

Judges: in Jewish law courts, II. 184–190, 197–198, 334–335.

Judges, biblical book: inclusion in canon, II. 317–318n.

Judgment: penal, at Qumran, II. 431, 432–433, 577, 579; divine, II. 465–466, 492, 494, 496, 512, 26–529, 540–544, 544–546, III. 761–762, 790, 794; by Messiah, II. 517, 526–529; the last, II. 539, 540–544, 544–546; internal Jewish, see Council; Sanhedrin.

Judiciary, Jewish: see under Jews; Council; Sanhedrin.

Judith, biblical book: III. **216–222**; story and character of, III. 216–218; date of composition, III. 217–219; portrayal of the woman Judith, III. 217; identity of author, III. 219; Semitic text of, III. 219–220; Greek, Latin, Syriac and Ethiopic texts, III. 220–221; literature on, III. 221–222; translation into Greek, III. 505.

Julia (= Livia), wife of Augustus: territorial bequests from Salome I, I. 92, 109, 110, 168, 335; Julias (= Livias) founded in her honour, I. 342, II. 177; gifts to Jerusalem Temple, II. 313, III. 78n.

Julia, daughter of Augustus: Julias founded in her honour by Philip, I. 339, II. 171–172; banished by Augustus, II. 172.

Julia Severa: built synagogue in Acmonia, III. 30–31.

Julianus, Antonius: procurator of Judaea, non-extant writings on war of Vespasian, I. 33–34.

Julianus, Laodicaean Jew: in rabbinic legend about 'Day of Trajan', I. 533.

Julias (= Livias, formerly Bethramphta), city: **II. 176–178**; founded by

Herod Antipas in honour of Julia, I. 342, II. 93, 177–178; location, II. 178; whether it was a *polis*, II. 182.

Julias (= Livias, formerly Bethsaida), city: **II. 171–172**; founded by Philip, I. 339, II. 93, 171, 172, 179; given to Agrippa II by Nero, I. 473; location, II. 171–172, 195n.; whether it was a *polis*, II. 172, 182; as toparchy, II. 194–195.

Julius Caesar: see Caesar, Julius.

Jupiter Capitolinus, temple of in Rome: precious gift of Aristobulus II to, I. 237; Jewish tax to, II. 272–273, III. 122–123.

Jurisprudence, internal Jewish: see under Jews; Council; Sanhedrin.

Justice: divine, see under Judgment.

Justin Martyr: use of *Enoch*, III. 261; use of the Additions to *Daniel*, III. 725–726.

Justus of Tiberias: **I. 34–37**; conflict with Josephus, I. 32–33, 35–36n., 53–54, III. 546; non-extant writings of, I. 32–33, 34–35, 36–37n., III. 590, 546; part played in the revolt, I. 34, 35, II. 131, 134; personal history, I. 34; use of his *Chronicle* by Africanus and others, I. 35, 36–37n., III. 546; expertise in Greek, II. 80.

Juvenal, satirist: writings against the Jews and Judaism, III. 152, 153, 164–165, 609, 615n.

K

Kabbalah: foreshadowed by mysticism of inter-Testamental era (see also under Mysticism), II. 353; for Kabbalistic texts, see under individual titles.

Kallah, minor talmudic tractate: position and subject treated, I. 80.

Kanata: whether town of this name existed distinct from Kanatha, **II. 138–139**, 142.

Kanatha, city: **II. 140–142**; member of Decapolis, II. 126, 141; whether the same as place called Kanata, II. 138–139, 142; inscriptions from, II. 140–141; location, II. 140; constitution, II. 141; history, II. 141–142; later called 'Septimia', II. 142.

Kanawâ: see Kanatha, Kanata.

Karaites: theory identifying them with the Qumran community, II. 585; antipathy to *Hekhalot* material, III. 274.

Karmon, river: III. 319n.

Karo, Joseph: author of *Shulḥan 'Arukh*, I. 80.

Kathedra: 'of Moses', in synagogues of Palestine, II. 442n.

Katoikoi/Katoikia: **III. 42, 89**; meaning of term, III. 42, 89, 90; use of term to describe community of Jewish settlers, III. 89, 91. See also Colonies; Cleruchies.

Kelim, Mishnah tractate: position and subject treated, I. 74.

Kerithoth, Mishnah tractate: position and subject treated, I. 73.

Kethubbah, marriage contract: see Marriage.

Ketubim: see under Bible; *Megilloth*; and individual titles.

Ketuboth, Mishnah tractate: position and subject treated, I. 72.

Kibotos: name for various places, III. 29.

Ḳiddushin, betrothal practice: see under Marriage.

Ḳiddushin, Mishnah tractate: position and subject treated, I. 72.

Kila'im, Mishnah tractate: position and subject treated, I. 71.

Kings, biblical book: and process of canonisation, II. 317–318n.; relation to *Chronicles*, II. 347.

Kingship, Jewish: priestly kingship of Hasmonaeans (see also under individual names), I. 281, II. 203–204, 215, 216, 227–228; royal power of the High Priests (see also under High Priests), II. 227–228;

earthly power of the Messiah (see also under Messianism; Messiah), II. 518–519.

Ḳinnim, Mishnah tractate: position and subject treated, I. 74.

Kiryath Arabaya: in administration of Bar Kokhba, I. 546.

Kittim: **I. 241–242n.**, **III.** 434–435; in the book of *Daniel*, I. 152n.; identification with the Romans, I. 241–242n., III. 403–404, 425–426, 431, 434–435; in Qumran writings, I. 241–242n., II. 554, 588, III. 403–404, 425–426, 431, 434–435.

Ḳodashim, fifth order of Mishnah: details of constituent tractates, I. 73–74.

Kohath, Testament of: III. 333.

Koheleth, biblical book (*Ecclesiastes*): and process of canonisation, II. 317–319n; reading of in synagogue, II. 452n.; association with Solomon, III. 241; *Midrash Koheleth*, see below.

Koheleth Rabbah (*Midrash Koheleth*): I. 91, 95.

Kokhba: see Bar Kokhba.

Ḳol-wa-ḥomer: exegetical principle attributed to Hillel, II. 344, 345n.

Ḳorban: sacred vow/offering, II. 486.

Kos, Edomite god: III. 45.

Koziba: see Bar Kokhba.

L

Laberius Maximus: I. 515.

Laconia: evidence for Jews living there, III. 66.

Lactantius: use of the *Sibylline Oracles*, III. 651; on the eschatological writings of Hystaspes, III. 654–655.

Lamentations, biblical book: midrash on (*Midrash Ekhah*), I. 91, 95; and process of canonisation, II. 317–318n.; reading of in synagogue, II. 452n.; see also *Megilloth*.

Lamia: see Aelius Lamia.

Lampon, Alexandrian anti-semite: embassy to Claudius against the Jews, I. 40, 398, 472n.; executed by Claudius, I. 394.

Lamps: and rules of Sabbath observance, II. 470.

Language: see Aramaic, Greek, Hebrew, Latin. Also under Jews and Judaea.

Laodicea: evidence for Jews living there, III. 27.

Laos: use of term to denote Jewish community, III. 20, 24, **89–90**, 91, 114n. See also under Community.

Larcius Lepidus (Sulpicianus), commander under Titus: I. 501, 502n.

Larissa in Thessaly: evidence for Jews living there, III. 66, 89.

Latin: **II. 80**; knowledge and use of by Jews in Roman Palestine, II. 53, 80; loan-words in Mishnah, II. 53, 60, 67–73; on coins of Palestine, II. 62–66; personal names among Jews, II. 73–74; representations of Jews and Judaism in Latin literature, III. 150–153.

Law, The Jewish: see Torah. For Jewish internal administration of, see Council; Sanhedrin. For particular rules of, see under Commandments and individual subjects. For its development by the Sages and the transmission of oral law, see *Halakhah*; Rabbis. In general see also under Jews and Judaism.

Legatio ad Gaium, work by Philo: see under Philo, Writings of.

Legions: see Military.

Lentulus Crus, consul: III. 22, 120.

Lentulus Marcellinus, governor of Syria: **I. 245**.

Leontopolis, Jewish Temple of: **III. 47–48, 145–147**; closed in time of Vespasian, I. 512, III. 146; history of building of by Onias, III. 47–48, 145–147; location, III. 146n.; not regarded as legitimate by Palestinian sages, III. 146–147.

Lepcis Magna in Tripolitania: evidence for Jews living there, III. 63.

Lepers, in Jewish law: separated from congregation in synagogue, II. 448; uncleanness of, II. 475; purification ritual, II. 477.

Lepidus: see Larcius Lepidus.

Levi, patriarch: eponymous head of tribe (Levites), II. 253; Testament of, see *Testament of the XII Patriarchs.*

Leviathan: to be eaten in messianic age, II. 534n.

Levies: see under Military.

Levirate Marriage: see *Halizah.*

Levites: **II. 250–256**; as subordinate officers in local courts, II. 187; division into courses, II. 247, 254–256, 292–293; distinct from priests after Ezekiel, secondary role, II. 250–252, 254; at Qumran, II. 251n.; closed hereditary circle, II. 253; later affiliated with Temple singers and door-keepers: duties, II. 253–254, 255, 282, 284, 286, 288, 289–291, 303, 307; numbers of, time of Ezra, II. 254–255, 256; Levitical cities, II. 256; places of residence, II. 256; tithes due to, II. 258, 259, 263; precedence in synagogue, II. 450; tribe of Levi given pre-eminence in *Jubilees,* III. 311–312; Levitical priesthood extolled in *Testament of XII Patriarchs,* III. 768.

Leviticus, biblical book: *Wayyikra Rabbah* (midrash), I. 91; in *Melchizedek Midrash* from Qumran, III. 449–450.

Libertinoi (Libertines): settlement of in Jerusalem, II. 428; Jewish community in Rome, III. 132–133.

Licinius Crassus: see Crassus, M. Licinius.

Licinius Mucianus, governor of Syria: **I. 265–266**; history of his term of office, I. 265–266; privileges for Jews, III. 121.

Life of Adam and Eve: see under Adam.

Lights, Festival of: see *Hanukkah.*

Lilith: exorcism of in Jewish magical practice, III. 353, 354.

Limyra, town in Lycia: evidence for Jews living there, III. 32.

Linen: wool and linen industries of Palestine, II. 70–71; used for priests' clothing, II. 293–294.

Linus: Jewish verses under name of, III. 669–670.

Lishkath ha-gazith, meeting place of Great Sanhedrin: II. 223–224, 225, 304.

Liturgy, Jewish: of synagogue, **II. 447–454**. See also Prayer.

Livia: see Julia.

Livias, city founded in honour of empress: see Julias (= Livias, formerly Bethramphtha).

Livy: life and works, **I. 66**.

Lod: see Lydda.

Logos: doctrine of in writings of Philo, III. 881–885.

Longinus: see Cassius and Pompeius.

Lots, casting of: **II. 287n.**; daily service of priests determined by, II. 287, 304, 305; officer of in Temple, II. 287.

Lucian, presbyter from Antioch: his recension of the *Septuagint,* **III. 484–486**.

Lucilfius Bassus, governor of Palestine: reduction of Palestinian fortresses, I. 511, 515.

'Lucius, Consul of Rome': **I. 195–197**; authenticity of letter on behalf of Jews in time of Simon Maccabee, I. 194–197, III. 4n., 120; identity, I. 195, 197.

Lucius Quietus: see Quietus.

Lucuas: leader of Jewish revolt in Cyrene, I. 531, 532.

Lucullus, Roman general: victory over Tigranes, I. 135, 231; settles Jewish disturbances in Cyrene, III. 60.

Luke, the Evangelist: account of census at birth of Jesus, I. 399, 405–427.

Lupus: see Rutilius Lupus.

Lycaonia: evidence for Jews living there, III. 34.

531–532; dated according to Seleucid era, source for Seleucid chronology, I. 17–19, 126, 127 *et passim*; use of by Josephus, I. 50, III. 183; dating of Egyptian campaigns of Antiochus IV, I. 128–129n.; various documents presented there, authenticity, I. 171–172n., 178–179n., 193–194, 195–196n., III. 4n., 531–532; about the author, III. 180–181; theology of, III. 180–181; date of composition, III. 181; original language of, III. 181–182; sources used, III. 181, 531; about the Hebrew title, III. 182–183; Christian use of, III. 183; editions, literature on, III. 183–185; and the 'History of John Hyrcanus', III. 185; translation into Greek, III. 505; relation to the *Letter of Aristeas*, III. 682.

Maccabees, Second Book of: **III. 531–537**; as source for Maccabaean revolt, compared with *I Macc.*, I. 17–18, 152n., 157n., 161n., III. 181, 531–532; dating of Egyptian campaigns of Antiochus IV, I. 128–129n.; various documents presented there, authenticity, I. 162, III. 532, 533–534; based on non-extant work of Jason of Cyrene, III. 60, 531–537; anti-Hasmonaean bias, III. 532, 533; date of composition, III. 532; purpose and style of work, III. 532–533, 534; letters to the Egyptian Jews regarding Hanukkah, III. 533–534; references to in later writings, III. 534–535; manuscripts, editions, literature on, III. 535–537; source for *IV Macc.*, III. 589.

Maccabees, Third Book of: **III. 537–542**; account of hostilities toward Jews by Ptolemy Physcon, III. 115n.; account of Jews' delivery from Ptolemy Physcon, III. 145; fictional character of the work, III. 537–539; date of the author, III. 539–540;

relation to Greek *Esther*, III. 539–540, 720; references to in later writings, III. 540–541; manuscripts, editions, literature on, III. 541–542.

Maccabees, Fourth Book of: **III. 588–593**; Josephus not the author, I. 55, III. 590, 591; contents of according to Sixtus Senensis, III. 185–186; dependence on *II Macc.*, III. 534, 589; style and content, III. 588–589, 590; use of various Greek philosophical schools, III. 589–590; date and place of composition, III. 590–591; manuscripts, editions, literature on, III. 591–593.

Macedonia: evidence for Jews living there, III. 5, 64, **66–68**.

Macedonians: towns in Palestine garrisoned by, period of Diadochi, I. 144.

Machaerus, fortress: **I. 511n.**; built by Alexander Jannaeus, I. 228n., 345n., 511n.; demolished by Gabinius, I. 268, 269, 511n.; location, I. 268n., 345n., 511n., II. 12n.; re-fortified by Herod the Great, I. 307–308, 315, 345n., 511n.; flight there of daughter of Aretas IV, I. 343; John the Baptist imprisoned there, I. 345, 346, 348n.; Roman garrison there, I. 365; siege of by Bassus, I. 511.

Macro, Naevius Sutorius: I. 389, 391n.

Magdola in the Fayûm: evidence for Jews living there, III. 51–52.

Magic, Jewish: **III. 342–347**, *et passim*; association of magical books with Noah, III. 333, 342; character and practice, III. 342–343, 345–346; Solomon regarded as greatest magician, III. 342, 375–379; literary and magical texts (see also under individual titles), III. 343–347, *et passim*; formulae and incantations, III. 347–348, 350–351, 352, 353–354, 357–358, 361–362, 376–377; incantation bowls and amulets, III. 348, 352–357,

Medeba, city in Transjordan: captured by Hyrcanus I, I. 207, II. 11; location, I. 207n.; as part of territory of Aretas IV, II. 12n.

Media: Jews resident there, III. 5, 7n., 10.

Medicine: see Doctors; Magic.

Megillah, Mishnah tractate: position and subject matter, I. 72.

Megillath Antiochus (= *Megillath Beth Hashmonai; Sepher Bene Hashmonai*): date, language of, editions, etc., I. **116**.

Megillath Taanith (Scroll of Fasting): date, authorship, literature on, etc., I. **114–115**, III. 186n.

Megilloth, the five: midrashim on, I. 93, 94–96; reading of in synagogue, I. 591, 593, II. 452n. See also under individual titles.

Me'ilah, Mishnah tractate: position and subject matter, I. 73.

Meir, R.: and compilation of proto-Mishnah, I. 77.

Mekhilta: I. **90–92**; nature of, I. 90–91; of R. Ishmael, I. 90, 91–92; of R. Simeon b. Yohai, I. 90, 92.

Melchireša, king of evil: in writings from Qumran, II. 526, **553–554**, III. 336n., 450.

Melchizedek: in writings from Qumran, II. 526, **553–554**; the *Melchizedek Midrash* from Qumran, III. 449–451; legend of in *II Enoch*, III. 450, 749.

Meleager the Poet: II. 49–50.

Melos: evidence for Jews living there, III. 71.

Memphis: evidence for Jews living there, III. 39, 40; colony of Phoenicians there, III. 44; Idumaeans living there, III. 45–46.

Menahem, an Essene in the time of Herod: II. 574, 587.

Menahem, son (?grandson) of Judas the Galilean: leader in revolt, AD 66, I. 382n., 441, II. 600, 601, 602.

Menahoth, Mishnah tractate: position and subject matter, I. 73.

Menander: Jewish verses under name of, III. 656, 657, 668–669, 692–694.

Menelaus, High Priest: I. **149–151**; loots the Temple treasures, I. 149, 151; relation to the Tobiads, I. 149–151n.; seizes high priesthood from Jason, I. 149; of the tribe of Benjamin, I. 149n.; murders Onias III, I. 150; not high priest under Judas Maccabaeus, I. 168n.

Menippus the Cynic: II. 50, 135.

Menorah (Jerusalem Temple): II. **297–298n.**; chief spoil in Titus' triumph, and subsequent history, I. 510; as Jewish symbol, II. 297–298n.; maintenance for use in the cult, II. 297–298, 303, 305, 306, 307.

Mercenaries (military): Jewish, under the Ptolemies, I. 179n., II. 475n., III. 41, 42, 48–49, 51, 52; use of by Hyrcanus I, I. 207; use of by Herod, I. 315, II. 76; organised as *politeumata* in various cities, III. 88–89n. See also under Military.

Merchants: Jewish, Greek influence on, II. 62; guild of in Tiberias, II. 181. See also under Trade.

Meris: administrative unit, time of Herod, II. 186n.

Merkabah (mysticism): III. **361–363**; development of, II. 353, 354, 381; the *Angelic Liturgy* from Qumran, II. 581, III. 462–464; and *III Enoch*, III. 270, 273; in *Apocalypse of Abraham*, III. 288–289; techniques and purpose, III. 360–361; and *Hekhaloth* literature, III. 361–364; physiognomic treatises, III. 367–368. See also *Hekhalot* literature and under individual titles.

Mesene: Jews of, III. 9, 10.

Mesopotamia: literature on chronology of (see also under Chronology; Calendar), I. 8; Jewish revolt in time of Trajan, I. 532, III. 8; Jews resident there, III. 5, 7, 8, 9.

Messalla, M. Corvinus, governor of Syria: I. 254.

Messenia (Greece): evidence for Jews living there, III. 66.

Messiah, the: **II. 488–554**; to come from the House of David, I. 528, II. 493, 499, 503–504, 518, 536, 550, 552; to sit in judgment over the Gentiles, II. 493, 494, 526–529; development of concept, II. 497–498, 499, 501, 503, 504, 505, 510–511, 512, 513, 514 *et passim*; 'mother' of, II. 501; regarding the expression 'Son of Man', II. 505, 520–523; called *Taheb* by Samaritans, II. 513; and Elijah, II. 515–516; time of coming, II. 517, 523–524; titles of, II. 517–518, 520–523; regarded as an earthly king and ruler, II. 518–519; pre-existence of, II. 519, 520–523; and Anti-Christ, II. 525–526; a light to the nations, II. 532–535; doctrine of the Suffering Servant, II. 547–549; notions of at Qumran, II. 550–554, 576, 582; hope in, see below under Messianism/Messianic hope; regarding Jesus, see Jesus Christ.

Messianism/Messianic hope: **II. 488–554**; and the Zealots, I. 382, II. 509–510, 601; mood following fall of Jerusalem, I. 527–528, II. 510–513; persecution of Davidic line by Rome after AD 70, I. 528; and Bar Kokhba, I. 543–545; development of concept, II. 492–549; ideas of universality, II. 493–494, 498, 502; Irananian influence on, II. 496; in *Daniel*, II. 497–498; in literature of the inter-testamental period, II. 497–507, 510–512, 514–549, III. 243–244, 252–253, 255–256, 256–259, 280–281 283–284n., 295, 297, 751–752, 768, 769–770, 775; in age of Jesus, II. 507–509, 549, 553; in Philo and Josephus, II. 507–510; among the Samaritans, II. 513; upheavals to precede Messianic age, II. 514–515; timing of Messianic age, II. 523–524, 537–538; character of Messianic kingdom, II. 529–537; duration of Messianic Age, II. 536–537, 538; resurrection of dead (see also Resurrection), II. 540–544; at Qumran (see also under Qumran Community), II. 550–554, 576, 582, III. 446–447, 457–458, 465; among diaspora Jewry, III. 149; doctrine of retribution, III. 295, 297, 761–762, 763, 790. See also *Ha'olam ha-ba'*; Messiah above.

Metatron: in the Book of *Enoch*, III. 270–273, 274; association with Yaoel, III. 289n.

Metellus Scipio, governor of Syria: I. **247**, 270.

Mezuzah: **II. 479–480**; description and purpose, II. 479, 480–481; discovered at Qumran, II. 479n.; language permitted to be written in, III. 143.

Mezuzah, minor talmudic tractate: position and subject treated, I. 80.

Mia: see Zia.

Micah, biblical book: fragmentary commentary on from Qumran, III. 430.

Micah, prophet: in *The Lives of the Prophets*, III. 783–784.

Michael, archangel: dispute with Satan about the body of Moses, II. 351, III. 278, 281; in writings from Qumran, identical with heavenly Melchizedek, II. 553, 554, III. 284n.; in *Testament of Abraham*, III. 761–762.

Michmash, town: location, I. 177n.; site of rival government under Jonathan the Maccabee, I. 177.

Middoth (rules of rabbinic exegesis): in *halakhah* (Hillel, Ishmael), II. 344, 377; in *haggadah* (Eliezer), II. 354.

Middoth, Mishnah tractate: position and subject matter, I. 74.

Midrash: **I. 90–99, II. 339–355**; nature of, mode and method of exegesis, I. 70, 90, II. 339–340, 342, 343–344, 346–354, 493, 496–497; the midrashim, specific works, I. 90–99;

material, I. 71; language of (mishnaic Hebrew), I. 71, II. 23, 27–28; names and subjects of constituent tractates, I. 71–74, II. 345; dates of rabbis most quoted, I. 74–76; codification of, I. 76–77, II. 369, 378; of the Hasmonaeans, I. 77n; of R. Akiba, I. 77n; relationship to Tosefta, I. 78–79; editions, literature on, I. 80–83; Aramaic sayings in, II. 21–22, 23; Greek loan words in, II. 53–73, 77.

Mishneh Torah (*Yad ha-Hazakah*): I. 80.

Mithras: cult of in Roman empire, III. 157–158; anti-Mithraic traits in *Liber Antiquitatum Biblicarum*, III. 327.

Mithridates of Parthia: war with Demetrius II, I. 197.

Mithridates of Pergamum: aided by Antipater in his Egyptian campaigns, I. 271; journey in support of Caesar, III. 48; seizure of Jewish funds from Cos, III. 69.

Mitzvot (religious duties): see Commandments.

Mizpah, place near Jerusalem: centre for army of Judas Maccabaeus, I. 159; location, I. 159n.

Mnaseas: **III. 597–598**; author of anti-Jewish work utilised by Apion, III. 597–598; identification of, other works by, III. 598; refutation of by Josephus, III. 610 *et passim*.

Moabites: forced to pay tribute by Alexander Jannaeus, I. 223, II. 11.

Modad, *Book of Eldad and Modad*: III. 783.

Modein, native town of the Maccabees: sepulchral monument there, I. 156n., 173, 188n.; regarding its location and name, I. 158n.

Modius: see Aequus Modius.

Mo'ed Katan, Mishnah tractate: position and subject matter, I. 72.

Mo'ed, second 'Order' of Talmud: contents, I. 72.

Moesia Inferior: evidence for Jews living there, III. 72.

Monobazus of Adiabene: conversion to Judaism, III. 163–164.

Monotheism, Jewish: daily affirmation of in the *Shema'*, II. 454–455.

Moon: eclipse of at time of Herod's death, I. 327n.; regarding new moon, see New Moon.

Moses: **II. 350–351**; midrash about conflict with Jannes and Jambres, I. 350, III. 781–782; Jewish legends concerning death of, I. 351, III. 284–285; and the Sanhedrin, II. 200, 202, 210, 215; depicted as father of all science and culture, II. 350–351, III. 582, 611, 876, 878; inventor of alphabet, II. 350, III. 518, 611; Moses and Mosaic law in the writings of Philo, II. 350, III. 542, 543, 840–841, 855, 875–876, 878; perfection of his revelation (Torah), II. 315–316, 324, 350–351; presented as founder of Egyptian religion in Artapanus, II. 350, III. 138, 521–523; institution of synagogue ascribed to him, II. 427; 'seat of' in synagogues, II. 442n.; custom of reciting the *Shema'* ascribed to him, II. 455; importance of for Essenes, II. 572; portrayal of in Egyptian anti-Jewish writings, III. 151, 595–596, 608n., 611; portrayed as a leper in anti-Jewish Egyptian legend, III. 151, 608n., 611; in account of Strabo, III. 154; *Assumption of Moses*, III. 278–288, 505; *Apocryphon of Moses*, III. 285; in *Jubilees*, III. 309–310; fragments of biblical exegesis on from Qumran, III. 324–325; *The Sword of Moses* (*Harba de Mosheh*), III. 345, 350–352; in drama by Ezekiel the Tragic Poet, III. 564; as portrayed in the writings of Aristobulus, III. 582; *Apocalypse of Moses*, III. 757–760; *Life of Moses*, III. 854–855.

Moses ben Maimon: see Maimonides.

Moses of Chorene: on Ariston of Pella, I. 38.

Moso: woman to whom origin of Jewish law is ascribed by Polyhistor, III. 512.

Mourning: forbidden to priests, II. 242–243. See also Burial Practices; Death.

Mucianus, governor of Syria: see Licinius Mucianus.

Munatius Plancus, governor of Syria: **I. 252–253**.

Murabba'at, documents from: concerning Bar Kokhba, I. 118, 543, 546–547; literature on, I. 122; Aramaic finds, II. 22–23, 25, 27; Greek texts, II. 78–79.

Murcus, governor of Syria: see Statius Murcus.

Music: performance of Greek music in Jerusalem, II. 60.

Music, sacred: at Temple in Jerusalem, II. 288–291, 303, 307; at Qumran, II. 290.

Myndus, city in Caria: evidence for Jews living there, III. 4n., 24, 25.

Mysteries, The Book of: see *Sefer ha-Razim*.

Mysticism, see under *Merkabah; Kabbalah*.

N

Nabataea, kingdom of: **I. 574–586**; defeat of Alexander Jannaeus, I. 226, 577; hostilities with Rome, I. 244, 245, 267, 579; parts of given to Cleopatra by M. Antonius, I. 298; battles against Herod, I. 300–301, 322–323, 580, II. 141; conflict with Herod Antipas, I. 342, 350; literature on, I. 574; coinage, inscriptions, I. 575; ethnic origin of Nabataeans, I. 575–576; conflict with Antigonus, I. 576; under Aretas I, I. 576–577; defeat of Antiochus XII, I. 577, 578; friendly attitude to Maccabees, I. 577; under Aretas IV, I. 578–579, 581–583; limited subjugation of under Pompey, I. 579; in time of Rabel II, I. 584–585; becomes Roman province, I. 585–586; evidence for Jews living there, III. 16, 17.

Nabonidus, Prayer of: see Qumran Community, writings from.

Nag Hammadi: gnostic discoveries there, III. 760–761.

Naḥal Ḥever: documents discovered there (see also Judaean Desert), I. 26, 27, 543, 546–547, 549, II. 78–79, III. 16.

Naḥal Ẓe'elim: documents discovered there (see also Judaean Desert), I. 543, 546–547.

Nahum, biblical book: commentary on from Qumran, III. 430–433.

Nahum, prophet: in *The Lives of the Prophets*, III. 783–784.

Name, the Divine: uttering of by priests in Temple (see also under God), II. 306–307n.

Names: Greek and Latin, among Jews of Palestine, II. 73–74; of the angels and others in magical formulae, III. 347–348, 350–351, 357, 361–362, 373.

Nannacus: see Annacus.

Naphtali, patriarch, Testament of: see *Testaments of the XII Patriarchs*.

Naples: evidence for Jews living there, III. 83.

Nashim: third order of Mishnah, subjects treated, I. 72.

Nasi, title: of President of Sanhedrin / Head of Nation, II. 215, 217.

Nationalism, Jewish: see Israel; Jews; Messianism.

Nawe: see Nineve.

Nazarenes: cursing of by Jews, II. 462–463.

Nazareth, town: journey whence of Joseph and Mary at time of census, I. 413, 426; synagogues of, II. 445.

Nazir, Mishnah tractate: position and subject matter, I. 72.

Nazirite: vow of Queen Helena, III. 163–164.

Neapolis, city near Shechem: **I. 520–521**; foundation of and location, I. 520, II. 183; predominantly a Gentile city, I. 521, II. 40.

Nebuchadnezzar: in *Judith*, III. 216, 218; in *Daniel*, III. 245–246.

Nedarim, Mishnah tractate: position and subject matter, I. 72.

Nega'im, Mishnah tractate: position and subject matter, I. 74.

Nehardea: major Jewish centre in Babylonia, III. 8; collection there of diaspora dues for Jerusalem Temple, III. 148.

Nehemiah, biblical book: and process of canonisation, II. 317–318n.; relation to *I Esdras*, *Chronicles*, *Ezra*, III. 708, 710–713.

Nemesis: cult of at Gerasa, II. 38.

Nero, emperor: governors of Syria during his reign, I. 264–266; gives parts of Galilee and Peraea to Agrippa II, I. 472–473; death, I. 499; deprived Jews of Caesarea of civic rights, II. 117; his reign generally favourable to Jews, III. 78, 122; symbolised as eagle's wing in *IV Ezra*, III. 299; portrayed as satanic figure in the *Sibylline Oracles*, III. 641, 644.

Neronias, city: Caesarea (Panias) renamed such by Agrippa II, I. 474, 475, II. 170; for history of city, see Caesarea Philippi and Panias.

Nethinim, temple servants: **II. 290–291**; relation to the Levites, II. 253, 291; duties of, II. 290–291.

Neve: see Nineve.

New Moon, Jewish feast of: observance of new moon essential for Jewish calendar reckoning (see also under Calendar), I. 590–593; High Priestly sacrifice on, II. 276, 308; Torah read on, II. 454; celebration of by diaspora Jewry, III. 144.

New Testament: Aramaic terms and names in Greek text, II. 22, 23; use of Jewish exegesis, II. 354–355. See also under Christianity.

New Year, Jewish feast of: High Priestly sacrifice on, II. 276, 308; horns blown on, II. 446; different calendar at Qumran (see also Qumran; Calendar), II. 581.

Nezikin: fourth order of Mishnah, subjects treated, I. 73.

Nicanor, Gate of, in Jerusalem Temple: II. 57–58.

Nicanor, Syrian general: **I. 169–170**; campaigns against Judas Maccabaeus, I. 159, 160n., 169–170; death, day of fixed as Jewish festival, I. 170.

Nicephorium (Callinicum): evidence for Jews living there, III. 9.

Nicharchus: author of work hostile to the Jews, I. 42, III. 608.

Nicolaus of Damascus: **I. 28–32**; source for Josephus, I. 26, 30–31, 32, 50–52; education and personal history, I. 28; in service of Herod, I. 28–29, 310, 312, 323; 'Nicolaus-dates', I. 29; supports Archelaus in Rome after Herod's death, I. 29, 331, 333; writings of, I. 29–32; guides Greek education of Herod, I. 310, 312; not author of drama about Susanna, III. 563.

Nicomachus: philosopher from Gerasa, II. 50.

Nicomedia: evidence for Jews living there, III. 36.

Nicopolis (formerly Emmaus), city: **I. 512–513**; foundation of in time of Elagabal, I. 512–513n., 521, II. 183; location, I. 512–513n.; whether military colony established here under Vespasian, I. 512–513n. See also Emmaus.

Nicopolis, city near Actium: building projects of Herod, I. 308.

Niddah, Mishnah tractate: position and subject matter, I. 74.

Nike: cult of in various cities of Palestine, II. 35, 36, 37, 43.

Nineve, Jewish fortress in Batanaea: location, II. 15n.

Nisibis, city in Northern Mesopotamia: **III. 8**; Jewish settlement there, III. 8, 9; location, III. 8n.; collected diaspora dues for Jerusalem Temple held there, III. 148.

Nisibis, town in Babylonia: **III. 8**; Jews resident there, III. 8; location, III. 8n.

Nittai of Arbela: see Mattai of Arbela.

Noah: **III. 28–30, 332–333**; legend of at Apamea, III. 28–30; in Qumran writings and *Enoch*, III. 253–254, 260, 319, 332–333, 465, 747, 749; association with medicine and magic, III. 332,333, 342; in writings of Philo, III. 846.

Noarus = Varus, son of Soemus: see Varus.

Numenius, Jewish ambassador: envoy to Rome and Sparta, time of Jonathan, I. 184; delegate to Rome in time of Simon Maccabee, I. 194–195.

Numenius, philosopher: knowledge of Jewish tradition, III. 696–697, 781–782.

Numidia: evidence for Jews living there, III. 63–64.

Numismatics: literature on Seleucid coins, I. 9–10; literature on city coins of Palestine, I. 10–11; literature on Jewish coins, I. 11; use for reckoning Seleucid chronology, I. 126–127 *et passim*; used for reckoning Herodian chronology, I. 327–328. See also Coins; Chronology.

Nymphidius: in *IV Ezra*, III. 299.

Nysa: name of several towns, including Scythopolis, II. 38; in Asia Minor, evidence for Jews living there, III. 24, 89–90.

O

Oaths: community oath of Essenes, II. 565; oaths by God's name rejected by Essenes, II. 568.

Obadiah, prophet: regarding settlement of Jews in 'Sepharad', III. 20–21; in *The Lives of the Prophets*, III. 783–784.

Obodas I, Nabataean king: I. 223, **577, 578**.

Obodas II, Nabataean king: I. 580.

Obodas III, Nabataean king: **I. 580–581**.

Octavian: relations with M. Antonius, I. 250, 253–254, 289; battle of Actium, I. 253; for later history, see Augustus.

Odes of Solomon: **III. 787–788**.

Oea in Tripolitania: evidence for Jews living there, III. 63.

Oenomaus of Gadara, Cynic: II. 50, 135.

Oenoparas, river: battle there between Ptolemy VI and Alexander Balas, I. 181.

Oescus on the Danube: evidence for Jews living there, III. 72.

Offerings, Jewish: see Sacrifice; Temple; and under separate titles of the various offerings.

Oholoth, Mishnah tractate: position and subject matter, I. 74.

'*Olam haba*': see *Ha'olam haba*'.

Olympias, sister of Archelaus: I. 349n.

Onias I, son of Jaddua, High Priest: I. 139n.

Onias II, son of Simon the Just, High Priest: I. 139n., 149–150n.

Onias III, son of Simon II, High Priest: in office on eve of Maccabaean revolt, I. 139n., 148; deposed by Jason, I. 148; death, I. 150; whether to be identified with Qumran Teacher of Righteousness, I. 150n., III. 436n.

Onias IV, son of Onias III, High Priest: and temple at Leontopolis, I. 168n., III. 47–48, 145–147; whether acting High Priest under Judas Maccabaeus, I. 168n.; whether his circle wrote *Jubilees*, III. 313; whether author of non-extant work entitled *Saga of the Oniads*, III. 558.

named tetrarch of, I. 336–338, 362; as part of Ituraean kingdom, I. 337–338n., 564, 566; mixed population of, I. 338, II. 169.

Pannonia: evidence for Jews living there, III. 72–73.

Panticapaeum: evidence for Jews living there, III. 36–37, 90, 105–106, 166.

Pappus, Laodicaean Jew: and rabbinic story about the 'Day of Trajan', I. 533.

Paradise: **II. 541–542, 546n.**; place for souls of righteous dead, II. 541–542, 545–546; view of according to New Testament, II. 542–543, 546n.; usually rendered as Garden of Eden in rabbinic Hebrew, II. 546n. See also After-life; Resurrection.

Parah, Mishnah tractate: position and subject matter, I. 74.

Parents: duty to educate children, II. 418, 420; Honour of, biblical command, II. 486.

Parmenides, philosopher: held in high esteem by Philo, III. 872.

Paros: evidence for Jews living there, III. 71.

Parthia: Jews resident there, III. 4, 7, 10.

Parthians: and death of Antiochus IV, I. 128; campaigns against by Crassus and Cassius Longinus, I. 246, 247; invasion of Syria, I. 251–252, 278–280, 282–283; relations with Rome, time of Tiberius, I. 350–351.

Pashur, priestly course of: II. 245–246.

Passover, Feast of: as celebrated at Temple, I. 522, II. 290, 292, 308, 473; sacrifice ceased after destruction of Temple, I. 522–523; method of calculating when feast should occur, I. 590, 591, 593; reckoning of according to Qumran calendar, I. 600–601, II. 581; difference in observance between Galilee and Judaea, II. 14; reckoning of in *Jubilees*, III. 310, 312; explanation

of in Aristobulus, III. 583.

Pater Synagogae, honorific title: III. 101.

Patriarch: **III. 125**; title of president at Yavneh, power of (see also Sanhedrin; Yavneh), I. 526; receives dues from diaspora Jewry, III. 34, 67, 124–125; authority of as highest Jewish official over Jews in days of the later Roman empire, III. 125.

Patriarchs, Testaments of: see *Testaments of the XII Patriarchs*.

Paul the Apostle: preaching in Jerusalem, I. 366, II. 74; appeals as Roman citizen, I. 369n., 370n., 378, 467; imprisonment of under Felix, I. 369n., 370n., 372, 378, 465–466; trial before Sanhedrin, I. 378, II. 219, 222; mistaken for 'the Egyptian', I. 463n.; meeting with Drusilla, I. 465; meeting with Agrippa II and Berenice, I. 475; follows a trade whilst preaching, II. 328; claims maintenance whilst preaching, II. 329; taught by Gamaliel I, II. 368; preaching in synagogues, II. 434, 445, III. 162; criticises Pharisees, II. 466, 486; whether held citizenship of Tarsus, III. 33–34, 126, 133; persecution of Christians, III. 119; travels of, III. 119, 141; familiar only with Greek Bible, III. 143; mission to the gentiles, III. 159; *Apocalypse of Paul*, III. 764; use of *Testament of Abraham* in the Pauline writings, III. 764; use of *Apocalypse of Elijah* in the Pauline writings, III. 799–801.

Pe'ah, Mishnah tractate: position and subject matter, I. 71.

Peki'in (Beki'in): location, II. 374n.

Pella, city in Peraea: **II. 145–148**; foundation of, I. 144, II. 146; destroyed by Alexander Jannaeus, I. 226, 228, II. 147; 'liberated' by Pompey, I. 240, II. 147; location, II. 12, 145–146; member of the Decapolis, II. 126, 127, 147; Christians take refuge there during first Jewish revolt, II. 147–148; coins of, II. 147; conquered by Antiochus III, II. 147; wrongly named among toparchies of Judaea by Josephus, II. 147, 190–191.

Pella on the Orontes: see Apamea.

Pelle, as toparchy of Judaea: see Bethletepha.

Pelusium: capture of by Mithridates, I. 271.

Pentateuch: see Torah; Bible; and under names of individual books.

Pentecost, Feast of: as celebrated at Temple, II. 290, 292, 308; special importance for Qumran community, II. 582, 595; chief feast among Therapeutae, II. 592, 595; reckoning of in *Jubilees*, III. 310.

Peraea: Antipas named tetrarch of, I. 326, 333, 341; fortified by Antipas, I. 342; ministry of John the Baptist there, I. 345, 346; boundary dispute with Philadelphians, I. 455; parts of given to Agrippa II, I. 473–474n.; subjugated by Vespasian, I. 498; boundaries of Jewish Peraea according to Josephus, II. 6n., 12, 145; and Judaization programme of Hasmonaeans, II. 10–13; name means 'beyond the Jordan', II. 12–13; population mainly Jewish in Roman-Herodian period, II. 12, 13; internal Jewish organisation (see also Courts; Council, etc.), II. 184–198; Roman toparchies of, II. 194–195. See also Palestine.

Perdiccas: statue of at Gerasa, II. 150; re-foundation of Samaria, II. 160.

Perek Shalom, minor talmudic tractate: position and subject treated, I. I.

Pergamum: evidence for Jews living there, III. 4, 5, 18–19; decree of friendship with Jews, time of Hyrcanus I, III. 18.

Persephone: worship of at Gaza, II. 30; worship of in Batanaea, Auranitis, etc., II. 43.

Perseus: siting of myth of at Joppa, II.

33–34; on coins of Ptolemais, II. 36.

Perutah, smallest copper coin in Palestine: II. 63, 64, **66**.

Pesah: see Passover.

Pesahim, Mishnah tractate: position and subject matter, I. 72.

Pesher, mode of exegesis: at Qumran (see also under Qumran Community), **II. 580n.**, 586, **III. 420–421**.

Pesikta (of Rab Kahana): character, composition date, editions, **I. 96**.

Pesikta Hadatta: I. 97.

Pesikta Rabbati: character, composition date, editions, **I. 97**.

Pesikta zutarta (Lekah Tob): wrongly labelled *Pesikta*, editions, I. 97.

Peter, disciple of Jesus: flees from Agrippa I, I. 448, 451; trial before Sanhedrin, II. 219.

Petra, Nabataean capital: flight there by Hyrcanus II, I. 542; renamed Hadriane Petra, I. 542, 586; besieged by Antigonus, I. 576; principal Nabataean city, I. 585, 586; road built between it and Bostra by Trajan, I. 586, II. 157, 158n.

Petronius, governor of Egypt: **I. 290n.**

Petronius, P., governor of Syria: **I. 263, 394–397**; chronology of his governorship, I. 263; negotiates with Jews over edict of Caligula, I. 361n., 370n., 394–397; supports Jewish religious freedom in Dora, II. 120; wary of provoking Mesopotamian Jews, III. 7.

Phaene: evidence for Jews living there, III. 14.

Phanasus, High Priest: see Phannias.

Phanni, High Priest: see Phannias.

Phannias, son of Samuel: appointed high priest time of John of Gischala, I. 496–497, II. 232, 234; various forms of his name, II. 232n.

Pharaton, town: location, I. 175n.; Syrian garrison there, I. 175.

Pharisees: **II. 381–403**; and the *Hasidim*, I. 157n., 212, II. 400–401; seats in the Sanhedrin, I. 204, 206,

210, 213, 215, 331; views on Providence, I. 206, 296, II. 572, 392–394, 395; as upholders of Torah, I. 211–213, 388–391, II. 464, 466; breach with Hyrcanus I, I. 211–215, II. 390, 394, 401; origins of sect, I. 211–213, II. 400–402; conflict with Alexander Jannaeus, I. 221–224, II. 401, III. 432; power restored under Alexandra, I. 229–232, II. 390, 394, 401–402; relations with Herod the Great, I. 296, 312–314, II. 206, 395, 505; and emergence of the Zealots/Fourth Philosophy, I. 382, II. 395, 599, 603n.; friendly relations with Jesus and Jewish Christians, I. 441; relations with Agrippa I, I. 446–447, 452; activities in revolt against Rome, I. 486, 489, 497, II. 395; replace Sadducees as leaders after AD 70, I. 523–525, II. 369, 402–403; adherence of the 'scribes' to the Pharisees, II. 329, 388; literature on, II. 381–382; evidence from Josephus, II. 382–383, 392–394; evidence of the Mishnah, II. 384–387; separation from '*am ha'arez*, II. 386–387, 396–400; attitude to the Oral Law, II. 389, 390–391; belief in resurrection, II. 391–392, 540, 541, 542n., 543n.; politics of in general, II. 394–395; called themselves *ḥaverim*, II. 396–400; meaning of name, II. 396–398; strict understanding of the laws of ritual purity, II. 396–400, 475n.; relations with Sadducees, II. 404–405, 409–410, 413, 414; criticised by Jesus for being over zealous, II. 468, 474n., 486, 549; practice of frequent fasting, II. 483; identification with Qumran community, II. 585; proselytising of, III. 159–160; whether authors of the *Psalms of Solomon*, III. 193, 194–195; authorship of *Assumption of Moses*, III. 283; whether to be ascribed authorship of *Jubilees*, III. 313.

Pharnaces, king of Pontus: hostilities with Caesar, I. 248.

Pharnapates, Parthian commander: I. 251.

Pharos, island: annual festival there to mark translation of bible into Greek, III. 476, 480, 684.

Pharsalus, battle of: I. 247.

Phasael, brother of Herod: **I. 278–280**; nominated *strategos* of Jerusalem by Antipater, I. 275; made tetrarch by M. Antonius, I. 278; capture of by Parthians, I. 279; death, I. 280; Herod founds Phasaelis in honour of, I. 306, II. 168.

Phasael, tower on palace of Herod: I. 487, 508.

Phasaelis, city: **II. 168–169**; founded by Herod in honour of Phasael, I. 306, II. 93, 168; bequeathed to Salome I by Herod, I. 333, II. 92, 168; palm groves of, I. 355n., II. 168; whether an independent *polis*, II. 182.

Phaselis, city in Lycia: evidence for Jews living there, III. 4n., 32.

Pheroras, brother of Herod: made tetrarch of Peraea by Herod, I. 292, 319; death, I. 294, 324; refortifies Alexandrium, I. 307n.; supports Antipater against Herod, I. 322, 324; promised power by the Pharisees, II. 505.

Phiabi, high priestly family of (see also under names of individual priests): II. 234.

Phiale, reputed source of the Jordan: I. 339.

Philadelphia (= Rabbah of the Ammonites), city: **II. 155–158**; conflict with Peraean Jews, I. 455, II. 12, 157; Hellenistic cults there, II. 37, 39, 48; member of the Decapolis, II. 126, 127, 156–157; continued use of ancient name, II. 155; location, II. 155, 158; conquered by Antiochus III, II. 156; renamed Philadelphia by Ptolemy II, II. 156; as part of province of Arabia, II. 157–158; as part of province of Syria, II. 157.

schools, III. 865, 866, 871–872, 882–883, 885, 887; literary style of, III. 871–872; doctrine of God, III. 880–885; doctrine of intermediary beings and the *logos*, III. 881–885; dualism, III. 881–888; doctrine of the nature of man, III. 886–888; his view of ethics, III. 887–888.

His writings in detail:

(1) *Quaestiones et Solutiones in Genesim, ... in Exodum* III. 825–830.

(2) Allegorical commentaries on select portions of Genesis (*Legum Allegoriae* and others under own headings) III. 588, 830–840, 842–844, 845.

(3) Systematic Exposition of the Mosaic Law (the whole of the Pentateuch) III. 542–543, 832, 840–854.

(4) *De Vita Mosis* III. 543, 854–855.

(5) *Quod omnis probus Liber* III. 856.

(6) *De vita contemplativa* III. 612n., 856–858.

(7) *De aeternitate mundi* III. 858–859.

(8) On the persecutors of the Jews (Sejanus, Flaccus, Caligula) III. 543, 859–864.

(9) *De providentia* III. 588, 864–865.

(10) *De animalibus* III. 865–866.

(11) *Hypothetica (Apologia pro Iudaeis)* III. 606–610, 616, 866–868.

(12) Lost works III. 609, 868.

(13) Non-genuine works (*De mundo; De Sampsone et Jona; Interpretatio Hebraicorum nominum; Liber antiquitatum biblicarum; Breviarium temporum*) III. 868–870.

Philo the Elder: **III. 555–556**; non-extant work on the kings of the Jews, III. 555; date, III. 556; possible identification with Philo the epic poet, III. 556, 559, 560.

Philo the Epic Poet: **III. 559–561**; possible identification with Philo the Elder, III. 556, 559, 560; Greek poem 'About Jerusalem', III. 559–560; literature on, III. 560–561.

Philocrates, Letter to: see Aristeas, Letter of.

Philodemus of Gadara, philosopher: II. 49, 135.

Philosophy: the Fourth, development and character (see also Judas of Gamala, son of Ezekias), II. 599–606; Jewish, character of in the Hellenistic period (see also under individual authors and titles), III. 567–568.

Philostephanus, Egyptian general: I. 220.

Philostorgius: use of Justus of Tiberias' *Chronicle of the Jewish Kings*, I. 37.

Philoteria, town on the lake of Gennesaret: I. 144, 228n.

Phinehas: as prototype of the Zealots, II. 604, 605; taken as ancestor of Hasmonaeans, II. 604; in rabbinic literature, II. 605n.

Phocaea: evidence for Jews living there, III. 19, 104.

Phocylides, gnomic poet from Miletus: **III. 687–688**, *et passim*; character of his writings, III. 687–688; Jewish (?) ethical verses written under his name, III. 688–692.

Phoenicia: coinage of, I. 10–11, II. 62–63, 66–67; as administrative district under Ptolemies, I. 141; conquered by Parthians, I. 251–252; parts of gifted to Cleopatra by M. Antonius, I. 253, 288, 298; adoption of Phoenician alphabet by the Greeks, II. 60; trade, II. 60; evidence for Jews living there, III. 4; Phoenician settlements overseas, III. 44, 107–108, 109, 110.

Photius: description of *Chronicle* of Justus of Tiberias, I. 35–36, 37; regarding so-called work of

Josephus, I. 55.

Phrygia: evidence for Jews living there, III. 17, 27–32, 89; settlement of Jews there by Antiochus III, III. 17, 27, 42; and localisation of Noah legend, III. 28–30.

Phylacteries: see *Tefillin*.

Pilate: see Pontius Pilate.

Pinḥas, High Priest: see Phannias.

Pirḳe de-Rabbi Eliezer (= *Baraitha de-Rabbi Eliezer*): character, composition date, editions, **I. 98**.

Pirqe 'Aboth, Mishnah tractate: **III. 214–215**; position in Mishnah, I. 73, III. 214; *Aboth de-Rabbi Nathan*, addition to, I. 80; literature on, I. 81–82, III. 215; character of, III. 214–215.

Piso, Cn. Calpurnius, consul 7 BC: as governor of Syria, conflict with Germanicus, I. 260–261.

Piso, L. Calpurnius, *pontifex* consul, 15 BC: whether he was legate of Syria, 4–1 BC, I. 258.

Pistus, father of Justus of Tiberias: I. 34.

Pitholaus, supporter of Aristobulus, Antigonus and Alexander against Rome: I. 270.

Placidus, Roman commander under Vespasian: leader of garrison in Sepphoris, I. 492; subjugation of Peraea, I. 498.

Plancus: see Munatius.

Plato: use of Platonic tenets by Jewish thinkers, III. 568, 571–572, 579, 583, 589; use of Platonic ideas in writings of Philo, III. 871, 872, 882, 884–885, 886.

Plato, rhetorician from Gaza: II. 50.

Pliny the Elder: his evidence regarding the location of the Essene community, II. 560, **563**, **584**, 589.

Pliny the younger: correspondence with Falco, I. 517.

Plutarch: **I. 65**; use of Posidonius of Apamea, I. 20; life and works, I. 65.

Pluto: worship of in Batanaea, Auranitis, etc., II. 43.

Poetry, Jewish, under Gentile pseudonyms: III. 656–671.

Polemon I of Pontus: I. 449n.

Polemon II of Pontus: I. 448, 449–450n.

Polemon of Cilicia: marriage to Berenice II, I. 474, 475.

Politeuma: **III. 88**; of Jews in Alexandria (see also under Alexandria), III. 88, 92–94; of Jews in Berenice (Cyrenaica), III. 88, 94–95; meaning of term, III. 88, 90, 91. See also under Community.

Pollio (Abtalion), a Pharisee: **II. 362–363**; serving under Herod, I. 296, 313, II. 362–363; refuses oath of allegiance to Herod, I. 313, 314n., II. 362; identification with Abtalion, II. 363.

Pollio Asinius, consul: see Asinius.

Pollio, prefect of Egypt: see Vitrasius.

Poll-tax: see   Taxation;   Tribute; Provinces; Palestine.

Polybius: **I. 63–64**; life and works, I. 63–64; as friend of Demetrius I, I. 129–130; characterisation of Antiochus IV, I. 146–147.

Polygamy: condemned by Qumran community, II. 579n., III. 390n., 413.

Polyhistor: see Alexander Polyhistor.

Pompeii: evidence for Jews living there, III. 82.

Pompeius Falco, governor of Judaea: **I. 516–517**.

Pompeius, Longinus, governor of Judaea: **I. 515–516**.

Pompeius Sextus: I. 252.

Pompey: **I. 236–241**; wars in the east, I. 135, 136, 236; makes Syria a Roman province, I. 136, 240, 244–248; gift of golden vine from Aristobulus, I. 236–237; relations with Aristobulus II and Hyrcanus II, subjugation of the Jews, I. 236–241, II. 148; siege of Temple Mount, I. 238–239; enters Holy of Holies, I. 240; liberates Hellenistic cities of Palestine from Jewish

Presbyteroi: **III. 102**; different from *archisynagogoi*, II. 435; inscriptional references to from various diaspora communities, III. 11, 14, 23, 26, 72, 88, 92, 98, 102n.; use and meaning of title *presbyteros*, III. 102. See also Elders.

Priene: evidence for Jews living there, III. 24.

Priests: **II. 237–313**; Hellenisation of in time of Jason, I. 148–149; dues, tithes, sacrificial portions etc. owed them, I. 523–524, 527, II. 257–274, 283, 345, III. 312; withdrawal from public life after AD 70, I. 523–524; literature on, II. 237–238; power of, II. 238–240, 257; exclusive right to sacrifice, II. 239–240, 251; in the Qumran community, II. 239n., 243–244n., 244–245n., 248, 251n., 252–253n., 294, 323n., 342n., 575–576, 588–589, 591, III. 408, 409; hereditary class, genealogies, II. 240; special marriage laws, II. 240–242, III. 175; required ritual cleanness, II. 242–243, 294–295; age of admission to office, II. 243; ceremony of consecration, II. 244; division into twenty four courses, II. 245–250; to be distinguished from Levites, II. 250–252; 'sons of Aaron', II. 252–253; 'sons of Zadok' (see also under Sadducees), II. 252–253n.; number of, II. 256; wives and daughters of, permitted to eat offerings, II. 261, 266, 270; daily Temple duties and sacrifices, II. 279–287, 287–291, 292–308, 304–307; vestments, II. 280, 281, 286, 293–294; as guardians of the Torah, time of Ezra, II. 322–323; priestly benediction in synagogue, II. 448, 450, 453–454; given precedence in synagogue, II. 450; Sabbath observance and sacrifice, II. 473, 474; priestly white vestments worn by Essenes, II. 564n., 569, 593; emphasis upon the Levitical priesthood in *Testaments of*

XII Patriarchs, III. 768; high priests, see High Priest; Teacher of Righteousness and the Wicked Priest of Qumran writings, see under Qumran Community. See also Sacrifice; Temple; Levites; and under names of various types of offerings, dues etc.

Priscillian: use of *Enoch*, III. 263.

Procurator, Roman office of: **I. 358–359**; later confusion with title *praefectus*, I. 358–359; title derived from original function as financial administrator, I. 358, 360, 372; title for governor of equestrian rank, I. 358; title of governors of Judaea from time of Claudius, I. 358; judicial authority, I. 350, 367–372; military arrangements in areas governed by, I. 359, 362, 367. See also under Governors; Provinces; and below.

Procurators of Judaea: **I. 357–387, 455–470, 485–486**; subordinate to governors of Syria, I. 257, 360; history of the title *procurator*, I. 358–360; place of residence, I. 361, II. 171; military arrangements in the province, I. 362–367; judicial authority, I. 367–372; administration of finances, I. 372–376; extent of Jewish self-government under, I. 376–381, II. 219–223; list of governors, AD 6–41, I. 382–383; procurators during the period AD 44–66, I. 455–470. See also Judaea, and under individual names.

Property: rabbinic method of settling disputes, II. 516; common ownership of among Essenes, II. 565–566; common ownership of at Qumran, II. 577.

Prophets, biblical books: canonisation of, II. 317–318n.; status lower than that of Torah, II. 319–321; reading of in synagogue, II. 448, 450, 452, 453, 454; for individual prophets and writings, see under separate names and titles.

Prophets, The Lives of: **III.** **783–786**; original language of, date, III. 705–708, 784; contents, III. 783–784; Jewish work, later Christianised, III. 784–785; editions, literature on, III. 786.

Prosbol: see *Prozbul.*

Proselytes, Jewish: **III.** **150–176**; proselytizers expelled from Rome, 131 BC, I. 197; conversion to Judaism punished by Domitian, I. 528, III. 122; number of decreased after 135 AD, I. 556; travel to Jerusalem for feasts, II. 76; forbidden in marriage to priests, II. 241; prayer for in the *Shemoneh 'Esreh*, II. 461; Lydia of *Acts* 16, III. 19; conversion to Judaism forbidden by Septimius Severus, III. 123; Christian converts to Judaism, III. 125; Jewish missionary literature, III. 158–162, 548, 552, 617–618 *et passim*; need to be circumcised, III. 164, 165, 169, 170, 173, 174; distinct from God-fearers, III. 169, 171; history of term *proselutos*, III. 169–171; given instruction in Jewish tenets and ritual, III. 172–173; baptism of, III. 173, 174, 642; need to take Hebrew name, III. 174–175; particular laws regarding female proselytes, III. 175; religious duties and rights of, III. 175–176; forced conversion of various peoples, see Conversion. See also 'God-fearers'.

Proseuche: inscriptional references to from various diaspora communities, III. 46–47, 52, 55, 73; use of term for pagan places of worship, III. 107.

Prostitutes: forbidden in marriage to priests, II. 240.

Proverbs, biblical book: process of canonisation, II. 317–318n.; as Wisdom Literature, III. 198; association with Solomon, III. 241.

Providence: **II.** **392–394**; doctrine of among Pharisees, I. 206, 296, II. 572, 392–394, 395; doctrine of among Sadducees, II. 392, 394, 572; general belief in, II. 494; doctrine of among Essenes, II. 571–572; doctrine of according to Philo, III. 865.

Provinces, Roman: **I.** **255, 357–376, 401–404**; different classes of, power and function of governors, I. 255, 357–376, 378; taxation of, I. 372–376, 401–404, II. 93–94, 96, 197n.

Prozbul: **II.** **366–367**; Greek loan word, II. 54; formula of, II. 185n., 366; instituted by Hillel, II. 366; meaning of term and its provisions, II. 366–367.

Psalms, Apocryphal and in Syriac from Qumran: III. 188–192, 203.

Psalms, biblical book: **III.** **187–197**; singing of in Temple, II. 303–304; process of canonisation, II. 317–318n., III. 187–188; so-called Maccabaean psalms, III. 187–188; use of Ps. 30 for Hanukkah, III. 187n.; Psalms Scroll from Qumran, III. 188; claim of Davidic authorship, III. 241; commentaries on from Qumran, III. 438–439, 448–449.

Psalms of Solomon: **III.** **192–197**; messianic hope, II. 503–504, 505, 517, 519, III. 194–195; anti-Hasmonaean content and stance, III. 193–194; authorship, III. 193, 194–195; original language of, III. 195; literature on, editions, translation, III. 196–197; translation into Greek, III. 505; whether source for *I Baruch*, III. 736, 737n.

Pseudepigrapha, the so-called: **II.** **348–355, III. 177–180** *et passim*; haggadic historiography, character and theology, II. 348–355, III. 177–180 *et passim*, 241–244, 279, 308, 505, 733ff, 746ff; messianic hope of, II. 501–507, 514–547; fragments of pseudepigraphic prophesies found at Qumran, III. 306–307; Jewish writings under

proseuche near Alexandria, III. 46–47.

Ptolemy IV Philopator: death, II. 89; defeats Antiochus III at Raphia, II. 98; portrayal of in *III Maccabees*, III. 537–539.

Ptolemy V Epiphanes: marriage to Cleopatra, daughter of Antiochus III, II. 98.

Ptolemy VI Philometor: supports claims of Alexander Balas to Syrian throne, I. 130, 177n., 180, 181; death, I. 181; friendly attitude to the Jews, III. 47, 49, 135–136; with Jews builds *proseuche* in Athribis, III. 49; allows Jewish temple to be built in Leontopolis, III. 115, 145–146; and the Jewish philosopher Aristobulus, III. 579, 586.

Ptolemy VII Physcon: opposes Demetrius II, I. 132; hostile attitude to Jews, III. 115.

Ptolemy VIII Lathyrus: conflict with Cleopatra and Alexander Jannaeus, I. 220–221, II. 173, 124.

Ptolemy VIII Physcon: legend about tossing Jews to elephants, III. 539.

Ptolemy Auletes: reinstated as king by Gabinius, I. 245–246.

Ptolemy, brother of Nicolaus of Damascus: not author of biography of Herod, I. 27; at court of Herod, I. 310–311.

Ptolemy, finance minister of Herod: I. 311.

Ptolemy, general of Antiochus Epiphanes: I. 159.

Ptolemy Mennaeus, king of the Ituraeans: I. 564–565.

Ptolemy, son in law of Simon Maccabee: kills Simon and his sons, I. 199; conflict with Hyrcanus I, I. 202.

Ptolemy, son of Antony and Cleopatra: acquisition of much of Syria, I. 253.

Publicans, tax collectors: **I. 374–376**; in Palestine, I. 374–376; opprobrium heaped on, I. 376.

Publicius Marcellus, governor of Syria:

sent to Judaea to put down Bar Kokhba revolt, I. 518–519, 547, 549.

Purim, Feast of: method of calculating when feast should fall, I. 591, 593; reading of scroll of *Esther* on, II. 450.

Purity, laws of ritual cleanness: **II. 475–478**; as practised by the Pharisees, II. 475–478; contact with Gentiles and their possessions to be avoided, II. 83–84; of priests, II. 239–244, 294–295, 299; corpse uncleanness, II. 242, 475; laws regarding access to Temple courts, II. 285n.; washing before prayer, II. 441; concept of, II. 475; types of water used to purify, II. 475, 477–478; extensions of according to *halakhah*, II. 476; of utensils, II. 476–478; among the Essenes, II. 564, 569n., 570; in Qumran community, II. 569n., 577n., 582, III. 399–400. 408–409, 410–411, 413–414; of Jews in Media and Mesene suspect, III. 9, 10.

Puteoli, city in Italy: Christian community there, III. 81n.; evidence for Jews living there, III. 81; settlement of Tyrians there, III. 110–111.

Pydna in Macedonia: worship of Zeus Hypsistos there, III. 68.

Pythagoras: use of Pythagorean teachings by Jewish thinkers, III. 568, 579, 583; view of Josephus and others that Pythagoras got his philosophy from Judaism, III. 696; influence of his teachings on Philo, III. 872.

Pythodoris, wife of Polemon I of Pontus: I. 449n.

Q

Quadrans, coin: II. 66.

Quadratus, Iulius Bassus, governor of Judaea: I. 516.

183, 195, 422, 431–432; prayers, III. 456–464. See also Essenes, and for further details of all of the above under Writings below.

Qumran Community, Writings from: **I. 118–122, III. 380–469**; literature on, editions etc. (for details regarding specific scrolls, see below), I. 118–122, III. 380 *et passim*; identity of the 'Wicked Priest', I. 188n., 224n., II. 552, III. 338n., 434–435, 438; identity of the 'Furious Young Lion', I. 224–225n., III. 431, 432; calendar reckoning in the scrolls, I. 592n., II. 245n., 581, 595, III. 313–314, 460, 466–467; close connections with the book of *Jubilees*, I. 592n., III. 308, 313–314; language of in general (for details of specific works see below), II. 23–24, 26, 27, 78–79; musical instruments, II. 290; exegetical methods of, II. 348, 354n., 580n., 586, III. 392, 420–421, *et passim*; 'Sons of Light' (doctrine of the two ways), II. 517n., 536n., 554, 578, 581, 583, III. 172–173n., 364, 382, 398, 399–400; Melchizedek and Milkireša', II. 526, 553–554, III. 336n., 449–451; fragments of Hebrew *Ben Sira*, III. 203–204, 507; *Tobit* fragments, III. 229; fragments of pseudepigraphic prophecies found there, III. 244, 306–307; fragments of *Daniel* discovered there, III. 248; Aramaic fragments of *Enoch* discovered there, III. 251–252, 254, 255, 256, 257–258, 260; Hebrew fragments of *Jubilees*, III. 309, 313–314; fragments of a *Book of Noah* found there, III. 332–333; *Testament of Kohath*, III. 333; *Testament of Amram*, III. 334; fragments of a *Samuel Apocryphon* found there, III. 335; authorship of *Martyrdom of Isaiah*, III. 338; apocryphal fragments from, III. 341; magical astrological texts (horoscopes), III. 364–366, 367,

464–466; Teacher of Righteousness not author of various scrolls, III. 384, 388, 396, 401n., 404, 417, 454–455; various commentaries and fragments of biblical exegesis, III. 421–469; angelology, III. 462–463; fragments of the Greek Bible found there, III. 478, 487–488; figure of the Teacher of Righteousness, III. 548, 551–552, 580, 587, III. 338n., 421, 434, 436, 438, 439, 453; similarities between Qumran documents and *Sibylline Oracles*, III. 642; fragment of the *Letter of Jeremiah*, III. 744, 745; fragments of the *Testaments of the XII Patriarchs*, III. 769–770, 772, 773–774, 775, 776; links with the Christian *Odes of Solomon*, III. 787.

Writings in detail:

(1) *Damascus Rule (Zadokite Fragments)*: **III. 389–398**; advocates calendar of *Jubilees*, III. 308, 311, 323, 392; content, III. 389–392; manuscript history, III. 389; exegetical method, III. 391–392, 420, 421; composition, structure, III. 392–395; date of composition, III. 395–396; editions, translations, literature on, III. 396–398; not written by Teacher of Righteousness, III. 396.

(2) *Community Rule (Manual of Discipline)*: **III. 381–386**; similarities with *Jubilees*, III. 314; scroll and fragments, III. 381–382; content, III. 382; structure and content, III. 382–384; editions, translations, literature on, III. 384–386; not written by Teacher of Righteousness, III. 384.

(3) *Thanksgiving Hymns (Hodayoth)*: **III. 451–456**; similarities with *Jubilees*, III. 314;

R

Ramathaim, district of Samaria: joined to Judaea under Jonathan Maccabee, I. 141, 142, 182, II. 2; predominantly Jewish population, I. 142, II. 1–2.

Rambam: see Maimonides.

Rammius Martialis, prefect of Egypt: I. 530, 531.

Raphana (=Raphon), city: **II. 137–138**; member of Decapolis, II. 126, 138; location, II. 137.

Raphia, city: **II. 97–98**; captured by Alexander Jannaeus, I. 221, II. 6, 98; 'liberated' by Pompey, I. 240, II. 6, 98; gentile city, Hellenistic culture, II. 3, 6, 30; coins of, II. 30, 98; Greek foundation myth, II. 51; battle of, 217 BC, II. 89, 98; rebuilt by Gabinius, II. 92, 98; location, II. 97–98.

Ravenna: evidence for Jews living there, III. 84.

Redemption (sacrifice): of first-born males, animal and human, **II. 265–266**, 268, 269–270n.

Refuge, cities of: II. 94–95.

Reges Socii, constitutional position of: see under Rome.

Reshith ('the best' of the offerings): to be given to priests, II. 258, 259.

Resurrection: **II. 494–495, 539–547**; belief among Pharisees, II. 391–392, 540, 541, 542n., 543n.; denied by Sadducees, II. 391–392, 411, 540; development of belief in, II. 494–495, 498, 500–501; doctrine of in *Daniel*, II. 498, 500–501; in apocryphal writings, II. 500–501, 502 *et passim*; in Messianic Age, II. 536, 539–540, 540–544, 544–547. See also Messianism; Immortality; After-life; etc.

Retribution, doctine of: see Judgment; Messianism; Resurrection.

Reuben, patriarch, Testament of: see *Testaments of the XII Patriarchs*.

Revolt, Jewish, against Rome, AD 66–74: **I. 484–513**; rival factions, civil war in Jerusalem, I. 181,

486–487, 489, 501, 502–503, II. 601, 602; activities of Josephus, I. 489–491, 492–494; activities of the Zealots, I. 496–498, 499, 600, 501, 511–512, II. 600, 601, 602, 603–604; siege and fall of Jerusalem, I. 503–508; siege of Masada, I. 511–512; coins of, I. 605–606, II. 603; Messianic fervour (see also under Messianism), II. 509–510; causes of according to Josephus, II. 510, 600, 602–603, 604; settlement in Judaea after revolt, II. 514; activities of the Essene/Qumran community, II. 588; Mesopotamian Jews assist in Revolt, III. 7; involvement of Jews of Cyrene, III. 61.

Revolt, of Bar Kokhba: see Bar Kokhba.

Reward: see After-life; Judgment.

Rhodes: evidence for Jews living there, III. 4n., 69–70.

Ritual (Jewish): baths and ablutions (see also Purity), II. 475, 477, 478, 564, 569, 570, 577n., 582; *zizith, mezuzah, tefillin*, II. 479–481; surrounding prayer, II. 481–483; fast-days, II. 483–484; feast-days, see under individual names. See also Commandments; Judaism, Temple, etc.

Rome: literature on calendar / chronology, I. 9; treaty with Jews, time of Judas Maccabaeus, I. 171–172, III. 74; treaty of friendship with Jonathan Maccabee, I. 184, III. 74; *senatus consultum* in respect of Simon the Maccabee, I. 194–197, III. 4, 18, 74–75; Jews expelled for proselytising, 139 BC, I. 197, III. 74–75; *senatus consultum* in favour of Jews to Antiochus VII, I. 204–205; conquest and organisation of Judaea by Pompey (see also under Pompey), I. 240–241, II. 91–92; called *Kittim* in the Dead Sea Scrolls, I. 241–242n., II. 588, III. 425–426, 431, 434–435; history and extent of Jewish community there,

conflict between Jesus and Pharisees concerning, II. 468, 474n.; legislation concerning 'Erubin', II. 472–473, 484–485; activities permitted on, II. 473–474; observance of among Essenes, II. 569, 572; as observed by Therapeutae, II. 591, 592, 593; toleration of Rome with respect to Sabbath observance, III. 120, 121; importance of observance in diaspora communities, III. 140, 141, 144; mocked by non-Jews as time of indolence, III. 152; observance of by non-Jews, III. 161; discussion of in Aristobulus, III. 582, 583; and cult of Sambethe, III. 624–626; worship of by pagans, III. 624, 625n.; Jewish writings about under Greek pseudonyms, III. 658, 659, 669–670.

Sabbath, Mishnah tractate: position and subjects treated, I. 72.

Sabbatical year: dates of according to *I. Macc.* and Josephus, I. 18–19; and siege of Temple mount, 162 BC, I. 167; safeguards for creditors, introduction of *prozbul*, II. 54, 366–367.

Sabbe: see Sambethe.

Sabinus, procurator of Judaea: I. 331–332.

Sabinus, soldier in army of Titus: I. 505.

Sacrifices, at Jerusalem Temple: **II. 292–313**; for the emperor, I. 379–380, 469n., 486, 522, 536n., II. 311–312, III. 613; ceased after AD 70, I. 505, 521–523, III. 328; as discussed by Josephus, I. 521–522; as discussed in Mishnah, I. 524–525, II. 345; exclusive right of priests (see also Priests), II. 239–240, 251, 252; at priests' consecration ceremony, II. 244; priests' dues, II. 257–270, 294, 345; the daily, II. 295–296, 299–301, 307; on Sabbaths and feast-days, II. 307–308, 473; by Gentiles, II. 309–313; for foreign foreign rulers other than the emperor, II. 311; use for

removal of personal uncleanness, II. 475, 477; among the Essenes, II. 570, 572, 588–589; not legitimate at Leontopolis Temple, III. 147; good thoughts better than, III. 200; according to Qumran *Temple Scroll* (see also under Qumran Community), III. 408, 409, 415; prescriptions for in *Testaments of the XII Patriarchs*, III. 768. See also Temple; Priests; and under various types of offering.

Sadducees: **II. 404–414**; dependence of John Hyrcanus upon, I. 211, 213–214, 413; origin and history of the name, I. 211–213, II. 405–407; priestly aristocracy, I. 212, II. 404, 412–413; rejection of the oral law, I. 212, II. 407–409, 410–411; in Sanhedrin, I. 213, 230, II. 202, 204, 210, 213, 215–216, 331, 412; in time of Alexandra, I. 230–231, II. 413; under Herod, I. 296, 313; disappearance of after AD 70, I. 523, II. 369, 370, 413; and Torah scholarship, II. 329; no belief in resurrection, II. 391–392, 411, 540; relations with the Pharisees, II. 404–405, 413, 414; rejection of Pharisaic rules of purity, II. 409–410, 475; teaching of compared with Pharisees, II. 409–411; their exegesis regarding the law of festivals, II. 410–411; belief in human free will, II. 411–412, 572; identification with Qumran community, II. 585; authorship of *Assumption of Moses*, III. 283.

Sagan (captain of the Temple): position and duties, **II. 277–278**, 286.

Sages: see Rabbis; Scribes.

Sala: evidence for Jews living there, III. 26.

Salamis, capital of Cyprus: destroyed in Jewish revolt of AD 116, I. 532, III. 68; evidence for Jews living there, III. 141.

Salampsio, daughter of Herod: concerning the name, I. 320n.

Salome (I), sister of Herod: **I. 302–304, 321–322, 335**; execution of first husband Joseph, I. 288, 303; denounces her second husband Costobar, I. 289, 303–304; intrigues against Mariamme, I. 302; planned marriage with Syllaeus, I. 313; intrigues against Alexander and Aristobulus, I. 321, 322; receives land and money according to Herod's will, I. 333, II. 92, 107, 109, 110, 168; bequeaths property to Livia, I. 335, II. 109, 110, 168.

Salome (II), daughter of Herodias: **I. 348–349**; marriage to Philip, I. 339, 344, 349n.; dancing before Antipas, I. 348; date of birth, I. 349n.; marriage to Aristobulus, I. 349n.

Salome Alexandra: see Alexandra.

Salvation: see Resurrection; After-life; Messianism.

Samaias: see Sameas.

Samareia, village so-called in Egypt: III. 45, 59.

Samaria (= Sebaste), city: **II. 160–164**; destroyed by John Hyrcanus, I. 209–210, II. 39, 162; 'liberated' by Pompey, I. 240, II. 91, 162; rebuilt and renamed Sebaste by Herod, I. 290–291n., 306, II. 39, 93, 162–163; given to Herod by Augustus, I. 302, II. 162; temple to Augustus, I. 306n.; did not take part in war against Varus, I. 332, 417; population mainly Gentile, II. 15–16; Macedonian colonists settled there by Alexander the Great, II. 16, 29, 39, 160–161; restored by Gabinius, II. 16, 39, 92, 162; Hellenism of, II. 29, 39–40; coins of, II. 39–40, 163; laid waste by Demetrius Poliorcetes, II. 161; razed by Ptolemy Lagus, II. 161; inhabitants called 'Gabinians', II. 162; becomes Roman colony, II. 163–164; given to Archelaus, II. 163; supported Rome during revolt, AD 66–70, II. 163; soldiers of, see Sebastenes.

Samaria, district: **I. 141, II. 16–20**; as separate administrative unit under Ptolemies and Seleucids, I. 141, II. 162; three *nomoi* of given to Judaea by Demetrius II, I. 141, 142, 182; whether given to Judaea as tax-free zone by Alexander the Great, I. 141, 142, III. 672, 673, 675n.; predominantly Jewish in south in time of Maccabees, I. 142; conquest of by John Hyrcanus, I. 209–210, II. 18–19; assigned to Archelaus by Augustus, I. 333, II. 163; description of Jewish province in Josephus, II. 6–7n., 10; population of province mainly Samaritan, II. 15–16, 17; Assyrian colonists (Cuthites), II. 17; occupied by Antiochus the Great, II. 162; subordinated to Sebaste, II. 163; Jewish expectation that an anti-Christ will come from there, III. 640; soldiers of, see Sebastenes; for troubles there under Pilate, Cumanus, etc., see under Samaritans. See also Samaria, city; Samaritans.

Samaritans: **II. 16–20**; destruction of sanctuary by John Hyrcanus, I. 207, II. 18–19; troubles under Pilate, I. 386–387, 439, II. 163; troubles in time of Cumanus, I. 459; said to have objected to rebuilding of Temple, time of Hadrian, I. 535; and Roman ban on circumcision, I. 539; regarded by Josephus as Jewish, II. 6–7n., 17; literature on, II. 16–17n.; centre of worship at Mt. Gerizim, II. 17, II. 161; origin of and history of Schism, II. 17–19; religion of, II. 17, 19; attitude of Pharisaic Judaism towards, II. 19–20, III. 59, 327; 'council of', time of Pilate, II. 163; meeting-houses of, II. 444; messianic doctrine of, II. 513; settlement in Egypt, III. 42, 45, 59–60; on Delos, synagogue of, III. 60, 71, 103; in Thessalonika, synagogue of, III. 60,

Sarapion, Egyptian Greek: III. 50.

Sarapis: see Serapis.

Sardis: **III. 20–22**; synagogue of, II. 443n., III. 21–22, 167; evidence for Jews living there, III. 20–22, 120, 167; Jews have own *synodos*, III. 21, 90, 120, 130.

Satan: see Belial; Melchireša.

Saturninus: see Sentius Saturninus; Volusius Saturninus.

Saul, relative of Agrippa II: banditry of, time of Albinus, I. 469.

Saxa: see Decidius Saxa.

Scaurus, M. Aemilius, governor of Syria: **I. 244–246**; campaigns against Aretas, I. 236, 244, 267; appointment as governor, I. 240, 244; coins of, I. 244; takes skeleton of sea-monster from Joppa to Rome, I. 244–245, II. 33.

Schedia in Alexandria: synagogue of, III. 104.

Schools: see Education.

Scipio: see Metellus Scipio.

Scopas, Egyptian general: II. 169.

Scribes (*soferim*): **II. 322–325** *et passim*; as interpreters of the law and spiritual leaders following Ezra, I. 143, II. 238–239, 322–324, 329; in Sanhedrin, II. 204, 212–213; and priests' income, II. 257; high esteem of, II. 323, 325, 327; various titles for, II. 324–325, 325–327; later known as sages, II. 325; adherence to Pharisees, II. 329; for later and general activities of, see Rabbis.

Scripture: see Bible.

Scroll of fasting: see *Megillath Taanith*.

Scrolls: see *Megilloth*.

Scrolls (Torah): render hands unclean, II. 318, 320; Ark of, II. 446, 450. See also Torah; Bible.

Scythians: in Palestine, and origin of name Scythopolis, II. 143.

Scythopolis (Beth-Shean), city: **II. 142–145**; Hellenistic culture of, I. 144, II. 29, 38, 45, 48; occupied by John Hyrcanus, I. 210, II. 9n., 16, 144; 'liberated' by Pompey, I.

240, II. 92, 144; location, II. 10, 142; mainly gentile population, II. 15–16; coinage of, II. 48, 144; origin of name Scythopolis, II. 51, 143–144; linen industry, II. 68n.; Christian community there, II. 75n.; language spoken there, II. 75; independent from time of Gabinius, II. 92, 144; right of sanctuary, II. 94–95, 144; member of Decapolis, II. 126, 127, 142, 144; ancient name Beth-Shean, II. 142–143; massacre of Jews during revolt against Rome, II. 144–145; territories of, II. 145.

Sebaste: see Samaria (= Sebaste), city.

Sebastenes (troops recruited from Sebaste/Samaria): number and history of activities, **I. 363–365**, 451, II. 95, 163.

Sects, Jewish: see Essenes, Pharisees, Sadducees, etc.

Secundus: see Aemilius Secundus.

Seder 'Olam Rabbah: date, editions, I. **115**.

Seder 'Olam Zuṭṭa: date, editions, I. **116**.

Sederim ('Orders' of Mishnah): names, number and contents, I. **71–74**.

Sefer ha-Malbush: III. 345.

Sefer ha-Razim (Book of Mysteries): **III. 347–350**; date of composition, III. 345, 348–349; cosmology and magical formulae, III. 347–348, 349; literature on, III. 349–350; orthodoxy of, III. 349.

Sefer ha-Zikhronoth (= *Chronicles of Yerahmeel*): I. 117.

Sefer Raziel: III. 344.

Sefer Torah, minor talmudic tractate: position and subject treated, I. 80.

Sejanus: hostility to Jews, I. 343n., III. 76; Antipas accused of collusion with, I. 352; lost work on by Philo, III. 543, 862n., 863.

Sela', coin: value, currency in Palestine, II. 64, 65n.

Selene: see Cleopatra Selene.

Seleuceia in Babylon: evidence for Jews living there, III. 9.

490; literature on, III. 491–493; decline in popularity of in favour of other Greek translations, III. 493; translation of *Esther*, III. 505–506; inclusion of books not in Hebrew canon, III. 706–708 *et passim*; use of by Philo, III. 873–874.

Serapis: worship of in Greek cities of Palestine, II. 35, 36, 38; worship of in Athens, III. 156; worship of in Rome, III. 157.

Sermon: in synagogue service, II. 336, 425–427, 435, 448, 453; whether *IV Maccabees* was written as such, III. 589; homiletical style of some of Philo's writings, III. 818.

Seventy (70): importance of in Jewish legend generally, II. 351n.; the law originally recorded in 70 languages, II. 351; on *gerousia* of Alexandrian community, III. 94; 72 scholars took 72 days to translate the Pentateuch, III. 678.

Severus, Claudius, govenor of Arabia: II. 153–154n., 157.

Severus, Julius, general under Hadrian: commander during Bar Kokhba revolt, I. 549; given a Triumph, I. 553.

Severus, Sextus Iulius, governor of Judaea: **I. 519**.

Sexual intercourse: forbidden on fast days, II. 484.

Shabbath, Mishnah tractate: position and subject treated, I. 72.

Shaliaḥ: representative of synagogue congregation in prayer, II. 438, 449.

Shammai: **II. 363–365**; with Hillel, one of the *zuggot*, II. 358, 361, 363; religious zeal of, II. 363–364, 365; whether Sameas to be identified with, II. 363.

Shammai, School of: **II. 365–366**; compared with that of Hillel, II. 342, 365–366; views on divorce, II. 485.

Shebi'ith, Mishnah tractate: position and subject matter, I. 71.

Shebu'oth, Mishnah tractate: position and subject matter, I. 73.

Shechem, city: conquered by John Hyrcanus (see also Samaria), I. 207, II. 19; Neapolis came to be identified with, I. 520; chief city of the Samaritans, II. 29, 161; in revolt of AD 66–70, II. 163; history of by Hellenistic poet Theodotus, III. 561–562.

Sheḳalim, Mishnah tractate: position and subject matter, I. 72.

Sheḳel, coin: use for sacred dues, II. 28, 266, 270n., 272; value, Phoenician-Hellenistic standard, II. 62, 63n., 64, 272n.; for tax to Jerusalem Temple, see Half-Shekel Tax.

Shem, Treatise of: **III. 369–372**.

Shema', the: **II. 454–455, 481–482**; may be recited in Greek or Hebrew, II. 23n., 77n., III. 142; women, slaves and children need not recite, II. 420n., 455; in synagogue liturgy, II. 448–449, 450; preceded by a benediction, II. 449, 573, 455; which texts comprise it, II. 449, 454–455; antiquity of, II. 455; when said, II. 455, 481–482.

Shemaiah (Sameas?), Pharisee: **II. 362–363**; member of sanhedrin time of Hyrcanus, II. 216; one of the 'pairs', II. 357, 362–363; identification with Sameas, II. 362–363. See also Sameas.

Shemoneh 'Esreh: **II. 455–463**; women and children obliged to recite, II. 420, 456; as used on Sabbath, II. 448, 449, 459; history of, II. 456, 459, 462, 481; known simply as 'The Prayer', II. 456; literature on, II. 456–457n.; nineteen *berakhoth* in Babylonian recession, II. 456–459; when said, II. 456, 481; eighteen *berakhoth* in Palestinian recession, II. 459–462; prayer against heretics, II. 461, 462; mention of Christians, II. 462–463; messianic hope in, II. 462, 499–500, 512, 531; permitted to recite it in Greek, III. 142.

Sin-offering: **II. 260**; dues to priests, II. 258, 260; on Day of Atonement, II. 276; on feast-days, II. 295–296, 308; not accepted from Gentiles, II. 310; water fit to be mixed with, II. 477.

Sirach: see *Ben Sira, Wisdom of.*

Sixtus Senensis: on *IV Macc.*, III. 185–186.

Slaves: mode of manumission in Jewish diaspora communities, III. 36, 37, 56–57, 65, 90, 105; rights of the manumitted in Rome, III. 133.

Slaves, Jewish: in time of Antiochus IV, I. 159; in aftermath of Bar-Kokhba revolt, I. 553; exemption from commandments, II. 420n., 421., 455; obliged to recite *Shemoneh 'Esreh* and *Berakhoth* before meals, II. 456, 482; none among the Essenes, II. 568; taken by Pompey to Rome, III. 75, 133; laws about captured women, III. 411; in Temple, see *Nethinim.*

Smyrna: **III. 19–20**; evidence for Jews living there, III. 19–20, 90, 106; hostility of Jews to Christians, III. 19–20.

Soaemus: king of independent Ituraeans, AD 38–49, I. 338n., 472n., 563, **569–570**.

Soemus, an Ituraean at court of Herod: I. 302–303.

Soemus, king of Emesa: supplied Vespasian with auxiliary troops, I. 449n., 492, 570.

Soferim: see Scribes.

Soferim, minor talmudic tractate: position and subject treated, I. 80.

Soldiers: see Military.

Solomon: **III. 375–379**; *Song of Solomon* and process of canonisation, II. 317–318n.; Psalms of, III. 192–197, 505, 736, 737n.; named as author of *Wisdom of Ben Sira* by Clement of Alexandria, III. 207, 208; association with various biblical books, III. 241; association with magic and medicine, III. 342, 375–379; *Testament of Solomon*, III. 372–375;

seal of ('Magen David'), III. 376; *Wisdom of Solomon*, III. 568–579; *Odes of Solomon*, III. 787–789.

'Son of Man', meaning of the phrase: II. 505, **520–523**, III. 252–253, 256–259.

Song of Solomon: and process of canonisation, II. 317–318n.

Song of Songs, biblical book: midrash on (*Shir ha-Shirim Rabbah*), I. 94–95; and process of canonisation, II. 317–318n.; render hands unclean, II. 318–319n.; reading of at Passover, II. 452n; association with Solomon, III. 241. See also *Megilloth.*

'Sons of Darkness' (Qumran): see 'Sons of Light'.

'Sons of Light': doctrine of the Two Ways at Qumran, II. 517n., 536n., 554, 578, 581, 583, **III. 172–173n.**, 398, 399–400. See also under Qumran Community.

Sophocles: Jewish poetry under name of, III. 656, 657, 661, 667–668, 676.

Sophronius of Damascus, Patriarch of Jerusalem: on Nicolaus of Damascus, I. 28.

Soreg, of Jerusalem Temple: whether demolished by Alcimus, I. 175–176n.

Sosates, the 'Jewish Homer': III. 559n.

Sosius, C., governor of Syria: **I. 252**; installs Herod and is awarded a Triumph, I. 252, 283–286; gifts to Jerusalem Temple, II. 313.

Sosus, philosopher from Ascalon: II. 49.

Soṭah, Mishnah tractate: position and subjects treated, I. 72.

Soul: various Jewish beliefs in immortality of, II. 539–540, 541, 542, 543, 544, 546, 574, III. 590; notion of in *Wisdom of Solomon*, III. 572; doctrine of in Philo's theory of man, III. 886–888; for belief among various sects, see under names of sects. See also After-life; Resurrection.

T

378–379, 380; not to be identified with Justin's Tryphon, II. 379.

Tarsus: evidence for Jews living there, III. 33–34; home-town of Paul the Apostle, III. 34, 126, 133.

Taxes, in Palestine: **I. 372–376, 405–427**; farming of, I. 140, 374–376; under Ptolemies and Seleucids, I. 140, II. 89–90; the Herodian taxation system, I. 317, 416–420; customs levies, I. 372–375; under Rome, as imperial province, I. 372–376, 405 *et passim*; and census of Quirinius, I. 405–427, II. 603; as collected by the *dekaprotoi*, II. 180n.; as collected by Jerusalem Sanhedrin, II. 197; the *Fiscus Iudaicus*, II. 272–273, III. 54, 58, 122–123; priests' dues, see Tithes; Priests; monies to Temple, see Half-Shekel Tax. See also under Tribute.

Taxes, other: customs duties at Palmyra, I. 373, 375n.; system and types of Roman taxation in general, I. 401–404, II. 92–94, 96, 197n.; the *Fiscus Iudaicus*, II. 272–273, III. 54, 58, 122–123; payment of *Laographia* (poll-tax) by Egyptian Jews, III. 50, 55; Jewish tax-farmers in Egypt, III. 57; monies to Jerusalem Temple, see Half-Shekel Tax.

Taxo, in the *Assumption of Moses*: III. 280, 282.

Teacher of Righteousness: see under Qumran Community.

Teachers / Teaching: see Rabbis; Education.

Tebah: see Ark.

Tebtynis in Egypt: evidence for Jews living there, III. 52.

Tebul Yom, Mishnah tractate: position and subject treated, I. 74.

Tefillah: see *Shemoneh 'Esreh*; Prayer.

Tefillin (Phylacteries): **II. 480–481**; women and children exempt from wearing, II. 420; origin, content and ritual, II. 479, 480–481; discovered at Qumran, II. 480n.; use to drive away evil spirits, II.

480, III. 352–357, 357–358, 377; defile hands, II. 481; language permitted to be written in, III. 143.

Tefillin, minor Talmudic tractate: position and subject treated, I. 80.

Tekoa, town: in Bar Kokhba revolt, I. 546, 547.

Temple at Jerusalem:

(1) History: looting of by Antiochus Epiphanes, I. 151; 'abomination of desolation' under Antiochus Epiphanes, I. 155; rededication of by Judas Maccabaeus, I. 162–163; demolition of inner court walls by Alcimus, I. 175, 175–176n.; entered by Pompey, I. 239–240, 269; robbery of treasures by Crassus, I. 269; reconstruction of by Herod, I. 292n., 308, 308–309n., 313, II. 57–58; eagle of Herod over Temple gate, I. 313, 325, II. 58; burning of in 4 BC, I. 331; plunder of by Sabinus, I. 331; use of treasure by Pilate to build aqueduct, I. 385; move to erect statue there by Caligula, I. 394–397; overlooked by Agrippa II, I. 475; plan to strengthen foundations by Agrippa II, I. 476; robbed by Florus, I. 485; siege and destruction of, AD 70, I. 505–506, III. 122; spoils of displayed in Titus' Triumph, I. 510; after AD 74, Temple tax extracted for Jupiter Capitolinus, I. 513, 528, II. 272, III. 122–123; whether permission given by Hadrian to rebuild Temple, I. 535–536, 546; yearly lamentation by Jews on site of (9 Ab), I. 556–557; sacrifice offered by Alexander the Great, II. 310; sacrifice offered by Antiochus VII, II. 310; votive offerings by Agrippa, II. 310, 313; gifts

from Antiochus the Great, II. 311; gifts presented by Ptolemy II, II. 312–313; Feast of Dedication, see Hanukkah.

(2) Cult: Gentiles forbidden to enter inner courts, I. 175–176n., 378, II. 80, 222, 284–285; sacrifices for emperor (see also Sacrifices), I. 379–380, II. 311–312, III. 613; half-shekel tax, I. 513, 528, II. 67n., 270–272, 282, 295, III. 443; in rabbinic discussion, I. 521–523, 524–525, II. 345; pilgrims journeying to for festivals, II. 76; High Priests, II. 227–236, 275–276; purity and privilege of priesthood (see also Priests), II. 238–244, 251–252; priestly and levitical courses, II. 245–250, 254–256, 292; Levites (see also Levites, Priests), II. 250–256; door-keepers, II. 253–254, 255n., 256, 284–286, 303, 307; singers and musicians, II. 253–254, 255n., 288–291, 303, 307; offerings: priestly dues and Temple maintenance, II. 257–274, III. 140, 147–148; great wealth of, II. 274, 279–281, III. 147–148, 162; Captain of the Temple, II. 277–279; treasurers, II. 281–284; slaves (*Nethinim*), II. 290–291; details of daily sacrificial worship (see also Sacrifice), II. 292–308, 473; worship and sarifice by gentiles there, II. 309–313; sacrifices for pre-Roman gentile authorities, II. 311; attendance by children, II. 420–421; laws of personal purity (see also Purity), II. 285n., 475n.; whether treasure of is referred to in Qumran Copper Scroll, III. 467–468.

(3) Other: architectural lay-out of (see also Court, *Soreg*, etc.), I.

175–176n., 308–309n., II. 284–285, 296–299; seat of Sanhedrin, I. 224; overlooked by citadel (Antonia), I. 366; stationing of Roman guards at festivals, I. 366; state supervision of AD 6–66, I. 379; topography of immediate environs, I. 503; exclusion of Essenes, II. 475n., 570, 572, 588–589; in World to Come, II. 502, 536–536; attitude of Qumran community towards, II. 535, 552, 570n., 582, 588–589; layout and rules regarding according to Qumran *Temple Scroll*, III. 407–409, 414; fortress of as described by Aristeas, III. 681.

Temple at Leontopolis: **III. 47–48, 145–147.** See also under Leontopolis; Onias III.

Temple on Mount Gerizim: I. 521, II. **17–19,** 161. See also Gerizim; Samaritans.

Temple to Yaho at Elephantine: III. 39–40. See also Elephantine.

Temples, pagan in Palestine: foundations in honour of Augustus by Herod, I. 304–306; of Jupiter Capitolinus on former Temple site in Jerusalem, I. 537, 540, 542, 554, III. 122–123; of various gods in gentile cities, II. 30–52. See also under names of individual deities.

Temurah, Mishnah tractate: position and subject treated, I. 73.

Ten: committee of *dekaprotoi* in Greek cities of Palestine, II. 152, 180, 213–214; men needed for synagogue service, see *Minyan*.

Teos: evidence for Jews living there, III. 22.

Tephon, town: Syrian garrison there under Bacchides, I. 175.

Termessos: evidence for Jews living there, III. 33.

Tertullian: on the imperial edict

forbidding Jews entry to Jerusalem, I. 38; use of *I Maccabees*, III. 183; use of *Judith*, III. 220; on *Enoch*, III. 262; references *Wisdom of Solomon*, III. 574; use of the Additions to *Daniel*, III. 726.

Terumah: see Heave-offering.

Terumoth, Mishnah tractate: position and subject treated, I. 71.

Testament of Moses: see *Assumption of Moses*.

Testaments of the XII Patriarchs: **III. 767–781**; contacts with *Enoch* and *Jubilees*, III. 261, 777; contents, teachings of, III. 767–768; Jewish or Christian authorship of, III. 767, 768–772; discoveries of at Qumran, III. 769–770, 772, 773–774, 775, 776; original language of, III. 772–774; date and provenance, III. 774–775; editions, translations, literature on, III. 778–781.

Tetragrammaton, the Ineffable Name: II. 306–307n. See also under God.

Tetrarch: meaning and history of term, **I. 333–335n.**

Tetrarchy: meaning and history of term, **I. 333–335n.**

Teucer of Cyzicus, writer: I. 40.

Teucheira, city in Cyrenaica: evidence for Jews living there, III. 61.

Textiles: products and imports of Palestine, II. 68n., 70–71.

Thaenae in North Africa: evidence for Jews living there, III. 63.

Thallus, Hellenistic writer: **III. 543–545**; whether same person as the freedman mentioned by Josephus, III. 81, 544; world-chronicle of, III. 543–544; whether a Samaritan, III. 544; literature on, III. 545.

Thammatha, town: location, I. 175n.; Syrian garrison under Bacchides, I. 175.

Thamna, town: **II. 192–193**; people sold into slavery by Cassius, I. 277; slaves freed by M. Antonius, I. 278; as a toparchy, II. 190, 192–193, 196; burial place of Joshua, II.

192n., 193; location, II. 192n., 193n.; other places of same name, II. 193n.

Thank-offering: see Sacrifice.

Theatres: in Jerusalem built by Herod, I. 304–305, II. 55; in various cities of Palestine, II. 46–48, 55. See also Games; Hellenism.

Thebes in Egypt: evidence for Jews living there, III. 41, 55.

Theodoret: allusions to *Liber Antiquitatum Biblicarum*, III. 329.

Theodorus of Gadara, orator: II. 50, 135.

Theodorus, tyrant of Amathus: II. 91.

Theodotion: **III. 499–504**; Greek translation of the Bible (in the Hexapla), III. 481, 482, 493, 499–504; personal history, III. 493, 499, 501; not to be identified with Jonathan ben Uzziel, III. 499, 502; use of his translation of *Daniel* by Church, III. 727–728.

Theodotus, poet: **III. 510, 561–563**; non-extant poem on Shechem, III. 561; whether Samaritan or Jew, III. 561–562; literature on, III. 562–563; not to be identified with the Theodotus cited by Josephus, III. 562.

Theodotus, Ptolemaic general: II. 123.

Theophilus of Antioch: use of the *Sibylline Oracles*, III. 638–639.

Theophilus, writer: I. 42, **556–557**.

Theophrastus: use of the *Story of Ahiqar*, III. 236.

Theos Hypsistos: Jewish *vs* pagan character of worship, III. 32, 68, 169; occurrences on inscriptions, III. 37, 38, 49, 67, 70, 72, 106, 109.

Theosebeis: see 'God-fearers'.

Thera: evidence for Jews living there, III. 71.

Therapeutae: **II. 591–597**; etymology of name, II. 559; life-style and organisation, II. 571, 591–593, III. 857; importance of Feast of Pentecost, II. 592, 595; similarities with Essenes, II. 593–597; compared with Qumran community, II. 594–595; evidence of Philo, II. 595–596, III. 856–858; and authorship of *Testament of Job*, III. 553; close affinity with Christian monks, III. 857.

Thessalonika: Samaritan synagogue there, inscription, III. 60, 66–67; evidence for Jews living there, III. 65, 66–67, 141.

Thessaly: evidence for Jews living there, III. 5, 64, 66, 68, 89.

Theudas, pseudo-prophet: I. 427, 439, **456**, II. 509.

Thmuis: evidence for Jews living there, III. 40.

Thrace: evidence for Jews living there, III. 72.

Thyatira: evidence for Jews living there, 'Sabbath House', III. 19.

Tiberianus: whether ever a governor of Judaea of this name, **I. 517–518**.

Tiberias, city: **II. 178–182**; palace with animal images destroyed by rebels, I. 40n., 490–491, II. 342–343; foundation of, I. 342–343, II. 93, 178–179; location and site, I. 342, II. 178; mixed population, I. 342, II. 179; Hellenistic constitution, I. 343, II. 179–180; under Agrippa I, I. 443, II. 97, 180; under Agrippa II, I. 473, II. 174–175, 181; attitude and fortunes during great revolt, I. 476, 490–491, 494, II. 179, 181; no pagan temple there until second century, II. 40; as capital of Galilee, II. 174, 180; coins, II. 179, 180, 181; as centre of rabbinic scholarship, II. 181, 369; commercial importance, II. 181; as toparchy of Galilee, II. 194–195.

Tiberius, emperor: administration and history of Syria during his reign, I. 260–263; Tiberias built in his honour, I. 342–343, II. 178; attitude towards Jews, I. 343n., III. 76; death, I. 350; supports Antipas against Aretas, I. 350; allows

provincial governors long period in office, I. 383; orders Pilate to remove offensive shields from Jerusalem, I. 386; imprisons Agrippa I, I. 444; Jamnia and Azotus his private possessions, II. 92, 110; expels Jews from Rome, III. 75–76, 78n.; symbolised as eagle's wing in *IV Ezra*, III. 299.

Tiberius Gemellus, grandson of Tiberius: death, I. 389; friend of Agrippa I, I. 444.

Tiberius Julius Alexander: see Alexander, Tiberius Julius.

Tigranes, king of Armenia: as ruler of Syria, I. 134, 135, 231, II. 124, 129; defeated by Lucullus, I. 135, 231; threatens Judaea in time of Alexandra, I. 231; submission to Pompey, I. 236; transports Jews to Armenia, III. 6, 10.

Timagenes of Alexandria, historian: I. **22–23**; life and works, I. 22–23; indirect use of by Josephus, I. 23.

Timochares, writer: I. 42.

Timotheus, leader of the Ammonites: I. 140n., 165.

Tineius, Rufus, governor of Judaea at time of Bar Kokhba revolt: **I. 518**, 547–549, 551.

Tirathana, village at foot of Mt. Gerizim: I. 386.

Tithes: **II. 257–274**; of cattle, II. 257, 258, 259, 265–267; of field and fruit, II. 257, 258, 259, 262–263, 265, III. 312; the second, II. 259, 264; II. 262–270; for the poor, II. 265n., 383; redemption (sacrifice) of first born males, II. 265–266, 268, 269–270n.; to what extent diaspora Jews contributed, II. 269–270; enjoyed by priests and their relatives, II. 270.

Titius, M., governor of Syria: I. 257, 420.

Tittius Frugi: see Frugi, M. Tittius.

Titus: **I. 477–480, 501–510**; friendship with Agrippa II, I. 477; games to celebrate conquest of Jerusalem, I.

477, 509, II. 47, 48; affair with Berenice, I. 479, III. 79n.; on coins of Agrippa II, I. 480n.; military activities during Jewish revolt, I. 492, 493, 494–495, 495–496, 501–508; travels to pay homage to Galba, I. 499; siege and capture of Jerusalem, I. 501–508, II. 74–75; burning of Jerusalem Temple, I. 505–507; hailed as Imperator by legions, I. 507; Arch of, I. 509n., 510n.; Triumph of, I. 509–510; protects rights of Jews of Antioch, III. 127, 129; death, III. 299; symbolised as eagle's head in *IV Ezra*, III. 299.

Tlos in Lycia: burial place for Jews there, III. 32–33; Jewish epitaphs from, III. 33, 106.

Tobiads, the: **I. 149–150n.**; account of in Josephus, I. 50, 149n., 151.; family members, history, I. 149–150n.; relations with Menelaus and high priestly family, I. 149–150n., 151n.; fortress, east of the Jordan, I. 150n., II. 59; in *The Saga of the Tobiads* preserved in Josephus, III. 558. See also under individual names.

Tobit, Book of: **III. 222–232**; language of, II. 26, III. 224–225; messianic hope, II. 500; story and character, III. 222–223; date of composition, III. 223–224; theology, III. 223; whether written in Palestine or diaspora, III. 223; fragments of discovered at Qumran, III. 225, 229; parallels with other similar tales, III. 226–227; Greek text, recensions, III. 227–229; use of in Christian Church, III. 227; Latin version, III. 229–230; Syriac, Aramaic, etc. versions, III. 230; literature on, III. 231–232; use of the *Story of Ahiqar*, III. 232, 235; translation of into Greek, III. 505.

Tohoroth, Mishnah tractate: position and subject treated, I. 74.

Tohoroth, Sixth Order of the Mishnah:

constituent tractates, I. 74.

Tombs: rock-cut at Marisa, art and inscriptions, II. 4–5n.; of the House of Adiabene in Jerusalem (=Tombs of the Kings), III. 164. See also Burial Practices.

Toparchies: Judaea divided into eleven, I. 372, II. 7, 186, **190–196**.

Topography, of Jerusalem: see under Jerusalem; Akra; etc.

Torah: midrash on, I. 90–99; Aramaic translation of (see also Targums), I. 99–105 II. 452–453; rabbinic study and interpretation of (see also Oral Law, *Halakhah*; *Haggadah*; Rabbis, etc.), I. 143, 524–525, II. 238–239, 322–324, 330–336, 337–355; focus for people after great revolt, I. 513, 524–525, 527, 555–556; Samaritan Pentateuch, II. 18; priestly code, II. 258–260, 315; divine authority and canonicity, II. 314–321; observance of (see also Commandments), II. 314–315, 464–466, 467 *et passim*, 492, 524; meaning of the term Torah, II. 321, 324; knowledge of and instruction in (see also Education), II. 332–335, 415–416, 417–422, 424–427, 464–466; Ark of the Scrolls, II. 446, 450; reading of in synagogue service, II. 448, 450–452; in World to Come, II. 535–536; identified with divine wisdom for first time by Ben Sira, III. 199–200; non-Septuagint translations into Greek (Aquila and Theodotion), III. 493–504; Greek translation of, see *Septuagint*. See also Bible.

Tosefta, the: **I. 77–78, 83**; structure and character, I. 77–78; compared with Mishnah, I. 78; editions, translations, literature on, I. 83–84; compared with Midrashim, I. 90; language of, II. 23.

Towns, Jewish in Palestine: **II. 184–198**; internal organisation, II. 184–188; authority over smaller towns and villages, II. 188–190;

distinction between city, town, and village, II. 188–189, 196–197. See also Cities; Palestine; Judaea; and under individual names.

Trachonitis, district of: **I. 337–338**; given to Herod by Augustus, I. 256, 291, 319; given to Philip as tetrarch, I. 326, 333, 336–339; location, I. 337–338n.; establishment of colony there by Herod, I. 338, 419, 479n., II. 14; mixed population, I. 338, II. 14–15; tetrarchy given to Agrippa II, I. 472, 479n., II. 7n.; advance of Hellenism, II. 14–15, 41–44.

Tractates, constituent of Mishnah: number and names, **I. 71–74**.

Trade in Palestine: **II. 60–72**; business transactions with Gentiles proscribed in Jewish law, I. 82–84; customs duties (tariffs, tolls), I. 373–376; weights and measures, II. 14; influence of Hellenism on terminology, II. 60–72; evidence of the Zenon papyri, II. 61–62, 100; with Greece and Athens, II. 61, 99, 108; export-import commodities, II. 67–72; at Gaza, II. 99, 100; importance of Ascalon as trading city, II. 108; importance of Joppa as a port, II. 111; merchants of Tiberias, II. 181.

Trajan, emperor; martyrdom of Simeon son of Cleopas, I. 516; whether hunted down Jews of Davidic descent, I. 528; Jewish rebellion in his reign, I. 529–533, III. 8, 58, 68; Day of, in Jewish legend, I. 533; *Via Traiana* built between Bostra and Petra, I. 586, II. 157, 158n.

Tralles: evidence for Jews living there, III. 24, 167.

Trastevere, quarter in Rome: Jewish community there, III. 75, 79.

Treasury / Treasures of Jerusalem Temple: see under Temple.

Tribes, the twelve: leaders of headed post-exilic community, II. 201; symbolic division of Qumran community (see also under Qumran Community), II. 201n.; gathering of in Messianic Age, II. 530–531; of Judah and Benjamin settled in Babylonia, III. 5, 8; the ten did not return from exile, III. 5; the ten, area deported to by Assyrians, III. 8; in *Testaments of the XII Patriarchs*, III. 768, 772.

Tribute, payment of in Palestine: **I. 401–406, 407** *et passim*; to Syrians abolished under Demetrius II, I. 179n., 190; not paid to any Syrian king after Antiochus Sidetes, I. 209; as imposed by Pompey, I. 240, 413; not paid by Herod to Rome, I. 317, 413, 416, 417, 420; imposed by Rome after AD 6, I. 372, 399–400, 401 *et passim*; as collected by the *dekaprotoi*, II. 180n. See also Taxes.

Tripolis, city: I. 308, II. 89.

Triumvirate, first: I. 246, 247.

Trogus, Pompeius: universal history of, epitomized by Justin, I. 68.

Trophimus, a Greek of *Acts* 21: I. 378n.

Trumpets: cultic use of, II. 290, 446–447.

Tryphaena, Antonia, mother of Polemon II of Pontus: I. 450.

Tryphon: **I. 130–131, 183** *et passim*; sets self up as king, dates, I. 130–131; defeated and killed by Antiochus VII, I. 131, 197–198, II. 112, 119–120; sets up Antiochus VI as pretender, I. 183, 184–186; supported by Jonathan, I. 183–184, 185–186; capture and murder of Jonathan Maccabee, I. 186–187; Justin's Tryphon, see Tarphon.

Turbo: see Marcius Turbo.

Tyche: worship of in cities of Palestine, II. 30, 35, 36, 37, 38.

Tyrants: setting themselves up in cities of Palestine as Seleucid power weakens, II. 91. See also under individual names.

Tyre, city: tyrant Marion seizes parts of Galilee, I. 277, 278; and building projects of Herod, I. 308;

celebration of games there by Alexander the Great, II. 44; public games, II. 44, 45n., 47; coinage of, use for Jewish Temple dues, II. 63n., 66–67, 266, 272; era and calendar, II. 88, 91, 103; ruled Ascalon in Persian period, II. 105–106; hostility to Jews, II. 123; evidence for Jews living there, III. 14, 15; settlement of Tyrians in Delos, III. 108; community of Tyrians in Puteoli, III. 111.

Tyre, Ladder of: I. 183n.

Tyropoeon, ravine dividing Jerusalem: I. 503.

U

'Ukzin, Mishnah tractate: position and subject addressed, I. 74.

Ulatha, district of: given to Herod by Augustus, I. 319.

Ummidius Quadratus: see Quadratus.

Underworld: see *Sheol*.

Universalism: growth of concept in Jewish thinking, II. 493–494, 498, 502, 532–533, 546–547, III. 159–160. See also Messianism; Proselytes.

Universitas: use of term to denote Jewish community, III. 91. See also under Community.

Uriel, angel: in *IV Ezra*, III. 294–296.

Usha, town: rabbinic academy there, II. 331, 369.

Utensils, household: importation of to Palestine, II. 71; laws of ritual cleanness, II. 83, 476–478.

Utica, in North Africa: evidence for Jews living there, III. 63.

Uzziah, king of Judah, funerary epigraph of, II. 25.

V

Valerius Gratus, governor of Judaea: dates of administration, I. 382; High Priests appointed by, II. 230.

Valerius Maximus: on the Jews, III. 74.

Varro (M. Terentius?), governor of Syria: **I. 256**.

Varus (= Noarus), son of Soaemus, ruler in the Lebanon: territory of given to Agrippa II by Claudius, I. 472; Agrippa delegates administration of his kingdom to, I. 477n.; endowed with small territory on death of Soaemus, I. 570.

Varus, P. Quinctilius, governor of Syria: **I. 257–258**; dates of administration, I. 257–258; puts down Jewish rebellion following death of Herod ('War of Varus'), I. 331–332, II. 173; and census of Quirinius, I. 420, 424–425; war of in *Assumption of Moses*, III. 279, 280n., 282.

Veiento, *legatus* in Syria, time of Bibulus: I. 247.

Venosa in southern Italy: Jewish catacomb there, III. 83.

Ventidius Cumanus: see Cumanus.

Ventidius, P., governor of Syria: I. **251–252**; campaigns against the Parthians, I. 251–252, 282–283.

Vergil: whether influenced by *Sibylline Oracles* in his fourth Eclogue, III. 647–649.

Vespasian, emperor: I. **491–496, 498–501**; memoirs of (*commentarii*), use by Josephus, I. 32–33; Josephus prophesies his elevation to the throne, I. 44–45, 494, II. 370, 510; appointed *legatus* in command of Jewish War, I. 265, 491; use of troops from Caesarea (*Sebasteni*), I. 364; subjugation of Judaea, I. 365–366, 498–501; military rearrangements in Judaea following the revolt, I. 367; relations with Agrippa II, I. 477–478, 494;

Wisdom literature: character of, III. 178–179, 567–568 *et passim*; III. 198–199; for specific works, see under individual titles.

Wisdom of Solomon: **III. 568–579**; content and purpose, III. 568–570, 571; use of Greek philosophical traditions, III. 568, 571–572; on the question of multiple authorship, III. 569n.; hypostatized wisdom, III. 570–571; date and place of composition, III. 572–573; references to in later writings, III. 573–575; manuscripts, editions, literature on, III. 575–579.

Women (Jewish): eighty hanged at Ascalon, I. 231; number of wives permitted to kings and commoners, I. 320n.; followers of Jesus, I. 349n.; of Alexandria during AD 38 pogrom, I. 391; liable to Roman poll-tax, I. 403, 412; those permitted in marriage to priests and High Priests, II. 240–242; wives of priests not mourned by husbands, II. 242–243; priestly, entitled to eat of offerings, II. 261, 266, 270; sacrificial offerings by following child-birth, II. 261n., 310; access to Temple courts, ritual impurity, II. 285–286n.; forecourt of in Temple, II. 285n., 296; trial by ordeal for suspected adulteress abolished after AD 70, II. 370; exemption from certain commandments, II. 420n., 421n., 455; obliged to recite *Shemoneh 'Esreh* and grace at table, II. 420n., 456, 482; various honorific titles bestowed upon in synagogue, II. 435–436, 448n., III. 25, 101, 107; segregation of men and women in synagogue, II. 447–448; permitted to assist a woman in child-birth on the Sabbath, II. 473; law of divorce, II. 485–486; in World to Come, II. 534; attitude towards among Essenes, II. 570, 578, 593, 594; at Qumran, II. 578, III. 409, 461–462; in community of the Therapeutae, II. 591, 592, 593, 594; from Arabia allowed to wear veil on Sabbath, III. 16; obliged to pay two-drachma tax imposed by Rome after AD 70, III. 54, 122–123; laws concerning female proselytes, III. 175; virginity suits, III. 175; laws about female slaves, III. 411; assertion by Polyhistor that Jewish law derived from a woman, III. 512; command to honour father and mother, see Parents. See also under Marriage, Divorce.

Women (non-Jewish): particularly attracted to Judaism, III. 162–163.

Wood-offering: II. 273.

Work: not permitted on the Sabbath, II. 439, 447.

World to Come: see *Ha'olam haba*; Messianism.

Worship: of gods in Hellenistic cities of Palestine (see also names of individual deities), II. 29–52; sacrificial, at Temple (see also Sacrifice; Temple), II. 287–308; in the synagogue (see also Synagogue), II. 438, 447–454; among Essenes (see also Essenes), II. 570–571, 572–573; at Qumran (see also Qumran), II. 581–582, 588–589; of emperor, see Emperor; Sacrifice. See also Sabbath; Prayer; Priests; etc.

Writings, the (*Ketubim*): targum on, I. 99, 113–114, III. 720; process of canonisation, II. 316–318; divine origin but lower than Torah, II. 319–321; only the five *megilloth* used in synagogue service, II. 452n. See also Bible; Megilloth; and under individual titles.

X

Xenophon (? of Lampsacus): whether author of Syrian topometry, I. 42.

Xiphilinus, epitomizer of Cassius Dio: I. 66.
Xystus, square so-called in Jerusalem: I. 486, 508.

Yose the Galilean, R.: II. 380.
Yose the Priest, R.: II. 370.
Yosippon (= *Joseph ben Gurion*), work attributed to Josephus: I. 117–118.

Y

Yad ha-Ḥazaḳah (Mishneh Torah): I. 80.
Yadayim, Mishnah tractate: position and subject treated, I. 74.
Yakim: see Alcimus.
Yalḳuṭ ha-Makhiri, midrash: date, editions, literature on, I. 99.
Yalḳuṭ Shim'oni, midrash: date, editions, literature on, I. 99.
Yaoel, angel: in *Apocalypse of Abraham* and other writings, III. 288–289.
Yavneh: see Jamnia.
Yeb the fortress: see Elephantine.
Yebamoth, Mishnah tractate: position and subject treated, I. 72.
Yehoḥanan Coins, the: I. 210–211n., **604**.
Yelammedenu (Tanḥuma), midrash: date, editions, literature on, **I. 98**.
Yeraḥmeel ben Solomon, Chronicles of (= *Sefer ha-Zikhronoth*): I. 117.
Yoḥanan ben Beroka, R.: II. 379–380.
Yoḥanan ben Nuri, R.: II. 379.
Yoḥanan ben Zakkai, Rabban: **II. 369–370**; legend regarding questioning by 'Hegemon Agnitus', I. 519; life and legal ordinances of, I. 525, 526n., II. 369–370, 372, 373, 374; given title *Rabban*, II. 326n.; prophesy regarding Vespasian's elevation, II. 370, 510; views on exorcism, III. 343.
Yom Kippur: see Atonement, day of.
Yom Ṭob (Bezah), Mishnah tractate: position and subject matter, I. 72.
Yoma, Mishnah tractate: position and subject treated, I. 72.
Yose ben Halafta, R.: ascribed authorship of *Seder 'Olam*, I. 115.
Yose ben Yoezer: II. 361.
Yose ben Yoḥanan: II. 361.

Z

Zabadaeans, Arabian tribe: I. 185.
Zabim, Mishnah tractate: position and subject treated, I. 74.
Zacchaeus, tax-collector of Jericho: I. 374, 376.
Zacharias ben Baruch: I. 497–498.
Zadduk, the Pharisee: with Judas the Galilean, founds the party of Zealots, I. 381–382, II. 599.
Zadok, R.: II. 371.
Zadok, sons of: priestly leaders of Qumran community, I. 212n., II. 252–253n., 323n., 390, 580; distinction between them and other Levites in time of Ezekiel, II. 251, 252–253. See also Sadducees.
Zadokite Fragments: see Qumran Community, Writings from.
Zamaris, Babylonian Jew: leader of Jewish colony in Batanaea, time of Herod, I. 338n.
Zealots, the: **I. 382, II. 598–606**; emergence of, time of Quirinius, I. 381–382, 426, II. 599, 603–604; involvement of Judas' descendants in the movement, I. 382n., II. 600–601; regarding the name 'Zealot', I. 382n., II. 604; association of Jesus with, I. 426, 439n., 441; characterised as bandits by Josephus, I. 441, 462n., II. 600, 604; activities under Felix, I. 462–463, II. 601; civil war in Jerusalem, AD 67–70, I. 496–498, 501, 502, 503, II. 211, 601, 602; last stand and suicide at Masada, AD 74 (Sicarii), I. 511–512, II. 441n., 588, 601, 604, 606; whether to be identified with Qumran sectarians, II. 585, III. 463; and the Fourth Philosophy, II.

599, 600, 601, 602–604; relationship to the Sicarii, II. 602–603, 605n.; beliefs, II. 603–604, 605; authorship of *Assumption of Moses*, III. 283; see also John of Gischala; Judas the Galilean; Sicarii.

Zebaḥim, Mishnah tractate: position and subject treated, I. 73.

Zeba'oth (Sabaoth): III. 74.

Zebulun, patriarch, Testament of: see *Testaments of the XII Patriarchs*.

Zechariah, prophet: in *The Lives of the Prophets*, III. 783–784.

Zeno Cotylas, tyrant of Philadelphia: II. 91, 156.

Zeno, philosopher: held in high esteem by Philo, III. 872.

Zenobius, author: III. 30.

Zenodorus, tetrarch: I. 292, 319, 337n., **565, 566**, II. 169.

Zenon / Zenon papyri: evidence for commercial and agricultural activity in Palestine, II. 61–62; evidence for Ptolemaic possession of Gaza, II. 100; contains earliest reference to Straton's Tower, II. 115; evidence fo Jews living in the Fayûm, III. 52.

Zephaniah, biblical book: commentary on from Qumran, III. 437.

Zephaniah, prophet: *Apocalypse of*

Zephaniah, III. 803–804.

Zera'im, First Order of Mishnah: constituent tractates, **I. 71–72**.

Zerubbabel: brought four priestly families back from exile, II. 245–246, 247; number of Levites who returned with, II. 254.

Zeus Hypsistos: see *Theos Hypsistos*.

Zeus, worship of: in Jerusalem at time of Antiochus Epiphanes, I. 155; on Mt. Gerizim, time of Hadrian, I. 521, II. 19n.; in various Hellenistic cites of Palestine, II. 36, 37, 38, 40, 43, 51.

Zia, village: II. 157, 158.

'Zion', in Jerusalem: to be identified with the Temple Mount, I. 154–155n.

Zizith: II. 479, 480–481.

Zizith, minor talmudic tractate: position and subject treated, I. 80.

Zodiac, signs of: in mosaic decorations of synagogues, II. 443.

Zoilus, tyrant of Straton's Tower and Dora: II. 91, 115, 120.

Zonaras: epitomato of Cassius Dio, I. 66; use of *Jubilees*, III. 308–309, 316.

Zuggot ('Pairs'): **II. 356–369**; not heads of the Jerusalem Sanhedrin, II. 215; names, order of succession, etc. II. 357–358 *et passim*.

GREEK WORD LIST

The following is not an exhaustive list of the Greek words used or referenced in the text. Only those words which appear in the original language (rather than transliteration or translation) and which receive significant or explicit discussion are listed. Similarly only the (principal) page(s) on which the word actually appears are cited. For full treatment of a given subject, the reader should consult the Main Index. Proper nouns are listed only if their form or etymology is discussed.

ἀθεότης (charge levelled at Jews) III.612, 613

Ἄκη   II.121n.

ἀκρόπολις (of Jerusalem)   I.154n.

ἀμήν   II.450n.

ἀμιξία (charge levelled at Jews) III.614

ἀνάθεμα   II.432

Ἀντιοχεῖς   II.123n., 150, 151

ἀπογραφαί I.403–406, 418–419, 422–423

ἀποκαλύπτω, ἀποκάλυψις   III.242n.

ἀπομνημονεύματα   I.27

ἀποτίμησις   I.405, 406, 418–419

ἀρχίατρος   III.23

ἀρχιγερουσιάρχης (as Jewish official) III.81, 98

ἀρχιερεῖς   II.212–213, 233–236

ἀρχισυνάγωγος (ראש הכנסת) II.434–436, III.100–101

ἄρχοντες (Jewish officials) II.212, III.92, 98–99, 100

Ἀσαμωναῖοι (חשמונאי)   I.194n.

Ἀσιδαῖοι (חסידים)   I.145, 157

βδέλυγμα τῆς ἐρημώσεως   I.155

Βελχειρά, Βεχειράς   III.336n.

Βερέαν, Βερεθ   I.173n.

Βηθσάν, Βαιθσάν   II.142

βῆμα (בימה)   II.446

βουλευταί   II.214

βουλή II.86, 185, 206, 207, 208, 212, 214ff, 224

γαζοφυλάκια, γαζοφύλακες II.281, 282

Γαλιλαία (הגליל)   II.7–8

γέεννα (גיהנום)   II.545n.

γενέσια, γενέθλια   I.346–348n.

Γέρασα   II.149–150

γερουσία (in Jerusalem) II.202–204, 206

γερουσιάρχης (as Jewish official) III.98

γραμματεῖς   II.212–213, 324

δέκα πρῶτοι   II.213–214

Δεκάπολις   II.125

δεξιολάβοι   I.366

δευτέρωσις, δευτεροῦν (משנה, שנה) I.70

δηνάριον   II.65

διδάσκαλε (רבי)   II.326

Δῶρα, Δοῦρα, Δῶρος   II.118n.

Ἑβραϊστί   II.28n.

ἔθνος (use for Jewish community) III.90, 114n.

ἐκκλησία (distinct from συναγωγή) II.429–430n.

ἐπαρχία (as applied to Judaea) I.359n., 360n.

ἔπαρχος   I.358, 359

ἐπικρίσις   I.404

ἐπιμελητής   I.359n.

II.459n.	הבדלה
II.346	הגדה (אגדה)
II.53	הגמון (ἡγεμών)
II.53	הגמוניא (ἡγεμωνία)
II.339, 341, 342	הלכה
II.452	הפטרה (אפטרה)
II.191	הר המלך (ἡ ὀρεινή)
II.258, 261, 295	זבחי שלמים
II.215	זוגות
II.249	זקני בית אב
II.184–185	זקני העיר
II.249	זקני כהנים, זקני בית אב
I.211n. (Jewish congregation)	חבר
I.211n.	חבר העיר
II,398–399 (Pharisees)	חברים
II.418, 438	חזן
III.198	חכמה
II.325	חכמים
II.265	חלה
I.163n.	חנוכה
I.157	חסדים
II.268, 432	חרם
I.201–202n ('Υρκανός)	חרקנוש
I.194n.	חשמונאי
I.587–588	טבת
II.480	טוטפרת
II.479n.	טלית
II.306	יהוה
	(ineffability of the Name)
II.430n., 575	יחד
	(Qumran community)
I.347n (γενέσια)	יום גיניסיא
I.347n.	יום הלידה
I.533	יום טריגוס
I.170n.	יום נקנור
I.239n.	יום צור (צומא רבא)
I.310n.	יוני הרדסיות
II.275	כהן גדול (כהנא רבא)
	(ἀρχιερεύς)
II.551, 552 (Qumran)	כוהן הרשע
I.543	כוסבה (כוסבא, כסבה)
II.17	כותים
II.344	כיוצא בו במקום אחד
	(rule of rabbinic interpretation)

I.190n. (crown-tax)	כלילאי
II.344	כלל ופרט ופרט וכלל
	(rule of rabbinic interpretation)
II.289, 290 (κινύρα)	כנור
II.429, 439	כנסת (כנישתא)
	(συναγωγή)
II.358	כנסת הגדול
I.587–588	כסלו
II.316	כתובים
	('Writings', process of canonisation)
II.53 (legiones)	לגיונות
II.224	לשכת הגזית
II.214, 224n.	לשכת פלהדרין
II.339	מדרש
II.344	מדות
	(rules of rabbinic interpretation)
I.373n., 376n.	מוכסין
II.217	מופלא
II.551, 552 (Qumran)	מורה הצדרק
II.296	מזבח הזהב
II.479–480	מזוזה
II.248–249	מחלקות
II.462–463	מינים
III.336n.	מלכי רע
II.297n.	מנורה
	(candelabrum of Jerusalem temple)
II.62 (μονοπώλης)	מנפול
II.293	מעמד
II.289 (κύμβαλα)	מצלתים
I.158n (Μακκαβαῖος)	מקבה
I.70n., II.341n.	מקרה (מקרא)
I.587–588	מרחשון
II.353	מרכבה
II.517	משיח (משיחא)
II.245–250, 254–256, 292–293	משמרות
	(Priestly, Levitical and Israelite Courses)
I.70, II.33	משנה
	(δευτέρωσις, repetition)
I.70n.	משנה ראשונה
I.71	משניות
II.289	משררים
II.316	נביאים
	(Books of the Prophets, process of canonisation)
II.289, 290 (νάβλα)	נבל